The Medieval Clothier

WORKING IN THE MIDDLE AGES

Series Editor
James Davis (Queen's University, Belfast)

This series aims to provide authoritative, accessible guides to medieval trades, offering surveys of their origins and development, alongside the practicalities of the occupation. It will cover both those who were concerned with the material needs of society, and those who contributed to cultural life and the professions.

New proposals are welcomed; they should be sent to the series editor and/or to the publisher at the addresses below.

Dr James Davis, School of History, Anthropology,
Philosophy and Politics
Queen's University Belfast
25 University Square
BELFAST
BT7 1PA

James.davis@qub.ac.uk

The Editorial Director (Medieval Studies), Boydell and Brewer Ltd,
PO Box 9, Woodbridge, Suffolk IP12 3DF, UK;
editorial@boydell.co.uk.

The Medieval Clothier

JOHN S. LEE

THE BOYDELL PRESS

First published 2018
The Boydell Press, Woodbridge

ISBN 978 1 78327 317 1

The Boydell Press is an imprint of Boydell & Brewer Ltd
PO Box 9, Woodbridge, Suffolk IP12 3DF, UK
and of Boydell & Brewer Inc.
668 Mt Hope Avenue, Rochester, NY 14620–2731, USA
website: www.boydellandbrewer.com

A CIP catalogue record for this book is available from the British Library

This publication is printed on acid-free paper

IN MEMORY OF RICHARD BRITNELL (1944–2013)
FELLOW OF THE BRITISH ACADEMY
PROFESSOR OF HISTORY, UNIVERSITY OF DURHAM

Contents

List of Illustrations ix
List of Tables xii
Acknowledgements xiii
Abbreviations xv
A Note on Money, Weights and Measures, and Places xvi

Introduction 1
The period 1350 to 1550 3
Cloth-making 8
Why did English cloth-making expand after 1350? 12
Entrepreneurs and capitalists 17
Historical sources 30

1 Making cloth 39
Processes in the making of cloth 39
Organising cloth production 65
Timescales and profits 72

2 Marketing cloth 77
Clothiers' customers in the provinces 78
Clothiers' customers in London 81
Buyers from overseas 91
Cloth markets 96
Selling cloth 107

3 Identifying Clothiers 115
Locating cloth-workers and clothiers 115
Why did the cloth industry develop in particular areas? 144

4 Clothiers and government 157
Developing legislation 157
Regulating cloth production 161
Responding to political protests 178

5 Clothiers in society 191
Family backgrounds 191
Houses and workshops 195
Farming and landholding 205
Religious and commemorative practice 209

6 Famous clothiers 226
Thomas Paycocke of Coggeshall 226
The Springs of Lavenham 239
The Winchcombes of Newbury 250
William Stumpe of Malmesbury 262

Conclusion 272
The rise of the medieval clothier 273
The skills of the medieval clothier 276
The environment of the medieval clothier 277
The medieval clothier and government 279
The medieval clothier as an early capitalist 280

Appendices
1. Cloths taxed by county 282
2. Cloths taxed by locality 284
3. Cloth types, as defined by statute in 1552 290
4. Will of Thomas Paycocke of Coggeshall 292
5. Will of Thomas Spring III of Lavenham 297
6. Will of John Smallwood the elder alias John Winchcombe I of Newbury 300
7. Will of William Stumpe of Malmesbury 302

Gazetteer of surviving buildings 304
Glossary 313
Bibliography 318
Index 338

Illustrations

COLOUR PLATES
(between pages 172 and 173)

I Stages in the production of cloth illustrated in the fifteenth-century cloth-workers' window in the church of Notre-Dame, Semur-en-Auxois, Burgundy, France. © Sonia Halliday Photo Library.

II Woman feeding chickens while holding a distaff and spindle. © The British Library Board (Luttrell Psalter, 1325–40: BL, Add MS 42130, fol. 166v).

III Women spinning with a hand wheel and carding. © The British Library Board (Luttrell Psalter, 1325–40: BL, Add MS 42130, fol. 193r).

IV Weaving using a treadle loom, c.1350–75. © The British Library Board (Egerton Genesis Picture Book: BL, Egerton MS 1894, fol. 2v detail).

V Cloth Market in 's-Hertogenbosch, Brabant, c.1530, Dutch School. Reproduced by permission of Collection het Noordbrabants Museum, 's-Hertogenbosch.

VI The Hanseatic merchant Georg Gisze (1532) by Hans Holbein the Younger (c. 1497–1543). Reproduced by permission of Gemäldegalerie, Staatliche Museum, Berlin. bpk / Gemäldegalerie, SMB / Jörg P. Anders.

VII Portrait of Thomas Bell (d. 1566), clothier and capper of Gloucester. Reproduced by permission of Gloucester City Museums Service, GLRCM: Art01069.

VIII Paycocke's House, Coggeshall, Essex (author's photograph).

IX Brass of John Wyncoll (d. 1544), clothier, Little Waldingfield church, Suffolk. Photograph reproduced courtesy of Martin Stuchfield.

X Portrait of John Winchcombe the Younger ('Jack of Newbury') (c.1489–1557), dated 1550. Photograph by Ruth Bubb Conservation Ltd. and courtesy of Newbury Town Council.

BLACK AND WHITE PLATES

1 Medieval spindle whorl. Reproduced courtesy of the Portable Antiquities Scheme/The Trustees of the British Museum (SWYOR-54017C). 48

2 Fulling stocks depicted in John Lane's aisle, Cullompton church, Devon (author's photograph). 55

3 Tenters, Otterburn Mill, Northumberland (author's photograph). 56

4 Teasel frames or handles depicted in John Lane's aisle, Cullompton church, Devon (author's photograph). 58

5 Cloth finisher with tools at Spaxton church, Somerset. © Historic England Archive. 60

6 Thomas Kitson's 'Boke of Remembraunce' or account book. Reproduced by kind permission of the Syndics of Cambridge University Library (CUL, Hengrave Hall MS 78(2)). 88

7 Marginal sketch of a ship from Thomas Kitson's account book. Reproduced by kind permission of the Syndics of Cambridge University Library (CUL, Hengrave Hall MS 78(2), fol. 220v). 90

8 The George Inn, Norton St Philip, Somerset (author's photograph). 106

9 Castle Combe, Wiltshire (author's photograph). 124

10 Medieval and post-medieval cloth seals. Reproduced courtesy of the Portable Antiquities Scheme/The Trustees of the British Museum. 162

11 Westwood House, Wiltshire, home of clothier Thomas Horton (d. 1530) (author's photograph). 202

12 Brass of John Compton (d. 1505), wife Edith and five sons in Beckington church, Somerset. Reproduced courtesy of Martin Stuchfield. 213

13 Corpus Christi Guildhall, Lavenham, Suffolk (author's photograph). 215

14 Merchant's mark detail from decorated fascia of Paycocke's, Coggeshall (author's photograph). 227

15 Wyvern detail from decorated fascia of Paycocke's, Coggeshall (author's photograph). 236

16 Church of St Peter and St Paul, Lavenham, Suffolk (author's photograph). 241

17 Detail of brass of Thomas Spring II, Lavenham church, Suffolk. Photograph reproduced courtesy of Martin Stuchfield. 247

18 Detail of the Spring parclose screen, Lavenham church (author's photograph). 249

19 Panelling from John Winchcombe's house, Newbury (author's photograph). 261
20 Thomas Kitson's purchases from William Stumpe of Malmesbury, 1535. Reproduced by kind permission of the Syndics of Cambridge University Library (CUL, Hengrave Hall MS 78(2), fol. 142). 268

FIGURES

1 English cloth exports, 1350–1544 9
2 Clothiers, cloth-makers and cloth-men appearing in Court of Common Pleas cases, 1410–1550 23
3 Stages in the production of woollen cloth 40
4 Simplified diagram of fulling mill machinery. © Rob Martin, Isle of Wight History Centre 54
5 Different types of organisation within the cloth industry 66
6 The clothier's customers 78
7 The clothier's markets 97
8 Paycocke family tree 228
9 Spring family tree 240
10 Winchcombe family tree 252
11 Stumpe family tree 263

MAPS

1 The main centres of cloth-making in late medieval England and other places discussed in the text. xvii
2 The main centres of cloth-making in Essex and Suffolk. xviii
3 The main centres of cloth-making in Gloucestershire, Somerset and Wiltshire. xix
4 Cloth-workers in the poll taxes of 1377–81 117
5 Clothiers in the Court of Common Pleas, 1453 118
6 Clothiers in the Court of Common Pleas, 1549 119

Tables

1 Estimates of English cloth produced from 1311–15 to 1541–45 9
2 Cloth-making crafts assessed in the poll tax returns, 1377–81 40
3 Principal dyestuffs used in medieval English cloth 62
4 Estimated timescales and labour costs of cloth-making in 1540s 73
5 Costs of making russet cloth, c.1391 75

Acknowledgements

I first encountered the clothiers of late medieval England while working on a Masters degree at the University of Durham with Richard Britnell, who was kind enough to share with me his work on the clothiers Thomas Paycocke and Thomas Spring, as well as his research on the medieval textile industry in Colchester and its hinterland. Clothiers were evident, although in the background, during my doctoral research at Corpus Christi College, Cambridge, with the support of John Hatcher as my supervisor. As I explored Cambridge and its economic region in the period 1450–1560 for my thesis, I discovered Suffolk cloth-makers attending Cambridge's Stourbridge Fair, alongside leading Coventry drapers and London merchants. Later, while preparing an article for *Urban History* on John Leland's observations of towns in his mid-sixteenth-century *Itinerary*, I encountered his descriptions of notable clothiers and their wealth. When Alex Brown invited me to contribute to *Crises in Economic and Social History: A Comparative Perspective*, I was able to revive these interests and offer a chapter on crises in the late medieval English cloth trade.

During the research for this book, it has been a pleasure to discuss aspects of this work with other historians, including Nicholas Amor, Catherine Casson, James Davis, Jordan Claridge, John Hatcher, Christian Steer, and Christopher Thornton. I am particularly grateful to Milan Pajic, whose doctoral research on the immigration of Flemings has provided me with many new insights, and to Sam Gibbs for sharing details from his poll tax database. I am greatly indebted to the late Eleanora Mary Carus-Wilson, Professor of Economic History at the University of London, for use of her unpublished material and am very grateful to John Hatcher for providing me with access to this.

It was very helpful to present seminar papers on the leading clothiers of the late Middle Ages during 2015 at the International Congress on Medieval Studies at the University of West Michigan, Kalamazoo, the International Medieval Congress at the University of Leeds, and the Fifteenth Century Conference at the University of Kent. I am grateful to the audiences and also to the organisers of these sessions, Peter Larson and Philip Slavin, for their helpful input. The participants on my course

'Making and Marketing Cloth in Medieval England' at the Centre for Lifelong Learning at the University of York have provided many useful ideas as well as stimulating questions.

Working as an 'independent researcher' outside academic employment is not always easy and I am most grateful to the Centre for Medieval Studies at the University of York who have enabled me to retain academic links as one of their Research Associates. John Henderson of the Northallerton Local History Society's Latin Group has kindly helped with translating trickier aspects of clothiers' wills and other documents. Karen Marchlik at the National Trust has provided me with unpublished research on Paycocke's, Coggeshall, and Sarah Orton at Gloucester City Museums Service supplied details about Sir Thomas Bell. Elizabeth Fathi, Chief Executive of Tiverton Almshouse Trust, willingly arranged my visit to Greenway's Almshouse chapel in Tiverton, and Penny Fussell access to consult Thomas Howell's ledger at the Drapers' Hall. Martin Stuchfield generously provided images of monumental brasses. The Pasold Research Fund kindly awarded a grant towards the cost of publishing some of the images used in this book. My thanks too to staff at The National Archives, the British Library, North Yorkshire County Council, and other libraries and repositories, who have supplied documents and books. Caroline Palmer, Rob Kinsey, Nick Bingham and their colleagues at Boydell and Brewer have been unfailingly helpful in preparing this book. James Lee has helped when I have struggled with spreadsheets and IT.

As noted above, my interest in clothiers began under the supervision of Richard Britnell. Richard, who died in December 2013, was one of the foremost historians of medieval economy and society at the turn of the twenty-first century. It was a great privilege to have known him as a supervisor and friend. This book is dedicated to his memory.

Abbreviations

AALT	Anglo-American Legal Tradition website image
BL	British Library, London
BRO	Berkshire Record Office, Reading
CHWT	*Cambridge History of Western Textiles*, vol. i
CPR	*Calendar of Patent Rolls*
CUHB	*Cambridge Urban History of Britain*, vol. i
CUL	Cambridge University Library
EcHR	*Economic History Review*
HMC	Historical Manuscripts Commission
HoP	*The History of Parliament online*
Itinerary	*The Itinerary of John Leland in or about the Years 1535–1543*, ed. Lucy Toulmin Smith, 5 vols, 2nd edn (London, 1964)
KHLC	Kent History and Library Centre, Maidstone
LMA	London Metropolitan Archives
LP	*Letters and Papers, Foreign and Domestic, of the Reign of Henry VIII*, eds J.S. Brewer, J. Gardiner and R.H. Brodie (21 vols and *Addenda*, London, 1862–1932)
NHLE	National Heritage List for England, Historic England, List entry number
ODNB	*Oxford Dictionary of National Biography online*
OED	*Oxford English Dictionary online*
SR	*Statutes of the Realm*
TED	*Tudor Economic Documents*, eds R.H. Tawney and E. Power, 3 vols (London, 1924)
TNA	The National Archives, London
VCH	*Victoria County History*
YBIA	Borthwick Institute for Archives, York,
YELA	York Explore Library and Archive

A Note on Money, Weights and Measures, and Places

The monetary system used in medieval England remained in use until 1971. £1 contained 20 shillings (s) or 240 pence (d). The mark was a sum of money worth two-thirds of £1, or 13s 4d. Price inflation since the Middle Ages makes direct comparisons meaningless, but as a guide, a skilled building craftsman earned 4d per day in 1400 and 6d per day in 1500.

Weights and measures are given in the units usually used in the Middle Ages. Cloth was measured by the yard (3 feet, or 0.9 metres) or the ell, which was often as long as a yard and a quarter (1.1 metres). Wool was sold in tods of 28 pounds (28 lb equals 13 kilograms) and sacks of 364 lb (165 kilograms). Distances are given in miles (1.6 kilometres) and areas of land in acres (0.4 hectares). The size of a cloth varied according to its type, but a statute of 1465 fixed a standard English broadcloth at 24 yards long by 1¾ yards wide.

Places are identified by their historic counties, although the Gazetteer includes reference to the modern administrative counties, established during the twentieth century, where these differ.

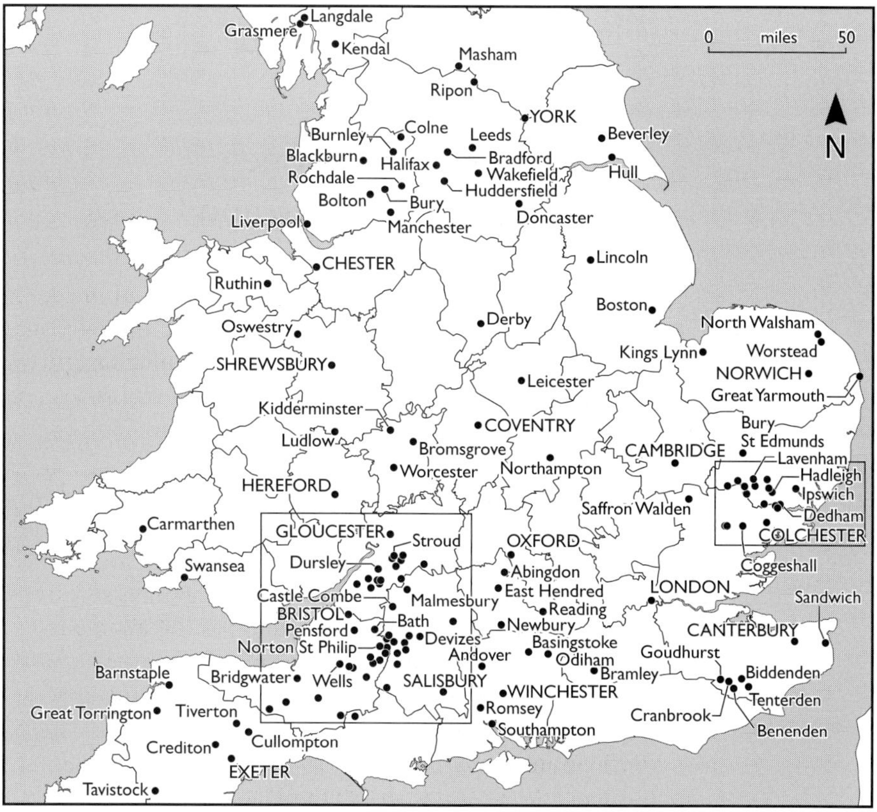

Map 1 The main centres of cloth-making in late medieval England and other places discussed in the text.

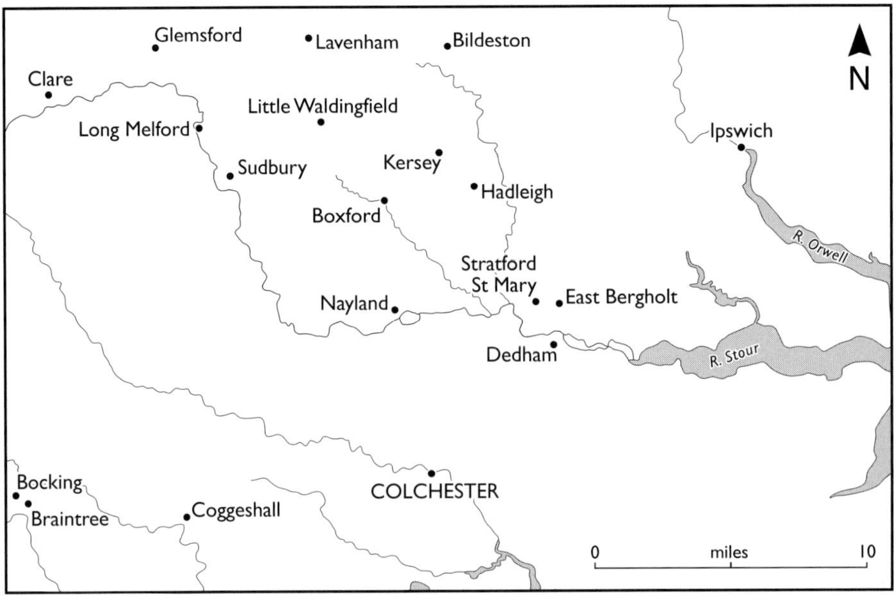

Map 2 The main centres of cloth-making in Essex and Suffolk.

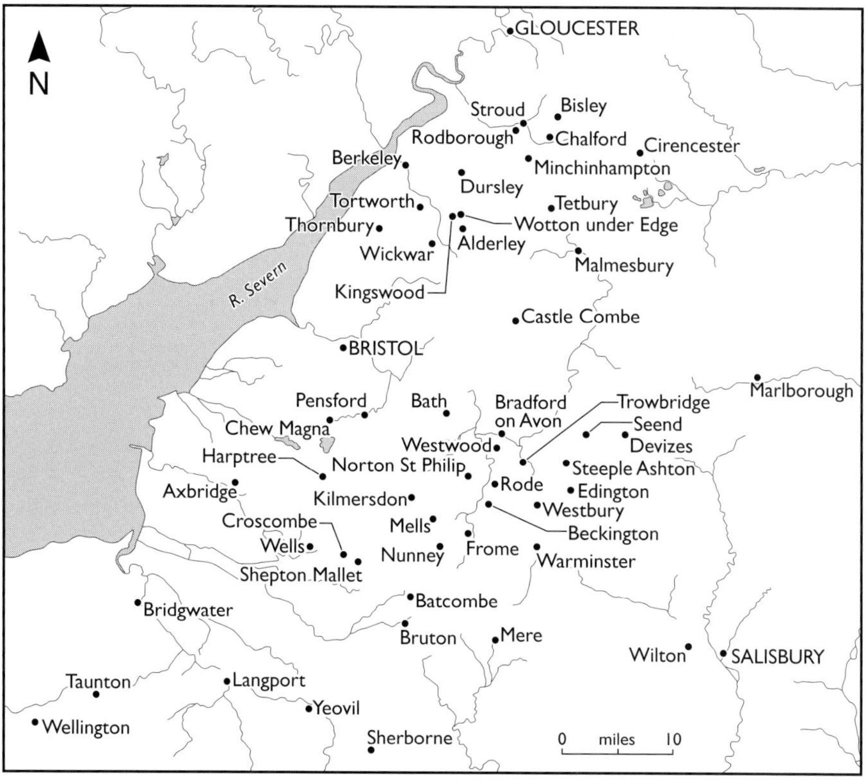

Map 3 The main centres of cloth-making in Gloucestershire, Somerset and Wiltshire.

Introduction

> This was a gallant clothier sure,
> Whose fame for ever shall endure.
>
> Thomas Deloney, *Jack of Newbury* (1597)[1]

A handful of clothiers earned vast fortunes making and marketing cloth in the later Middle Ages. Thomas Paycocke of Coggeshall, the Springs of Lavenham, William Stumpe of Malmesbury, and John Winchcombe of Newbury are still remembered in their communities, five centuries after their birth. These were the multi-millionaires of their day, often rising from humble origins to fame and fortune. In some cases, their children even joined the ranks of the gentry. Such rapid social mobility intrigues us even today. These clothiers extended, enlarged and rebuilt parish churches, and left instructions for elaborate remembrance practices to ensure that they and their families were commemorated after their deaths. Their names were celebrated in verse: the poet of the royal court John Skelton wrote of his contemporary, 'Good Spring of Lavenham', while two generations later Thomas Deloney celebrated the life of John Winchcombe as 'Jack of Newbury', a pioneer of factory production. This book examines these individuals, together with their less prominent and prosperous contemporaries, the far more numerous group of clothiers who might be described as the 'jacks of all trades'. What were their origins and how did they accumulate their fortunes? To what extent were they responsible for transforming the cloth industry and their wider communities?

The *Oxford English Dictionary* defines a clothier as 'one engaged in the cloth trade'. The entry in the dictionary also includes 'a maker of woollen cloth', 'one who performs the operations subsequent to the weaving', and 'a seller of cloth and men's clothes'. [2] For the purposes

[1] Thomas Deloney, *Jack of Newbury*, in *An Anthology of Elizabethan Prose Fiction*, ed. Paul Salzman (Oxford, 1987), p. 336.

[2] *OED*: 'clothier'.

of this book though, we need to define the term more precisely. The clothier was involved in both the *making* and *marketing* of woollen cloth. He, or occasionally she, was not usually a maker of clothes, which was the role of the tailor. Both contemporaries and historians have seen clothiers as a distinctive group of entrepreneurs who emerged during the later Middle Ages to coordinate the different stages of production within the textile industry, and to control an increasing share of the cloth trade. Around 1400, many workers in the cloth industry operated independently, financing their own production, although they depended on merchants to sell their cloth. By 1500 though, the organisation of many parts of the industry had been transformed. Clothiers were now putting out raw materials to workers who processed them in their own homes and returned products to the clothier to sell. These clothiers were acting as merchant capitalists, for as well as organising this putting-out system of production, they were providing the finance to enable it to function. In a handful of cases, clothiers even centralised different processes of production within buildings which we might describe as factories. Some historians have therefore identified clothiers as early capitalists.

In the years after 1350, cloth-making became England's leading industry, both in terms of the total employment that it generated and the value of its output. Cloth-making provided a major source of demand for agricultural commodities, notably wool, but also for products used in the cloth-making process, including dyestuffs, butter and oil, fuller's earth, and teasels. Of high value relative to its weight, and neither fragile nor perishable, cloth was readily tradable. Woollen textiles were the leading manufactured product entering regional and overseas trade, and in addition to the finished textiles, there was significant international exchange in the essential raw materials of wool, dyestuffs and alum.

Cloth-making stimulated economic growth in particular localities, and some individuals amassed huge fortunes as a result of the trade. Between the late fourteenth and early sixteenth centuries, the small cloth-making communities of Lavenham, Newbury and Hadleigh grew to become among the thirty wealthiest towns in England, overtaking, in terms of total taxable wealth, established towns such as Southampton, Stamford and Cambridge. The cloth industry in parts of Suffolk in the 1520s had generated a concentration of wealth that was unequalled anywhere outside London.[3] Some of these centres of textile production largely escaped later redevelopment and retain their medieval street plans and buildings today. Places such as Castle Combe in Wiltshire and Lavenham in Suffolk, with their picture-postcard streets, have become

[3] *CUHB*, pp. 765–6; J.C.K. Cornwall, *Wealth and Society in Early Sixteenth Century England* (London, 1988), p. 72.

sanitised from their industrial past. Other medieval cloth-making centres, such as Stroudwater, Leeds or Basingstoke, have changed out of all recognition through subsequent periods of industrial expansion.

THE PERIOD 1350 TO 1550

> By means of an industrial revolution hardly less momentous than the later and more familiar one, England had transformed herself, between 1350 and 1450, into a large-scale producer and exporter of woollen cloth.
>
> *Cambridge Urban History of Britain*[4]

This book covers the period 1350 to 1550, spanning two centuries of economic, social and political change. In economic terms, the period begins with the catastrophic outbreak of plague known as the Black Death, covers an era of major growth in the production and export of cloth, and concludes with the collapse of the cloth trade in Antwerp. In political terms, the period opens with the reign of Edward III, marked by military conquests in France and the beginning of the Hundred Years War, and closes with the reign of Edward VI, son of Henry VIII. In religious and social terms, England moved from a deeply Catholic country to one undergoing a Protestant Reformation. Historians often categorise the earlier part of the period 1350–1550 as late medieval and the later part as early modern but there is no consensus on where the dividing line should be drawn. Some might argue that 1485 forms the watershed, with the victory of Henry Tudor at the battle of Bosworth marking the beginning of the Tudor dynasty, while others might point to Henry VIII's break from the authority of the Pope and the Roman Catholic Church during the 1530s as a more significant turning point. Those looking from an international perspective might choose the fall of Constantinople in 1453, marking the end of the eastern Roman Empire, or Christopher Columbus' first transatlantic expedition to the Americas in 1492.

There were significant changes within the English economy and society between the years 1350–1550, but such transitions are often difficult to pinpoint to a specific year. Many of these changes had significant implications for the cloth industry. They can be grouped under three main headings – land, labour and capital. These are the terms that economists use to identify the three basic factors of production that are all needed in some combination to produce a commodity. Entrepreneurs such as clothiers combined these three resources in order to make a profit, refining their products as well as their methods of production.

[4] *CUHB*, p. 478.

Land

The Black Death of 1348–49 probably reduced the English population by around half, and it did not begin to recover until the later fifteenth or early sixteenth century.[5] The impact of plague mortality was exacerbated by climate change bringing colder weather and more violent storms in the first stage of the Little Ice Age, so that agricultural activities in more marginal areas were reduced or abandoned.[6] Land became relatively abundant and labour relatively scarce. These trends favoured extensive rather than intensive agriculture, particularly sheep farming. This required little labour and met a growing demand for livestock, dairy produce and clothing. Wool had already been exported from England to the cloth-producing towns of Flanders in the twelfth and thirteenth centuries, initially by Flemish merchants and later by Italians. After the Black Death, English wool supplied both overseas markets and the growing domestic cloth industry.

From the later fourteenth century, institutional landowners like monasteries and the nobility, who had previously cultivated their rural estates directly using customary labour, now rented their lands out to a variety of tenants, including gentry and peasant farmers. These new tenants left far fewer records than major institutions. While some historians suggest that these changes created a less market-oriented and more self-sufficient economy, others argue that they led to a greater focus on producing for the market rather than for the needs of large noble and ecclesiastical households.[7] Earlier institutional barriers to personal mobility and the transferability of property reduced with the decline of tenurial servility, known as villeinage, and personal servility, known as serfdom, and the terms on which peasants held land became more commercialised. These changes created new opportunities for smaller peasant farmers to accumulate holdings, and for larger farmers to employ wage labourers. Some historians see these trends as marking the beginnings of agrarian capitalism.[8] They also provided the precondi-

[5] J. Hatcher, *Plague, Population and the English Economy, 1348–1530* (London, 1977).

[6] B.M.S. Campbell, 'Nature as Historical Protagonist: Environment and Society in Pre-Industrial England', *EcHR* 63 (2010), pp. 281–314.

[7] M.M. Postan, 'The Fifteenth Century', *EcHR* 9 (1938–39), pp. 160–7; Christopher Dyer, *An Age of Transition?: Economy and Society in England in the Later Middle Ages* (Oxford, 2005), pp. 173–210.

[8] See the discussion in R. Britnell, 'Commerce and Capitalism in Late Medieval England: Problems of Description and Theory', *Journal of Historical Sociology* 6 (1993), pp. 359–76; C. Dyer, 'Were There Any Capitalists in Fifteenth-century England?', in C. Dyer, *Everyday Life in Medieval England* (London, 1994), pp. 316–20; John Hatcher and Mark Bailey, *Modelling the Middle Ages: The History and Theory of England's Economic Development* (Oxford, 2001), pp. 175–83.

tions that enabled rural cloth-making to develop more readily through the amassing of land and capital. The end of sheep farming by the large monastic houses broke the direct link that had existed previously between these major wool producers and merchants as exporters. Consequently leading wool dealers took an increasingly key role in collecting wool from smaller landholdings to sell to merchants and to cloth producers.

Labour

England's population probably reached its lowest level of between 2 and 2½ million in the middle of the fifteenth century. It finally began to recover at some point in the later fifteenth or early sixteenth century, but the timing and extent of this growth is uncertain. The smaller population after the Black Death made labour scarce. Despite attempts to hold them down, wage rates increased, and those earning their living primarily from wages saw their standards of living rise. During the sixteenth century, though, wages began to lag behind price increases, causing real earnings to start to fall. While these general trends are accepted, the degree to which individuals and families relied on wages for their income is uncertain. Some historians have therefore questioned the scale of the rise in living standards in the fifteenth century, while others have challenged the extent of the fall in living standards in the sixteenth century. Although few would dispute that there were some gains in living standards after the Black Death, which enabled more consumers to purchase more cloth of better quality, it is the extent of these gains that is debated, and whether they were sufficient to generate a 'consumer revolution'.[9] When labour became scarce, there were potentially greater opportunities for women within the workforce, particularly around 1400. Although some of these opportunities appear to have been relatively short-lived, much of the work in the growing cloth industry, particularly processing wool and spinning, relied on female labour.[10]

[9] Hatcher, *Plague*, pp. 68–9; D. Woodward, 'Wage Rates and Living Standards in Pre-industrial England', *Past and Present* 91 (1981), pp. 28–46. Recent debates are summarised in J. Hatcher, 'Unreal Wages: Long-Run Living Standards and the "Golden Age" of the Fifteenth Century', in B. Dodds and C.D. Liddy, eds, *Commercial Activity, Markets and Entrepreneurs in the Middle Ages: Essays in Honour of Richard Britnell* (Woodbridge, 2011), pp. 1–24, and Christopher Dyer, 'A Golden Age Rediscovered: Labourers' Wages in the Fifteenth Century', in M. Allen and D. Coffman, eds, *Prices, Money and Wages* (London, 2014), pp. 180–95.

[10] P.J.P. Goldberg, *Women, Work, and Life Cycle in a Medieval Economy: Women in York and Yorkshire c.1300–1520* (Oxford, 1992); Jennifer Ward, 'Townswomen and their Households', in Richard Britnell, ed., *Daily Life in the Late Middle Ages* (Stroud, 1998), p. 40.

Capital

By 1350 England had already developed a network of towns, transport, markets and credit. While the halving of the population through the Black Death led to a reduction in the size of many towns, and a fall in the number of functioning markets, English society retained its commercialised character. The most heavily urbanised region of Europe was in northern Italy, comprising the cities of Milan, Venice, Florence and Genoa, but there was a second concentration of urban development in north-western Europe, which included London together with Paris, Ghent and Cologne. As Britain lay on the periphery of this urban region of north-western Europe, the commercial opportunities were greatest around London and the southern and eastern parts of England, where there was ready trade with continental towns across the English Channel and North Sea. By contrast, in north-western England, Wales and Scotland, urban populations were much smaller and markets less well-developed. The distribution of the textile industry largely reflected this.[11]

The English population was overwhelmingly rural, with less than 20 per cent of the population living in towns of any size. London, with both England's leading port and the centre of government at Westminster, was by far the largest town, with perhaps between 50,000 and 70,000 people. The second-largest urban centre was Norwich, with around 10,000 inhabitants. Together with forty other towns with over 5,000 people, there were about 800 smaller places that possessed urban characteristics: their residents were engaged in activities outside agriculture and needed to buy foodstuffs, and they had markets and fairs to serve them.[12] Many of these urban centres were known as boroughs, with charters granted by the Crown or a lord to the townspeople to exercise certain rights and privileges. Most trade was local, with townspeople supplying manufactured and imported goods to villagers in exchange for food and raw materials. The medium-sized provincial town of Cambridge, with perhaps 3,500 residents, drew most of its grain supplies from within ten miles.[13] Some of this trade used the formal marketing infrastructure of weekly markets and annual fairs, although many deals were achieved by private negotiations outside such venues. Trading disputes could be settled at courts of the manor, borough or central government, depending on their value and complexity; these courts also regulated the quality, price and supply of many commodities. Certain manufactured goods though, depended

[11] Ben Dodds and Richard Britnell, eds, *Agriculture and Rural Society after the Black Death: Common Themes and Regional Variations* (Hatfield, 2008), pp. 5–6.

[12] Richard Britnell, *The Closing of the Middle Ages? England, 1471–1529* (Oxford, 1997), pp. 210–11.

[13] John S. Lee, *Cambridge and its Economic Region, 1450–1560* (Hatfield, 2005).

on mercantile connections over long distances. England's overseas trade principally consisted of exports of wool, cloth, lead, tin and pewter, in return for imports of raw materials, foodstuffs and manufactured goods. The most important markets were Flanders and the Low Countries, but there were other major trading links with the Baltic, France, Spain, Portugal and the Mediterranean.[14]

Once considered primitive, the transport infrastructure has been shown by recent research to have benefitted from significant investment in the Middle Ages, which funded the construction of bridges, navigation improvements and port facilities. The road network was regularly utilised, with carts running at least weekly between the port of Southampton and the towns of Salisbury, Winchester and London. The cloth industry sparked further improvements, such as bequests to repair highways, or investment in cranes at cloth-exporting ports like Hythe near Colchester.[15]

As the volume of the medieval English coinage (no more than £2.3 million) had to finance an economy at least twice as large (with a gross domestic product of £4–6 million), various forms of credit were needed to fill the shortfall. The amount of cash in circulation declined in the fifteenth century, and there seem to have been particular difficulties during the middle years of the century, when the flow of precious metal across Europe was reduced. The extent to which credit could circumvent these problems with the money supply has been debated.[16] It is clear though that the use of credit was ubiquitous throughout the medieval economy, and ranged from peasants entering into debts with their neighbours, to international systems that allowed merchants to transfer money through bills of exchange. As the only banks were those focused on financing overseas trade, and run by foreign merchants in London, domestic credit relied on the financial resources of local people, or urban traders. Local and central courts allowed these debts to be registered and

[14] J.L. Bolton, *The Medieval English Economy* (London, 1980), pp. 287–95; Richard Britnell, *Britain and Ireland 1050–1530: Economy and Society* (Oxford, 2004), pp. 326–33.

[15] David Harrison, *The Bridges of Medieval England: Transport and Society, 400–1800* (Oxford, 2004); Michael Hicks, ed., *English Inland Trade 1430–1540* (Oxford, 2015), pp. 43–52; R.H. Britnell, *Growth and Decline in Colchester, 1300–1525* (Cambridge, 1986), p. 69.

[16] J.L. Bolton, *Money in the Medieval English Economy 973–1489* (Manchester, 2012); Pamela Nightingale, 'The Impact of Crises on Credit in the Late Medieval English Economy', in A.T. Brown, Andy Burn and Rob Doherty, eds, *Crises in Economic and Social History: A Comparative Perspective* (Woodbridge, 2015), pp. 261–82.

debtors to be pursued if they defaulted.[17] All parts of the cloth-making process could be financed on credit, as could major purchases of raw materials and sales of finished cloth, which might involve transactions with overseas merchants.

CLOTH-MAKING

The industry before 1350

From the eleventh and twelfth centuries, several regions of western Europe developed prominent cloth industries. These included parts of north-west France, particularly the counties of Flanders and Artois, the Low Countries, the Rhineland, Normandy, Languedoc, Tuscany, Lombardy, Catalonia and Aragon, as well as several English towns.[18] By the early thirteenth century, the leading centres of production in England seem to have been Lincoln and York, with other important centres at Newcastle-upon-Tyne, Beverley, Leicester, Northampton and Winchester. At least some of this cloth was supplying wider markets than the purely local, including the royal court and markets overseas.[19]

During the later thirteenth century though, England's cloth industry appears to have declined, or at best failed to expand. This seems to have been largely due to competing imports from Flanders. Textile production in several English towns faced difficulties, while in some rural areas expanded. In Yorkshire, for example, the weavers' guild of York frequently failed to make any payment to the Crown for their privileges, and by 1309 had amassed a deficit of £780.[20] Meanwhile cloth-making was being practised in many small towns and rural communities, from Halifax in the western Pennines to Hedon on the east coast, and from Wakefield in the south to Whitby on the north-east coast. In many of these small communities, cloth-making was just one of a range of industrial trades. In 1304 the small town of Masham in lower Wensleydale, home to a few hundred residents at most, possessed a fulling mill for processing cloth, alongside a corn mill, tannery and a coal mine.[21] The

[17] Chris Briggs, *Credit and Village Society in Fourteenth-Century England* (Oxford, 2009).

[18] *CHWT*, p. 218.

[19] Edward Miller and John Hatcher, *Medieval England: Towns, Commerce and Crafts 1086–1348* (London, 1995), pp. 100–4.

[20] Edward Miller, 'The Fortunes of the English Textile Industry during the Thirteenth Century', *EcHR* 18 (1965), pp. 64–82; *VCH Yorkshire: The City of York*, p. 44.

[21] Herbert Heaton, *The Yorkshire Woollen and Worsted Industries from the Earliest Times up to the Industrial Revolution*, 2nd edn (Oxford, 1965), pp. 4–7; John S. Lee, 'Medieval Local History from Published Records: A Case-study of the Medieval Manor, Market and Church of Masham, Yorkshire', *The Local Historian* 45

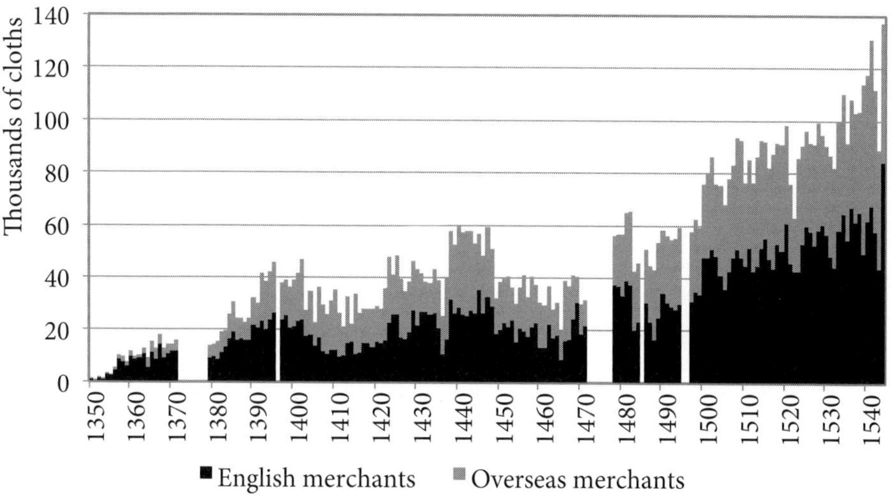

Figure 1 English cloth exports, 1350–1544
Source: A.R. Bridbury, *Medieval English Clothmaking: An Economic Survey* (London, 1982), pp. 118–22.

Table 1 Estimates of English cloth produced from 1311–15 to 1541–45

Numbers of cloths produced	*1311–15*	*1441–45*	*1541–45*
Domestic market	160,000	140,000	190,000
Export market	3,900	56,500	118,100
Total	163,900	196,500	308,100
Average cloth weight (lb)	38	46	64
Total cloth produced (lb)	6,228,200	9,039,000	19,718,400
Population	4,690,000	1,950,000	2,830,000
Pounds of cloth produced per capita	1.3	4.6	7.0

Source: Oldland, 'Economic Impact', p. 235.

English cloth industry had already experienced both rural and urban growth before the mid fourteenth century.

The main product of the cloth industry was also changing by 1350, from worsteds to woollens. Worsteds were lighter, coarser cloths, that could be readily made in the home on a narrow loom, and did not need to be fulled or finished. Woollens were heavier and costlier to produce,

(2015), p. 59.

requiring greater preparation and treatment of the wool and the woven cloth. Cloth-making became more labour-intensive and it became far more difficult for a single household to produce woollen cloth of an acceptable quality.[22]

The industry after 1350

The English cloth industry grew dramatically between the mid fourteenth and mid sixteenth centuries, serving both home and overseas markets. Table 1 provides estimates of the total amounts of cloth produced during this period. The primary source of demand was the export market, recorded in the customs accounts. The amount of English cloths exported increased over fourteenfold between 1311–15 and 1441–45, and a further twofold over the following century. Exports grew dramatically from around 8,000 cloths in 1360 to over 50,000 by 1440, to 75,000 by 1500, and nearly 120,000 by 1540 (see Figure 1). These figures may even underestimate the size of the export market, as cheap narrow cloths were not subject to customs. By the mid fourteenth century the English textile industry had virtually captured the home market, and aided by customs duties imposed by the Crown on wool exports, English cloth-makers gradually penetrated the overseas markets of Gascony, the Mediterranean, the Baltic and the Low Countries. Customs payable on wool exports were initially introduced in 1275, but raised significantly in the 1330s to finance the war with France, and by the later fourteenth century they markedly discouraged the export of English wool and enabled English cloth-makers to source wool more cheaply than their foreign competitors.[23]

Domestic demand is harder to quantify due to a lack of statistical records, but the evidence generally points to a growing and widening market in cloth, particularly in the later fourteenth century. Although the total domestic consumption of cloth probably fell slightly in the century after the Black Death, this reflected the drop in the total population, which had fallen by over 50 per cent (Table 1). Rising living

[22] John Oldland, 'The Economic Impact of Clothmaking on Rural Society, 1300–1550', in Martin Allen and Matthew Davies, eds, *Medieval Merchants and Money. Essays in Honour of James L. Bolton* (London, 2016), pp. 230–1. See below, Chapter 1, for an explanation of cloth-making processes.

[23] These fiscal policies gave the English cloth industry a cost advantage of 25–30 per cent: J.H. Munro, 'The Symbiosis of Towns and Textiles', *Journal of Early Modern History* 3 (1999), pp. 37–40; Britnell, *Britain and Ireland*, pp. 327–9.

standards and increased consumer spending, explored below, meant that the consumption of cloth per head of population increased.[24]

This growth in output was even greater than that suggested by the increase in the number of cloths produced for domestic and overseas markets. This is because the average weight of woollen cloth increased over the period too (Table 1). Woollen cloths became heavier as the market moved from light worsteds to heavier broadcloths, and then continued to increase in weight as wool prices fell and quality expectations rose, and as English merchants used their cost advantage in obtaining wool more cheaply to capture continental markets.[25]

In the later fourteenth century, cloth production centred on a few major towns, including Coventry, Colchester, Norwich, Salisbury and York. Each town made its own speciality fabric and used a readily accessible port for its cloth exports. York produced broadcloths exported through Hull; Norwich manufactured worsted shipped via Yarmouth; Coventry specialised in blue woollen cloths exported through the ports of the Wash; Salisbury made rays (cloths with stripes woven into the pattern) shipped through Southampton; and Colchester specialised in middle-grade russet cloth, shipped from its own port of Hythe and from Ipswich.[26]

During the second half of the fifteenth century, cloth production moved out of the larger towns and became increasingly centred on rural localities, most notably in the Stour valley of Suffolk, the Stroud valley of Gloucestershire, western Wiltshire, the Aire and Calder valleys of the West Riding of Yorkshire, east Devon, and parts of Kent, Hampshire and Berkshire. There was also growth around Kendal in the Lake District, and along the Welsh border. Many of these localities also developed their own specialities. Western Wiltshire became noted for white woollen broadcloths, the Stroud region was known for Bristol red, and Newbury developed as a centre for making shorter cloths known as kerseys. More and more the new cloth-making centres sold and exported their cloth through London, as merchants in the capital increasingly dominated networks of marketing and credit. Following disruption to other overseas markets, cloth exports became further directed to the London–Antwerp market, and increasingly focused on higher-priced, heavier cloths.[27]

[24] C. Dyer, *Standards of Living in the Later Middle Ages: Social Change in England, c.1200–1520* (Cambridge, 1989), pp. 176–7; C. Dyer, *A Country Merchant, 1495–1520: Trading and Farming at the End of the Middle Ages* (Oxford, 2012), p. 17. See also John Oldland, 'Wool and Cloth Production in Late Medieval and Early Tudor England', *EcHR* 67 (2014), pp. 39, 41.

[25] Oldland, 'Economic Impact', pp. 230–1.

[26] Britnell, *Britain and Ireland*, p. 352.

[27] Oldland, 'Wool and Cloth Production', pp. 35–6.

WHY DID ENGLISH CLOTH-MAKING EXPAND AFTER 1350?

The expansion of the English cloth industry in the two centuries after 1350, while not constant, was so dramatic that it is important to consider briefly the dynamics influencing this growth and forming the environment in which the clothier emerged. Here we explore the factors responsible for the expansion of the industry; the causes of growth in particular localities are examined later, in Chapter 3.

Consumer spending

Demand for cloth was stimulated by the enhanced incomes that many peasants and wage earners enjoyed after the Black Death. This enabled them to buy better-quality clothing that many contemporary observers regarded as unbefitting to their status. After 1350 peasant clothing was transformed by changes in fashion, including the introduction of closer-fitting clothing, loose outer garments, and more vivid colours. Complaints that lower classes were wearing expensive cloth and luxurious ornaments were first raised formally in sumptuary legislation in 1363, which attempted to regulate clothing according to social status. Referring to the 'outrageous and excessive apparel of many people, contrary to their estate and degree', this statue restricted the servants of lords to wear clothing made from cloth of not more than 2 marks in value, and craftsmen and yeomen to cloth worth not more than £2. Agricultural workers were to wear only coarse cloth known as blanket or russet.[28]

Such legislation reflected the views of contemporary writers. The monastic chronicler Henry Knighton (d. *c.*1396) bemoaned 'the elation of the inferior people in dress and accoutrements in these days, so that one person cannot be discerned from another, in splendour of dress or belongings'.[29] The poet John Gower (d. 1408) looked back nostalgically to when labourers wore clothing of plain grey. Geoffrey Chaucer (c.1340–1400) expressed similar sentiments in his poem, 'The Former Age', of c.1380:

> No mader, welde, or wood no litestere
> Ne knew; the flees was of his former hewe

[28] 2 marks = £1 6s 8d; *The Black Death*, ed. R. Horrox (Manchester, 1994), pp. 340–2.

[29] *Chronicon Henrici Knighton vel Cnitthon, monachi Leycestrensis*, ed. Joseph Rawson Lumby, 2 vols (London, 1889–95), ii, p. 299. John Hatcher, 'England in the Aftermath of the Black Death', *Past and Present* 144 (1994), p. 18.

(No madder, weld, or woad no dyer knew;
the fleece was of its former hue)[30]

The late medieval peasant could afford to dress more colourfully than his or her predecessors, with blues, greens and reds replacing whites and russets.

Inventories reveal the extent of individual ownership of clothes. John Jackson of Grimston in Yorkshire, a peasant with a modest landholding, owned three garments, a tunic and two gowns worth 7s 4d, as well as sheets and a coverlet. Although peasants like this owned only a relatively small number of garments, they must have been forced to replace at least some of them on a regular basis. Wealthier farmers and traders might own as many as nine garments, and bought higher-quality cloth at 3s per yard. The aristocracy bought the most expensive woollen cloth at 5s or 6s per yard, as well as cheaper materials for liveries for their servants and followers. By 1500, it has been estimated that domestic demand accounted for almost 4 million yards of cloth, or 160,000 whole cloths, twice the total of exports.[31]

Another stimulus behind the increasing consumer demand for cloth was the changing climate of the late Middle Ages. Longer and colder winters increased demand for warmer, heavier broadcloths, which required more wool than the lighter fabrics that had dominated production in the thirteenth century. Falling temperatures may even have prompted the growing fashion for darker, heat-absorbing colours during the fifteenth century.[32]

Wool supplies

English wool ranged widely in quality and price, but from the twelfth to the sixteenth centuries certain varieties were considered the finest in Europe, particularly those from Shropshire and Herefordshire, parts of the Cotswolds, and Lincolnshire.[33] The years after the Black Death saw a major shift in agriculture from cereal growing to pastoral farming. Animal husbandry required less labour than cultivating the fields, and the collapse of grain prices in the late fourteenth century and persistently low prices and high wages in the early fifteenth century further

[30] *eChaucer: Chaucer in the Twenty-First Century* website, http://echaucer.machias.edu/formage/

[31] Dyer, *Age of Transition*, pp. 78–9, 175–7.

[32] N.R. Amor, *From Wool to Cloth. The Triumph of the Suffolk Clothier* (Bungay, 2016), p. 59. For alternative explanations for the fashion for darker fabrics, see John Munro, 'The Anti-Red Shift—To the Dark Side: Colour Changes in Flemish Luxury Woollens, 1300–1550', in Robin Netherton and Gale R. Owen-Crocker, eds, *Medieval Clothing and Textiles* 3 (Woodbridge, 2007), pp. 87–91.

[33] *CHWT*, pp. 185–6. See also below, Chapter 1, pp. 43–4.

encouraged the conversion of arable land into pasture in most parts of the country. In Staffordshire, for example, the percentage of pasture recorded in conveyancing documents known as final concords rose from 3 per cent to 31 per cent between the middle of the fourteenth century and end of the fifteenth.[34] Across the country, the balance between arable and grassland probably shifted from being equal in 1300 to two-thirds grassland by 1500, although pasture was used to feed cattle as well as sheep.[35] The number of wool producers expanded rapidly in the late fourteenth and early fifteenth centuries as increasing numbers of larger estates were leased out and many smaller-scale producers entered the market. For a growing number of farmers, sheep farming proved a more attractive proposition than cereals, but it was not necessarily lucrative for all these producers. The average price that an English grower received for a stone of wool fell from 4.2s in the first decade of the 1400s to 2.3s by the 1450s, and remained depressed for much of the century. Growers devoted time and money searching for potential customers, even offering extended credit to would-be purchasers.[36] This buyers' market helped English cloth-makers. They were supported further by customs duties on wool exports, which kept the cost of wool to English cloth producers lower than to their foreign competitors.

A group of intermediaries emerged linking this growing network of buyers and sellers. They bought from a range of different producers and sold to local clothiers and merchant exporters of wool. Wool exports were more tightly controlled than cloth, and sales of wool had to be made through a staple town, periodically in England, and periodically abroad, to aid the collection of customs duties. From 1363, the wool Staple was usually at Calais. Many of the wool exporters became affiliated to the Company of the Staple of Calais, a monopolistic enterprise with responsibility for trade and ordinances restricting the export of bullion.[37] These Merchant Staplers, as they became known, included the Cely family (c.1450–c.1500) of London, who relied largely on wool supplies from wool trader William Midwinter of Northleach, and Thomas Betson (d. 1486), who entered into partnership with Sir William Stonor (c.1449–94), owner of sheep-runs in the Chilterns and Cotswolds. The letters of the Cely and Stonor families have survived and provide a

[34] E. Miller, ed., *The Agrarian History of England and Wales*, iii: *1348–1500* (Cambridge, 1991), p. 79.

[35] Oldland, 'Wool and Cloth Production', p. 28.

[36] John Hatcher, 'The Great Slump of the Mid-Fifteenth Century', in R.H. Britnell and J. Hatcher, eds, *Progress and Problems in Medieval England: Essays in Honour of Edward Miller* (Cambridge, 1996), pp. 249–51.

[37] Nigel Saul, 'The Wool Merchants and their Brasses', *Transactions of the Monumental Brass Society* 17 (2006), pp. 315–35.

detailed picture of the organisation of the wool trade, which the cloth industry lacks.[38] Another notable Merchant Stapler was John Barton (d. 1491), who enlarged the churches of Holme and North Muskham near Newark-on-Trent.[39]

Government policies: customs duties

Customs payable on wool exports were first introduced in 1275 at 6s 8d per sack for both English and foreign merchants. From the 1330s though, these levies were increased to fund the war with France. English merchants now paid £2 on a sack of wool and alien merchants paid £2 3s 4d, but rates for the latter group rose to nearly £4 by the end of the fifteenth century, placing them at an increasing disadvantage compared to native merchants. In the long term these customs duties discouraged the export of English wool and enabled English cloth-makers to source wool more cheaply than their foreign competitors.[40] Raw wool still comprised about one-third of all exports from English ports around 1470, but by c.1540 had shrunk to nearer 5 per cent. These customs duties did not discriminate between different qualities of wool, so they were more of a disincentive for the export of cheaper wools than for finer wools. It appears that it was the king's need for money that drove this policy, and 'the benefit that accrued to the English cloth industry was almost an accidental by-product'.[41]

Government policies: settlement of Flemish textile workers

The Crown, however, also made more deliberate attempts to promote the English textile industry through legislation. Edward II's Ordinance of the Staple in 1326 promised the grant of suitable franchises to weavers, fullers, dyers and other cloth-workers, and his son Edward III enacted that any man or woman in the realm could produce cloth; no foreign textiles were to be imported except for the royal family, the nobility or the rich; and suitable franchises would be conceded to all overseas cloth-workers wishing to establish themselves in England. Another strand of this policy was put into practice in 1331 when Edward granted letters of

[38] Christine Carpenter, 'Stonor family (*per. c.*1315–*c.*1500)', and George Holmes, 'Cely family (*per. c.*1450–*c.*1500)', *ODNB*; E. Power, 'Thomas Betson: A merchant of the Staple in the Fifteenth Century', in E. Power, *Medieval People* (London, 1924), pp. 120–51; A. Hanham, *The Celys and their World: An English Merchant Family of the Fifteenth Century* (Cambridge, 1985).

[39] John S. Lee, '"Tis the sheep have paid for all": Merchant Commemoration in Late Medieval Newark', *Transactions of the Monumental Brass Society* 19 (2017), pp. 301–27.

[40] Britnell, *Britain and Ireland*, pp. 327–9.

[41] Michael Prestwich, *The Three Edwards: War and State in England 1272–1377* (London, 1980), p. 243.

protection to the Flemish weaver John Kempe and his men to exercise and teach their trade.[42] This was followed in 1333 by collective grants to all textile workers from Flanders and Brabant coming to England, and between 1336 and 1343 to specific immigrants in York, Winchester, Huntingdonshire and Berkshire. After the forced departure in 1351 of nearly 1,500 rebels, mostly textile workers, from the county of Flanders, Edward III issued letters of protection to all those who wished to establish themselves in his kingdom. Flemish weavers, fullers and dyers could be found in London, Winchester, Norwich, Bristol, Abingdon and York during the fourteenth century.[43]

Earlier generations of historians credited Edward III with stimulating the English textile industry through this policy of encouraging the immigration of Flemish cloth-workers, but later historians have been more sceptical about its impact. In Yorkshire and Essex the number of Flemings in the cloth industry has been seen as minimal, and their influence in rural areas as negligible.[44] Noting the wider influence of Flanders on the economy and society of Suffolk through overseas trade and some stylistic similarities in architecture, it has been suggested that Suffolk textile manufacturers copied the latest fashions in patterns and warps, producing cheap cloths in the Flemish style: 'Flemish weaves exercised a greater influence upon Suffolk cloth-making than Flemish weavers.'[45]

Recent research, however, is reappraising the role of Flemish immigrants in the development of the English cloth industry in the later fourteenth century, revealing how they provided labour, expertise and financial resources to support the development of the cloth industry in London, Colchester, Great Yarmouth and elsewhere. A small group of prosperous Flemings and Brabanters successfully established a separate guild of foreign weavers in London in 1362. This guild was sufficiently influential to negotiate, in 1380, a working compromise with the English cloth-workers in London and resolve a long-standing tension over the payment of the annual sum owed to the king by the city's weavers. Around fifty Flemish artisans, predominantly weavers, are known to have resided in London in the third quarter of the fourteenth century. In the fifteen years after 1351, at least 126 people from the Low Countries migrated to Colchester. In several cases, these immigrants were described by the

[42] *CPR 1330–4*, p. 161.

[43] E. Lipson, *The Economic History of England*, i: *The Middle Ages*, 12th edn (London, 1959), pp. 451–3; Bart Lambert and Milan Pajic, 'Drapery in Exile: Edward III, Colchester and the Flemings, 1351–1367', *History* 99 (2014), pp. 733–53.

[44] Heaton, *Yorkshire Woollen*, pp. 13–20; L.R. Poos, *A Rural Society after the Black Death: Essex, 1350–1525* (Cambridge, 1991), p. 70.

[45] Mark Bailey, 'Technology and the Growth of Textile Manufacture in Suffolk', *Proceedings of the Suffolk Institute of Archaeology and History* 42 (2009), p. 14.

family name 'Flemyng' in the Colchester court records. Twenty Flemings in cloth-making crafts entered the freedom of York between 1341 and 1361. Flemish weavers in Bristol were fined for taking excessive amounts for their work in 1363, and in Bath they were among those weavers taxed in 1381.[46] The cloth industry in Flanders was more integrated than that in England, with a more sophisticated organisation: weaver-drapers operated a domestic or putting-out system of production, in which materials were put out to workers in return for payment.[47] Some of these Flemish immigrants appear to have operated as weaver-drapers in England, stimulating the expansion of the putting-out system and the associated rise of the clothier.[48]

ENTREPRENEURS AND CAPITALISTS

In economic terms, an entrepreneur is an individual who organises production, bringing together the factors of production, land, labour and capital, in the most feasible way to produce goods or services.[49] The manufacture of cloth requires several different stages of production, and from an early date some of these processes, as well as the marketing of cloth, were being co-ordinated by merchants or other craftsmen through a putting-out system. From these entrepreneurs, the clothier eventually emerged.

The expansion of the cloth industry in north-western Europe during the eleventh and twelfth centuries demanded new arrangements to co-ordinate a larger group of trained and specialised workers. Historians from earlier generations, such as Henry Pirenne, argued that by the thirteenth century, merchant-entrepreneurs came to dominate the import of wool and other raw materials and the production of cloth, 'gaining vertical control of the product virtually from sheep to sales hall', and imposing a form of industrial capitalism on textile trades. Subsequent research has questioned many of these certainties. Jehan Boinebroke of Douai

[46] Lambert and Pajic, 'Drapery in Exile'; Bart Lambert and Milan Pajic, 'Common Profit versus Corporate Protectionism: The London Weavers and the Crown's Economic Immigration Policy in the Fourteenth Century', *Journal of British Studies* 55 (2016), pp. 633–57; Milan Pajic, 'The Migration of Flemish Weavers to England in the Fourteenth Century: The Economic Influence and Transfer of Skills 1331–1381', University of Strasbourg and University of Ghent, Docteur thesis, 2016; Milan Pajic, *Immigration and Economic Development. Flemish Textile Workers in England 1331–1400* (forthcoming).

[47] *CHWT*, p. 219.

[48] See below, pp. 19–20.

[49] For differing perspectives on entrepreneurship, see Mark Casson and Catherine Casson, *The Entrepreneur in History from Medieval Merchant to Modern Business Leader* (Basingstoke, 2013), pp. 12–41.

(d. 1286), for example, has often been highlighted as an early industrial capitalist. He was, however, principally a wool merchant, providing wool on credit to drapers. Most of his wage-earning employees worked in the wool trade, and there is no evidence that he directly supervised the main processes of cloth production.[50] Merchants trading in wool, dyestuffs and finished cloths often took a key role but a large amount of production was undertaken by weaver-drapers. They were usually subordinate to merchants, from whom they bought wool and other raw materials on credit, and sold manufactured but unfinished cloths to other merchants. These weaver-drapers became known as *drapier* in France and the Low Countries and *lanaiuoli* in Italy.[51] In the 1390s, Francesco di Marco Datini operated large wool-processing workshops in Prato, where over eighty workers engaged in carding and combing wool, but this wool was put-out to spinners living within the town and surrounding countryside and when the yarn was returned to the workshop it was then distributed to weavers who also worked at home.[52]

In England too, there are examples of entrepreneurs engaging with several aspects of cloth production. Regulations dating from the late twelfth century indicate that manufacturing craftworkers in Beverley, Lincoln, Marlborough, Oxford and Winchester had become economically dependent on leading citizens who controlled production and access to markets. In response, these craftworkers, with royal backing, established their own associations, known as guilds. They paid between £2 and £12 yearly to the king for various privileges that gave them a monopoly on cloth-making in their areas.[53] In the 1250s, two Leicester citizens, Henry Houhil and Richard of Shilton, were dyeing wool, paying fullers to finish their cloths, and trading at Boston Fair. Thirteenth-century Londoners who produced coarse and cheap woollen cloth known as burel employed weavers to work for them, and paid them for piece-work. In 1348, it was reported that many citizens of Lincoln kept hired weavers making cloths

[50] James M. Murray, *Bruges, Cradle of Capitalism, 1280–1390* (Cambridge, 2005), p. 278. For older interpretations, see Henri Pirenne, *Economic and Social History of Medieval Europe* (London, 1936), pp. 188–91; E.M. Carus-Wilson, 'The Woollen Industry', in Edward Miller, Cynthia Postan and M.M. Postan, eds, *The Cambridge Economic History of Europe*, ii: *Trade and Industry in the Middle Ages*, 2nd edn (Cambridge, 1987), pp. 639–40.

[51] *CHWT*, pp. 218–20.

[52] Francesco Ammannati, 'Francesco di Marco Datini's Wool Workshops', in Giampero Nigro, ed., *Francesco di Marco Datini. The Man the Merchant* (Florence, 2010), pp. 489–514.

[53] E.M. Carus-Wilson, 'The English Cloth Industry in the Twelfth and Early Thirteenth Centuries', *EcHR* 14 (1944), pp. 32–50, reprinted in E.M. Carus-Wilson, *Medieval Merchant Venturers*, 2nd edn (London, 1967), pp. 235–8; *VCH Wiltshire*, iv, p. 118; Miller and Hatcher, *Medieval England*, pp. 104–6.

for sale.[54] Some rural industry was also being encouraged by urban entrepreneurs, who provided capital and commercial services to support production and distribution. A group of weavers at Beckley, Cowley and Islip stated in 1275 that their looms had been delivered to them by a group of Oxford merchants active in the wine, wool and cloth trades. Complaints were made in 1260 that Leicester merchants had fulling mills for finishing cloth outside the town.[55] There are even occasional examples of a factory system of production. A writ of 1339 stated that Thomas Blanket and other burgesses of Bristol had set up instruments for weaving cloth and employed weavers and other workmen in their own houses. Yet generally in the mid fourteenth century, the English textile industry consisted of craftsmen working as their own masters.[56]

By the late fourteenth century, the growing market for cloth both at home and abroad, and the booming cloth industry in towns such as Colchester, Exeter, Winchester and York, encouraged many urban families to dabble in the cloth trade. Many people who had some spare money invested in cloth production. Some employed craftsmen to work up materials, hoping to profit on the final product. Among these earlier entrepreneurs were some of the Flemish weavers who had migrated from the Low Countries, where capitalist relationships between merchants and cloth-workers were much more evident. Many of these immigrants had enjoyed a high economic status before leaving Flanders, and a number became active wool exporters from Yarmouth and London, so it is likely that some had the resources to organise the whole production process. In Yarmouth and Colchester, Flemish weavers were contracting with other immigrants to buy wool, full and dye it, and in the 1370s in Yarmouth they attracted frequent fines from the borough court for selling cloth. In London, the amounts of cloth that the Flemings took to be taxed between 1374 and 1377 were consistently higher than those brought by their English counterparts over the same years. Five of the Flemish exiles are referred to in the London sources as merchants or merchant-drapers.[57] John Kempe had received protection for 'his men, servants and apprentices' in 1331, and in 1343 John Bruyn was described as a 'burgess of Ghent, now making stay in Abingdon, making woollen cloth there and trading in other wares within the realm, and his men and

[54] *CPR 1348–50*, p. 120; Carus-Wilson, 'English Cloth Industry', pp. 228–35.

[55] Miller, 'Fortunes', p. 73

[56] *Calendar of Close Rolls, 1339–41*, p. 311; Lipson, *Economic history*, i, p. 469; R.H. Britnell, *The Commercialisation of English Society, 1000–1500*, 2nd edn (Manchester, 1996), p. 149.

[57] Pajic, 'Migration of Flemish Weavers', pp. 210–39.

servants'.[58] These early Flemish entrepreneurs may have stimulated more coordinated production in the English cloth industry.

Perhaps influenced by their Flemish immigrant neighbours, some English weavers also coordinated the cloth-making process, like William Okle of Colchester. He brought a court case in 1388, claiming that he had organised the manufacture of a broadcloth on behalf of Matilda Westoneys, who now owed him 10s 6d. He itemised his costs to have the wool spun, dyed and woven, and in having the cloth fulled. William claimed that he had lent Matilda part of the wool, and he had paid for hanging the cloth on tenterhooks after washing and fulling. On the basis of the low production costs revealed in this legal case, it has been argued that it was not only the cheapness of the wool but also the level of manufacturing costs that allowed English towns like Colchester to compete successfully in continental Europe.[59]

Merchants could also be found funding and employing cloth-workers, supplying yarn to weavers, and cloth to shearmen, fullers and dyers. Piecemeal evidence for these business relationships usually emerges only when problems arose: in Exeter in 1390, John Grey prosecuted weaver Michael Cartere for failing to place Grey's cloth in his 'Webtakel' at the time Grey wanted. John Grey also claimed damages from Philip Touker for tearing his cloth during the fulling process. Another Exeter merchant, Richard Swan, accused Peter Yurle of replacing nearly half of the 51 lb of white yarn that he had supplied him with weaker yarn, damaging Richard's cloth to the value of 100s. These merchants also dominated the import of dyestuffs, servicing dyers across east Devon and west Somerset. On the basis of such examples, it has been argued that in Exeter the capitalist clothier had emerged by the late fourteenth century from this mercantile background.[60] Similar examples can be found in York, where a handful of merchants coordinated cloth-making between wool producers, weavers, fullers and dyers. Walter de Kelstern was reported to have bought ten sacks of wool at Scotton and carried them to York to make cloth in 1338. Some of the city's merchants who traded overseas left testamentary bequests to their workers, including artisans who lived in towns and villages beyond York. Robert Holme of York (d. 1396) made bequests to five dyers, including one from Pontefract. In 1439 Thomas Clynt of York left money to fullers in Tadcaster and fullers and weavers in York and its suburbs who had worked for him,

[58] *CPR 1330–4*, p. 161; *CPR 1343–5*, p. 115.

[59] R.H. Britnell, *Growth and Decline in Colchester, 1300–1525* (Cambridge, 1986), pp. 60–3. See also below, pp. 74–5.

[60] Maryanne Kowaleski, *Local Markets and Regional Trade in Medieval Exeter* (Cambridge, 1995), pp. 150–2, 272–3.

and Thomas Curtas made gifts to fullers in Stamford Bridge and York in 1461. Robert Collinson (d. 1458) probably bought wool directly from rural producers, and co-ordinated the finishing of cloth from dyeing to shearing. He left bequests to unnamed individuals scattered across the northern counties who may have been his wool suppliers, spinners and weavers, as well as to 'dyers, fullers, shearmen and weavers working with me, from whom I have had any goods, a good breakfast and 12d each'.[61]

The ulnage accounts, recording tax paid on cloths sold, reveal a few sellers in some communities paying subsidies on more cloths than they could possibly have produced themselves, even as full-time cloth-workers. At Barnstaple in Devon in 1396–97, John Parman paid ulnage on 1,080 narrow cloths and Richard Burnard on 1,005. In an account of the following year though, the closest equivalents to these names, John Parkman and Richard Barnard, were responsible for only 12 and 24 cloths, leading one historian to conclude that if the accounts were reliable, these individuals were merchants buying the cloth for export, rather than clothiers organising its production.[62] Generally though, the size of production was typically very small. In Colchester, eighty-three sellers sold 10 cloths or fewer; only four sellers sold 100 or more cloths. There must remain a strong suspicion that some returns simply amalgamated smaller producers into the totals of their wealthier neighbours. What is also not clear from these records is the extent to which these individuals had financed the entire process of cloth production from spinning to finishing, and to what extent they bought cloth at various stages of its making. The owner of the finished cloth who was offering it for sale was liable to pay the ulnage, regardless of who had produced it. Only about half those selling cloth at Winchester, for example, appear to have been actively involved in producing it themselves. At York it seems to have been more usual for merchants and drapers to buy cloth from independent producers and to pay the tax on it when they had it sealed.[63] Even so, in the 1390s, only around 30 per cent of the merchants from York and Beverley who were exporting cloth through Hull were also presenting cloth for sealing. Most exporters from these Yorkshire towns must have been buying cloth from small producers or from middlemen.[64]

[61] YBIA, York Prob. Reg. 1, fols 100v–3v (Holme); Prob. Reg. 3, fols 378–80 (Collinson), 438–9 (Curtas), 567–8v (Clynt); Jennifer Kermode, *Medieval Merchants: York, Beverley, and Hull in the later Middle Ages* (Cambridge, 1998), pp. 205–6; *VCH Yorkshire: The City of York*, p. 88.

[62] E.M. Carus-Wilson, 'The Aulnage Accounts: A Criticism', *EcHR* 2 (1929), pp. 39–60, reprinted in Carus-Wilson, *Medieval Merchant Venturers*, p. 285.

[63] Phoebe Merrick, 'Taxing Medieval Cloth', *The Local Historian* 32 (2002), pp. 230–2; *VCH Yorkshire: The City of York*, p. 88.

[64] Kermode, *Medieval Merchants*, p. 204.

The rise of the clothier

While there were undoubtedly entrepreneurs organising cloth production during the later fourteenth century in some towns, who might be seen as forerunners to the clothier, this book argues that the clothier emerged in the particular economic conditions of the fifteenth century, and that they were a notable feature of cloth-making in small towns and villages, rather than larger towns, as is explored in Chapter 3. We can chart the rise of the clothier in the use of the term and the frequency with which references to clothiers appear in the historical sources. This is not foolproof because the Latin term *pannarius* can be translated as either 'clothier' or 'draper', but fortunately one particular series of documents, the cases brought to the Court of Common Pleas in Westminster, records the occupations of the plaintiff and defendant in English. The *Middle English Dictionary* notes that the word is first recorded as an occupational surname in the late thirteenth century and its earliest recorded use as a noun is in William Langland's *Piers Plowman* of the late fourteenth century, possibly around 1370. In this work, Langland refers to clothiers preparing their wool before spinning by carding and combing it, and suggests that the virtues of wisdom and wit are similarly only valued if they have been sorted out by greed to serve the user's purpose:

> Wisdom and wyt now is not worþ a risshe
> But it be cardit wiþ coueitise as cloþeris don here wolle.
>
> (Wisdom and wit now are not worth a rush
> Unless they're carded with covetousness as clothiers card wool).[65]

The earliest known use of 'cloth-maker' also dates from this period. The Wycliffite Bible, dating from before 1382, translates a passage from the first book of Samuel as, 'Your daughters he shall make to him oynement makers, and fier makers, and cloth-makers.'[66]

The terms 'clothier', 'cloth-maker' and 'cloth-man' seem to have been used interchangeably and without any discernible distinction. Indeed sometimes, the same individual could even be described on separate

[65] *Middle English Dictionary*, eds Hans Kurath, Sherman M. Kuhn and Robert E. Lewis (Ann Arbor, 1952–2001): 'clothier'. *OED*: 'clothier'. William Langland, *Piers Plowman. A Parallel-Text Edition of the A, B, C and Z Versions*, ed. A.V.C. Schmidt, 2 vols (London, 1995), i, pp. 398–9 (Version B, Passus X, lines 17–18; Version A, Passus XI, lines 17–18; Version C, Passus XI, lines 14–15), and ii, p. 281 for dating the versions of the text. William Langland, *Will's Vision of Piers Plowman. An Alliterative Verse Translation by E. Talbot Donaldson*, eds E.D. Kirk and J.H. Anderson (New York, 1990), p. 88.

[66] 1 Samuel viii, v. 13. *Middle English Dictionary*: 'cloth-maker'; *OED*: 'cloth-maker'. The King James Bible translates the same passage as: 'And he will take your daughters to be confectionaries, and to be cooks, and to be bakers.'

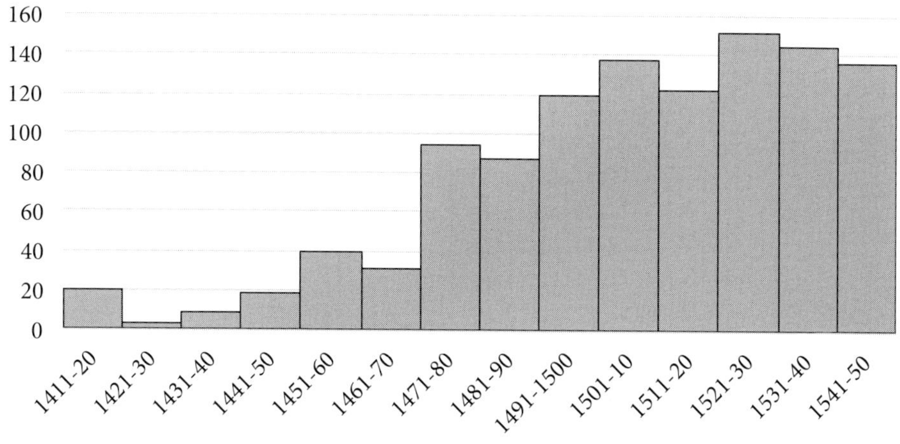

Figure 2. Clothiers, cloth-makers and cloth-men appearing in Court of Common Pleas cases, 1410–1550

Note: Numbers are an average for each decade.

Source: AALT indexes.

occasions by each of these three titles, like the entries for John Stokton of Frome in Somerset in the plea rolls in 1465.[67]

The cases in the Court of Common Pleas show the growing role of the clothier within society. This was a court held in Westminster to which litigants from around the country came to recover debts worth £2 or more. About 70 to 80 per cent of pleas concerned debts while other actions included titles to land and alleged trespass, including infringement of legislation.[68] Of those plea rolls that have now been indexed, the clothier is first recorded in 1418, in Croscombe and Wells in Somerset.[69] Growing numbers of clothiers were involved in cases over the course of the fifteenth and the first half of the sixteenth century (Figure 2).

The evidence from the Court of Common Pleas points to the emergence of the clothier during the fifteenth century. Other historians, generally focusing on a single region, have differed in their dating of the clothier's first appearance. The activities of Exeter merchants cited above led Maryanne Kowaleski to argue that clothiers had emerged in this city

[67] Amor, *From Wool to Cloth*, p. 190, citing TNA, CP 40/814, m. 24, 211d, 351d (AALT 50, 1392d, 1663d).

[68] Amor, *From Wool to Cloth*, pp. 8–10; Jonathan Mackman and Matthew Stevens, 'Introducing Common Pleas', *Court of Common Pleas: The National Archives, CP40 1399–1500* (London, 2010), British History Online website, http://www.british-history.ac.uk/no-series/common-pleas/1399-1500/introducing-common-pleas

[69] See below, p. 123.

by the end of the fourteenth century. Looking at the late-fourteenth-century ulnage accounts, Louis Salzman suggested that this evidence 'seems to limit the spheres of influence of the capitalist clothiers to a few definite towns prior to the beginning of the fifteenth century'.[70] Richard Britnell found clothiers appearing in Colchester in the late fifteenth century, while George Ramsay and Herbert Heaton saw the capitalist clothiers of Wiltshire and Yorkshire developing mainly in the Tudor period.[71] It is, of course, entirely possible that clothiers became visible in some places earlier than others: Chapter 3 explores the rise of the clothier in different cloth-making regions.

Were clothiers early capitalists?

Clothiers have fascinated many generations of historians, and several have identified them as early examples of capitalists. Capitalism is a difficult term as it has been used in different ways by different writers. Some historians, notably Robert Brenner, have placed greater emphasis on capitalist developments in agriculture rather than commerce, and have focused on social and property relationships between landlords and tenants.[72] Several historians though, have considered that the leading clothiers of the later Middle Ages were early capitalists, as they controlled labour, owned capital and property, and concentrated production within their hands. This has wider implications for economists and other social scientists, as one of the major questions in studies of pre-modern economies has been the causes and timing of the transition from a feudal to a capitalist economy. This change was marked by the concentration of the means of production (that is, the facilities and resources for producing goods) in the hands of a few entrepreneurs, and by a labour force working for contractual wages and separated from the means of production. This was occurring in some parts of the English cloth industry by the later Middle Ages, as some clothiers owned resources for cloth-making, such as looms, fulling mills and dye pans, and employed workers on their premises.[73] More frequently though, clothiers coordinated the separate

[70] Kowaleski, *Exeter*, p. 150; L.F. Salzman, *English Industries of the Middle Ages*, 2nd edn (London, 1923), pp. 226–8.

[71] Britnell, *Colchester*, pp. 184–5; G.D. Ramsay, *The Wiltshire Woollen Industry in the Sixteenth and Seventeenth Centuries*, 2nd edn (London, 1965), pp. 6–30; Heaton, *Yorkshire Woollen*, pp. 89–101.

[72] R. Brenner, 'Agrarian Class Structure and Economic Development in Pre-Industrial Europe', *Past and Present* 70 (1976), pp. 30–75. Brenner's model is examined in Jane Whittle, *The Development of Agrarian Capitalism: Land and Labour in Norfolk 1440–1580* (Oxford, 2000), and Hatcher and Bailey, *Modelling*, pp. 106–20.

[73] Britnell, 'Commerce and Capitalism'; Dyer, 'Were There Any Capitalists', pp. 305–7, 325.

activities of artisans who worked semi-independently at home through a putting-out system, which Karl Marx viewed as a transitional form in the move from a feudal to capitalist mode of production.[74] Other historians, however, have taken different views, and it is important to consider the clothier in relation to these varying historiographical interpretations.

William Cunningham (1849–1919), writing his textbook in 1890 that went through six editions and laid the foundation for the study of economic history at the University of Cambridge, saw late-fifteenth-century clothiers as capitalists and the cloth trade as driving economic growth: 'In Edward IV's reign it [cloth-making] was carried on by capitalists, very much as it was in the eighteenth century, and the difficulties between the clothier and those whom he employed were very similar at these two periods.'[75] Cunningham's publications became standard works of reference on the industrial history of England and economic histories written in the early twentieth century, such as those by Ephraim Lipson and George Unwin, stressed the importance of the clothier.[76]

The origins of merchant capitalism before industrialisation were explored by Eileen Power (1889–1940), a leading medieval and economic historian of the inter-war period, who described areas of cloth-making as 'pockets of capitalism in a pre-capitalistic world'.[77] Her popular and enduring biographical account of the clothier Thomas Paycocke of Coggeshall, first published in 1924, ran to ten editions. Using the individual personality of Paycocke to explore wider trends within the cloth trade, Power drew on the textual evidence of Paycocke's will and the material evidence of his house, where she resided while working on her longer study *The Paycockes of Coggeshall*.[78] Her work was developed further by Eleanora Carus-Wilson (1897–1977), who made significant contributions to the early history of the textile industry, including a comprehensive assessment of the surviving customs accounts, investigations into the commercial structures of the Merchant Adventurers, and

[74] K. Marx, *Capital*, 3 vols (1867–94), iii, p. 227, https://www.marxists.org/archive/marx/works/download/pdf/Capital-Volume-III.pdf

[75] W. Cunningham, *The Growth of English Industry and Commerce during the Early and Middle Ages* (Cambridge, 1890), pp. 392–3.

[76] Gerard M. Koot, 'Cunningham, William (1849–1919)', *ODNB*; George Unwin, *Industrial Organization in the Sixteenth and Seventeenth Centuries*, 2nd edn (London, 1957); E. Lipson, *The History of the Woollen and Worsted Industries* (London, 1921); Lipson, *Economic History*.

[77] E. Power, *The Wool Trade in English Medieval History: Being the Ford Lectures* (Oxford, 1941), p. 6.

[78] E. Power, 'Thomas Paycocke of Coggeshall: An Essex Clothier in the Days of Henry VII', in Power, *Medieval People*, pp. 152–73. E. Power, *The Paycockes of Coggeshall* (London, 1920).

detailed regional studies, as well as a more provocative article tracing the introduction and diffusion of the fulling mill.[79]

Maurice Dobb (1900–76) noted the activities of clothiers in his landmark work on Marxist economic development, *Studies in the Development of Capitalism*, published in 1946. He identified clothiers as examples of merchant capital taking increasingly close control over production in the textile trades, mainly through extending handicraft production and breaking down urban monopolies. Dobb also noted a few examples of 'manufactory-capitalists', like John Winchcombe and William Stumpe who employed large numbers of workers in central workshops or factories. For Dobb, these men were 'considerable capitalists who were imbued with a desire to invest in industry'.[80] Those establishing capitalist enterprises in the textile industry were among the individuals identified by Richard Henry Tawney (1880–1962) as he sought to explain major shifts in attitude towards economic behaviour in this period.[81] The use of simple machinery, the introduction of workers from overseas, and particularly the move from towns to the countryside, were seen by J.D. Mackie in his *Oxford History of England* volume as the capitalist attitudes of 'men who understood competition better than custom'. Furthermore,

> The new clothier found a natural ally in the grazier who supplied wool in bulk and in their alliance may be seen the close connexion between the 'revolution' in industry and that in agriculture.[82]

Clothiers were prime examples of an increasingly capitalist mentality developing within sixteenth-century society, characterised by individualistic and acquisitive attitudes.

Such views were increasingly questioned, however, during the post-war period, as economic history started to focus more on quantifying growth and less on human agency. The expansion and decline of population was now seen as the key factor in explaining changes within the medieval economy. By the 1970s a new scepticism about the role of clothier could be found in the literature. According to D.C. Coleman,

[79] E.M. Carus-Wilson and O. Coleman, *England's Export Trade, 1275–1547* (Oxford, 1963); Carus-Wilson, 'The Woollen Industry'; E.M. Carus-Wilson, 'An Industrial Revolution of the Thirteenth Century', *EcHR* 11 (1941), pp. 39–60, reprinted in Carus-Wilson, *Medieval Merchant Venturers*, pp. 183–210; E.M. Carus-Wilson, 'Evidences of Industrial Growth on Some Fifteenth-Century Manors', *EcHR*, 2nd series 12 (1959), pp. 190–205; *VCH Wiltshire*, iv, pp. 115–47.

[80] Maurice Dobb, *Studies in the Development of Capitalism* (London, 1946), pp. 127–34, 138.

[81] R.H. Tawney, *Religion and the Rise of Capitalism* (Harmondsworth, 1938), pp. 79–80, 141–2.

[82] J.D. Mackie, *The Oxford History of England*, vii: *The Earlier Tudors 1485–1558* (Oxford, 1952), p. 463.

John Winchcombe and William Stumpe were 'boom-time freaks'. A.R. Bridbury saw the same individuals as 'men intoxicated by a sort of *folie de grandeur*', and wittily described the exceptional nature of Thomas Spring's wealth as 'one Spring does not make summer'.[83] Eric Kerridge queried historians' accounts of William Stumpe's large textile workshop in Malmesbury, which he felt were hardly justified by Leland's original description, and dismissed the scale of John Winchcombe's production as poetic licence.[84] F.F. Mendels put forward a model of proto-industrialisation in which the rural industries of the early modern period were seen as containing the conditions for subsequent factory-based manufacturing. While Mendels saw this process as creating an accumulation of capital in the hands of merchant entrepreneurs, his examples were drawn from the seventeenth and eighteenth centuries.[85] Even J.W. Gough, who thought that William Stumpe's weaving workshop at Malmesbury Abbey was 'the most authentic forerunner of the factory system', acknowledged that 'it would be a mistake to regard Stumpe as the inaugurator of an industrial revolution … for it seems quite clear that his establishment was quite exceptional, if not actually unique'.[86]

Studies of medieval trade and towns began to gain more prominence during the 1970s and 1980s. Clothiers were analysed by Richard Britnell as he examined the ways in which changes in commercial institutions and practices had important long-term implications for economic development. His work established commercialisation as an explanation of economic and social change, highlighting the importance of markets, urban growth and expanding trade.[87] While earlier generations of historians had identified the later Middle Ages as the key period in which commercial developments encouraged the emergence of capitalism, Britnell argued that the commercialisation of the economy occurred more rapidly between 1000 and 1300 than between 1300 and 1530. He

[83] D.C. Coleman, *Industry in Tudor and Stuart England* (London, 1975), p. 27; A.R. Bridbury, *Medieval English Clothmaking: An Economic Survey* (London, 1982), p. 11; A.R. Bridbury, 'English Provincial Towns in the Later Middle Ages', *EcHR*, 2nd series 34 (1981), p. 19.

[84] Eric Kerridge, *Textile Manufactures in Early Modern England* (Manchester, 1985), pp. 192, 196.

[85] F.F. Mendels, 'Proto-Industrialization: The First Phase of the Industrialization Process', *Journal of Economic History* 32 (1972), pp. 241–61; Michael Zell, *Industry in the Countryside: Wealden Society in the Sixteenth Century* (Cambridge, 1994), pp. 228–46.

[86] J.W. Gough, *The Rise of the Entrepreneur* (London, 1969), pp. 36, 42; John Gaisford, 'Elizabethan Entrepreneurs: Three Clothiers of the Frome Valley, 1550–1600', in J.P. Bowen and A.T. Brown, eds, *Custom and Commercialisation in English Rural Society: Revisiting Tawney and Postan* (Hatfield, 2016), pp. 207–8.

[87] Christopher Dyer, Richard Britnell obituary, *The Guardian*, 26 December 2013.

identified the increasing dependence on organisation by merchant clothiers in some parts of the cloth industry as one of the few significant moves towards capitalism in the later Middle Ages.[88]

Britnell was wary though, of over-exaggerating the role of clothiers in wider economic change. In his study of the region around Colchester, he warned against assuming that all the cloth-making villages of the region were enjoying industrial growth solely on the basis of 'evidence of an increasingly capitalist organisation', particularly in the absence of figures relating to output or sales.[89] His biographical entry for Thomas Paycocke speaks of an 'unremarkable career'.[90] He argued that the structural changes within the late medieval cloth industry, placing workers into dependence on merchant clothiers, could not have affected more than a few thousand people by 1500. He also noted that local economic development, like that arising from cloth-making, was often the outcome of entrepreneurial restructuring in trade and industry, rather than of net economic growth.[91] Nonetheless, Britnell argued that in particular localities, such as parts of Suffolk, wage labour in the cloth industry was so extensive by the 1520s that it made these areas peculiarly vulnerable to fluctuations in overseas markets, and the prospects of underemployment and unemployment.[92] His work has also informed much recent analysis of aspects of marketing networks in the Middle Ages, including credit, marketing infrastructure and market ethics: he noted that the grouping of textile towns in particular regions implied that such clusters offered advantages in mercantile organisation and credit, although these could be difficult to define.[93]

Recent years have seen a renewed interest in the textile industry. John Munro's research has helped to place the English industry within the context of wider European production and trade. He describes English clothiers as weaver-drapers, who, like their continental counterparts, organised production by putting out raw materials to workers

[88] Britnell, *Commercialisation*, pp. 233–5; Britnell, 'Commerce and Capitalism', pp. 359–69.

[89] Britnell, *Colchester*, p. 192.

[90] R.H. Britnell, 'Paycocke, Thomas (d. 1518)', *ODNB*.

[91] Britnell, 'Commerce and Capitalism', p. 369; Britnell, *Commercialisation*, p. 234; R.H. Britnell, 'The English Economy and the Government, 1450–1550', in J.L. Watts, ed, *The End of the Middle Ages? England in the Fifteenth and Sixteenth Centuries* (Stroud, 1998), pp. 89–97.

[92] Richard Britnell, 'The Woollen Textile Industry of Suffolk in the Later Middle Ages', *The Ricardian* 23 (2003), pp. 86–99.

[93] *CUHB*, pp. 319–20; Richard Britnell, 'Urban Demand in the English Economy, 1300–1600', in James A. Galloway, ed., *Trade, Urban Hinterlands and Market Integration* c.*1300–1600*, Centre for Metropolitan History Working Paper Series 3 (London, 2000), pp. 1–21.

in their own homes and collecting their finished products. John Oldland has cogently argued that historians have seriously underestimated the extent of employment in cloth-making and its role in promoting wider economic growth. He sees the rural clothier as taking a leading role through using capital and labour more effectively than the urban draper.[94] Craig Muldrew's work on the role of spinning, while focusing on the period after 1500, also emphasises the wider economic impact of the textile industry.[95] Nicholas Amor's detailed study of the Suffolk cloth industry has traced the rise of the Suffolk clothier to the period between 1470 and 1500.[96] There have been important studies of the economies and societies of particular textile regions, including western Berkshire, the Kentish Weald, Suffolk and Wiltshire.[97] Some cloth-making towns, and even a few individual clothiers, have been examined.[98] There is valuable information on cloth-making localities within the *Victoria County History*, and on individual clothier families within the *Oxford Dictionary of National Biography* and the *History of Parliament*.[99] Other studies have highlighted the role of fairs as outlets for cloth sales, and the role of London merchants in cloth purchases.[100] Less has been published on the social, political and religious dimensions of clothiers, but a few recent studies have looked at other groups of merchants. Jennifer Kermode

[94] *CHWT*, p. 218; Oldland, 'Economic Impact', p. 232.

[95] Craig Muldrew, '"Th'ancient Distaff" and "Whirling Spindle": Measuring the Contribution of Spinning to Household Earnings and the National Economy in England, 1550–1770', *EcHR*, 2nd series 65 (2012), pp. 498–526; Craig Muldrew, 'An Early Industrial Workforce: Spinning in the Countryside, *c.*1500–50', in Richard Jones and Christopher Dyer, eds, *Farmers, Consumers, Innovators. The World of Joan Thirsk* (Hatfield, 2016), pp. 79–88.

[96] Amor, *From Wool to Cloth*, p. 217.

[97] Margaret Yates, *Town and Countryside in Western Berkshire, c.1327–c.1600: Social and Economic Change* (Woodbridge, 2007); Zell, *Industry in the Countryside*; N.R. Amor, 'Merchant Adventurer or Jack of all Trades? The Suffolk Clothier in the 1460s', *Proceedings of the Suffolk Institute of Archaeology and History* 40 (2004), pp. 414–36; J.N. Hare, *A Prospering Society: Wiltshire in the Later Middle Ages* (Hatfield, 2011); Gaisford, 'Elizabethan Entrepreneurs'. Studies of individual towns include A. Betterton and D. Dymond, *Lavenham: Industrial Town* (Lavenham, 1989), and D.G. Shaw, *The Creation of a Community: The City of Wells in the Middle Ages* (Oxford, 1993).

[98] C. Jackson, 'Boom-Time Freaks or Heroic Industrial Pioneers? Clothing Entrepreneurs in Sixteenth- and Early Seventeenth-Century Berkshire', *Textile History* 39 (2008), pp. 145–71; David Peacock, 'The Winchcombe Family and the Woollen Industry in Sixteenth-Century Newbury', University of Reading, Ph.D. thesis, 2003.

[99] *VCH*; *ODNB*; *HoP*.

[100] John S. Lee, 'The Role of Fairs in Late Medieval England', in M. Bailey and S. Rigby, eds, *Town and Countryside in the Age of the Black Death: Essays in Honour of John Hatcher* (Turnhout, 2012), pp. 407–37; John Oldland, 'Making and Marketing Woollen Cloth in Late-Medieval London', *London Journal* 36 (2011), pp. 89–108.

analysed all levels of merchant society in the towns of York, Beverley and Hull. Pamela Nightingale and Anne Sutton have traced the social origins of the London Grocers and Mercers alongside commercial and constitutional developments.[101] Other recent research has suggested that there was a distinctive merchant outlook on life and death, and a class consciousness.[102] The examination of historic buildings and artistic analysis is also making important contributions. Detailed surveys of surviving buildings in Coggeshall and Lavenham have provided new information about these cloth-making communities. Close scrutiny of the stylistic influences of the carving on the Spring parclose screen in Lavenham church and Paycocke's house in Coggeshall has also shed important new evidence on the social aspirations of these families.[103] Such studies have drawn on a range of historical evidence, and it is to these sources that we now turn.

HISTORICAL SOURCES

Wills

Wills provide valuable insights into many aspects of economy, society, religion and culture. They follow a standard format, in which the man or woman making the will (the testator or testatrix) set out instructions regarding burial, made bequests to individuals, appointed executors and listed witnesses. Officials in ecclesiastical courts granted probate (the power for an executor to make the disbursements named in the will) and copied the wills into their registers. Wills, however, have their limitations. They tend to cover a limited period and are generally restricted to the wealthier. While they may include elaborate preambles and detailed concerns for the afterlife, it is very difficult to know the extent to which

[101] Kermode, *Medieval Merchants*; Pamela Nightingale, *A Medieval Mercantile Community: The Grocers' Company & the Politics & Trade of London, 1000–1485* (New Haven, 1995); Anne F. Sutton, *The Mercery of London: Trade, Goods and People, 1130–1578* (Aldershot, 2005).

[102] C. Burgess, 'Making Mammon Serve God: Merchant Piety in Later Medieval England', in C.M. Barron and A.F. Sutton, eds, *The Medieval Merchant* (Donington, 2014), pp. 183–207.

[103] D.F. Stenning, *Discovering Coggeshall. Timber-framed Buildings in the Town Centre* (Coggeshall, 2013); David Andrews, ed., *Discovering Coggeshall 2: The 1575 Rental Survey and the Dated Buildings* (Coggeshall, 2013); Leigh Alston, 'The Old Grammar School. The Finest Merchant's House in Lavenham', *Historic Buildings of Suffolk: The Journal of the Suffolk Historic Buildings Group* 1 (1998), pp. 31–49; C. Tracy, H. Harrison and L. Wrapson, 'Thomas Spring's Chantry and Parclose at Lavenham, Suffolk', *Journal of the British Archaeological Association* 164 (2011), pp. 221–59; L. Alston, 'Paycocke's Coggeshall, Essex. Historical Analysis of Structure', unpublished report, 2005; C. Thornton, 'Paycocke's House, Coggeshall. Historical Report', unpublished report for the National Trust, 2011.

these reflected the personal piety of the individual rather than established practice: 'They are less windows on to the soul than mirrors of social convention.'[104] Wills often reveal little about the good works that the testator performed during his or her lifetime, which may have been more important than the provisions made in the will. It is also difficult to know if the provisions of a will were actually carried out.

Nonetheless, the surviving wills of clothiers are particularly valuable. They tell us about family relationships, in an age before parish registers recorded baptisms, marriages and burials. They show the bequests that clothiers made, including gifts to parish churches, monastic houses and guilds. In some cases, we can even identify economic relationships between clothiers and other textile workers, as with the bequests that Thomas Paycocke of Coggeshall (d. 1518) made to his spinners, fullers, weavers and shearmen.[105] Where they survive, inventories can reveal details about the tools and stock that clothiers held.

Taxation records

In the absence of census records, taxation returns provide approximate indications of the size of towns and villages and their relative wealth. The most useful taxation records for this purpose are the lay subsidies of 1334, the poll taxes collected between 1377 and 1381, and the lay subsidies and other taxes levied during the 1520s. As these taxes were assessed on different bases, direct comparisons between the fourteenth-century and sixteenth-century assessments cannot be made. They can be used, though, to explore *relative* changes in the numbers of tax payers and levels of taxable wealth in different communities over the century and a half between the two assessments.[106] Similarly, examining changes in wealth across the country reveals that the principal areas of growth included cloth-making districts in Gloucestershire, Wiltshire and the south-west, Essex and Suffolk, the West Riding of Yorkshire, and the Kentish Weald.[107]

Where they survive, the returns of individual taxpayers can provide

[104] A.D. Brown, *Popular Piety in Late Medieval England: The Diocese of Salisbury, 1250–1550* (Oxford, 1995), pp. 21–3.

[105] See below, Appendix 4.

[106] *CUHB*, pp. 755–70; W.G. Hoskins, 'English Provincial Towns in the Early Sixteenth Century', *Transactions of the Royal Historical Society*, fifth series 6 (1956), pp. 2–6. For an example of comparisons using tax records over wider areas see John S. Lee, 'Tracing Regional and Local Changes in Population and Wealth during the Later Middle Ages Using Taxation Records: Cambridgeshire, 1334–1563', *Local Population Studies* 69 (2002), pp. 32–50.

[107] H.C. Darby, R.E. Glasscock, J. Sheail and G.R. Versey, 'The Changing Geographical Distribution of Wealth in England: 1086–1334–1525', *Journal of Historical Geography* 5 (1979), pp. 257–61.

valuable evidence of employment and household structure. The poll tax of 1377 required all lay people over fourteen years of age to pay 4d each, while the subsequent taxes granted in 1379 and 1380 were assessed partly on a graduated basis according to status. By 1381, there was intense opposition to the taxes, culminating in the Peasants' Revolt, and they were abandoned. The recording of trades is absent from the records of the first poll tax, and is more consistent in the 1381 returns than in those for 1379. The extent of survival is, however, mixed.[108] The lay subsidies of 1524–25 also recorded the wealth of individuals, enabling us to see, for example, that Alice Spring, the widow of Thomas Spring III, was the second-wealthiest person in Suffolk in 1524 and paid over one-third of the total taxes collected in Lavenham, and that Thomas Horton of Bradford-on-Avon in Wiltshire contributed 70 per cent of his town's subsidy payment.[109]

The accounts of the ulnage tax, levied on sales of cloth, help to quantify the extent of the shifts in the production and marketing of cloth during the later Middle Ages.[110] The ulnage, introduced in 1353, comprised two parts – a subsidy or basic charge of 4d per woollen cloth, and an ulnage or measuring fee of ½d per cloth – which in practice were usually collectively called the ulnage. Sometimes the official collecting the tax, the ulnager, recorded the names of the payers in each locality and the number of cloths on which each person paid the subsidy, but at other times he noted only the number of persons and saleable cloths in each district. The returns offer the potential to trace changes in the output of localities and the scale of enterprise of individuals, but need to be used cautiously. Eleanora Carus-Wilson examined a series of ulnage accounts for the West Country from 1467 to 1478 and found they contained names that bore no relation to those paying the ulnage fees and had presumably been fabricated or taken at random from other lists. Other returns, however, can be used with greater confidence. About half the names recorded on the ulnage returns for Winchester in the 1390s appear in other city records. In Essex and Suffolk, administrative reforms in the 1460s helped to increase the sums collected.[111]

The ulnage returns are valuable in showing the changing location

[108] Carolyn C. Fenwick, *The Poll Taxes of 1377, 1379 and 1381*, 3 vols (Oxford, 1998–2005).

[109] Phillipp R. Schofield, 'Spring family (*per. c.*1400–*c.*1550)', *ODNB*; Hoskins, 'English Provincial Towns', pp. 6–7.

[110] Also spelled as aulnage or alnage: *OED*.

[111] E.M. Carus-Wilson, 'The Aulnage Accounts: A Criticism', *EcHR* 2 (1929), reprinted in Carus-Wilson, *Medieval Merchant Venturers*, pp. 279–91; A.R. Bridbury, *Economic Growth: England in the Later Middle Ages* (London, 1962), pp. 33–5; Britnell, *Colchester*, pp. 187–8; Merrick, 'Taxing Medieval Cloth'.

of cloth production, highlighting the varying relative importance of different cloth-making regions across the country, as well as highlighting change within these regions.[112] In Yorkshire for example, the ulnage accounts show that between the 1390s and the 1470s, Bradford, Leeds, Wakefield, Halifax and Huddersfield had expanded at the expense of York, Beverley and Ripon. It should be noted though, that they record where cloth was sold and not necessarily where it had been produced.

The ulnage accounts also document the types of people who were selling cloth, and the growing concentration of the trade in fewer hands. As described above, they reveal that even in the 1390s, some people were paying ulnage on more cloths than they could possibly have produced themselves, even as full-time cloth-workers. Particularly in the later fourteenth century, many individuals dabbled in the cloth trade. They may have bought semi-finished cloths at varying stages of production, as only the owner of the finished cloth who was offering it for sale was liable to pay the ulnage.[113]

Records of trade

Very few accounts survive from medieval merchants, and there are no known examples from contemporary clothiers. There are, however, a few examples from men who traded with clothiers. The account book of John Heritage of Moreton-in-Marsh in Gloucestershire, discovered in the 1990s, reveals how this wool trader supplied the prominent clothiers Thomas Spring of Lavenham and Robert, brother of Thomas Paycocke of Coggeshall.[114] The accounts of Thomas Kitson, London merchant and Merchant Adventurer, record purchases from clothiers, as do the accounts of the London draper Thomas Howell and Bristol mercer John Smythe.[115]

While English overseas trade was recorded in detail in the customs accounts,[116] medieval inland trade is generally much harder to identify. A few toll records survive providing direct evidence of inland trade. The most important series is the Southampton brokage books, covering twenty-seven years between 1430 and 1540, and recording tolls on goods and carts entering or leaving the town. The accounts do not cover coastal

[112] See below, Appendices 1–2.

[113] Heaton, *Yorkshire Woollen*, pp. xiii–xiv, 84–8; Merrick, 'Taxing Medieval Cloth', pp. 230–2; Britnell, 'Woollen Textile Industry', pp. 92, 99.

[114] Dyer, *Country Merchant*, pp. 117–18.

[115] Drapers' Company, London, Ledger of Thomas Howell; CUL, Hengrave Hall MS 78(2). G. Connell-Smith, 'The Ledger of Thomas Howell', *EcHR*, 2nd series 3 (1950–1), pp. 363–70; *The Ledger of John Smythe, 1538–1550*, eds John Angus and Jean Vanes, HMC, Joint Publication Series 19 (London, 1974).

[116] Carus-Wilson and Coleman, *England's Export Trade*.

shipping or river trade, few packhorses or herded animals are listed, and there is nothing about the commodities carried by hand by men like pedlars and chapmen. Incoming goods seem to be incompletely documented: cloth figures, for instance, show little relationship to the records of cloth exported in the respective years. Nonetheless, study of the brokage books highlights important long-term trends as well as short-term fluctuations in the trade of Southampton and its region, which extended into much of southern and midland England.[117]

Much of the evidence for trade relies on the indirect sources of debt cases and trade disputes. Debt litigation reveals patterns of credit. Manorial and borough courts could be used for debts of up to 40s and so recorded predominantly local and small-scale trade, mostly in food, clothes, leather goods and other necessities. Cases relating to trade on a larger scale or over long distances were usually heard in larger borough courts, while many creditors sought recovery of debts in London courts. Records of debts may only state the names of individuals involved and their place of residence, and not the reason for the debt, which might arise not only from sales, but also from rents, services, loans, pledges or damages.[118] About three-quarters of pleas within the Court of Common Pleas, which sat at Westminster, were actions for debt. Few of these actions were tried: a writ was often issued simply to draw the defendant into arbitration. The plea rolls have been used to examine the cloth trade in Salisbury and Exeter, and most recently by Nicholas Amor, who extracted data from 1480 to 1500 to study the changing fortunes of thirty specific cloth-making centres. The pleas recorded can also reveal the extent of London's economic hinterland and the role of London creditors.[119] The cataloguing and photography of many of these rolls on the Anglo-American Legal Tradition website has made these records far more accessible.[120] Another useful source of information on trade disputes are the early Chancery proceedings.[121] These were petitions to the chancellor complaining of alleged wrongs and requesting that the offender be summoned to answer, because the courts of common law

[117] Hicks, ed., *Inland Trade*. See also the Overland Trade Project website, http://www.overlandtrade.org

[118] Kowaleski, *Exeter*, pp. 202–8; Britnell, *Colchester*, pp. 100–1, 108–9, 208.

[119] Bridbury, *Clothmaking*, pp. 70–2; Kowaleski, *Exeter*, p. 280; Amor, *From Wool to Cloth*, pp. 8–11, 21–52; Derek Keene, 'Changes in London's Economic Hinterland as Indicated by Debt Cases in the Court of Common Pleas', in Galloway, ed., *Trade*, pp. 59–81; Matthew Stevens, 'London Creditors and the Fifteenth-century Depression', *EcHR* 69 (2016), pp. 1083–1107.

[120] http://aalt.law.uh.edu/

[121] TNA, series C1.

were unable to resolve the matter. They can often be dated only approximately, by the title of the chancellor addressed in each bill.

Literary, material and artistic evidence

Literary evidence includes Thomas Deloney's poem, 'Jack of Newbury', loosely depicting the career of clothier John Winchcombe II, and the description of the Wife of Bath within Geoffrey Chaucer's *Canterbury Tales*, who has been seen as a West Country clothier.[122] Particularly valuable are the writings compiled by the antiquarian John Leland (c.1503–52) as he travelled across England between 1539 and 1545. A poet and antiquary, among his research notes Leland included remarks on buildings, markets and industries, findings that were intended to provide the background for a series of works that were never produced. The notes are not complete – only fragments survive for Essex and Suffolk, for example, and even in counties where more detailed records survive, Leland did not visit every town. Nonetheless, as Leland took an interest, arguably unparalleled by earlier writers, in the state of towns, markets and commercial and industrial ventures, they can be used to chart the changing distribution of the cloth industry.[123]

Several of the houses of the leading clothiers survive, including those of Thomas Paycocke at Coggeshall (Plate VIII), Thomas Horton at Westwood (Plate 11), and William Stumpe at Malmesbury, as well as other properties in cloth-making towns such as Lavenham. Evidence of cloth-making processes within buildings such as these is more difficult to trace. All cloth-making processes required a large amount of storage space, but these rarely left any distinguishing features in the architecture. Weaving needed good light. Attic storeys at houses such as Paycockes in Coggeshall (later removed) were intended for storage. It also seems likely though, that much spinning and weaving was carried out in ordinary houses lacking special or identifiable workspaces. Looms and spinning wheels could be set up without leaving physical traces in the building. Craft activity was often conducted on a part-time basis, supplementing farming income.[124]

[122] Deloney, *Jack of Newbury*; Geoffrey Chaucer, *The Wife of Bath*, ed. Peter G. Beidler (New York, 1996).

[123] John S. Lee, 'The Functions and Fortunes of English Small Towns at the Close of the Middle Ages: Evidence from John Leland's *Itinerary*', *Urban History* 37 (2010), pp. 3–25. Leland's notes were published verbatim and in original form by Lucy Toulmin Smith in *Itinerary*, and reordered and set out in modern English by John Chandler, *John Leland's Itinerary: Travels in Tudor England* (Stroud, 1993).

[124] P.S. Barnwell, 'Workshops, Industrial Production and the Landscape', in P.S. Barnwell, M. Palmer and M. Airs, eds, *The Vernacular Workshop: From Craft to Industry, 1400–1900*, Council for British Archaeology Research Report 140 (York, 2004), p. 180.

The visibility of industry through archaeology is mainly dependent on infrastructure that leaves traces in the ground, such as tanks, vats, furnaces and water channels, or on discarded residues. This tends to skew the archaeological record towards 'metal-bashing' industries such as smelting and smithing, as well as other activities such as tanning and tile-making that required similar infrastructure.[125] As a consequence of this, dyeing can be readily identified, like the fifteenth-century dyer's workshop excavated at Westwick Street in Norwich.[126] Fulling mills can leave remains of water-supply systems, timber and masonry structures and wheel-pits, like those found in the Lake District and Northumberland.[127] Other cloth-making evidence relies on much smaller finds. These include spindle whorls (Plate 1), which provided a weight for spinning using a distaff; tenterhooks, which held cloths to dry and stretch on tenters; harbicks, which were hooks to secure cloth to boards for shearing; and seals, attached to cloth as an assessment of quality and denoting payment of tax (Plate 10). Although archaeology has tended to focus on the making of cloth rather than its marketing, excavations in Guildhall Yard have uncovered the remains of Blackwell Hall, the cloth market for late medieval London.[128]

In addition to their homes and workplaces, wealthier clothiers have left material evidence in their contributions to the rebuilding or extending of churches, notably those of Lavenham (Plate 16), Dedham and Newbury. Monumental brasses, comprising engravings on sheets of metal inlaid in matrices cut into the stone, also provide a memorial to those buried inside churches (Plate IX).[129] Many clothiers chose to be commemorated in this way, and some included their merchants' marks on their brasses. Other artistic evidence includes the contemporary portrait of John Winchcombe II and later portrait of Thomas Bell (Plates

[125] Nigel Baker, 'The Archaeology of the Larger Medieval Towns', *West Midlands Regional Research Framework, Research Papers* (Birmingham, 2003), available at http://archaeologydataservice.ac.uk

[126] Brian Ayers, *Norwich: 'a fine city'* (Stroud, 2003), p. 133.

[127] Peter Schofield and Alastair Vannan, *Windermere Reflections: Fulling Mills in Easedale, Grasmere, Elterwater, Great Langdale and Graythwaite*, Oxford Archaeology North (Lancaster, 2012); Richard Carlton and David Jones, 'A Medieval Fulling Mill at Barrowburn on the River Coquet: Evidence and Context', *Archaeologia Aeliana* 43 (2014), pp. 221–40.

[128] Geoffrey Egan, 'Provenanced Leaden Cloth Seals', University of London, Ph.D. thesis, 1987; Stuart F. Elton, *Cloth Seals. An illustrated Reference Guide to the Identification of Lead Seals Attached to Cloth* (Oxford, 2017); Nick Bateman, 'From Rags to Riches: Blackwell Hall and the Wool Cloth Trade, *c.*1450–1790', *Post-Medieval Archaeology* 38 (2004), pp. 1–15.

[129] For a general introduction see the website of the Monumental Brass Society, http://www.mbs-brasses.co.uk/

VII and X) and the carved wooden panelling that came from Winchcombe's home (Plate 19).

*

Drawing on the historiography and sources outlined above, this book examines the clothiers of late medieval England over six chapters. Chapter 1 looks at the methods by which clothiers organised production, often by providing workers with raw materials in their own homes and collecting the processed products from them (known as the putting-out system). It explains the different processes of cloth-making, from buying, preparing and sorting, combing and carding wool, through spinning, weaving and fulling, to finishing. These processes were coordinated by the clothiers, who might carry out some stages of production themselves. Chapter 2 explores the clothier's key role in selling cloth, whether at fairs, Blackwell Hall in London, or through informal markets such as inns. Clothiers dealt with English and overseas merchants, frequently relying on credit to fund their transactions. Trading links are placed within the context of the growing importance of London. Chapter 3 looks at the locations of clothiers, and the principal cloth-making regions in England in the later Middle Ages. It will examine how the industries in these regions changed over the period and assess the evidence regarding the relative numbers and work of clothiers in these regions. Central and local government developed legislation to respond to these changes in production and their impact. Chapter 4 examines this legislation, and the role of clothiers in shaping and responding to it. Clothiers in the wider society, their religious practices, and their landownership, are explored in Chapter 5. Like other wealthy members of medieval society, clothiers often left elaborate instructions for commemoration after their deaths, including endowing chantries and funding the rebuilding of churches. Four famous clothiers are the focus of Chapter 6, who dominated production in their localities and bequeathed major legacies to their families and communities. Appendices contain county and locality totals for cloths taxed for ulnage, details of the types of cloth defined by statute in 1552, and extracts from clothiers' wills. Lastly there is a gazetteer of sites connected with medieval clothiers.

By examining the medieval clothier, this book seeks to address several broader questions. What were the particular economic circumstances in which the clothier emerged? Tracing the rise of the clothier across different regions helps to illuminate the pace of economic development in England over the course of the later Middle Ages. What skills did the clothier require to succeed in the competitive economic environment? These were the means through which the clothier organised the processes of cloth-making, engaged with the market, sought finance, and brokered deals. How did the clothier affect the landscape in which he or she worked? The cloth industry impacted on both the natural and built environments. How did the clothier interact with local and national governments? Clothiers lobbied to influence legislation as well as being themselves the subject of regulation. Finally, as outlined above, the medieval clothier is often seen as one of England's first capitalist entrepreneurs, employing workers and even establishing early factories. This book explores how appropriate this description might be. It also examines the implications of the ways in which clothiers organised their production and engaged their workers, considering how this impacted on the wider economy and society of late medieval England.

1

Making cloth

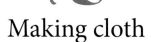

Anyone producing a piece of cloth from raw wool needs to undertake several different activities (Figure 3). Specialised cloth-workers including carders, combers, spinners, weavers, fullers and dyers emerged during the Middle Ages, skilled in specific aspects of cloth-making. We still use terms from cloth-making processes in our everyday speech, when we talk of being 'dyed in the wool' or 'on tenterhooks'. Spinster originally denoted someone who practised spinning, but from the seventeenth century, unmarried women have been designated in legal terms as spinsters.[1] Common surnames reflect the processes carried out by various textile workers, including Weaver, Webb, Webber, and Webster (weavers), Fuller and Walker (fullers), and Dyer and Lister (dyers). This chapter explores these activities, taking a step-by-step approach from the buying of wool to the finishing of the fabric. Clothiers coordinated these processes, and in some cases carried out stages of production themselves.

PROCESSES IN THE MAKING OF CLOTH

The main product of the medieval textile industry was broadcloth, made from short staple wool, which was densely woven and heavily fulled. By the later Middle Ages this had been standardised at 26 to 28 yards long and 1¾ yards wide, produced by two weavers working on a broadloom. The type and price varied according to the quality of the wool used, the dye and the degree of finish. Some cloths were woven on a narrower loom, requiring only one person to weave. These were half the width of a standard broadcloth and known as straits. Worsted, made from long staple wool, was made mainly for the home market and was far less heavily legislated. Linen was produced from flax, and harden cloth from hemp or flax.[2]

[1] *OED*.
[2] Heather Swanson, *Medieval Artisans* (Oxford, 1989), pp. 26–7.

Sourcing wool	Buying Grading
Preparing wool	Sorting Scouring (short staple wools) Beating (Dyeing in the wool) Carding (short staple wools) / Combing (long staple wools)
Spinning	Spinning (Yarn dyeing)
Weaving	Weaving
Fulling and tentering	(Piece dyeing) Fulling Burling Washing Tentering Wet napping and shearing
Finishing	(Fabric dyeing) Dry napping and shearing Folding and pressing

Figure 3 Stages in the production of woollen cloth

Table 2 Cloth-making crafts assessed in the poll tax returns, 1377–81

	Average tax paid (d)	*Range of tax paid (d)*
comber	10	4–24
spinster	8	4–36*
weaver	10	4–120
fuller	12	4–108
shearman	11	4–36
dyer	16	6–80

Source: Database compiled by Samuel Gibbs from Fenwick, *Poll Taxes*.

Note: * Excludes one spinster assessed on £12 in Wormhill, High Peak, Derbyshire in 1381.

Sourcing wool

The clothier's first task was to obtain wool. Its quality, its source and the frequency with which clothiers bought it varied according to the resources at their disposal. A document of 1615 shows how clothiers procured their wool in different ways according to the money they had available. The wealthiest bought from wool producers in wool counties, made their provision for the whole year beforehand, and had the wool spun, woven and fulled by their own employees. Less affluent clothiers travelled little to wool-producing counties but borrowed money to buy wool, mostly at the market, had it made into cloth to sell, and then borrowed more money. The poorest bought little or no wool, purchasing instead yarn on a weekly basis in markets, and had it made in to cloth.[3]

A few clothiers could source wool from their own flocks of sheep. John Flower of Potterne (Wiltshire) owned over 800 sheep, and John Winchcombe II of Newbury had a flock of some 450 sheep in 1558.[4] Many clothiers left bequests of sheep in their wills, presumably from their own flocks. Dealing in wool may have provided the initial entry into cloth-making for several families of clothiers. Thomas Paycocke of Coggeshall, for example, had a father and grandfather who were both butchers, and possibly traded in cattle and sheep.[5]

Most clothiers though, had to buy their wool, and looked to several different sources, including farmers, middlemen, and other clothiers who dealt in wool as a sideline to their cloth-making businesses. Some clothiers bought wool from local farmers, like James Towker or Terumber of Trowbridge, who bought £40 of pure white wool in 1468–69 from the clip of the Hungerford estates at nearby Farleigh Hungerford castle.[6] The quality of wool varied across the country though, and local fleeces were not always adequate. Some clothiers made direct contracts with large-scale producers of wool, who resided at a considerable distance, such as William Durston of Wilton in Wiltshire who contracted with John Mathewe of Yarcombe in Devon during the 1540s to buy all his wool.[7] Roger Townshend II had over 18,000 sheep in 1516 and supplied wool to the cloth industry in Norwich, Hadleigh and Lavenham.[8] Sometimes wool was to be paid for in cloth, like that supplied by Sir William Carewe to Ralph Typpyng of Lavenham in the early 1500s.[9]

3 TNA, SP 14/80, fol. 19; *Calendar of State Papers Domestic James I*, No. James Vol. LXXX, 13, p. 271, quoted in Unwin, *Industrial Organisation*, pp. 234–6.

4 Ramsay, *Wiltshire*, p. 12; Jackson, 'Boom-time Freaks', p. 149.

5 See below, Chapter 6.

6 *VCH Wiltshire*, iv, p. 135.

7 TNA, C 1/1117/33.

8 Britnell, *Britain and Ireland*, p. 419.

9 TNA, C 1/364/19.

Clothiers also secured supplies from middlemen, known as woolmen, woolmongers or wool broggers, who collected wool from the growers and sold it to cloth producers. These dealers assumed a greater importance after the Black Death when the great ecclesiastical landlords withdrew from sheep farming, breaking the link that had previously existed between grower and exporter. Some woolmen accumulated large fortunes, such as William Greville of Chipping Camden (d. 1401) or John Tame of Fairford (d. 1500), but others such as John Heritage of Moreton-in-Marsh, in Gloucestershire, ran far more modest operations. Heritage kept an account book of his trade in wool in the first and second decades of the sixteenth century. This book lists the producers from whom Heritage purchased his fleeces, and the merchants to whom he sold them, which included the clothiers Robert Paycocke of Coggeshall, brother of Thomas, and Thomas Spring III of Lavenham, two of the most prominent clothiers in early sixteenth-century England. Heritage did not, however, appear to have supplied the flourishing cloth-making industry that was developing much closer to his home, around Stroud. London merchants, who exported through Calais, and a variety of more local middlemen also bought Heritage's wool. Most of his suppliers came from within eight miles of Moreton, and many were relatively small-scale producers, with flocks of less than one hundred sheep.[10] In Suffolk, a cluster of woolmen resided at Bury St Edmunds, including William Copynger, who recorded debt pleas with four clothiers and two fullers from Suffolk at the end of the fifteenth century.[11] Woolmen also operated in Yorkshire, and York council tried to regulate their activities in 1428 and 1460.[12] National legislation passed in 1465, and re-enacted in 1489 and 1531, forbade wool dealers from purchasing unshorn wool between March and August each year.[13]

Wool traders might also operate as clothiers, drapers and dyers, just as some clothiers kept flocks of sheep. The Fortey family had a senior branch of dyers residing in Cirencester, and a junior branch of wool traders in Northleach.[14] Emmot, widow of Thomas Fermor of Witney (Oxfordshire), and previously married to woolman Henry Wenman, also traded in wool and cloth. On her death in 1501, she had more than £1,000 in debts owing to her, from London traders and Italian merchants,

[10] J.J. Simpson, 'The Wool Trade and the Woolmen of Gloucestershire', *Transactions of the Bristol and Gloucestershire Archaeological Society* 53 (1931), pp. 65–97; Dyer, *Country Merchant*; Peter Bowden, *The Wool Trade in Tudor and Stuart England* (London, 1962), pp. 77–84.

[11] Amor, *From Wool to Cloth*, pp. 102–16.

[12] Swanson, *Medieval Artisans*, p. 140.

[13] 4 Edward IV, c. 4; 4 Henry VII, c. 11: *SR*, ii, pp. 410, 535–6.

[14] Saul, 'Wool Merchants', pp. 322–4.

including over £275 owed by the Bonvisi family, and left wool stocked in her 'wool houses' at Witney and Northleach. Emmot may have been arranging the manufacture of six 'unwrought' broadcloths, which she also bequeathed.[15]

The smaller cloth producers of Calderdale in Yorkshire were dependent on making small purchases of wool from middlemen in Halifax known as wooldrivers. A statute of 1555 described how these clothiers, who could not afford to buy large quantities of wool, or to keep a horse to carry their wool, relied on wooldrivers to purchase

> some a stone, some two, and some three or four, according to their ability, and to carry the same to their houses, some three, four, five and six miles off, upon their heads and backs, and so to make and convert the same either to yarn or cloth, and to sell the same, and so to buy more wool of the wooldriver.[16]

The statute of 1555 allowed wool dealers and other middlemen to continue to operate in the area around Halifax, although their activities had been forbidden elsewhere by an earlier statute of 1552.[17] Subsequent legislation offered similar privileges to clothiers in Lancashire, Richmondshire, Westmorland, Cumberland and Durham in 1585, and to Rochdale clothiers in 1590.[18] Some Halifax clothiers though, sold coarse Yorkshire wool to Rochdale clothiers, as they apparently preferred to use finer wool from Lincolnshire for their narrow kerseys. In 1526, two Lancashire clothiers were in Halifax and bought 30 stones of wool from the Halifax clothier John Hardy.[19]

Markets and fairs provided clothiers with another source of wool or yarn. Some textile-producing towns had notable wool fairs, such as those at Coggeshall in Essex. The Orlandini and Cambini firms of merchants from Florence bought wool at the Cotswold fairs of Burford and Northleach in the early fifteenth century, which they then exported. Writing in 1402, a buyer for the Orlandini noted that the wools sold at fairs were of better quality and weight than those in 'common markets', and a Cambini merchant noted in 1403 that the valuation of wools at Burford Fair determined prices in the whole of the Cotswolds.[20]

Wool varied considerably in quality, reflecting differences in climate,

[15] *VCH Oxfordshire*, xiv, p. 78.

[16] 2 & 3 Philip and Mary, c. 13: *SR*, iv (1), p. 288.

[17] 5 & 6 Edward VI, c. 7: *SR*, iv (1), pp. 141–2.

[18] Heaton, *Yorkshire Woollen*, p. 94, 120–2.

[19] TNA, C 1/639/43; Royal Commission on Historical Manuscripts, *The Manuscripts of Lord Kenyon*, HMC 14, Appendix, Part 4 (London, 1894), p. 573.

[20] Britnell, *Colchester*, p. 45; E.B. Fryde, *Peasants and Landlords in Later Medieval England*, c.1380–c.1525 (Stroud, 1996), pp. 88–9, 96–8.

pasture and husbandry. The finest English wools were considered to be firstly those from the Welsh marches of Shropshire and Herefordshire, secondly from the adjoining Cotswold districts of Worcestershire, Gloucestershire and Oxfordshire, and thirdly, from the Lindsey, Kesteven and Holland districts of Lincolnshire. Medium-grade wools came from southern Yorkshire, East Anglia, and Essex, Kent, Sussex and Hampshire. By the later fourteenth and fifteenth centuries, the northern wools of Westmorland, Cumberland, Lancashire, Cheshire, Northumberland, Durham and the North Riding of Yorkshire, and those from the far south-west counties of Cornwall and Devon, were considered inferior.[21] Yet even within these regions there were important local variations. In Yorkshire in 1357, for example, lower-quality wools came from Holderness, Craven, Spaldingmoor, Cleveland, Blackmoor and Richmondshire, while better-quality wools, worth nearly two-thirds more, came from the districts of Elmet, Burghshire, the Liberty of Ripon, *Walde* and Ryedale.[22] The clothier had to take all these differences into consideration, carefully selecting the wool available that most closely met his needs.

Preparing wool

> At first, the Parter, that doth neatly cull
> The finer from the coarser sort of wool
>
> R. Watts, *The Young Man's Looking Glass* (1641)[23]

Before it can be spun, wool needs to be sorted and prepared (Plate I, top left). Wool from different sections of the fleece varies in quality and length. If a fleece was used without sorting, the resulting yarn would be faulty and uneven and dyeing would be patchy. The length of the wool was referred to as the staple, and this could range from very short curly wool about two inches long, to fine wool of five to six inches in length. Clothiers used culling baskets and boards to sort and select their wool, and a few even had rooms described as a 'culling chamber' or 'culling shop' for this purpose. John Winchcombe II of Newbury's house contained workrooms for picking, sorting, carding and weighing wool, and storage

21 *CHWT*, pp. 186–7; John Munro, 'Wool-price Schedules and the Qualities of English Wools in the Later Middle Ages *c.*1270–1499', *Textile History* 9 (1978), pp. 118–69.

22 John Munro, 'The 1357 Wool-price Schedule and the Decline of Yorkshire Wool Values', *Textile History* 10 (1979), pp. 211–19. Several of these areas formed the names of local government administrative districts in the 1970s; others are now less familiar but were identified by Munro, although *Walde* may have been in one of three different locations within the county.

23 Quoted from Lipson, *Woollen and Worsted Industries*, p. 128.

lofts for wool and dyestuffs.[24] According to an act of parliament of 1554, the true sorting of wool was 'the perfect and principal ground of cloth-making' and experience of this 'consisteth only in women, as clothiers' wives and their women servants'.[25]

The cloth-maker had to decide whether or not to scour and remove the natural oils in the wool. Historians have categorised these different treatments as wet and dry draperies. Longer staple wools usually went unscoured and were used for worsteds. Short staple wools, used for broadcloth, kerseys and straits, used the wet drapery process, where the wool was scoured in water and urine. After drying, this wool might be spread on hurdles or 'fleyks' where it was beaten with 'swinging sticks' or rods to remove gritty particles and knots.[26] The wool was then re-greased and lubricated to replace the natural oils lost, initially with butter, but by the fifteenth century usually with olive oil, which was imported from Spain and purchased from merchants. London merchant Thomas Kitson sold 'Seville oil' or olive oil to the clothiers John Clevelod of Beckington and Roger Tanner of Westbury in 1532. About 8 to 10 lb of oil was used with the 60 or 70 lb of wool in each cloth.[27] Tuns and vats often appear among clothiers' goods, suggesting that these processes were often carried out by the clothier or his servants.[28]

Carding and combing straightened the fibres, separating the shorter from the longer strands, and removed imperfect fibres and dirt. This was a demanding process as all the knots in the wool had to be removed. Combing was used particularly for longer staple wool. Wool combs were generally warmed and dipped into a pot of grease to lubricate the wool and prevent the fibres from becoming damaged. Combs were commonly used in pairs, with a lower comb resting on the comber's knee or fixed to a wooden post known as a combing stock.

Carding was an alternative technique for preparing short-fibred wools, particularly the weft threads. It was a technique probably borrowed from the Islamic cotton industries of Spain or Sicily during the later thirteenth century. Like combing, carding disentangled and straightened the wool fibres and removed impurities, but separated the strands without removing the short fibres. It also provided a way of blending together

[24] Jackson, 'Boom-time Freaks', p. 150.

[25] 1 Mary, c. 7: *SR*, iv (1), p. 232.

[26] W.B. Crump and Gertrude Ghorbal, *History of the Huddersfield Woollen Industry*, Tolson Memorial Museum Publications 10 (Huddersfield, 1935), pp. 34–5.

[27] C.J. Brett, 'Thomas Kytson and Somerset Clothmen 1529–1539', *Somerset Archaeology and Natural History Society: Proceedings* 143 (2001), p. 38; C.J. Brett, 'Thomas Kytson and Wiltshire Clothmen, 1529–1539', *Wiltshire Archaeology and Natural History Magazine* 97 (2004), p. 49.

[28] Muldrew, 'Th'ancient Distaff', p. 502; Zell, *Industry*, p. 164.

a variety of wools. Hand cards were rectangular wooden boards with handles, one side of the board being pierced with rows of iron hooks or teeth. Wool was placed on one card and the other card was drawn across it repeatedly until the wool was suitable for spinning. Stock-cards, where a wool-card was fastened to a stock or support, were also used (see Plate I, top right). The work was initially done with teasel heads, and the term 'card' comes from *carduus*, the Latin word for thistle.[29] Teasels were mostly collected locally, but occasionally were supplemented by imports, like those carried from Southampton to the cloth-making towns of Salisbury, London, Winchester, Newbury, Romsey and Basingstoke in the later fifteenth and early sixteenth centuries.[30]

Carding and combing both had their advantages. Yarn that was combed was stronger than that which had been carded, but combing was more wasteful than carding because shorter fibres were discarded. Combing required more upper body strength, so was often done by men, who might expect higher wages than women. During the fifteenth century, combed yarn was sometimes used for the warp with carded yarn for the weft. By 1500, as the spinning wheel became more extensively used, both the warp and weft yarn were generally carded.[31]

Carding and combing, like spinning, were activities that required little capital investment, and were often undertaken by workers in their own homes for piece-rate wages. In 1393, Katherine, wife of James Sadler of York, worked at 'kempstercraft' or wool-carding, in addition to assisting her husband with his work.[32] Clothiers and other textile entrepreneurs who controlled production might employ their own carders and spinners. In his will of 1466, York dyer William Crosseby remembered 'the poor women of custom working and travailing in carding and spinning my wool'. Thomas Paycocke of Coggeshall left bequests in 1518 to 'my combers, carders and spinners'.[33]

[29] *CHWT*, pp. 197–200; Patricia Basing, *Trades and Crafts in Medieval Manuscripts* (London, 1990), p. 78.

[30] Hicks, ed., *Inland Trade*, p. 159.

[31] Amor, *From Wool to Cloth*, pp. 118–21.

[32] Goldberg, *Women*, p. 118.

[33] YBIA, York Prob. Reg. 4, fol. 70; see below, Appendix 4.

Spinning

> If she have no wool of her own, she may take wool to spin of cloth-makers, and by that means she may have a convenient living, and many times to do other works.
>
> John Fitzherbert, *The Boke of Husbandry* (1533) describing the general duties of a wife[34]

The clothier divided the wool into consignments and delivered it to spinners, who twisted together the fibres into long threads or yarn by spinning. There were two different methods of spinning, using either a hand spindle or a spinning wheel. The hand spindle was the older method and the more precise. Threads were drawn out and twisted by a free-hanging short wooden stick known as a spindle. A weight or whorl, of clay, stone, wood or lead, was attached to the bottom of the spindle to improve its rotation, and the wool would spin as it fell towards the ground (Plate 1). A cleft staff about three feet long, known as the distaff, was placed under the left arm to hold the prepared but unspun wool. The wool fibres were drawn from the distaff through the fingers of the spinner's left hand, and twisted spirally by the forefinger and thumb of their right hand, with the aid of the suspended spindle, round which the thread, as it was twisted or spun, was wound. The spinner twisted and wound the finished thread around a tapered part of the spindle. The distaff and spindle enabled the spinner to carry their work with them around the home or even into the fields.[35] The early-fourteenth-century Luttrell Psalter depicts a woman feeding chickens and an enormous hen while holding a distaff and spindle under her arm (Plate II). This type of spinning was slow but accurate because the spinner had more control over the strength of the yarn, and the finest yarn was spun on the distaff.

The hand-operated spinning wheel appeared in Europe in the late twelfth and early thirteenth centuries. In England it was also known as the wool wheel, broad wheel, walking wheel, or great wheel. A spindle attached to the wheel pulled out the thread or yarn on to a bobbin. The spinner manipulated the thread with the left hand and rotated the wheel with the right, often using a small stick (Plate III). Although still turned by hand, this was a faster process and probably tripled productivity compared to hand spinning. The yarn produced, though, could vary in strength and was liable to break because the spinner often had to stop to wind the finished yarn onto the spindle. An improved spinning wheel,

[34] John Fitzherbert, *The Boke of Husbandry* (London, 1533), STC (2nd edn)/10995.5, p. 62v.

[35] Basing, *Trades*, p. 80.

Plate 1 Medieval spindle whorl.
This lead alloy spindle whorl was found in Grimston near Tadcaster, Yorkshire. It would have been added to the bottom of a wooden spindle to help it rotate when spinning yarn. (Portable Antiquities Scheme SWYOR-54017C).

with a mechanically driven flyer and bobbin to twist the yarn into thread, and a treadle with crank and axle to power the wheel by foot, emerged in the fifteenth century. Known as the Saxony wheel, this new spinning wheel was at least twice as productive as the old.[36] The pace at which the new technology of the spinning wheel was adopted is difficult to trace. Isabella Whelespynner lived at Bishopthorpe near York in 1379 and her surname suggests that the spinning wheel was still relatively uncommon in the area at this time.[37] Nicholas Amor found only nine references to spinning wheels in his extensive research into the Suffolk cloth industry in the fifteenth century. He suggested that this paucity may reflect the lack of wills made by spinners, or that spinning wheels belonged to clothiers who employed them and did not bother to have such low-value items recorded in their wills.[38]

Spinners supplying yarn for producing broadcloths had to spin both warp (the yarn stretched lengthways when weaving on a loom), which was spun close and twisted for strength, and weft (the yarn inserted sideways when weaving), which only had to be loosely spun as it was

[36] Muldrew, 'Th'ancient Distaff', pp. 503–4; Steven A. Epstein, *An Economic and Social History of Later Medieval Europe, 1000–1500* (Cambridge, 2009), pp. 193–4; *CHWT*, pp. 202–3.

[37] Goldberg, *Women*, p. 145.

[38] Amor, *From Wool to Cloth*, p. 123.

pounded together during the fulling process. The long warp threads had to be measured out to the exact length of the piece of cloth to be produced, using a warping frame. Sockets in the internal timbers of houses probably held these frames along with pegs to wind the warp, and examples survive in Lavenham.[39]

Spinning was commonly carried out by women in the home, and for many women, unmarried or widowed, it must have been their sole source of income. John Fitzherbert's *The Boke of Husbandry* (1533) noted spinning as one of the tasks that a wife should undertake, either using wool from her own family's sheep, or supplied by a clothier. Children, who generally lacked the skill and patience to apply themselves to finer work, could have been employed in wool picking, carding, and the spinning of loose yarn.[40] For poorer families, spinning was often a necessity, but even in better-off households it provided a useful supplement to income, and in the wealthier households it was an activity undertaken by resident female servants. Agnes Stubbard of Bury St Edmunds employed two female servants to whom she bequeathed wool combs, combing stocks, spinning wheels and cards in 1418. Some weavers did their own spinning, like Robert Woolpit of Fornham St Genevieve in Suffolk, described in the late fourteenth century as 'an habitual spinner and weaver of woollen and linen cloth', who employed an apprentice and female servant.[41]

The status of spinners appears to have deteriorated during the fifteenth century. In the poll taxes of 1377–81 their per capita contribution was only slightly less than that of weavers and fullers (Table 2), but the role appears to have become downgraded during the fifteenth century. A similar trend has been identified in the brewing industry, where the independent female labourer was replaced by a male-dominated, more capital intensive, and extensively organised system of production.[42] Clothiers frequently paid spinners in arrears, often for work over considerable periods.[43] However, at least some employers remembered the spinners they employed in their wills. In 1435 the York draper William Shipley made bequests 'to each poor woman who was accustomed to work and spin for me'. York textile entrepreneur Thomas Clynt (d. 1439) and merchant's widow Alice Chellow (d. 1466) also made bequests to

[39] Muldrew, 'Th'ancient Distaff', p. 501; Betterton and Dymond, *Lavenham*, pp. 30–1, 61.

[40] Muldrew, 'Th'ancient Distaff', p. 502.

[41] Amor, *From Wool to Cloth*, p. 120; Mark Bailey, *A Marginal Economy?: East Anglian Breckland in the Later Middle Ages* (Cambridge, 1989), p. 174.

[42] Amor, *From Wool to Cloth*, pp. 127–8.

[43] See below, p. 71.

spinsters.[44] John Golding of Glemsford left 12d to each of his spinners in 1497, and in 1520 Thomas Christmas of Colchester left an ell of linen worth 6d 'to every of my spinners that of old long time have continued within'.[45]

It was crucial for the clothier to organise spinning efficiently in order to achieve sufficient speed and profitability within the cloth-making process. This was because it would have taken an average spinner about a day to convert 1 lb of wool into yarn. Working a six-day week, the same spinner would have taken about fourteen weeks to produce sufficient yarn for a single broadcloth. No clothier, however wealthy, could afford to wait that long, and had to rely on a large group of spinners. It has been calculated for example, that the yarn needed for Kent's annual output of cloths in the 1560s required around 5,000–6,000 spinners, each working at least 150 days per year, or about one person in five from the entire population of the Kent Weald.[46] Such a proportion was probably only achieved because so many women undertook spinning. It was in the interests of clothiers that as many people as possible, within travelling distance of their residence, were willing to spin, even if not full time.

Weaving

Clothiers would gather together the yarn produced by their many spinners and put it out again to weavers to make up into cloth. A piece of cloth is made up of threads running lengthways laid parallel to each other known as the warp, crossed by threads inserted sideways known as the weft. Weaving consists of inserting the threads of the weft between the alternate threads of the warp on a loom to produce cloth. Weaving looms need to hold the warp tense and take up or roll the finished cloth. Although early looms had vertical frames in which the warp thread was held tense by loom weights, it was the horizontal framed loom that was in use by the thirteenth century. This enabled the production of wider, firmer cloth with a variety of patterns. The warp threads were attached to heddles, or small cords, which could be raised and lowered alternately, usually by treadles controlled by the weaver's feet. Using a shuttle, the weaver passed the short thread, or weft, through the opening (known as the shed) made in the threads of the warp by the heddles. After each pass of the shuttle, the weft threads were beaten together using a reed or slay, a moveable wooden frame like a comb (Plate IV). A single weaver could

[44] YBIA, York Prob. Reg. 3, fol. 437 (Shipley), fols 567–8 (Clynt); Prob. Reg. 4, fol. 72 (Chellow).

[45] G.A. Thornton, *A History of Clare Suffolk* (Cambridge, 1928), p. 185; Britnell, *Colchester*, p. 184.

[46] Zell, *Industry*, p. 166.

work a narrow loom producing narrow cloths by throwing the shuttle with his right hand and catching it at the other side with his left but two weavers were needed to produce broadcloth at least 1¾ yards wide on the broadloom – one at each end, to receive and return the shuttle thrown by his partner.[47]

Like the spinning wheel, the horizontal loom probably tripled productivity. Using data from late medieval Flanders, it has been calculated that a typical team of weavers could produce ten broadcloths in a year – a rate of productivity not surpassed until major advances in technology in the eighteenth century.[48] It has been estimated that a loom could process about 6 lb of yarn per day, the work of six full-time spinners. Weavers produced about 2 yards of cloth each day, so it would take a weaver and his assistant nearly two weeks to produce a typical broadcloth. On this basis, it has been estimated that at least 650 looms were operating in Kent in the 1560s, requiring a labour force of about 1,300 people.[49]

In contrast to spinners, who were often of low status, weavers varied considerably in wealth and social standing (Table 2). In the poll taxes of 1377–81, while the majority of weavers paid tax of only 6d, a few had very high assessments, like John Welles of Salisbury, assessed on 10s, and retaining four servants; William Ore and John Beneyt of Canterbury, each assessed on 9s, and each keeping one apprentice and two servants; and John Denton of Oxford, assessed on 8s, who had two servants.[50] These weavers are likely to have operated substantial businesses, but other weavers supplemented their income through farming. Indeed many weavers held dual occupations, which allowed their families to survive in periods when there was little or no income to be gained from weaving. Those weavers who had no land to work and had to sustain themselves as labourers were in a particularly precarious position.[51] Wives and daughters of weavers helped operate the loom and many women weavers who worked independently were widows of weavers. Twenty-two female weavers were recorded as working in Wakefield and surrounding villages in 1399, and the York weavers' ordinances made in 1400 permitted women to work in the trade if they could demonstrate their skill.[52] By the later fifteenth century however, when several large cloth-making towns were facing decline, employment opportunities for women appear to have contracted. A weavers' ordinance at Bristol in

[47] Basing, *Trades*, pp. 80–1; Lipson, *Woollen and Worsted Industries*, pp. 136–8.

[48] Epstein, *Economic and Social History*, pp. 194–6.

[49] Zell, *Industry*, pp. 169, 179.

[50] Fenwick, *Poll Taxes*, i, p. 420; ii, p. 340; iii, p. 123.

[51] Zell, *Industry*, pp. 169–79.

[52] *Calendar of Inquisitions Miscellaneous*, 7 vols (London, 1916–68), vi: *1392–9*, pp. 242–9; Goldberg, *Women*, pp. 120–1.

1461 referred to wives, daughters and maids working on their own looms or employed by other weavers, causing many men, who were skilled in the craft, to live as vagrants. Female labour was therefore to stop, except in the case of the weaver's wife, who was able to work for her husband as long as he lived.[53]

Weavers needed more plant and capital than spinners, but these requirements were still minimal in comparison with the capital that a clothier needed to function. A loom and a pair of shuttles could be obtained for around £1 in Colchester in the later fourteenth century.[54] Start-up costs were therefore relatively modest. Weavers generally tended to accept low piece-rates and payment long in arrears rather than leave looms idle for extended periods. Looms were often bequeathed in wills. Henry Borham, cloth-maker of Clare, in 1523 left his son his small pair of looms, and to his wife his 'broad looms'.[55]

Some individuals operated as both clothiers and weavers, and some clothiers owned looms that weavers must have rented in their own homes, or travelled to the clothier's workshop to use. Weaver Roger Crytott of Lavenham was a clothier in all but name, who with his kinsman Thomas, presented more broadcloth to the ulnager in the 1460s than any other cloth producer in the town. Crytott owned two dye-houses and tenters for stretching cloth, traded with merchants in King's Lynn, and exported cloth from Ipswich.[56] The clothier John Flower of Potterne owned four looms around 1550, and William Stumpe created a workshop for his weavers in the former abbey buildings at Malmesbury.[57] The Weavers Act of 1555 prohibited rural clothiers from operating more than two looms, although some weavers continued to use three or four looms, apparently without penalty.[58]

Several clothiers left bequests to weavers, including Thomas Christmas of Colchester, who bequeathed 6s 8d in 1520 'to every of my tenants that be my fullers, weavers and shearmen'. Although only five weavers and two shearmen were recorded in the list that was attached to the will, Christmas may have employed others who were not his tenants.[59] William Gilbert of Clare in his will of 1547 bequeathed 'that

[53] *The Little Red Book of Bristol*, ed. F.B. Bickley, 2 vols (Bristol, 1900), ii, pp. 127–9.

[54] Britnell, *Colchester*, pp. 75–6.

[55] Thornton, *Clare*, p. 186.

[56] Amor, *From Wool to Cloth*, p. 147.

[57] Ramsay, *Wiltshire*, p. 17.

[58] See below, p. 171.

[59] Britnell, *Colchester*, p. 184.

every of my weavers being the chief weaver in the looms shall have 6s 8d, and that every spinner of mine shall have 12d.'[60]

Fulling and tentering

> Cloth that comes from weaving is not comely to wear
> Till it's fulled under foot or in fulling-frames,
> Washed well with water, and with teasels combed,
> Stretched on tenters, and tinted, and placed in tailor's hand
>
> William Langland, *Piers Plowman* (1370s)[61]

Clothiers collected their cloths from weavers and took them to fullers to cleanse and thicken the fabrics. Fulling had two functions, scouring, which cleansed the cloth of the oils used in preparing the yarns, and thickening, which matted the fibres together to give strength and increase waterproofing. The cloth was scoured with cleaning agents such as fuller's earth (a soft clay-like substance that occurs naturally as hydrous aluminium silicate) and urine. While soaked, the cloth was pounded. Initially this was done by simply trampling the cloth underfoot (Plate I, middle left). From the late twelfth century onwards though, water-power was increasingly harnessed to pound the cloth by moving large and heavy wooden hammers, driven by a tappet wheel attached to a water wheel (Figure 4 and Plate 2). Cloth was usually subjected to this immersion and pummelling twice, and in between, the cloth was hung over a pole or frame for burling – the removal of any knots or defects.

The earliest known English fulling mills were at Paxton in Huntingdonshire in 1173 and at Temple Newsam in Yorkshire and Barton in Gloucestershire in 1185. In an influential article, Eleanora Carus-Wilson argued that the water-powered fulling mill provided an 'industrial revolution of the thirteenth century', enabling the English cloth industry to outperform its foreign rivals and leading to a shift from urban to rural production, although subsequent studies have questioned the impact of this new technology. Even so, the mechanisation of fulling transformed a process that had taken three to five days to a task that could be achieved in a few hours. Using evidence from sixteenth-century Brabant, estimates for the productivity gains achieved from fulling using a mill compared to fulling with feet suggest that there was a 70 per cent saving for mill-fulling and a 3.3-fold productivity gain.[62]

[60] Thornton, *Clare*, p. 185.

[61] Langland, *Piers Plowman*, i, p. 600; Langland, *Will's Vision*, p. 175 (B, Passus XV, lines 451–4).

[62] Carus-Wilson, 'Industrial Revolution', pp. 183–210; Bridbury, *Clothmaking*, pp. 16–25; *CHWT*, pp. 204–9, 271–3.

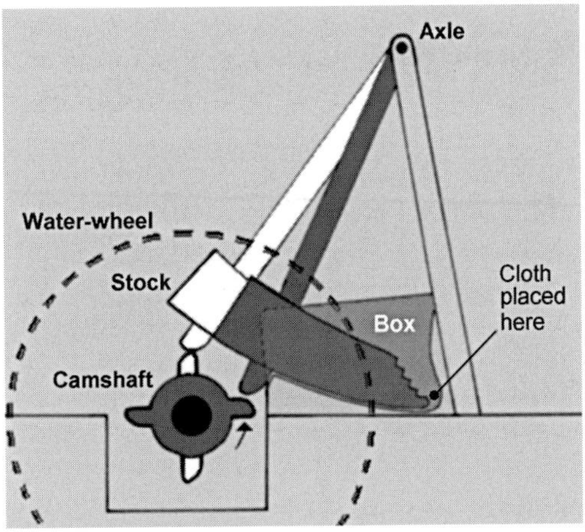

Figure 4 Simplified diagram of fulling mill machinery

Fulling was generally undertaken by independent craftsmen who were paid piece rates by the clothiers. These fullers were also known as tuckers in the west of England and walkers in the north of England.[63] There are also a few known examples of fulling mills being bequeathed to widows and of widows being licensed to trade as fullers.[64] A fulling mill was a major capital investment, much larger than the amount that a clothier usually invested in fixed plant. The construction of a new fulling mill in 1545 at Otham, near Maidstone, for example, with two 7½-foot wheels, cost £88.[65] A few fullers owned their own mills but many were tenants or employees of owners, or lessees of the mills. Roger Smith, who leased a fulling mill at Rolvenden in Kent in the early 1530s, had at least one male servant and was able to provide £20 for his daughter.[66] Many fulling mills were owned by the gentry, and up to the dissolution of the monasteries, a number were held by religious houses. The last abbot of Cirencester constructed two fulling mills within the town. Mary's Mill, newly built in 1533–34, and comprising a house, four stock mills and one gig mill, was leased by the abbey to clothier Robert Fowler of Stonehouse.[67]

Some clothiers though, had sufficient capital to acquire fulling mills, thereby ensuring that their cloths were finished when they required them. In Suffolk, a handful of wealthy clothiers held fulling mills in the

63 E.M. Carus-Wilson, 'The Significance of the Secular Sculptures in the Lane Chapel, Cullompton', *Medieval Archaeology* 1 (1957), p. 106.

64 Goldberg, *Women*, p. 122.

65 KHLC, U1044/F1, pp. 55–61.

66 Zell, *Industry*, pp. 180–1.

67 Gloucestershire Archives, D674b/T8; *Itinerary*, i, p. 129.

Plate 2 Fulling stocks depicted in John Lane's aisle, Cullompton church, Devon.
Large wooden hammers, usually powered by a water wheel, pounded the cloth to scour and thicken it during the fulling process.

late fifteenth century, including John Horrold of Clare, Hugh Turnour of Stoke-by-Clare, and Richard Davy of Nayland.[68] In Wiltshire, William Stowford acquired a lease of four fulling mills at Stowford in 1459, and by the Tudor period, clothiers generally controlled fulling mills either by

[68] Amor, *From Wool to Cloth*, p. 156.

Plate 3 Tenters, Otterburn Mill, Northumberland.
After fulling, cloth was stretched and hung to dry on tenters. This mill claims to have the last surviving set of tenters.

owning or leasing them, although this was much less evident in the Kent Weald.[69] If they could not afford to buy a fulling mill, some clothiers leased one. Thomas Christmas of Colchester leased Newbridge Mill in West Bergholt, and left bequests in his will to his fullers, while his father had leased two fulling and grain mills.[70] Clothiers occasionally made bequests to fullers, like those of John Tyler, cloth-maker of Wells, who in 1512 left 'to my weavers and tuckers to every man of them 4d'.[71] In the absence of other evidence, it is unclear whether these fullers were employees of the clothier, his tenants, or simply independent craft-workers with whom the clothier had worked.

After the fuller had removed the wet cloth from the vat, it was hung on a tenter to dry the cloth, remove any wrinkles, make repairs, and restore some of the size lost through shrinkage. These tenters were wooden

[69] *VCH Wiltshire*, iv, p. 136; Ramsay, *Wiltshire*, p. 19; Zell, *Industry*, p. 180.

[70] Britnell, *Colchester*, pp. 184–5.

[71] *Somerset Medieval Wills 1501–1530*, ed. F.W. Weaver, Somerset Record Society (1903), p. 159.

frames up to 30 yards long, with closely spaced tenterhooks on the top and bottom bars, on which the cloth was hung by its edges (Plate 3). The lower bar was adjustable so that cloth could be pulled and stretched to its proper shape and width. Tenters were usually placed outside and the process generally took about two days in summer and four days in winter.[72] Clothiers commonly owned their own tenter grounds – all those mentioned in Lavenham wills were bequeathed by clothiers. As it was difficult to handle and move long lengths of wet cloth, it has been suggested that fullers often worked on the clothiers' premises.[73] Robert Barker of Colchester's will of 1503 refers to a gate through which his son is to have access to a pasture 'to dry wool and to tenter his own cloths'.[74] John Winchcombe I of Newbury (d. 1520) bequeathed all the 'racks and tenters as there now stand within a close called the culverhouse', situated on the town's Bartholomew Street.[75] Field names such as Tenter Croft and Tenter Field in Coggeshall mark the sites where tenters would have stood.[76]

While the wet cloth hung on the tenter, fullers gave the cloth a preliminary 'wet napping' with teasels. The heads of the fullers' teasel have hooked prickles between the flowers, which were used to raise the nap (the rough layer of projecting threads or fibres on the surface of the cloth). These teasels were fitted into hand-held wooden frames, known as handles, which were drawn across the cloth, picking up loose or protruding fibres that could then be cut with shears, a process known as wet shearing. These handles are depicted in the carvings of John Lane's chapel at Cullompton, Devon (Plate 4), and on bench ends at East Budleigh and Spaxton, Somerset (Plate 5), as well as in one of the panels of the cloth-workers' window in Semur-en-Auxois church in Burgundy (Plate I, middle right).[77]

This process, described as raising the nap, napping, rowing or teasing, was a laborious task: it might take up to eight hours for initial raising on a high-quality woollen cloth. The water-powered gig mill reduced this process to minutes, by placing teasels in a rotating cylinder that was drawn across the moving cloth placed on a revolving belt. The earliest

72 *CHWT*, p. 209.

73 Betterton and Dymond, *Lavenham*, p. 36.

74 James A. Galloway, 'Colchester and its Region, 1310–1560: Wealth, Industry and Rural–Urban Mobility in a Medieval Society', University of Edinburgh, Ph.D. thesis, 1986, p. 222.

75 See Appendix 6. A culver was a dove or pigeon: *OED*.

76 Andrews, ed., *Discovering Coggeshall* 2, p. 31.

77 Carus-Wilson, 'Lane Chapel', pp. 109–13. See also Michael L. Ryder, 'Fascinating *Fullonum*', *Circaea, The Journal of the Association for Environmental Archaeology* 11 (1994 for 1993), pp. 23–31.

Plate 4 Teasel frames or handles depicted in John Lane's aisle, Cullompton church, Devon.
Teasels fitted into hand-held wooden frames, known as handles, were drawn across the cloth, picking up loose or protruding fibres that could then be cut with shears.

known example in England was that established by William Haynes (d. 1435) at Castle Combe in Wiltshire. By 1533, there was a gig mill at Bishopstrow in Wiltshire leased from the nuns of Lacock Abbey and another at Cirencester leased from the abbey there.[78] A seventeenth-century report suggested that a gig mill could achieve a nine-fold gain in productivity.[79] Yet despite this, the technology was very slow to be adopted, as there were concerns that gig mills might damage the cloth, particularly if teasels were replaced with iron cards. Parliament banned the use of iron-tooth cards in 1465, and gig mills in 1552.[80]

Finishing

> The Rower next his arms lifts up on high,
> And near him sings the Shearman merrily
> The Drawer, last that many faults doth hide
> (Whom merchant nor the weaver can abide)
>
> R. Watts, *The Young Man's Looking Glass* (1641)[81]

The shearer carried out the finishing processes of dry napping and shearing, which were essentially the same as those performed on the wet cloth while it had been hanging on the tenter, but were far more vigorous and thorough. The shearer again raised the nap with teasels and cropped it with shears, often repeating the process several times, and then pressed the cloth. The surplus nap was cut off the woollen cloth to give a smooth surface appearance, the shearman using huge cloth shears (Plate I, bottom left). The cloth was draped over a padded bench, one area at a time, using copper alloy hooked clasps, known as harbicks, to secure the cloth. This process was also known as barbing, shearing or cropping. Any imperfections in the cloth would be repaired by workers known as drawers. Finally the cloth was pressed, usually without heat, in a wooden vice or with a wooden press (Plate I, bottom right, and Plate 5). Shears were an important asset, often bequeathed in wills. Gilbert Waterhouse of Halifax left 'all my looms, walker shears, cloth presses and shear boards' to his sons Laurence and John in 1541.[82] In the late fifteenth century, the Suffolk merchant William Smyth of Higham complained that he lent a pair of shears for two days to a shearman who kept them

[78] Gloucestershire Archives, D674b/T8; Carus-Wilson, 'Evidences of Industrial Growth', p. 201; *VCH Wiltshire*, iv, pp. 130–1, viii, p. 10.

[79] *CHWT*, pp. 209–10.

[80] 4 Edward IV, c. 1: *SR*, ii, p. 406; 5 & 6 Edward VI, c. 22: *SR*, iv (1), p. 156.

[81] Quoted from Lipson, *Woollen and Worsted Industries*, p. 128.

[82] *Halifax Wills: Being Abstracts and Translations of the Wills Registered at York from the Parish of Halifax. Part I, 1389 to 1514*, ed. J.W. Clay (Halifax, 1904), pp. 147–8.

Plate 5 Cloth finisher with tools at Spaxton church, Somerset.
This decorates the end of a sixteenth-century pew. The finisher is brushing or pressing cloth. In the pieces of cloth are holes made by tenterhooks. To the left of the cloth finisher is a burling knife, used to remove knots in the cloth, and to the right is a pair of cloth shears. Above the cloth finisher on the left is a teasel frame and on the right a comb.

for more than five years without paying anything. Cloth shears are represented in churches. They are carved in Seend church, Wiltshire, and in the Lane chapel at Cullompton, Devon, and illustrated in the Christ of the Trades painting in Hessett church, Suffolk, on a misericord stall in Brampton church, Huntingdonshire, on a pew end at Spaxton, Somerset (Plate 5), and in the window at Semur (Plate I, bottom left).[83]

While clothiers would usually arrange these processes, some merchants bought cloths unfinished from clothiers and organised the finishing themselves. John Smythe, mercer of Bristol, in 1539 and 1541 employed a tucker, Richard Tippar of Bristol, for 'rowing' the cloths that Smythe had bought from the clothiers John Yerbery, Thomas Hasche and William Buchar. Smythe also paid Tippar for 'bringing up' of 'northern' cloth (probably a similar process of raising the nap), which he had purchased from Thomas Abel of Manchester. Smythe relied on a Bristol shearman, Davy Hart, for 'barbing and shearing' cloths.[84] Another fuller who like Richard Tippar also finished cloth, was Roger Benet (d. 1546), who leased the West Mills in Newbury. His workshop contained fourteen sets of handles and six pairs of shears, a press and boards.[85]

Dyeing

Cloth could be dyed at any stage in its manufacture. Dyeing of the wool might be carried out before weaving, like Lavenham blue broadcloth, which was 'dyed in the wool'. Alternatively, undyed yarn could be woven to produce cloths known as 'whites', which were dyed after completion locally, in London, or overseas. Raw wool, yarn, or lengths of cloth were immersed in boiling liquids that contained the dyeing agents – admixtures of plants and chemicals that could require hours of preparation. Dyers needed to generate heat and dispose of water, requiring furnaces, stoke pits, wells and drains, like the fifteenth-century dyer's workshop uncovered at Westwick Street, Norwich in the medieval *Letestere Row*.[86] The brick-built culverts running under some of the main streets in Lavenham may have been to supply water to dyers and fullers and remove their effluent.[87] Dyers also needed cisterns, vats and coppers, like the two great brass pans called dyers' pans that Thomas Creswell, cloth-man, in 1500–01 discussed buying from the London grocer

[83] Carus-Wilson, 'Lane Chapel', pp. 105–8; Amor, *From Wool to Cloth*, plate 5.3.

[84] *Ledger of John Smythe*, pp. 92–3, 183, 198–9.

[85] BRO, D/A1/39, fol. 32a.

[86] Ayers, *Norwich*, p. 133.

[87] Betterton and Dymond, *Lavenham*, p. 34; Michael Fradley, 'Water Street, Lavenham, Suffolk. A Desk-based Assessment of a Brick Culvert', *English Heritage Research Department Report Series* 7/2007, 10–11.

William Bene in exchange for kerseys.[88] Two tools used in the dyeing process form the merchant's mark of the Hall family, carved into the clerestory of St Margaret's church, Ipswich. These are the dyer's posser, a handled tool for agitating cloth in a vat, and a pair of tongs for removing the cloth. On his death in 1503, John Hall left his son William his woad store or 'woad house'.[89]

Table 3 Principal dyestuffs used in medieval English cloth

Dyestuff	*Colour*	*Source*
Woad	blue, green, violet and black	Mediterranean, especially Tuscany and Piedmont; Toulouse and south-western France; the Azores
Madder	red	Germany and the Baltic
Weld	yellow	Germany and France
'Grain' – red dye	scarlet	Mediterranean red dye from the dried bodies of female insects popularly referred to as kermes or grain living on the kermes oak
Cinnabar	vermillion	From the Red Sea and purchased via Italian merchants
Vegetable and fruit dyes, such as saffron for yellow	various	Obtained locally, from elsewhere in England, or imported

Source: Thornton, 'Paycocke's House', p. 58; Hicks, ed., *Inland Trade*, pp. 134–6.

Table 3 shows the principal dyestuffs used in the medieval cloth industry. The shade of colour was determined by the quality of the dyestuff and the strength of the dyeing solution. Mixing different dyestuffs produced other colours: russets, sanguines, murreys and violets, for example, were produced by colouring wool with a weak solution of woad and then dipping it in a weak solution of madder.[90] Other dyestuffs could also be used, like brasil, gallnuts, litmus, saffron and

[88] TNA, C 1/238/66.

[89] John Blatchly and Peter Northeast, 'Discoveries in the Clerestory and Roof Structure of St Margaret's Church, Ipswich', *Proceedings of the Suffolk Institute of Archaeology* 38 (1996), p. 396; N.R. Amor, *Late Medieval Ipswich: Trade and Industry* (Woodbridge, 2011), pp. 10, 252.

[90] Britnell, *Colchester*, p. 55.

orchil (a purple dye), transported from Southampton.[91] Many dyestuffs were imported, although demand may have stimulated the cultivation of the saffron crocus in north Essex and south Cambridgeshire from the late fifteenth century. This expensive commodity was used for dyeing, cooking and as a medicine. Trade in saffron centred on the small Essex town of Walden, which during the sixteenth century adopted saffron both as its emblem and as the prefix to its name.[92]

Woad was generally imported in casks in dry balls, which were then broken up, moistened with water, and fermented for several weeks, with the temperature carefully regulated to ensure that all the woad underwent the same degree of fermentation. Potash was then added as the alkali and a temperature of about 50 degrees celsius needed to be maintained for two to three days.[93] Thomas Spring III of Lavenham left ten half-balls of woad in his will to his apprentice Peter Gauge in 1523.[94] Woad did not require a mordant but needed an alkali such as potash to extract the indigo pigment.

Most dyes though, needed alum, a fixing agent or mordant, to set the dyes to the cloth. Initially it was sourced from Asia Minor and traded by the Genoese, and there were also smaller quantities brought from southern Spain. The Genoese trade was disrupted by the capture of Foglia by the Turks in 1455, but new sources were discovered at Tolfa in the Papal States in 1462. The alum trade was dominated by a small wealthy elite, mostly Londoners, and by the Italians.[95] It was not until the early seventeenth century that alum was extracted within England, from quarried shale along the Yorkshire coast.

While some dyers were independent craftsmen, others were employed by clothiers, who may have carried out dyeing themselves. Clothiers' workshops were often designated as the 'dyehouse', and the mysteries of dyeing probably formed part of the core of the cloth-maker's special technical knowledge and taught through an apprenticeship. Dyeing was a skilled process and dyers paid the highest average amount of tax of all textile workers in the poll taxes of 1377–81 (Table 2). Their skills could add significant value to wool: in the 1580s it increased its price by between 25 per cent and 150 per cent.[96] Dyehouses could be valuable assets. Clothier John Winchcombe II's dye-house was valued at £40 in

[91] Hicks, ed., *Inland Trade*, p. 156.

[92] Lee, *Cambridge*, pp. 107–12.

[93] John Edwards, *The History of Woad and the Medieval Woad Vat* (Chalfont St Giles, 1998), pp. 6–7; David Peacock, 'Dyeing Winchcombe Kersies and Other Kersey Cloth in Sixteenth-Century Newbury', *Textile History* 37 (2006), pp. 192–3.

[94] See below, Appendix 5.

[95] Hicks, ed., *Inland Trade*, pp. 157–8.

[96] Zell, *Industry*, pp. 164–5.

1558.[97] Dyehouses could also be referred to in wills as parts or shares, which may reflect joint investment, or the division of inheritance. The clothier Thomas Wyllymot of Lavenham, for example, when he died in 1460 left to his two sons his part in a dye-house, and when one of these sons, Robert, died in 1502, he left 'the fourth part of the dyehouse' to his wife Elizabeth.[98] Servants, often women, helped to wash and prepare the cloth. A York case of 1411 refers to the servants of a man called Usburn, probably John Usburn (d. 1428), who cleaned cloth by the banks of the River Ouse.[99]

Some clothiers chose to sell their cloths undyed to merchants who either organised the dyeing themselves, or exported the undyed cloth overseas. The London draper Thomas Howell paid the London dyer Thomas Hoocke to colour some of the cloths he had purchased undyed from clothiers. In 1522, Hoocke dyed cloths red, blue, brown-blue, pewke, violet, tawny and green for him.[100] The Bristol mercer John Smythe owned a dyeing vat at the premises of John Lawrence in Bristol, where he paid William Shipman 2d per lb for dyeing cloths weighing 88 lb. He also employed Bristol dyers for colouring green cloth, for 'refreshing of the colours of two old gowns', and for 'woading, maddering and pewking' of a kersey. Smythe often supplied alum and dyestuffs to the dyers in part payment for their services.[101]

Linen making

While we have focused predominately on woollen cloth, it should also be noted that linen was produced from flax, and a coarse fabric known as harden was made from hemp or flax. Flax was a field crop, and as it was regarded as exhausting to the soil, long intervals were left between sowing on the same patch. Hemp, however, could be grown year after year on well-manured plots. Both crops need to be immersed in water to separate the fibres from the outer part of the stem, a process called retting. This often led to complaints about the polluting of water sources. Local courts, like those of the Honour of Knaresborough, forbade the steeping of flax or hemp in springs or running streams, and national legislation in 1541 prohibited the soaking of flax in water that served cattle.[102] The hemp or flax was then dried over fire. If this drying was

97 Jackson, 'Boom-time Freaks', p. 149.

98 Betterton and Dymond, *Lavenham*, p. 35.

99 Goldberg, *Women*, p. 192.

100 Drapers' Company, Ledger of Thomas Howell, fols 18*, 23v–24.

101 *Ledger of John Smythe*, pp. 35, 49–50, 79–80, 312–13, 330. 'Pewkyng' was to dye cloth to produce pewke or puke, a very deep bluish black or dark brown colour.

102 Bernard Jennings, ed., *A History of Harrogate and Knaresborough* (Huddersfield, 1970), p. 207; 33 Henry VIII, c. 17: *SR*, iii, p. 853.

done inside the house, it could create a serious fire hazard as well as a noxious smell, so the practice was often forbidden, as at Liverpool in 1540.[103] Once dried, the fibres were beaten and then combed or carded into long strands, usually with a tool known as a heckle. William Caype of Northallerton owned a heckle together with quantities of hemp, linen and linen seed in 1497.[104] After spinning, the yarn was bleached and woven into linen. Some weavers worked with both woollen and linen cloth, even in towns. In 1498 Robert Dacres of Beverley bequeathed one woollen-loom, and two 'bastard looms', one for broadcloths and kerseys, and one for linen and hempen cloth. Even the London weavers' guild stipulated in 1492 that no linen weaver should take any woollen yarn to weave unless he could work it himself and had the necessary gear.[105]

ORGANISING CLOTH PRODUCTION

> The custom of our country is to carry our wool out to carding and spinning and put it to divers and sundry spinners who have in their houses divers and sundry children and servants that do card and spin the same wool
>
> Petition from Suffolk clothiers (c.1575)[106]

During the medieval and early modern period, industrial activities were broadly organised in three different ways (Figure 5). Firstly, in many crafts the unit of production was the individual skilled worker, from the village carpenter to the city goldsmith. Secondly, there was the domestic or putting-out system in which merchant-entrepreneurs organised and financed production that was carried out in the homes of workers. Many textiles were produced in this way, as were some small metalwares. Thirdly, there were a few examples of centralised production, such as iron smelting using the blast furnace, where workers undertook different processes on the same site.[107] Examples of all three types of organisation could be found within the medieval English cloth industry. Initially cloth-making was carried out by the individual craftsperson. From an early date, some of these individual cloth-workers grouped together, although certain skilled craftworkers, such as some dyers and shearmen,

[103] Norman Lowe, *The Lancashire Textile Industry in the Sixteenth Century* (Manchester, 1972), pp. 43–6.

[104] Christine M. Newman, *Late Medieval Northallerton* (Stamford, 1999), p. 111.

[105] YBIA, York Prob. Reg. 5, fol. 515; Salzman, *English Industries*, pp. 239–40.

[106] TNA, SP 12/106/1, fol. 106; *Calendar of State Papers, Domestic Series, of the Reigns of Edward VI, Mary, Elizabeth, 1547–1580*, No. Eliz Vol. CVI, 48, p. 511.

[107] D.C. Coleman, *Industry in Tudor and Stuart England* (London, 1975), pp. 17–49.

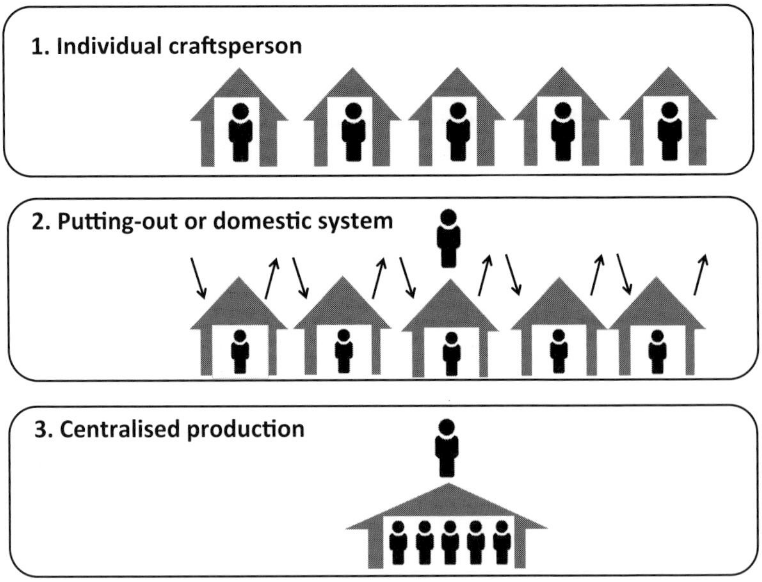

Figure 5 Different types of organisation within the cloth industry

continued to remain as individual family businesses throughout the medieval period. Increasingly during the course of the later Middle Ages, clothiers organised cloth production through the putting-out or domestic system, supplying raw or semi-processed materials to workers and marketing the finished products. Centralised production was established by William Stumpe of Malmesbury, John Winchcombe of Newbury, and a handful of other sixteenth-century clothiers, who appear to have brought together the different processes of cloth-making on a large scale at a single site.[108] In all three types of organisation, the clothier increasingly controlled the stages of production, from the buying of wool to the finishing processes.

The domestic or putting-out system[109] developed where the market for manufactured goods became sufficiently large and the techniques of production allowed manufacturing to be carried out in workers' homes. Merchant-entrepreneurs such as clothiers 'put out' materials to workers who returned them after completing their work for payment on a piece-work or wage basis. The workers neither bought their materials nor sold

[108] See below, Chapter 6.

[109] Also known as the *Verlagssytem* or *Verlagswesen*, using terms coined by German historians: Fernand Braudel, *The Wheels of Commerce* (London, 1982), pp. 316–20.

their products, relying on the merchant-entrepreneurs for both these activities. The cloth industry was particularly suitable for this system of industrial organisation as it required several different processes thus allowing the division of labour, used materials that were readily transportable, and consisted of processes that mostly (with the exception of fulling and dyeing) could be readily undertaken in households once basic skills had been acquired (such as spinning) and tools purchased or loaned (such as looms). Within the domestic system, the clothier benefitted from lower wage costs and increased efficiency due to a more extensive division of labour within the craft. Piece-rates were paid only for work carried out. As employers, they incurred no overheads for work done in the homes of their employees. If the market slumped, they had no ongoing costs apart from their materials and possibly their equipment, while if the market boomed they could readily expand without encountering shortages of plant or machinery. The worker enjoyed the independence to work in his or her own house, generally free from restraint and supervision, and could engage their family, choose their own hours of work, and combine their craft with farming or housework.[110]

The factory[111] brought the advantage of employing workers under direct supervision, reducing the opportunities for fraud, regulating the productivity of labour, maintaining uniform standards, and cutting the time spent moving materials between different processes. Yet until water-powered machinery capable of mechanising spinning and weaving was introduced during the eighteenth century, the factory system did not offer any significant benefits over the cottage-based industry of the domestic system. A lack of surplus labour willing or able to devote time solely to manufacturing rather than combining their work with agricultural or household tasks was another reason why factories were rarely to be found in the later Middle Ages. The initial cost of erecting a large building was also a deterrent, although some clothiers could obtain buildings in situ in the 1540s by acquiring parts of dissolved monasteries and friaries. The domestic system survived for many centuries, and hand looms could still be found producing cloth in homes in the nineteenth century.[112]

Wage labour accounted for a smaller proportion of work in the late Middle Ages than today. The characteristic form of organisation in towns was the individual craftsperson. Self-employed, and often assisted

110 Heaton, *Yorkshire Woollen*, pp. 90–1, 347–51; Bridbury, *Clothmaking*, p. 11.

111 Some historians apply the term 'manufactory' to workshops where articles are handmade and 'factory' to enterprises using machinery: Braudel, *Wheels of Commerce*, p. 329.

112 Heaton, *Yorkshire Woollen*, pp. 90–1, 351–2, 358; Bolton, *Medieval English Economy*, p. 282.

by family members, this independent artisan, such as a weaver, dyer or fuller, might employ apprentices or journeymen as extra hands. Apprentices were employed under contract for long periods, up to seven years, usually receiving in exchange board and lodgings, but very little cash. Journeymen had served apprenticeships but were unable or unwilling to become masters themselves, and worked on a contracted longer-term basis. Servants were also employed. If they were household servants, any craft work that they undertook was probably subsidiary to their main household duties, but it has been suggested that the term may have been used to describe journeymen too.[113] Independent artisans also drew on casual wage-labour to supplement their efforts. Indeed the distinction between the independent craftsperson and the wage-earner could be blurred, as some combined contract work with trading on their own account. Richard Silvester of Colchester, for instance, claimed debts for cloths he sold, but in 1373 was alleged to have woven cloths on contract.[114] Employment arrangements, and particularly apprenticeships, were regulated in larger towns through guilds and borough governments, and even national government occasionally intervened in such matters.[115] Clothiers might employ apprentices and journeymen, like John Briggs of Salisbury in 1491 and John Benet of Cirencester in 1497, who each had thirteen servants and apprentices, but the wealthier clothiers, particularly in newer centres of cloth-making, relied largely on casual wage-labour organised through the putting-out system.[116]

It was not uncommon for richer clothiers to have numerous dependent workers but estimating the extent of the putting-out system is difficult. Richard Britnell's suggestion that this form of organisation was 'unlikely to have affected more than a few thousand workers' in the later Middle Ages was based on estimates for cloth production that have subsequently been revised upwards.[117] Based on estimates of lump sums left in bequests to their workers, Thomas Paycocke of Coggeshall may have had between 80 and 240 workers, and Thomas Spring II anywhere between 220 and 3,900 workers, although these clothiers were exceptional in their wealth, and probably in the size of their operations.[118] Assessments of wealth made in the 1520s suggest that wage earners predominated in a number of cloth-making areas. More than a quarter of the weavers in the Babergh hundred of Suffolk in 1522 were too poor

[113] Galloway, 'Colchester and its Region', p. 182.

[114] Britnell, *Colchester*, p. 75, n. 27.

[115] See below, Chapter 4.

[116] Dyer, *Age of Transition*, p. 230.

[117] Britnell, 'Commerce and Capitalism', pp. 359–60; Britnell, *Commercialisation*, p. 234; Oldland, 'Economic Impact'.

[118] See below, pp. 232, 244–5.

to have their goods assessed in the military survey, and almost another quarter were assessed at the lowest rate of £1. Similarly, many weavers and other cloth-workers in Worcestershire in 1525 had their goods valued for taxation at the same lowest threshold. Very high proportions of taxpayers were being assessed on wages in the cloth-making centres of Stroudwater in Gloucestershire (46 per cent) and Kidderminster in Worcestershire (44 per cent).[119]

A few clothiers brought wage earners together in single workplaces in centralised systems of production. A small, early example may have been the eleven servants, probably Flemish cloth-workers, at Bildeston in Suffolk in 1483, working for John Stanesby.[120] Based on estimates of their output, John Winchcombe II of Newbury must have engaged at least four hundred workers, and possibly more than eight hundred, and William Stumpe of Malmesbury may have employed similar numbers. These leading clothiers were long celebrated as pioneers of factory production, although how many of these workers were actually based in centralised workshops, rather than working in their own homes, is unclear.[121]

It would be misleading to equate clothiers and their workers with employers and employees, as crucial features of modern employment relationships cannot be found in the links between these two groups.[122] Many of the dependent cloth-workers were outworkers, working away from their employer's premises, commonly at home, and often using their own equipment. They had no right to a regular wage, but depended on being offered work by the clothiers. Such wage labour was often very casual, with very short periods of work. This was not necessarily to the disadvantage of many wage earners, who might work for more than one master, undertake different occupational tasks, combine agricultural or household duties, or show a high preference for leisure and a reluctance to commit to fixed hours of employment.[123]

There is some evidence, though, that the putting-out system placed at least some workers at a disadvantage. A complaint of 1539 by the weavers of Suffolk and Essex, including those of Ipswich, Hadleigh, Lavenham,

119 *The Military Survey of 1522 for Babergh Hundred*, ed. John Pound, Suffolk Records Society 28 (Woodbridge, 1986), p. 133; Dyer, *Age of Transition*, pp. 230–1.

120 Amor, 'Jack of all Trades', pp. 426–7; England's Immigrants 1330–1550, https://www.englandsimmigrants.com. Tax assessors recorded the Bildeston cloth-workers as Italians, perhaps swayed by Stanesby's Italian trading connections, but the names suggest Flemish origins.

121 See below, pp. 258, 264–6.

122 G.D. Ramsay, *The English Woollen Industry, 1500–1750* (London, 1982), p. 24; Amor, *From Wool to Cloth*, p. 210.

123 Richard Britnell, *The Closing of the Middle Ages? England, 1471–1529* (Oxford, 1997), pp. 223–4.

Bergholt, Colchester and Dedham, protested that clothiers now possessed looms, had weavers and fullers working in their own houses, and were driving down the price of weaving, leading to the impoverishment of independent weavers. The complaint also suggested that the clothiers were colluding to agree a price for weaving:

> For the rich men, the clothiers, be concluded and agreed among themselves to hold and pay one price for weaving of the said cloths, which price is so little, that your said supplicants the weavers cannot … sustain and maintain their poor households although they should work incessantly night and day, holy day and work day.[124]

The evidence available for cloth-making in Essex and Suffolk reflects the position described, with the disappearance of small independent artisans, and the increasing role of clothiers in exercising direct control over the manufacturing process. Half the weavers living in the Suffolk hundred of Babergh in 1522 were either 'of no substance', or assessed at the very lowest level, with only £1 in goods.[125] Around 1536, Kentish weavers compiled a similar list of complaints, requesting no cloth-maker keep and use more than one loom for weaving in his own house, that clothiers pay for the work of spinners and weavers in ready money, not in goods, and that a procedure be established to arbitrate in disputes between clothiers and weavers.[126] Earlier disputes between the cloth-makers and the weavers, fullers and tuckers in Reading led to an agreement between the two parties issued in the Court of Star Chamber in 1520.[127] Grievances were also voiced about clothiers paying their workers in truck, that is in foodstuffs or goods instead of money wages. Successive national and local legislation, including an act of parliament in 1464, tried to stop these payments.[128] The borough court at Colchester, for example, was informed in 1483–84 that a town bailiff and cloth-maker was carrying out these practices:

> Richard Plomer is in the habit of buying one bushel of wheat flour for 9d and sells it to fullers for their labour for 15d [and also] the said Richard buys one weight of cheese for 10s and sells it to fullers and weavers for their labours for 16s.[129]

In some cases though, the payment of wages in goods rather than in

124 TNA, SP 1/151, fol. 70; *LP*, xiv (1), no. 874, p. 408.
125 *Military Survey*, p. 133.
126 BL, Cotton MS Titus B.1, no. 59, fol. 193.
127 BRO, R/IC2/1.
128 See below, pp. 170–1.
129 Galloway, 'Colchester and its Region', p. 190; Britnell, *Colchester*, p. 184.

money might have reflected a shortage of coinage or concerns about its quality.[130]

Another way in which clothiers might exploit their workers was by delaying payment of their wages. Debts recorded in wills and inventories suggest that spinners in particular were frequently paid in arrears, often for work over considerable periods, and there appear to have been no commonly accepted conventions about how frequently outworkers should be paid. John Bawden, a clothier of Horsmonden, Kent, in 1564 owed 'Mother Richards' £2 10s for spinning, which must have amounted to wages for at least two hundred days' work. Spinners bore a disproportionate share of the credit that sustained the clothier's business, although clothiers also left independent artisans, such as weavers, fullers and shearmen, waiting for payment, thereby increasing their own liquidity.[131]

Indeed credit underpinned all aspects of cloth-making. The supply of wool on credit to cloth-makers was recognised in fifteenth-century legislation. A statute of 1465 restricted sales of wool in advance of shearing to spinners and cloth-makers for the next two years in eighteen principal wool-growing counties, and a subsequent statute of 1488–89 applied a blanket ban on the buying of 'wool unshorn' except for those making yarn and cloth in England.[132] On the other hand, wool producers could demand payments in earnest (initial instalments) of up to 40 per cent of the total agreed price, and might refuse to deal with smaller buyers, like the wool dealer John Heritage, who were unable to provide them.[133] Clothiers might exchange cloth for wool, as in the agreement made in June 1496 between William Brograve and William Dormer, woolman of West Wycombe in Buckinghamshire. Dormer was to deliver 69 sacks of wool and Brograve to supply in return 126 broadcloths of puke colour, to be provided in five instalments over the next year and a half, with a penalty of £7 for every cloth undelivered.[134]

Many of the other raw materials required for cloth production like dyes and mordants might also rely on credit, often supplied by merchants who were buying the finished cloth. The London draper John Brikles sold thirty bales of woad worth £48 to John Person of Lavenham cloth-maker, who was to deliver to him in exchange twenty-four blue cloths of his own making, or ready money. John Bigge of Goudhurst in Kent supplied the London draper Thomas Howell with a russet broadcloth in 1528 for £5

[130] See below, pp. 151–2, 170.

[131] TNA, PROB 11/47/178; M. Zell, 'Credit in the Pre-Industrial English Woollen Industry', *EcHR*, 2nd series 49 (1996), pp. 680–1; Amor, *From Wool to Cloth*, p. 125.

[132] 4 Edward IV, c. 4; 4 Henry VII, c. 11: *SR*, ii, pp. 410, 535–6.

[133] Dyer, *Country Merchant*, pp. 97–8, 101–2.

[134] TNA, C 1/308/15.

16s 8d, of which nearly half was paid in woad.[135] Equipment could also be supplied on credit, like the loom that John Grom constructed in his home in Colchester in 1375, for which he was still alleged to owe money several years later, or the spinning wheel leased to the wife of Richard Taillour, a fellow townsman, in 1391.[136]

In the putting-out system, the clothier put out materials to workers to work on and then to return in exchange for a money payment. In 1477, William Smyth of Colchester claimed that he had delivered to Robert Sympson 400 lb of white wool with 500 lb of 'waide' (woad) for it to be dyed, for which Sympson was to receive 20s for his labour. Through Sympson's negligence, the wool and woad were totally ruined. Sympson denied this charge, claiming that he had dyed the wool well and sufficiently in his 'wode house'.[137] In this case, and indeed in most cases, the materials were put out to workers in their own homes or workshops. Some workers though, may have used equipment on the clothier's premises. Some clothiers, for example, owned several broadlooms. Robert Rychard of Dursley had three looms in his house in 1492 and William Cuff of Salisbury had three broadlooms and two other looms in his weaving house in 1500.[138] Poorer clothiers probably distributed and collected materials themselves, while richer clothiers were likely to have used agents. In eighteenth-century Yorkshire, women supplemented their income as spinners by receiving commission for putting out and collecting wool.[139] Most textile workers engaged by clothiers were probably based in the local area, although some employees might reside a considerable distance away. John Stoby of Cirencester had thirty-six 'Bristol red' cloths woven and dyed in Cirencester and then delivered by packhorse to six fullers at Stroud, eight miles away. After watering, washing, fulling, teasing and shearing the cloths, they were returned to Stoby at Cirencester ready to be transported onwards to markets.[140]

TIMESCALES AND PROFITS

How long did it take to produce a piece of cloth? Clearly this depended on the size and quality of the cloth, but mechanically fulled broadcloth is estimated to have taken 978 hours to produce in the sixteenth century (Table 4). As 978 hours were just under half a year's work, it clearly made

[135] TNA, C 1/70/102; Drapers' Company, Ledger of Thomas Howell, fols 64v–65.
[136] Britnell, *Colchester*, pp. 75, 102.
[137] Galloway, 'Colchester and its Region', p. 184.
[138] TNA, PROB 2/57 (Rychard); PROB 2/174 (Cuff).
[139] Heaton, *Yorkshire Woollen*, p. 336.
[140] Carus-Wilson, 'Evidences of Industrial Growth', p. 195.

Table 4 Estimated timescales and labour costs of cloth-making in 1540s

Process	*Hours to produce one cloth*	*Daily wage or income (d)*	*Total labour cost (d)*	*Notes*
Wool sorting	50	1.5	8	
Yarn preparation	572	2	114	
Weaving	130	3.9	51	(1)
Fulling/tentering	30	3	9	
Cleansing	60	3	18	
Finishing	120	4.2	50	
Dyeing	8	6.5	5	(2)
Packing and transport	8	4	3	
Total	978		258	

Source: Based on the estimates provided by Oldland, 'Economic Impact', pp. 236–41, which are drawn from W. Endrei, 'Manufacturing a Piece of Woollen Cloth in Medieval Flanders: How Many Work Hours?', in E. Aerts and J. Munro, *Textiles of the Low Countries in European Economic History* (Leuven, 1990), pp. 14–33.

Notes: There are no detailed accounts of English cloth production in this period so several assumptions have been made. These include assuming a working day of 10 hours, and a working year of 230 days. It is also assumed that yarn preparation was mostly carried out by women who gave about 40 per cent of their time to cloth-making. Cloth-workers were often paid piece rates for work done.

(1) Weaving costs assume that a master weaver received 4.9d per day and the assistant was paid half this and did half the total work.

(2) Dyeing costs assume that the master dyer obtained 10d and his two assistants 3d, and the master did half the total work.

sense for the different parts of the manufacturing process to be carried out by different workers.

The longest task, and therefore the most labour intensive, was the yarn preparation, involving combing, carding and spinning, which took up over half the total time taken to make the cloth (Table 4). A proposal to establish cloth-making in Skipton in 1588 estimated that of the sixty people that would need to be employed to make a single broadcloth of 86 lb, thirty would be needed for spinning and carding.[141] It was in the clothier's interest to find as many spinners as possible, to avoid this task becoming a bottleneck and delaying completion of the cloth. This might

[141] Royal Commission on Historical Manuscripts, *The Manuscripts of Lord Kenyon*, p. 573.

entail using spinners residing at some distance. In 1493, the Lavenham clothier Thomas Sturmyne bequeathed 2d to each of his spinners who lived at Glemsford and Stoke-by-Clare, the latter fifteen miles from Lavenham.[142] When a cloth-maker called Tucker of Burford tried to acquire the site of Abingdon Abbey in 1538, it was claimed that 'Weekly need constrains him to send to Abingdon his cart laden with wool to be carded and spun', and 'likewise he sendeth to Stroudwater', over thirty miles from Burford.[143] It was also in the clothier's interest though, to hold down the cost of spinning as far as possible. While spinning took up 58 per cent of the total time, it only accounted for 44 per cent of the total labour costs. Spinning at 2d a day was a good wage compared to men's winter wages, or servants on annual contract. In the 1590s, a married woman who spent half her time spinning would have earned just under one-third of a labourer's wage.[144]

The most expensive craft, because it demanded the greatest skill, was dyeing, averaging 6½d per day (Table 4). Those clothiers who had the expertise to dye wool or cloth themselves would have been at an advantage, providing that they could obtain the raw materials and equipment at the same costs or less than specialist dyers. It is likely that they could source raw materials at competitive prices through their trading relationships, as the merchants to whom they supplied cloth often imported or distributed dyestuffs. Clothiers also sold cloth to merchants undyed, who then arranged dyeing and finishing. Finishing was also an expensive craft, again reflecting the skill and responsibility involved.

The total amount paid in labour, on average, to produce one cloth, was 258d, or just over £1 (Table 4). If it is assumed that the average cloth retailed at around £4 in the early 1540s, production wages accounted for about a quarter of the final price.[145] Wool was, on average, 35 per cent of the manufacturing cost.[146] If we compare these percentages with the costs of producing russet cloth in Colchester in the late fourteenth century (Table 5), when labour accounted for about half the total cost, it suggests that sixteenth-century clothiers had been able to drive down their labour costs.[147] The comparison is not exact, because the Colchester example is not based solely on labour costs, but presumably included some allowances for the costs of procuring raw materials

[142] Betterton and Dymond, *Lavenham*, p. 27.

[143] TNA, SP 1/129, fol. 154; *LP*, xiii (1), no. 415, p. 154.

[144] Oldland, 'Economic Impact', p. 243; Muldrew, 'Th'ancient Distaff', p. 510.

[145] Oldland, 'Economic Impact', p. 247.

[146] Oldland, 'Wool and Cloth Production', p. 34.

[147] For earlier estimates, not directly comparable, of producing cloth at Beaulieu Abbey and Laleham (Middlesex) in the late thirteenth century, see Miller and Hatcher, *Medieval England*, p. 96.

for the different cloth-making processes (such as oil, fuller's earth and dyestuffs), for transport, and for carding or combing, which may have been included in the spinning costs. Wool costs too had fallen by the sixteenth century, because although wool comprised just over one-third of the total production costs at both dates, the late-fourteenth-century russet cloth used 26 lb of wool but by the sixteenth century the standard broadcloth required 84 lb. of wool.[148] Colchester cloths had been able to compete in European markets in the late fourteenth century not simply because of the cheapness of the wool from which they were made, but because of the level of manufacturing costs. The sixteenth-century clothier could reduce these labour costs further, largely through the putting-out system.

Table 5 Costs of making russet cloth, c.1391

	s	*d*	%
Wool (26 lb @ 4d per lb.)	8	8	36
Spinning	1	7	7
Dyeing	3	10	16
Weaving	4	0	17
Fulling	3	0	12
'Lyste' or border to hold cloth on tenterhooks		2	1
Sealing		2¼	1
Total production costs	21	5¼	90
Entrepreneur's costs and margin	2	6¾	10
Sale price	24	0	

Source: Britnell, *Colchester*, pp. 58–62.

Note: Based on a case brought to Colchester borough court by weaver William Okle in 1388, who had organised the manufacture of a cloth for Matilda Westoneys. The russet cloth was 37½ feet long by 6 feet wide and this measure was known as a *decena*. Using the average price of broadcloths recorded in the town, Britnell suggested that the entrepreneur earned a profit of approximately 10 per cent.

Applying the estimates for the hours required to make one cloth to the estimates of total cloth produced in England, John Oldland has calculated approximately how many people were engaged in cloth-making across the country. As noted in the Introduction, total English cloth production may have risen from just under 200,000 cloths in the 1440s

148 Oldland, 'Economic Impact', p. 230.

to 308,000 by the 1540s. Oldland suggests that this latter figure would have taken around 264,000 cloth-workers, or about 15 per cent of the adult workforce.[149] A different calculation by Craig Muldrew suggests that by the same decade, spinning provided earnings for about 25 per cent of households in the country, working on average, for two-thirds of the year. The population began to grow again in the sixteenth century, and by the 1540s the birth rate was higher than at any time before the early nineteenth century. This may have provided the additional labour to enable the industry to expand, and extra family earnings from cloth-making may have supported a higher birth rate.[150]

CONCLUSION

Cloth-making involved several different processes that were initially undertaken separately by individual craftsmen, but increasingly during the later Middle Ages, were being coordinated by clothiers. Technological developments within the cloth industry brought major gains in productivity. Spinning using a wheel rather than by distaff and spindle probably tripled productivity. Gains of similar magnitude came from weaving using a horizontal loom instead of a vertical loom, and fulling in a mill rather than by foot.

Clothiers required a range of technical knowledge, from buying wool to dyeing. Throughout the cloth-making processes they had to monitor quality and ensure that products were completed and delivered on time. They sought to drive down production costs, particularly for labour, as the estimates show and complaints like those of the weavers of Essex and Suffolk also illustrate. This was mainly achieved through the widespread adoption of the putting-out system. Clothiers invested the majority of their capital, which was mainly circulating capital, in the form of raw materials, semi-finished goods and stocks. In some cases they also invested in fixed capital, such as looms and dye-houses. The clothier generally provided the working credit to cover the completion of the various processes up to the sale of the cloth. Once manufacture of the cloth was completed, the clothier's work was not over. His livelihood, and that of his dependent workers, relied upon him being able to sell his cloth in one of many competing markets.

149 Oldland, 'Economic Impact', p. 235. This is based on estimates of full-time work for fulling and finishing cloth, and part-time work for weaving and yarn production.

150 Muldrew, 'Early Industrial Workforce', pp. 85–7.

2

Marketing cloth

> I occupy with divers cloth-men in Suffolk, and in other places. The which have weekly some of them, as they send up their cloths, must have their money. And if they fail of their money, they say, they cannot set the poor folks to work. There are divers cloth-men, the which I buy all their cloths that they make … I was wont to sell for most part every year 400 or 500 cloths to strangers, which was worth to the king's grace in his customs, more than though I had shipped myself five times so many. I was wont betwixt Christmas and Whitsuntide to sell most part of them.
>
> Humfrey Monmouth, London draper (1528)[1]

The clothier was distinguished by his activities not only in organising the making of cloth, but also in marketing it. In the passage quoted above, Humfrey Monmouth, a London draper and cloth exporter, explains how clothiers, which he calls cloth-men, supply him with textiles to sell overseas. The clothiers send their cloth weekly to be sold in London, and are reliant on the money that Monmouth pays them to employ their workers. Monmouth provided this explanation in May 1528, while he was imprisoned on suspicion of heresy, so we may need to allow for some overstatement of his case to support the petition he was making to Cardinal Thomas Wolsey for his release. Even so, it seems a realistic picture of the commercial environment in which clothiers relied on London merchants to sell their cloths, who in turn were largely dependent on buyers in overseas markets.

Cloth was a relatively flexible commodity. It could be sold on at any stage in the manufacturing process, in any quantity. Clothiers sold cloths both finished and unfinished, with the latter being completed by cloth-workers, possibly in London or overseas. Cloth retained its value over time as, unlike foodstuffs, it was not perishable. It was also easily transportable. Officials and organisations acting on behalf of national and

[1] J. Strype, *Ecclesiastical Memorials Relating Chiefly to Religion*, 3 vols in 6 parts (Oxford, 1822), i, part 2, no. 89, p. 367, quoted in Britnell, 'Woollen Textile Industry', p. 94.

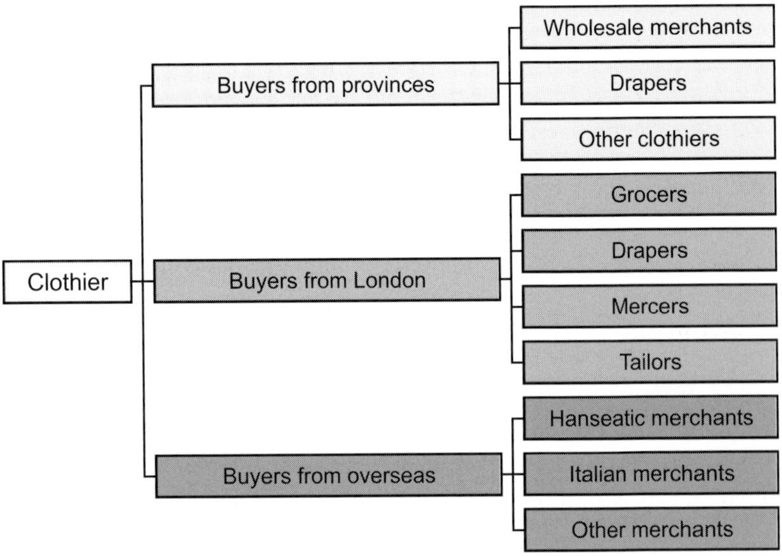

Figure 6 The clothier's customers

local governments regulated quality.[2] Clothiers could choose to sell their cloth locally, in a provincial town, or in London, and to a wide variety of buyers including specialist traders and overseas merchants (Figure 6). The larger and wealthier clothiers had the resources to enter the London market, and find a buyer who was supplying the home market or exporting overseas, such as the Merchant Adventurers, Hanseatic or Italian merchants. Both the home and overseas markets were significant: around 1560, the annual value of textiles for export has been assessed as worth about £1 million (about £170 million in today's prices), and the annual value of textiles for the home market as worth about half that.[3] The clothier's willingness to confront the market required his personal labour, judgement, and an acceptance of risk, but potentially brought reward in the form of profit.

CLOTHIERS' CUSTOMERS IN THE PROVINCES

Wholesale merchants within the provinces were potential buyers from clothiers, particularly if they could provide ready money or raw materials. In turn these merchants sold the cloth on to provincial drapers and tailors, sent it for sale in London, or arranged for the cloth to be exported. The merchants of some provincial towns organised cloth

[2] See below, Chapter 4.
[3] Ramsay, *Woollen Industry*, pp. 53, 76.

production during the later fourteenth century, and might be seen as forerunners to the clothier.[4] Most provincial merchants who exported cloth though, had bought it from others rather than arranging for its production themselves.

In the later fourteenth and early fifteenth centuries, much of the cloth sold by clothiers was shipped by merchants from provincial ports to overseas markets. Bristol served the west of England, Coventry and the Welsh marches, and had seafaring connections along the Atlantic seaboard from Ireland to Brittany, Gascony, Spain, Portugal and the Mediterranean. Southampton drew trade from much of southern England and was an important centre for Italian galleys. Dartmouth and Plymouth handled south Devon cloth and probably also some of Exeter's production, and provided shipping routes to Gascony. Hull served Yorkshire and supplied Scandinavia, the Baltic, the Low Countries and Gascony, while Ipswich and Hythe provided a similar outlet for East Anglian cloth. These ports also provided raw materials for the cloth industry, including teasels and dyestuffs from various parts of western Europe and alum from Asia Minor and Tolfa.[5] Provincial merchants, however, faced increasing competition from London as the later Middle Ages progressed.

William Mucklowe of Worcester (d. 1530) provides an example of a wealthy provincial merchant exporting English cloth. His account book of 1511 survives, revealing that he took 478 cloths to the spring and summer fairs in the Low Countries that year. These were mostly short cloths, including short whites, as well as 'draperies of diverse marks'. The accounts do not state where these cloths had been manufactured, but it may have been in Worcester where Mucklowe was based and where he served as bailiff on three occasions. Mucklowe sold cloth mostly to men from Antwerp, but occasionally from Brussels. From the proceeds of these sales he bought a wide range of cloth, mercery and grocery goods, including such varied items as 8,000 swan feathers, 18 barrels of green ginger and 146 lb of treacle, which he had carried in six ships back to London. He accumulated a large fortune, bequeathing land, cash and plate to his family. Mucklowe may have begun as a clothier, who became drawn into exporting and then into dealing in mercery and grocery goods, or he may have started out as a mercer and then become a cloth exporter.[6] John Greenway (d. 1529) of Tiverton probably had similar

[4] See above, Introduction.

[5] Carus-Wilson, 'Woollen Industry', pp. 681–2.

[6] Birmingham Archives and Heritage, Library of Birmingham, Z Lloyd 51/1; TNA, PROB 11/23/259; Alan D. Dyer, *The City of Worcester in the Sixteenth Century* (Leicester, 1973), pp. 106–7.

origins. He became a member of the London Drapers' Company and Merchant Venturers, and engaged in exporting cloth from Devon ports and London.[7]

John Smythe of Bristol (d. 1556) exported cloth from clothiers in Somerset, Wiltshire and Manchester. In return he supplied the clothiers with wool oil, alum, woad, madder and other dyestuffs. Smythe also obtained leather from the Forest of Dean and the Welsh borders, and exported hides, wheat and lead, and imported Gascon wine from Bordeaux and iron from northern Spain. His surviving ledger, detailing his business between 1538 and 1550, shows that his main supplier of cloth was John Yerbery of Bruton in Somerset, who supplied about 70 cloths a year on average, mostly described as 'penny hewes' and 'truckers'. Thomas Abeck of Manchester supplied Manchester 'cottons' in 1542, and his widow Ann supplied a further 150 cloths in 1547. Smythe often arranged the dyeing and finishing of these cloths to be carried out by Bristol craftworkers himself.[8]

Some of these provincial merchants were known as chapmen. They generally supplied cloth to London in exchange for luxury and imported goods, which they distributed locally. Henry Selwood, for example, a chapman of Wells, bought goods in London from grocer Thomas Lane in 1438. Chapmen were of higher status than pedlars and it seems that traders who were known in their home districts as merchants or mercers would sometimes be described as chapmen by Londoners, on account of their perceived subordinate status.[9] Among two hundred chapmen from thirty-one counties appearing in pardons of outlawries that concluded prosecutions for debts by London mercers between 1400 and 1490, those counties with the most chapmen as debtors were the cloth-making shires of Suffolk, Somerset, Yorkshire, Norfolk and Devon.[10]

Provincial tailors and mercers also purchased cloth produced by clothiers, either buying it from them directly, or more usually through drapers and other wholesale merchants. York tailor John Carter (d. 1485) had separate workshops for western cloth and for southern cloth. The workshop for western cloth included woollen cloth of Halifax and Craven, such as Halifax tawny, Halifax green, Halifax russet, Halifax

[7] A.E. Welsford, *John Greenway 1460–1529 Merchant of Tiverton and London. A Devon Worthy* (Tiverton, 1984), pp. 4–5; Carus-Wilson, 'Lane Chapel', pp. 115–16.

[8] *Ledger of John Smythe.*

[9] Keene, 'Debt Cases', pp. 74–6; James Davis, '"Men as March with Fote Packes": Pedlars and Freedom of Movement in Late Medieval England', in P. Holden, ed., *Freedom of Movement in the Middle Ages: People, Ideas, Goods* (Donington, 2007), pp. 137–56; Nightingale, *Medieval Mercantile Community*, pp. 365–8, 439–40; Shaw, *Wells*, pp. 92–3.

[10] Sutton, *Mercery*, pp. 213–14, 217–20.

black kersey, and 'Kentish Kendal'. The places of origin of the materials in the workshop for southern cloth, which included black, blood-red, crimson and green coloured cloth, were not specified. None of Carter's cloth was explicitly listed as having been produced in the city itself, and Carter owed £2 to a Halifax man called Bothe, possibly a clothier.[11] Retail woollen drapers in Kent purchased cloth produced in the Weald from wholesale merchants or drapers based in the county's principal market towns.[12] Other retailers such as mercers and grocers sold fabrics, threads, trimmings and accessories. Knaresborough mercer James Willinson (d. 1555) kept a range of hats and embellishments such as 'Venis golde' and possibly obtained much of his stock from 'a merchant man of London' to whom he owed £5 10s.[13]

Some clothiers conducted their own retail trade within their localities. William Forthe of Hadleigh (d. 1504) was the second-largest cloth producer in Suffolk in the late 1460s. Between 1440 and 1504 he engaged in at least ninety disputes in the Court of Common Pleas, nearly always as the claimant. His cases were of high value, with over half being worth at least £10. Although he acquired property in London, he traded mainly through the small towns and villages of Essex, Norfolk and Suffolk, dealing with a wide variety of people, including an ash burner, glover and pewterer, although nearly half his cases were with husbandmen and yeomen. This appears to have been a very successful trading strategy, reflecting the greater bargaining power that such clothiers probably enjoyed in the provinces in contrast to London.[14]

CLOTHIERS' CUSTOMERS IN LONDON

London's share of English overseas trade grew substantially during the fifteenth and sixteenth centuries. In the 1390s around 50 per cent of England's cloth exports had passed through London, by the 1470s this share had risen to around 60 per cent, by the 1540s it had reached 85 per cent, and by the 1560s it exceeded 90 per cent. Ships carried out cloth and other exports and brought back consumer goods and supplies for the textile industry. London merchants were no longer dependent solely on distributing luxury imports and increasingly supplied provincial markets with imported raw materials as well as products manufactured

[11] *Probate Inventories of the York Diocese 1350–1500*, eds P.M. Stell and Louise Hampson (York, 1998), pp. 287–94.

[12] Zell, *Industry*, p. 217.

[13] Susan North, '"Galloon, incle and points": Fashionable Dress and Accessories in Rural England, 1552–1665', in Richard Jones and Christopher Dyer, eds, *Farmers, Consumers, Innovators. The World of Joan Thirsk* (Hatfield, 2016), pp. 104–23.

[14] Amor, *From Wool to Cloth*, pp. 206–7.

in London. This two-way trade, which has been likened to a 'centrifugal force', drew clothiers and other provincial traders away from local ports, and concentrated trading links, wealth and population in London.[15] Increasingly, it was Londoners who bought cloths for export from the clothiers, and many of these exporters belonged to the Company of Merchant Adventurers, who had monopoly rights over English trade with the Netherlands.

The lack of merchants' account books and detailed customs accounts for London makes it difficult to discover what London merchants bought and sold. The London merchant's account book of the ironmonger Gilbert Maghfeld (d. 1397) is an exceptional survival, but he appears to have been typical in combining a significant trade in iron with more general business in wool, cloth and wine. He imported woad and alum, selling some to London grocers for resale and one consignment to a merchant of Bristol, but most of these raw materials were sold to drapers and dyers in Hadleigh and Salisbury. These included John Kempston of Hadleigh, who operated between around 1379 and 1410, and sold cloth worth over £213 to Maghfeld between August 1390 and September 1392. Kempston paid ulnage on 30 dozens in 1394/5. Kempston entered into several high-value transactions with customers from London, Colchester, Ipswich and Pulham Market in Norfolk before running into financial difficulties, and by 1395 he owed Maghfeld and others £80 in debts.[16]

London traders, to a much greater degree than their counterparts in the provinces, specialised in particular commodities. London's occupations were organised into over 100 guilds or companies, each named after a craft or merchandise that they traditionally represented and over which they exercised control. In principle, however, wholesale trade was open to all citizens. Company affiliation could therefore be little more than a formality, and many successful London merchants traded in goods other than those associated with their company. Many members of the largest companies traded in cloth, as well as in goods relating to their particular specialism. Grocers imported spices, dyes and mordants, and exported wool and cloth. Mercers imported silks, linens and small merceries, and exported cloth and worsteds. Drapers dealt in cloth, initially mainly imported fabrics, but during the fifteenth century they handled more provincial cloth, which they also began to export. The share of London's cloth exports traded by different companies therefore

[15] Ramsay, *Woollen Industry*, p. 39; Justin Colson, 'Commerce, Clusters and Community: A Re-evaluation of the Occupational Geography of London, *c.*1400–*c.*1550', *EcHR* 69 (2016), pp. 105–6.

[16] Margery K. James, 'A London Merchant of the Fourteenth Century', *EcHR*, 2nd series 8 (1956), pp. 364–76; Elspeth Veale, 'Maghfeld, Gilbert (d. 1397)', *ODNB*; Britnell, 'Woollen Textile Industry', p. 88; Amor, *From Wool to Cloth*, p. 194.

changed over the period. The fishmongers, for example, had distributed 30 per cent of total cloths exported from London in 1390–91, but handled less than 3 per cent of the total in 1502–03.[17]

A handful of provincial clothiers even joined London merchant guilds. The Suffolk clothiers John Stanesby and John Motte of Bildeston were both admitted to the London company of fishmongers and traded as stockfishmongers. Stanesby had Italian trading connections and Motte had trading links with Spain. In the 1460s they were the first- and fifth-largest cloth producers in Suffolk. John Kyng (d. 1469), who was born in Hadleigh, based his cloth-making in the nearby village of Shelley, but was a member of the Grocers' Company and resided in London.[18] John Thomas (d. 1514) became a London mercer but left large sums to two Worcester weavers and a fuller who may have been his employees, as well as £10 towards repairing the highway from Worcester towards London. He may have operated a clothier's business in Worcester while exporting from London.[19]

London grocers

The London Grocers' Company probably derives its name from the Latin, *grossarius*, one who buys and sells in the gross, or a wholesale merchant. Initially its members were wholesale dealers in spices and foreign produce, but increasingly they advanced credit to dyers, fullers, shearmen and drapers connected with the cloth industry, from whom they purchased cloth.[20] Grocers supplied raw materials to clothiers, like the two bales of madder Mark Walker sold in 1494 to John Beauchamp, cloth-maker of Sudbury, which Beauchamp never paid for, and Walker had to claim through the Court of Common Pleas six years later.[21] Grocers even occasionally sold consignments of wool to clothiers, like that purchased by William Twyne of Newbury in 1551.[22]

London drapers

In the early fourteenth century, the leading London drapers had exported wool and imported luxury continental cloth, which they sold in London and the provinces, but as domestic production increased and cloth imports declined, they substituted domestic for imported cloth.

[17] Colson, 'Commerce', pp. 114, 117–18; Oldland, 'Making and Marketing'.
[18] Amor, *From Wool to Cloth*, pp. 71, 194–5.
[19] TNA, PROB 11/17/607; Dyer, *Worcester*, p. 108.
[20] Nightingale, *Medieval Mercantile Community*, pp. 222, 298.
[21] TNA, CP 40/953, rot. 127d, published in Mackman and Stevens, *Court of Common Pleas*, http://www.british-history.ac.uk/no-series/common-pleas/1399-1500/trinity-term-1500
[22] Yates, *Town and Countryside*, p. 89.

Increasingly they became reliant on provincial clothiers rather than London producers for their cloths. The stock held by London draper John Olyver in 1406 illustrates this. Only half of his 22 rolls of frieze and less than 10 per cent of his 156 cloths had been made in London; the rest of the cloth came from Essex and Guildford, terms used to describe counties north-east and south-west of the city, and from Salisbury, Winchester, Reading and Colchester, while the remaining frieze was Welsh. Much of the cloth that London drapers bought was unfinished, and they put it out to fullers, shearmen and dyers working in London. Some of this cloth the drapers then exported themselves, and some they sold to other merchants. Drapers became the second-largest exporters of cloth in London, after the Mercers, and successfully transferred their cloth trade from southern Europe to Antwerp during the mid-fifteenth-century depression.[23]

By the later fifteenth century, the drapers had become more involved in exporting cloth and importing raw materials, taking over some of the distributive roles previously dominated by the London grocers as they imported oils, dyes and alum as raw materials for cloth-making, and exchanged these with clothiers. Chancery petitions illustrate the growing commercial relationships between London drapers and provincial clothiers. In 1472, draper John Brickles claimed that he had sold thirty bales of woad to a cloth-maker from Lavenham, to be repaid either in money or in twenty-four blue cloths, and in the 1480s another Lavenham cloth-man claimed to have bought certain unspecified wares from William Calley, draper, partly in money and partly in cloth.[24] In 1478, John Swetyng, a Coggeshall dyer 'alias cloth-maker', was pardoned after being locked up in the Fleet prison for owing nearly £100 to two London drapers and a haberdasher. Between 1499 and 1504, three drapers bought 800 marks worth of cloth in Croscombe, Somerset, from the clothier Richard Mawdleyn.[25]

Drapers also consolidated their control over the marketing of cloth in London. In 1364 they secured a royal charter that prevented dyers, weavers and fullers from meddling with the buying and selling of cloth, and ordered that all cloth for sale in the city or its suburbs must be sold to enfranchised drapers. This was aided by the city's centralised cloth market at Blackwell Hall, established in 1396. From 1404, drapers appointed the keeper of the hall, and from 1439 they appointed ulnagers,

[23] Eleanor Jane Powys Quinton, 'The Drapers and the Drapery Trade of Late Medieval London, *c.*1300–*c.*1500', University of London, Ph.D. thesis, 2001, pp. 209–81; Oldland, 'Making and Marketing'.

[24] TNA, C 1/70/102, C 1/122/58. Quinton, 'Drapers', pp. 146–7.

[25] TNA, C 1/244/13; *CPR 1476–85*, p. 130.

who had the right to inspect all cloth before it was sold. Later in the 1520s, drapers secured the office of metership, which involved the measurement of all cloths sold within the city.[26]

Thomas Howell (c.1480–1537), London draper

We have a detailed record of the business of one London draper, Thomas Howell, thanks to the survival of his ledger.[27] Recording transactions made between 1517 and 1528, the ledger shows that Howell bought his cloth mainly from clothiers in several locations spread across southern England, including Biddenden, Cranbrook and Goudhurst in Kent; Bildeston, Boxford, Hadleigh, Ipswich, Nayland and Stoke-by-Nayland in Suffolk; and Dedham and Colchester in Essex. Howell exported a variety of types of cloth to Spain, including whites, scarlets, russets, medleys, light tawney, fine blues, kerseys and Kentish cloths. He imported raw materials for cloth-making, including alum, woad, oil, soap, and the valuable red dyestuff known as grain, together with damask, black satin, wine and raisins. Like John Smythe of Bristol, Howell purchased some cloths unfinished and then paid for them to be dyed and finished himself. A chancery case of 1515–18 reveals that Howell sold his cloth to other London merchants and then offered to sell the same cloth abroad, charging a premium for carrying the risk of the overseas sale: a London merchant tailor, Thomas Smyth, bought £80 worth of cloths from Howell, paying 6s 8d per cloth more than they were selling for in London, as Howell promised to 'bear the adventure' of them in Andalusia.[28] Howell was the son of a Bristol merchant family that seems originally to have come from Monmouthshire. He moved to London by 1507 and became a freeman of the Drapers' Company. In 1528 he took up permanent residence in Spain, stating that he had been there on and off for about twenty-six years.[29]

London tailors

The London tailors were another company, incorporated in 1408, that became increasingly involved in the cloth trade in the fifteenth century. Disputes erupted in the 1430s and 1440s as the Tailors' Company threatened the Drapers' dominance of cloth retailing in London. The tailors

[26] Oldland, 'Making and Marketing', p. 95; Penelope Hunting, *A History of the Drapers' Company* (London, 1989), pp. 67–70.

[27] Drapers' Company, Ledger of Thomas Howell. An abstract is published in A.H. Johnson, *The History of the Worshipful Company of the Drapers of London*, 5 vols (Oxford, 1914–22), ii, pp. 44–5, 251–7.

[28] TNA, C1/443/29.

[29] Glanmor Williams, 'Howel, Thomas (*c*.1480–1537)', *ODNB*; Connell-Smith, 'Ledger'.

received the right to inspect their own cloth in 1440, traditionally the exclusive preserve of the drapers. Conflict also flared in the major London textile market of St Bartholomew's Fair, where the tailors challenged the drapers' rights to inspect their cloth. Like the drapers, the tailors also used Blackwell Hall in London to purchase cloth, and the tailors' court minutes for 1486 record an agreement between the two guilds for regulating trading activities there. Tailors could assemble large stocks of cloth in their warehouses, some of which would have been made into garments, and some sold on to other craftsmen. Roger Shavelock was said to have had cloth worth £1,000 in his shop at his death in 1489.[30]

The London tailors established links with cloth producers in the provinces and with cloth finishers. Tailor Bartholomew Donne bought 'as many cloths of various colours as comes to £72' from William Hewet, a Colchester dyer. Merchant Taylor Richard Allen purchased fifteen cloths from the Cranbrook clothier Richard Courthop during the mid 1530s for £100, but Allen claimed that several of the cloths were defective and refused to pay the full amount.[31] By the close of the fifteenth century, members of the Company were regularly exporting large quantities of cloth, and a number had become members of the society of Merchant Adventurers.

London mercers

Mercers, who had traditionally dominated the sale of silks, linen, small mercery items, and worsted cloth produced mostly in Norfolk, also took an increasing share of the cloth trade during the fifteenth century. In the Court of Common Pleas, the mercers had only four debtors in the textile trades in 1424, but this had risen to twenty-four in 1484, or 8 per cent of their total cases. Suffolk clothiers were associated with debt claims with London mercers more frequently than with any other London company in the later fifteenth century, and these twenty-eight disputes involved clothiers from sixteen towns or villages.[32] Unlike the grocers, the mercers were not major dealers in raw materials for the cloth industry, although they supplied some madder. It has been suggested that the mercers travelled to cloth-making areas to buy their cloth, as the Hansards did, and the flow of apprentices into the Mercers' Company may have followed the fortunes of local cloth industries, as some clothiers sent their sons to work in London. During the fifteenth century, mercers originated from

[30] Matthew Davies and Ann Saunders, *A History of the Merchant Taylors' Company* (Leeds, 2004), pp. 64–5.

[31] Davies and Saunders, *Merchant Taylors*, p. 65; Zell, *Industry*, p. 219.

[32] Sutton, *Mercery*, p. 220; Amor, *From Wool to Cloth*, pp. 202–3.

cloth-producing areas of Colchester, Coventry, Essex, Suffolk, Kent and Devon.[33]

The mercers came to dominate the London cloth trade through their role as leading members of the London Company of Merchant Adventurers, which is considered in more detail below. By 1534–35, the mercers handled almost 50 per cent of London's cloth exports, but even this trade was passing into the hands of the wealthy few, with a mere twenty-five shippers taking almost half the total trade. The accounts of cloth merchant Frans de Pape of Antwerp for 1538–45 show him purchasing cloths from twenty-five English merchants, of whom ten were mercers. The cloths that they sold de Pape included Castlecombes, Worcesters, Coggeshalls and fine whites, indicating the wide geographical areas from which clothiers were selling their cloth to the mercers.[34]

Merchant adventurers

The Fellowship of Merchant Adventurers originated from organised trading groups to the Netherlands, Prussia and Scandinavia, with delegated authority from the English crown. The term had originally been applied to any overseas trader not exporting wool, but the merchant adventurers came to concentrate primarily on the export of cloth. By cooperating together in their shipments to the Low Countries, merchants benefitted from uniform freight rates and the protection of convoys, and could present a common view on policy matters.

The London organisation, dominated by the mercers, was formalised by a grant of 1486. Its members were chiefly mercers, grocers, drapers, skinners and haberdashers. Other English towns had similar trading fellowships, notably the Merchant Adventurers of York and Newcastle. The York merchants' fraternity had built a hall between 1357 and 1361, which still stands in the city today. While these provincial groups of adventurers equipped their own fleets for the quarterly markets in the Low Countries, the London adventurers increasingly sought to control and exclude adventurers from other English ports and other merchants outside their company who traded within their territory. The mercers of York, Hull, Beverley and Scarborough protested in 1478 that John Pickering, mercer of London and governor of the company, was making unjust demands upon them. The merchants of Norwich complained in 1509 that 'we suppose the merchants of the city of London will bind all merchants of England at their will and pleasure … to the intent to

33 Sutton, *Mercery*, pp. 220–3.

34 Sutton, *Mercery*, p. 412. *De Engelse Natie te Antwerpen in de 16e Eeuw (1496–1582)*, ed. O. De Smedt, 2 vols (Antwerp, 1950–4), ii, pp. 341–7.

worry us, that we should come no more to the marts.'[35] Increasingly, any provincial merchant wanting to participate in the lucrative cloth trade had to join the London-based Merchant Adventurers of England and pay a large entry fee. By the 1550s the dominance of the London adventurers over their provincial rivals was complete.[36]

Thomas Kitson, London mercer and merchant adventurer (1485–1540)
Thanks to the survival of his account book (Plate 6), we have details of the business activities of one London merchant, Thomas Kitson, and the clothiers whom he purchased from, over the years 1529 to 1539. Born in Warton, Lancashire, Thomas Kitson became apprenticed to Richard Glasyer, a mercer and merchant adventurer of London. On completing his apprenticeship, Kitson was admitted into the Mercers' Company

Plate 6 Thomas Kitson's 'Boke of Remembraunce' or account book. (CUL, Hengrave Hall MS 78(2)).
This records shipments of cloth to the annual fairs, and purchases of cloth from clothiers and prices paid by this London merchant between 1529 and 1539.

[35] *York Mercers and Merchant Adventurers, 1356–1917*, ed. M. Sellers, Surtees Society 79 (Durham, 1918), p. 122.

[36] E.M. Carus-Wilson, 'The Origins and Early Development of the Merchant Adventurers' Organisation in London as Shown in Their Own Medieval Records', in Carus-Wilson, *Medieval Merchant Venturers*, pp. 143–82; Sutton, *Mercery*, pp. 413–14; G.D. Ramsay, 'The Cloth Trade at London in Mid-sixteenth Century: The Merchant Adventurers and Their Rivals', in M. Spallanzani, ed., *Produzione, commercio e consume dei panni di lana* (Florence, 1976), pp. 377–83.

and he subsequently became a member of the Merchant Adventurers' Company, dealing extensively in cloth exported to marts in Flanders.[37]

Kitson mainly bought unfinished broadcloths or 'whites' from Somerset and Wiltshire, but he also purchased kerseys, Castlecombes, Kentish russets, Cheshire penistones, coarser Lancashire cottons and Welsh friezes. Over the ten-year period covered by his account book, over forty cloth-men in Somerset and nearly seventy in Wiltshire supplied Kitson. His largest suppliers were based in Somerset: John Clevelod of Beckington, supplying 3,340 cloths, Roger Blackdon of Farleigh Hungerford, supplying 680 cloths, and John Kent of Bath, supplying 560 cloths. His principal suppliers in Wiltshire were Richard Batt, Roger Tanner and John Lawrens of Westbury, each supplying more than 400 cloths. Other prominent clothiers supplying Kitson with cloths were William Stumpe of Malmesbury, Alexander Langford (senior and junior) and Thomas Bailey of Trowbridge. Occasionally, clothiers promised to deliver all their production to Kitson over a defined period, such as in this ledger entry regarding Richard Batt of Westbury:

> Memorandum that the said Richard Batt hath promised my master all his cloths which he shall make between this and Hallowtide next coming in the said cloths to be as good in wool, spinning and making as these before received
> Received 17 October 1533 40 whites
> 12 Nov 1533 15 whites
> Total £346 13s 4d.[38]

Kitson also supplied some clothiers with raw materials. He sold woad for dyeing to James Bysee and John Horner of Stoke Michael or Stoke Lane and to Roger Adlam and John Norinton of Devizes. To John Clevelod of Beckington and Roger Tanner of Westbury he sold 'Sevile oil' or olive oil to use in spinning wool.

When recording transactions in his account book, Kitson often included a representation of the clothier's mark, together with a note of its colour. He also recorded the prices of the cloths that he bought in a cipher. This practice may have been to protect him from his competitors should the account book have fallen into the wrong hands, but it could also have been a personal precaution against any inquiry regarding government legislation that banned the export of unfinished cloth above a certain value.[39]

[37] CUL, Hengrave Hall MS 78(2); Brett, 'Somerset Clothmen'; Brett, 'Wiltshire Clothmen'; *ODNB*.

[38] CUL, Hengrave Hall MS 78(2), fol. 99.

[39] Sutton, *Mercery*, pp. 337–8.

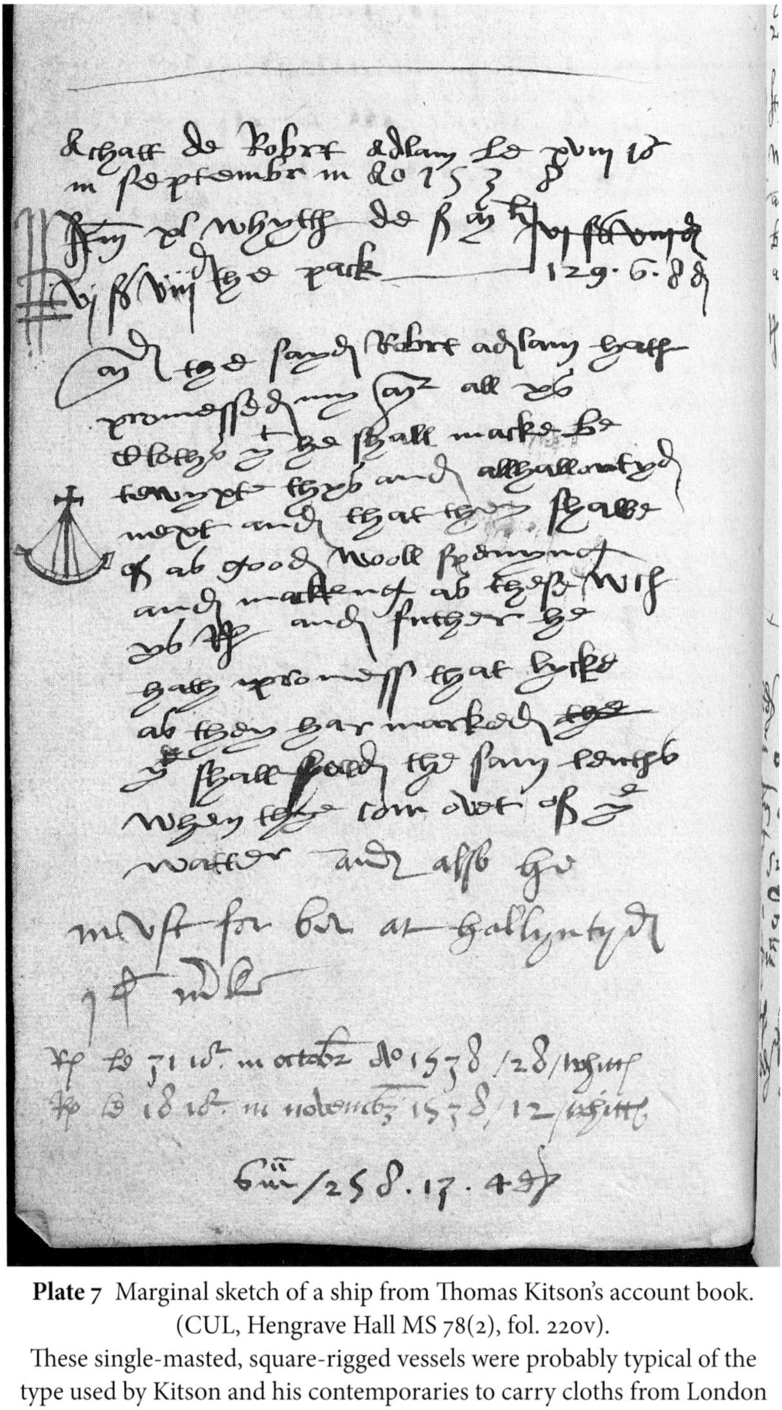

Plate 7 Marginal sketch of a ship from Thomas Kitson's account book. (CUL, Hengrave Hall MS 78(2), fol. 220v).
These single-masted, square-rigged vessels were probably typical of the type used by Kitson and his contemporaries to carry cloths from London to the fairs in the Low Countries.

Kitson's account book includes two marginal sketches of single-masted, square-rigged ships (Plate 7), probably the type of ships used to carry his cloths from London to the fairs in Flanders, a sea journey of a day and half.[40] During the year 1534–35, when Kitson exported 625 cloths, only ten merchants exported larger quantities. Kitson recorded his shipments of cloth to the four annual marts in Flanders. These were the *Pask* or the Easter mart at Bergen-op-Zoom, beginning on Maundy Thursday; the *Sinxten* mart or Pentecost fair at Antwerp, commencing on the second Sunday before Whitsuntide; the *Bamis* mart or St Bavo's Fair at Antwerp, starting on the second Sunday after the Assumption (15 August); and the Cold mart at Bergen-op-Zoom, opening on the Thursday before All Hallows Eve (31 October).[41] A similar, but smaller cloth fair that London merchants would have attended at 's-Hertogenbosch, Brabant, was illustrated around 1530 in a painting showing St Francis in the foreground (Plate V).

Kitson's gross annual profit on his business has been calculated as 25 per cent, or 20 per cent net over the years 1520–30.[42] He certainly accumulated a large fortune, being assessed on goods worth 4,000 marks in 1535, the seventh-highest assessment in London. Kitson used part of his wealth to construct Hengrave Hall near Bury St Edmunds in Suffolk, spending more than £3,500 (or over £2 million in today's money) on building works there between 1525 and 1539. The mansion still survives with its showpiece bay window over the main doorway, fan vaulting above the bay window in the hall, and a chapel with stained glass probably imported from France.[43] Hengrave Hall stands as a monument to the wealth that some London merchants could achieve through their trade with provincial clothiers.

BUYERS FROM OVERSEAS

Hanse merchants

The Hanseatic League was an organisation founded by north German towns and German merchant communities abroad to protect their mutual trading interests. Its members, known as the Hanse or Hansards, attempted to organise and control trade by winning commercial privileges and monopolies and by establishing trading bases overseas. Their principal base was in Lübeck, but they established commercial enclaves, known as *kontor*, in cities across the Baltic, including Bruges

[40] Brett, 'Somerset Clothmen', pp. 44–5.
[41] Brett, 'Wiltshire Clothmen', p. 36.
[42] Sutton, *Mercery*, p. 467.
[43] *ODNB*.

in Flanders, Bergen in Norway, and Novgorod in Russia.[44] Their main centre in England was the Steelyard in Thames Street, London, where Hans Holbein the Younger painted the Hanseatic merchant Georg Gisze (1497–1562) in 1532 (Plate VI). The Hanse also traded from Ipswich, King's Lynn, Boston, Hull and Newcastle.[45] The Hanseatic Warehouse in King's Lynn survives; this quadrangular complex built around 1475 consists of two long parallel warehouses connected at the east end by a domestic wing that was rebuilt in the mid eighteenth century, and a shorter warehouse wing to the west.[46] The League brought grain, timber, furs, tar, honey and flax from Russia and Poland to England, and exported wool, cloth and pewter eastwards. The Hansards enjoyed freedom of trade and preferential tariffs in England. In the early Tudor period, for example, they paid only 24d in customs duties on dyed cloth, compared to 28d for English merchants and 66d for other overseas merchants, the latter of whom also paid a subsidy of 12d in the pound.[47] By the mid sixteenth century though, the Merchant Adventurers had succeeded in persuading the Crown to end these Hanseatic privileges.[48]

Two main groups of Hanseatic merchants traded in English cloth. The Hanse of the Baltic and Prussia operated through the east coast ports, notably Boston, Lynn and Hull. Merchants from Cologne imported and exported through London, Ipswich and Colchester, distributing English cloth to Germany and central Europe. They bought from clothiers in the provinces, at Blackwell Hall in London, and from London mercers. During the fifteenth century, the Cologners trade outgrew that of the north Germans, and there was a dramatic shift in the location of Hanseatic cloth exports, from the east coast ports to London. Boston for example, had accounted for 60 per cent of cloth exports by Hansards from England during the years 1382–87, but by the end of the fifteenth century the port accounted for less than 1 per cent of Hanseatic cloth exports. This was in part a consequence of the complex series of disputes between English merchants and the Hanseatic League, which included diplomatic

[44] M.M. Postan, 'The Economic and Political Relations of England and the Hanse from 1400 to 1475', in E. Power and M.M. Postan, eds, *Studies in English Trade in the Fifteenth Century* (London, 1933), pp. 91–153; John D. Fudge, *Cargoes, Embargos, and Emissaries: The Commercial and Political Interaction of England and the German Hanse, 1450–1510* (Toronto, 1995).

[45] Sally Badham and Paul Cockerham, eds, *'The beste and fayrest of al Lincolnshire': The Church of St Botolph, Boston, Lincolnshire, and its Medieval Monuments*, British Archaeological Reports, British Series 554 (Oxford, 2012), pp. 11–26; Amor, *Late Medieval Ipswich*, pp. 114–38; Britnell, *Colchester*, pp. 168–71, 175–6.

[46] NHLE 1195393 (Hanse House, King's Lynn).

[47] Lipson, *Economic History*, i, p. 537.

[48] Sutton, *Mercery*, pp. 422–3; Ramsay, 'Cloth Trade'.

disputes, piracy and eventually naval warfare, and saw merchants arrested and goods detained in 1385–88, 1405–08, 1431–37, 1449–50 and 1468–74.[49] Clement Armstrong (c.1477–1536), a London grocer writing around 1533, suggested that the Hanse 'out of the cold countries in the east parts, where is frost and snow on eight months in the year', carried 'needful commodities' to England such as pitch, tar, and wax, as well as gold and silver to buy woollen cloth. The German Hanse, on the other hand, brought 'strange alien merchandises of all countries' and shipped large quantities of cloths from England, which were commonly bought 'white only', that is spun, woven and fulled, but unfinished.[50]

Some clothiers sold directly to the Hansards. In 1458 Thomas Peverell of East Bergholt in Suffolk bound himself to full four blue cloths known as vesses and two grey cloths on behalf of Eberhard Kryt of Cologne. In 1468 Henning Buring of Cologne claimed debts in Dedham, Stratford St Mary, Stoke-by-Nayland, Lavenham and Colchester. John Horndon contracted in Colchester in 1459 to make for an English client two broadcloths called murray greys, 'like the ones he used to sell to merchants of the Hanse'.[51] In 1468 the cloth-workers of Gloucestershire petitioned the Crown on behalf of the German merchants when a breakdown between England and the Hanseatic League appeared inevitable, complaining that they were 'right grievously hurt lacking utterance and sale of their cloth'.[52] Cologne merchants complained in 1462 about their associates, who, they claimed, bought cloth from English clothiers in the provinces on credit, rather than for cash or goods, and who depended on a system of obligations and sureties on which they could readily default. The Cologne merchants argued that these practices were inflating the price of cloth.[53] Bristol men, though, stated in 1486 that they preferred to sell their cloth to the Hanse rather than to London merchants. The Hanse bought cloth for ready money whereas the Londoners 'buy none but for days and therefore do make payments in cards, tennis balls, fish-hooks, bristles, tassels, and such other simple wares'. If the Londoners did pay in cash, they insisted on a discount of 8s or 10s on each cloth, arguing that the cloth was too short or poorly made.[54] Clement Armstrong, however, made similar complaints about the Hanse paying cloth-makers

[49] Badham and Cockerham, eds, *The Church of St Botolph*, pp. 23–5; Sutton, *Mercery*, pp. 277–84; Britnell, *Britain and Ireland*, p. 454.

[50] *TED*, iii, pp. 108–9. For the dating, see S.T. Bindoff, 'Clement Armstrong and his Treatises of the Commonweal', *EcHR* 14 (1944), pp. 64–73.

[51] Britnell, *Colchester*, pp. 172–3.

[52] Fudge, *Cargoes*, p. 229.

[53] Sutton, *Mercery*, p. 283.

[54] *Acts of Court of the Mercers' Company, 1453–1527*, eds L. Lyell and F.D. Watney (Cambridge, 1936), pp. 294–5.

in money and wares, resulting in the cloth-makers 'pestering all poor common people with wares and little money'.[55]

Italian and Spanish merchants

The English cloth industry also attracted Italian merchants. Venetian state galleys visited London and Southampton from the 1390s until the 1530s, bringing spices and taking back English cloth. Independent trading voyages were also made by private merchants. Genoese carracks called at Southampton from the late fourteenth century, bringing raw materials for the cloth industry and collecting English cloth. Florentine state galleys first came to England in 1425 and continued until the 1470s, loading cloth, wool and tin for export at Southampton and Sandwich. The Italians took English cloth into the Middle East: cloth from Salisbury and the surrounding area, called 'westerns', were known in Damascus in 1413, Beirut in 1417, and Alexandria in 1424; 'Southamptons' were to be found in Damascus in 1416 and Acre in 1439; and Essex cloth sold in Damascus by 1416. English cloth producers relied on Italian merchants for many mordants and dyestuffs, particularly in the fifteenth century, including alum, woad, and grain used to obtain scarlet.[56]

Italian merchants operated in a far more sophisticated way than their English or Hanseatic counterparts. By the mid fifteenth century, there were representatives of some twenty or thirty companies from Venice, Genoa, Florence, Milan and Lucca in London, forming parts of wider organisations with other branches across Europe. They developed bookkeeping, particularly the use of Arabic numerals and double entry accounting, which was not widely used in northern Europe until the sixteenth century. They acted as both merchants and bankers, accepting deposits, making ledger transfers across customers' accounts, and using bills of exchange to move money across Europe.[57] The Marcanova had a London employee, the Venetian-born draper John Manwyche, who bought 450 cloths directly from John Gawter of Beckington in Somerset in 1442. Manwyche and his colleagues paid over £180 per year in 1461 to farm the ulnage of Wiltshire and Salisbury with Somerset and Dorset.[58] The clothier James Towker or Terumber of Bradford-on-Avon and Trowbridge sold twenty-nine white cloths to Venetian merchant, Bernard Justinian, at Bridport in 1463. The cloths were confiscated from Justinian's house in London as it was claimed that they had been put for sale

[55] *TED*, iii, p. 109.

[56] Hicks, ed., *Inland Trade*, pp. 73, 154–8. For the uses of these mordants and dyes, see above, Chapter 1.

[57] Bolton, *Medieval English Economy*, pp. 311–15.

[58] Hicks, ed., *Inland Trade*, p. 73.

without being viewed by the ulnager, but Justinian declared that they had been made by James Towker at Bradford, inspected by the Wiltshire ulnager, and then taken to Bridport, from where Justinian had conveyed them to London. James confirmed this and said that he had done the same with one hundred other cloths he had made.[59]

The sixteenth century saw a reduction in the number of resident Italians, and the number of branches of large companies operating in London, as many companies switched their focus to Antwerp. Instead, specialist commission agents emerged, who bought large quantities of English cloth. Kerseys were often bought while still on the loom. An example of these specialist commission agents dealing in cloth is Martino de Federico, an Italian merchant resident in London, who worked as an English agent of Italian merchants and of an Antwerp commission house. He was a major exporter of English cloth in the 1530s. He became bankrupt in 1541 and records from a subsequent legal dispute show that Italian merchants sent him bills of exchange to be drawn on Italian firms in London, from which he was to purchase kerseys. Federico was sent detailed instructions of the colours and qualities needed. Federico may have bought most of the kerseys at Blackwell Hall but he sometimes sent a representative into the country to buy them and he also dealt directly with the clothier John Winchcombe II.[60]

Some Italians became involved in aspects of cloth manufacturing in England. The Genoese imported unfinished cloth, from England and the Netherlands, through Southampton and despatched it to Romsey to be fulled and dyed, before exporting the finished cloth to the Mediterranean. Over a thousand broadcloths had been carried to Romsey and then back to Southampton in 1441. Romsey was also used as a centre where cloth could be sent for repair to any flaws in the weave.[61] The Genoese-born Antonio Spinola brought 160 dozen kerseys from Newbury to Southampton in 1477–78. In 1483 he was given royal licence to bring twenty masters 'from any part of the world' to 'make and dye cloths in another fashion to those now made in the realm, so that the king's subjects may be able to learn the art'. His agent, John Stanesby, although based mainly in London, had eleven cloth-workers, probably Flemings, working for

[59] *VCH Wiltshire*, iv, pp. 134–5.

[60] M.E. Bratchel, 'Italian Merchant Organization and Business Relationships in Early Tudor London', *Journal of European Economic History* 7 (1978), pp. 30–1; Florence Edler, 'Winchcombe Kerseys in Antwerp (1538–44)', *EcHR* 7 (1936), pp. 57–62.

[61] A.A. Ruddock, *Italian Merchants and Shipping in Southampton 1270–1600* (Southampton, 1951), pp. 162–86; I.M.W. Harvey, *Jack Cade's Rebellion of 1450* (Oxford, 1991), pp. 127–8.

him at Bildeston, Suffolk, in 1483.[62] Antonio Bonvisi (1470x75–1558), a merchant from Lucca, resided at Crosby Place, Bishopsgate Street in London. He dealt mainly in fine woollen cloth, although he also purchased Berkshire kerseys. Leake, in his *Treatise on the Cloth Industry*, written in 1577, stated that Bonvisi had introduced the making of 'Coxall' cloths using finely spun yarn produced with a distaff.[63]

Spanish merchants exported cloth and imported dyes, wool oil and soap for cloth-making, together with iron ore, wine and foodstuffs. They traded mainly through London, Bristol, Southampton and Sandwich, although some could be found elsewhere. Francisco Dyes bought cloths worth £130 from an Essex dyer, as well as from London drapers, during the 1450s.[64] Two Spanish merchants carrying western cloth brought from Bradford fair, including coarse blankets that had not been sealed, were apprehended by officers of the mayor of York in 1506.[65] Fernando de Ibarra had been married and settled in Chester for fifteen years when he was imprisoned by the mayor in 1535 for contravening the city's marketing regulations. According to the mayor, when merchants from Spain or other foreign parts came to the city with merchandise or money, Fernando bargained with them and

> rideth to all parties near adjoining to the said city as well to markets and fairs as to other towns and villages where no markets or fairs are and that with the said merchant strangers' money buyeth to their uses all such cloths and other merchandises mete for the said merchant strangers as he can find.[66]

CLOTH MARKETS

Clothiers sold their cloth in a variety of different markets, both formal and informal (Figure 7). In formal markets, transactions are transparent, governed by regulations, and take place at fixed hours. Trust between buyers and sellers is based upon trust in the system, rather than (or as

62 *CPR 1476–85*, p. 342; Hicks, ed., *Inland Trade*, p. 73. For Stanesby, see above pp. 69, 83.

63 Hicks, ed., *Inland Trade*, p. 73; *TED*, iii, p. 211. The idea that Bonvisi introduced a new method of spinning into the Devonshire cloth trade, as stated in the *ODNB*, is based on the misreading by a seventeenth-century topographer, Thomas Westcote, of the loosely worded passage in Leake's *Treatise*. See H.P.R. Finberg, *Tavistock Abbey, A Study in the Social and Economic History of Devon* (Cambridge, 1951), p. 152, n. 4. See also below, p. 233, 235.

64 Wendy R. Childs, *Anglo-Castilian Trade in the Later Middle Ages* (Manchester, 1978), pp. 61, 105–11, 226.

65 YELA, Y/COU/1/1, vol. 9, fol. 36v.

66 TNA, SP 1/99, fol. 22; *LP*, ix, no. 794, p. 268.

well as) personal knowledge. Transactions are usually concentrated at specific locations like marketplaces, fairgrounds and cloth halls, where infrastructure is provided. By contrast, an informal market can be based at any convenient place, such as the farm gate or the street corner. Informal transactions tend to be small, lightly regulated, dispersed over a range of locations, and dependent on personal trust, rather than on trust in the system.[67]

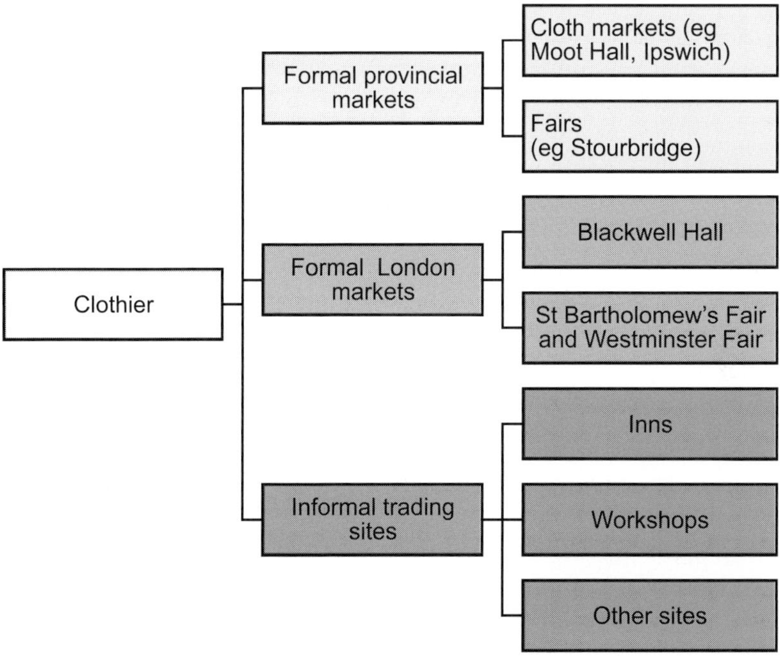

Figure 7 The clothier's markets

Formal provincial markets: cloth markets

Markets were held at least weekly, and more frequently in larger towns, which often established dedicated locations for the sale of cloth, in the form of specific marketplaces or covered halls. These included the 'Worsted Seld' at Norwich, the Thursday Market at York, the Moot Hall at Ipswich, and the Draperies at Coventry, Northampton and Winchester.[68] The city government of Norwich acquired a large site north of the marketplace in 1384 to act as a 'clothseld' or public hall for the sealing

[67] Mark Casson and John S. Lee, 'The Origin and Development of Markets: A Business History Perspective', *Business History Review* 85 (2011), p. 14.

[68] Lipson, *Economic History*, i, p. 465.

of cloth. An ordinance of 1388 prohibited the sale of any cloths from Norfolk or Norwich except at this location. The hall raised at least £18 on average each year during the late 1390s, but by 1414 there were complaints that it had been abandoned and sales were being made elsewhere in the city.[69] Shortly afterwards, Bristol petitioned for a common hall to receive foreign cloth merchants, and to hold a weekly market for them to sell their cloth, as was done at Blackwell Hall, as the king was losing custom through the secret selling of cloth by these traders.[70] Hull had a sale hall for cloth by 1498–99.[71] Even some very small cloth-making centres developed dedicated marketing facilities for the sale of cloth, like Kersey in Suffolk, which had an open cloth market and a cloth hall standing within it in 1398–99. There were also formal wool markets, such as that set up in the cellar of Colchester Moot Hall in 1373.[72]

Such facilities helped buyers and officials to inspect goods more easily as well as allowing the ready collection of royal and municipal levies on items sold. The bailiffs of Colchester were instructed to appoint supervisors of wool sales in the Moot Hall cellar in 1438. In 1492 the city government in York ordered cloth traders from outside the city, whom they described as 'foreign drapers of the country', to 'have tables set openly in Thursday market and there sell their cloths by retail'. This was so that the cloths could be properly inspected by searchers appointed by the city's tailors and drapers.[73] In mid-fifteenth-century Ipswich, fullers and clothiers were required to sell their cloth only on market day at the Moot Hall.[74]

Some of these markets acquired reputations for the sale of cloth. In the late 1530s, John Leland observed that Bolton market in Lancashire stood mainly by cottons and coarse yarn and that 'the market for woollen cloth is very well-known' at Kendal in Westmorland. It is not clear from his comments whether these cloth markets were for wholesale or retail trade, although Leland noted that the market at Grinton near Reeth in the Yorkshire Dales provided linen cloth and corn for the men of Swaledale.[75]

[69] Penelope Dunn, 'Trade', in Carole Rawcliffe and Richard Wilson, eds, *Medieval Norwich* (London, 2004), pp. 216–17; Ayers, *Norwich*, p. 111.

[70] TNA, SC 8/96/4789.

[71] *VCH Yorks ER*, i, p. 55.

[72] Britnell, 'Woollen Textile Industry', p. 86; Britnell, *Colchester*, pp. 72–4.

[73] YELA, Y/COU/1/1, vol. 7, fol. 76v. Britnell, *Colchester*, p. 219.

[74] Amor, *Late Medieval Ipswich*, pp. 149–50, 170–1.

[75] Lee, 'Functions and Fortunes', p. 25.

Provincial fairs

Medieval fairs were usually annual events, established primarily for trade rather than entertainment. They provided the opportunity to buy and sell goods of higher value than those available at weekly markets. By the fourteenth century, English fairs such as Boston and Winchester, which had formerly enjoyed an international reputation, attracting traders from many parts of England and overseas, were rapidly contracting into small, local events. English merchants increasingly diverted their trade from these fairs to towns, particularly London, where they could buy and sell the same range of goods throughout the year. These fairs had also been heavily dependent on foreign merchants coming to England to collect wool for export, and wool was increasingly handled by English merchants. The major international fairs of the later fifteenth century were at Antwerp, Bergen-op-Zoom, and Middelburg, which were frequented by English merchants.

The new mercantile networks that linked consumers with areas of specialised production after the Black Death of 1348–49 led to the growth of regional fairs, which provided outlets for the changing marketing networks for livestock, fish, consumer and luxury goods, and particularly the cloth trade. When the textile industry expanded in the later fourteenth and early fifteenth centuries, fairs of cloth-producing towns such as Colchester and Salisbury provided outlets for locally produced cloth. Colchester's two fairs were reorganized in 1374 and their duration extended to bring more merchants into the town to sell their cloth. The ulnage accounts show that June and July, when the cloth fairs were held, was the busiest period of cloth sales in Colchester. The borough court heard the case of Richard Hykeman who had worked briefly for a fuller in September 1398, and was still owed by his employer 5s for his work and a further 1s for carrying cloth to various fairs.[76]

As cloth production became increasingly dominated by smaller towns and rural areas during the later fifteenth century, regional fairs such as those in Somerset and Yorkshire attracted cloth producers. A fair at Exeter drew a chapman from Bradford in Somerset to sell narrow cloths in 1436.[77] Cloth-makers and traders from Wells and north Somerset and merchants from Bristol attended a regional cycle of fairs in the West Country. A Dulverton clothier disputed the price of kerseys sold at St James' Fair, Bristol, in the 1530s.[78] At York's Ascensiontide Fair in 1502, streets were specified for the sale of cloth from Leeds, Wakefield, Halifax and Bradford, and from Kendal, Ripon and Knaresborough. Two

[76] Lee, 'Role of Fairs'; Britnell, *Colchester*, pp. 68, 80, 102, 181.

[77] TNA, E 159/212, Trinity, m. 4.

[78] TNA, C 1/886/25.

Spanish merchants brought western cloth from Bradford fair to York in 1506. John Stede of Norland near Halifax bequeathed 20s to his brother Thomas in 1540 to assist John's wife and daughter 'to sell their cloth in the fairs in Yorkshire'.[79] Several London companies, including the mercers and the grocers, prohibited their members from attending provincial fairs. In theory, this forced provincial merchants to travel to London, but the impact of these measures seems to have been limited, and by the late fifteenth century the Haberdashers Company had become successful through trading at fairs.[80] Some of the fairs that operated in cloth-making areas were not successful though. Wool and cloth had been sold at Wentford Fair at Clare, Suffolk in the later fourteenth century, but in 1425 it was reported that the fair had not been held for the last three years because no one came to trade there.[81]

By the beginning of the sixteenth century, two fairs had become major cloth markets – St Bartholomew's Fair, London (considered in the next section), and Stourbridge Fair, Cambridge. At Stourbridge Fair, held on the outskirts of Cambridge, the ulnage accounts of 1464–66 record London and Leicester cloth dealers at the fair, and Suffolk traders selling cloth at a nearby fair at Ely. By the 1520s, a regular contingent of cloth-makers from south Suffolk were attending Stourbridge Fair. Known as the 'Hadleigh men', they included cloth-makers William Jacob of Sudbury and Robert Glaswright of Great Waldingfield, shearman Thomas Holton of Nayland, and weavers John Colman of Great Cornard and William Turnour of Hadleigh. Kendalmen Adam Wolford and Patrick Bryket, who attended the fair in 1523–24, probably brought cloth that had been manufactured in the Lake District. Drapers of Coventry, including mayors Julian Nethermill, Thomas Banwell, Christopher Waren and Thomas Ryley held booths at the fair, as did other provincial and London merchants. Matthew Goodwyn of Ipswich, who possessed a Hadleigh booth in Stourbridge Fair for at least twelve years, and Richard Cary of Bristol, fined at the fair for selling kerseys, were also recorded as cloth sellers at the main London cloth market at Blackwell Hall in 1561–62.[82] The prominence that fairs like Stourbridge and St Bartholomew's enjoyed in the cloth trade was reinforced by a statute of 1554–55 that prohibited anyone living in the country to sell by retail 'woollen cloth, linen cloth, haberdashery wares, grocery wares, mercery wares' in any towns except in open fairs.[83]

[79] YELA, Y/COU/1/1, vol. 8, fol. 131; Y/COU/1/1, vol. 9, fol. 36v. *Halifax Wills*, i, p. 143; Heaton, *Yorkshire Woollen*, pp. 71, 75, 145.

[80] Lee, 'Role of Fairs', pp. 426–7.

[81] Thornton, *Clare*, pp. 177–8.

[82] Lee, *Cambridge*, pp. 124–8.

[83] 1 & 2 Philip and Mary, c. 7: *SR*, iv (1), pp. 244–5.

Formal London markets: Blackwell Hall

> This Bakewell Hall ... hath been long since employed as a weekly marketplace for all sorts of woollen cloths broad and narrow, brought from all parts of this realm, there to be sold.
>
> John Stow, *A Survey of London* (1598), describing Blackwell Hall[84]

Blackwell Hall was the London market where country cloth-makers brought their packs of cloth to be sold to merchants. It was established in the late fourteenth century when increasing quantities of provincial cloth entering London had prompted the city authorities to confine cloth sales to specific locations. In 1380, the city government decreed that all cloths made in 'Essex, Shropshire or elsewhere beyond the liberties of the city' could only be sold at the Stocks market or at the Guildhall, and in 1387 the sale of 'foreign' cloth (i.e. not belonging to a citizen) was restricted to three locations within the city. The mayor and commonalty purchased Blackwell Hall in 1396, a thirteenth-century private hall and its associated buildings lying close by the city's guildhall, to form a dedicated cloth market for London, and in 1397–98 all 'foreign' (non-citizen) merchants were required to bring their cloths there for sale. Merchants could rent chambers, cupboards, or chests in the hall by the year, month or even for a day. The rents from these lettings were collected by the keeper of Blackwell Hall, who paid them to the city chamberlain.[85] In 1557 the management of this market, and the collection and receipt of fees, was handed over as an endowment to Christ's Hospital.[86] The hall was rebuilt in 1588 and again after the Great Fire of 1666. Intermediaries, known as the Blackwell Hall factors, came to dominate trade, but business declined in the eighteenth century and the hall was demolished in 1820.[87]

Blackwell Hall enabled London citizens to retain control of most of the transactions made with textile manufacturers from outside the city, and helped them to collect the income levied on the sale of each cloth. The city government required all those who were not freemen of London to warehouse at Blackwell Hall all woollen cloth brought to the city to be sold, and restricted the times at which strangers could sell cloth there to between 11a.m. on Thursday and 11a.m. on Saturday. From

[84] John Stow, *A Survey of London*, ed. C.L. Kingsford, 2 vols (Oxford, 1908), i, p. 288.

[85] *Calendar of Letter-books Preserved Among the Archives of the Corporation of the City of London at the Guildhall*, ed. R.R. Sharpe (London, 1899–1912), vol. H, pp. 145, 301, 449–50; Caroline M. Barron, *London in the Later Middle Ages: Government and People, 1200–1500* (Oxford, 2004), p. 53.

[86] D.W. Jones, 'The "Hallage" Receipts of the London Cloth Markets, 1562–c.1720', *EcHR* 25 (1972), pp. 567–87.

[87] Bateman, 'From Rags to Riches', pp. 11–13.

1404, the Drapers' Company appointed a keeper of the hall who swore not to allow any merchant stranger to sell any cloth within the hall to another merchant stranger. In practice, there was some flexibility, and it was noted by the city government in 1518 and endorsed by statute in 1523 that cloths sent to London to fulfil bargains made in the country could be delivered directly to the warehouse of the purchaser without being brought to Blackwell Hall. Foreign merchants could buy cloths at Blackwell Hall, but only after eight days from their delivery to the market. They were to pay for their purchases in ready money or goods within one month.[88] Writing around 1533, London grocer Clement Armstrong suggested that the use of Blackwell Hall had grown since the 1470s, and that before this time, merchants had generally bought their cloths from cloth-makers in the provinces:

> For a sixty years ago old merchants bought all their cloths of cloth-makers in the country by the whole sorts in packs brought home to their houses in carts and in waines, when then all sailing cloths came never to Blackwell Hall to no Easterlings hands.[89]

Blackwell Hall made it easier for provincial clothiers to market their cloth, for London and alien merchants to buy it, including the Easterlings (Hanseatic merchants) mentioned by Armstrong, and for Londoners to supervise. It was 'a catalyst for London's growing pre-eminence in the nation's cloth trade'.[90]

Excavations in the Guildhall Yard between 1987 and 1998 found substantial medieval remains of Blackwell Hall. These revealed an open-arcaded building with large chambers and undercrofts, and the former thirteenth-century private hall, where cloth was displayed and stored. The adjoining private chapel of St Mary-in-the-Jewry was also retained.[91] By the early sixteenth century, the hall had specialised sales-rooms, including 'Colchester Hall within Blackwell Hall', where John Boswell, cloth-maker of Colchester, had taken cloths to sell in 1528.[92] The importance of Blackwell Hall to the English cloth trade by the 1520s is highlighted by the concerns of Henry VIII's government when the London cloth market collapsed in the expectation of a trade war with

[88] LMA, COL/CC/01/01/011 (Microfilm X109/053): Journal of the Court of Common Council of London, vol. 11 (1507–19), fol. 366v; 14 & 15 Henry VIII, c. 1: *SR*, iii, pp. 206–7; Ramsay, *Woollen Industry*, pp. 40–1.

[89] *TED*, iii, p. 108.

[90] Oldland, 'Making and Marketing', p. 98.

[91] Bateman, 'From Rags to Riches', pp. 5–6.

[92] TNA, SP 1/47, fol. 162; *LP*, iv (2), no. 4145, p. 1831.

the Netherlands, and by Cardinal Wolsey's attempts to force the London merchants to continue buying from the clothiers.[93]

London fairs

Cloth could only be sold wholesale in London at the cloth market in Blackwell Hall or at the fairs of St Bartholomew, Southwark and Westminster. London draper Henry Chacombe bought nine woollen cloths from Thomas Wolf, draper of Coventry, at St Bartholomew's Fair in 1456, and later in the century a Norwich dyer, William Ferrour, attended the fair.[94] Yorkshire clothiers bequeathed booths at St Bartholomew's Fair to their children: these included William Hardy of Heptonstall in 1518, Henry Farrer of Halifax in 1542 and John Crossley of Huddersfield in 1562. In 1558 it was reported that 'divers clothiers of sundry parts of the realm' sold coarse cloths and kerseys at the fair, and the Privy Council conferred about cloth statutes with representatives from Bewdley in Shropshire; Halifax, Manningham and Selby in Yorkshire; Hemyock, Morebath and Tiverton in Devon; and Abergavenny in Monmouthshire.[95] Clothiers sold their cloths to London buyers like Robert Tallmage, merchant tailor, who would 'bestow and pay great sums of money at the said feast of Saint Bartholomew' during his 'great business' at the fair in the 1530s. London mayor Sir John Allen suggested that about £20,000 worth of goods would come to the fair in 1535, at a time when he thought that cloth sellers would have very slack sales.[96] The Venetian Alessandro Magno visited London in 1562 and remarked that 'Cloth and wool of every sort are the main commodities and our goods sell very well at this fair.'[97] According to the late-sixteenth century antiquarian John Stow, it had been a fair to which 'the clothiers of all England, and drapers of London repaired' or assembled.[98]

Informal trading sites

Despite the existence of cloth markets and fairs, many transactions must have taken place outside these formal arenas, in places such as shops, inns and houses. It has been suggested that generally, less than half of all commercial transactions in the Middle Ages passed through formal

[93] See below, Chapter 4.

[94] TNA C 1/25/119, C 1/64/580.

[95] TNA, PC 2/8, fols 146–7; *Acts of the Privy Council of England*: vi: *1556–1558*, pp. 379–80; Heaton, *Yorkshire Woollen*, pp. 146–8; *Halifax Wills*, i, pp. 53, 156.

[96] TNA, C1/905/3, SP 1/95, fol. 131; *LP*, ix, no. 152, p. 44.

[97] Caroline Barron, Christopher Coleman and Claire Gobbii, 'The London Journal of Alessandro Magno 1562', *London Journal* 9 (1983), p. 148.

[98] Stow, *Survey*, ii, p. 27.

markets and fairs.[99] While many clothiers took cloth directly to London to be marketed there, merchants also travelled to clothiers to inspect their cloth, make purchases or place advance orders. Articles relating to the operation of Blackwell Hall agreed by the city government in 1518 acknowledged that merchants were buying from clothiers outside the formal market, although they were supposed to bring these cloths to the hall after making the purchase.[100]

The Colchester borough court rolls provide evidence of trade from private houses in a range of items, including equipment, materials for cloth-making, and finished cloth. John Prentys leased a spinning wheel to the wife of Richard Taillour from his house in North Ward in 1395. In the same year, Thomas Leyham, at his home, allegedly gave three 'tens' of woollen cloth on credit to Thomas Exyng and Matilda his wife. John Savey sold a pipe of oil from his home to John Reve, weaver, in 1404.[101] Such transactions raise the question of the extent to which the houses of leading clothiers, like Paycockes of Coggeshall, were constructed to impress potential customers. Like the shops and houses of other merchants, they probably provided for both the storage and display of goods, serving as showrooms in which samples could be displayed, and with decoration to impress visitors when business negotiations were being conducted.[102]

Inns

Inns provided rest and refreshment for travellers, offered safe storage of goods overnight, and, at places where the mode of transport changed, they could provide storage until boats, carts, or pack animals were available. They often also developed as informal centres of trade outside formal marketplaces, selling commodities such as grain and firewood.[103] Some were even legally recognised as centres for marketing, such as the Eagle and New Inn at Exeter for cloth sales, and Blossom's Inn in St Laurence Old Jewry, London, for worsted sales to citizens.[104] In Colchester, it was alleged in 1394 that Richard Pypere had sold fifty pieces of cloth of various colours to Robert Chapman of Coggeshall in the house of John

[99] Richard H. Britnell, 'Markets, Shops, Inns, Taverns and Private Houses in Medieval English Trade', in Bruno Blondé, Peter Stabel, Jon Stobart and Ilja Van Damme, eds, *Buyers and Sellers: Retail Circuits and Practices in Medieval and Early Modern Europe* (Turnhout, 2006), p. 121.

[100] LMA, COL/CC/01/01/011, fol. 366v. See below, pp. 107–8.

[101] Britnell, 'Markets, Shops', p. 120.

[102] See below, Chapter 5.

[103] J.N. Hare, 'Inns, Innkeepers and the Society of Later Medieval England, 1350–1600', *Journal of Medieval History* 39 (2013), pp. 477–97; Casson and Lee, 'Origin and Development of Markets', p. 31.

[104] Hare, 'Inns', p. 482; Sutton, *Mercery*, p. 224.

Aylemar, brewer, who is known to have kept an inn in Colchester in this period.[105] Cloth sales in London, which should have taken place at Blackwell Hall, might occur at inns, like the twenty pieces of Bridgwater cloths that Somerset cloth-man Thomas Budde of Wellington confessed that he had brought to an inn in Holborn to sell to a merchant stranger in June 1515.[106] The need for merchants or their factors to travel around buying cloth generated a particular demand for accommodation and a prevalence of inns at cloth-making centres, such as Bradford-on-Avon (with three medieval inns), Trowbridge (two), Warminster (three) and Wilton (four). A Southampton inn even possessed a Kendalmen's chamber, reflecting the long-distance journeys made to bring Kendal cloth to this south-coast port. Kendalmen bringing woollen cloth to York in 1492 were ordered to sell in gross in their inns and lodgings and by retail in the Thursday Market. Some innkeepers were personally engaged in the cloth trade, including five innkeepers of Winchester in the 1395 ulnage accounts, and Richard Kingsmill, innkeeper at Basingstoke, who marketed cloth in 1467. John Belchamber of Basingstoke was variously documented as a mercer, an innkeeper, and even as a clothier after his death in 1542, but in later life he moved out of Basingstoke to the neighbouring village of Cliddesden.[107]

The George Inn at Norton St Philip in Somerset (Plate 8), with fabric dating back to the 1370s, is one of the best preserved medieval inns in England, and was closely connected with the cloth trade. Adjoining a marketplace and fairground, this inn provided storage for goods prior to and after the fairs, offered accommodation during these events, and probably served as a place of trade outside the prescribed times of the operation of the markets and fairs. The George seems to have formed part of a planned settlement created by the Carthusian monks of Hinton Charterhouse to generate income from trade in the neighbouring parish of Norton St Philip. The main road from Bath to Salisbury widens into a triangular marketplace, known as the Plain, and the George Inn was constructed here to accommodate travellers and merchants attending two fairs in the village. The monks obtained grants of these fairs on the feast of St Philip and St James (1 May), extended from three to five days in 1353, and at the end of August. Two weekly markets were also granted

[105] Britnell, 'Markets, Shops', p. 118.

[106] LMA, COL/CA/01/01/003 (Microfilm X109/129): Court of Aldermen Repertory, vol. 3 (1515–19), fol. 28v.

[107] YELA, Y/COU/1/1, vol. 7, fol. 77v. Hare, 'Inns', pp. 487, 491–3; Hicks, ed., *Overland Trade*, p. 110.

Plate 8 The George Inn, Norton St Philip, Somerset.
With the earliest surviving parts dating to around 1370, altered and adapted over the subsequent three centuries, and little changed since the end of the seventeenth century, the George retains much of its medieval appearance.

to the prior and convent.[108] The fairs at Norton specialised in wool, cloth and sheep, drawing buyers and sellers from a wide area. The ulnager for Somerset, Thomas Newton, was attacked and wounded at the fair in 1400, where one of his servants was killed and others chased away.[109] The Cotswold woolman John Chapman of Minchinhampton, left money to churches at Norton St Philip, Priddy, Binegar and Maiden Bradley, all places where he may have bought wool at fairs. An ordinance for the drapers of Bristol made in 1370 prohibited merchants from leaving the city to sell or buy cloth on a Friday or Saturday unless it was to the fairs of Norton St Philip, Binegar, Midsomer Norton, Priddy, Wells, Cosham and

[108] Ferguson Mann Architects and Kirsty Rodwell, *The George Inn Norton St Philip Somerset* (Bristol, 1999), pp. 4–5. Colin J. Brett, 'The Fairs and Markets of Norton St Philip', *Somerset Archaeology and Natural History Society: Proceedings* 144 (2002 for 2000), pp. 165–7, 184.

[109] Merrick, 'Taxing Medieval Cloth', p. 223.

Bradley. Local clothiers like John Compton, buried and commemorated on a brass at Beckington church, three miles south of Norton St Philip, probably used the Norton fairs to conduct much of their business.[110] John Leland described Norton as 'mostly maintained by clothing'. In the mid sixteenth century, Bristol merchant John Smythe arranged for customers to pay debts to him at the fair.[111]

The George Inn was altered or rebuilt several times between the late fourteenth and late seventeenth centuries, including the addition of galleries in the fifteenth century which may have related to the commercial use of the building, possibly allowing bales of wool to be hauled up to the first and second floors by a hoist. A survey of the building in 1638 mentions a fair loft 'where the linen cloth is sold at the fair times'. An inquiry of 1595 provides a vivid description of the inn's role at the time of the fairs. Linen packs were brought into the 'great house or inn called the George' up to three weeks before, and for thirty-eight years the tenants of the inn had regularly prepared their rooms to receive the packs of cloth. This involved removing 'tables and household stuff out of the hall, kitchen, two parlours, cellars and chambers' to make space. Those bringing cloth were given tickets or notes of receipt: 'The bailiffs or their deputies have attended usually at the gate of the said inn at the fair times and received of the buyers and sellers sums of money for the linen cloth there sold.'[112]

SELLING CLOTH

We know relatively little about the trading practices used for selling cloth. In London, the city government agreed in 1518 that the lawful buying and selling of woollen cloth could include:

> Cloths bought in the country and scantillons [samples] taken or sealed by the buyer.
>
> Cloths bought beforehand by indenture, to be paid either in money, wares or days. [These could be for a certain number of cloths, or as many cloths as the clothier made during a certain period of time, of such sorts as were agreed according to scantillons or samples agreed by the same parties].
>
> Cloths bought beforehand without indenture or scantillon, the freeman paying any money or wares in earnest [as an initial

[110] Brett, 'Fairs and Markets', p. 182. For John Compton see below, pp. 212–14, 221, 304.

[111] *Itinerary*, v, p. 98; *Ledger of John Smythe*, pp. 43, 164.

[112] Brett, 'Fairs and Markets', p. 187.

> instalment] beforehand for certain cloths, and noting the agreement in their books 'as divers freemen do use between the clothiers and the said freemen', knowing their usual wools, wool making, colour, length, breadth and weight.
>
> Any freemen agreeing with a clothier to make him any number of cloths or writing to him or sending him word knowing his making and price, all cloths to be brought to the house of the freeman that has bought the said cloths.
>
> Every man's cloth lawfully bought according to these articles ought to be brought to Blackwell Hall and the freeman declare the truth of the purchase to the master or his deputies by his word or oath.
>
> If any freemen received into his house any cloth which was not made according to his bargain and refused them, these cloths were to be conveyed to Blackwell Hall.[113]

The account books of Thomas Howell and Thomas Kitson provide surviving examples of the books used between freemen and clothiers. Rare surviving cloth samples, which a buyer provided to show the standard he required, are fixed in the register of the notary who recorded the agreement of a merchant of Toulouse to buy four pieces of English cloth from a merchant of Limendous in 1458.[114] Clothiers might also work together to sell their cloth. In the early sixteenth century, John and William Appulford of Thaxted had approached William Manhode of the same town, 'knowing him to be a very poor man', and having one cloth of his own and four cloths of another Thaxted resident to sell in London, and asked him to help sell three cloths belonging to them. All the cloths were sold to John Parle, merchant of London.[115]

Credit

Clothiers made extensive use of credit, which was a major consideration when negotiating cloth sales. As noted in the previous chapter, clothiers tried to pay in arrears those supplying wool to them and those undertaking work for them. This helped clothiers to maximise their working capital. When it came to sales though, large-scale clothiers did not follow normal business practice by demanding payment as quickly as possible. Instead they offered credit to their major customers, the wholesale

113 LMA, COL/CC/01/01/011, fol. 366v–367; COL/AD/01/013 (Microfilm X109/028), Letter Book N (1515–26), fols 95v–96.

114 Philippe Wolff, 'Three Samples of English Fifteenth-Century Cloth', in N.B. Harte and K.G. Ponting, eds, *Cloth and Clothing in Medieval Europe. Essays in Memory of Professor E.M. Carus-Wilson* (London, 1983), pp. 120–5.

115 TNA, C 1/546/60.

merchants. This meant that they could obtain a better price than poorer clothiers, who often had to sell for immediate payment so that they could continue in production. Poorer clothiers therefore generally looked to local markets, or to wealthier clothiers, to sell their cloth. In contrast, the leading clothiers had sufficient capital to purchase and hold finished cloth in stock, they maintained large supplies of raw materials, which could be bartered for finished cloth, and they had regular commercial links with London cloth merchants.[116]

The best prices could be obtained by offering delivery before payment, and the larger clothiers sold on these terms, particularly to London cloth buyers. The Cranbrook clothier Richard Barre sold sixteen broadcloths to London grocer Thomas Maynard about 1515–18, and many months later, Barre sued Maynard, who admitted that he had sold the cloths overseas and not yet paid Barre, but claimed that three of the cloths were defective.[117] Clothiers supplying Bristol mercer John Smythe in the 1540s similarly accepted payment in deferred instalments. Payment was sometimes made by a 'circular' or 'giro' method. For example, Smythe supplied wine to William Northe or Stevyn Chick of Bruton, who then paid John Yerbery of Bruton for the cloth that Yerbery had sent cloth to Smythe.[118] Terms of credit seem to have been influenced by the wealth and status of the clothier and the merchant. London mercer Thomas Kitson always paid established suppliers in cash on receipt of the cloths, and by doing so must have offered an advantage over other cloth dealers. He also offered some customers extended credit, but on terms that could result in them paying interest at rates of 23 or even 51 per cent.[119] The clothier William Stumpe of Malmesbury allowed Thomas Gresham, mercer and merchant adventurer of London, to pay £500 in five instalments of £100 between 1548 and 1552. Other clothiers might expect a down payment of one-half or one-third of the purchase price, with the balance paid off in three or six months. Gresham appears to have paid his debts to greater clothiers more promptly than to lesser ones. It has been suggested that this may reflect the fact that wealthier clothiers had permanent agents in London to collect debts as they fell due, whereas smaller clothiers would have to wait until the next time that they visited London in person.[120]

Some London merchants who purchased cloth from clothiers found overseas buyers for the fabrics even before they had taken delivery of them. A chancery case from the late fifteenth or early sixteenth century

[116] Zell, *Industry*, p. 218.
[117] TNA, C 1/427/40.
[118] *Ledger of John Smythe*, pp. 19–20.
[119] Brett, 'Somerset Clothmen', p. 42.
[120] Peter Ramsey, *Tudor Economic Problems* (London, 1963), p. 89.

relates how John Baker, merchant of London, claimed that he had bought twenty cloths from Robert Beste of Essex, cloth-maker, to be delivered within fourteen days of making the bargain, as he had in times past. Baker went to Zeeland, leaving his factor to receive the cloth, and sold the cloth in Zeeland to a merchant there as he had with other cloths made by Beste, trusting to have the cloths when his factor came to Zeeland as he had previously. Beste, however, supplied cloths 'not of his own mark and making', and worth only half as much in value to Baker's factor, and the merchant refused them and had Baker arrested. The plaintiff emphasised that his business relationship with the cloth-maker was longstanding.[121]

Clothiers also extended credit to overseas merchants. A scrivener's book of 1458–59 records two German merchants in February 1459 entering a bond with John Harding, cloth-man of Tidbury, Gloucestershire, to pay him £12 at the following Whitsun, £11 in November, and £11 6s 10d in February of the next year. The transaction is unspecified, but probably relates to cloth sales.[122] Following complaints that English merchants were unable to sell cloth to overseas traders after an act of 1430 prohibited the offer of credit to aliens, a period of six months was subsequently allowed.[123] The wills of the Lavenham clothiers John Hunte (1539) and Robert Grome (1540) refer to debts owing to them 'as well beyond the sea as on this side'.[124]

Credit was available in a variety of forms, as a recent examination of London creditors in the Court of Common Pleas has shown. If a small amount of money was needed, a creditor might offer a cash loan, to around £5. Sales of goods on credit tended to be for medium-sized transactions of around £10. When the amount of credit required was larger than this, or the potential debtor's creditworthiness was unclear, a bond would be used, a formal written instrument with the debtor's seal. This stated the agreed dates of payment, and as payments were made they were recorded on the back of the bill. Interest was usually calculated as part of the agreed debt value as for much of the period it was technically illegal to take interest on a loan.[125] Historians have questioned the flexibility of credit arrangements in the Middle Ages, and particularly whether written credit instruments were assignable (passing a debt owed to yourself in order to pay off a debt that you owed to a third party) and

[121] TNA, C 1/121/57.

[122] Bolton, *Medieval English Economy*, p. 303.

[123] 8 Henry VI, c. 24: *SR*, ii, p. 257; 9 Henry VI, c. 2: *SR*, ii, p. 264.

[124] Betterton and Dymond, *Lavenham*, p. 26.

[125] Stevens, 'London Creditors', pp. 1091–5, 1101. During the years 1546 to 1553, interest of up to 10 per cent was legal: 37 Henry VIII, c. 9: *SR*, iii, p. 996; 5 & 6 Edward VI, c. 20: *SR*, iv (1), p. 155.

negotiable (selling the debt to a third party for less than its face value).[126] A chancery case of 1521 suggests that bills obligatory were being used flexibly in the cloth trade to pay debts to others or to raise cash. Thomas Alake of Tewkesbury bought ten cloths from Robert Bydfeld of the same town for 40 marks (£26 13s 4d), to be paid at various dates. This was agreed by a bill obligatory, 'which bill has frequently been bargained and sold by both parties by way of merchandise at home and overseas'. At a final reckoning in June 1521, Robert was found to owe Thomas £5 10s and should have returned the bill obligatory but refused to do so.[127]

The most successful clothiers were those who could carry their customer's debts. The clothiers Walter Mayow of Croscombe (d. 1482) and Robert Rychard of Dursley (d. 1492) were owed hopeful debts that made up over 30 per cent of the value of their total inventories, and in the case of the leading clothier in Cranbrook, Stephen Draner (d. 1539), they comprised 77 per cent. Of those owing money to Draner, Londoners owed £500, over half the total, and at least three were drapers. Other debtors included four cloth-makers and a Cranbrook merchant.[128] Some of these may have been personal loans rather than trade debts, but they nonetheless reveal the complex web of credit that underpinned the wealthier clothier's business. Carrying large amounts of debt brought high levels of risk, as debtors might default. In 1522, Thomas Spring III had debts owing to him of £2,200, of which only £1,400 were described as 'sperate', meaning that they were likely to be recovered.[129] Spring, with £1,800 in moveable goods plus landholdings valued at over £100, could afford to write these debts off, but others might have to engage in lengthy legal processes to try to recover them, particularly if they had debts themselves owing to other creditors who were pushing for payment.

Transport

The clothier had to arrange transport for his raw materials, semi-processed products and finished goods. He could use his own transport, commission a private carter, or use a common carrier. Reflecting their reliance on road transport, several clothiers made bequests in their wills for the maintenance of highways and bridges.[130]

Carts commissioned privately by one or more owners to convey their personal cargoes are recorded in the Southampton brokage books carrying raw materials for cloth-making and finished cloth, as well as

126 These issues are discussed in Bolton, *Money*, pp. 274–93.

127 TNA, C 1/378/40.

128 TNA, PROB 2/10 (Mayow); PROB 2/57 (Rychard); PROB 2/525 (Draner). Oldland, 'Merchant Capital', p. 1062; Zell, 'Credit', p. 683.

129 *Military Survey*, p. 75; *OED*: 'sperate'.

130 See below, Chapter 5.

a range of other products. Departing Southampton at least weekly for Salisbury, Winchester and London, the brokage books indicate that journeys took two days to Salisbury and four days to London. The carts operated throughout the year, with trips at their peak in the winter months, giving the lie to the traditional assumption that roads were then impassable.[131] Carts that had brought cloth to Southampton, London or another cloth-exporting port would not return empty, but were loaded with bulky commodities to be sold in the local area. Wool merchant John Heritage of Moreton-in-the-Marsh, for example, brought from London barrels of tar, preserved herring and sprats, as well as luxury goods such as hats, gunpowder, and a pewter salt cellar. Heritage then engaged in small-scale retailing himself, like selling the herring from one barrel to several customers. Clothiers may similarly have been drawn into trading general merchandise.[132]

Packhorses were less efficient than carts. When packhorses operated to or from Southampton in the mid fifteenth century, they carried only one-tenth of the load carried by carts. Packhorses remained useful though, in times of inclement weather or over difficult terrain, like the Westmorland cloth brought by packhorse from Kendal to Southampton in the early sixteenth century.[133] The gateways of some clothiers' houses, such as the Old Grammar School in Lavenham, are too narrow for carts to pass through, suggesting that pack animals were used, particularly in locations where carts would have difficulty negotiating inclines.[134] London mercer Thomas Kitson received six cloths from John Clevelod of Beckington 'by horse' in 1532.[135]

Common carriers, recognised as bound to serve the public, existed by the fifteenth century. A number seem to have operated to and from London, although the extent to which these providers offered regular services, taking the goods of a variety of customers along a specific route, on a consistent schedule, is unclear. John Paston wrote in 1465 that 'The bearer of this letter is a common carrier', and an act of parliament for street-paving in Holborn in 1533 referred to 'The poor carriers ... repairing weekly and monthly to your city of London.'[136] Clothiers

131 Hicks, ed., *Inland Trade*, pp. 43–51.

132 Dyer, *Country Merchant*, p. 119.

133 John Langdon, 'Horse-hauling: A Revolution in Vehicle Transport in Twelfth- and Thirteenth-Century England', *Past and Present* 103 (1984), pp. 60, 64, n. 72; B.C. Jones, 'Westmorland Pack-Horsemen in Southampton', *Transactions of the Cumberland and Westmorland Antiquarian and Archaeological Society* 59 (1960), pp. 65–6.

134 Alston, 'Old Grammar School', p. 44.

135 Brett, 'Somerset Clothmen', p. 43.

136 *OED*: 'common' and 'carrier'.

utilised common carriers, sometimes with unfortunate consequences. During the late 1510s, John Richardson, a common carrier of Chippenham, sent ten fine white cloths to London with his servant William Goodbarne, on behalf of Henry Long of Steeple Ashton. After selling the cloths, Goodbarne absconded to Appleby-in-Westmorland.[137] During the early 1530s Oliver Truxton, a common carrier operating between Ludlow and London, carried broad white cloth 'of like making as long Worcesters' for the clothier Walter Nicholls of Burwood in Shropshire. This cloth was found was found to be deficient in length and weight at Blackwell Hall in London and Truxton had to pay the fine.[138] The Colchester court rolls record the commissioning of a carrier in 1531 to take a short azure cloth to London to be delivered to William Cowpere at the sign of the Bell in Gracechurch Street. In the same year, the London mercer Thomas Kitson bought Devonshire cloths from John Chasty, a carrier from Exeter.[139] On his death in 1559, the carrier William Parks of Worcester owed debts to at least five London merchants, including a mercer, salter and pewterer. Three Worcester clothiers owed debts to him, one of which was specifically for the carriage of two cloths to London, and the bishop of Worcester also owed him four separate debts. Parks clearly took cloths from Worcester to London and returned with imported and luxury goods. His house contained a shop with scales, weights and baskets, probably used for the collection and delivery of goods in transit.[140]

CONCLUSION

Just as the term clothier encompassed individuals with varying degrees of wealth and involved with cloth-making to varying extents, it embraced individuals who engaged in marketing cloth in different ways. A few clothiers built up extensive retail trading links within their regions, like William Forthe of Hadleigh, or shipped their own products overseas, like John Lane of Cullompton, who exported on average forty-three cloths each year between 1506 and 1528.[141] The majority of clothiers though, sold their cloth wholesale to merchants. Many of these cloths were then shipped overseas. Clothiers traded with provincial, London and overseas merchants, but it was increasingly the Londoners, and within this group the Merchant Adventurers, who monopolised cloth exports. Records

[137] TNA, C 1/439/36
[138] TNA, C1/1387/55.
[139] CUL, Hengrave Hall MS 78(2), fol. 38; Britnell, *Colchester*, p. 178.
[140] Dyer, *Worcester*, p. 59.
[141] Carus-Wilson, 'Lane Chapel', pp. 114, 116.

tend to emphasise the sales made in formal markets and fairs, but inns, shops and homes were also places where clothiers sold their fabrics. Underpinning both the manufacturing and marketing processes was an extensive network of credit, also increasingly dominated by London lenders.

Cloth sales could be a risky business. The Southampton brokage books occasionally record unsold or unshipped cloth, like Thomas Osemond of Frome's cloth in 1443–44 'that could not sell here', or Master Nycolyne's cloth sent back to be loaded at London in 1539–40.[142] Clothiers bore these risks on behalf of their workers. A long chain of cloth-making and marketing potentially connected sheep farmers, spinners, weavers, fullers, dyers, carriers and merchants, with the clothier providing the common link.

142 Hicks, ed., *Inland Trade*, p. 74.

3

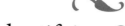

Identifying Clothiers

LOCATING CLOTH-WORKERS AND CLOTHIERS

Evidence for the extent and distribution of cloth-workers and clothiers in the late Middle Ages can be drawn from a range of sources, including the poll tax returns of 1377–81, the ulnage accounts recording subsidies paid for cloth sold, the rolls of the Court of Common Pleas, and from the travel writings of John Leland, the Tudor antiquarian. These sources each present their own challenges of interpretation.[1]

The ulnage accounts, despite their many limitations, can be used to explore the changing distribution of the cloth industry. In 1356–58, the leading counties for cloth production were, in descending order, Hampshire, Gloucestershire, London and Middlesex, Somerset (including Dorset), Lincolnshire and Kent (see table in Appendix 1). The industries were predominantly urban based, and these county totals mainly reflect production in Winchester, Bristol, London, Wells, Bath, Lincoln and Canterbury, which together with Salisbury and York, were the leading centres of cloth-making at this time. The south-west region, stretching from Southampton and Winchester through Salisbury to Bristol and Gloucester, and comprising the five counties of Hampshire, Wiltshire, Dorset, Somerset and Gloucestershire, accounted for over half the total cloth sold in England. By 1394–98, Somerset had become the leading county for cloth production, followed by Wiltshire, Gloucestershire, Yorkshire and Warwickshire. Although the large towns of Salisbury, Bristol, York and Coventry still comprised one-third of the total cloth sold, many smaller towns and rural communities were now supplying cloth for sale, perhaps accounting for up to half of all output. The south-western counties still made up over half of the total sales in the country, and the other major textile-producing areas comprised the Suffolk–Essex border, the city of York and the growing industry of the West Riding, the city of Coventry, and Berkshire. By 1468–73, the ulnage totals suggest that Suffolk had become the leading county, with Somerset close behind,

[1] See above, Introduction.

followed by Yorkshire, Gloucestershire and Wiltshire. The industry was now becoming increasingly based in small towns and rural communities. While the general trend was for cloth production to increase during the fifteenth century, the 1460s were a period of downturn, so a comparison of the total cloth sales recorded in the ulnage accounts between 1394–98 and 1468–73 shows a fall of 20 per cent. To some extent this may reflect increasing evasion of the payment of ulnage, as annual average cloth exports in 1468–71 were only 10 per cent smaller than in 1396–99.[2] It is safer therefore, when comparing fourteenth- and fifteenth-century figures, to compare *relative* changes in totals, rather than to compare the same totals directly.[3] Even then, the figures need to be treated with caution. Kerseys, straits and other narrow cloths were not included in the 1350s ulnage accounts, so counties like Suffolk and Yorkshire, which produced large quantities of narrow cloths, are under-represented in the mid-fourteenth-century figures. In contrast, narrow cloths were included in the ulnage accounts of the 1390s.[4] It has also been argued, that as the West Country accounts become fraudulent and understated during the fifteenth century, it is unlikely that Suffolk production was ever greater than the counties of Gloucestershire, Somerset and Wiltshire, whose average totals in 1468–73 were, in any case, very close to those of Suffolk.[5]

The poll tax returns of 1377–81 provide an indication of cloth-making in the late fourteenth century (Map 4), although it should be acknowledged at the outset that many returns are fragmentary or missing. The occupations recorded in the poll taxes that have been identified as cloth-workers are cardmaker, comber, draper, dyer, fuller, shearman, spinster and weaver.[6] Occupational surnames have not been used to identify trades, although some other studies have done so.[7] Major concentrations of cloth-workers could be found in urban centres, including Canterbury, York, Oxford, Derby, Salisbury, Bath, Worcester and Coventry, but some rural communities also had major clusters of textile workers, including

[2] Bridbury, *Clothmaking*, pp. 118–22.

[3] A similar approach can be used to compare other taxation records: Lee, 'Tracing Regional and Local Changes'.

[4] Amor, *From Wool to Cloth*, pp. 219–21.

[5] John Oldland, 'Book Reviews: Nicholas Amor, *From Wool to Cloth*', *EcHR* 70 (2017), pp. 662–3.

[6] From a database compiled by Samuel Gibbs from the transcribed records in Fenwick, *Poll Taxes*. Further details about the database are provided in Samuel Gibbs, 'The Service Patterns and Social-economic Status of English Archers, 1367–1417: The Evidence of the Muster Rolls and Poll Tax Returns', University of Reading, Ph.D. thesis, 2015. I am extremely grateful to Dr Gibbs for sharing this data with me.

[7] P.J.P. Goldberg, 'Urban Identity and the Poll Taxes of 1377, 1379, and 1381', *EcHR* 43 (1990), pp. 194–216.

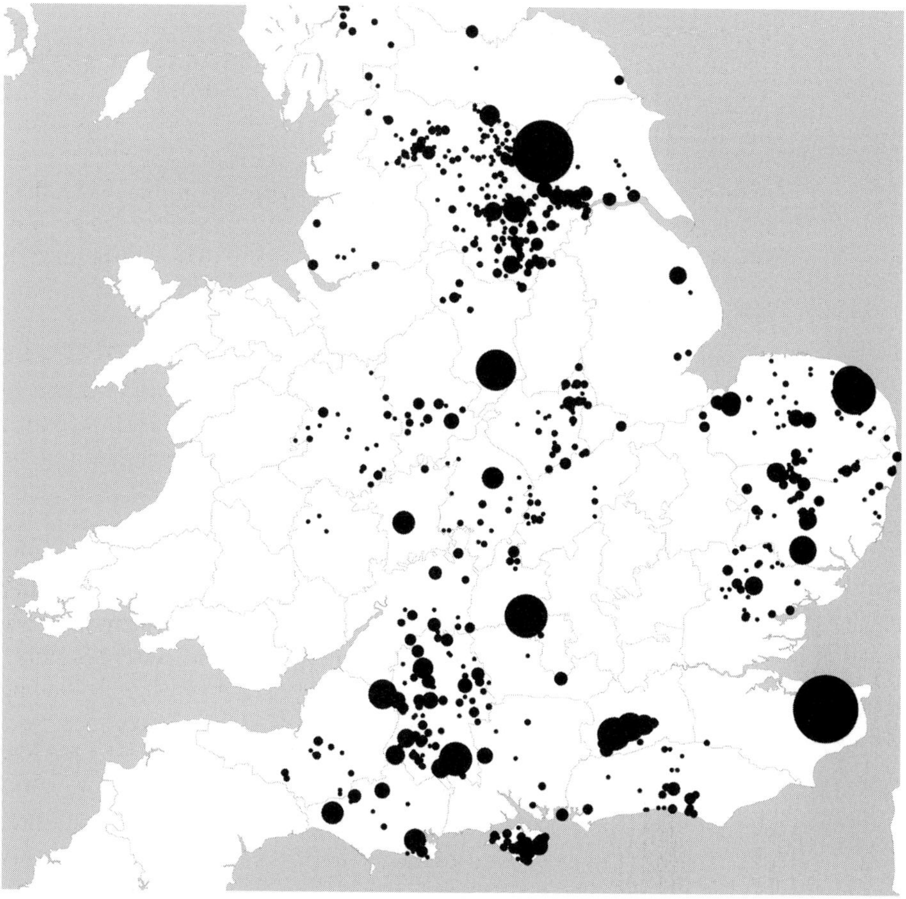

Map 4 Cloth-workers in the poll taxes of 1377–81
Source: Database compiled by Samuel Gibbs from Fenwick, *Poll Taxes*.
Note: Circle sizes represent 1–4, 5–19, 20–49, 50–99 or 100+ individuals.

North Walsham and Worstead in Norfolk, the centre of the worsted industry. The clusters in Wiltshire, north Essex and Suffolk, and the West Riding of Yorkshire, three of the leading cloth-producing areas in the fifteenth century, are also already evident.

While the ulnage accounts and poll tax returns show that cloth-making occurred in many counties, albeit with variations in the extent of production, clothiers were more geographically clustered. In the Introduction, we traced the rise of the clothier in cases brought to the Court of Common Pleas, to which litigants from around the country came to recover debts worth £2 or more. Taking two snapshots of cases in the Court of Common Pleas in 1453 and 1549 involving clothiers, cloth-makers and cloth-men, we can see that in the mid fifteenth century (Map

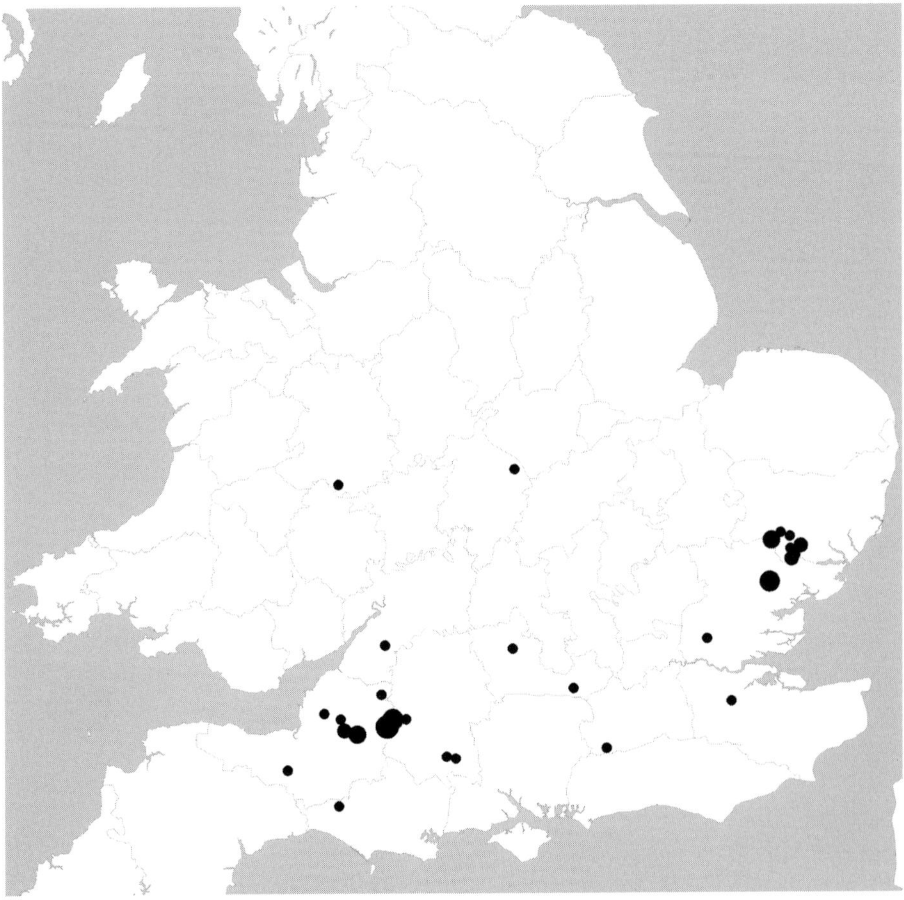

Map 5 Clothiers in the Court of Common Pleas, 1453
Source: AALT index compiled from CP 40/768.
Note: Circle sizes represent 1, 2–3, or 4+ individuals.

5) clothiers involved in Common Plea cases were concentrated in just two main areas, Somerset, particularly in Beckington and Frome, and south Suffolk and north Essex, notably in Long Melford and Coggeshall. A century later though (Map 6), clothiers had become more dispersed across other south-western counties, particularly Wiltshire and Gloucestershire, and also emerged in the Weald of Kent, and at Halifax and Wakefield in Yorkshire.

A larger sample from ten plea rolls from the Court of Common Pleas between 1480 and 1500 shows similar trends.[8] Clothiers resided in three

[8] Extracted by Nicholas Amor from ten plea rolls of the Court of Common Pleas between 1480 and 1500 and published in his book *From Wool to Cloth*, pp. 222–39. My thanks to Dr Amor for sharing this data with me.

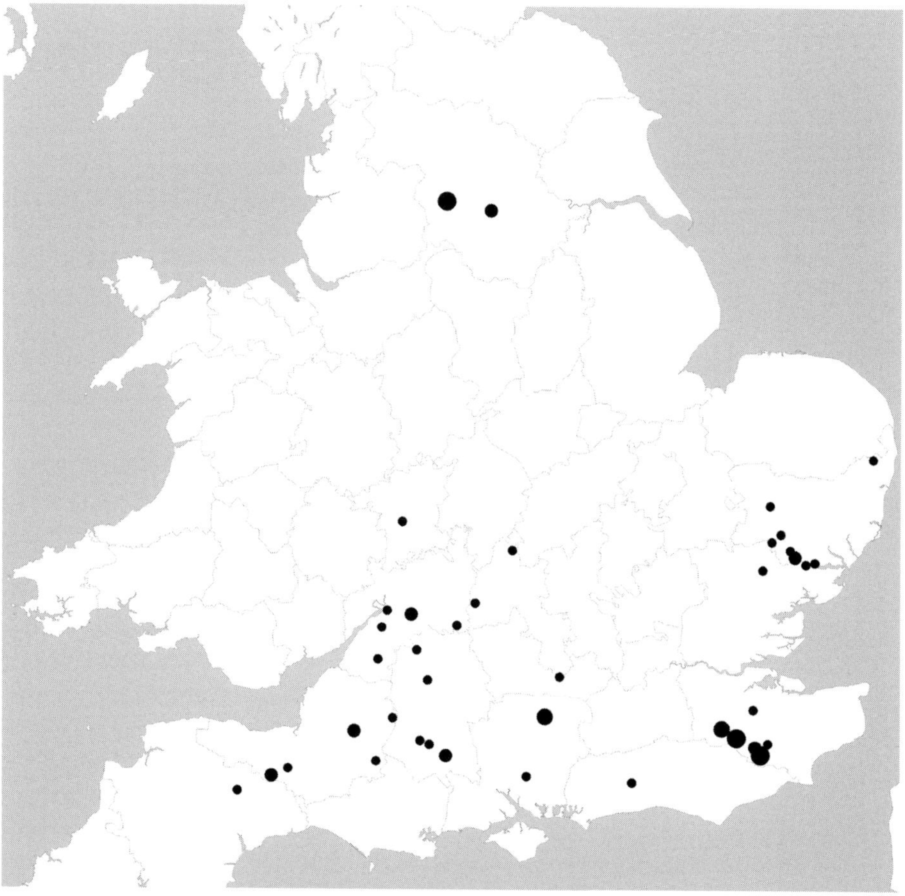

Map 6 Clothiers in the Court of Common Pleas, 1549

Source: AALT index compiled from CP 40/1139.

Note: Circle sizes represent 1, 2–3, or 4+ individuals.

main clusters, in the south-west, in the three counties of Gloucestershire, Wiltshire and Somerset; in Suffolk and in neighbouring Essex; and in the Kentish Weald. Some cloth-making areas had few clothiers. In Devon, for example, 117 cloth-workers appeared in the plea rolls, but only 5 of these were clothiers. Clothiers were not generally based in established cloth-making towns and cities. The plea roll sample from 1480 to 1500, for example, include 44 cloth-workers from Coventry but only 2 clothiers, and 34 cloth-workers from York with not a single clothier from the city. A few established cloth-making towns were home to groups of clothiers, including Bath, Bury St Edmunds, Winchester, Worcester, and most notably Colchester. Other cloth-workers lived in towns in greater proportions than clothiers. In the plea roll sample of 1480–1500, one-third of cloth finishers (dyers and shearmen) lived in the twenty-four greater medieval English towns, and one-fifth of cloth producers (spinsters, weavers and fullers), but only one in twelve clothiers did so.[9]

We need to explain, therefore, not only why cloth-making tended to locate in certain places and not others, but also why clothiers tended to cluster in particular communities. Economists and geographers have examined the success of modern entrepreneurial clusters, most notably the concentration of high-tech enterprises in the San Francisco Bay Area of the United States known as Silicon Valley. We can identify three 'Silicon Valleys' of entrepreneurship in the late medieval English textile industry: the West Country (east Somerset/west Wiltshire and Gloucestershire); the Stour valley of north Essex and south Suffolk; the Kentish Weald. We need to examine the work of clothiers within these and the other main areas of cloth-making in late medieval England, before looking at potential explanations for why the industry grew in some regions but not others in this period.

The West Country: cloth-making centres

The West Country cloth-making region stretched from Gloucester south-westwards and was described in 1576 as comprising 'the rivers of Fromewater, Kingswood water, the rivers of Avon, Willibourne [Wylye] and Salisbury bournes, and Stroudwater in the said counties of Somerset, Wiltshire and Gloucester and the branches of the same waters'.[10] The ulnage accounts illustrate the dramatic shift from urban to rural textile production that took place between the late fourteenth and mid fifteenth centuries in this region. In the 1390s, Bristol accounted for 92 per cent of the cloths sealed in Gloucestershire, Salisbury for 89 per cent of Wiltshire cloths, Sherborne for 87 per cent of Dorset cloths, and Winchester for 77 per cent of Hampshire cloths, although the towns of Bath, Bridgwater, Taunton and Wells together only comprised 24 per cent of the cloths sealed in Somerset. Cloth-making was developing in the countryside, in places like Pensford, where the largest single proportion of cloths was sealed in Somerset. Pensford was an entirely new settlement, not even recognised as a place for taxation purposes in 1334, which had grown up at a ford on the edge of two adjoining parishes. The predominantly rural area of west Wiltshire accounted for nearly 11 per cent of the county's cloths sealed in 1394–95, and this rose to 26 per cent in 1414–15 and 77 per cent by 1467.[11]

[9] Amor, *From Wool to Cloth*, pp. 54–5.

[10] 18 Elizabeth, c. 16: *SR*, iv (1), p. 626.

[11] J.N. Hare, 'Growth and Recession in the Fifteenth-century Economy: The Wiltshire Textile Industry and the Countryside', *EcHR* 52 (1999), pp. 3–5; John Hare, 'Pensford and the Growth of the Cloth Industry in Late Medieval Somerset', *Somerset Archaeology and Natural History Society: Proceedings* 147 (2003), pp. 173–80. See also below, Appendix 2.

By the time that John Leland visited in 1539–45, cloth-making in the Cotswolds was mainly to be found in small towns and villages. In the Vale of Gloucester, he passed through Dursley, 'a pleasant clothing town', with fulling mills and a market established only nine years before; Wotton-under-Edge, where 'a fair number of its inhabitants are clothiers'; Kingswood, with 'some clothiers'; Alderley, 'a clothing village'; Tortworth, 'where some good clothiers live'; and Wickwar, 'an attractive little clothing town'. Further west, however, the cloth trade was not as important as it had previously been at Berkeley, and at Thornbury 'idleness much reigns there'.[12] Along the river Avon in west Wiltshire, Leland found one of the most intensively developed areas of cloth-making in the country. He noted that Bradford-on-Avon 'stands by cloth-making', Trowbridge 'flourishes by drapery', and Steeple Ashton 'depends largely on its cloth trade'. Leland also recorded the importance of cloth-making at Devizes and Westbury, but did not comment on the flourishing industry at Castle Combe.[13] Moving into Somerset, Leland described Frome as situated in a valley where 'a number of good clothiers live, with fine houses and fulling mills', and noted the importance of cloth-making at Norton St Philip, Bruton, Wells and Chew Magna. At the larger town of Bath, Leland described three clothiers, Thomas Chapman, John Kent and Thomas Style, 'by whom the town of Bath then flourished', and after their deaths 'it has somewhat decayed'. London mercer Thomas Kitson had traded with all three families during the 1530s.[14] At Pensford, Leland found a 'pleasant little cloth-making town' and several fulling mills. His assertion that 'Browne of London in Limestreet' owned the village is questionable, as the settlement lay across at least two manors, making title by a single person unlikely. The statement does, however, suggest that the Londoner had forged prominent links with this cloth-making town. The industry in neighbouring Dorset was less significant, and Leland found that Sherborne 'stands partly by making of cloth, but most by all manner of crafts'.[15]

Within this region were distinct areas of specialised production. Western Wiltshire and eastern Somerset concentrated on heavily fulled white broadcloth, increasingly supplying the London market and merchants like Thomas Kitson,[16] although their reputation was already known when the 'western blanket' of Devizes and Beckington was specifically referred to in a parliamentary petition of 1429. Castle Combe, where in the early fifteenth century cloth-makers from Cirencester and Bath sent cloths to be dyed, and Stroudwater, became

[12] *Itinerary*, v, pp. 95–6, 100–1.
[13] *Itinerary*, v, pp. 82–3.
[14] *Itinerary*, i, pp. 143, 145, 149; v, pp. 97–8, 103; Brett, 'Somerset Clothmen', p. 32.
[15] *Itinerary*, i, p. 152; v, p. 103; Hare, 'Pensford', pp. 173–80.
[16] See above, Chapter 2.

renowned for producing fine red cloths.[17] Salisbury and the river valleys that surrounded it concentrated on lighter rays, or medleys, which were made from dyed wool. In and around Marlborough in Wiltshire, and at Andover, Alton and Basingstoke in north Hampshire, kerseys were produced in industries that linked with the Thames valley areas.[18] The knitting of woollen caps was established in Gloucester by 1481, and by the 1530s it appears to have become the town's principal industry.[19]

The West Country: cloth-workers and clothiers

Salisbury was probably the leading centre of cloth production in England in 1400. The city's poll tax returns are unfortunately incomplete, but include seven weavers sufficiently wealthy to have servants residing in their households, and one, Henry Bonde, employing five male servants. They also show a concentration of weavers and fullers in the Wyle valley to the west of the city. In 1421, 112 master weavers, 208 journeymen weavers, 53 master fullers and 27 journeymen fullers are recorded in Salisbury. Major cloth-makers from the city in the fifteenth century were Henry Swayne (d. 1479), who supplied the mayor of Salisbury with jackets for soldiers in 1464, and left a dye-house, wool and cloth; John Briggs (d. 1491), who employed thirteen servants and apprentices; and William Cuff (d. 1500), whose inventory of household goods and business items totalled £595 and included five looms.[20]

The shift of the textile industry from larger towns to smaller rural locations appears to have first occurred in Somerset, where as noted above, the larger towns comprised only a quarter of the county's total production in 1396–97. Cloth producers in these villages were concentrating production. The ulnage accounts of the 1390s suggest that the average seller in Croscombe offered 43 dozens per year for sale, in Pensford they supplied 84, and in Frome as many as 118, compared to less than 25 in the larger centres of Wells, Bridgwater and Bath. The largest cloth market in the county at this date was Pensford. Its merchants included Thomas Prysshton and John Prysshton, the two largest dealers in the county, bringing 795 and 570 dozens respectively to be taxed.[21] It is not

[17] *VCH Wiltshire*, iv, pp. 130, 139; Carus-Wilson, 'Evidences of Industrial Growth', pp. 192, 196, 200.

[18] Hare, *Prospering Society*, pp. 177–9; Hare, 'Pensford', p. 177; John Hare, 'Regional Prosperity in Fifteenth-century England: Some Evidence from Wessex', in M. Hicks, ed., *Revolution and Consumption in Late Medieval England* (Woodbridge, 2001), p. 114.

[19] *VCH Gloucestershire*, iv, pp. 52–3.

[20] TNA, PROB 2/174 (Cuff); Amor, *From Wool to Cloth*, p. 30; Bridbury, *Clothmaking*, pp. 78–9; Dyer, *Age of Transition*, p. 230.

[21] Shaw, *Wells*, p. 82; Hare, 'Growth and Recession', pp. 3–5.

surprising therefore, that the earliest recorded references to clothiers in the indexed Court of Common Plea records are to be found in Somerset.[22] In 1418, two men from Croscombe, both described as 'clother', defended debts. John Harryes defended a debt for £6 brought by William Armeys, and Robert Bomer defended a debt of 6 marks brought by John Isard. In the same year, Margery Horewood of Wells, widow of John, 'clothester' defended a plea of 40s. John Harryes and John Horewood both had cloths sealed in the ulnage accounts of 1402–03.[23] Other early cases in the Court of Common Pleas involve a Croscombe clothier in 1422 and a Croscombe cloth-maker and Wells clothier in 1430.[24] Croscombe and Wells continued to be centres of cloth production at the end of the century: three London drapers bought 800 marks worth of cloth at Croscombe from Richard Mawdleyn. John Mawdleyn, described by Leland as 'late a great clothier in Wells', had been assessed at £200 of moveable goods in 1524, and served four times as master of the borough of Wells.[25]

While Croscombe and Wells can currently claim the oldest-known documentary references to clothiers, at the same date, and within the same plea roll, are the first known documentary references to 'clothmaker'. In 1418, the executors of Walter Colbrond of Gussage St Michael in Dorset brought three debt cases against groups of cloth-makers from Coventry, Worcester and Wolverhampton, and several villages in Dorset, Somerset and Wiltshire.[26] These cases are important reminders that the clothiers and cloth-makers were urban, as well as rural figures.

'Castlecombes' and 'Stroudwaters' became household words for fine cloth manufactured in two rural locations in the Cotswolds, which expanded dramatically during the fifteenth century. At Castle Combe (Plate 9) there was a tradition recorded by the surveyor in 1458 that the first inhabitants to be artificers of wool and cloth were three members of the Touker family, and that Roger Young had lived in the village as a clothier in Edward III's reign. Indeed the Touker family first appear in the court rolls in 1349 and a Thomas Touker paid the large entry fine of over

[22] At the time of consulting the AALT website, there were no rolls indexed between 1399 and 1418.

[23] TNA, CP 40/629, m. 15d (AALT 906d); CP40/629, m. 214d (AALT 1311d); CP 40/629, m. 329d (AALT 1542d); E 101/344/4.

[24] CP 40/627, m. 13d (AALT 457d); CP 40/677, m. 404, 388d (AALT 806, 1644d).

[25] TNA, C1/244/13; *Itinerary*, i, p. 145; Shaw, *Wells*, pp. 72–3, 293.

[26] TNA, CP 40/629, m. 275d (AALT 1435d, 1436d); CP 40/629, m. 399d (AALT 1685d). The cloth-makers in the first case came from North Bradley, Westbury and Tilshead(?) in Wiltshire; Beckington, Somerset; and Wolverhampton. In the second case the cloth-makers were from Orcheston, Canning Marsh (All Cannings), Cheltenham and High Swindon in Wiltshire; Coventry and Worcester. In the third case they were from (Sixpenny) Handley and Tarrant Hinton in Dorset.

Plate 9 Castle Combe, Wiltshire.
This village boomed as a cloth-making centre during the early fifteenth century, stimulated by regular cloth purchases from its lord, Sir John Fastolf.

£10 for a fulling mill in 1374. The surveyor noted how Sir John Fastolf, who had acquired the estate in 1409, and had had a distinguished military career in France, purchased every year a hundred-pounds' worth of cloth from the villagers, and attributed these purchases as the principal cause of Castle Combe's wealth. By 1447 there were three fulling mills and a gig mill, for raising the nap on cloth. Fifty new houses were built between 1409 and 1454.[27] Stroudwater, like Castle Combe, underwent a remarkable boom from cloth-making, and developed as a specialised fulling, dyeing and finishing centre where clothiers could be found by the 1470s. These industrial centres developed along a stretch of the river Frome from Chalford running westwards to the modern town of Stroud.

[27] Carus-Wilson, 'Evidences of Industrial Growth', p. 198; M.W. Beresford and J.K.S. St Joseph, *Medieval England. An Aerial Survey*, 2nd edn (Cambridge, 1979), pp. 267–9.

The population of Stroud increased threefold, from about seventy households in 1327 to more than two hundred in 1551, while the two dozen manorial tenants in Rodborough in the early fourteenth century swelled to more than forty households by 1522.[28] In these two parishes and at Bisley, fulling mills and houses for cloth-workers were built. John Benet of Cirencester (d. 1497) had houses in Stroud, King's Stanley and Rodborough, where his mill 'and all shears called Shermansheris and lez handelles' were to be found.[29] Also in Rodborough was the house, mill and dye-house of Edward Haliday, cloth-maker (d. 1519), the son of a fuller, and commemorated by a brass in Minchinhampton church. His family remained in business for several generations.[30] In contrast to Castle Combe, later industrial developments have meant that there are now few physical remnants of this medieval growth in the Stroud valleys.

Thirteen clothiers from Stroud were recorded in Court of Common Plea records between 1480 and 1500, and fourteen from Dursley. The clothier Robert Rychard of Dursley (d. 1492) had goods and furnishings amounting to the enormous sum of £700 in his inventory. He possessed a house in the market town of Berkeley, and properties in Dursley, as well as a warehouse, wool loft, dye-house and shop. His will refers to an apprentice, three servants, and at least nine other employees.[31] Two later Dursley clothiers enjoyed an unenviable reputation: Webb, a 'great clothier dwelling in Dursley in the days of Queen Mary', and his father, who had resided there during Henry VIII's reign. They allegedly:

> Using to buy very great quantities of wool out of most counties of England; at the weighing whereof both father and son (the better to draw on their ends) would even promise out of that parcel a gown-cloth, petticoat cloth, apron or the like to the good wife or her daughters, but never paid anything.[32]

The Webbs' empty rhetoric became part of folklore and by the 1630s had given rise to a proverb, '"He'll prove, I think, a man of Dursley", i.e. a man that will promise much but perform nothing.'[33]

[28] Dyer, *Age of Transition*, p. 227; C. Dyer, 'Villages and Non-villages in the Medieval Cotswolds', *Transactions of the Bristol and Gloucestershire Archaeological Society* 120 (2002), p. 32.

[29] TNA, PROB 11/11/94.

[30] Carus-Wilson, 'Evidences of Industrial Growth', pp. 195–6; R. Perry, 'The Gloucestershire Woollen Industry, 1100–1690', *Transactions of the Bristol and Gloucestershire Archaeological Society* 66 (1945), pp. 78–9.

[31] TNA, PROB 2/57; PROB 11/9/7.

[32] John Smyth, *The Berkeley Manuscripts, A Description of the Hundred of Berkeley in the County of Gloucester and of its Inhabitants*, ed. John Maclean, 3 vols (Gloucester, 1883), iii, pp. 26–7.

[33] Smyth, *Berkeley Manuscripts*, iii, pp. 26–7.

In west Wiltshire, John Leland recalled a notable group of clothiers during his visits in 1539–45. James Terumber (d. 1488) had become legendary over half a century after his death:

> one James Terumber, a very rich clothier, built a fine impressive house in the town, which at his death he gave with other property as an endowment for two chantry priests in Trowbridge Church. He also built a small almshouse next to the church.[34]

Leland encountered a 'large clothier in Trowbridge by the name of Alexander'. This was Alexander Langford (or Longford) (d. 1545), who had fulling mills in Trowbridge and Freshford (Somerset), which he passed to his sons Alexander and Edward. All three members of the family sold cloth to the London mercer Thomas Kitson. Thomas Bailey (d. 1543) of Trowbridge, described by Leland as 'Old Bayllie', also sold broadcloths to Thomas Kitson, and to merchants of the Hanse. He acquired a house, garden and fulling mills at Stowford and invested in houses and lands in several other places. His sons continued in cloth-making, William at Keevil and Christopher at Trowbridge and Stowford.[35] Another 'rich clothier', Thomas Horton (d. 1530), held fulling mills at Bradford and Iford, and his house at Westwood still survives. At Steeple Ashton, the clothiers Robert Long and Walter Lucas had built the church aisles.[36]

Following the dissolution of the monasteries, William Stumpe (c.1497–1552) of Malmesbury, described by Leland as 'an exceeding rich clothier', established weaving workshops in buildings formerly part of the abbey, as well as gifting the former abbey church to the town. Leland found that 3,000 cloths were being produced every year.[37] In another religious house, in Gloucester, the capper, cloth-maker and alderman Thomas Bell (1485/6–1566) (Plate VII) had converted the house of the Blackfriars into a weaving-house and his residence, and in 1538 reportedly provided employment to over three hundred people.[38] The impact of the dissolution of the monasteries on the region's cloth industry must have been mixed, as some monastic lords had provided significant investment. Leland recorded that the last abbot of Cirencester had invested 700 marks (£466) in building two fulling mills in his town, and these were 'wonderfully necessary, because the town stands all by

[34] *Itinerary*, i, p. 136.

[35] *Itinerary*, i, p. 136. *VCH Wiltshire*, iv, pp. 142–3; Brett, 'Wiltshire Clothmen', pp. 39–40.

[36] *Itinerary*, i, p. 135; v, p. 83. See also below, pp. 310–12.

[37] *Itinerary*, i, p. 132; see also below, Chapter 6.

[38] *Itinerary*, ii, p. 58; *VCH Gloucestershire*, iv, pp. 53–4, 376; see also below, p. 307.

clothing'. Abbot Selwood of Glastonbury had rebuilt one street of houses at the cloth-making centre of Mells.[39]

The Stour valley of Suffolk and Essex: cloth-making centres

We move now to the river Stour, forming most of the county boundary between Suffolk and Essex, in the area that was later home to the landscape painter John Constable. The industry was concentrated in the small towns and villages along this river, including Dedham, East Bergholt, Sudbury, Long Melford and Clare, and in other settlements on tributaries of the Stour, such as Hadleigh and Lavenham. The latter was home to three generations of the Spring family of clothiers, including Thomas III, who by his death in 1523 was one of the wealthiest commoners in the country. Industrial production extended south into Essex, notably to Braintree and Coggeshall, where the striking half-timbered house of the clothier Thomas Paycocke (d. 1518) still stands.[40]

The cloth industry in Colchester expanded in the later fourteenth century, creating significant growth within the town. The town's population may have grown from below 3,000 before the Black Death of 1348–49 to a medieval peak of over 8,000 by the second decade of the fifteenth century. Colchester specialised in the production of russets, a grey-brown coloured cloth, exported during the later fourteenth century to Gascony and Prussia through the town's port of Hythe. There were also links with London, where Essex cloths were acquired by Italian and Hanseatic exporters. Cloths produced in Colchester could compete in European markets not simply because of the cheapness of the wool from which they were made, but also because of the low manufacturing costs. During the mid fifteenth century, both the Baltic and Gascon markets declined, and Colchester become more reliant on London trading links.[41] Colchester was also the foremost centre for marketing cloth produced in Essex, and unlike many other larger towns, it enhanced this role over the course of the fifteenth century. Comparing the ulnage accounts for the county from the 1390s and 1460s, one can see that Colchester not only remained the principal town for the sale of cloth, but had increased its lead relative to other centres in Essex. The distribution of rural clothmaking in Essex was concentrated within the northern part of the county, north of a line from Chelmsford to Maldon and east of a line from Chelmsford to Saffron Walden.

Growth also occurred on the Suffolk side of the Stour valley from the later fourteenth century, with new centres of production such as

[39] *Itinerary*, i, p. 129; iii, p. 101; v, p. 505. See below, p. 309.

[40] See below, Chapter 6, for more on the Spring and Paycocke families.

[41] Britnell, *Colchester*, pp. 61–71.

Hadleigh, Lavenham and Long Melford emerging alongside older industries in Bury St Edmunds, Sudbury and Clare. Although the Suffolk ulnage accounts of the 1390s do not record the distribution of the cloth trade between these different localities, other evidence points to the growing importance of these new manufacturing centres. At Hadleigh, about one-fifth of the male inhabitants were working in textiles in 1381. Kersey, which had given its name to a type of narrow fabric by 1376, possessed a cloth market and cloth hall in 1398–99. Lavenham was counted equivalent in wealth to Bath, Derby, Whitby, Plymouth and Lichfield in 1397, when a loan was raised from seventy towns.[42] Cloth-making in Suffolk grew faster than anywhere else in England between the 1390s and 1460s, by which time it was the leading county for cloth production. The ulnage account of 1467–68 shows that Lavenham, Bildeston and Hadleigh were now the most important marketing centres, accounting for half of recorded sales in the whole county (Appendix 2).

Merchants of Ipswich and Colchester imported raw materials and exported finished cloth for the Suffolk textile industry until at least the 1440s, when the cloth producers increasingly turned to Londoners. Even in the late fourteenth century though, some Suffolk cloth-makers were dependent on London merchants, like the Hadleigh draper John Kempston, who had sold over £200 in cloth to Gilbert Maghfeld in the early 1390s.[43]

The industry within Essex and Suffolk produced a variety of cloths. In the early fifteenth century, Colchester diversified from its traditional russets to a wider range of cloths of higher quality, including musterdevillers, blue cloths and grey cloths.[44] Many of the cloths produced in Suffolk in the later fourteenth and early fifteenth centuries were lighter and less costly types, such as straits and kerseys, aimed at the lower end of the market. Lower-grade cloths tended to be made from local wool, which was usually coarser and lighter in weight. From the 1460s onwards, however, production in many parts of Suffolk and Essex moved to heavier and slightly higher-quality broadcloths. While straits could be woven on a rudimentary loom by a single weaver, broadcloths needed larger looms operated by two people, and required more wool, so broadcloth production was more capital intensive. These encouraged entrepreneurs rather than small producers, who could minimise their overheads and deal in bulk.[45] Suffolk products ranged from vesses or

[42] Bailey, *Medieval Suffolk*, pp. 269–72; Britnell, 'Woollen Textile Industry', p. 86.

[43] Britnell, 'Woollen Textile Industry', pp. 87–8. See above, p. 82.

[44] Musterdevillers were a mixed grey cloth, modelled on the fine grey cloths produced in the town of Montivilliers in Normandy: *OED*.

[45] Bailey, *Medieval Suffolk*, pp. 271–2, 276; Amor, *From Wool to Cloth*, pp. 216–18.

set-cloth, a lower-quality woollen woven as both straits and broadcloths, to very fine Glemsford whites, but its coloured cloth seems to have been most successful. Slightly heavier than most of the cloth made in western England, but probably made from slightly coarser wools, these dominated markets in south Europe in the early sixteenth century. After the Reformation, Suffolk repositioned itself to make blue cloths for northern European markets.[46]

The Stour valley of Suffolk and Essex: cloth-workers and clothiers

By the late fourteenth century, textile workers formed the largest number of persons employed in Essex after those working in agriculture. When the cloth-workers of Essex, Suffolk and parts of Norfolk presented a parliamentary petition in 1393 they claimed that 'Many and the greater part of the people of the said districts ... are able to do nothing else but work in that craft.'[47] The bailiffs of Braintree stated in 1452 that weaving was practised in their town more than any other craft and had been so from time beyond memory.[48] In both rural Essex and Colchester, many textile workers operated on a small-scale basis, often engaged in only one or two stages of the cloth-making process. These activities could be combined with other crafts or agricultural work. So while in Hinckford Hundred, in the centre of the cloth-making region of Essex, five per cent of those households whose occupations were recorded in the poll tax returns of 1381 were making cloth, it is likely that there were many others who were not recorded, because they would have worked in the textile industry on a part-time or secondary basis.[49]

In later-fourteenth-century Colchester, some fullers were coordinating several of the cloth-making processes, including putting-out wool to dye and yarn to be woven. Others accepted unfinished cloth to full and sell, paying the weaver later. But this was not a very advanced form of organisation, and the units of organisation were typically small. Ulnage accounts for Colchester in 1395–97 show that cloth-making remained in the hands of small producers during this period of rapid growth. Only 10 of the 189 cloth sellers listed in the accounts are known to have been exporting cloth. Over 80 cloth sellers sold ten cloths or fewer, and 6 sold only one cloth each.[50]

By the later fifteenth century, the ulnage accounts show that cloth

[46] John Oldland, 'The Variety and Quality of English Woollen Cloth Exported in the Late Middle Ages', *Journal of European Economic History* 39 (2011), pp. 226–9; Oldland, 'Book Reviews', p. 662.

[47] Poos, *Rural Society*, p. 59.

[48] *VCH Essex*, ii, p. 330.

[49] Poos, *Rural Society*, p. 59.

[50] Britnell, *Colchester*, pp. 77–9.

sales were becoming concentrated in fewer hands. In 1477/8, the top quartile of sellers in Colchester accounted for just over one third of all the cloths being taxed there, although in Lavenham they brought more than three-quarters of all the cloths taxed. Most weavers, fullers and dyers recorded in the Colchester court rolls were not selling cloth, but depended on other entrepreneurs. It was not until the last quarter of the fifteenth century that Colchester's wealthiest townspeople began to describe themselves as cloth-makers.[51]

Across Suffolk, the cloth industry in the 1460s was still predominantly characterised by a large number of small producers, many of whom had other interests, including farming. In a few places though, control over production was becoming concentrated in the hands of wealthy clothiers. In Hadleigh, for example, six clothiers accounted for over two-thirds of cloth sales in the town. In the late 1460s, the foremost clothier in Suffolk, responsible for over 10 per cent of the county's total production, was John Stanesby at Bildeston, a member of the London company of fishmongers. John Motte (d. 1473) was the other major cloth producer in this Suffolk village and a member of the same London company. He remembered spinners, fullers and weavers in his will who probably worked for him, and left £240 for roads linking Bildeston to Semer, Rattlesden and Ipswich, and Colchester to London. The county's other leading clothiers at this time were William and Robert Forthe, Thomas Fulsnape and John Clerke, all based in Hadleigh, and Thomas Spring II of Lavenham.[52]

Between the 1470s and 1520s, further changes in the Suffolk cloth industry saw a small number of centres becoming even more prominent and control of production being concentrated in the hands of fewer clothiers, as trade increasingly focused on London. In Lavenham in Suffolk, for example, the percentage of sales by the leading five cloth sellers rose from 35 to 83 per cent between 1463 and 1478, while the total number of cloth sellers halved. The departure of the Hanseatic merchants from Colchester and Ipswich triggered major changes in the organisation of the Suffolk textile industry. The more substantial weavers increasingly titled themselves as clothiers and many others became their workers.[53] By 1522, 21 of the 32 settlements in the Suffolk hundred of Babergh had people engaged in cloth-making or finishing, with clothiers to be found in 18 of these locations. The largest concentrations of clothiers were located in Lavenham, Glemsford and Nayland, with 34, 20 and

[51] Britnell, *Colchester*, p. 184.

[52] Amor, 'Jack of All Trades', pp. 420, 426–7; Amor, *From Wool to Cloth*, pp. 194–5.

[53] Britnell, 'Woollen Textile Industry', p. 99; Amor, *From Wool to Cloth*, p. 143.

14 clothiers respectively.[54] By the 1520s the industry in Suffolk was at its peak, and when the rich clothier Thomas Spring III of Lavenham died in 1523, he left a personal estate larger than that of any other commoner.[55]

Yorkshire

We now move further north to examine the textile industry in Yorkshire. The poll tax returns of 1379 record clusters of 'drapours' in market towns such as Doncaster, Pontefract and Wakefield, as well as in smaller villages.[56] Accumulation of resources among the wealthier peasantry may have enabled some to become wool dealers and clothiers.[57] By the 1390s the York Weavers' Guild complained that weavers and dyers in rural communities and small towns such as Wakefield in the West Riding were competing with them illegally.[58] York remained a major centre of cloth production though until well into the fifteenth century. The city, which had at least sixty-nine weavers in 1381, still had some 111 broadlooms operational in the 1450s, and a surviving weavers' apprentice book suggests an active employment market until the 1470s.[59] There is scattered evidence in York of a few merchants acting as clothiers through coordinating cloth-making between wool producers, weavers, fullers and dyers. Some of the city's merchants who traded overseas left bequests to their workers, including artisans residing in towns and villages outside York.[60]

The movement in cloth production from the urban industries of York, Beverley and Ripon westwards to the rural industries of the Aire and Calder valleys was well underway when Leland toured the county in the early 1540s. Leland visited the small towns of Bradford and Leeds which 'stands most by clothing', and Wakefield, where 'the whole profit of the town stands by coarse drapery'. The ulnage accounts show that between the 1390s and the 1470s, these three West Riding towns together with Halifax and Huddersfield had expanded at the expense of the established centres of York, Beverley and Ripon, and rural parts of the North Riding. Leland found that 'There was good cloth-making at Beverley: but that is now much decayed.' At Ripon, 'idleness is sore increased in the town, and cloth-making almost decayed'.[61] The vacant tenter plots

[54] *Military Survey*, p. 128; John Patten, 'Village and Town: An Occupational Study', *Agricultural History Review* 20 (1972), pp. 11–12.

[55] See below, Chapter 7.

[56] Fenwick, *Poll Taxes*, iii, pp. 323–6, 347–51, 380–1.

[57] Swanson, *Medieval Artisans*, p. 143.

[58] *Calendar of Inquisitions Miscellaneous*, vi: 1392–9, pp. 242–9.

[59] Swanson, *Medieval Artisans*, pp. 30–6.

[60] See above, pp. 20–1.

[61] *Itinerary*, i, pp. 47, 82.

that he saw in Ripon are listed in an account of 1532. Fulling mills in the North Riding had closed during the fifteenth century and those at Knottingley and Hillam near Selby were no longer operating in 1537.[62] In 1564, the Boroughbridge fulling mill and the older mill at Knaresborough, previously let for 66s 8d per year, were 'utterly decayed eight years past'.[63] Another indicator of the distribution of production across the West Riding is provided by a list of offenders found to be weaving cloth with weft made of flocks (waste wool and cloth shearings), following a commission established in 1533. The list includes 542 clothiers, and the document is incomplete. Over half belonged to the parishes of Halifax, Heptonstall and Elland, the rest coming from places like Huddersfield, Almondbury, Dewsbury, Wakefield, Leeds and Bradford.[64]

The typical figure in the West Riding industry, however, was the small independent clothier. Farmer-weavers can be found in wills and inventories in Nidderdale and the Forest of Knaresborough from the mid sixteenth century onwards, operating a mixed economy of farming and cloth-making. At Harrogate, for example, Elizabeth Kirkby (d. 1521) left yarn and a pair of combs, while John Lindley (d. 1541) left a woollen loom and a pair of wool combs. In 1558, John Keighley of Scriven near Knaresborough had cattle, sheep, pigs, poultry, bees and five different arable crops, as well as a spinning wheel, wool combs, hemp, linen yarn, harden yarn, wool and kersey cloth.[65] Such clothiers employed little labour beyond their own families, and production was often limited. In 1551 the city of York relaxed its rules for the sale of cloth for the benefit of 'any husbandman or other poor creatures of the country being unfranchised that make a piece or two of woollen cloth in a year within his own house and bring to this city to sell … by retail'.[66] The Halifax clothiers operated on a particularly small scale, even compared to their counterparts in nearby Leeds, and the 'Halifax Act' of 1555 allowed wool dealers and other middlemen to operate in the area around Halifax, whose activities had been forbidden elsewhere in an earlier statute.[67]

[62] Heaton, *Yorkshire Woollen*, p. 75; A.J. Pollard, *North East England during the Wars of the Roses: Lay Society, War, and Politics, 1450–1500* (Oxford, 1990), p. 73; R.B. Smith, *Land and Politics in the England of Henry VIII. The West Riding of Yorkshire: 1530–1546* (Oxford, 1970), pp. 24–7.

[63] Bernard Jennings, ed., *A History of Nidderdale*, 3rd edn (York, 1992), p. 76.

[64] Heaton, *Yorkshire Woollen*, pp. 133–5. The Almondbury, Huddersfield and Kirkheaton names are listed in Crump and Ghorbal, *Huddersfield Woollen Industry*, pp. 38–42.

[65] Jennings, ed., *Harrogate and Knaresborough*, pp. 204–7; Jennings, ed., *Nidderdale*, pp. 162–71.

[66] YELA, Y/COU/1/1, vol. 20, fol. 63v.

[67] See above, p. 43.

Thames valley

Another prominent area of cloth production was the Thames valley of Berkshire and Oxfordshire. In the 1390s, the ulnage accounts suggest that the main centre of production was in the north of this region at Steventon, East Hendred and Abingdon.[68] In the mid fifteenth century, a 'cloth-man' (also 'kerseyman') of Hendred called John Hatter, and London mercer William Hatter, were owed £20 by a man from Wallingford. East Hendred church contains a memorial brass of 1479 to William Whitwey (clothier or draper and woolman), and brasses with merchant's marks to two brothers who were merchants, Henry and Roger (d. 1439) Eldysley.[69] Leland described Abingdon as 'standing by clothing', although by the sixteenth century production there was dwarfed by that of Newbury and Reading.[70] The clothier Thomas Braybrooke, Abingdon's wealthiest resident in 1524–25, was taxed on goods worth £80, little more than one-third of the assessment of John Winchcombe, Newbury's wealthiest inhabitant and clothier. A cloth-maker from Burford put forward a scheme to re-invigorate textile production in Abingdon in 1538, but nothing became of the proposal.[71]

At Reading, Leland described the channels of the river Kennet as, 'very commodious for dyers, well occupied there, for the town chiefly stands by clothing'.[72] The town appears to have specialised in cloth finishing, as significantly more fullers and dyers from Reading appear in the plea rolls at the end of the fifteenth century than clothiers.[73] Increasing trade within the borough necessitated appointing two officials in 1512, known as cofferers, to collect rents and charges from the wharf and the public scales known as the wool beam and yarn beam. A third officer was added in 1529, and a fourth in 1535.[74] Walter Barton of Reading left a substantial inventory of goods worth £436 in 1538, including £200 of wares in his workshop.[75] Reading specialised in the production of the very heaviest broadcloths, like Kent and Sussex. An agreement was made between the cloth-makers of Reading on the one part, and the weavers, fullers and tuckers on the other, in the court of Star Chamber in 1520. This set out the approved weights of yarn required for a broadcloth, the size of the

[68] See below, Appendix 2.
[69] Yates, *Town and Countryside*, pp. 82–3.
[70] *Itinerary*, i, p. 122.
[71] Christine Jackson, 'Clothmaking and the Economy in Sixteenth-Century Abingdon', *Oxoniensia* 67 (2002), pp. 59–78. See also below, p. 176.
[72] *Itinerary*, i, p. 111.
[73] Amor, *From Wool to Cloth*, pp. 38, 222.
[74] *VCH Berkshire*, iii, p. 349.
[75] TNA, PROB 2/220.

finished broadcloth, prices for weaving, penalties for poor workmanship, and required all cloths made in the town to be marked with a seal.[76]

Newbury became the main centre for cloth-making in the region by the later fifteenth century, when twelve clothiers from the town were recorded in the plea rolls, and Newbury merchants accounted for between 15 and 22 per cent of the cloths sealed in Berkshire and Oxfordshire.[77] Kerseys, smaller and lighter than a broadcloth, were the main type of cloth produced, and this was exported and raw materials brought in through Southampton.[78] During the sixteenth century, Newbury became home to the famous clothiers John Smallwood alias John Winchcombe I (d. 1520) and his son John Winchcombe II (d. 1557), immortalised in Thomas Deloney's poem *Jack of Newbury*, and Thomas Dolman (d. 1575). The size of Winchcombe's enterprise is demonstrated by the 1,000 kerseys supplied to Thomas Cromwell in 1539 and an annual average of 1,200 kerseys sold to the London mercer Thomas Gresham between 1546 and 1549. Both Winchcombe and Dolman may have manufactured kerseys in centralised workshops.[79]

The Thames valley industry extended into north Hampshire, where Basingstoke, Odiham and Andover also concentrated on the production of kerseys. At Basingstoke, the growth of the cloth industry is revealed through fines for breaking the assize, which were in effect payments for pursuing occupations within the town. The numbers involved in cloth production or marketing rose from only five in 1454 to sixty-seven in 1524. The town's leading cloth trader in 1467 was Nicholas Draper, also known as Nicholas Bayly, who marketed nearly 60 per cent of the cloth from Basingstoke and Odiham. Fined successively in Basingstoke as a tailor, draper and mercer, he served as bailiff in 1465–66, and leased the rectory there in 1470–71.[80] London mercer Thomas Kitson bought kerseys from Robert and Edmund Smith in Odiham in 1531.[81]

Devon

In the late fourteenth century, cloth sales within Devon were highest in the areas of north and mid Devon, particularly at Barnstaple on the northern coast, which with its ready coastal access to Bristol may have

[76] BRO, R/IC2/1.

[77] Amor, *From Wool to Cloth*, pp. 38, 222; Yates, *Town and Countryside*, p. 84.

[78] Hicks, ed., *Inland Trade*, pp. 107–8.

[79] Yates, *Town and Countryside*, pp. 93–5. See also below, Chapter 6.

[80] TNA, E 101/344/17, m. 18; Hare, 'Regional Prosperity', pp. 114–15; John Hare, *Basingstoke: A Medieval Town, c.1000–c.1600* (forthcoming). My thanks to John Hare for sharing a draft of his chapter on the town's economy in advance of publication.

[81] CUL, Hengrave Hall MS 78(2), fols 44–5, 51v–52.

also drawn in cloth manufactured in Somerset to the west of Taunton. During the fifteenth century, the Culm and Exe River valleys of east Devon became more prominent centres of production, and Exeter, its commercial hub, had its own significant textile industry. Textile production made Crediton, Cullompton and Tiverton sufficiently prosperous to be ranked among the hundred wealthiest towns in England by 1524–25, as measured by their taxation assessments.[82] Leland observed fulling mills at Fenny Bridges near Ottery St Mary and noted that most of the inhabitants of Crediton earned their living by making cloth, as they also did, he reported, in north Devon at Great Torrington and Pilton near Barnstaple.[83] Another centre of production was around Tavistock, where by 1500 there were no fewer than sixteen fulling mills in operation within two miles of the town.[84] The main types of textiles woven in Devon were dozens and straits, which were narrower than the standard broadcloth. Using Devon's poor-quality wools, these were coarse, cheap cloths sold at home and overseas in Brittany, Normandy, Gascony and Spain. The production of kerseys, a lighter cloth of better quality, replaced dozens, particularly in east Devon during the fifteenth century.

There was a notable textile industry in Exeter by the late fourteenth century, and as in Colchester, Winchester and York there is piecemeal evidence for the multifaceted involvement of the city's merchants in the production and sale of cloth. Merchants supplied wool yarn to weavers to produce cloth, and hired the services of fullers, shearers and dyers.[85] On the basis of this evidence, Maryanne Kowaleski has suggested that clothiers had emerged in Exeter by the end of the fourteenth century, that they came primarily from a merchant background, and that they funded and employed artisans to produce cloth. There were also individuals in Barnstaple in the 1390s who were paying ulnage on over 1,000 cloths each. As has been noted in the introduction, however, it is unclear from this evidence whether these men were financing all aspects of cloth production from start to finish, or only taking a partial role in the production process.

There seem to have been relatively few prosperous clothiers in Devon in the later Middle Ages. Only five clothiers from the county are recorded in the sample of plea rolls between 1480 and 1500, and Leland did not note the names of any during his perambulations there in 1542. One notable exception was John Lane (d. 1529) of Cullompton who both produced and exported cloth. He had at least fifty standard-size cloths

[82] *CUHB*, p. 766.
[83] *Itinerary*, i, pp. 170, 172, 239–40.
[84] Finberg, *Tavistock Abbey*, p. 154.
[85] Kowaleski, *Exeter*, pp. 128, 151. See also above, p. 20.

on his premises when he died. The chapel that he endowed within the parish church is decorated with cloth-making images, including teasel frames, cloth shears and fulling stocks (Plates 2 and 4).[86]

While recent comparisons of debt cases made in the fifteenth and sixteenth centuries have suggested that Devon retained a measure of independence from London, there were important marketing links with the city, as the career of John Greenway of Tiverton illustrates. Often labelled as a clothier, Greenway is more accurately described as a provincial draper and merchant, for although much of his fortune was probably made from cloth, it seems to have been through the sale of textiles rather than their manufacture.[87] Greenway exported cloth, tin and hides from Devon ports and London, and imported wine, iron, salt, dyestuffs and linen. By 1482, he had acquired his own ship, trading from Dartmouth, and he later owned three merchant ships. In 1497, Greenway purchased admission into the Drapers' Company of London, and was later admitted into its livery and governing body. He probably also joined the Merchant Adventurers, as he included their arms on his chapel. He obtained the farm of customs of cloth in Devon and Cornwall in 1514. Like many of his counterparts who were wealthy clothiers, Greenway provided endowments, including a chantry chapel and an almshouse.[88] Tiverton also benefitted from a later clothier, Peter Blundell (c.1520–1601), who made extensive benefactions to his local community, including the creation of a free grammar school. Blundell apparently built his fortune from nothing by purchasing a single kersey, which a carrier took to London for him. It sold for great advantage, and after buying and selling others, Blundell eventually had sufficient kerseys to load a horse, and went to London with them himself. He was employed there by those managing the kersey trade, and continued until he was wealthy enough to set up making kerseys himself in Tiverton.[89] This folk memory demonstrates the importance of London marketing links within the region's cloth industry. A generation earlier, London mercer Thomas Kitson had made occasional purchases of 'Devonshires' and 'western dozens' from Austin Horton of Cullompton and a carrier from Exeter.[90]

[86] Carus-Wilson, 'Lane Chapel', pp. 114–16.

[87] Keene, 'Changes in London's Economic Hinterland', p. 67; Britnell, *Closing of the Middle Ages?*, pp. 217–18.

[88] Welsford, *John Greenway*; Carus-Wilson, 'Lane Chapel', pp. 115–16; John Prince, *Danmonii orientales illustres: or, the worthies of Devon* (Exeter, 1701), pp. 324–5.

[89] Prince, *Worthies of Devon*, p. 89; Joyce Youings, 'Blundell, Peter (*c.*1520–1601)', *ODNB*.

[90] CUL, Hengrave Hall MS 78(2), fols 38, 80v.

Kent

Kent remained an important, but second-ranking region of cloth production, over the late fourteenth, fifteenth and sixteenth centuries.[91] Canterbury was a notable centre of production in the late fourteenth century, with more than forty spinners, weavers and fullers recorded in the poll tax assessments. Although Canterbury, together with Dartford and Tunbridge Wells appear to have remained as cloth-finishing centres, cloth-making developed in more rural areas. Two main types of cloth were produced in Kent: kerseys of low value and narrow width in several areas of the North Weald and adjacent parishes, and heavy high-quality broadcloth manufactured in about six parishes around Cranbrook. It was the latter industry that produced greater volumes and values of output, employed larger numbers, and had a more capitalist structure. Wealden broadcloths were the longest and heaviest type of cloth recognised by statute: in 1552, Kent broadcloths had to be at least 28 yards long, 1¾ yards in width, and to weigh at least 90 lb. The weight was modified to 86 lb for coloured broadcloth of Kent by another statute of 1557.[92]

Cranbrook and neighbouring villages became the centre of the Kentish broadcloth industry. This is highlighted in the proportion of the county's cloth sealed in this area in the mid 1470s, and in the concentration of clothiers found in the plea rolls of the late fifteenth century. Similarly a survey of a range of sources compiled between the 1480s and 1540s found 167 clothiers across the Kentish Weald, of which the largest concentrations were in the parishes of Cranbrook (54), Biddenden (20), Benenden (19) and Goudhurst (19).[93] Cranbrook and Tenterden had already been among the one hundred largest towns in England in 1377 for which records survive.[94] The taxation records of the 1520s show wealthier clothiers rated at a similar level to the local gentry. These included Stephen Draner, rated at £300 in goods, Richard Courthop at £200, Alexander Courthop at 200 marks, and William Lynch at £160. Stephen Draner of Cranbrook (d. 1539) left the enormous sum of £1,834 in his will, although two-thirds of this consisted of hopeful debts.[95] Kentish cloths found a market in London, with draper Thomas Howell and mercer Thomas Kitson buying russets, greys, tawneys and azure-coloured cloth in the 1520s and 1530s.[96]

[91] Zell, *Industry*, p. 158.

[92] See below, Appendix 3.

[93] Zell, *Industry*, p. 155.

[94] *CUHB*, p. 759.

[95] TNA, PROB 2/525; Zell, *Industry*, p. 153, n. 3.

[96] Drapers' Company, Ledger of Thomas Howell, fols 18v, 39v, 52v; CUL, Hengrave Hall MS 78(2), fols 19, 19v, 24v, 25, 25v, 32v, 33, 116v, 123, 151; Zell, *Industry*, pp. 160–3.

Lancashire

The main products made in Lancashire were rugs, friezes, kerseys and cottons, all narrow cloths produced on a narrow loom operated by one man, as opposed to broadcloth made on a broadloom, requiring two men to work it. Rugs and friezes were coarse cloths made mainly in the areas around Manchester, Bury, Bolton and Rochdale. Kerseys were shorter and lighter, manufactured mostly in the north-eastern part of Lancashire in Colne, Burnley, Padiham, Blackburn and Preston. Cottons, which consisted solely of wool, were produced in Manchester, Bolton, Bury, Blackburn, and surrounding areas, and linen was woven almost everywhere in the county.[97] John Leland noted that 'Bolton on the Moor market stands most by cottons and coarse yarn. Several villages on the moors about Bolton do make cottons.'[98] Cloth-making had become so important to Manchester by 1541 that the privilege of sanctuary allowed to the town, by which a fugitive from justice was entitled to forty days of immunity from arrest, had to be moved to Chester. This was because the sanctuary had been attracting 'divers light and evil disposed persons' who stole linen yarn as it lay outside bleaching, and woollen cloth as it hung on tenterhooks drying. The act of parliament obtained for moving the sanctuary described the inhabitants of Manchester as 'well set awork in making of cloths, as well of linen as of wool'.[99]

The textile industry in Lancashire relied not only on local wool but also on raw wool and linen yarn brought over from Ireland. Although the Irish parliament prohibited the export of wool in 1522, this embargo was circumvented by smuggling and by licences granted by the English crown. Leland noted in 1535 that a great deal of Irish yarn was bought at Liverpool by Manchester men, where the customs rates were low.[100] As the preamble to the act of 1541 stated,

> Many strangers as well of Ireland as of other places within this realm have resorted to the said town [Manchester] with linen yarn wools and other necessary wares for making of cloths.[101]

London was one of the main destinations for Lancashire woollens. In 1531, Thomas Kitson bought 177 cottons from John Brown of Manchester and 170 Cheshire cottons from Gilbert Saricold, or Sorocould, of Manchester.[102] Another member of this family, Edmund Sorocould, sold

[97] Lowe, *Lancashire Textile Industry*, pp. 3–5.
[98] *Itinerary*, v, p. 43.
[99] 33 Henry VIII, c. 15: *SR*, iii, p. 850.
[100] *Itinerary*, v, p. 41; Lowe, *Lancashire Textile Industry*, pp. 10–11.
[101] 33 Henry VIII, c. 15: *SR*, iii, p. 850.
[102] CUL, Hengrave Hall MS 78(2), fols 36, 39v, 52v.

three packs of cottons for £20 to a citizen and haberdasher of London in 1543. Richard Thornton of Ashton-under-Lyme sold ten packs of friezes in London in 1553, making sales enroute of six packs of friezes at Loughborough and another six packs at Stourbridge Fair.[103]

Other markets are known only from passing references. Some coarse woollens made in north-east Lancashire were taken to Halifax. In the early 1540s, Christopher Mitchell, a Colne clothier, sold cloth worth £31 to John Banester of Halifax. The long-distance trade from northern England to Southampton, frequented by merchants from Kendal, also had links with Lancashire. Richard Tetley or Tetlow brought woad and oil for cloth-making, together with wine and bowstaves, from Southampton to Manchester in 1461–62, and 'Mr Browtun' of Manchester brought ten horse-loads of cloth into Southampton in 1535.[104]

A study of the inventories of Lancashire textile workers in the sixteenth century has shown that many producers were relatively poor and worked at home, assisted by the rest of their family. They owned one loom and possibly a spinning wheel, and usually combined their cloth-making with farming. Buying wool in small quantities, probably on credit, from wool dealers, they were generally not obliged to return the cloth to the dealer who had supplied them with their raw materials, but could freely sell their product to the buyer offering the best price. Inventories in north-east Lancashire indicate that several cloth-making processes, including carding, combing, spinning and weaving, were often undertaken in the same household.[105] There were, however, a few cloth producers who carried out several of the processes of cloth-making, could afford to buy large stocks of raw materials in bulk, and were not compelled to sell every piece of cloth as soon as it was finished in order to buy food or pay for the raw materials used. John Nabbs (d. 1570) of Manchester described himself as a cloth-maker. His goods were worth around £105, of which over half was made up of industrial capital, including 180 stones of wool and 19 pieces of cloth. He could carry out every cloth-making process except fulling and dyeing, as he owned stock cards, hand cards, spinning wheels, a loom, a board for cloth shearing and cloth shears. He employed six people, whom he described as servants, and left them 5s each and requested that two fullers have 12d each. There is little evidence, even among the larger producers, of operating a putting-out system. Instead of putting-out raw materials, cloth producers

[103] Lowe, *Lancashire Textile Industry*, pp. 59–60.

[104] Lowe, *Lancashire Textile Industry*, pp. 59–61; Hicks, ed., *Inland Trade*, p. 110.

[105] Lowe, *Lancashire Textile Industry*, pp. 26, 35; John T. Swain, *Industry Before the Industrial Revolution: North-east Lancashire, c.1500–1640*, Chetham Society, third series 32 (Manchester, 1986), p. 110.

brought in extra labour when required, or on a semi-permanent basis as a servant or apprentice.[106] Even by the close of the sixteenth century, the Lancashire woollen and linen industries still comprised predominantly small and independent spinners and weavers, rather than the putting-out system in which workers were dependent on clothiers and drapers for obtaining their raw materials and for marketing their cloth.

Other cloth-making centres

Cloth-making developed in the southern Lake District, where the industry centred on Kendal, Langdale and Grasmere. There were only two fulling mills in the parish of Grasmere in the late fourteenth century, but this had risen to six by 1453, at least ten in 1493–94, and eighteen by 1506–07. The Benson family dominated weaving and fulling and built up a landholding in Grasmere and Langdale. Some Kendal cloth was carried as far as Southampton in return for woad and raisins, with eleven men recorded in 1492–93, fourteen in 1527–28 and twenty-eight in 1552–53.[107] Kendal cloth-man James Striklond was trading with London grocer Edward Savage in the late fifteenth century, and London mercer Thomas Kitson purchased cloth from ten different suppliers in and around Kendal in 1530/1, mostly of 'penistones', made from a coarse type of wool. Leland described Kendal as very well-known for its cloth market.[108]

Cloth-making emerged across the marcher lordships of late medieval Wales, and clusters of fulling mills could be found in Swansea, Carmarthen, and in the lordship of Dyffryn Clwyd, around Ruthin, in Denbighshire. This cloth was sold through English ports, notably Bristol, and the markets of border towns such as Ludlow, Shrewsbury, Hereford and Oswestry, where Leland noted in 1539 that 'the town stands mostly by sale of cloth made in Wales'.[109] Shrewsbury merchants often brought Welsh cloth back to their town for finishing before transporting it to London. The number of burgesses admitted as shearmen there rose from just 1 per cent at the end of the fourteenth century to 16 per cent between 1500 and 1524. Shrewsbury also had its own cloth industry though, with

[106] Lowe, *Lancashire Textile Industry*, pp. 29, 31; Swain, *Industry*, p. 115.

[107] M.L. Armitt, 'Fullers and Freeholders of the Parish of Grasmere', *Transactions of the Cumberland and Westmorland Antiquarian and Archaeological Society*, new series 8 (1908), pp. 139–41, 179–80; Hicks, ed., *Inland Trade*, p. 110; Jones, 'Westmorland Pack-Horsemen', pp. 65–6.

[108] TNA, C 1/46/74; CUL, Hengrave Hall MS 78(2), fols 43v, 45, 45v, 46v; *Itinerary*, v, p. 46.

[109] *Itinerary*, iii, p. 75; Ian R. Jack, 'The Cloth Industry in Medieval Wales', *Welsh History Review* 10 (1980), pp. 443–60; J. Geraint Jenkins, *The Welsh Woollen Industry* (Cardiff, 1969), pp. 100–1.

a craft fellowship of forty-one master weavers in 1397–98, falling to twenty-nine by 1525.[110] Welsh frieze and cottons found another market in London. In August 1531, Thomas Kitson bought 45 pieces of frieze from William Davy of Haverfordwest in Pembrokeshire and 7 pieces from William Chans of Pendine in Carmarthenshire.[111]

Worsted was produced in Norwich and in several villages lying in a compact area between the city and the north Norfolk coast, including Worstead, from where the cloth derives its name. In 1379, there were weavers taxed in nineteen parishes in Tunstead hundred, including 45 weavers in Worstead and 29 at North Walsham. They were among the most prosperous group of weavers recorded anywhere in the poll tax returns, with over 40 per cent of them paying more than 12d in tax. By the late fifteenth century though, the plea roll evidence suggests that production in the hundred had declined sharply, a picture matched by reductions in taxation made to these communities in 1449. Analysis of a dozen sixteenth-century wills found a contrasting picture in two neighbouring Norfolk villages. Weavers in Scottow were usually wealthy men with large landholdings who owned their own looms, while weavers in nearby Marsham were poorer, do not appear to have owned any looms, and so were possibly employed as outworkers.[112]

In Norwich, the making of worsteds became crucial to the economic success of the city from 1400 to 1550, and replaced the manufacture of woollen cloth as the town's main industry. The development of high-quality double worsted, woven and finished to give it qualities like silk, became an important export in the later fifteenth century. Production only started to decline in the second quarter of the sixteenth century in competition from cheaper, continental fabrics.[113] Norwich tightly regulated and supervised the worsted industry within the county to maintain quality. The city established a right of search throughout the county in 1442, which was extended to Suffolk and Cambridgeshire in 1467, when all weavers were required to mark their cloths. Acts for shearing and dyeing worsteds were passed during the early sixteenth century. In 1511, Norwich worsted weavers were each limited to holding no more than four broadlooms and a single narrow loom, and county weavers to two broadlooms and a single loom, all of which had to be located within the weaver's home. The city's weavers were also restricted to taking four apprentices and county weavers to two. These regulations did allow

[110] *VCH Shropshire*, vi (1), p. 111.

[111] CUL, Hengrave Hall MS 78(2), fols 72, 78.

[112] Amor, *From Wool to Cloth*, pp. 42–7; Whittle, *Agrarian Capitalism*, pp. 247–52.

[113] John Oldland, '"Fyne worsted whech is almost like silke": Norwich's Double Worsted', *Textile History* 42 (2011), pp. 181–99.

weavers to operate reasonably large workshops and for production to concentrate among a few better-capitalised weavers.[114]

Several other large towns were prominent cloth-making centres. Coventry and Winchester had been among the leading cloth-making towns in the late fourteenth century, but declined in the century that followed. Cloth-making at Winchester waned after about 1430, when its fulling mills gradually ceased to function, and the fullers, who dominated the organisation of the finishing processes in the city, faced financial difficulties.[115] In the case of Coventry, the textile industry appears to have stagnated from the mid fifteenth century, and by the 1520s the city faced crisis, compounded by a local slump and grain shortages. Twenty years later, Leland remarked that 'The town rose by making of cloth and caps, that now decaying the glory of the city decayeth.'[116] Although the designation clothier is rarely found in Coventry, many dyers, drapers and merchants acted in a similar capacity, buying wool and handing it out for spinning and carding, distributing yarn to weavers, and putting cloth out for dyeing, fulling, teasing and shearing, before selling the finished product. The scope for those coordinating cloth production to widen their activities, though, was restricted by the regulations enforced by the city's leet court, which interfered continuously while the industry was depressed during the early sixteenth century. Clothiers were restricted to using craftworkers based in the city: in 1518, they were to 'put no cloth to weaving into the country but to their own neighbours within this city', and to 'put no cloth to any walker to full but if he will burl it and "wranghalf" it within the city'. By 1544 though, when clothiers were beginning to set up looms in their own houses, and bringing in employees to work on them, the leet finally gave permission for clothiers to weave their own cloth, as long as they made an initial payment of 3s 4d to the weavers' guild.[117]

More successful was Worcester, where Leland thought that 'the wealth of the town of Worcester stands most by drapering, and no town of England at the present time makes so many cloths yearly as this town does'. He also found nearby Kidderminster 'stands most by clothing' and that Bromsgrove was also dependent, although to a lesser extent, on its

[114] Oldland, 'Fyne worsted'.

[115] Derek Keene, *Survey of Medieval Winchester*, 2 vols (Oxford, 1985), pp. 305–9.

[116] *Itinerary*, ii, p. 108; Charles Phythian-Adams, *Desolation of a City. Coventry and the Urban Crisis of the Late Middle Ages* (Cambridge, 1979); John S. Lee, 'Grain Shortages in Late Medieval Towns', in Dodds and Liddy, eds, *Commercial Activity*, pp. 63–80.

[117] *The Coventry Leet Book*, ed. M. Dormer Harris, Early English Text Society, O.S., 4 vols, 134, 135, 138, 146 (London, 1907–13), pp. 659, 661, 776–7; *VCH Warwickshire*, viii, pp. 157–8.

cloth trade.[118] Worcester specialised in manufacturing very high-quality broadcloth, both white and coloured, while Bromsgrove and Kidderminster produced mainly narrow cloths. The textile industry at Worcester was dominated by independent artisans and the putting-out system was rarely found. The clothiers within the city were differentiated from the weavers by their greater wealth, and their larger reserves of capital. This enabled the clothiers to buy and store large quantities of raw materials, and to maintain continuous production from their looms, with cloth waiting for sale, while weavers were dependent on selling their cloth before they could buy their next consignment of wool or yarn. Clothiers might also act as middlemen for the sale of the independent weaver's cloth. The urban industry was closely regulated and rural competition discouraged, particularly through the Worcestershire cloth act of 1534, which limited production within the county to Worcester and the four market towns of Bromsgrove, Droitwich, Evesham and Kidderminster. In 1575, the city's corporation argued that the protection given by the act had enabled its citizen clothiers to grow rich.[119]

London had been an important cloth-making centre in the twelfth and thirteenth centuries, and entrepreneurs known as burellers put out wool to weavers, fullers and dyers. By the later fourteenth century, London had moved from producing cheap woollens to making some of the country's finest broadcloths, using both alien and native weavers. There was a large cloth industry in Southwark in 1381, where 11 per cent of the workers taxed were involved in textile production, particularly as spinsters. During the fifteenth century, London weavers lost most of their markets for local cloth to competition from provincial clothiers. London now became primarily a cloth-finishing centre, and its fullers, dyers and, particularly, shearmen prospered from dyeing, finishing and packing provincial cloth for merchants from the city and overseas.[120] During the 1520s for example, the London draper Thomas Howell purchased cloths unfinished from provincial clothiers and then paid shearman and draper Thomas Pettor to arrange for them to be rowed, sheared and packed in London.[121]

118 *Itinerary*, ii, pp. 87, 91, 95.

119 Dyer, *Worcester*, pp. 93–119.

120 Barron, *London*, pp. 65–8; Oldland, 'Making and Marketing', p. 103.

121 Drapers' Company, Ledger of Thomas Howell, fols 17*, 21v–22; John R. Oldland, 'London Clothmaking, *c.*1270–*c.*1550', University of London, Ph.D. thesis, 2003, pp. 116–19.

WHY DID THE CLOTH INDUSTRY DEVELOP IN PARTICULAR AREAS?

As this chapter has shown, there was a strong regional dimension to the textile industry in the late Middle Ages. Why then did cloth-making develop in some areas but not others, and at differing times and with differing rates of success? In the introductory chapter, we explored the factors that influenced the growth of the English cloth industry in the two centuries after 1350. These included increasing consumer demand for cloth, plentiful wool supplies, and customs duties that discouraged the export of English wool and enabled English cloth-makers to source wool more cheaply than their foreign competitors.[122] These influences, though, were relatively uniform across the country. The English government also encouraged Flemish cloth-workers to migrate to England and this may have provided a stimulus to the expansion of cloth-making in certain communities, such as Colchester, during the later fourteenth century.[123] We will now explore a range of other potential factors that may have stimulated the development of cloth-making in particular localities during the later Middle Ages, and examine why clothiers and cloth-workers tended to be found more frequently, although not exclusively, in rural rather than urban environments.

Access to raw materials and water supplies

While many industries locate close to available sources of raw materials and power, these do not appear to have been significant considerations for the cloth-making of medieval England. Wool, while bulky, was relatively light, and could be readily transported by packhorse or cart. There is no correlation between areas that produced wool of the highest quality and areas of cloth-making. Fifteenth-century price schedules, for example, list areas such as Herefordshire and Shropshire as producing the most expensive wool of the highest quality, but these counties did not have significant cloth-making industries. In many instances, as Thomas Fuller noted in the seventeenth century, counties 'who had most of the wool, had least of clothing'.[124] Many dyestuffs were imported. Access to a local port was not vital, because cloth, like wool, could be readily transported by road. Kendal cloth was regularly carried to Southampton, for

[122] See above, Introduction.

[123] Lambert and Pajic, 'Drapery in Exile'; Pajic, 'Migration of Flemish Weavers'. See above, Introduction.

[124] Munro, 'Wool-Price Schedules', p. 141; Thomas Fuller, *The History of the Worthies of England* (London, 1662), p. 279, quoted in Betterton and Dymond, *Lavenham*, pp. 2–3.

example.[125] Fuller's earth was dug locally in the Stroud Valley but had to be imported to Suffolk from Kent.[126] Firewood heated dye vats and provided potash used for dyeing. Several manors in north-central Essex developed a trade in wood and firewood in the later fourteenth century, including Kelvedon, which sold faggots to consumers in the cloth-making centres of Colchester and Coggeshall. These manors, together with adjoining parts of Suffolk and Cambridgeshire, which met demand from the university town of Cambridge, may also have supplied the textile industries of the Stour valley of Suffolk. Competing industrial uses made firewood a limited and valuable commodity, and concerns about shortages were voiced at Worcester in the 1540s, due to salt-making, and in the Kentish Weald in the 1570s, when the clothiers complained about the quantities of firewood being consumed by iron-making.[127]

Access to a good water supply was important, as water was required for washing wool, for dyeing, and for disposing of waste from the manufacturing process. The production of a coloured cloth of standard measure required around two cubic metres of water in thirteenth-century France. Unsurprisingly, most English textile centres were in river valley locations, at less than 100 metres above sea level, providing plentiful supplies of water.[128] Water also powered machinery, and the introduction of the water-powered fulling mill has been seen as an explanation for the shift of the English textile industry from towns to the countryside. Unfortunately, the spatial distribution of fulling mills on a regional and local scale does not correlate particularly well with the location of major centres of cloth-making.[129] Broadcloths could be easily carried for fulling elsewhere. The Leeds township of Headingley-cum-Burley provides an interesting example of an area with watercourses that by the sixteenth century had attracted a series of fulling mills operated by clothiers based in other townships. There were no clothiers, dyers or cloth finishers residing in Headingley-cum-Burley itself. This seems to have been because Headingley, like other townships adjoining Leeds situated to the north of the river Aire, enjoyed good arable land, while villages to the south and west

[125] Jones, 'Westmorland Pack-Horsemen'.

[126] Joan Thirsk, 'Industries in the Countryside', in F.J. Fisher, ed., *Essays in the Economic and Social History of Tudor and Stuart England* (London, 1961), p. 72; Carus-Wilson, 'Evidences of Industrial Growth', p. 92.

[127] James A. Galloway, Derek Keene and Margaret Murphy, 'Fuelling the City: Production and Distribution of Firewood and Fuel in London's Region, 1290–1400', *EcHR* 49 (1996), p. 466; John S. Lee, 'Feeding the Colleges: Cambridge's Food and Fuel Supplies, 1450–1560', *EcHR* 56 (2003), pp. 253–6; Dyer, *Worcester*, pp. 53–6; Zell, *Industry*, pp. 200–1, 236–7.

[128] Amor, *From Wool to Cloth*, pp. 60–1.

[129] Carus-Wilson, 'Industrial Revolution'; Bridbury, *Clothmaking*, pp. 16–25; *CHWT*, pp. 271–3.

of the river, which were steeply sloping and poorly suited to grain production, became cloth manufacturing areas. The town of Leeds, at the river crossing, acted as the principal interface between these two zones.[130]

Pastoral farming

An explanation for the tendency of rural industries to develop in pastoral rather than arable areas, as suggested by the land use around the hinterland of Leeds, was first put forward by Joan Thirsk. She argued that animal husbandry demanded less time than cultivating crops, giving time to spare for other activities. In pastoral areas, where farm labour was less intense, land less valuable, and manorial institutions often weaker, farms remained small. These farmers engaged in industrial by-employments to supplement agriculture, as their profits from the land alone were not sufficient to provide income beyond subsistence. Other historians subsequently developed these ideas as the concept of proto-industrialisation. Certainly, some of the main cloth-making areas of the later Middle Ages were in regions of predominantly pastoral farming, including the West Riding of Yorkshire and the Kentish Weald, as were other industrial areas such as the metalworking regions of the Black Country and south Yorkshire. In northern Essex and north-east Norfolk, however, textile industries developed in regions characterised by highly productive arable sectors, and even in Wiltshire, the most prosperous cloth-making centres were to be found in the west, within an area of mixed farming, rather than in one specialising in dairying.[131]

Lordship

Thirsk suggested that rural industries tended to locate in areas of weaker lordship. Such characteristics have been identified in the Kentish Weald, where seigneurial institutions were weak and landownership fragmented, and in the Agbrigg and Morley wapentakes of the West Riding of Yorkshire, where smallholders had unusually light manorial customs.[132] In some areas of weak lordship, entirely new settlements might emerge as cloth-making centres, such as Pensford, at the edge of two adjoining parishes, or Stroud, which grew between the two manors of Bisley and Minchinhampton, both with absentee lords.

Lordship could also, however, stimulate industrial and economic development. In the twelfth and thirteenth centuries, lords had acquired

[130] John Louis Cruickshank, *Headingley-cum-Burley, c.1540–c.1784*, Thoresby Society, 2nd series 22 (Leeds, 2012), pp. 255–6, 259, 263–4.

[131] Thirsk, 'Industries', pp. 70–86; Zell, *Industry*, pp. 1–6, 228–46; Poos, *Rural Society*, pp. 63–4; Whittle, *Agrarian Capitalism*, pp. 248–9; Gaisford, 'Elizabethan Entrepreneurs', p. 210.

[132] Zell, *Industry*, pp. 230–1; Smith, *Land and Politics*, pp. 120–2.

market charters, laid out building plots, redirected streets, and introduced burgage tenure to attract settlement and stimulate commercial development and manufacturing. They established small medieval boroughs that have recently been considered as 'enterprise zones', possessing distinct commercial or industrial sectors within a managed agrarian and manorial economy.[133] Similar attempts can be found to promote cloth-making. Most of the Suffolk textile towns, for example, were to be found on the manors of major landholders, including Long Melford (a manor of the abbey of Bury St Edmunds), Lavenham (earl of Oxford), Glemsford and Needham Market (bishop of Ely), and Hadleigh (Canterbury Cathedral Priory). These powerful landlords offered patronage, security, more effective manorial courts, and greater stability than lesser lords could provide.[134]

Lavenham may have benefitted from the efforts of successive generations of the de Vere family, earls of Oxford, who held a deer park and lodge on the manor. The family acquired a market charter for Lavenham in 1257, and in 1329 an exemption for their tenants from paying tolls throughout England. John de Vere, the thirteenth earl, inspired the rebuilding of Lavenham church, donating at least £40 himself, and leaning on clothiers to contribute to the rebuilding, including William Jacob, John Newton and Thomas Risby, the latter donating £200.[135] The de Vere family may have provided the Spring family with contacts to the Flemish craftsmen who had worked on royal commissions and produced the parclose screen that protected Thomas Spring III's tomb in Lavenham church. The marriage of Margaret Spring, a niece of Thomas III, to Aubrey de Vere, second son of the fifteenth earl of Oxford, cemented the links between the two families.[136] The de Vere's links though, seem to have been with the leading clothiers, rather than promoting cloth-making more generally. While it is often suggested that the carved corner post on Lavenham's Corpus Christi guildhall displays an effigy of John, the fifteenth earl, who granted the guild its charter in 1529, this carving is more likely to be of a mythical figure. The staff in the figure's right hand is similar to one held by the man of the woods, who supports the ceiling in the nearby Bull Hotel in Long Melford.[137]

[133] Richard Goddard, 'Small Boroughs and the Manorial Economy: Enterprise Zones or Urban Failures?', *Past and Present* 210 (2011), pp. 3–31.

[134] Bailey, *Medieval Suffolk*, p. 299.

[135] Alston, 'Old Grammar School', p. 32; Betterton and Dymond, *Lavenham*, pp. 9–11; James Ross, *John de Vere, Thirteenth Earl of Oxford 1442–1513 'The foremost man of the kingdom'* (Woodbridge, 2011), p. 213 and n. 40, and p. 215.

[136] Tracy and Harrison, 'Thomas Spring's chantry'; *ODNB*. See also below, Chapter 6.

[137] National Trust, *Guildhall of Corpus Christi Lavenham* (Swindon, 2004), p. 18.

Sir John Fastolf (d. 1459), helped the expansion of the cloth industry in Castle Combe in Wiltshire, and possibly also in Dedham in Essex. Fastolf ordered large quantities of cloth for his soldiers in France between 1415 and 1440, and according to his steward, bought over £100 of red and white cloth every year from his tenants at Castle Combe. These purchases were one of the 'principal causes of the augmentation of the common wealth and store of the said town and of the new buildings raised in it'. Fastolf also obtained a new grant confirming the market and fair and an exemption for his tenants from contributing to the payment of their members of parliament and the royal right of prise (the compulsory purchase of provisions to supply troops or the king's household). The manorial court was the only regulating body in the village, and clothiers could introduce new methods like the gig mill that raised the nap on cloth mechanically. Sir John still drew substantial income from his tenants, however. When William Haynes died in 1436, his goods and chattels were initially valued at 3,000 marks, and although this was challenged and reduced to £40, his widow Marjorie paid a further £100 for permission to remarry and to possess all William's property, including fulling, gig and corn mills.[138] Dedham in Essex may also have benefitted from the attentions of John Fastolf, who held the manor from 1428. This small town was the fourth-largest centre for cloth sales in Essex in the 1390s, and the third-largest centre in the 1460s. Dedham certainly experienced industrial growth in the 1430s and 1440s when its cloth, like that of Colchester, was supplying Hanseatic and German markets, and land values rose, but when this trade collapsed in the 1450s, Dedham, like Colchester, faced economic decline for much of the latter part of the century.[139]

Urban versus rural manufacturing

The migration of cloth-making from the town to the countryside, and the associated new form of organisation with a labour force working for contractual wages, independent of guild control, have long been seen as changes brought about by capitalist clothiers. Tawney wrote of

> the commercial capitalist ... hampered by the defensive machinery of the gilds, with their corporate discipline, their organized torpor restricting individual enterprise, and their rough equalitarianism, either he quietly evaded gild regulations by withdrawing from the corporate towns ... or he ... developed a system under which the craftsman, even if nominally a master, was in effect the servant of an employer.[140]

[138] Carus-Wilson, 'Evidences of Industrial Growth'; Bolton, *Medieval English Economy*, pp. 269, 272.
[139] Britnell, *Colchester*, pp. 14, 168, 172, 251–2.
[140] Tawney, *Religion*, p. 141.

Similarly, Herbert Heaton described the weavers of York and Beverley as 'overtaxed and over-regulated … unable to withstand the competition which came from the rural areas'.[141] Some historians have even identified a wider 'urban crisis' of the later Middle Ages but there is little agreement on how such a concept should be defined or exactly when it occurred.[142]

Indeed, similar explanations based on freedom from urban government and guild regulations, and lower rural labour costs, have been used to explain the growth of rural cloth-making in the late thirteenth century. It should be noted though, that not all cloth-making moved to the countryside, and even in the sixteenth century, towns such as Exeter, Worcester and Reading retained important textile industries. Urban locations offered potential advantages in terms of congregating, training and supervising skilled labour, ensuring quality controls in the weaving, fulling, dyeing and finishing processes, and in providing access to commercial and marketing facilities, and finance.[143]

Nonetheless, there are strong grounds to argue that the restrictive legislation promulgated by civic governments and craft guilds in larger towns increased production costs and encouraged industry to relocate to smaller and less heavily governed places.[144] Civic legislation restricted working hours, fixed wage rates, controlled quality, and tended to reinforce small units of production, restricting attempts to agglomerate urban manufacturing that would have brought down costs. Regulations could restrict the use of craftworkers from outside their respective boroughs.[145] This insistence on exacting standards by the guilds made urban products expensive in competition with cloths produced in the countryside. This was particularly damaging at the cheaper end of the market, where products could be supplied by country competitors who were less tightly organised and supervised.

In contrast to the larger boroughs, smaller towns and villages were constrained only by national regulations and local manor courts. There were generally no restrictions on working hours, on the fixing of wage rates, and there was no expense of civic or guild pageantry. Guilds and guildhalls in places such as Lavenham were social and religious organisations with no authority over craft production.[146] These rural environments offered attractions to both clothiers, who saw the prospect of

[141] Heaton, *Yorkshire Woollen*, p. 44.

[142] Alan Dyer, *Decline and Growth in English Towns 1400–1640* (Cambridge, 1991).

[143] *CHWT*, p. 275.

[144] *CUHB*, pp. 332–3, although cf. Swanson, *Medieval Artisans*, pp. 30, 112–13.

[145] For examples of such legislation, see below, Chapter 4.

[146] Bolton, *Medieval English Economy*, pp. 265–7; Britnell, *Closing of the Middle Ages?*, p. 224.

cheaper labour, and to cloth-workers, who enjoyed greater freedoms to practise their trade. Smaller market towns probably proved particularly attractive because they offered many of the benefits of larger boroughs, such as the convenience of regular markets, easy access to commercial networks, readily available accommodation, and a regulatory framework to provide an effective means of redress in the event of disputes with other traders, without the overheads or restrictive legislation of their larger neighbours.[147]

Residents in the larger established towns faced heavier charges of self-government to maintain their urban fabric, including streets, bridges, marketplaces, gates and walls, guildhalls, and public water supplies. The administrative apparatus of the borough carried a cost, as did maintaining representation in parliament, and making gifts and displays to noble and royal visitors to cultivate good lordship and influential friends in government.[148] Craft guilds too required contributions for membership, feasts and entertainments. These costs could be more easily avoided in villages and smaller towns, where living expenses were also generally likely to be lower. When explanations for the decline of cloth-making in York were given to the city government there in 1561, this was attributed to the convenience of water mills in the West Riding, and the relative costs of labour, food and fuel in that area compared to prices in the city:

> the lack of cloth-making in the said city as was in old time accustomed, which is now increased and used in the towns of Halifax, Leeds, and Wakefield, for that not only the commodity of the water mills is there nigh [at] hand, but also the poor folk as spinners, carders and other necessary workfolks for the said weaving, may there besides their hand labour, have cows, fire and other relief good cheap, which is in this city very dear and wanting.[149]

Access to labour

Labour costs in the countryside may have been lower than in large towns not only due to fewer restrictions, but because there was a greater availability of labour. Rural areas, it is suggested, had a pool of under-employed labourers who could be engaged at low wages in the textile industry to supplement their income from agriculture. This extensive rural labour force probably helped to sustain the growth of the cloth industry during

[147] James Davis, 'Selling Food and Drink in the Aftermath of the Black Death', in Bailey and Rigby, eds, *Town and Countryside*, pp. 351–406.

[148] *CUHB*, p. 333; Dyer, *Decline and Growth*, p. 42.

[149] YELA, Y/COU/1/1, vol. 23, fol. 20.

the sixteenth century, but it does not necessarily offer an explanation for the growth of the rural cloth industry before the population began to recover from successive outbreaks of plague. Rising wage rates after the Black Death may have given rural cloth-making a more significant cost advantage over urban producers, but without evidence of productivity, quality controls, and transaction costs in competing urban and rural industries that produced comparable textiles, there is no way of measuring this.[150]

The growth of rural cloth-making was based largely on the putting-out system. This enabled the network of supply and distribution to expand while the basic unit of production remained small. While putting out was adopted to some extent by the mercantile elite in larger towns such as York, it remained a characteristically rural system. It appears to have thrived more in rural than in urban areas, and this seems to have been due to the greater availability of capital and easier access to key markets.

Access to capital

The extension of pastoral farming and the accumulation of holdings and livestock by more prosperous peasant farmers in the wake of the Black Death may have provided the growth of capital necessary for rural cloth-makers to become established. The poll tax returns of the 1370s reveal the presence of cloth-workers in many small towns and rural communities. These include clusters of drapers in Bocking in Essex, Bramley in Surrey, Hadleigh in Suffolk, and several parts of the West Riding of Yorkshire, some of whom may have acted like clothiers, taking a role in both the manufacturing and marketing of cloth. This source of agricultural capital meant that rural industries were no longer dependent on urban merchants, and the products of these rural industries could be distributed by local traders, provincial chapmen, and increasingly by London merchants.

In terms of access to credit too, the countryside may have offered an advantage over the town. It has been suggested that the initial move of cloth-making in Somerset, Wiltshire, and Yorkshire out of towns into the countryside in the late fourteenth and early fifteenth centuries reflected a shortage of silver coinage, as in rural areas there was less need for coin for wages as workers could be paid in kind. These advantages may have become even more important when coinage became scarcer during the mid-fifteenth-century slump. Cloth-workers, it is argued,

[150] Swanson, *Medieval Artisans*, pp. 142–3.

could live more easily in the countryside with less coin than in towns.[151] Prosperous yeomen farmers and landowners in the countryside became more willing to supply credit on easier terms, particularly to village clothiers with whom they had close ties. Other potential sources of finance for clothiers were provincial chapmen, who supplied London merchants with cloth in return for luxury and imported goods, as well as the Londoners themselves.

Historians have related changes in the volume of debt cases to wider economic trends. From the early 1400s, increasing numbers of provincial chapmen owed debts to London merchants, which they often paid for by deliveries of cloth. The 1420s saw a marked increase in credit transactions between merchants of cloth-making centres, such as Long Melford, Norwich, Coventry, Salisbury, Exeter, Frome, Bradford-on-Avon and Wells, with London mercers, drapers and grocers.[152] During the particularly difficult trading conditions between the 1440s and 1460s, which historians have labelled the 'great slump', London lenders withdrew credit, possibly in response to a shortage of coinage. Their lending practices became more restrictive, as they moved from extending credit on fixed terms to payment on request, and offered relatively smaller sales of goods on credit and larger loans. This had a trickle-down effect on those buying from Londoners, including clothiers, who must have been forced to provide similar terms to their customers.[153] This contraction did not, however, prevent some London merchants from continuing to finance provincial cloth production. Between 1449 and 1451, Henry Archer of London gave over £156 in credit to a dyer to establish a dye-house in St Neots, and supplied materials from London as well as vessels and implements for the craft.[154] In the 1470s John Kendall, cloth merchant of Bridgwater, with a business associate from Dorset, borrowed £60 from William Collet, London mercer, and subsequently extended smaller sums of credit to traders including a Welsh tailor and merchant from Melcombe Regis.[155] Even when trading conditions improved from the 1470s, and the supply of silver increased again in the 1490s, a greater proportion of London creditors were to be found. Londoners' 'over-

[151] Pamela Nightingale, 'Gold, Credit, and Mortality: Distinguishing Deflationary Pressures on the Late Medieval English Economy', *EcHR* 63 (2010), p. 1091; Pamela Nightingale, 'The Rise and Decline of Medieval York: A Reassessment', *Past and Present* 206 (2010), p. 40.

[152] Nightingale, 'Gold', pp. 1094, 1097–8.

[153] Stevens, 'London Creditors', p. 1105.

[154] Nightingale, *Grocers' Company*, p. 486.

[155] R. Goddard, 'Surviving Recession: English Borough Courts and Commercial Contraction: 1350–1500', in R. Goddard, J. Langdon and M. Muller, eds, *Survival and Discord in Medieval Society: Essays in Honour of Christopher Dyer* (Turnhout, 2010), p. 76.

whelming domination of the money market and of the export trade, particularly in cloth, were symbiotic'.[156]

Innovation

The economic historians A.R. Bridbury and D.C. Coleman both argued that the growth of the textile industry in the later medieval and early modern periods was driven by the continued emergence of new products: 'new fabrics, new designs, different colours, different finishes; changes in yarn, in weaves, in patterns. They were, in essence, mutations; and most of them were continually disseminated by imitation.'[157] Coleman proposed that this imitation was fostered by migrations of craftsmen, and by the increasing range of international contacts between merchants selling textiles. Our tour of the cloth-making regions has shown an array of assorted products, often linked to specific localities, from Salisbury rays to Colchester russets, and Suffolk vesses to western blankets. Some became trade names, known across the continent as well as in England, like Castlecombes and Stroudwaters.

The clothier responded to market opportunities and local specialisms. Until the middle of the fifteenth century, many producers concentrated on lower-quality broadcloth and narrow cloths, but in the later fifteenth century the range of English cloths widened, and the price and quality of most cloths increased. More luxurious cloths and a wide range of kerseys, comparable in price to broadcloth, were now exported, as well as inexpensive narrow cloths, cottons and frieze.[158]

In the fourteenth century, much of the broadcloth that was manufactured in England was not of full length, but half-cloth, known as *duodenum* or dozens. Production of full-length cloths seems to have been concentrated within London, York, Salisbury and Bristol, where finer cloths were manufactured. Outside these major cities, many other cloth-making centres, including those in Devon, Essex, Suffolk, Somerset, Warwickshire and Kent, produced half-cloths and narrow short cloths, known as straits. Cloths exported in the fourteenth century were mostly dyed and finished, and trade was largely from Bristol and London to Gascony, Iberia and Ireland.

Trade disruptions with Flanders in the 1380s and 1390s encouraged Italian and Hanseatic merchants to purchase more cloth in England, mostly lower-quality broadcloths and cheaper narrow straits and kerseys.

[156] Nightingale, 'Gold', p. 1100.

[157] D.C. Coleman, 'Textile Growth', in N.B. Harte and K.G. Ponting, eds, *Textile History and Economic History. Essays in Honour of Miss Julia de Lacy Mann* (Manchester, 1973), p. 9; Bridbury, *Clothmaking*, p. 103.

[158] Oldland, 'Variety and Quality of English Woollen Cloth', pp. 215–29.

Venetian merchants were looking for lower-priced English cloth to sell to the Levant, such as the west country cloths known as westerns and bastards. Florentine merchants too bought only cheaper English cloths, as they were purchasing the finest English wools for their own high-value cloth industries. Many of these cloths came from Somerset, Wiltshire and Essex, while Coventry, Kentish and Guildford cloths (produced in Surrey and Sussex) were also exported. Colchester sold russet cloths to markets in Gascony and the Baltic. It made sense for clothiers to focus at this time on these inexpensive cloths. They could meet demand, at both home and abroad, from the fastest-growing part of the market, the lower ranks of society, as their rising living standards rose. In contrast, the fashion in dress among the aristocracy at this time was for silk rather than woollens.

During the course of the fifteenth century though, the market changed as wool prices fell, export duties on wool increased as a percentage of wool prices, and the Low Countries' draperies weakened. Antwerp developed as a market for English cloth, and by the later fifteenth century, the Italians and Spaniards, and probably also the Hanse, were exporting mostly higher-quality cloth. Suffolk and Essex moved from producing straits to making quality broadcloth, and in Hampshire and Devon from straits to kerseys. By the sixteenth century, English clothiers were exporting some of the finest cloths made anywhere, notably fine white Worcesters, coloured Kentish cloths, Coggeshalls from Essex and Castlecombes from Wiltshire, for which merchants paid 100s or more. Unfinished broadcloth from Somerset, west Wiltshire and Gloucestershire was the main cloth sold in Antwerp and Bergen. Coloured Suffolk broadcloths were sold too, to London merchants like Thomas Howell. Cheaper broadcloths also proliferated. These included Suffolk vesses or setcloth, westerns or bastards from the western counties, Bridgwaters, Totnes dozens, Tavistocks and Moltons from Devon; northern dozens and Penistone dozens from the West Riding, Lancashire and Cheshire; and Kendals from Westmorland. Kersey production stretched across southern England from eastern Devon to the Kentish Weald, as well as the West Riding of Yorkshire and Lancashire. The average kersey was a much higher-quality product than in the fourteenth century. They were mostly dyed, and they were now worth, on average, as much by surface area as a broadcloth. Kerseys became the main cloth export for Italians and Spaniards, and the Merchant Adventurers were shipping more kerseys than broadcloths by 1535.[159]

[159] Oldland, 'Variety and Quality of English Woollen Cloth'; *CHWT*, pp. 273–5, 410–11.

Access to markets

The development of increasingly specialised and niche products required good access to major markets and longer-distance trade, often conducted through merchant intermediaries such as chapmen. These mercantile networks made it advantageous for cloth-workers and other artisans to live in particular towns and industrial villages, as it gave them easier access to such networks for the distribution of their goods. This created major changes in marketing patterns during the later Middle Ages. Some local marketing centres like Lavenham or Newbury became the focus of regional migration and industrial growth in a period that was generally unfavourable to small market towns. London trading links were particularly evident, and cloth production responded to the demands of the capital. In similar ways, London investment and demand stimulated the emergence of the small towns of Saffron Walden as a hub for saffron cultivation, Thaxted as a centre for the cutlery production, and Royston as a market for malt barley.[160] The growth of the putting-out system also increased the direct dependence of craftworkers on merchants as employers. This created a particularly volatile system, because it depended on overseas markets, and on mercantile calculations as to where labour or other factors of production were cheapest at any given moment.[161]

Crises in the cloth trade

Periods of severe dislocation in the cloth trade hastened structural changes within the textile industry. These included a sharp and prolonged depression from around 1445 to 1465 in which English cloth exports virtually halved, and a period of market disruption with a fall of over 20 per cent in cloth exports during the 1520s. During the most difficult trading years, the higher relative costs of manufacturing cloth in larger towns, compared to production in smaller urban centres, became more apparent. It was also during the crisis years that the lower production costs of the larger cloth-makers, who tended to locate in the smaller urban centres, gave them the greatest competitive advantages over smaller producers. These lesser manufacturers declined as their profits became more difficult to achieve. Lower costs of production enabled larger producers to survive the crises better than smaller producers, prompting the concentration of production in the hands of wealthier

[160] Lee, *Cambridge and its Economic Region*, pp. 105–12.
[161] Britnell, 'Urban Demand', pp. 14–21.

clothiers. The trade crises provided the economic environment in which entrepreneurs such as the leading clothiers could thrive.[162]

CONCLUSION

Single or simplistic explanations of any type of economic or social change are usually inadequate, as such changes are generally highly complex processes involving a range of variables acting together. In examining the development of the cloth industry in medieval England, it is helpful to distinguish between *conditions* for growth and *causes* of growth. The former might include a system of pastoral agriculture and a prevalence of smallholdings, while the latter could incorporate available markets, product innovations and local expertise.[163] Ultimately it was the decisions of individual clothiers that determined where they would locate their trade. Cloth-making in the later Middle Ages was increasingly based in small towns and villages rather than in cities and boroughs. The poll tax returns of 1377–81 show that cloth-workers were already located in many parts of the countryside, as well as in towns, and comparison of the ulnage accounts or the common pleas reveal the increasing preference for rural locations. The clothier was largely a rural figure.

The key conditions that encouraged cloth-making to grow in rural areas and that enabled the clothier to emerge and flourish appear to have been access to labour, capital and markets. The rural labour force could engage in cloth-making as a part-time activity, and the putting-out system required little capital on the part of the worker, who could undertake tasks in their own home. The capital accumulated in rural communities could be used to support cloth-making, while marketing networks provided links to London merchants and overseas markets. Places like Coggeshall, Lavenham, Newbury and Malmesbury provided ideal environments for the leading clothiers of the age to flourish. Indeed, the Spring family may have migrated from County Durham and the Winchcombes from south Essex.[164] It is unlikely that similar entrepreneurs would have emerged within the cloth industry in, for example, Lincolnshire or Staffordshire at this time. Entrepreneurial calculations as to where labour, capital or markets were most easily accessible led to a more volatile economic environment, and one that national and local governments, aware of the damaging impact of recession in the cloth industry, became increasingly keen to influence.

[162] John S. Lee, 'Crises in the Late Medieval English Cloth Trade', in A.T. Brown, Andy Burn and Rob Doherty, eds, *Crises in Economic and Social History: A Comparative Perspective* (Woodbridge, 2015), pp. 325–49. See also below, Chapter 4.

[163] Bailey, *Medieval Suffolk*, p. 301.

[164] See below, Chapter 6.

4

Clothiers and government

English central and local government legislated extensively for the cloth industry as they sought to standardise goods, protect consumers, and monitor quality. In fact, cloth-making attracted so much attention from these authorities that one historian memorably described the industry as the 'favourite child of the legislature'.[1] This chapter explores this legislation, examining how clothiers helped to shape these policies, and how they operated within this regulatory framework. Governments became increasingly anxious to protect markets and employment within the textile industry. The cloth trade was a major contributor of revenue to the Exchequer, primarily through customs duties on cloth exports, but also through the subsidy levied on cloth sales known as ulnage. Governments were also aware though, that disruptions to overseas cloth sales created unemployment and unrest, and in the face of political protests by textile workers, they looked to clothiers to maintain production.

DEVELOPING LEGISLATION

Responsibility for regulating the making and marketing of cloth was divided between the Crown and local communities. While all places were subject to national legislation unless specifically exempt, the degree of regulation at the local level could vary considerably from place to place. Boroughs, with charters granted by the Crown or a lord to townspeople to exercise rights and privileges, issued a multiplicity of regulations. Guilds representing specific crafts might also have regulatory powers. In smaller towns and villages, where craft guilds were absent and control was exercised through the local court, there could be little or no intervention. It has been suggested that entrepreneurial ambition was deterred by the amount of regulation in many late medieval boroughs, and certainly most of the leading clothiers of the early sixteenth century were to be found in smaller urban settlements and rural areas which generally lacked these local regulatory institutions.

[1] Lipson, *Woollen and Worsted Industries*, p. 5.

Borough governments and craft guilds

Many boroughs had liberties of tenure, trade, and local administration granted by the king or another lord to a defined group of members known as burgesses or freemen, who were distinct from the main body of inhabitants. These privileges varied from borough to borough, but generally included trading privileges derived from borough charters, ordinances and by-laws. Many borough governments regulated trade to promote opportunities and provide safeguards for their burgesses, and to restrict outsiders, whether unfranchised inhabitants of the town, 'foreigners' from another town, or 'aliens' from another country. In twelfth-century Bristol for example, no foreign merchant could sell cloth retail except at fairs and could only buy hides, cloth or wool from the burgesses. Weavers and fullers in London and Beverley could only sell their cloth to merchants of the city and not to foreigners. In reality though, boroughs had to allow outsiders to trade and operate within their markets, while much trade was conducted outside formal borough markets. Borough governments were also aware that if they appeared to go too far in promoting their own interests at the expense of the whole town, they could face tension and conflict.[2]

The role of craft guilds varied between towns due to local politics and cultural traditions.[3] Many had their roots in religious fraternities, and provided important religious and social functions, as well as having an economic role. They consisted of confraternities of both employers and employees, masters and apprentices, and included searchers overseeing the conduct of a particular trade. Borough councils often delegated the policing of trades to craft guilds, which provided quality assurance and upheld standards of production but also maintained profits for their members. These aims were expressed in ordinances of the craft guilds of Bristol:

> diverse ordinances have been made on the working of woollen cloths to the intent that good and true cloth shall be made in the town, as well for the preservation of the good fame of the same as for the profit which they shall take on the sale of their cloth.[4]

Public interests therefore often blurred with sectional interests, as those in positions of authority, such as the burgesses of a borough, or the master craftsmen of a guild, sought to strengthen their own privileges at

[2] James Davis, *Medieval Market Morality: Life, Law and Ethics in the English Marketplace, 1200–1500* (Oxford, 2011), pp. 159–62.

[3] Craft guilds were not formed in some medieval boroughs, such as Ipswich, or in most English small towns.

[4] *The Little Red Book of Bristol*, ed. F.B. Bickley, 2 vols (Bristol, 1900), ii, p. 40 quoted in Davis, *Medieval Market Morality*, p. 216.

the expense of others outside these organisations. It has been suggested that the increasing number of restrictive rules protecting towns' own interests may have helped to drive capital and enterprise away from established cloth-making towns to smaller and less heavily governed centres.[5] Clothiers within borough governments, though, may have tried to modify regulations that hampered their urban businesses. Where they resided in boroughs, wealthier clothiers were often elected or appointed to serve in civic offices. Robert Youle (c.1497–1561) of Worcester, for example, held the offices of auditor, chamberlain, alderman, bailiff, bridgemaster, and member of the Twenty-Four in his city's government. Thomas Bell (1485/6–1566) of Gloucester (Plate VII) served as sheriff, alderman, three times as mayor, and represented the city in parliament on four or five occasions.[6]

Parliament

Parliament was the forum in which the Crown obtained consent for taxation and local grievances were presented, potentially resulting in new legislation in response. By the mid fourteenth century, representatives of the counties (knights of the shire) and of the towns (burgesses), forming the House of Commons, had become a permanent part of Parliament. During the fifteenth century though, English boroughs were increasingly represented by county gentlemen, and the overall proportion of resident burgesses elected to the Commons fell from two-thirds to less than half.[7] The extent to which clothiers represented their communities as members of parliament therefore varied between constituencies and over time. From 1386 to 1411 the parliamentary representation of Winchester, for example, was dominated by merchants and men with interests in the cloth industry, but thereafter seats were also occupied by members of the legal profession. The cloth-making county of Wiltshire was particularly well represented in parliament, for with the city of Salisbury and its fifteen parliamentary boroughs, it returned more members than any other county. These were represented in the early sixteenth century by clothiers including William Stumpe, Matthew King and John Hedges as MPs for Malmesbury, William Allen, MP for Calne, and the Coventre family of Devizes, and it was not until the 1560s that these seats were increasingly taken by the gentry of the county.[8]

In developing legislation relating to the cloth industry, the state faced

[5] Britnell, *Commercialisation*, p. 176; *CUHB*, p. 332.

[6] A. Davidson, 'YOULE, Robert (*c*.1497–1561), of Worcester', A.D.K. Hawkyard, 'BELL, Thomas (1485/86–1566), of Gloucester', *HoP, 1509–1558*.

[7] *CUHB*, p. 284.

[8] *VCH Wiltshire*, v, pp. 112–13. L.S. Woodger, 'Winchester', *HoP, 1386–1421*; N.M. Fuidge, 'Wiltshire', *HoP, 1509–1558*; Ramsay, *Wiltshire*, pp. 46–7.

sectional interest groups with potentially conflicting agendas. As we have noted, provincial towns and cities had members of parliament in the House of Commons, although the extent to which burgesses and clothiers were represented varied. London merchants were regulated by livery companies, whom the Crown could influence through the city's political structure. Major wholesale cloth merchants were represented by the wealthy and influential Merchant Adventurers' Company. Most clothiers though, were based in small towns and villages, often lacking specific parliamentary representation beneath the level of the county, and operating without the regulations of any guild or borough. The loose structures of the putting-out system meant that textile workers often had no masters who could be held responsible for their behaviour.[9]

Much of the legislation concerning the cloth industry that emerged from the late fourteenth century onwards reflected the concerns of the Commons, and the shared interests of cloth producers. In many cases, measures relating to cloth-making introduced by borough governments were adopted by central government a few years later, reflecting no doubt the influence and experience of members from parliamentary boroughs.[10] The concerns of specific localities can also be seen, as in the handful of statutes regulating the cloth industry in Worcestershire. The Act for Clothiers within the Shire of Worcester of 1534 required cloth to be made within the county only at Worcester and four other towns; the 1552 Act for the Making of Woollen Cloth specified separate lengths and weights for 'long and short Worcesters'; and a further act in 1558 reduced the weight of 'long Worcesters' after the corporation had sent three deputations to the Privy Council. The sale of wool to Worcestershire clothiers was also controlled by an act of 1531, renewed in 1545. Other bills for cloth-making in the county though, put forward in 1542, 1547 and 1555, failed to secure parliamentary assent.[11] Devon interests unsuccessfully tried to introduce bills for the manufacture of straits in 1515 and 1547, but two acts regulating cloth production in the early 1550s included reference to these types of cloth. The Commons Journal records that 'divers Clothiers of Devon' exhibited a bill in 1549 for modifying an act of taxation made the previous year, which failed, but was subsumed in a later petition for a release of taxation on cloth and sheep, from which another

[9] Michael Zell, 'Parliament, the Textile Industry and the Mid-Tudor Crisis', in Charles Carlton, ed., *State, Sovereigns & Society in Early Modern England: Essays in Honour of A.J. Slavin* (Stroud, 1998), pp. 73–4.

[10] Other legislation may have developed in a similar way: the census of people, grain, bakers and brewers drawn up in Coventry in 1520 was followed by a national survey of grain stocks in 1527: Lee, 'Grain Shortages'.

[11] N.M. Fuidge, 'Worcestershire', *HoP, 1509–1558*; Dyer, *Worcester*, pp. 113–14.

act emerged in 1550.[12] The capacity of individual clothiers to influence policy is more difficult to discern, although in 1541 John Winchcombe II of Newbury was able, with other clothiers, to secure the repeal of regulations in the 1536 act that fixed the length and breadth of cloth.[13] In 1558 the clothier Thomas Wild, MP for Worcester, was accused of slandering John Marshe, one of the members for London, by saying 'that he had unburdened the clothiers from the search of cloths and laid it upon the buyers'.[14]

REGULATING CLOTH PRODUCTION

Size and quality standards

Despite attempts at standardisation by governments, consumers faced a bewildering array of products. The names of different types of cloth might be derived from their colour, their place of manufacture, their method of production, or the purpose for which they were intended. Products associated with particular places could provide an early type of local branding, such as the cloths called Halifax, Ripon and Middleham whites on board the *Marie* of Hull in 1467, or even the 'Molton whites' sold by the merchant Philip Burges of North Molton in the early 1500s.[15] Such terms were used inconsistently though, as a place-name might indicate the place of marketing or export, rather than the location of production, as with many of the 'Bristols' and 'Southamptons'. Some cloths that appear to be based on a place-name might reflect a characteristic of production, like the 'Stamfords', which may have been cloths 'of strong warp thread' (*staminis fortis*). Even by the thirteenth century these were no longer exclusively associated with the Lincolnshire town, like the 'Milanese Stamfords of Monza' found in Venice in 1265.[16]

Attempts to regulate the size and quality of cloth date back to the late twelfth century. The Crown attempted to enforce standard weights and measures and the Assize of Measures of 1197 established that woollen cloths should all have the same width, measured by a standard ell. Magna Carta in 1215 fixed the width of fine and expensive weaves of dyed cloth as well as russet, which at this time was a cheap, undyed cloth, much worn by country-people.[17] While such standards enabled consumers

[12] N.M. Fuidge, 'Devon', *HoP, 1509–1558*; *Journal of the House of Commons*, i: *1547–1629* (London, 1802), p. 11.

[13] See below, p. 259.

[14] A. Davidson, 'WILD, Thomas (by 1508–59), of The Ford and Worcester, Worcs.', *HoP, 1509–1558*.

[15] TNA, E 159/246 Trinity, m. 17d, 18. C 1/287/27, C 1/466/45.

[16] Salzman, *English Industries*, p. 199.

[17] Britnell, *Commercialisation*, pp. 90–1.

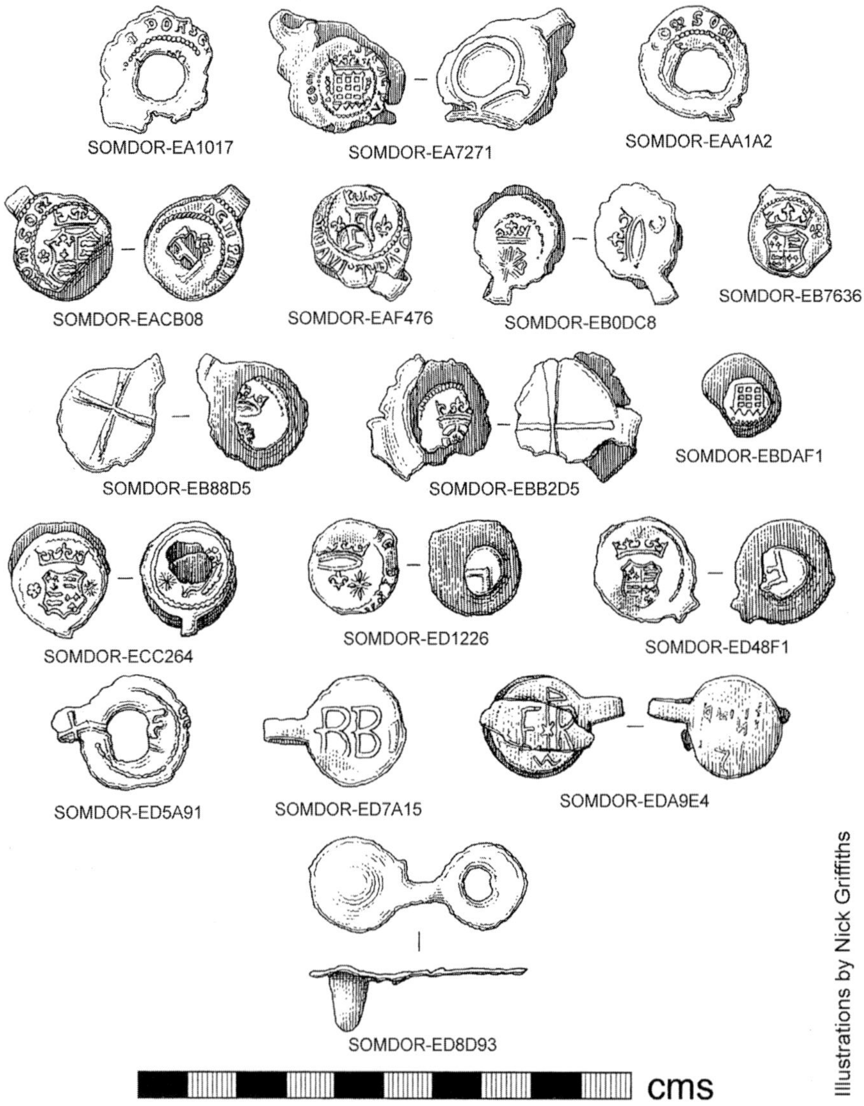

Plate 10 Medieval and post-medieval cloth seals.
Examples from a group of twenty-two lead cloth seals discovered in a field in Cerne Abbas, Dorset. They include a seal with the initials 'RB' of a clothier or weaver, and an unused example, which has not been folded together or stamped (Portable Antiquities Scheme).

to receive a more uniform product, and to maintain the reputation of English cloth in home and overseas markets, they also made it easier to ensure, once subsidies had been introduced on the sale and export of cloth, the collection of revenue.

The length for cloths was fixed for the first time in 1278 and to enforce this the Crown appointed officials charged with checking the measurements and quality of every piece of cloth sold, affixing a seal (Plate 10) when the cloth was sound and confiscating it when it was found to be defective. These officials became known as ulnagers. From 1353 onwards they collected a subsidy and fees, which varied according to size and type of cloth. A whole cloth of assize paid a subsidy of 4d and an ulnager's fee of ½d. Ulnage accounts record the quantities of cloth sealed and the subsidies paid.[18] By the sixteenth century, the ulnage was let out to farm. Lessees paid a fixed rent to the Crown for collecting this tax, usually on a county basis, and then sometimes sub-leased the collection in localities to clothiers. The farmers of the ulnage in Surrey and Sussex for example, Thomas Jonys and Christopher More, in 1510 sub-let to John Perkyns of Guildford, clothier, the profits of the ulnage in the town of Guildford and hundred of Woking. The deputy ulnager for Sussex, John Morrys, made an agreement with William Yonge of Petworth, clothier, in 1544, that Yonge was to seal all cloths made or bought by him in Petworth, Tillington and Lodsworth.[19] The ulnage system offered officials half the value of all confiscated goods and was thus particularly open to abuse. Several Wiltshire accounts drawn up in the fifteenth century contain fictitious names and totals. In sixteenth-century Lancashire, ulnagers took fees for sealing cloths without having seen the actual cloths that were supposed to be inspected, and even sold the wax seals so that clothiers could apply their own seals without official examination. Ralph Trafford, son of Margaret, ulnager for Lancashire, began to act as ulnager illegally in 1550, forging his own seal.[20]

The inspection of cloths increased further in 1549 when a proclamation required town officials and magistrates to check quarterly the premises of every clothier, cloth-worker and draper to see that their cloth had been properly made and dyed. These provisions were repeated in a statute of 1550, but mayors and justices of the peace were now ordered to appoint overseers to conduct inspections of all premises where cloth was made, in all towns and villages that were not incorporated. Records

[18] Egan, 'Cloth Seals'; Elton, *Cloth Seals*, pp. 20–33; Merrick, 'Taxing Medieval Cloth'; Heaton, *Yorkshire Woollen*, pp. 126–9.

[19] Surrey History Centre, LM/1535, LM/1536/1.

[20] Carus-Wilson, 'Aulnage Accounts'; Lowe, *Lancashire Textile Industry*, pp. 86–92.

of cloths seized in London and provincial cloth-making centres were recorded on rolls sent to the Exchequer.[21] In 1552, mayors of boroughs were to appoint two or more cloth searchers to examine all cloths dyed or dressed in their towns.[22] A new system of enforcement had been established that reflected the fact that much textile production was now taking place away from the oversight of urban craft guilds.

These national attempts to standardise the sizes and quality of cloth inevitably faced opposition from regional groups of cloth-makers who felt disadvantaged by these regulations. In 1376 for example, the commons of Essex and Suffolk successfully petitioned parliament to exclude cogware, kerseys and other narrow cloths from statutory control, and this was reconfirmed in 1381. The commons of Essex, Suffolk and Norfolk presented another petition in 1394 asking to have licence to make short cloths of 12 yards in length and 1 yard in width of coarse wool as they had in the past, arguing that 'the bulk and majority of people' from the three counties 'do not know how to do anything else except work in the said craft'.[23] When the size of all cloths was fixed by statute at 28 yards long in 1405–06, this completely disregarded narrower rayed cloth (cloth with stripes woven into the pattern).[24] Consequently, the cloth-makers of Salisbury found that their rays were confiscated when they attempted to sell them at Westminster Fair because they were not of the statutory width. An extraordinary meeting of the City Convocation assembled in January 1412 to discuss this issue, comprising thirty-five Salisbury citizens, 'many other makers of cloth within the city', and the mayor, draper William Doudyng. Two citizens were sent to London to negotiate, and when the delegates later reported that the king and his council were insistent about the standardised size of rays, it was agreed to send examples of Salisbury rays at different stages of production to demonstrate to the council that they could not be made of the required

[21] *Tudor Royal Proclamations*, eds Paul L. Hughes and James F. Larkin, 3 vols (New Haven, 1964–69), i, no. 328, pp. 453–5; 3 & 4 Edward VI, c. 2: *SR*, iv (1), pp. 101–2; Zell, 'Parliament', pp. 78–9; Michael Zell, 'The Exchequer Lists of Provincial Cloth-makers Fined in London during the Sixteenth Century', *Bulletin of the Institute of Historical Research* 57 (1984), pp. 129–30; G.D. Ramsay, 'The Distribution of the Cloth Industry in 1561–2', *English Historical Review* 57 (1942), pp. 361–9.

[22] 5 & 6 Edward VI, c. 2: *SR*, iv (1), p. 139.

[23] *Rotuli Parliamentorum*, 6 vols (London, 1777–1832), ii, p. 347, iii, p. 320, quoted in Amor, *From Wool to Cloth*, pp. 219–20.

[24] Makers of ray cloths initially obtained exemption from this legislation in 1407, but the provisions were revived in 1409–10 and confirmed in 1411: 7 Henry IV, c. 10, 9 Henry IV, c. 6, 11 Henry IV, c. 6, 13 Henry IV, c. 4: *SR*, ii, pp. 154, 160, 163–5, 168.

width.[25] The specific nature of Devonshire wool was recognised in 1467 thanks to the efforts of the residents of the Devon hundreds of Lifton, Roborough and Tavistock. They were permitted to add flocks or waste wool to their wool, a practice that had been prohibited nationally in 1464.[26] In 1523 the clothiers of Suffolk secured an exemption from regulations governing cloth sizes for their fabrics known as vesses or set-cloths. Another act of 1536, while maintaining this proviso, fixed the breadth of ordinary cloth, and the Suffolk clothiers argued that unless the act was at least postponed they would give up making cloths as they could not keep the regulations for fabric breadth and the weavers were too poor to acquire new looms and slays. Following lobbying from clothiers in the southern counties, certain provisions within the act were repealed in 1541, described as being prejudicial to kersey makers, especially in Berkshire, Southampton, Oxfordshire, Surrey, Sussex and Yorkshire.[27]

Perhaps it was the experience of these regional challenges to previous national statutes that in 1552 prompted the House of Commons to appoint a committee of clothiers and merchants to help draft the first act to define the sizes and weights of regional cloth types. This act specified the minimum dimensions (when fully wet and shrunk) and weight (when thoroughly cleaned and dry) of around forty different types of cloth after 'scouring, thicking and drying' (Appendix 3). These cloths were mostly known after their original county of manufacture, sometimes even after a town or village. The products ranged from Kent, Sussex and Reading broadcloths of 28 yards in length weighing at least 90 lb each, to Devonshire kerseys only 12 yards long and weighing just 14 lb. Essentially though, all these different sorts of cloth fell into two main types, broadcloths and kerseys, the latter being smaller and lighter fabrics. Cloth-makers were to be fined for each deficient cloth offered for sale.[28]

The same statute also regulated the colours permitted in English broadcloths. Only the following colours were allowed: scarlet, red, crimson, murrey, violet, puke, brown blue, black, green, yellow, blue, azure, orange, tawney, russet, marble grey, sad new colour, sheeps colour, watchet, lion colour, motley and iron grey.[29] As in other aspects

[25] *VCH Wiltshire*, iv, p. 125; Bridbury, *Clothmaking*, pp. 68–9, 109.

[26] 7 Edward IV, c. 2: *SR*, ii, pp. 421–2. Finberg, *Tavistock Abbey*, p. 153.

[27] 14 & 15 Henry VIII, c. 11, 27 Henry VIII, c. 12, 33 Henry VIII, c. 18: *SR*, iii, pp. 217, 545, 854; Salzman, *English Industries*, p. 218. See also below, p. 259.

[28] 5 & 6 Edward VI, c. 6: *SR*, iv (1), pp. 136–8; Zell, *Industry*, pp. 158–9.

[29] Puke: produced by galls and copperas and so probably a very deep bluish black or dark brown colour. Murrey: mulberry-coloured, reddish purple or blood red. Sad: dark or deep. Watchet: light blue. Motley: cloth woven from threads of two or more colours (*OED*).

of the act, novelty was associated with a loss of quality, rather than with new market opportunities. The extensive range of shades listed though, does suggest that broadcloths were being made in a wider assortment of colours than a generation before.[30] Nonetheless, despite the detail in the 1552 act, just six years later it was reported that 'diverse clothiers found themselves aggrieved, alleging that it is impossible for them to observe the same Act in all points', and the weights of some cloths were modified by another statute. This act also permitted the sale of cloth in additional colours – friar's grey, crane-colour, purple, and old medley.[31] In addition to these national regulations, town authorities and guilds also attempted to standardise products. In Coventry in 1451, for example, weavers were ordered not to make a 'dozen' cloth with less than 30 lb of yarn.[32] In Reading, an agreement of 1520 required every cloth owner to deliver 48 lb of yarn for warp and 65 lb of yarn for weft for each cloth, and every weaver was to deliver a cloth that when fulled was 26 yards in length.[33]

Clothiers usually marked the cloths that they had produced with their own distinctive mark. Such makers' marks were commonly adopted by other trades including bakers, coopers, metal and tile workers, and wool merchants.[34] These marks could be used to identify the ownership of goods, liability for taxation, and to trace responsibility for substandard work. In some circumstances, they may also have identified commercial premises as shop signs. A statute of 1389–90 instructed weavers, cloth-workers and fullers to put their 'signs' on cloths, which may have been marks inked or sewn on to the fabric.[35] In an attempt to enforce quality standards, a statute of 1535–36 made this an essential requirement:

> every clothier within this realm shall weave, or cause to be woven, his or their several token or mark in all and every cloth, kersey and other cloths, whatsoever they be, made and wrought to be uttered and sold.[36]

Some urban governments had already introduced local legislation to ensure quality through the marking of cloth, notably Coventry. In 1468 every fuller in Coventry was required to set his own mark on his

[30] Zell, *Industry*, p. 163.

[31] 4 & 5 Philip & Mary c. 5: *SR*, iv (1), pp. 323–5. Crane-colour: ashy-grey. Medley: mixed or blended colour (*OED*).

[32] Britnell, *Commercialisation*, p. 176.

[33] BRO, R/IC2/1.

[34] Salzman, *English Industries*, p. 325; F.A. Girling, *English Merchants' Marks. A Field Survey of Marks Made by Merchants and Tradesmen in England between 1400 and 1700* (London, 1964), p. 9.

[35] 13 Richard II, c. 11: *SR*, ii, p. 64.

[36] 27 Henry VIII, c. 12: *SR*, iii, p. 544.

cloth.[37] Searchers inspected newly made cloths in the city, and in 1518 it was ordered that good-quality cloths were to be sealed with the city arms; cloth that failed to meet this standard could be offered for sale but without the backing of the city's 'kitemark'. This prevented the sale of inferior goods from other places under the name of Coventry cloth. The city's reputation for dyeing its Coventry blue cloth was also protected when, in 1529, it was ordered that cloth dyed musters or medleys was not to bear the city's seal.[38] Clothiers' marks were a convenient means by which buyers could identify the origin of products they were purchasing. The mercer Thomas Kitson drew the relevant mark, and noted its colour, next to his records of transactions with clothiers in his account book, presumably so that he could cross-check this against the actual consignments of cloth.[39] As well as being placed on the cloth that they produced, clothiers used such marks as if they were heraldic emblems, inserting them on their seals and monuments. The Webbs of Dedham in Essex, for example, applied their mark to a fireplace lintel in one of their houses, to their funerary monuments, and to church-building work that they had funded.[40] In this sense, clothiers' marks often became family rather than personal emblems, although the most socially ambitious merchants were keen to acquire a proper coat of arms.[41]

There could be complaints about quality at any stage of the cloth-making process. The act of 1552, for example, remarked that 'Clothiers study rather to make many than to make good cloths' and described various abuses, including mixing the yarns of various spinnings in one cloth; mixing of fell wool, lambs' wool, and fleece wool; taking cloth out of the mill before it was fully thickened; over-stretching cloths on the tenter; stopping breaks in the cloth with flocks; and 'using so many subtle sleights and untruths' that when cloths were put in water, they came out with neither the length or the breadth that they should.[42] These concerns were not new. Cloths made in the counties of Somerset, Devon, Bristol and Gloucester were apparently put to sale tacked and folded, frequently concealing poor workmanship, and so in 1389–90 it was ordered that cloths were to be sold open, so that buyers could see them.[43] A cloth statute of 1483 prohibited various illicit practices, including the re-stretching of fulled cloth, dry shearing of cloth, private and secret tenter yards, and putting flocks on cloth, mirroring regulations that

37 *Coventry Leet Book*, p. 338.
38 *VCH Warwickshire*, viii, p. 164.
39 See below, Plate 14.
40 *VCH Essex*, x, p. 161, n. 19, p. 182.
41 Saul, 'Wool Merchants', p. 335.
42 5 & 6 Edward VI, c. 6: *SR*, iv (1), p. 136.
43 13 Richard II, c. 11: *SR*, ii, p. 64.

the city and crafts of London had introduced after 1470.[44] The 1552 act though, introduced new penalties. The clothier must repay the purchase price to anyone who had bought a faulty cloth that had been sealed by him and an ulnager. A merchant who had shipped a cloth overseas that was found there to be defective could recover the cost of shipping back to England from the clothier as well. The same parliament also prohibited the use of gig mills, which were claimed to impair the quality of cloth, although their use never seems to have been very widespread.[45]

Urban craft guilds also sought to protect the consumer against defective goods and maintain profits for producers. Regulations could set out in minute detail specifications for production and draconian punishments for those who failed to meet these quality standards. The regulations of the weavers of Bristol in 1346, for example, fixed the width of cloth and directed that if the threads were deficient in the cloth or were too far apart, the cloth and the instrument on which it had been worked was to be burnt. Dyers at York producing faulty work were to be fined 40d for their first offence, 6s 8d for their second, and were to be expelled from the city on their third offence. When in 1517 the wardens of the craft of fullers at Nottingham discovered a fault of workmanship in the kersey that William Nicholson had fulled, sheared and scoured on behalf of Robert Mellors, William was to lose all his work on the kersey and receive nothing for his labour.[46]

Powerful interest groups could circumvent the law. Both parliament and the civic government of London sought to prevent the export of unfulled cloth, believing that the finishing process added value and provided additional employment. Exporters though, particularly the Merchant Adventurers, wanted the freedom to export finished or unfinished cloth, depending on their customers' needs. Several statutes decreed that no cloth should be exported unless it had been barbed, rowed and shorn. In practice, many Merchant Adventurers bought licences to sidestep these restrictions.[47]

Fraudulent practices in cloth-making

Measures to prevent fraudulent practices by employers or employees were also introduced through parliament. An act of 1512 described the potential for such deception by clothiers and their workers during each stage of cloth-making through the putting-out system:

[44] 1 Richard III, c. 8: *SR*, ii, pp. 484–9; Oldland, 'Making and Marketing', p. 101.

[45] 5 & 6 Edward VI, c. 6, 22: *SR*, iv (1), pp. 138–9, 156. See also above, pp. 57–9.

[46] Lipson, *Economic History*, i, pp. 329–32; Bolton, *Medieval English Economy*, p. 266.

[47] Oldland, 'Making and Marketing', pp. 102–3.

> First that the wool which shall be delivered for or by the clothier to any person or persons for breaking, combing, carding or spinning of the same the delivery shall be the even just and true poise and weight …
>
> That the breaker or comber to deliver again to the said clothier the same wool so broken and kempt[48] and the carder and spinner to deliver again to the said clothier yarn of the same wool by the same even, just and true poise and weight, the waste thereof excepted, without any part thereof concealing or any more oil, water, or other thing put thereunto deceivably …
>
> The weaver … shall weave, work and put into the web[49] for cloth to be made thereof as much and all the same yarn as the clothier or any person for him shall deliver to the same weaver … without changing or any parcel thereof leaving out of the same web …
>
> That the walker and fuller shall truly walk, full, thick and work every web of woollen yarn which he shall have … without any flocks[50] or any other manner of deceit … and shall not row nor work any cloth or web with any cards on the right side nor of the wrong side …
>
> The clothier nor other person whatever … shall not put any cloth to sale which when it shall be full wet shall shrink more than one yard in all the length and one quarter of a yard in the breadth …[51]

Clothiers who transgressed were to be fined, and textile workers were to be placed in the pillory or cucking-stool. Local legislation, such as the repeated ordinances requiring the use of standard wool weights at Colchester, Coventry and Worcester, reflected similar attempts to prevent fraud and exploitation. At Colchester, it had become the custom by 1452 that any cloth-maker who wished to put wool out to be combed in another household should use a 5 lb weight called a 'kembyngston', and anyone putting wool out for spinning should use a 4½ lb weight known as a 'spynnyngston'. The bailiffs could imprison and fine employers who exploited women by using over-large weights.[52]

[48] Kempt: combed (*OED*).

[49] Web: a whole piece of cloth in the process of being woven or after it comes from the loom (*OED*).

[50] Flocks: the coarse tufts and refuse of wool and cloth shearings (*OED*).

[51] 3 Henry VIII, c. 6: *SR*, iii, p. 28.

[52] Britnell, *Colchester*, p. 241.

Protection of artisans

The practice of truck, with clothiers paying their workers in goods rather than in money, was also legislated against. A statute of 1464, made in response to a complaint addressed to parliament, described how labourers in cloth-making were 'driven to take a great part of their wages in pins, girdles, and other unprofitable wares', and ordered cloth-makers to pay labourers in any part of the trade in lawful money for all their wages.[53] This may in part reflect an inadequate supply of coinage, although there could also have been an element of exploitation by the clothiers. The anonymous writer of 'A Trade Policy', who may have worked in the cloth industry, writing shortly before 1464, complained that silver was in such short supply that manufacturers paid their workers half in money and half in goods at inflated prices, which the workers were then supposed to sell to make up their earnings.[54] Local by-laws against the payment of truck wages were made for weavers at Colchester in 1411–12, at Norwich in 1460, and at Worcester in 1467.[55] A parliamentary statute of 1512 instructed clothiers to pay wool-breakers, combers, carders, spinners, weavers and fullers for their workmanship in ready money and not any part in wares or victuals.[56] Clothiers paying their workers in wares was a concern in the city and soke of Winchester in 1517, although this may have been related to anxiety about the quality of the coinage, particularly the 'taking and refusing of pennies'.[57] Weavers were to be paid in ready money by cloth-makers in Reading in 1520 as part of articles agreed to regulate cloth-making in the town.[58] Clement Armstrong, a London grocer, complained around 1533 that cloth-makers told their workers 'if they will have any work, therefore they must take both wares and money', making it very difficult for poor people to pay their lord's rents.[59] Kentish weavers made demands around 1536 for clothiers to pay spinners and weavers in ready money and not in goods.[60] Clothiers were accused in

[53] *Rotuli Parliamentorum*, v, pp. 501–3; 4 Edward IV, c. 1: *SR*, ii, p. 406.

[54] *Political Poems and Songs Relating to English History, Composed During the Period from the Accession of Edw. III to that of Ric. III*, ed. T. Wright, 2 vols (London, 1859–61), ii, p. 285; Bolton, *Money*, p. 270.

[55] Lipson, *Economic History*, i, p. 481.

[56] 3 Henry VIII, c. 6: *SR*, iii, p. 28.

[57] *Letters of Richard Fox, 1486–1527*, eds P.S. Allen and H.M. Allen (Oxford, 1929), pp. 98–9, 102.

[58] BRO, R/IC2/1.

[59] *TED*, iii, p. 109. For dating Armstrong's text, see Bindoff, 'Clement Armstrong'.

[60] BL, Cotton MS, Titus B.1, no. 59, fol. 193.

1549 of paying poor labourers with 'soap, candles, rotten cloth, stinking fish and such like baggage' instead of money.[61]

The weavers of cloth-making centres in Suffolk and Essex petitioned parliament in 1539 that they felt wholly dependent on rich clothiers for their work, and the clothiers had agreed a fixed price for weaving cloths. Similar complaints made by weavers to parliament in 1555, that the wealthy clothiers oppressed them by setting up and keeping divers looms in their homes, and maintaining journeymen and unskilled persons, led to the Weavers' Act. This legislation required clothiers living outside towns to keep no more than one loom, and weavers no more than two looms.[62] It echoed earlier legislation by craft guilds and borough governments to maintain small units of production and prevent the agglomeration of manufacturing. At Coventry in 1449, it had been ordered that wool should be handed out to spinners in quantities of not more than 2¼ lb, and in 1452 it was laid down that if any spinner was given more than 2½ lb she was to take it to the sheriffs, who would ensure that she was paid the correct wage. In 1447 the weavers of Bury St Edmunds were prohibited from possessing more than four looms each.[63]

Apprenticeship

Apprenticeship was another measure that central and local governments promoted during the later Middle Ages to regulate production. Entry to a craft guild was usually through a long apprenticeship. As these apprenticeships were recognised by the civic authorities, masters could prosecute apprentices who failed to work satisfactorily during their term. William Wytham sought the judgement of Colchester borough court in 1387–88 on the behaviour of his bound apprentice John atte Lane, who had spent his time, it was claimed, 'playing at dice, spoiling cloth, and committing fornication with William's maid'.[64] Although a statute of 1363 required each craftsman to confine himself to one craft, the legislation was treated as permissive by urban authorities, to be made effective when they chose. In Colchester, for example, apprenticeship rules were not formulated until 1418, when the fullers' craft secured the enactment that apprenticeships in weaving and fulling should be at least five years long, and no burgess should practice the craft of weaving and fulling

[61] John Hales, 'Defence', printed in Thomas Smith, *A Discourse of the Common Weal of this Realm of England*, ed. E. Lamond (Cambridge, 1893), p. lxvi.

[62] TNA, SP 1/151, fol. 70; *LP*, xiv (1), no. 874, p. 408. 2 & 3 Philip and Mary, c. 11: *SR*, iv (1), p. 286.

[63] Royal Commission on Historical Manuscripts, *The Manuscripts of Lincoln, Bury St Edmunds and Great Grimsby Corporations*, HMC, Fourteenth Report, Appendix, Part 8 (London, 1895), p. 135; *VCH Warwickshire*, viii, pp. 158, 160.

[64] Galloway, 'Colchester and its Region', p. 141.

together. These ordinances sought to restrict entry into the textile crafts under the premise that poor workmanship was undermining the town's reputation. Workers could no longer switch into new occupations in the time that it took them to learn the new skills.[65] The number of apprentices that a master might supervise was often restricted too. In Hull for example, no weaver could take more than two apprentices into his charge at the same time. Anyone setting up a loom in their house who had not been an apprentice for seven years was to be fined £10 by the same guild. Having completed their term, an apprentice was examined by several masters and if found suitable, could join the guild as a master, and thereby employ others, or as a journeyman, who was employed by another master. Guilds charged entry fees: at York, a weaver paid £1 to set up his loom and a dyer paid the same for his own vat, a shearman 6s 8d and a fuller 3s 4d.[66]

The government, concerned about quality standards, and probably encouraged by representations from boroughs, which possessed detailed apprenticeship regulations, and from established clothiers, who wanted to limit new competition, introduced wider regulations on apprenticeship in the cloth industry during the sixteenth century. In 1550, established clothiers voiced their concerns to the Privy Council about newcomers to the industry:

> Finding great fault with the multitude of clothiers lately increased in the realm, affirming that as long as every man that would have liberty to be a clothier, as they have now, it was impossible to have good cloth made in the realm, for he that is not bred up in that faculty must trust his factors, and so is commonly deceived … wherefore it was concluded that some devise should be had for a law that none should meddle with cloth-making but such as had been apprentices to the occupation.[67]

In 1550 journeymen clothiers, weavers, fullers and shearmen who had served an apprenticeship but had not established their own business, were to be hired for not less than a quarter of a year. From 1552, weavers were required to serve a seven-year apprenticeship.[68] A subsequent act of 1554 explained that this was disadvantaging clothiers who had made cloth for five or six years, or who married clothiers' wives who had practised cloth-making for twenty years, and this restriction was therefore relaxed for inhabitants of cities, boroughs or market towns.

[65] Britnell, *Colchester*, pp. 139, 186, 239–40.
[66] Heaton, *Yorkshire Woollen*, pp. 35–6.
[67] *Acts of Privy Council 1550–2*, p. 20; *TED*, i, pp. 184–5.
[68] 3 & 4 Edward VI, c. 22; 5 & 6 Edward IV, c. 8: *SR*, iv (1), pp. 121, 142.

Plate I Stages in the production of cloth illustrated in the fifteenth-century cloth-workers' window in the church of Notre-Dame, Semur-en-Auxois, Burgundy, France. Shown from left to right, from the top, are sorting and cleaning the fleece; carding; washing; weaving; fulling; napping; shearing; and pressing.

Plate II Woman feeding chickens while holding a distaff and spindle. (Luttrell Psalter, 1325–40: BL, Add MS 42130, fol. 166v).

Plate III Women spinning with a hand wheel and carding. (Luttrell Psalter, 1325–40: BL, Add MS 42130, fol. 193r).

Plate IV Weaving using a treadle loom, c.1350–75. (Egerton Genesis Picture Book: BL, Egerton MS 1894, fol. 2v detail).

Plate V Cloth Market in 's-Hertogenbosch, Brabant, c.1530, Dutch School. (Het Noordbrabants Museum, 's-Hertogenbosch).
One of several fairs in the Low Countries attended by London merchants, and although on a smaller scale similar to those at Antwerp, Bergen-op-Zoom and Middelburg.

Plate VI The Hanseatic merchant Georg Gisze (1532) by Hans Holbein the Younger (c.1497–1543). (Gemäldegalerie, Staatliche Museum, Berlin). Hanseatic merchants exported English cloth to the Baltic, Prussia, Germany and central Europe. Gisze was based in the London Steelyard and Holbein has depicted his chamber with its correspondence, seals, wax, and scales for weighing coins.

Plate VII Portrait of Thomas Bell (d. 1566), clothier and capper of Gloucester. (Gloucester City Museums Service). Thomas Bell acquired the Gloucester house of the Black Friars at the dissolution. He converted the church into his mansion and used the other buildings as workshops for his weavers. This portrait is one of a set depicting mayors of Gloucester, probably produced around the turn of the seventeenth century.

Plate VIII Paycocke's House, Coggeshall, Essex. Built in 1509 for clothier Thomas Paycocke, whose prosperity and commercial success is reflected in the elaborate decoration, both inside and out.

Plate IX Brass of John Wyncoll (d. 1544), clothier, Little Waldingfield church, Suffolk.
Wyncoll directed in his will to have laid over his tomb in the parish church 'a marble stone with my picture and a Scripture graven in plate for the better memorial of the time of my decease'.

Plate X Portrait of John Winchcombe the Younger ('Jack of Newbury') (c.1489–1557), dated 1550.

John Winchcombe II of Newbury, a major producer of smaller cloths known as kerseys, was long celebrated as a pioneer of factory production. This portrait can be viewed at the Town Hall, Newbury.

The seven-year apprenticeship for weavers was repeated in 1555 though, when the crafts of weaving and fulling were also separated, no weaver being permitted to have a fulling mill, and no fuller to have a loom.[69] Statutes relating to the apprenticeship of weavers were enforced, with twenty-seven prosecutions made in Lancashire between 1563 and 1603 for example, but the prosecutions did not in practice necessarily restrain craftworkers from continuing their occupations once their fines had been paid.[70]

Restricting cloth-making to towns

Several town governments introduced legislation forbidding their burgesses from employing workers from the countryside. Winchester seems to have been one of the earliest towns to do so, stating in the thirteenth century that no citizen should manufacture burel cloth outside the city. At Bristol, permission to weave woollen cloth in country districts was withdrawn in 1381. Colchester prevented townspeople taking wool for spinning outside the liberty in 1411–12. At Norwich, it was decreed in 1421 that no inhabitant should employ a weaver or fuller who did not live or carry out his craft within the city. Ordinances of Worcester in 1467 prevented citizens from putting out wool, as there were sufficient persons to dye, card, spin, weave and full within the city. At Coventry in 1518 it was ordered that no one was to put out cloth to be woven or fulled in the country, or, in an ordinance of 1549, send yarn outside the town to be worked up.[71] Such legislation generated an ongoing conflict of interest between textile craftworkers operating within towns who faced reduced opportunities for employment and urban-based textile producers who looked to rural workers for cheaper labour and to evade the oversight and regulation of craft guilds and borough governments.

Parliamentary legislation supplemented civic legislation in the sixteenth century as corporate towns made renewed attempts to curtail industrial activities in their hinterlands. Norwich successfully promoted measures for the protection of the worsted industry in the city, including assuming responsibility for supervising the worsted trade of East Anglia in 1523, and the right to dye, colour and calendar all worsted cloths made in the surrounding area in 1534. Cloth-making in Worcestershire was confined to its five principal towns in 1534, and York received a monopoly of the manufacture of coverlets in 1543.[72] Although promoting

[69] 1 Mary c. 7; 2 & 3 Philip and Mary, c. 11: *SR*, iv (1), pp. 232, 287.

[70] Lowe, *Lancashire Textile Industry*, pp. 84–5.

[71] Lipson, *Economic History*, i, p. 502; Britnell, *Colchester*, p. 139.

[72] 14 & 15 Henry VIII, c. 3; 25 Henry VIII, c. 18; 26 Henry VIII, c. 16; 34 & 35 Henry VIII, c. 10: *SR*, iii, pp. 211, 459, 513, 908–9.

local interests, such bills reflected wider concerns in government about the state of provincial towns. Many corporate towns were struggling to pay their fee farms, annual payments made to the Crown in return for holding privileges of self-government. Some eighty towns were named in rebuilding acts passed by parliament between 1536 and 1544, ordering owners to restore dilapidated buildings and vacant sites, and giving urban corporations powers to rebuild them.[73]

Parliamentary legislation also reflected the argument being made by some influential commentators that cloth-making standards could be enforced more rigorously in towns, and that clothiers should be placed under their jurisdiction. Sir Thomas Smith (1513–77), in his *Discourse of the Common Weal* suggested:

> every artificer dwelling out of all towns ... as fullers, tanners, clothiers, such should be limited to be under the correction of one good town or another; and they to sell no wares, but such as are first approved and sealed by the town they are limited unto.[74]

This argument was also put forward in John Coke's 'Debate between the Heralds' of 1549, a translation of a late medieval French text adapted for an English readership. In response to the boasts of the French herald, the English herald noted that:

> If our clothiers were commanded to inhabit in towns, as they do in France, Flanders, Brabant, Holland, and other places, we should have as many good towns in England as you have in France, and cloth more finer and truly made.[75]

Four bills were introduced between 1547 and 1553 for clothiers and other artificers to operate from towns, but these did not become legislation.[76] The cloth-making act of 1552, however, required mayors to appoint two or more cloth searchers to examine all cloths dyed or dressed in their towns. No cloth was to be sold in any towns without the seals applied by these searchers. The weavers' act of 1555 forbade the making of woollen cloth except in cities, corporate or market towns, or in places where cloth had been made continually for the previous ten years. Another act followed in 1557, restricting the making of cloth to cities, towns, or places

[73] Charles Phythian-Adams, 'Urban Decay in Late Medieval England', in Philip Abrams and E.A. Wrigley, eds, *Towns in Societies: Essays in Economic History and Historical Sociology* (Cambridge, 1978), p. 178; Bridbury, 'English Provincial Towns', pp. 23–4; Dyer, *Decline and Growth*, pp. 35–7.

[74] Smith, *Discourse of the Common Weal*, p. 130. For Smith's authorship of the *Discourse*, see Ian W. Archer, 'Smith, Sir Thomas (1513–1577)', *ODNB*.

[75] *TED*, iii, p. 8.

[76] Zell, 'Parliament', p. 75.

where cloth had been made for the last twenty years. An interesting catalogue of exemptions, listing places where cloths could be made outside market towns, was appended to this statute. These included not only impoverished upland areas where coarser cloths were produced, such as Lancashire, Westmorland and Wales, but also major centres of rural production, notably Suffolk, Kent, Godalming in Surrey, Yorkshire not within twelve miles of York, and towns and villages near Stroudwater in Gloucestershire, which must reflect pressure by local interests during the drafting of the bill. Nearly twenty years later, another bill also exempted clothiers in Wiltshire, Somerset and Gloucester from these restrictions.[77] Another strand of this policy was to confine retail sales of cloth to towns. A statute of 1554–55 stated that towns were being exploited by linen and woollen drapers, haberdashers and grocers residing in the countryside and practising their occupations there, who only came into towns to sell their wares. Retailing trade was therefore restricted to urban centres, and countryfolk were permitted to sell retail only at the time of fairs.[78]

Economic stimulus

The sixteenth century saw several schemes to stimulate cloth-making in specific localities. John Veysey (formerly Harman), (c.1464–1554), bishop of Exeter, set up the making of kerseys at Sutton Coldfield in Warwickshire, 'in imitation of Devonshire' which he saw had 'much enriched that county'. This formed just part of the support that Vesyey gave to his home town, as he also built fifty-one stone houses, a moot hall and prison, improved the parish church, endowed a grammar school, laid out the marketplace, paved the town, and secured its borough privileges. His kersey-making scheme, however, 'in the end came to small effect'.[79] The mayor of Lincoln invited a clothier to his city in 1516 to supervise a stock for setting up the cloth trade, and wool spinners and cloth-makers were offered their freedom if they resided there. These policies may have been ineffective as further efforts were made in 1551, when the disused church of the Holy Rood, its churchyard and other land was handed over to clothiers to create a fulling mill and dye-house, without rent, providing that they make at least twenty broadcloths a year. Young people and others who were idle were to be taken on by clothiers for eight or nine

[77] 2 & 3 Philip and Mary, c. 11; 4 & 5 Philip and Mary, c. 5; 18 Elizabeth, c. 16: *SR*, iv (1), pp. 286, 325–6, 626.

[78] 1 & 2 Philip and Mary, c. 7: *SR*, iv (1), pp. 244–5; Phythian-Adams, 'Urban Decay', pp. 178–9.

[79] P.B. Chatwin and E.G. Harcourt, 'The Bishop Vesey Houses and Other Old Buildings in Sutton Coldfield', *Birmingham Archaeological Society Transactions and Proceedings* 64 (1941–42), p. 2; Nicholas Orme, 'Veysey, John (*c.*1464–1554)', *ODNB*; Lee, 'Functions and Fortunes', p. 16.

years. Tolls on wool, dyestuffs and on persons coming to buy cloth were suspended for seven years.[80]

Several cloth-making schemes were proposed after the dissolution of the monasteries and friaries released urban sites. The clothier and capmaker Thomas Bell of Gloucester, who reportedly did 'much good in that town among the poor people setting many on work above 300 daily', acquired the Blackfriars site in the town. He converted the church into his mansion and used the monastic buildings for cloth-making.[81] Richard Rich, reporting to Thomas Cromwell about the decline of the town and abbey at Abingdon in 1538, advised that it was likely to decay further unless the inhabitants were set to work to 'drape' (weave) cloth. Rich reported that Tucker, a cloth-maker from Burford, was willing to spend 100 marks a week providing employment in cloth-making in Abingdon in return for a grant of the abbey fulling mill, floodgates, fishing and a farm. Tucker already employed five hundred people and sent wool to Abingdon for carding and spinning, but had undertaken to provide work for the inhabitants of Abingdon, so that in a few years they would earn more than they had done 'in twenty years past'.[82] Dr John London described the decay within the town of Northampton in 1539 and proposed, with Thomas Cromwell's help, 'to set the poor people now being idle and of no small numbers in occupation of carding, spinning, weaving, fulling, and dyeing', as, 'in the Friars also be goodly rooms meet for clothiers'.[83] Later the same year, it was reported that the king wanted a clothier called Bathhurst to live in Canterbury, 'for erection there of cloth-making'. The king had offered Bathhurst the house previously belonging to the Grey Friars, although if he or 'another of the best clothiers in Kent were disposed to set up cloth-making in Canterbury', Cromwell was informed that the Blackfriars would be sufficient for the purpose.[84] Another proposal was to establish a cloth-making workshop at Osney Abbey in 1546, which the borough government of Oxford hoped would provide work for two thousand people.[85]

Few of these projects seem to have been successful. Although centralised cloth-making workshops were occasionally established, notably

[80] Royal Commission, *Manuscripts of Lincoln*, pp. 26, 44.

[81] BL, Cotton MS, Cleopatra E IV, fol. 302v, printed in Joyce Youings, *The Dissolution of the Monasteries* (London, 1971), pp. 178–9; *LP*, xiii (1), no. 1109, p. 405, xiv (1), no. 1354 (48), p. 590; *Itinerary*, ii, p. 58; C.F.R. Palmer, 'The Friars-Preachers, or Black Friars, of Gloucester', *Archaeological Journal* 39 (1882), pp. 296–306.

[82] TNA, SP 1/129, fols 83, 154; *LP*, xiii (1), no. 332, pp. 113–14, no. 415, p. 154; Jackson, 'Clothmaking', pp. 64–5.

[83] TNA, SP 1/142, fol. 31; *LP*, xiv (1), no. 42, p. 21.

[84] TNA, SP 1/144, fol. 13; *LP*, xiv (1), no. 423, p. 170.

[85] *VCH Oxfordshire*, ii, p. 244.

by William Stumpe at the former abbey of Malmesbury, most clothiers relied on putting out materials to dependent workers in their own homes. The scheme at Osney Abbey never materialised, nor did that at Abingdon, where the fulling mill was still in disrepair in 1548. The cloth-making initiatives proposed for redundant religious houses may have prompted the initial drafting of a parliamentary act in 1539 to set 'idle people' to work on making linen cloth.[86] Such efforts also foreshadowed municipal ventures of the later sixteenth century, where the legacies of local benefactors were lent out by town councils on favourable terms to contracting clothiers, to encourage them to establish new branches of cloth-making, and thereby provide employment for the poor.[87]

We noted in the Introduction how the Crown encouraged Flemish cloth-workers to migrate to England in the fourteenth century. A similar but less successful attempt was made in 1551. Nearly seventy households of weavers of northern French or Walloon origin, fleeing Catholic persecutions on the Continent, were invited to settle at Glastonbury by the Lord Protector, Edward Seymour, Duke of Somerset. Valérand Poullain, Protestant theologian and church leader, was appointed superintendent of the fledgling community, known as the Stranger Church at Glastonbury. Although these weavers of worsted cloth were reported to be 'godly and honest folk, ready to teach their crafts and likely soon to bring great commodity to those parts', Poullain's church did not survive the accession of Queen Mary, and in 1553 the community left England.[88] More enduring was the settlement during Elizabeth I's reign of immigrants from the Low Countries, who established the manufacture of finer fabrics known as the 'new draperies' in several towns, notably Norwich, Colchester, Southampton and also in London, where they practised silk-weaving.[89]

[86] TNA, SP 1/151, fol. 65; *LP*, xiv (1), no. 872, p. 408.

[87] Unwin, *Industrial Organisation*, p. 93; Kerridge, *Textile Manufactures*, pp. 232–4.

[88] Chris Linsley, 'A Stranger Church at Glastonbury, 1551–1553', England's Immigrants 1330–1550, https://www.englandsimmigrants.com/page/individual-studies/a-stranger-church-at-Glastonbury-1551-1553

[89] Lipson, *Economic History*, i, pp. 494–501.

RESPONDING TO POLITICAL PROTESTS

> The clothier played a very important part in the English commonwealth. On his prosperity, and ability to give work to the poor, depended the social tranquillity of England from the fifteenth to the eighteenth century.
>
> Astrid Friis, *Alderman Cockayne's Project and the Cloth Trade* (1927)[90]

During the later Middle Ages, English governments became increasingly anxious to protect employment within the textile industry. For as the English cloth industry grew, it became increasingly dependent on overseas markets, and on clothiers and other merchants making investment decisions based on where labour and other production costs were cheapest. Increasing numbers of people were becoming dependent on the clothiers for work. Interruptions to cloth sales placed many of these textile workers at risk of underemployment and unemployment. Overseas markets, which probably accounted for about half of all sales, were particularly vulnerable to such disruptions through failed diplomacy and warfare. Unemployment quickly led to unrest. In 1449 for example, Parliament was informed of the effects of a ban on English cloth imports in Burgundy:

> many cloth-makers, men weavers, fullers, dyers, and women combers, carders, and spinners, and other buyers and sellers thereof ... such of them as cannot do none other occupations, become as idle people, which provokes them to sin and mischievous living.[91]

A century later, in his *Discourse of the Common Weal*, Sir Thomas Smith presents economic analysis as a dialogue between a knight, a doctor, a merchant, a capper, and a husbandman, as representatives of different social groups, who each put forward their interpretation of the causes of inflation. The knight must have echoed the fears of many when he stated that numerous wise men blamed the clothiers for outbreaks of unrest:

> all these insurrections do stir by occasion of all these clothiers; for when our clothiers lack vent overseas, there is great multitude of these clothiers idle, and when they be idle, then they assemble in companies, and murmur for lack of living, and so pick one quarrel or other to stir the poor commons, that be as idle as they, to a commotion... it were better there were none of them in the realm at all, and consequently that the wool were uttered unwrought overseas.[92]

[90] Astrid Friis, *Alderman Cockayne's Project and the Cloth Trade: Commercial Policy of England in its Main Aspects, 1603–1625* (Copenhagen, 1927), p. 22.

[91] *Rotuli Parliamentorum*, v, p. 150, no. 20.

[92] Smith, *Discourse of the Common Weal*, pp. 88–9.

The doctor though, rebukes the knight and stresses that the cloth industry maintains employment and brings in treasure. This dialogue reflects the debate within government circles as well as wider society. The dependence of particular areas on cloth-making made them especially vulnerable to underemployment and unemployment when cloth markets were depressed. Disruptions to the cloth trade troubled the country's politicians, as well as its manufacturers, and prompted legislation aimed at regulating and restoring the textile industry.

Cade's revolt, 1450

Although primarily a protest against Henry VI's insolvent and corrupt administration, Cade's revolt in 1450 was fuelled by the slump in the cloth trade, reflecting both a widespread European economic depression, and specific trade embargoes.[93] Cloth-making communities such as Castle Combe, Trowbridge and Hindon in Wiltshire experienced falling rents and lower receipts from their manorial courts.[94] A short-lived uprising saw rebels temporarily occupy London and outbreaks of violence in several parts of southern England, including the murder of William Aiscough, bishop of Salisbury, at Edington in Wiltshire. Political and religious grievances merged with economic concerns about disruption to the cloth trade. The bishop of Salisbury was one of the most hated men in the royal circle, and there had been long-running struggles between the citizens of Salisbury and their lord, the bishop, and between the residents of Sherborne and their lord, the abbot.[95]

Many of the areas of disorder were areas of cloth production, such as the west Wiltshire textile centres of Devizes, Wilton and Malmesbury, Sherborne (Dorset), Crawley (Hampshire), Newbury and Hungerford in the Thames valley, the area around Gloucester, Wells, the Kent Weald, Essex including Colchester, Hadleigh in Suffolk, Norwich, and probably Winchester and Coventry.[96] Textile workers were prominent among the rebels. The list of villagers in Smarden, Kent, who were pardoned in July 1450 for having risen with Cade is particularly full, and of the 101 names recorded, 22 were employed in the cloth industry and 5 were described as cloth-makers.[97] Of those indicted in Wiltshire, 23 per cent were from the cloth industry in Edington and 17 per cent from Salisbury. Also indicted was James Touker of Bradford, yeoman. This was probably James Terumber or Touker, who became a wealthy clothier, trading with

93 Britnell, *Britain and Ireland*, p. 321.
94 Hare, 'Growth and Recession', p. 20.
95 Harvey, *Cade*, pp. 121–4.
96 J.N. Hare, 'The Wiltshire Risings of 1450: Political and Economic Discontent in Mid-Fifteenth Century England', *Southern History* 4 (1982), pp. 25–7.
97 *CPR 1446–52*, pp. 363–4.

a Venetian merchant at Bridport in 1463, and later endowing an almshouse. However at this stage in his career, he may have been a relatively small producer. It has been suggested that Terumber was a self-made man who rose from humble origins, possibly as a Bristol fuller.[98] Textile workers in Romsey (Hampshire), who fulled, dyed and mended cloth for Genoese merchants, and had established a cloth-finishing industry there, marched on Southampton to wreak vengeance on their Italian masters. Over in Suffolk and Essex, textile workers were also protesting, like the four fullers, three weavers and a mercer indicted at Hadleigh, and weavers from Great Tey and Bocking.[99] There does not, however, appear to be any reliable evidence to support Shakespeare's assertion that the rebel leader, John or Jack Cade, was a clothier: 'Jack Cade the clothier means to dress the commonwealth, and turn it, and set a new nap upon it.'[100] After Cade's death though, his corpse was beheaded and quarters were sent to be displayed at Norwich, Salisbury and Gloucester – three prominent cloth-making towns that were centres of the disturbances.[101]

Unrest continued to flare up during the decade, often involving clothworkers. Thomas Bright, a fuller from Canterbury, was accused of raising a rebellion in Kent in 1452. John Percy, a tailor from Erith in north-west Kent, led a revolt in 1456, and of those indicted, nearly a third were from the cloth trades, comprising tailors, weavers, fullers and clothiers. In 1453 the Percy family's cause in Yorkshire was supported by the citizens of York and rural textile workers, including tailors, fullers and dyers, whose interests had been damaged by the commercial recession.[102] Unrest against the newly established government of Edward IV in 1463–64 stretched across the west Cotswolds and the vale of Gloucester, including cloth-making centres such as Stroud and Tetbury, and one of the instigators was a fuller, Robert White.[103]

The Crises of the 1520s

The cloth trade experienced another series of disruptions during the 1520s. The industry was hit by falling demand following poor harvests across Europe in 1520 coupled with a trade embargo with the Low Countries. More difficulties followed in 1527, caused by grain shortages, and in 1528, with the expectation of a trade war with the Low Countries. The

98 Hare, *Prospering Society*, pp. 184–5, 204–5.

99 Harvey, *Cade*, pp. 118–19, 127–8; Poos, *Rural Society*, pp. 255–9.

100 2 Henry VI, Act IV, Scene 2, lines 4–6.

101 I.M.W. Harvey, 'Cade, John (*d.* 1450)', *ODNB*.

102 Lee, 'Crises', p. 331.

103 R.H. Hilton, *The English Peasantry in the Later Middle Ages: The Ford Lectures for 1973 and Related Studies* (Oxford, 1975), pp. 71–2.

impact of this period of disruption, while less severe than that of the mid fifteenth century, was still significant. Total cloth exports fell by 23 per cent between 1520 and 1521, by 17 per cent between 1521 and 1522, and by 5 per cent between 1525 and 1526, and these shocks led to unemployment and unrest in cloth-making districts. The greatest opposition arose in Suffolk, around the cloth-making centres of Lavenham and Sudbury, where clothiers had laid off their workers, but there was also passive resistance in Warwickshire, Berkshire, Wiltshire and Kent.[104]

By 1525, unprecedented levels of taxation were exacerbating the difficulties caused by the downturn in exports. Following loans in 1522, retrospectively converted into grants, and two subsidies assessed in 1524 and 1525, the Amicable Grant was to be levied on valuations of personal wealth compiled back in 1522 rather than on valuations made in 1525. The total raised in taxation between 1522 and 1527 has been estimated as accounting for one-third of the coinage in circulation.[105] Taxation reduced demand within the economy, and repeated taxation led to falling investment, unemployment and insolvencies. Even the wealthiest clothiers such as Thomas Spring III of Lavenham were affected.[106] The chronicler Edward Hall relates how after being assessed for the tax in 1525, the clothiers 'called to them their spinners, carders, fullers, weavers and other artificers … and said, sirs we be not able to set you a work our goods be taken from us'.[107] Shakespeare described the position a couple of generations later in his play, *Henry VIII*:

> for upon these taxations,
> The clothiers all, not able to maintain
> The many to them 'longing, have put off
> The spinsters, carders, fullers, weavers, who,
> Unfit for other life, compell'd by hunger
> And lack of other means, in desperate manner
> Daring th'event to th' teeth, are all in uproar,
> And danger serves among them.[108]

In Norwich it was feared that the tax would draw all the money out of

[104] A. Fletcher and D. MacCulloch, *Tudor Rebellions*, rev. 5th edn (London, 2008), p. 25; G.W. Bernard, *War, Taxation, and Rebellion in Early Tudor England: Henry VIII, Wolsey, and the Amicable Grant of 1525* (Brighton, 1986), pp. 136–48; D. MacCulloch, *Suffolk and the Tudors. Politics and Religion in an English County 1500–1600* (Oxford, 1986), pp. 291–7.

[105] R.W. Hoyle, 'Taxation and the Mid Tudor Crisis', *EcHR* 51 (1998), pp. 649–75.

[106] See below, Chapter 6.

[107] E. Hall, *The Union of the Two Noble and Illustre Famelies of Lancastre and Yorke* (London, 1809), p. 699.

[108] Henry VIII, Act 1, Scene 2, lines 30–6.

the city, preventing clothiers from paying their workers, and Warwickshire obtained a remission from the grant in April 1525.[109] The king was informed of the 'rebellious demeanour of the inhabitants of Lavenham, Sudbury and other towns thereabouts'.[110] Hall thought that the rebels numbered four thousand, but another chronicler, Ellis Griffith, reports that ten thousand gathered at Lavenham. Cardinal Wolsey was advised that 'a great part of this shire and of Essex … Cambridgeshire, the town of Cambridge and the scholars there' were ready to congregate on the ringing of bells, and twenty thousand people were thought to have assembled. Griffith suggests that the rebels in Lavenham had links with men in the towns of Kent. The dukes of Norfolk and Suffolk met with a group of the protestors from Lavenham and Brent Eleigh on 11 May. Dressed in their shirts and kneeling to demonstrate their obedience, the rebels explained to the dukes that their protests were 'only for lack of work so that they knew not how to get their living'.[111] The Crown issued a commission in July to inquire into 'all insurrections, riots, assemblies, confederations and illicit gatherings within the county of Berkshire', another centre of cloth-making.[112] Faced with this opposition, Henry VIII abandoned the grant, realising that his monarchy needed the support of the tax-paying classes, and probably also aware of contemporary events elsewhere in Europe, as following his account of the Amicable Grant the chronicler Hall remarked that 'in this troublous season the uplandish men of Germany … rose in a great number … and rebelled against the princes of Germany'.[113]

Over one-third of the rebels indicted for participating in the Suffolk uprising against the Amicable Grant in 1525 were textile workers, and the largest groups came from the cloth-making centres of Lavenham, Waldingfield and Long Melford. They included Thomas Sprunte, dyer of Lavenham, who had been assessed on goods of £30 and lands worth 10s. in 1522, but whose wealth had fallen to just £5 by 1524. The crisis in the cloth trade, combined with repeated taxation, had increased levels of poverty. In Lavenham, the proportion of the poor may have increased threefold in 1525. Wage earners numbered over half the taxable

[109] BL, Cotton MS, Cleopatra F.VI, fol. 268; Phythian-Adams, *Desolation*, p. 63.

[110] TNA, SP 1/34, fol. 174; *LP*, iv (1), no. 1319, p. 580.

[111] BL, Cotton MS, Cleopatra F.VI, fols 260–1; *LP*, iv (1), no. 1323, p. 583; Royal Commission on Historical Manuscripts, *Report on Manuscripts in the Welsh Language*, 2 vols (London, 1898–99), i, p. ii.

[112] TNA, STAC 10/4/144.

[113] Hall, *Union*, p. 702; Bernard, *War*, p. 147.

population there but owned less than 3 per cent of property, and many were probably out of work in 1525.[114]

With tax collections abandoned, the immediate crisis was averted but tensions increased again after another disastrous harvest in 1527. After disturbances in Stowmarket, the duke of Norfolk sought reassurance from the wealthier inhabitants of Lavenham that there was no similar unrest there.[115] In April 1528, Archbishop Wareham of Canterbury received a petition from the inhabitants of Kent asking for the king to repay the loan, which the archbishop undertook should be refunded to them as they were 'so impoverished by the great dearth of all manner of grains and corn'.[116] The Crown ordered a national survey of grain stocks and the few surviving returns show that shortages were particularly acute in Ballingdon (Essex), a poor suburb of the cloth-manufacturing town of Sudbury. Cloth-making centres that had moved away from arable cultivation and were more dependent on the grain market were particularly vulnerable at times of grain shortage, as demand for cloth fell when food prices rose. Such problems were to become especially acute during the severe harvest failures of the late 1590s in cloth-making areas of Essex, Devon and Westmorland.[117]

Another scare arose in 1528 when the London cloth market collapsed in the expectation of a trade war with the Netherlands.[118] Merchants withdrew from the market, and clothiers were again forced to lay off their employees. Hall describes how merchants had been unable to venture to Spain since the previous April, and consequently,

> the Clothiers of Essex, Kent, Wiltshire, Suffolk & other shires which use cloth-making, brought clothes into Blackwell Hall of London, to be sold as they were wont to do: few merchants or none bought any cloth at all. When the clothiers lacked sale, then they put from them their spinners, carders, tuckers & such other that live by

[114] J.F. Pound, 'Rebellion and Poverty in 16th Century Suffolk: The 1525 Uprising against the Amicable Grant', *Proceedings of the Suffolk Institute of Archaeology* 39 (1999), pp. 317–30.

[115] TNA, SP 1/45, fol. 266; *LP*, iv (2), no. 3703, p. 1659.

[116] TNA, SP 1/47, fol. 191; *LP*, iv (2), no. 4173, pp. 1843–4.

[117] Lee, 'Grain Shortages'; David Dymond, 'The Famine of 1527 in Essex', *Local Population Studies* 26 (1981), p. 37; P. Slack, 'Mortality Crises and Epidemic Disease in England, 1485–1610', in C. Webster, ed., *Health, Medicine and Mortality in the Late Sixteenth Century* (Cambridge, 1979), pp. 53–4.

[118] For the wider background, see S.J. Gunn, 'Wolsey's Foreign Policy and the Domestic Crisis of 1527–8', in S.J. Gunn and P.G. Lindley, eds, *Cardinal Wolsey: Church, State and Art* (Cambridge, 1991), pp. 149–77.

cloth-working, which caused the people greatly to murmur, and specially in Suffolk.[119]

The Colchester clothier John Boswell wrote to Thomas Sammys in March that he could not sell a cloth even at half the cost price, and had scant money to pay his spinners. Boswell was in debt to Sammys for wool and needed more time in which to pay. When trying to sell his cloth at Blackwell Hall, a London merchant had told him that he thought the only remedy would be if the commons rose and complained to the king that 'they be not half set awork'.[120] Humfrey Monmouth, London draper and cloth exporter, explained in May 1528 how the interruption of trade with Burgundy had hit his own sales and the cloth-men in Suffolk that he traded with, who would be unable to employ their workers.[121] Nationally, exports fell from 99,500 cloths in 1528 to under 82,000 by 1532, before recovering again. Yet despite these pockets of unrest, there were no major disturbances. The monarchy was in a far stronger position than in the 1450s, and was able to use the aristocracy in the provinces to prevent unrest spreading.

We can see much more clearly than in the 1450s that the uprisings in the 1520s were by cloth-workers rather than clothiers. Of the 118 cloth-workers indicted for the rebellion in Suffolk in 1525, only one was recorded as a clothier.[122] Sir John Spring and Thomas Jermyn, the son and son in-law of the clothier Thomas Spring III, acted to restrain the population in 1525. Hall noted that 'Master Jermyn took much pain in riding and going between the lords and commons'.[123] Clothiers were also supplying the government with intelligence about the situation, although not necessarily willingly. In May 1527, the king's council instructed Thomas More to observe the cloth trade at Blackwell Hall and 'to report the demeanour both of Londoners and clothiers in buying and selling'.[124] In May 1528, John Andrew of Cranbrook, clothier, was sent to Wolsey to tell 'the whole truth' about reports of seditious behaviour in Goudhurst and Cranbrook, and although two cloth-makers were implicated, they were not among those attainted in Rochester at Whitsuntide.[125]

Facing unrest in Suffolk, the duke of Norfolk suggested to Cardinal Wolsey that he might cause 'the merchants of London not to suffer so

119 Hall, *Union*, p. 745.

120 TNA, SP 1/47, fols 152, 163; *LP*, iv (2), no. 4129 (ii), p. 1826, no. 4145 (ii), p. 1831.

121 Quoted above, p. 77.

122 Pound, 'Rebellion and Poverty', p. 329.

123 Hall, *Union*, p. 700.

124 The Huntington Library, San Marino, California, Ellesmere MS 2652, fol. 12.

125 *LP*, iv (2), no. 4287, p. 1886, no. 4301, p. 1891, no. 4310, pp. 1893–4, no. 4331, p. 1903.

many cloths to lie in Blackwell Hall unbought', and the Gloucestershire gentry asked Wolsey to create an opportunity for cloth to be sold.[126] Wolsey tried to pressurise the London merchants to continue buying cloth despite the market downturn:

> where the Clothiers do daily bring cloths, to your market for your ease, to their great cost, and there be ready to sell them, you of your wilfulness will not buy them, as you have been accustomed to do: what manner of men be you said the Cardinal?[127]

Wolsey threatened to break the privileges of Blackwell Hall, saying that the king would buy all the stock and sell it to foreign merchants. The clothiers apparently tried unsuccessfully to profit from this situation:

> When the Clothiers heard that the Cardinal took their part, they waxed proud, and spoke evil of the merchants, and when the merchants came to buy cloths the clothiers set them higher than they were accustomed to be sold: but at length they were fain, both to abate the price, and also to seek of the merchant men, for all the Cardinal's saying.[128]

The French ambassador though, reported that although the merchants had 'conspired' not to buy from the peasants, after being threatened by Wolsey, they had promised that at the next Wednesday market 'there shall not remain a crown's worth of merchandise'.[129]

In 1528, leading noblemen monitored the textile industry in particular localities, and met with clothiers to persuade or even order them to retain their workforce. In March, the duke of Norfolk met with forty of the most substantial local clothiers of the area around Stoke-by-Nayland, and 'with the best words I could use persuaded them to continue the setting of their workfolks on work' and to take back servants they had laid off. The duke added that if he had not quashed rumours of the arrests of English merchants in Spain and Flanders, he would have had two or three hundred women suing him to make the clothiers set their husbands and children to work.[130] Yet by May, the duke reported to Cardinal Wolsey that local clothiers were complaining that unless they could sell their cloths in London, they would be unable to 'set their workfolks on work' for more than a fortnight or three weeks. The problem was compounded, the clothiers argued, by a scarcity of oil, which unless supplies came from Spain, would force them to give up making cloth.[131]

126 TNA, SP 1/47, fols 83v, 113; *LP*, iv (2), no. 4044, p. 1796, no. 4085, p. 1807.
127 Hall, *Union*, p. 746.
128 Hall, *Union*, p. 746.
129 *LP*, iv (2), no. 3930, p. 1749.
130 TNA, SP 1/47, fol. 83; *LP*, iv (2), no. 4044, p. 1796.
131 TNA, SP 1/48, fol. 1; *LP*, iv (2), no. 4239, p. 1868.

This suggests that the trade dispute had also hit imports of raw materials essential to the cloth-making process. Around the same time, Sir Henry Guildford also warned Wolsey that the clothiers of Kent were about to lay off workers due to the depressed state of the market:

> The clothiers as they say hath so ill utterance of their cloth so that they be not able to keep so many on work as they have done in times past. And if they be driven by necessity to leave their occupation a great company shall be set to idleness.[132]

With his brothers, he 'handled' the clothiers so that until harvest they would not 'slack any part of their occupation or put away any of their folk'. He hoped, however, that Wolsey would find some remedy, for the clothiers would not be able to continue for long.[133] Similar sentiments were expressed by Thomas Lord Berkeley and other gentry in Gloucestershire. William Lord Sandys advised that no clothiers would be permitted to discharge workers in Hampshire, and he hoped that Berkshire and Wiltshire would be equally well managed. Unlawful assemblies, however, were reported during spring 1528 at Westbury and Devizes, insurrections at Taunton and Bridgwater, and disturbances in Kent, before the government was able to agree a truce with the Low Countries in June.[134]

Other early-sixteenth-century crises

The fear of revolt by cloth-workers haunted leaders at times of unrest. Richard Fox (1447/8–1528), bishop of Winchester, warned Cardinal Wolsey in 1517 that following disturbances in Southampton, he thought that any commotion in Hampshire, Wiltshire, Berkshire or Somerset, 'shall be by the means of weavers, fullers, shearmen and other journeymen artificers and servants for cloth-makers'. Fox suggested that making proclamations in these counties would help prevent unrest:

> if there be proclamations sent and made in the said shires, that clothiers shall have their liberty in buying of wool, and that the said artificers and journeymen be paid for their labours and works by the said clothiers in ready money and not in wares, according to the statutes in both cases provided, I doubt not it shall put them in great quietness and comfort and avoid the occasions of all such commotions.[135]

Similar proclamations were probably made in Lincolnshire during the

132 TNA, SP 1/48, fol. 24; *LP*, iv (2), no. 4276, p. 1881.

133 TNA, SP 1/48, fol. 24.

134 TNA, SP 1/47, fols 82, 93, 113; *LP*, iv (2), no. 4043, p. 1796, no. 4058, p. 1799, no. 4085, p. 1807, no. 4141, p. 1830, nos. 4188–90, pp. 1850–1, no. 4377, p. 1919.

135 *Letters of Richard Fox*, eds Allen and Allen, pp. 98–9.

period of unrest that preceded the Pilgrimage of Grace in 1536. Fearful of the resentment by clothiers and workers at the act fixing the breadth of cloth,[136] the duke of Norfolk told the royal council in October that 'light persons rejoice at this business in Lincolnshire, and that if I had not come, and the proclamation for cloth-making been made, some business might have chanced'. He had been advised that 'the young clothiers are very light'. The following day, he recommended that if the earl of Oxford 'make sure of his town of Lavenham, the rest of these parts will be safe'. He would stop anyone from Boston 'trusting to the clothiers of Suffolk'. Norfolk was referring to cloth-workers rather than wealthy clothiers. Indeed, as in 1525, he relied on help from John Spring and Sir Thomas Jermyn, the son and son-in-law of the clothier Thomas Spring III.[137] Spring and Jermyn were to provide men to oppose the rebels, as were clothiers Stephen Draner of Cranbrook and John Winchcombe of Newbury.[138] In August 1536, Sir John Allen, mayor of London, even suggested that the government make a loan of £10,000 to promote the sale of goods at St Bartholomew's cloth fair. A mercer and merchant adventurer,[139] Allen warned that

> many sellers of cloth come to this city … they shall have very flat sale … by reason whereof they have showed unto me that they must be fain [obliged] to discharge their workmen for lack of money if some remedy in that behalf be not provided by the king.[140]

Such a sum of money, Allen argued, would 'cause many a man, women and children to be set awork, the which will beg or steal, if a remedy be not found'.[141]

A deeper depression hit the cloth trade in 1550, following nearly a decade of heavy taxation, forced loans and inflation. The drop in demand was accompanied by a rapid fall in the value of sterling, while from March to July 1551, sweating sickness caused many deaths. Trade and the exchange rate recovered from 1552 onwards, but the cloth industry never experienced such a peak again and became subject to severe fluctuations. The London Merchant Adventurers used the crisis to increase their dominance: between 1550 and 1564, they gained control of three-quarters of exports of English cloth from London. The privileges of the Hanseatic League were revoked and the trading rights of Italian

[136] See pp. 165, 259.
[137] TNA, SP 1/107, fols 83, 118; *LP*, xi, nos. 603, 625, pp. 243, 250.
[138] TNA, SP 1/107, fols 43, 47v, SP 1/113, fol. 209v; *LP*, xi, no. 580, pp. 223–4, App. 8, p. 594.
[139] Elizabeth Lane Furdell, 'Allen, Sir John (*c.*1470–1544)', *ODNB*.
[140] TNA, SP 1/95, fol. 131. *LP*, ix, no. 152, p. 44 misdates this letter to August 1535.
[141] TNA, SP 1/95, fol. 131.

merchants were restricted. The crown cooperated because new customs rates introduced in 1558 increased the duties payable on undyed cloths by English exporters from 14d to 6s 8d per cloth, and from 2s 9d to 14s 9d for exports by overseas merchants, securing the queen a customs' income of £30,000.[142]

In this instance, unrest preceded a slump in overseas trade, although possibly not in domestic trade, which cannot be readily quantified. Recent research has revealed that the rebellion led by Robert Kett in Norfolk in 1549, largely in response to the enclosure of land, was part of a wider crisis involving several cloth-making areas. Residents from Lavenham and Hadleigh supported the rebel camp at Bury St Edmunds. Some two hundred artificers threw down hedges and fences at the cloth-making centre of Frome, which led to disaffection spreading across Somerset and Wiltshire. The weavers of Kent complained that their wives and children could not get a living because clothiers had also become weavers. The journeymen weavers of Worcester protested that they had been laid off, despite a previous arrangement that each loom should be worked by one journeyman and one apprentice, because apprentices were cheaper to keep as they did not require wages to support their wives and children. Other complaints were that 'artificers and clothiers were now also ploughmen and graziers' and that clothiers were not paying poor labourers in money. The Council's instructions to Lord Russell when he was dispatched to the west in June 1549 was to ensure that clothiers, dyers, weavers, fullers and other artificers were kept occupied.[143]

The parliamentary legislation of the 1550s, including the cloth-making statute of 1552 and the weavers' act of 1555, were passed in response to this crisis. Reflecting many long-standing concerns, these statutes proposed many traditional remedies. The state once again attempted to insist that clothiers continue to operate their businesses. The act of 1552 legislated that no clothier may cease his business between 1 May and Michaelmas 1552 without licence from three JPs or borough officers, on pain of not being permitted to operate as a clothier in future.[144] Although there is no evidence that this specific provision was ever enforced, similar orders were issued in May 1556, when the council advised the Crown that

> in certain parts clothiers put out of their houses some of their servants, partly to reduce household costs in this dear harvest, partly because

[142] Sutton, *Mercery*, pp. 420–4; J.D. Gould, *The Great Debasement: Currency and Economy in Mid-Tudor England* (Oxford, 1970), pp. 114–60.

[143] Smith, *Discourse of the Common Weal*, pp. lxv–lxvi, 21, 48. MacCulloch, *Suffolk and the Tudors*, p. 305; Amanda Jones, '"Commotion time": The English Risings of 1549', University of Warwick, Ph.D. thesis, 2003, pp. 85–6, 91–2, 280–1.

[144] Zell, 'Parliament', p. 80.

> work (as all else) is so expensive, order is given to magistrates of all places where cloth is made to summon the cloth-makers and order them to retain their workers; which order, we understand, is obeyed in all places.[145]

Similar instructions had been given back in 1528, when the king ordered Lord Sandys to be vigilant that no cloth-maker discharge any artificer that they had 'put in occupation about the draping of their cloths by reason whereof any unlawful assembly might arise to the violation of the peace', and the duke of Norfolk had persuaded Suffolk clothiers to continue providing work to their labour force and to take back the servants that they had laid off.[146]

CONCLUSION

The role of the clothier in government reflected the range of wealth and backgrounds of these individuals. The urban-based clothier might find himself lobbying to safeguard the interests of his borough and promoting civic and parliamentary legislation to protect local industry. His interests might differ if he relied on rural labour or was based outside a major town, in which case he might find his operations conflicting with this legislation. All clothiers though, had to operate within the same legislative environment in the cloth industry. Some clothiers helped shape this legislation while others challenged national statutes that failed to take account of local peculiarities.

All clothiers were also affected by the periodic disruptions to markets, particularly in the mid fifteenth century, the 1520s and the 1550s, but it seems that very few clothiers joined other cloth-workers in armed protest, and some even supplied intelligence to the government about the uprisings or acted to restrain the local populace. The evidence does not suggest that the clothiers deliberately stirred up their workers into protesting in the hope that disturbances would lead to favourable concessions by the Crown, such as a reduction or cancellation of taxation being levied. There is no sign of any conspiracy between clothiers and their workers.

What is evident though during these political crises is the fragile nature of the clothiers' business operations. Clothiers offered credit to London merchants and other buyers, with sales usually secured by providing delivery of cloth before payment. When these relationships

[145] TNA, SP 11/8, fol. 83; *Calendar of State Papers, Domestic Series, of the Reign of Mary I, 1553–1558*, pp. 204–5.

[146] TNA, SP 1/47, fols 83, 93; *LP*, iv (2), no. 4044, p. 1796, no. 4058, p. 1799.

collapsed during crises, clothiers were unable to pay their cloth-workers. In 1528, for example, the king was informed that clothiers' servants and others had assembled in unlawful numbers around Westbury, 'by reason their masters have not payment of such sums as be owing unto them for their cloths in London and other places, they be expelled from their work, having no means to get their living'.[147] The putting-out system relied on outworkers, whom the clothier only paid when work was available, and on keeping labour costs low. John Green, who acted as a spokesman for the Suffolk rebels in 1525, explained to the duke of Norfolk that the clothiers 'give us so little wages for our workmanship, that scarcely we be able to live, and thus in penury we pass the time, we our wives and children'. He added that the clothiers had 'put all these people, and a far greater number [than were assembled there] from work'.[148] The crises illustrate the vulnerable nature of the textile industry, where a sudden shock could have a rapid and marked effect on employment. With the growth of the medieval clothier and the associated cloth trade, governments had to face the consequences of communities largely dependent on the fortunes of distant markets for their livelihoods.

[147] TNA, SP 1/47, fol. 82.
[148] Hall, *Chronicle*, p. 700.

5

Clothiers in society

This chapter examines the roles of clothiers in wider society. Their family backgrounds, houses and workshops, and activities as farmers and landowners are explored, as are their religious beliefs and commemorative practices. Historians have frequently attempted to categorise groups within medieval society and identify defining characteristics. They have considered merchants who traded in goods separately from craftworkers and artisans who likewise produced goods and traded. Similarly, those earning a living from the land have been categorised differently from those earning a living from crafts and industry. Medieval houses are differentiated in terms of urban and rural locations, agricultural and mercantile functions, and peasant and middling-class ownership. A specific merchant approach to life and death, and a distinctive merchant culture have been identified.[1] Clothiers, however, straddled all these boundaries. Any consideration of the role of clothiers within society, therefore, needs to range widely, viewing as broadly as possible the limited evidence at our disposal.

FAMILY BACKGROUNDS

The absence of detailed biographical information about many clothiers makes tracing their origins difficult. Michael Zell's detailed study of clothiers in the Weald of Kent around 1500 found that these clothiers tended to be the sons or nephews of clothiers, or the sons of relatively prosperous farmers, traders and artisans, whose families could afford the premium for apprenticeship and the capital needed to set up a cloth-making business. Inheriting a smallholding with a house and outbuildings to store materials and carry out some cloth-making tasks was also an advantage.[2] The backgrounds of the leading clothiers of the

[1] P.J.P. Goldberg, 'The Fashioning of Bourgeois Domesticity in Later Medieval England: A Material Culture Perspective', in Maryanne Kowaleski and Jeremy Goldberg, eds, *Medieval Domesticity* (Cambridge, 2008), pp. 124–44; Barron and Sutton, eds, *Medieval Merchant*; Dyer, *Standards of Living*.

[2] Zell, *Industry*, pp. 191–2.

later Middle Ages, who are among the best documented, suggest that many of these men came from families of farmers and artisans. Thomas Paycocke's father and grandfather were butchers, while Thomas Spring I may have been a sheep farmer; William Stumpe's father was a weaver and his brother a husbandman.[3]

Gervase Amyot (d. 1537) of Benenden in Kent provides a good example of a clothier of more modest wealth from an agricultural background. His grandfather Stephen Amyot of Benenden was a small farmer who left his son Thomas, Gervase's father, a house and lands in 1489. Stephen also had sufficient wealth to leave in his will £1 for repairs to highways and 5 marks to employ a chantry priest for half a year. Thomas Aymot, also a farmer, had two daughters and four sons, including Gervase, the eldest, who he apprenticed to a clothier. Thomas died in 1520 and bequeathed his house and lands to Gervase, who was instructed to pay £10 each to his three younger brothers over a period of thirteen years. Gervase was assessed at £3 per year in lands in the 1524/5 lay subsidy rolls, and his two younger brothers, who worked for him, were listed as servants. Gervase married Benet, the daughter of Matthew Hartrege, a freeholder and farmer in Cranbrook. When Gervase died in 1537, his business probably remained relatively small, as his main bequests were 10 marks to each of his three sons and his daughter, and £1 to his sole apprentice. He still owned land, but little more than his father had provided for him. Gervase had operated a modest, family-based cloth-making business.[4]

Even in more remote upland areas like the Lake District, over several generations some clothier families could expand their businesses and seize opportunities to acquire property. In 1480, when several new fulling mills were appearing in the parish, John Benson, a manorial reeve, bought a freehold tenement in Grasmere. He and two other members of his family paid rents for 'intakes', or enclosures of waste fell-land in Langdale in 1506–7, possibly to stretch and dry their cloths on tenters. The family bought the manor of Baisbrown and its mills in 1546 after the dissolution of Conishead Priory. William Benson, who made his will in 1568, had become a wealthy trader in Kendal, while three other family members are described as clothiers in 1575 when they bought much of Loughrigg.[5]

Some clothiers started as weavers, fullers, dyers or other cloth-workers. John Horrold, a clothier of Clare (d. 1478), began as a weaver. The career

[3] See below, Chapter 6.

[4] KHLC, PRC 17/5 fol. 177, PRC 17/14, fols 110v–111, PRC 17/21, fols 69–70v; Zell, *Industry*, p. 192.

[5] Armitt, 'Fullers and Freeholders', pp. 141–7; Schofield and Vannan, *Windermere Reflections*, p. 15.

of Laurence Dowe of Long Melford was similar: he was recorded as a weaver in 1475 and as a clothier five years later.[6] James Terumber of Bradford-on-Avon and Trowbridge, described by John Leland as 'a very rich clothier', may have been a Bristol fuller who migrated up the Avon to Bradford and Trowbridge to exploit the opportunities there, returning to reside at Bristol at the end of his life.[7]

Through apprenticeship, or training at home, a clothier would learn his craft. A young clothier may have begun his career at 14 or 15 years of age with an apprenticeship of up to seven years. As an apprentice, he would have learned the essential skills of his trade such as selecting and grading wool, weaving, dyeing and marketing. The apprenticeship also enabled the future clothier to develop useful business links. Unfortunately, there is little surviving evidence for apprenticeships other than bequests in wills of clothiers who died leaving under-age sons. In his will of 1527, Stephen Pattenden of Rolvenden in Kent requested that his son John attend school until he was fifteen years old, and then be apprenticed to John Sharpe of Cranbrook, 'or some other honest man to learn weaving and cloth-making'. Similarly George Fyllype of Tenterden, who died in 1551, directed that when his son George attained the age of fifteen, his executors should 'provide for him some honest master in the occupation of cloth-making and to dwell with and to serve him' for five years.[8] Other specialised cloth-workers often served apprenticeships, and larger boroughs established rigid rules for such trades.[9] Following their apprenticeship, cloth-workers might move to another part of the country, like William Ball, who lived at Dewsbury in Yorkshire in 1543, but who had learned his craft as a shearman as an apprentice in Suffolk.[10] When the training ended, a young clothier might set up alone, but in many cases they worked as journeymen for established clothiers for several years before starting their own business.

It was taken for granted that wives working within the household would help in their husband's craft or trade, although this is often difficult to identify from the records. Women took roles in marketing as well as manufacture. Women who worked independently, and working widows, were described as *femmes soles*, responsible for their own business and their own debts.[11] In his will of 1478, John Horrold of Clare stipulated

6 Amor, *From Wool to Cloth*, p. 193.

7 *VCH Wiltshire*, iv, pp. 134–6.

8 KHLC, PRC 32/15 fol. 32 (Pattenden), PRC 32/24, fol. 71 (Fyllype).

9 See above, Chapter 4.

10 A.G. Dickens, *Lollards and Protestants in the Diocese of York, 1509–1558* (Oxford, 1959), p. 27.

11 Ward, 'Townswomen', pp. 38–9; Caroline M. Barron and Anne F. Sutton, eds, *Medieval London Widows, 1300–1500* (London, 1994).

that his wife Agnes was to pay the executor for bills that she had incurred, including debts of £18 and £22 to two Londoners. John left Agnes his dwelling place in the market in Clare, with his goods, looms and wool, both worked and unworked.[12] Widows might continue their husbands' businesses. Some remained in business for only a short time, winding up their husbands' affairs and enabling a son or other family member to take over, while others continued for many years. In Wells, for example, the ulnage accounts of 1395–96 record sizeable cloth sales by the recently widowed Janna Shorthose, as well as by Agnes Schecher, who had been involved in business activities for many years since her husband died.[13] Account books provide examples of widows and relatives attempting to continue supplying cloth to merchants. Mary, the daughter of John Clevelod of Beckington, and the widows of John Kent of Bath and Roger Blackdon of Farleigh Hungerford, tried to supply Thomas Kitson after the deaths of their respective clothier husbands, but seem to have been unable to deliver the quantity this London mercer required. A widow Ann Abeck of Manchester provided 150 'Manchester' cloths to John Smythe of Bristol in 1547 after the death of her husband Thomas, who had previously supplied Smythe with the same types of cloth.[14]

The most famous cloth-making widow is the Wife of Bath, Alisoun, one of the fictional characters that Geoffrey Chaucer (c.1340–1400) included within his best-known work, *The Canterbury Tales*. Chaucer notes that she lived 'beside Bath' and describes her big hat, fine scarlet stockings, and five husbands. He writes, 'Of cloth-making she had such skill, She surpassed them of Ypres and Ghent'.[15] Through his work as a senior customs official, with responsibility for the trade in wool, hides and skins at the port of London, Chaucer would have developed a detailed knowledge of the wool and cloth trade, and indeed another of his characters, the merchant, is an exporter of wool. The precise nature of the Wife of Bath's role in the textile industry, though, has been much debated. The economic historian Eleanora Carus-Wilson described her as a 'west-country clothier, that redoubtable goodwife living near Bath', a view supported by the literature scholars Mary Carruthers and David Robertson.[16] Others, however, have seen the Wife as simply a weaver, interpreted the comparison to the great cloth-making centres of Ypres

[12] Thornton, *Clare*, pp. 181–2.

[13] Shaw, *Wells*, p. 72.

[14] Brett, 'Wiltshire Clothmen', pp. 39–40; *Ledger of John Smythe*, pp. 207, 297.

[15] Chaucer, *Wife of Bath*, p. 42 (General Prologue, lines 447–8).

[16] E.M. Carus-Wilson, 'Trends in the Export of English Woollens in the Fourteenth Century', *EcHR*, 2nd series 3 (1950), p. 177, reprinted in Carus-Wilson, *Medieval Merchant Venturers*, p. 262; Mary Carruthers, 'The Wife of Bath and the Painting of Lions', *PMLA: Publications of the Modern Language Association of*

and Ghent in Flanders as an empty boast or a mockery of her achievements, and suggested that Chaucer chose Bath not for its cloth-making, but as a pun.[17]

HOUSES AND WORKSHOPS

The clothier required a building appropriate for three purposes. Firstly, there needed to be space for cloth-making processes to be carried out and for storage of raw materials, processed and finished products; secondly, rooms for the display and sale of finished products; and thirdly, domestic accommodation for the clothier's family and servants. Although business and manufacturing were often undertaken within the home, not all of these activities were necessarily accommodated in one building, as much depended on the wealth of the individual clothier and the nature of his trade.

The small clothier, carrying out weaving himself, often simply created additional space for manufacture and storage within his house by extending the main living space, or adding an additional room. As these smaller producers lacked the resources and marketing contacts of the wealthier clothiers, their houses did not need to accommodate large storage spaces or rooms to display finished products. The main living room might be enlarged to provide extra space near the heat and light of the fire, but out of the way of domestic activities. A window, which could be the largest in the house, was often inserted. Alternatively, a separate room might be added as a work place.[18] Aisled houses with an additional room that may have been used for cloth-making purposes are found scattered across a wide area of West Yorkshire but overwhelmingly in the upper Calder valley, which forms the hinterland of Halifax. The majority of these aisled houses have been dated to the century between 1475 and 1575, and it has been suggested that these were related to the rapid expansion of the local cloth industry. The lower rooms of these aisled houses were used as workshops for cloth-making and for storage, and as these rooms tended to be sited on the north side of their houses, they would

America 94, No. 2 (1979), p. 210; D.W. Robertson, '"And for my land thus hastow mordred me?" Land Tenure, the Cloth Industry, and the Wife of Bath', *Chaucer Review* 14 (1980), p. 415.

17 In referring to Bath, as part of the diocese of Bath and Wells, Chaucer may have been alluding both to a bathhouse, a place of sexual encounters, and to the well where Jesus met a Samaritan woman, who like Alisoun had five husbands: Chaucer, *The Wife of Bath*, pp. 134–5; Stephen Rigby, ed., *Historians on Chaucer. The 'General Prologue' to the* Canterbury Tales (Oxford, 2014), pp. 321–2, and n. 10.

18 R.W. Brunskill, *Vernacular Architecture: An Illustrated Handbook*, 4th edn (London, 2000), pp. 180–1.

have provided a cool environment for the latter.[19] Bank House, Halifax, provides a notable example. It was probably built for the Waterhouse family, perhaps after 1534 when Robert Waterhouse bought the half share of the Bank House estate not already in his ownership. On his death in 1553, Robert owned a messuage called Bank House, a barn, fulling mill, and other property. The main living space of the sixteenth-century timber-framed aisled house is preserved within the seventeenth-century stone house. Another late medieval timber-framed aisled hall is encased in stone at Broad Bottom Old Hall, Mytholmroyd. This was held by the Draper family from the fourteenth century. The clothier Henry Draper (d. 1536) bought a fulling mill in 1517.[20] It has been questioned, however, if this type of house can always be associated with yeoman-clothiers, particularly as recent surveys have identified more aisled houses across a wider area.[21]

In urban locations, spaces to accommodate cloth-making processes, storage and marketing were generally found in shops fronting the street. Shops varied in form and function: some may have been little more than stalls opened on market day, while others served as showrooms for wealthy merchants. The majority, though, operated primarily as manufacturing workshops rather than retail premises, with production rather than selling being the main activity. These small, cramped spaces might be attached to domestic houses on the street and in rear yards, or could be lock-ups positioned in and around marketplaces. Many shops were probably used for the manufacture of cloth. Wealthier clothiers may have owned several of these units, while a poorer clothier may have based his business from one. A surviving example of a shop attached to a domestic house from the fifteenth or early sixteenth century is at 26 Market Place, Lavenham, Suffolk. This is a two-storey timber-framed and plastered building with a tiled roof. The upper storey is jettied on the front. The shop extended to 12 feet by 8 feet. It was lit by two wide openings that lacked glazing. Single hinged shutters, hooked to the ceiling during the day, would have been lowered at night (external hinged shutters were added later). While these windows could have provided retail display,

[19] Royal Commission for Historical Monuments England, *Rural Houses of West Yorkshire 1400–1830* (London, 1986), pp. 33–6; Ruth Harman and Nikolaus Pevsner, *The Buildings of England: Yorkshire West Riding: Sheffield and the South* (London, 2017), pp. 31–2.

[20] *Halifax Wills*, i, p. 189; *Rural Houses of West Yorkshire*, pp. 29, 33; Harman and Pevsner, *Yorkshire West Riding*, pp. 302, 414. NHLE 1313994 (Bank House, Bank House Lane, Salterhebble, Halifax), 1279330 (Broad Bottom Old Hall, Broad Bottom Lane, Mytholmroyd).

[21] Colum Giles, *Research Agenda: Historic Buildings in West Yorkshire (Medieval & Post-Medieval to 1914)* (West Yorkshire Joint Services, West Yorkshire Archaeology Advisory Service, 2013), p. 100.

their primary function was to admit as much light as possible into the workshop in the absence of adequate artificial lighting. A narrow door opened directly into the shop to the right of the windows, and another from inside the house. Wills sometimes describe tools and equipment left in shops. In Lavenham, Elizabeth Branch left two looms in her shop in 1501, and Roger Critoft left looms and equipment from his in 1537.[22]

The smallest of these types of spaces were single unit lock-up shops, constructed either as stand-alone units or within other public buildings. Guildhalls, market halls and court halls were usually located in prime commercial locations and to raise funds for their owners; they often had associated shop units on the lower storey and meeting halls above. Two bays of a chamber beneath the moot hall in the marketplace at Clare were let in 1386 to John Cardemakere, who presumably made and sold carding combs for straightening wool fibres. These shop units were as likely to be manufacturing workshops as retail outlets. Two medieval shop windows with internal oak shutters still survive in the passage of the fourteenth-century Trinity Guildhall in Felsted, Essex.[23]

Warehouses, and sometimes even workshops, were also to be found in the rear courtyards of the houses of wealthier clothiers, along with stables and kitchens. Although most courtyards were accessed through hall cross-passages, some were provided with separate street gateways. Six of these gateways survive in Lavenham. The courtyards often feature small 'lock-up' rooms with large open spaces above reached by wide stairs. The upper floors were probably used for storage of wool, dyestuffs and finished cloth, where these bulky items would have been less prone to damp, although some upper storey rooms had wide arched windows, suggesting that they were used for weaving or preparing yarn. At Dedham, the long rear range of the house that became the Marlborough Head Inn may have been used in connection with the cloth trade. Southfields, also in Dedham, has late-fifteenth- or early-sixteenth-century ranges that appear to be for industrial purposes attached to very high-status accommodation. This seems to have been a wealthy clothier's house, with warehouses and workshops constructed around a courtyard. By 1583, when the property was divided between the sons of the clothier John Wood (d. 1577), there was also a north range with a gallery and chamber over

[22] NHLE 1181069 (26 Market Place, Lavenham); D.F. Stenning, 'Timber-framed Shops 1300–1600: Comparative Plans', *Vernacular Architecture* (1985), pp. 16, 35–9; Alston, 'Late Medieval Workshops in East Anglia', pp. 39–41.

[23] NHLE 1146621 (Old School Room, Braintree Road, Felsted); Alston, 'Late Medieval Workshops in East Anglia', pp. 54–8; David Clark, 'The Shop Within?: An Analysis of the Architectural Evidence for Medieval Shops', *Architectural History* 43 (2000), pp. 75–6; Kathryn A. Morrison, *English Shops and Shopping* (London, 2003), pp. 24–5.

the gatehouse, as well as a weighing house and burling shop (to remove knots from cloth). A similar courtyard building, also in Essex, Penns at Boxted, belonged to a clothier family. The building no longer exists, but was depicted on a map of 1586 as a heated range with cross wings, and two additional ranges for warehousing or industrial premises, around an open courtyard.[24] Another surviving example is Alston Court, Nayland, which contains a fully enclosed sixteenth-century courtyard behind the hall, and on the west side, a service wing that included workshops and probably a dye-house. Many rear courtyards also contained tenter frames for broadcloth to be stretched and dried after fulling. Roofs extended from jetties to provide dry passages between courtyard doors. Robert Trippe, a clothier of Lavenham, bequeathed a tenter yard with a shop and access through his house in 1549.[25]

In some locations, watercourses were constructed or diverted to provide supplies for cloth processing and dyeing. Thomas Horton's house in Bradford-on-Avon, now forming the annex to a late-eighteenth-century building known as Abbey House, seems to have been constructed on a site with a stream running through. The brick culverts that run under some of the main streets in Lavenham are likely to have been used for cloth-making purposes, but a recent survey was unable to date the Water Street culvert securely to the later Middle Ages, and it is possible that this watercourse remained open or was lined, and only specific properties invested in building over the channel to enable them to encroach on to the street frontage.[26] Like some other urban craftsmen, clothiers occasionally constructed their own piped water supplies. In Colchester, Henry Webb obtained permissions in 1535 and 1545 to bring water to his house on North Street, probably to the building that is now the Marquis of Granby Inn, and in 1549 Nicholas Maynard had a water conduit running from the river Colne 'on certain pipes of lead or wood joined together' to the house in East Street where he worked 'dyeing and washing wool' for cloth-making. John Winchcombe II sold a conduit

[24] NHLE 1239285 (Loom House Marlborough Head Inn, High Street, Dedham), 1239217 (Southfields The Flemish Cottages, The Drift, Dedham); Bettley and Pevsner, *Essex*, p. 323; *VCH Essex*, x, pp. 57–8, 161–4; Thornton, 'Paycocke's House', p. 85.

[25] NHLE 1033571 (Alston Court, High Street, Nayland); James Bettley and Nikolaus Pevsner, *The Buildings of England: Suffolk: West* (London, 2015), pp. 417–18; Alston, 'Late Medieval Workshops in East Anglia', pp. 49–54.

[26] Betterton and Dymond, *Lavenham*, p. 34; Fradley, 'Water Street'; Bradford-on-Avon – History website, http://www.freshford.com/10_horton_house.htm

house and conduit leading from the river Kennet to serve a tenement in Newbury in 1557.[27]

Storage

Wills and inventories show that clothiers stored a range of raw materials and cloths on their premises. The clothier Robert Rychard of Dursley's items of highest value, totalling £121, were kept in his warehouse. Sixteen whole red cloths, three whole white cloths, madder, alum, a weigh beam and pulleys were listed in 1492, together with three packs of red cloth at London.[28] The Lavenham clothier Thomas Stansby (d. 1518) referred to 'my white wool within my house and all my woad and oil within my house', and John Barker, also from Lavenham, in 1544 left 'all my wool and yarn both white and coloured which I have this present day within my house'.[29] The Old Grammar School in Lavenham contains a first-floor hall chamber that was probably used as a purpose-built warehouse for the storage of cloth and wool. Its lack of daylight would have prevented dyed wool, yarn and cloth from fading in the sun, while its location on the first floor would have avoided damp.[30] Attics or sollars also provided storage. Paycockes at Coggeshall originally possessed a long storage loft at second-floor level over the entire range, which was later removed. Forming an additional storey to the house, this was the 'first known building to give architectural expression to the clothier's need for storage'.[31]

Wool stores, described variously as wool houses, wool lofts and wool cellars, were used by merchants, woolmongers, and producers with extensive flocks, as well as by clothiers. Examples have tentatively been identified in Burford and Northleach, standing in courtyards at the back of merchant houses, as barn-like structures. One example had slit windows that provided ventilation but retained security. Emmot Fermor of Witney, a major wool trader who may also have been involved in cloth-making, in 1501 had a wool chamber in her house at Witney and separate wool stores at Northleach and Witney. The Witney wool house contained 85 sacks of wool, a beam, two scales and various weights, requiring a floor space of more than 25 square metres.[32] Robert Rychard of Dursley had a wool loft with a beating hurdle, on which the

27 BRO, D/EW T49/3. Galloway, 'Colchester and its Region', p. 220; *VCH Essex*, ix, p. 104; John S. Lee, 'Piped Water Supplies Managed by Civic Bodies in Medieval English Towns', *Urban History* 41 (2014), p. 382.

28 TNA, PROB 2/57; PROB 11/9/7.

29 Alston, 'Old Grammar School', p. 42.

30 Alston, 'Old Grammar School', p. 42.

31 Stenning, *Discovering Coggeshall*, p. 78.

32 Dyer, *Country Merchant*, pp. 112–14; *VCH Oxfordshire*, xiv, p. 78.

wool would have been spread, and beating rods, used to remove impurities.[33] Some clothiers may have had rooms for storing particular equipment or for carrying out specific cloth-making processes. John Benet of Cirencester (d. 1497) left his 'messuage with appurtenances called Rodborough with the water mill and all shears called Shermansheris and lez handelles'; the latter were the frames or handles of the teasels used to raise the nap of cloth.[34] As clothiers often combined cloth-making with farming, their premises might need to accommodate agricultural activities too.[35]

Marketing

Although many clothiers' shops were primarily workshops for the production rather than the sale of their goods, wealthier clothiers, like other rich merchants, may have used premises to display goods to prospective buyers. These could have been furnished with counters and tables for laying out cloth for display, like the 'shewyng tables' and 'cowchebords' found in both the front shop and rear warehouse of a draper in Cornhill, London, in 1475.[36] Chests or coffers were also used to store goods and serve as counters.[37] While medieval shop windows were designed primarily to admit light rather than to display stock, many of those in urban and semi-urban locations had aesthetic features, including arched windows, 'regarded perhaps as a badge of commercial probity and permanence', and the use of close studding, a form of timber work in which vertical timbers, known as studs, are set close together.[38] Shops were usually entered directly from the street, but there was often another entry from the house, which may have allowed the owner to detect when a customer entered the shop, and also enabled him to take the customer into the house to celebrate the conclusion of a deal with food and drink. Such shops may have formed part of a suite of business rooms. The houses of wealthier clothiers, like Paycockes at Coggeshall and the Old Grammar School at Lavenham, had separate offices or counting chambers for the keeping of records. Similarly, the account book of the Ipswich merchant Henry Tooley (d. 1551) refers to his counting chamber. These rooms were probably furnished in a comparable way to the chamber depicted in Hans Holbein's portrait of

33 TNA, PROB 2/57; Crump and Ghorbal, *Huddersfield Woollen Industry*, p. 34.

34 TNA, PROB 11/11/94.

35 See below, pp. 205–6.

36 John Bennell, 'Shop and Office in Medieval and Tudor London', *Transactions of the London and Middlesex Archaeological Society* 40 (1989), pp. 189–206.

37 Morrison, *English Shops*, p. 28.

38 Alston, 'Late Medieval Workshops in East Anglia', p. 42.

Georg Gisze, a Hanseatic merchant based in the London Steelyard, with correspondence, seals, wax, and scales for weighing coins (Plate VI).[39]

Marketing and business considerations, rather than domestic comfort, appear to have lay behind a number of architectural features at Paycockes House in Coggeshall. The ground-floor hall has a ceiling with heavy moulded joists decorated with foliage and Gothic tracery, and carvings that include the Paycocke family's merchant's mark and the initials of Thomas and Margaret Paycocke. This was decoration to impress visitors, and was probably where business negotiations were conducted.[40] The existing brick stack in the hall is a later addition, and the room may originally have been unheated, which suggests use as show-rooms or mercantile premises. The west wall of the hall has evidence for a fireplace mantle but no space for a brick chimney and no evidence for a stack in the ceiling above, leading to the suggestion that an elaborate *trompe l'œil* may have been used to give the appearance of a painted fire where none existed. Alternatively, it may have been intended to erect a brick chimney stack at the western end of the site, but there was a change of plan during construction when it was found that the pre-fabricated house frame entirely filled the width of the site, and Paycocke was unable to acquire additional land for a chimney. The principal upper chamber, which lay above the hall, had another finely moulded ceiling and was probably used for the private reception of important guests. The east chamber on the ground floor was a small room with a moulded ceiling, subsequently extended and panelled, which probably formed Thomas Paycocke's business office. This was close by the principal entrance to the house and to the ground-floor hall and to its staircase, and within sight of the cartway and its pedestrian entrance.[41]

There may be similarities in function for sales and storage with the premises of the wealthiest cloth merchants, like the surviving timber-framed showroom of Dragon Hall, Norwich, owned by the mercer Robert Toppes (c.1405–67). This two-storey range, added to an earlier hall soon after 1427, provided a brick-vaulted undercroft, warehouse space and riverside access, together with an extensive upper hall. Oriel windows would have lit an impressive interior of carved and painted timbers, including the fine surviving painted carving of a dragon in a spandrel. The unheated southern bays of this hall probably served as a showroom and the heated northern bays may have been used more

[39] Clark, 'The Shop Within?', pp. 73–4. Alston, 'Old Grammar School', pp. 43–4; Bennell, 'Shop and Office', pp. 202–4; Thornton, 'Paycocke's House', pp. 87–8.

[40] The external carvings are examined in the following chapter.

[41] Thornton, 'Paycockes', pp. 86–9; Alston, 'Paycocke's Coggeshall', pp. 5–6; Stenning, *Discovering Coggeshall*, pp. 76–81.

Plate 11 Westwood House, Wiltshire, home of the clothier Thomas Horton (d. 1530).
Originally built in the fifteenth century, Thomas Horton added the parlour and panelled bedroom above, and oriel window, to create the west wing.

privately to entertain customers and strike deals. At the rear is a wider jetty supported by posts, which allowed a covered open-air arcade passage to run down to the river. Toppes is unlikely to have lived at Dragon Hall; his main dwelling house was near the Guildhall and parish church of St Peter Mancroft, which he endowed with glazing. Toppes owned shares in several boats sailing from Yarmouth to the Continent, taking wool and fine cloths and returning with fabrics, ceramics, metalwork, wines and spices. A list of debts due to his executors in 1492 record 116 sums owing in Norwich and in 51 towns and villages across Norfolk, and from Beccles, Bungay, Bury St Edmunds and Hadleigh in Suffolk.[42] On a smaller scale to Dragon Hall, the two late-fifteenth-century houses close to the churchyard at Headcorn, Kent, with handsome upper rooms, one originally open from end to end, have been suggested as clothiers' showrooms.[43]

[42] NHLE 1051236 (The Old Barge, 115–23 King Street, Norwich); Anthony Quiney, *Town Houses of Medieval Britain* (London, 2003), p. 212; Ayers, *Norwich*, pp. 113–15; Dunn, 'Trade', p. 229.

[43] NHLE 1344308, 1344312 (Shakespeare House, High Street, and Cloth Hall, North Street, Headcorn); John Newman, *The Buildings of England: Kent: West and the Weald* (London, 2012), pp. 43, 290; H.S. Cowper, 'Two Headcorn Cloth Halls', *Archaeologia Cantiana* 31 (1915), pp. 121–30.

Domestic accommodation

The extent of a clothier's domestic accommodation depended on his wealth. The residences of the very wealthiest clothiers, like Westwood, home of Thomas Horton (Plate 11), and Abbey House, owned by William Stumpe, may have been exclusively domestic accommodation, with no storage or workshops on site, but even in these cases, production was located close by, in the former abbey buildings at Malmesbury, and at the fulling mill at Hinton Charterhouse, the parish neighbouring Westwood.

Furniture was far more limited than today, with the principal items being objects like a table and chairs or benches and a chest in the hall, perhaps a stool and bench for work and accounting in another chamber, and beds elsewhere. The clothier William Martyn of Wokingham left all his 'household stuff' in his hall, parlour and chambers to his son in 1541, which he described as 'tables, boards, hangings, cupboards, bedsteads, coffers, stools, forms, featherbeds, bolsters and half my bedding as coverlets and blankets'.[44] Merchants often exhibited plate. In addition to displaying status, this was readily convertible to cash, acceptable as security for a loan, and often formed an inheritance in wills as it was convenient for distributing the assets of an estate. Robert Rychard of Dursley had over £10 in plate in 1492.[45] Spoons were conspicuous markers of wealth, symbolised good manners and some had devotional references. Drinking vessels and salt cellars were also popular. Among the forty-five wills of late medieval clothiers of Suffolk proved at the court of Canterbury, fifteen mention silverware, including bowls, mazers, plate, salters and spoons. Bourgeois homes also tended to contain a wider variety of soft furnishings.[46] Robert Rychard had a painted cloth of Robin Hood worth 5s in his parlour.[47] Thomas Spring III (d. 1523) left 'plate, ornaments and implements of household, as bedding, napery, hangings, brass, pewter and all other hustlements (household furniture) of house', to be divided between his wife and eldest son.[48]

Wealthier clothiers decorated their houses with personal embellishments of ownership. The house probably built by the clothier Henry Webb around 1525 on North Hill, Colchester, is now the Marquis of Granby Inn. The main room of the east wing includes a richly carved transom beam bearing his initials HW. Webb supplied London draper Thomas Howell

[44] BRO, D/EZ104/1/1–2.

[45] TNA, PROB 2/57.

[46] S.L. Thrupp, *The Merchant Class of Medieval London* (London, 1948), pp. 146–7; Goldberg, 'Fashioning of Bourgeois Domesticity', p. 135; Amor, *From Wool to Cloth*, p. 191.

[47] TNA, PROB 2/57.

[48] See below, Appendix 5.

with cloth.[49] At Westwood, Thomas Horton's initials likewise appear in stone spandrels above the fireplace in the dining room and in stained glass featuring his rebus, the barrel or tun, in the bedroom, as well as in the adjacent parish church. Again, at Malmesbury, Stumpe's coat of arms decorates the porch of his house.[50] Homes of wealthy clothiers were built to impress. Such was their splendour that they caught the attention of the traveller John Leland in the mid sixteenth century. He observed the 'very fine house' built by Thomas Horton at Bradford-on-Avon, the 'fine impressive house' built by James Terumber at Trowbridge, the buildings erected by Bailey there, and the 'fine houses' in the Frome valley inhabited by clothiers.[51]

Some houses may have been built by wealthy clothiers for their employees. Richard Halwey rebuilt his own home and built nine new houses at Castle Combe, which were among the fifty new houses erected there after 1409 and recorded in a survey of 1454.[52] At North Warnborough in Hampshire is a long terrace of timber-framed houses with jettied first floors. Built in 1476 as a range ninety-six feet long, it was extended by a further eighty-one feet in 1534–35. Given the rural setting, about a mile from Odiham market, and the apparent lack of monastic or institutional involvement, it has been suggested that this building could have been a row of weavers' cottages, only one of which, possibly for an overseer, had a fireplace. This may have been to reduce the fire risk in a building associated with cloth-making.[53] At Bildeston in Suffolk is an early-sixteenth-century row of four identical half-timbered houses that faced on to the medieval marketplace. Each house has a parlour lit by two windows which would have provided ideal workshops for cloth-workers, and it has been suggested that this row was built by 'a wealthy clothier as "tied-cottages" for his weavers'.[54] A rental of 1575 recorded six houses in Coggeshall on a plot belonging to John Paycocke at the end of East Street with frontages only a single perch long, which may have been intended to accommodate people who worked for the Paycockes in cloth-making.[55] While not a clothier himself, Abbot John Selwood of

[49] NHLE 1123534 (Marquis of Granby Inn, 24 North Hill, Colchester); *VCH Essex*, ix, p. 104. Drapers' Company, Ledger of Thomas Howell, fols 54v–55.

[50] See pp. 266, 308–9.

[51] Leland, *Itinerary*, i, pp. 127, 135–6; v, p. 98.

[52] Carus-Wilson, 'Evidences of Industrial Growth', p. 202.

[53] NHLE 1092183 (Castle Bridge Cottages, Bridge Road, North Warnborough); Edward Roberts and Daniel Miles, 'Castle Bridge Cottages, North Warnborough, Hampshire', *Vernacular Architecture* 28 (1997), pp. 117–18; Hare, *Basingstoke*.

[54] NHLE 1193247 (23–33 Chapel Street, Bildeston); Alston, 'Late Medieval Workshops', p. 46.

[55] Andrews, ed., *Discovering Coggeshall* 2, pp. 11, 72. As a measure of length, a perch varied locally but was later standardised at 16½ feet (5.03 metres).

Glastonbury (1456–92) rebuilt one street of houses at the cloth-making centre of Mells, and according to Leland, he had intended to build more, laid out in an Anthony Cross, or T shape.[56] His New Street survives, comprising two facing terraces of c.1490, although several of the houses have subsequently been rebuilt or altered, and the street extended southwards. Each house has a cross-passage linking the front and back doors and giving access on one side to a hall heated by a hearth, and a service room on the other. A semi-octagonal stair turret leads to two chambers and a closet. The houses were clearly built to attract, with a wide frontage, and spacious, having a total floor area of about 1,300 square feet (120 m^2).[57]

FARMING AND LANDHOLDING

Many clothiers combined farming with cloth-making. The Lavenham clothier John Place bequeathed three horses, grain, a cart and a tumbrel together with his woollen cloth, wool and yarn in 1440. Likewise John Harry, again from Lavenham, in 1473 left wheat, malt and two cows in addition to his wool and cloths.[58] Even wealthy clothiers might be engaged in agriculture. Thomas Spring III of Lavenham referred in his will to corn and malt in his solar, and John Winchcombe II left the lease on his farm at Greenham to his wife Christian, with a range of produce, equipment and livestock, including two hundred sheep.[59] Henry Goldney alias Fernell (by 1517–72/3) of Chippenham was the son of Nicholas Afternewell, who had sold white broadcloths to the mercer Thomas Kitson, and referred to three looms and a fulling mill in his will of 1538. Henry sued his mother and her second husband a year later over his expulsion from 240 acres in Chippenham and Longley, on which he had entered as his father's heir. Henry used this land as a farmer, rearing cattle and pigs, raising crops, and maintaining at least one grist mill, but he was also a clothier, with stocks of oil, wool and yarn. He was indicted for keeping a gig mill for mechanically raising the nap on cloth.[60] In

[56] *Itinerary*, v, p. 105.

[57] NHLE 1295803, 1058326, 1174367 (Nos. 4, 7 and 8, 9 New Street, Mells); Quiney, *Town Houses*, p. 267; E.H.D. Williams, J. and J. Penoyre and B.C.M. Hale, 'New Street, Mells. A Building Survey of an Uncompleted Late Medieval Planned Development', *Somerset Archaeology and Natural History Society: Proceedings* 130 (1985–6), pp. 115–25; W.A. Pantin, 'Chantry Priests' Houses and other Medieval Lodgings', *Medieval Archaeology* 3 (1959), p. 250.

[58] Betterton and Dymond, *Lavenham*, p. 3.

[59] TNA, PROB 11/40/283 (Winchcombe II); below, Appendix 5 (Spring III).

[60] T.F.T. Baker, 'GOLDNEY (FARNELL, AFFERNEWELL), alias FERNELL, Henry (by 1517–72/73), of Chippenham, Wilts.', *HoP, 1509–1558*; Ramsay, *Wiltshire*, p. 13.

the 'Debate between the Heralds', John Coke's 1549 translation of a late medieval French text, the French herald remarked to the English herald:

> your clothiers dwell in great farms abroad in the country, having houses with commodities like unto gentlemen, where as well they make cloth and keep husbandry and also grass and feed sheep and cattle, taking thereby away the livings of the poor husbandmen and graziers.[61]

Indeed cloth-makers were one of the occupational groups, along with merchant adventurers, goldsmiths, butchers and tanners, who were accused in 1514 of occupying more farms than they could cultivate. In some instances, it was claimed, they held up to sixteen farms, resulting in a scarcity of victuals. A bill instructed no person to keep more than one farm, and required them to dwell on it.[62]

The extent to which late medieval merchants invested in land rather than making other forms of business investment has attracted criticism from historians. Successful London merchants, for example, might invest a third to a half or more of their fortunes in land. Surplus wealth, it is argued, was invested in land to secure an income for families, to provide Masses for the good of their souls, or to turn their sons into country gentlemen, rather than being invested to develop trade or industry.[63] Medieval clothiers and merchants, however, would probably not have drawn such a sharp distinction between their property interests and their trading interests. Many of the most successful clothiers were also farmers and rentier landowners, who supplemented profits from cloth-making with income from agriculture and from lands and houses they rented out. Some clothiers, particularly in the Kentish Weald, acquired woodland to provide them with their own source of firewood for dyeing.[64] Clothiers could use the rents paid by their tenants to help finance their manufacturing businesses, and also invest part of the profits of their businesses in property that could be leased out. Property might be acquired in the routine course of business, with leases or rents accepted as security against deferred payment or collateral for loans. In 1382, the York draper Thomas de Kilburn accepted land in Little Ribston from John Blome against Blome's payment of 10 marks within ten years.[65] Some clothiers leased manors from major landowners, such as Robert Kyng, cloth-maker of Edwardstone, Suffolk, who with his wife and three

[61] *TED*, iii, p. 5.

[62] TNA, SP 1/9, fol. 223; *LP*, i (2), no. 3600, p. 1493.

[63] Thrupp, *Merchant Class*, pp. 103–30, 279–87; Bolton, *Medieval English Economy*, pp. 282–6.

[64] Zell, *Industry*, pp. 200–1.

[65] Kermode, *Medieval Merchants*, p. 289.

sons leased the manor of Borehouse within Edwardstone parish for £9 per annum for ten years from King's College, Cambridge in 1477.[66] Many clothiers held property, whether it was a smallholding like the 1½ acres that James Wrose of Horsforth (Yorkshire) acquired in his village in 1538, or dispersed holdings, such as the messuages in Colne in Lancashire and in Allerthorpe, Ardsley and Wakefield in Yorkshire bequeathed by John Mitchell of Colne in 1552. Some clothiers had an enormous portfolio, like the twenty-six manors in Cambridgeshire, Essex, Norfolk and Suffolk owned by Thomas Spring III on his death in 1523. Spring invested his money in comparable ways to the wealthiest of London merchants who bought large estates outside the city but also maintained town houses, shops and warehouses.[67]

There are examples of clothier families that joined the ranks of the gentry. William Allen (1511–72/76) of Calne, Wiltshire, was the grandson of a clothier from Suffolk. The younger William was also a clothier, but he was styled as 'gentleman' when assessed for taxation in 1547 and in the parliamentary returns from 1553 onwards. He paid £792 for former monastic lands around Calne in 1544.[68] The Springs of Lavenham, Stumpes of Malmesbury, and Winchcombes of Newbury all had sons who became gentlemen.[69] There are traditions that a couple of the leading clothiers were even graced by visits from the king, but no clear evidence to support this. Thomas Deloney's account of Jack of Newbury describes how he entertained Henry VIII and his queen while they were on progress in Berkshire, but there are no known references to the king visiting John Winchcombe at Newbury. Similarly, the account of William Stumpe entertaining Henry VIII and his retinue with an impromptu feast at Malmesbury may only be legendary, but Stumpe must have enjoyed royal favour to be appointed to the office of receiver for north Wales to the Court of Augmentations, and shortly after his appointment he acquired the leasehold of some property formerly belonging to Conway abbey.[70] The existing gentry did not always welcome these *nouveaux riches*. In the later sixteenth century, it was claimed that it was the clothier, 'Who doth most harm of all other degrees in this land by purchasing land or leases, or by maintaining his son in the Inns of Court like a gentleman or by

66 King's College, Cambridge, KCAR/3/3/1/1/1, fol. 74.

67 West Yorkshire Archive Service, Bradford, SpSt/4/11/66/53, SpSt/6/6/3/5. Oldland, 'Merchant Capital', p. 1076; Thrupp, *Merchant Class*, pp. 118–30.

68 T.F.T. Baker, 'ALLEN, William (by 1511–72/76), of Calne, Wilts.', *HoP, 1509–1558*.

69 See below, Chapter 6.

70 See below, p. 266.

buying offices for him'.[71] In 1576, future acquisitions of land in Wiltshire, Somerset and Gloucestershire were to be limited so that no clothier should own more than twenty acres, but there is no evidence to suggest that this legislation was ever enforced.[72]

A few members of the gentry and nobility engaged themselves in cloth-making, however. John Howard, later duke of Norfolk (d. 1485), owned a fulling mill, sold wool and woad to the local clothier Robert Sergeaunt, and presented twenty broadcloths for ulnage in Ipswich in 1466.[73] A group of gentry in the area around Huddersfield was sealing cloth at Almondbury in 1469–73. These were Thomas Beaumont (d. 1495) of Whitley Beaumont, who had succeeded to his estates in 1469, and married Elizabeth, daughter of Robert Neville of Liversedge, who himself had sealed 160 cloths in 1469–70. Robert's son John, who also brought cloth for sealing in 1471–73, later became a knight and high sheriff of Yorkshire. Laurence Kaye, another cloth seller in the same account, and later listed with other Almondbury clothiers in 1533, was a member of the Kaye family of Woodsome Hall.[74] Gentry families in other parts of the country participated in industrial and commercial activities as well as more profitable branches of agriculture.[75]

The dissolution of the monasteries and friaries brought a huge amount of property onto the market, and wealthier clothiers were keen to exploit these new opportunities. Clothiers acquired fulling mills previously owned by monasteries, like the house and fulling mills obtained by Thomas Bailey (d. 1543), described as 'four under one roof', at Stowford on the river Frome, formerly owned by Keynsham Abbey.[76] Occasionally, land purchases were used for new industrial purposes. Arthur Kaye of Woodsome Hall bought the house and manor of Denby Grange, formerly owned by Byland Abbey, expanded his manor of Slaithwaite by acquiring land at Lingards, and built two fulling mills there. His son John (1530–94) enclosed Farnley Moor, bought a fulling mill and the manor of Honley, and in partnership with two other men started iron smelting.[77] Some clothiers converted the buildings of religious houses into cloth-making workshops. The most well-known example is that of William Stumpe, who installed broadlooms in several of the former buildings of Malmesbury

71 Bodleian Library, Oxford, Rawlinson MS D, vol. 133, fol. 13, quoted in F.J. Fisher, 'Commercial Trends and Policy in Sixteenth-Century England', *EcHR* 10 (1940), p. 110.

72 18 Elizabeth, c. 16: *SR*, iv (1), p. 626; Ramsay, *Wiltshire*, pp. 45–6.

73 Amor, *From Wool to Cloth*, p. 83.

74 Crump and Ghorbal, *Huddersfield Woollen Industry*, pp. 29–30, 41.

75 Dyer, *Age of Transition*, pp. 103–5.

76 *VCH Wiltshire*, iv, p. 142.

77 Crump and Ghorbal, *Huddersfield Woollen Industry*, p. 43.

Abbey. The city of Oxford tried to establish a similar project with Stumpe at Osney Abbey, but nothing came of this.[78] Also unsuccessful was the proposal by a cloth-maker of Burford to use the fulling mills and property of Abingdon Abbey to develop cloth-making there. Thomas Bell converted the house of the Black Friars at Gloucester into a weaving-house, and the former friaries at Northampton and Canterbury were also proposed as places where cloth-making could be set up.[79]

Clothiers also created new residences on former monastic estates, sometimes adapting existing religious buildings. William Stumpe built Abbey House in the monastic precinct at Malmesbury, and Thomas Bell created a house in the former church of the Gloucester Black Friars. William Wotton, a clothier of Harberton near Totnes, and his son John, a merchant of Totnes, jointly paid £324 in 1546 for a lease of the neighbouring manor of Great Englebourne, formerly owned by Buckfast Abbey, which then became their family seat.[80] Thomas Wild (c.1508–59), clothier of Worcester, purchased the site of the Hospital of St Wulstan in the city, known as the Commandery, in 1544. Thomas' father had died as a clothier in 1528, and his own son Robert (d. 1607) gave up cloth-making to live on his rental income and farming. On his death, Thomas Wild's goods were valued in his inventory at £700 and his house at the Commandery had thirty-one rooms, one of them containing no fewer than twenty feather beds.[81] Both the Commandery at Worcester and Blackfriars at Gloucester still survive, although both have been much altered since the sixteenth century.[82]

RELIGIOUS AND COMMEMORATIVE PRACTICE

Late medieval religion was shaped by the belief that after death most souls went not directly to paradise but to the intermediate world of purgatory, from where they were purified by appropriate penance. This could be accelerated by the prayers, Masses and charitable acts of the faithful living. All groups in society strove to ensure that they would be commemorated after their deaths, from wealthy nobles who might endow colleges of priests to say Masses in perpetuity, to the poor making small donations to their local church, guild or friary. There was 'a cult

[78] See below, p. 265.

[79] See above, pp. 176–7.

[80] A.D.K. Hawkyard, 'WOTTON, John (by 1523–55 or later), of Totnes and Great Englebourne, Devon', *HoP, 1509–1558*.

[81] *VCH Worcestershire*, iv, pp. 390–4; Dyer, *Worcester*, pp. 101, 187; *HoP, 1509–1558*.

[82] NHLE 1390176 (The Commandery, Sidbury, Worcester), 1245989 (Blackfriars church and part of east range of friary, Gloucester). See also below, p. 309.

of living friends in the service of dead ones' and 'never … has God been bombarded with such a barrage of masses as rose from late medieval England'.[83] This commemoration varied in scale and form according to the wealth and interests of the believer, but often included an elaborate funeral and re-enactment of these rites at anniversary dates; the commissioning of funerary images, such as tomb chests or memorial brasses; leaving bequests to guilds and religious houses; providing church furnishings; and endowing almshouses and funding a range of public works such as repairs to roads.[84] By the later Middle Ages, the range of religious institutions to which benefactors could make gifts and entrust their commemoration had expanded significantly.

The wealthy arranged elaborate funerals, which included the *Placebo*, vespers for the dead recited on the night before the funeral, and the *Dirige* or dirge on the morrow, followed by the requiem Mass and interment of the body. Knells would be rung, candles and torches burned, and members of the poor required to attend, attired in clothes provided from the deceased's estate and given doles of bread.[85] The draper John Philipson of Doncaster directed in 1444 that four quarters of wheat for pounding into bread were to be distributed to the poor on the day of his death, together with five quarters of barley to convert into ale to enjoy on the same day.[86] Commemorations could include the re-enactment of aspects of these funeral rites. Many testators requested a monthly or yearly 'mind', when the deceased would again be commemorated with a requiem Mass. Some of these anniversaries, or obits, were endowed on a permanent basis, while others were limited to a number of years. Such ceremonies could include a solemn recreation of the funeral service: the parish hearse draped with a pall, torches or candles burned, bells rung, and the poor summoned to attend, as if the corpse was present once more. The clothier Thomas Paycocke of Coggeshall instructed in 1518 that a trental (a series of thirty requiem Masses) was to be said with repeated commemorations on the seventh day after his death and after

[83] Christopher Harper-Bill, 'The English Church and English Religion after the Black Death', in Mark Ormrod and Phillip Lindley, eds, *The Black Death in England* (Donington, 2003), p. 111.

[84] Clive Burgess, 'Obligations and Strategy: Managing Memory in the Later Medieval Parish', *Transactions of the Monumental Brass Society* 18 (2012), pp. 289–310. For examples of the varying commemorative practices within a single town, see Lee, 'Tis the sheep' and John S. Lee, 'Monuments and Memory: A University Town in Late Medieval England', in John S. Lee and Christian Steer, eds, *Commemoration in Medieval Cambridge* (Woodbridge, 2018).

[85] Burgess, 'Obligations and Strategy', pp. 296–7; E. Duffy, *The Stripping of the Altars. Traditional Religion in England 1400–1580*, 2nd edn (London, 2005), pp. 354–76.

[86] YBIA, York Prob. Reg. 2, fol. 83.

a month had passed. Payments were to be made on these three occasions to small children carrying wax candles, men holding torches, bell ringers, and for two sermons.[87]

Testators could choose from a variety of forms of remembrance, depending on their means. Maintaining an altar light, for example, usually required between 2s and 4s per annum, while a trental cost around 10s. Robert Hervey, cloth-maker (d. 1488) of Colchester, asked to be buried in the Jesus chapel at St Peter's church in the town. He bequeathed four torches, weighing 15 lb each, for the Jesus Mass, and one or two were to be lit every Friday when the host was elevated, and at the burial of every brother and sister. The torches were to be replaced every five years, when all guild members were to contribute.[88] The wealthy could afford to leave endowments to employ one or more priests to celebrate daily or weekly Masses for their souls, better known as chantries, which required provision for an income of around £6 per annum by the mid to late fifteenth century. While only one in four Suffolk clothiers who made wills in the lower church courts in the 1460s left bequests for a chantry priest, nearly three in four of the wealthy clothiers did so. The leading Suffolk clothiers in the 1460s, John Archer, Thomas Fulsnape, William Jacob and Thomas Spring, together paid for forty-seven years' worth of prayers at a total cost of over £280.[89]

Aside from parish churches, other religious institutions including monasteries, friaries and guilds received donations in return for providing commemorative functions. Some of these bequests may have reflected business connections. In 1450, the York mercer and clothier Robert Collinson made bequests throughout Cumberland, Westmorland, and the North and West Ridings of Yorkshire, and some of his beneficiaries, like the priories of Bolton-in-Craven and Richmond, may have sold him wool and bought goods from him, while other individuals may have been spinners and weavers of cloth. Collinson sold cushions and spices to Fountains Abbey in the 1450s.[90]

Funerary images

Funerary images were generally located near the grave and close to the altar, which was often the designated site for intercessory Masses for the deceased. They may have operated as part of their patron's anniversary services and as a minimum they provided a focus for those attending

[87] See below, Appendix 4.

[88] Jennifer Ward, 'Merchant Families and Religion in Later Medieval Colchester', in Barron and Sutton, eds, *The Medieval Merchant*, p. 258.

[89] Amor, 'Jack of all Trades', p. 428.

[90] Kermode, *Medieval Merchants*, p. 206.

the rites.[91] The clothier John Wyncoll (d. 1544) of Little Waldingfield in Suffolk, for example, directed in his will to be buried in the parish church and have laid there 'a marble stone with my picture and a Scripture graven in plate for the better memorial of the time of my decease'.[92] His brass still survives in the church (Plate IX). The funerary images of clothiers, together with those of wool merchants, form a remarkably coherent group: 'In the case of no other occupational grouping do we find so distinctive a commemorative profile'.[93] Memorial brasses rather than sculpted effigies, they usually depict the individuals in civilian attire and often include details of their trade and occupation. Most of these brasses were produced in London workshops rather than those of the provinces, reflecting the importance of London trading links to this group. Merchants' marks, which signified the ownership or origin of goods, and by association the reputation of the merchant, were frequently used like heraldic devices as a visual mnemonic to encourage remembrance.[94] These could be supplemented by other trading or occupational emblems. The brass of John Jay (d. c.1480) in St Mary Redcliffe, Bristol, includes two shields with carding combs, and the brass of John Greenway (d. 1529) in St Peter's, Tiverton, includes the arms of the Merchant Adventurers' and the Drapers' companies. A different image is presented at Lavenham on the memorial brass of Thomas Spring II, his wife Margaret and their children, where the family are shown in shrouds, emerging from two coffins at the Last Judgement (Plate 17). Brasses depicting the deceased as a corpse, either wearing a shroud or as a skeleton, became increasingly common during the last quarter of the fifteenth century. They were intended to move the spectator to concern for his or her own future and to commemorate the deceased. The Spring brass, originally affixed to the outside wall of the church vestry that he had provided, was produced by a London workshop and is considered to be an excellent example of its type.[95]

The ways in which a family of clothiers could combine a memorial brass with other elements of commemoration can be seen at St George's church, Beckington (Somerset). Compton's aisle, added to the south side of the chancel, was probably built for the clothier John Compton (d.

91 Burgess, 'Obligations and Strategy', pp. 300–1.

92 TNA, PROB 11/30/188. My thanks to Dr Amor for sharing Wyncoll's will with me.

93 Saul, 'Wool Merchants', p. 322.

94 Badham and Cockerham, eds, *The Church of St Botolph*, pp. 91–2.

95 M. Norris, *Monumental Brasses: The Memorials*, 2 vols (London, 1977), i, pp. 206–7, ii, plate 247. For an earlier fifteenth-century example, see David Harry, 'A Cadaver in Context: The Shroud Brass of John Brigge Revisited', *Transactions of the Monumental Brass Society* 19 (2015), pp. 101–10.

Plate 12 Brass of John Compton (d. 1505), wife Edith and five sons in Beckington church, Somerset.
Above the images of John and Edith Compton are roundels depicting angels holding Compton's rebus, a barrel or tun inscribed 'J.Com', and the family's merchant's mark.

1484). He left £8 to the church, 20s to the rector, 50 marks for a chaplain to pray for his soul for five years after his death, and a close of land to maintain a light before the image of the Holy Trinity. An enormous six-light straight-headed window fills the south wall, 'indication of a late date and an ambitious chantry bequest'.[96] Compton's son John (d. 1505), to whom he left a silver cup and two bales of woad, is also buried there, and commemorated by a brass depicting him, his wife Edith and their five sons, all in prayer (Plate 12). The inscription exhorts the reader to pray for the souls of John and Edith. On each side are angels holding Compton's rebus, a barrel or tun inscribed 'J.Com', while now separated from the rest of the memorial and placed in the south aisle is a brass with the family's merchant's mark, consisting of a gridiron with handle in the form of a cross and the initials JC.[97] The brass was the most visible means of remembrance, and clothiers, like others, were competing for fashionable memorials.

Guilds

The great majority of medieval guilds were not craft guilds, concerned with the organisation of trade, and generally confined to larger towns, but social and religious bodies.[98] These fraternities provided a surrogate extended family, and individuals were obliged to remember other members through prayers, Masses and memorials. Guild members were assured of a public funeral and regular commemoration as their collective funds could be used to hire priests. Guilds also provided a link between the individual and the Church, organising celebrations on the feast day of their patron saint, which perhaps involved plays or processions, and maintaining an image of the saint in the parish church. They also raised money to repair churches, often organising a church ale at which members brewed and sold ale. Members paid entry fees and subscriptions and in return could expect to borrow money from guild funds, or receive support when sick, injured or impoverished. As entry fees varied enormously, membership of certain guilds probably carried an element of social prestige. Initially, guilds met in private homes or in part of the parish church, but as their incomes increased, some were able to acquire their own purpose-built guildhalls. These guildhalls usually

[96] *Somerset Medieval Wills*, ed. F.W. Weaver, Somerset Record Society (1901), pp. 248–9; N. Pevsner, *The Buildings of England: North Somerset and Bristol* (Harmondsworth, 1958), p. 141.

[97] Michael McGarvie, *St George's Church Beckington* (Beckington, 1990), pp. 7–9.

[98] For craft guilds, see above, Chapter 4.

Plate 13 Corpus Christi Guildhall, Lavenham, Suffolk. A sumptuous timber-framed building erected c.1530 as the headquarters for one of Lavenham's medieval guilds, which were social and religious bodies. This was one of the last buildings to be constructed before this boom town of the early sixteenth century became an economic backwater.

contained at least one large room where all the members could assemble for meetings and feasts.[99]

Five guilds are known to have existed in Lavenham between 1416 and 1540, and at least four of them possessed their own halls. The Holy Trinity guild was left money in 1469 to endow a chaplain to celebrate Mass in the church on behalf of its members, and for six almshouses. The guild of Saints Peter and Paul had its own priest by 1446 and a hall at the top of the High Street. It also owned cooking equipment and a stall in the marketplace. Lavenham's Corpus Christi guildhall appears to have been constructed in 1529–30 (Plate 13). It was purpose-built, as shown by its lack of heating, and originally the main hall was only 12 feet in length. The Corpus Christi guild attracted very few bequests – only two have been traced in the surviving wills, a small sum of money from Robert Parsons in 1477 and a High Street tenement from Miles Wytton in 1520.

[99] Duffy, *Stripping*, pp. 141–54.

It was perhaps a particularly exclusive guild, taking members only from the merchant elite. This might explain its large attic space, which may have served as a warehouse.[100]

Benefactors left financial legacies to guilds, desiring their prayers and masses for themselves and their relatives after their deaths. In Lavenham, the clothier John Harry bequeathed 10 marks to the guild of Holy Trinity in 1473 to buy 'as much livelihood as will provide a chaplain to celebrate divine service in Lavenham church for the souls of the same fraternity'. The clothier John Rysby left 6s 8d to the guild of Saints Peter and Paul in 1493, desiring to become a brother and partaking in their prayers; Edmund Bownde donated his great mazer, twelve pieces of pewter and a table cloth to the same guild in 1504.[101] At least one clothier even established a new fraternity. The Reading clothier Henry Kelsall described himself in his will of 1493 as 'the first minder sustainer and maintainer of my devotion of the mass of Jesu' in St Laurence's parish. He bequeathed a tenor bell, dedicated to Jesus, to the parish church, which would have been rung for burials, and at monthly and yearly minds, including those that Kelsall established. His tombstone, which once lay in the church's north aisle next to the chancel where the altar for the Jesus Mass was sited, reflected this devotion with the words: 'J[es]hu tha in Bethelem was borne / save us that we be not forlone'. Kelsall's will refers to ten other individuals who were 'sustainers' of same fraternity, including a clothier and three drapers.[102] Often concentrated in markets, ports and urban areas, guilds provided a source of credit to finance commercial activities, a useful forum for the resolution of disputes, and centres of political and economic networking, although their primary focus was religious.[103]

Church embellishments and rebuilding

Clothiers, like other benefactors, might make bequests for specific devotional and commemorative items around the church, which included carving, glazing, statues, screens, metalwork, vestments and books, to promote reciprocal prayer and commemoration. Thomas Stansby for example, left donations for Lavenham church in 1518 to acquire an altar cloth of gold, a pair of organs to keep Our Lady's Mass, candlesticks for

100 National Trust, *Guildhall of Lavenham*, p. 12.

101 Betterton and Dymond, *Lavenham*, pp. 110–11.

102 Brown, *Popular Piety*, pp. 129, 139–40.

103 John S. Lee, 'Decline and Growth in the Late Medieval Fenland: The Examples of Outwell and Upwell', *Proceedings of the Cambridge Antiquarian Society* 104 (2015), pp. 6–7; R. Goddard, 'Medieval Business Networks: St Mary's Guild and the Borough Court in Later Medieval Nottingham', *Urban History* 40 (2013), pp. 3–27; Casson and Casson, *Entrepreneur*, pp. 85–6.

the high altar, and two copes for the rector.[104] In his will of 1537, John Clevelod of Beckington donated two service books, an antiphon and a gradual to the Dorset church of Okeford Fitzpaine, where he wished to be buried.[105] In 1528 Thomas Strete of Mells bequeathed to his parish church a pair of vestments of black velvet 'with white corses (corpses) rising out of the grave with a chalice'.[106] Such gifts often linked the donor with a significant aspect of the ceremonies observed within the church. Thomas Paycocke left 100 marks for the carving and gilding of the tabernacles of the Trinity at the high altar and of St Margaret in St Catherine's aisle, where he and his family were buried.[107] Parishes and guilds maintained bede rolls, carefully recording donations to the fabric or activities of the church, and thereby ensured that the benefactors received regular prayer and remembrance. The Devon clothier John Lane (d. 1529) left 6s 8d each to no fewer than one hundred parish churches 'next about Cullompton', for them to add his name to their bede rolls and to pray for him 'in their pulpits'.[108]

Enlarging or rebuilding parish churches was another charitable and commemorative act, and clothiers appear to have led or joined collaborative building works at many parish churches in the later Middle Ages. At Lavenham, between 1485 and 1540 fifty donors left a total of £2,287 to the fabric of the parish church, and at least thirty-five of these are known to have worked in the cloth industry.[109] The clothiers Richard Brickenden, Stephen Draner and Alexander Courthop gave the three largest donations (totalling £170) towards the rebuilding of the nave of Cranbrook church in 1520. Steeple Ashton church was rebuilt between 1480 and 1500, with clothier Robert Long and Edith his wife funding the north aisle, and clothier Walter Lucas and Matilda his wife bearing most of the cost of the south aisle.[110] In St Margaret's church, Ipswich, the late-fifteenth-century clerestory has the initials and monograms of the Hall family, and also their merchant's mark, formed of a dyer's posser and pair of tongs. These commemorate John Hall (d. 1503), dyer, his wife Katherine (d. 1506), and son William (d. 1526), a clothier and dyer. John's

104 Betterton and Dymond, *Lavenham*, p. 108.

105 *Somerset Medieval Wills 1531–1538*, ed. F.W. Weaver, Somerset Record Society 21 (1905), p. 36.

106 *Somerset Medieval Wills 1501–1530*, p. 269.

107 See below, Appendix 4.

108 Carus-Wilson, 'Lane Chapel', p. 114.

109 Betterton and Dymond, *Lavenham*, p. 12.

110 William Tarbutt, *The Annals of Cranbrook Church* (Cranbrook, 1870), pp. 8, 50; Brown, *Popular Piety*, p. 118.

donations to the church were so significant that he requested to be buried in the most privileged place in the nave, 'in front of the crucifix'.[111]

The bequests of clothiers probably funded most of the rebuilding of the parish church of St Mary the Virgin in Dedham, Essex. This took place in a single phase of construction between 1492 and about 1520. Nikolaus Pevsner described St Mary's as 'the visible proof of the flourishing cloth-trade of the town'. Mirroring the trading links of the Stour valley cloth industry, which extended from north Essex into south Suffolk, the church is 'more in a Suffolk than an Essex style'.[112] The leading family of clothiers at Dedham in the early sixteenth century were the Webbs. Brook House on Dedham High Street is probably the 'new house at the brook' that John Webb bequeathed in 1523, and has the Webbs' merchant's mark on a fireplace lintel. The Thomas Webb who served as vicar of Dedham (1516–23) was probably another member of this prominent family. John Webb erected a monument to his father Thomas (d. 1506), a traceried tomb chest, now in the north aisle of the church, which contains their initials and merchant's mark. Above the recess of the tomb is a framed stone panel with indents marking where a brass once depicted Thomas and his family. The vault of the church tower is panelled and decorated with their initials and merchant's mark, together with tracery, roses and portcullises. Two heads are also depicted, which may be those of Thomas and either his wife or John. The huge west tower of Dedham church, around 130 feet high, was completed by another clothier, Stephen Dunton, who left £100 for the battlements in 1518.[113] Church towers were often rebuilt to house bells, which by the late fifteenth century had become larger and more sonorous, and required more sophisticated frames that allowed bells to rotate 180 degrees. The sound of bells reminded parishioners of the need for intercession and would have been used for the death knell.[114]

These works were commissioned to inspire remembrance, and frequently identified the donor and sought prayers from the passing observer. John Lane's chapel at St Andrew's church, Cullompton, bears an external inscription dated 1526 asking the reader to remember with a *Paternoster* and an *Ave Maria* the souls of John Lane and Thomasyn his wife, the founders of the chapel who lie buried there. At Lavenham, the inscription on the south chapel seeks prayers for the souls of Thomas Spring III and his wife Alice, while that on the north chapel requests

111 Blatchly and Northeast, 'Discoveries in the Clerestory', p. 396.

112 James Bettley and Nikolaus Pevsner, *The Buildings of England: Essex* (London, 2007), pp. 319–20.

113 TNA, PROB 11/19/97; *VCH Essex*, x, p. 161 and n. 19, pp. 180–2.

114 Brown, *Popular Piety*, p. 129.

prayers for the souls of Simon Branch and his wife Elizabeth. Perhaps the most flamboyant surviving example of all is the carved decoration that John Greenway, Tiverton merchant and London draper, applied to the exterior walls of his chantry chapel at Tiverton. An upper frieze portrays scenes from the life of Christ, and a lower frieze depicts images of his own business. These include a whole fleet of ships, from three-masted galleons to slender row-barges, as well as anchors, ropes, wool sacks, and representations of his merchant's mark. There are also coats of arms, comprising Greenway's own arms, the Royal Arms, and those of the Drapers' Company and the Merchant Adventurers. Above the inner doorway of the south porch is the Assumption of the Virgin flanked by the kneeling donor John Greenway and his wife, Joan.[115] In the south-west corner of the chapel, placed strategically to catch the eye, are three memorable inscriptions:

> Of your charitie pray for the souls of John Greenway and his wife.
> O Lord o all grant John Greenway good fort'n and grace and in Heaven a place.
> God sped J.G.

Benefactors used initials, heraldry, rebuses and other marks to identify their contribution and promote reciprocal prayer and commemoration.[116] As they usually lacked a coat of arms, clothiers generally used their merchant's mark for this purpose, but were not afraid to include other symbols of the cloth trade. The south aisle that John Lane constructed at Cullompton has external buttresses decorated with references to his sources of wealth: ships, cloth shears, teasel frames and his cloth mark. Similar images, including fulling stocks and teasel frames, recur inside the building (Plates 2 and 4).[117] At Seend in Wiltshire, where the clothier John Stokes (d. 1498) asked to be buried in 'my newly built and constructed chapel', and which once contained painted glass with pictures of his children, the surviving window mouldings depict cloth shears on the inside, and shears and scissors on the carvings outside.[118]

Charitable bequests

Many testators in the Middle Ages also made provision in their wills for social welfare and public works, including almshouses, hospitals, schools, bridges, roads and water supplies, believing that they were

[115] Burgess, 'Making Mammon', pp. 202–3 and plates 4–7; Welsford, *John Greenway*.

[116] Burgess, 'Obligations and Strategy', pp. 303–4.

[117] N. Pevsner and B. Cherry, *The Buildings of England: Devon*, 2nd edn (London, 1989), p. 303; Carus-Wilson, 'Lane Chapel'.

[118] Brown, *Popular Piety*, p. 127.

performing a religious act through these bequests.[119] The funeral dole could develop into longer-term charitable relief provided weekly over a year or more. Thomas Spring I, in 1440, for example, left 12d each week to distribute among twelve paupers for four years. The prevalence of entries for alms to be distributed regularly over a long period in the wills of Lavenham residents in the mid fifteenth century, at least five of whom were engaged in cloth-making, has led one historian to dub this as 'the Lavenham project' – 'a co-ordinated campaign' of social welfare. Similar arrangements existed in the nearby cloth-making towns of Long Melford and Stoke-by-Nayland. Just over a quarter of the wealthiest Suffolk clothiers made provision for social welfare in the period between c.1470 and c.1520.[120]

A few clothiers made bequests for education. Robert Harset, clothmaker of Long Melford, in 1484 bequeathed part of his large house to be used as a school.[121] Thomas Horton founded a chantry in Bradford-on-Avon with a school attached, and the priest was to pay the clerk there 20s a year for teaching the children to sing for divine service.[122] The clothier Thomas Wild of Worcester bequeathed land in 1558 to re-establish the Worcester Free School 'for the bringing up of youth in their ABC, matins and evensong and other learning', and Robert Youle, another Worcester cloth manufacturer, provided a further endowment to the same school on his death in 1560, requiring the master and boys to come yearly to his grave in Worcester cathedral to pray for his soul and those of his family and all Christians.[123] Even university education was sometimes supported. Alan Sturmyn, cloth-worker of Lavenham, was a minor benefactor of Queens' College, Cambridge in the mid fifteenth century.[124] Thomas Spring III's executors paid 100 marks for the support of scholars studying at the universities of Oxford and Cambridge.[125]

Almshouses offered free housing, often requiring the residents to pray for the souls of the donors in the local parish church or in a dedicated chapel. The clothier James Terumber founded a chantry and almshouse

119 Duffy, *Stripping*, pp. 367–8; Brown, *Popular Piety*, pp. 103–4; Lee, 'Piped Water Supplies'.

120 Betterton and Dymond, *Lavenham*, p. 10; Christopher Dyer, 'Poverty and its Relief in Late Medieval England', *Past and Present* 216 (2012), pp. 58, 68; Amor, *From Wool to Cloth*, pp. 212–13.

121 Nicholas Orme, *Medieval Schools from Roman Britain to Renaissance England* (New Haven, 2006), p. 244; *VCH Suffolk*, ii, pp. 340–1.

122 *VCH Wiltshire*, iv, p. 142; vii, p. 26.

123 *HoP, 1509–1558*; Dyer, *Worcester*, pp. 244–5.

124 Anne Sutton, 'London Mercers from Suffolk c1200 to 1570: Benefactors, Pirates and Merchant Adventurers (Part II)', *Proceedings of the Suffolk Institute for Archaeology and History* 42 (2010), p. 165.

125 Betterton and Dymond, *Lavenham*, p. 100.

in Trowbridge in 1484. John Leland noted the almshouse and Terumber's own 'notable fair house', which he had given to form part of the endowment. Terumber named over forty people whose souls were to benefit from the Masses said by his chantry priest. The six residents of his almshouse were to assemble twice daily, at which time one member would announce, 'We shall specially pray for the souls of James Terumber, Johanne and Alice his wives, our founders, and of all the other benefactors.' Members would then proceed to the parish church to say the psalter of St Mary for all the souls commemorated.[126] At least two sets of almshouses founded by medieval cloth traders continue to offer charitable support today. Stephen Dunton's seven cottages for the use of the poor at Dedham were rebuilt as Dunton's Almshouses in 1806, and continue to provide housing.[127] John Greenway's almshouses, originally provided in 1517 for five men, who were to receive 8d weekly to pray daily for Greenway, his wife Joan and all Christian people, have also been rebuilt, and now form part of Tiverton Almshouse Trust. The chapel survives, once a richly decorated structure similar to the Greenway chapel at Tiverton church. Its Gold Street elevation still includes the text, 'have grace ye men and ever pray for the soul of John and Joan Greenway'.[128] Another surviving building erected by a clothier for charitable purposes is Thomas Horton's 'commodious church house, of squared stone blocks', as John Leland described it, in Bradford-on-Avon. This building, now a Masonic Lodge, contains original oak-timbered ceilings, an open stone fireplace and an oak gallery.[129]

Clothiers also made charitable contributions towards improving infrastructure. These included donations for bridges and causeways, like the contributions specified in 1450 by Robert Collinson, a mercer and clothier of York, to repair Catterick and Greatham bridges and the road from Ferrybridge to York. Likewise, in 1503 John Compton of Beckington contributed to a causeway called *Standewekes*. Thomas Horton left £5 to construct a new bridge at Freshford (Somerset) in his will of 1530, a bridge that Leland described as 'two or three fair new arches of stone' and that still spans the river Frome.[130] William Jacob (d. 1500) paid for the

[126] W.H. Jones, 'Terumber's Chantry at Trowbridge, with Deed of Endowment 1483', *Wiltshire Archaeological and Natural History Society* 10 (1867), pp. 240–52.

[127] *VCH Essex*, x, p. 185.

[128] NHLE 1384842 (Greenway's Almshouses and Chapel, Gold Street, Tiverton); Welsford, *John Greenway*, pp. 14–19; Pevsner and Cherry, *Devon*, pp. 814–15; Tiverton Almshouse Trust website, http://www.tivertonalmshouse.org.uk

[129] *Itinerary*, i, p. 135; NHLE 1036037 (Holy Trinity Church Hall, Bradford-on-Avon); Cherry and Pevsner, *Wiltshire*, p. 132.

[130] YBIA, York Prob. Reg. 3, fol. 379 (Collinson); TNA, PROB 11/14/740 (Compton), PROB 11/23/339 (Horton). NHLE 1158368 (Freshford Bridge).

market cross in Lavenham, stipulating that the design should be based on that in Cambridge marketplace.[131] The provision of piped drinking water in towns was seen as another charitable act: James Terumber left a legacy for the water conduit at Redcliffe, Bristol, in 1488.[132] Unsurprisingly, roads were the item of infrastructure most commonly mentioned in clothiers' wills. These routes would have been very familiar to the clothiers and their workers carrying wool and cloth. William Frere of Clare gave £40 for 'the highway between Clare and Yeldham', a route between Essex towns and London.[133] In Lavenham, seventeen donors left money for repairing roads before 1485, averaging just under £6 per person, but the eighteen bequests made for this purpose between 1485 and 1540, averaged over £25 per person, a remarkable figure. Most of these Lavenham donors were clothiers or the widows of clothiers.[134] Like other benefactors, clothiers believed that in making provision for these public works they were undertaking virtuous deeds as works of charity.

Despite the traditional beliefs of many clothiers, some historians have associated cloth-making areas with areas of dissent, and Lollard, Protestant and other nonconformist beliefs. Lollardy was a movement that emphasised vernacular Scripture and denied the efficacy of many late medieval Catholic teachings. Prosecuting authorities often chose to conflate Lollardy with more general anti-clericalism, so it is difficult to ascertain the precise impact of these beliefs. However, Lollard teachings seem to have been prevalent in textile-producing centres with their literate craftsmen who had established links with towns and ports. In 1431, there were gatherings in Abingdon and Salisbury at which subversive religious literature was distributed, and weavers from these two towns and Westbury, and a dyer from Frome, were among those implicated. The fuller Robert White, one of the ringleaders of the disturbances in the west Cotswolds in 1464, was accused of being a Lollard and spreading heretical opinions. The majority of those prosecuted for heresy in Coventry between 1486 and 1522 whose occupations were recorded worked in the cloth or leather trades, either in processing or creating the finished product.[135] Books and ideas could travel with the cloth trade. William Ball, a Yorkshire shearman, returned to his native Dewsbury in

[131] NHLE 1037179 (Market Cross, Lavenham). The stepped base remains at Lavenham with a later shaft. Betterton and Dymond, *Lavenham*, p. 20.

[132] Lee, 'Piped Water Supplies'; *VCH Wiltshire*, iv, p. 136.

[133] Thornton, *Clare*, pp. 190–1.

[134] Betterton and Dymond, *Lavenham*, pp. 16, 113–15.

[135] Harvey, *Cade*, pp. 23–7; J.F. Davis, 'Lollard Survival and the Textile Industry in the South-east of England', *Studies in Church History* 3 (1966), pp. 191–201; Hilton, *English Peasantry*, p. 72; S. McSheffrey and N. Tanner, eds, *Lollards of Coventry, 1486–1522*, Camden Fifth Series 23 (London, 2003), p. 25.

the early 1540s with radical ideas he had absorbed while working as an apprentice and journeyman in Waldingfield, Ipswich and Hadleigh.[136]

Areas of early industrial activity and those with significant exports in cloth, cattle, leather or grain have been identified as places where nonconformity was potentially more prevalent. Transport networks and trading links facilitated the dissemination of religious and political ideas between these regions and parts of Protestant continental Europe. It has even been suggested that there was more time for reading in pastoral areas than in those with a full-scale arable routine, and weavers could read while working at their looms.[137] The classic example often cited is that of William Tyndale (c.1494–1536), translator of the Bible and religious reformer, who was born in Gloucestershire, probably in one of the villages near Dursley, in the cloth-making area of the vale of Berkeley. A member of a prosperous family of landowners, wool merchants and administrators, Tyndale was supported by merchants in the cloth trade, notably his younger brother John and Humfrey Monmouth of London. Monmouth shared books Tyndale had sent him, including his translation of the New Testament, with Dr Thomas Stockhouse, rector of the Suffolk cloth-making town of Lavenham, who found no fault in them. Tyndale is said to have wanted 'the weaver at his loom' to sing a text of Scripture that would 'drive away the tediousness of time'.[138]

In the same part of Gloucestershire, John Smyth of Nibley recounted in 1639 the tale of a clothier who in Edward VI's reign removed a medieval wooden icon of a saint from Cam church. He placed it in a clothier's wain as he travelled towards Blackwell Hall, and carried the icon to a place called *Colbrooke*, fifteen miles from London, where a common inn called the George was subsequently established. Although Smyth does not name the clothier, one suggestion that has been put forward is Thomas Trotman (d. 1558), clothier of Cam. His father Henry had purchased a mill, possibly a fulling mill, in 1512. Thomas married the daughter of another leading clothier family in Cam, the Hardings. The Trotmans had connections with the Tyndales: Thomas' son Richard married Katherine Tyndale, William's niece.[139] Yet while there may

[136] Dickens, *Lollards and Protestants*, p. 48.

[137] A.G. Dickens, *The English Reformation* (London, 1964), pp. 56, 267, 369; Margaret Spufford, 'The Importance of Religion in the Sixteenth and Seventeenth Centuries', in Margaret Spufford, ed., *The World of Rural Dissenters, 1520–1725* (Cambridge, 1995), pp. 45, 47.

[138] David Daniell, 'Tyndale, William (*c*.1494–1536)', *ODNB*; David Rollison, *The Local Origins of Modern Society: Gloucestershire 1500–1800* (London, 1992), pp. 84–94; Betterton and Dymond, *Lavenham*, pp. 46–7.

[139] Smyth, *Berkeley Manuscripts*, iii, pp. 123–4; Rollison, *Local Origins*, pp. 97–101.

have been a correlation between cloth-making areas and radical ideas, a correlation does not necessarily imply a relationship. Local studies have shown a wide variety of different experiences, even in prominent cloth-making centres. In Halifax, for example, the textile trade had no more than marginal influence on religion, and in Hadleigh, opposition to reform in the parish was led by two clothiers, John and Walter Clerke.[140]

CONCLUSION

Clothiers included merchants and craftworkers, townspeople and countryfolk, farmers and artisans, and members of the gentry, peasantry and middling sorts. Clothiers therefore crossed the social groupings that historians have frequently used to categorise late medieval society. Our understanding of their backgrounds, their homes and their beliefs, must be sufficiently flexible to consider a wide range of approaches, and needs to bring together different forms of source material to provide a more rounded picture of clothiers in society.

The clothier potentially had to accommodate within his premises cloth-making and storage, the display and sale of goods, and domestic living space. The wealth of the individual clothier and the nature of his business determined the extent of these requirements. A poor rural clothier combining cloth-making with agriculture probably lived in a house similar to that inhabited by a yeoman farmer, with possibly an additional room to accommodate equipment and materials for cloth-making. A poor urban clothier probably occupied a single shop unit resembling those of other craftworkers. Where manufacturing, marketing and domestic accommodation needed to be provided on the same site, and where space and finance permitted, wealthier clothiers tended to favour courtyard arrangements, which allowed activities to be accommodated in different ranges, facilitated circulation between them, and could provide a sense of occasion to those entering. In this respect, the preferences of wealthier clothiers resembled those not only of other affluent merchants, but also of leading ecclesiastical and civic dignitaries, who also generally grouped their urban buildings within courtyards.[141]

Clothiers in late medieval England were part of a society much concerned with death, and which placed great emphasis on the powers of prayer and pious works to ease souls through purgatory. To the extent

[140] John Craig, 'Reformers, Conflict, and Revisionism: The Reformation in Sixteenth-Century Hadleigh', *Historical Journal* 42 (1999), pp. 1–23; William and Sarah Sheils, 'Textiles and Reform: Halifax and its Hinterland', in Patrick Collinson and John Craig, eds, *The Reformation in English Towns 1500–1640* (Basingstoke, 1998), pp. 130–43.

[141] Quiney, *Town Houses*, pp. 209–16.

to which their individual fortunes allowed, clothiers commissioned elaborate funerals, acts of remembrance and memorials, supported guilds, funded the embellishment and rebuilding of churches, and donated to a range of other public works, including almshouses, educational provision and charitable relief. Wealthier clothiers made extensive use of monumental brasses, a fashionable and affordable commemorative device for merchants and the gentry to utilise as part of a broader strategy of commemoration.[142] On these brasses, and on their other commemorative works including church extensions, clothiers and woolmen displayed the tools of their trade to a prodigious extent not generally found in other occupations.[143] Like merchants, the gentry and the aristocracy, clothiers were willing to invest in the liturgy and embellish the parish churches where they wished to be buried. More affluent merchants, including the wealthier clothiers, could commission impressive new buildings and obtain high-quality furnishings through their wealth, taste and connections. They could also bring financial and managerial expertise to assist with maintaining their endowments.[144] While heresy and dissent may have been active in some cloth-making areas, the fragmentary evidence suggests that it was cloth-workers, rather than clothiers, who tended to be sympathetic. Indeed, the practice of orthodox piety seems to have been particularly intense within textile-producing areas, as the wealth generated by the cloth trade provided funds to invest in church-building, chantries and guilds.[145]

[142] For other examples of mercantile commemorative practice, see Christian Steer, 'The Language of Commemoration', in Mary Carruthers, ed., *Language in Medieval Britain: Networks and Exchanges* (Donington, 2015), pp. 240–50; and '"For quicke and deade memorie masses": Merchant Piety in Late Medieval London', in Martin Allen and Matthew Davies, eds, *Medieval Merchants and Money: Essays in Honour of James L. Bolton* (London, 2016), pp. 71–89; and Lee, 'Tis the sheep'.

[143] Saul, 'Wool Merchants', p. 335.

[144] Burgess, 'Making Mammon', pp. 183–207.

[145] Brown, *Popular Piety*, pp. 222, 259.

6

Famous clothiers

This chapter focuses on four famous clothier families, whose members amassed huge fortunes and left lasting legacies to their communities. Thomas Paycocke of Coggeshall in Essex, who came from a family of butchers and cloth-makers, created a magnificent house which is now a National Trust property. The Springs were three generations of clothiers, all called Thomas, whose wealth made Lavenham in Suffolk one of the richest towns in England in 1524, and who were major contributors to the rebuilding of Lavenham parish church. Father and son John Winchcombe I and II of Newbury occupied a substantial house within the town, were large-scale producers of kerseys, and were commemorated a generation later in Thomas Deloney's poem 'Jack of Newbury'. William Stumpe set up looms in the buildings of the former abbey in Malmesbury, and gave the abbey church to become the town's parish church.

THOMAS PAYCOCKE OF COGGESHALL

> For his beautiful house still stood in West Street, opposite the vicarage, and was the delight of all who saw it. It stands there still, and looking upon it to-day, and thinking of Thomas Paycocke who once dwelt in it, do there not come to mind the famous words of Ecclesiasticus? 'Let us now praise famous men and our fathers that begat us …'
>
> Eileen Power, 'Thomas Paycocke of Coggeshall' (1924)[1]

With the pride and ostentation of a peacock, Thomas Paycocke's ornate timber-framed house at Coggeshall still catches the eye, five centuries after its construction (Plate VIII). The metaphor is apt as the family name Paycocke was variously spelt Peaycocke, Pecock, and Peacock, and this may be the species of bird carved on the exterior of his house. Indeed his merchant's mark, which also decorates the house, although described variously as a trefoil of pearls or berries, a two-stemmed clover, or an ermine tail, might, with a stretch of the imagination, be a stylised representation of peacock feathers (Plate 14). Paycocke's house

[1] Power, 'Thomas Paycocke', p. 168.

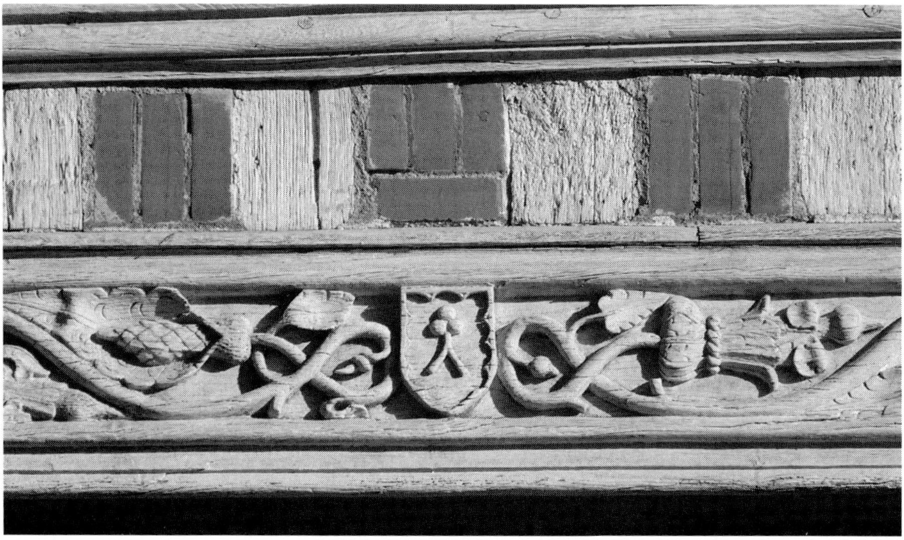

Plate 14 Merchant's mark detail from decorated fascia of Paycocke's, Coggeshall.
This may have been a stylised representation of peacock feathers, a two-stemmed clover, a trefoil of three pearls or berries on a stalk split at the base, or an ermine tail. Paycocke probably applied this merchant's mark to his cloth, and it also appears on his tomb.

has attracted generations of admirers, including Noel Buxton, who restored the property to its original timbered appearance and presented it to the National Trust in 1920. The architectural historian Nikolaus Pevsner described it as 'one of the most attractive half-timbered houses of England'; the economic historian Eileen Power thought it was 'the house of a man who was nouveau riche in an age when to be nouveau riche was not yet to be vulgar'.[2] Power examined the house, together with Paycocke's will, to sketch out the career of this clothier. In fact, what we know about Thomas Paycocke is still largely reliant on these two key pieces of evidence, although recent research has uncovered more information about this clothier, his business, and his remarkable house.[3]

Coggeshall is situated ten miles west of Colchester in the valley of the river Blackwater, which provided water for washing cloth and powering mills. A bend in the river encloses the site of an abbey, founded about 1140, which became a Cistercian foundation. The abbey's enormous

[2] Bettley and Pevsner, *Essex*, p. 252; Power, 'Thomas Paycocke', p. 154.

[3] Thornton, 'Paycocke's House'; Alston, 'Paycocke's, Coggeshall'; Stenning, *Discovering Coggeshall*; Andrews, ed., *Discovering Coggeshall 2*.

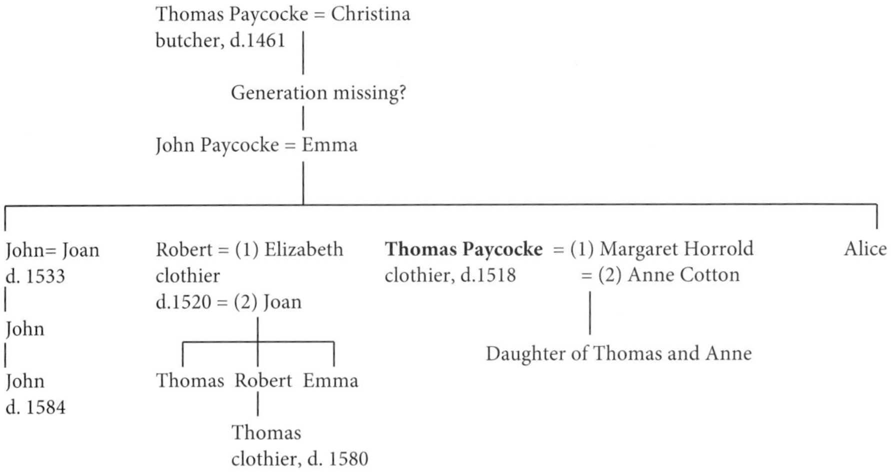

Figure 8 Paycocke family tree
Source: Power, *Paycockes*, p. 67.

timber-framed grange barn, constructed to store the produce of its estates, still survives, as does the gate chapel of St Nicholas, while some of the other monastic buildings have been incorporated into a Tudor house. The monks diverted the course of the river, developed the town's economy by obtaining grants of a fair and market, and probably reshaped the settlement pattern of the town. The abbey's role in promoting the development of the town's cloth trade is less certain. While many Cistercian abbeys were leading wool producers, and although Coggeshall exported wool to Italy, its flocks were never large and local wool was not of a particularly high quality, although the town did host notable wool fairs.[4]

Nonetheless, cloth-making appears to have been evident in Coggeshall by the late thirteenth century when the surnames of fuller and webbe (weaver) are recorded in the town. Cloths from Coggeshall are among those mentioned in a list of customs payable at Ipswich at the end of the thirteenth century. The town's cloth products had become distinctive enough for a Coggeshall cloak to be identified in the Leicester coroner's rolls in 1320.[5] In the 1390s Coggeshall was the third-largest centre for cloth sealed in Essex, producing mainly narrow cloths known as straits. By the late 1460s it had become the second-largest centre in the county,

[4] Andrews, ed., *Discovering Coggeshall* 2, pp. 6–7, 23, 67; Britnell, Colchester, p. 45, n. 48.

[5] Andrews, ed., *Discovering Coggeshall* 2, pp. 23–4; Britnell, *Colchester*, p. 14, n. 36.

although its output was less than a quarter of the output of Colchester.[6] Among the seventy people paying ulnage in Coggeshall around this time were Christina and John Paycocke.[7]

The Paycocke family had been based in Suffolk and Essex since at least the thirteenth century. The earliest known ancestor of the clothier Thomas Paycocke is his grandfather (or possibly his great-grandfather if a generation has been missed), also called Thomas. He died in 1461 and had a gravestone, now lost, inscribed with his occupation, as a butcher, in Coggeshall parish church. He was, however, also associated with the cloth trade. His widow Christina and 'sons' John senior and junior (the latter possibly her grandson) brought a case to the Court of Common Pleas in London in 1467 as the executors of Thomas' will. Robert Colman, fuller of Coggeshall, and William Skarlet, weaver of Coggeshall, had made a bond with Thomas Paycocke in London in 1451 for £20 payable at the following Michaelmas. The executors claimed that Thomas had never received the £20, but the defendants pleaded that they had offered the money to him at Yeldham in Essex, by the hand of William Dorewarde, but Thomas had only accepted £8. Two gentlemen from Colchester and another Robert Colman of Coggeshall, cloth-maker, acted as surety for the defendants.[8] Colman the fuller and Skarlet subsequently brought another case against John Fabiano, merchant of London, claiming he had unlawfully maintained the suit of the executors.[9] By revealing that Thomas had lent a large sum of money to two Coggeshall cloth producers, this case shows us that he had close associations with the local textile industry, and sufficient resources to loan money to other craftsmen working within it. Thomas Paycocke may also have been a tax commissioner in Coggeshall and landowner in Earls Colne (Essex) in the mid fifteenth century, again suggesting that he was able to accumulate some wealth.[10]

Like the elder Thomas, John, his son (or grandson) was a butcher, and both men may have been involved in the wool trade as graziers and dealers, as well as working as part-time cloth-makers. Christina, Thomas' widow, and John Paycocke paid ulnage in Coggeshall in 1464–65 on 3½ cloths each.[11] John appointed two fullers from the nearby villages of Little Coggeshall and Aldham to be witnesses to his will. He had accumulated sufficient means by his death in 1506 to make provision for the

[6] See Appendix 2.

[7] TNA, E 101/342/24.

[8] Court of Common Pleas, CP 40/822, rot. 284d, published at http://www.british-history.ac.uk/no-series/common-pleas/1399-1500/hilary-term-1467

[9] Court of Common Pleas, CP 40/823, rot. 345, published at http://www.british-history.ac.uk/no-series/common-pleas/1399-1500/easter-term-1467

[10] Thornton, 'Paycocke's House', p. 7.

[11] TNA, E 101/342/24.

commemoration of his soul and that of his parents in the parish church, as well as leaving bequests to his three sons. John owned a number of properties in Coggeshall and on the road to Colchester and his will referred to three principal houses that he left, one each, to his sons, including a house in West Street that he bequeathed to his youngest son Thomas.[12]

Thomas married Margaret Horrold, the daughter of a wealthy clothier from Clare in Suffolk. The Paycockes had family connections in Clare and Thomas may have been apprenticed to the Horrolds or even distantly related. Margaret's father, Thomas Horrold (d. 1504), had built up a cloth-making business and with his brother owed debts to London mercers in the 1480s. He was probably the younger son of John Horrold (d. 1478), who was described as a weaver and mercer in 1440, assessed for ulnage, and held lands in several Suffolk and Essex villages. Thomas and Margaret Paycocke seem to have enjoyed particular favour from Thomas Horrold in his will. Margaret received an estate and Thomas Paycocke was made the senior executor. It was also Thomas and Margaret Paycocke, rather than Horrold's own wife or son, who were given responsibility for Horrold's two younger daughters, Margaret's sisters, Margaret (II) and Margery.[13]

Thomas Paycocke's own will of 1518 reflected these family arrangements, giving prominence to the memory of his father-in-law, Thomas Horrold. It stipulated that Horrold was to be one of the main beneficiaries of the chantry to be established in Coggeshall church, and that a brass image of Thomas Horrold and his family was to be provided in Clare church.[14] Although his first wife Margaret had predeceased him, Paycocke left bequests to his former wife's younger sisters, Margaret (II) and Margery Horrold. Perhaps mindful though, of trouble ahead, he directed, 'if the said Margery make any business and trouble with mine executors I will her part be otherwise bestowed'. Unfortunately, as will be discussed below, he was to be proved correct.

When Thomas Paycocke died in 1518, his second wife Anne Cotton was pregnant. Thomas therefore left his unborn child 500 marks, and willed that if the child was male then he should also inherit the house and other property when he reached twenty-one. If the child was female, however, all the property was to descend to his brother John and his male heirs. In fact, the child was female, and Thomas' nephew, John Paycocke the younger (d. 1584), brought two Chancery petitions in 1529–32 to try

12 TNA, PROB 11/15/107. Power, *Paycockes*, pp. 24–6; Thornton, 'Paycocke's House', pp. 8–10.

13 TNA, PROB 11/14/319. Thornton, 'Paycocke's House', pp. 12–15.

14 See below, Appendix 4.

to secure the estate. Thomas' elder brother, John Paycocke, was assessed on £53 of goods in 1524, and his son John on £10.[15] Although the richest man in Coggeshall, John does not seem to have been a major clothier. Perhaps the bequests in Thomas' will had depleted the family's fortune.

Paycocke's cloth-making business

As noted above, Thomas's father and grandfather (or great-grandfather) were both butchers who were probably involved in the cloth trade, and members of the family were producing small quantities of cloth in the town by the mid fifteenth century. These could have provided the foundations for Thomas's business, together with the property he inherited on the site of Paycocke's House, and other holdings from his father John Paycocke in 1506. It was the Horrolds, however, who probably brought Thomas the greatest wealth. Margaret Horrold could have provided a substantial dowry on her marriage, and she inherited an estate on the death of her father in 1504. As executor to Thomas Horrold's will, Paycocke also had oversight of Horrold's two younger daughters, Margaret (II) and Margery, and their inherited lands, and other elements of Horrold's estate. Indeed, it was later claimed that Thomas Paycocke had misappropriated some of this income. Margery Horrold's husband, John Leman, made two petitions to the Court of Chancery between 1518 and 1529, claiming that the income from the lands left for Margaret (II) and Margery, worth £8 a year, had been illegally seized by Thomas Paycocke from 1504 until his death in 1518. Leman tried to obtain the money from Paycocke's executor, Thomas Perpoint, who responded by arguing that the money had been used towards supporting the two younger sisters in the Paycocke household. The outcome of the case is not known.[16] Paycocke may also have directly inherited or taken over Thomas Horrold's cloth-making business, as the bequests in Paycocke's will to repair local roads suggest that the main extent of his trade was between Clare to the north and London to the south.[17]

Most of what we know about Thomas as a clothier comes from his will. He required his executors to give a broadcloth to the abbot and convent of Coggeshall, and this may have been the type of cloth that he produced. He left legacies to two shearmen, Thomas and Edward Gooday and their families, and a former apprentice, Humphrey Stoner. Paycocke cancelled the debts owing to him from weaver John Beycham and fuller Robert Taylor, and left them additional bequests. He had seven other servants or tenants, including John Sponer, probably the son

[15] Thornton, 'Paycocke's House', pp. 17–19.
[16] TNA, C 1/536/8, 9; Thornton, 'Paycocke's House', pp. 13–15.
[17] *ODNB*.

of a Coggeshall weaver who had died in 1511.[18] Paycocke had close links with a London draper, Thomas Perpoint, whom he called his cousin and made his executor. Perpoint's will, made in 1544, reveals that he had a dye-house and another house in Coggeshall, as well as properties in and around London. Paycocke may well have been Perpoint's business partner, providing him with a reliable supply of undyed cloth that Perpoint dyed in Coggeshall and marketed in London.[19] Paycocke also made the following provisions, which reveal something about the scale of his cloth-making business:

> Item I bequeath to all my weavers, fullers and shearmen that be not afore rehearsed by name 12d apiece. And will they that have wrought me very much work have 3s 4d apiece. Item I bequeath to be distributed among my combers, carders and spinners total £4.

Thomas Paycocke was therefore a clothier, with workers who would comb, card and spin the wool, and weave, full and finish the cloth. If the bequest that totalled £4 quoted above was distributed evenly by giving 12d to each worker, 80 persons would benefit, but if each worker received only 4d, it would stretch to as many as 240 workers.[20] In any case, the scale of Paycocke's operations was significant.

What is not clear from the will is whether Thomas Paycocke employed any of these workers on his own premises, in a nascent factory system, as a small handful of clothiers later did, such as William Stumpe of Malmesbury and John Winchcombe of Newbury. The long, low room at the back of Paycocke's house is traditionally supposed to have been used for weaving.[21] In 1539, only twenty years after Paycocke's death, the weavers of Essex and Suffolk, including those of Ipswich, Hadleigh, Lavenham, Bergholt, Colchester and Dedham complained that master weavers were unemployed because clothiers now had looms, weavers and fullers working in their own houses.[22] In 1575, John Paycocke owned land containing six houses with narrow frontages at the end of East Street in Coggeshall, which may have accommodated the family's cloth-workers.[23]

It has been suggested that Paycocke introduced the distinctive handspun, undyed cloth known as 'Coggeshall whites', and it was to this that he owed his fortune. The yarn for the warp was handspun on the distaff

[18] Thornton, 'Paycocke's House', pp. 22–4; Poos, *Rural Society*, p. 65.
[19] TNA, PROB 11/30/159. I am grateful to Dr Thornton for this point.
[20] Thornton, 'Paycocke's House', p. 68.
[21] Power, 'Thomas Paycocke', p. 157.
[22] See above, pp. 69–70.
[23] Andrews, ed., *Discovering Coggeshall* 2, pp. 11, 72.

rather than on the spinning wheel, producing a finer quality cloth.[24] In the 1570s though, Anthony Bonvisi (1470x75–1558), a merchant belonging to an ancient family from Lucca in north Italy, was credited with introducing these 'Coxall' cloths to Coggeshall around 1539.[25] 'Coxhall whites' were being sold in Antwerp in 1538, and were recognised in the cloth-making statute of 1552.[26]

Thomas' brother, Robert, also ran a significant cloth-making business. Robert bought wool in 1502–03 from John Heritage, a wool trader from Moreton-in-Marsh in Gloucestershire. Robert purchased 2 sacks and 3 tods of *remys* wool, more than any of the other traders that year. It has been presumed that the sale was negotiated in London and Robert paid £3 and promised to pay the remainder of the total of £10 3s the following August.[27] A petition presented to the Court of Chancery c.1520 recounted that Robert had sold over £37 worth of cloth to John Parle, a London merchant. Robert had subsequently died and Parle claimed that he had already delivered two tons of oil worth £20 in part payment of the debt, but Robert's executors had taken a plea of debt against Parle in the sheriff of London's court to recover the full original amount.[28]

Paycocke's religious bequests

Thomas Paycocke's religious bequests, like those of many other wealthy clothiers and merchants, made detailed provisions for the benefit of his soul and those of his family. His funeral, if the executors followed the requests in his will, would have been an elaborate affair. A trental (a series of thirty requiem Masses) was to be said, with repeated commemorations on the seventh day after and a month after. Payments were to be made on these three occasions to small children carrying wax candles, men holding torches, bell-ringers, and for two sermons. Thomas Paycocke stipulated that he should be buried before St Katherine's altar in Coggeshall church and gave 100s for carving and gilding images in the aisle where it lay. Thomas founded a chantry in Coggeshall church, with a priest and six poor men, to pray for the souls of himself and his wife, his parents, and his father-in-law, Thomas Horrold of Clare.

The Paycockes were buried at the parish church of St Peter ad Vincula, Coggeshall, in the north aisle, which may have been built by earlier

[24] These cloths were known variously as Coggeshall whites, handwarps and baizes.

[25] *TED*, iii, p. 211; C.T. Martin, rev. Basil Morgan, 'Bonvisi, Antonio (1470x75–1558)', *ODNB*; Kerridge, *Textile Manufactures*, pp. 90–4.

[26] *De Engelse Natie te Antwerpen*, ii, p. 341; Appendix 3.

[27] Dyer, *Country Merchant*, p. 118. *Remys* was a lesser grade of wool.

[28] TNA, C 1/556/28. John Parle is described as a London merchant in C 1/546/60.

generations of the family. Although this aisle, much of the tower and the west end of the church were damaged by a bombing raid in 1940, the church has since been restored and the Paycocke tombs can still be seen in front of the altar rail. These comprise the tombs of Thomas Paycocke and his wives Margaret and Anne; his brother John and wife Joan; brother Robert and wives Elizabeth and Joan; and Robert's grandson Thomas. Brasses survive for John, Joan and the younger Thomas, who died in 1580. While the elder Thomas' brass has disappeared, his merchant's mark still survives, carved on his tomb stone, as does the mark of his brother Robert on his tomb. The fact that both brothers used the same symbol, only altering their initials, suggests that they were closely associated rather than rival business partners.

Thomas Paycocke's instructions for commemoration extended well beyond his parish church. The monks of Coggeshall Abbey were to provide a dirge and Mass and to ring their bells at his burial, and again on the seventh day and a month afterwards. Thomas was a brother of the Crutched Friars of Colchester and gave them £4 to pray for him. He made gifts to the Grey Friars of Colchester and the friars of Maldon, Chelmsford, Sudbury and Clare. Thomas also left bequests to churches at Bradwell, Pattiswick and Markshall, whose parishes were adjacent to Coggeshall; to Stoke-by-Nayland, Clare and Poslingford in Suffolk; to Ovington and Belchamp St Paul in Essex; and to St Paul in London. Thomas made special provision for his father-in-law, Thomas Horrold, to whom he appears to have owed so much. In addition to specifically naming him in his new chantry in Coggeshall church, he instructed his executors to obtain a stone and memorial brass for Thomas Horrold's grave in Clare church 'with his picture and his wife and children thereon'. He also left five cows or £3 in money to Clare church to maintain Thomas Horrold's obit.[29]

Paycocke's House

Thomas Paycocke's house on West Street in Coggeshall comprises a main range of five bays, facing the street, together with two rear wings. The main range is timber-framed and infilled with herringbone brickwork (known as brick nogging), and the upper storey is jettied with a fascia board with vine leaf decoration covering the ends of the projecting floor joists. Traditionally, the building has been interpreted as having been built by Thomas's father, John, and bequeathed to his son. Recent tree-ring analysis, however, has found that the street frontage of the house was built for Thomas Paycocke after his father's death in two phases, in 1509 and 1510 (the second phase comprising a fifth bay that provided the

[29] See below, Appendix 4.

gateway to the street frontage). There was a jettied half-storey with attic chambers possibly providing warehousing space, which was removed in 1588. It provided an imposing façade for another building adjoining it at the rear, presumably the older house that Thomas' father bequeathed to him in 1506, part of which may survive in the south-west range.[30]

The work of 1509–10 created a fashionable new front range with continental influences, perhaps acquired through Paycocke's connections in the cloth trade. The second jettied half-storey, with attic chambers, subsequently removed, was common in France at this time, but 'Thomas Paycocke was undoubtedly a pioneer' in including this structure, for it only became more popular in England later in the sixteenth century.[31] The fascia board with its foliage trails and grotesque faces is probably one of the earliest English examples of this style of ornament. There is very little to compare on the early-sixteenth-century merchants' houses that survive in Lavenham.[32] A similar combination of Gothic and Renaissance styles is found in the early-sixteenth-century roof of St David's cathedral in Wales, where it is suggested that Flemish craftsmen were involved. The oriel windows at Paycocke's, although modern replacements, seem to be based on similar originals that used a continental style of construction. There is no doubt that 'the external appearance of the new structure would have represented the height of fashion in 1509'.[33]

One of the most striking features of the house is the original moulded and carved wooden fascia, which together with other carvings on the building seems to have carried messages that were personal to the Paycockes. The vine trail motif that runs along the fascia includes various symbols and grotesques similar to those found in illuminated manuscripts. Recent work has shown that marginal drawings, even in functional medieval documents such as registers, had a meaning closely related to the text, and the decoration on Paycocke's House seems to have been symbolic to the family.[34] Thomas' initials are set either side of his merchant's mark in front of the parlour. His marriage to Margaret Horrold and inheritance from the Horrold family may be celebrated on the exterior by the carving of the upper halves of a king and queen holding

[30] Alston, 'Paycocke's Coggeshall'; Thornton, 'Paycocke's House', pp. 80–1.

[31] Alston, 'Paycocke's Coggeshall', p. 8.

[32] One exception is the Old Grammar School, Lavenham, a former clothier's house, which has some similar decorative features to Paycocke's: Alston, 'Old Grammar School', pp. 34, 45–7.

[33] Alston, 'Paycocke's Coggeshall', p. 4.

[34] M. Camille, 'At the Edge of the Law: An Illustrated Register of Writs in the Pierpoint Morgan Library', in N. Rogers, ed., *England in the Fourteenth Century. Proceedings of the 1991 Harlaxton Symposium* (Stamford, 1993), pp. 1–14.

Plate 15 Wyvern detail from decorated fascia of Paycocke's, Coggeshall. This image may suggest that Thomas Paycocke wanted to associate himself with the London Weavers' Company.

each other by the hand, as well as more clearly inside the house by their initials (TP and MP) on ceiling beams in the hall.[35] It also appears that Thomas Paycocke wanted to associate himself with the London Weavers' Company. The leopard and the rose on the house facade formed part of the Company's heraldic insignia, and the upside-down 'wyver' or wyvern, also carved on the fascia (Plate 15), was a visual pun or trade rebus that eventually became a supporter of the Weavers' Company arms in the early seventeenth century.[36] The bird perched on the vine may represent a pelican or peacock. The latter would have been a rebus for Paycocke, and appears on the seal of a later Thomas Paycocke, affixed to a document of 1564.[37] Paycocke's merchant's mark, also depicted on the house, might be a stylised representation of peacock feathers (Plate 14). Other suggestions for the mark are a two-stemmed clover (possibly

[35] Thornton, 'Paycocke's House', p. 11.

[36] Andrews, ed., *Discovering Coggeshall 2*, p. 59. 'Wyvern' derives from 'wyver': *OED*.

[37] TNA, DL 25/3371.

a pun on clothier), a trefoil of three pearls or berries on a stalk split at the base, or an ermine tail (an indication of cleanliness or quality of the cloth). The same symbol appears on Thomas and Robert Paycocke's tombs in Coggeshall parish church, and on a carved oak bedpost on display at Paycocke's House.[38]

The Paycockes used the house as a centre for their business. The carriageway doors enabled the movement of goods. The roof space and parts of the wings of the house were probably used to store both wool, before it was distributed to cloth-workers, and also the cloth that they produced. Much of the garden may have served as a tentering yard where cloths were stretched out to dry after fulling. Thomas's will refers to a dove house in the garden. The east chamber on the ground floor was probably a business office. The hall may have provided a showroom or merchant premises, as it appears to have initially been built unheated.[39]

The 'Discovering Coggeshall' project has organised a tree-ring dating programme combined with detailed building recording, which has enabled twenty-three buildings in the town to be dated. The chronological distribution of these dates shows a striking peak at the end of the fourteenth century and in the early fifteenth century, with building activity then declining during the mid fifteenth and early sixteenth centuries. This peak between the 1360s and 1460s is repeated in other tree-ring data for buildings across Essex. While the Coggeshall sample is limited, it arguably reflects the economic trends of rising standards of living and increased prosperity in the later fourteenth century followed by economic difficulties in the mid to late fifteenth century. Paycocke's House is the only building within the sample to fall within the first third of the sixteenth century, and no houses date from the final third of the fifteenth century. Admittedly a small sample, this nonetheless suggests that wealth and commercial expansion became more concentrated within the town after 1450 than in the previous century, when more houses appear to have been adapted to commercial requirements by having cross-wings added to provide workshop and storage space. It was also in this earlier period, between 1403 and 1429, that a market and court hall building were constructed in Coggeshall.[40]

Recent research has also shown how the Paycockes acquired an extensive portfolio of property within the town during the sixteenth century. This included the East Street houses which may have been built

[38] Victoria and Albert Museum, London, set of bed posts, museum no. W.22–1913, on loan to Paycocke's House, Coggeshall.

[39] See above, p. 201.

[40] Andrews, ed., *Discovering Coggeshall* 2, pp. 38–9, 221–6.

to accommodate textile workers,[41] as well as a fifteenth-century house of exceptional quality in the central location of Market End. This building comprised a single-storey hall, with handsome queen post roof, and adjoining cross-wing, jettied on both sides, forming the only known three-storey building of its time within the town. It now forms Cavendish House and part of the White Hart Inn. The name 'Paycok' has been incised on the fireplace lintel within another house, No. 14 East Street, which contains an impressive cross-wing, and possibly a shop at ground level.[42] The Paycockes owned most of the land south of their house in West Street towards the river. A rental of 1575 shows that this was held by Thomas and John Paycocke. The two men held 24 plots, totalling 28 acres, within the town. The main landholding, in an area of meadows and pasture, may have been built up by the butchers Thomas (d. 1461) and John (d. 1506) for grazing. Their descendants as clothiers would have found the land valuable because it provided them with access to water and space to carry out finishing processes involving washing and drying cloth on a relatively large scale. The Paycockes may have diverted a brook to benefit their land.[43]

Writing in 2004, Richard Britnell argued that the survival of Paycocke's attractive house, and the fact that he was commemorated by Eileen Power in her book *Medieval People*, 'brought him a fame that his unremarkable career would never otherwise have earned for him'.[44] Thanks to subsequent research, we now know more about the family business, and this statement needs to be reassessed. Members of the Paycocke family produced cloth in the mid fifteenth century, combining this with the butchery trade and lending money to other Coggeshall textile workers. Thomas' brother Robert bought a major consignment of wool on credit in 1502/3. By the 1570s the family had amassed a major property portfolio in the town, probably started by Thomas' predecessors. Thomas benefitted significantly from his marriage to Margaret Horrold and from the bequests from his father-in-law. He celebrated the marriage in the decoration outside and within his house and expressed his gratitude to his father-in-law in his will. Thomas may have aspired to associate himself with the London Weavers' Company. He built a new façade for Paycocke's House after his father's death, with innovative features and continental influences. As the majority of buildings in the town had been built in the late fourteenth and early fifteenth centuries, the house reflects the concentration of wealth in one community within

[41] See above, p. 204.
[42] Andrews, ed., *Discovering Coggeshall 2*, pp. 158–66.
[43] Andrews, ed., *Discovering Coggeshall 2*, pp. 15–17, 32.
[44] *ODNB*.

the hands of a single family, an increasing feature of the cloth industry during the early sixteenth century. While Richard Britnell suggested that 'Paycocke's chief claim to fame is perhaps his father's generosity',[45] given what we now know about the timber-dating of the house frontage and the provisions in Thomas Horrold's will, it would be more appropriate to say that Paycocke owed at least some of his fame to the generosity of his father-in-law.

THE SPRINGS OF LAVENHAM

> The rise of the family as clothiers, their accumulation of a vast family fortune, and their entry, through marriage, into the ranks of the nobility, encourage the perception of the Springs as an archetypal late medieval success story.
>
> 'Spring family', *Oxford Dictionary of National Biography*

It is difficult to imagine that five hundred years ago, the now predominantly rural and agricultural county of Suffolk was 'more urbanised and industrialised than probably any other area in England'.[46] About 30 per cent of the county's population were living in towns, and about one-third of its rural inhabitants earned a living primarily from crafts. Nowhere is this contrast between medieval industry and modern rurality more apparent than in Lavenham.

Lavenham lies five miles north-east of Sudbury on a ridge on the western bank of the river Brett. Today a village of less than 2,000 inhabitants, in 1524 it was the fifteenth wealthiest town in England, when the total tax contributions paid by its residents, and particularly Alice Spring, widow of the clothier Thomas, placed Lavenham above such prominent centres as Gloucester, Yarmouth and Lincoln.[47] Such a meteoric rise was short-lived, and within a generation cloth production was moving elsewhere and the town had become an economic backwater. An early-seventeenth-century source describes how the townspeople even began to demolish the larger houses that they could no longer afford to maintain. 'Lavenham may claim a place alongside any late-twentieth century industrial slum as a victim of economic boom and bust.'[48]

This fleeting prosperity has helped to preserve much of the late medieval townscape of Lavenham. Almost every corner of this small town still provides a vista of ancient timbers, coloured plaster, leaning gables and

[45] *ODNB*.

[46] Bailey, *Medieval Suffolk*, p. 293.

[47] *CUHB*, p. 765.

[48] Alston, 'Old Grammar School', pp. 31, 47; National Trust, *Guildhall of Lavenham*, pp. 3–11.

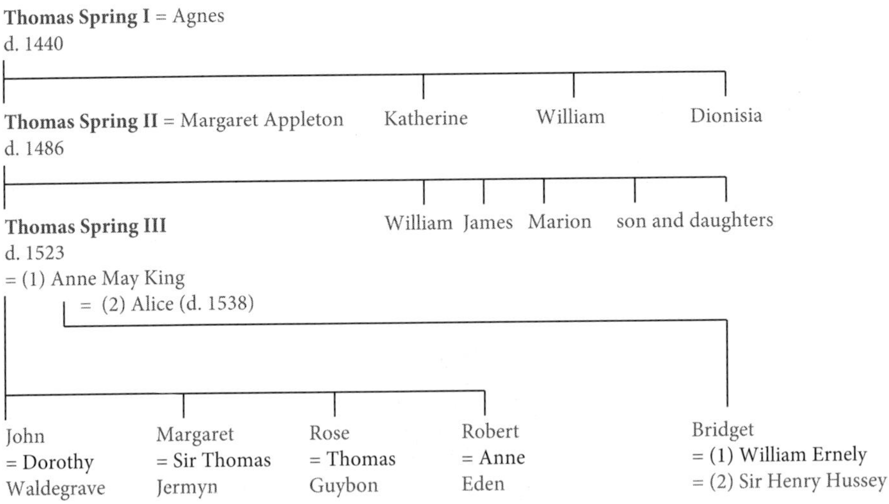

Figure 9 Spring family tree

Source: Betterton and Dymond, *Lavenham*, p. 51; McClenagham, *Springs of Lavenham*, p. 85.

lurching roofs. Buildings within the town made generous use of timber, often moulded and sometimes carved. The majority date from between about 1460 and 1530. One of the last buildings to be constructed during this boom period was the impressive two-storeyed, lavishly timbered guildhall, built for the Corpus Christi guild, one of five fraternities operating within the town (Plate 13). Yet if one building alone was to characterise the wealth and the instability of the late medieval cloth trade, Lavenham's parish church of St Peter and St Paul would usefully serve that task (Plate 16). Between 1485 and 1540, at least thirty-five donors with links to the cloth trade made bequests to the church fabric. They included legacies for the tower, standing 141 feet high, 'as mighty as its nave is noble', from the clothiers Thomas Spring II and Thomas III.[49] Around the plinth at the base of the tower are the merchant's marks of the Spring family, and the shields and stars of the de Vere family, but by the time that the tower parapet was added, Thomas Spring III could include shields bearing his family's newly granted coat of arms. The trade upon which this wealth was generated was volatile, and during the trade crisis of 1525, when unemployed cloth-workers rose in protest against the burden of repeated taxation, some of the rebels tried to ring the bells in this newly completed tower to summon support for their cause. A wealthy townsman, however, had removed the clappers, preventing

[49] Bettley and Pevsner, *Suffolk: West*, p. 351.

Plate 16 Church of St Peter and St Paul, Lavenham, Suffolk. Reflecting the wealth generated by cloth-making, this church was built in the late fifteenth and early sixteenth centuries by the efforts of local clothiers, chiefly the Springs, and the lord of the manor John de Vere, thirteenth earl of Oxford.

greater numbers from assembling and enabling negotiations to proceed. That wealthy townsman may even have been Thomas III's eldest son, Sir John, or Thomas' son-in-law, Thomas Jermyn, as these two men helped to restrain the local populace during the unrest.[50]

By the late fifteenth century, Lavenham was the leading centre of the cloth industry in Suffolk. Trade was becoming more concentrated: by 1477–78, the three leading merchants in Lavenham sold more than twice as many cloths as Colchester's leading seller.[51] In 1522, 21 out of the 23 wealthiest individuals in Lavenham, assessed on more than £50 in goods, were clothiers. At the larger town of Sudbury, there were only nine residents with more than £50, and only two of these were clothiers. Over thirty clothiers were recorded in Lavenham, of whom all but one

[50] *Manuscripts in the Welsh Language*, i, p. ii; *ODNB*. See also above, Chapter 4.
[51] Britnell, *Colchester*, p. 184.

were worth over £10, and more than one-third of all the trades listed in the town were in the textile industry.[52]

Lavenham was home to three generations of the Spring family, all called Thomas, and all clothiers. Thomas I, who died in 1440, is thought to have moved the family from Houghton-le-Spring in County Durham in the early fifteenth century. He may have been a sheep farmer who successfully adapted to making and marketing cloth in his new home.[53] By 1424–25, he was the largest producer in Lavenham. Thomas I accumulated sufficient wealth to be able to leave £100 in his will 'to be raised from my goods and debts', and four tenements in Lavenham and Preston to his four children. Thomas II, who appears to have been the eldest son and heir of Thomas I, inherited his capital messuage and expanded the business further.[54]

Under Thomas III, known as 'the rich clothier', the Spring family's fortunes in the cloth industry reached their peak. He married Anne King, daughter of a clothier of Boxford, and later a widow, Alice May. Anne may have supplied further business connections and Alice certainly provided additional wealth: Thomas' will records that Alice brought him 600 marks at the time of their marriage.[55] As we do not know where the Springs lived in Lavenham, the main indicator of Thomas III's business success is the personal wealth that he had accrued by the end of his life. He invested heavily in the land market, acquiring land in Suffolk and the adjoining counties of Norfolk, Essex and Cambridgeshire. Sometimes he appears to have challenged long-established landholding customs. On Westminster Abbey's manor of Birdbrook, he was admitted to six copyhold tenements 'free of any punishment, penalty or forfeiture for waste done or to be done in any home, homes or buildings upon these premises', and he may have 'bullied and bribed' the monks to obtain such a favourable concession.[56] By 1522, Thomas III possessed moveable goods worth £1,800 and debts owing to him of £2,200, far more than any other inhabitant in Lavenham. His landed estate in Suffolk, comprising seventeen holdings, and worth over £100, was the third-highest in value in the county.[57] His wealth attracted the attention of the poet of the royal court, John Skelton (c.1460–1529), who also held the rectory of Diss in Norfolk, just over twenty miles from Lavenham. In his satirical

52 *Military Survey*, pp. 19–29, 75–82, 128,

53 Tracy and Harrison, 'Thomas Spring's Chantry', p. 221.

54 *ODNB*; Betterton and Dymond, *Lavenham*, pp. 10, 12.

55 See below, Appendix 5.

56 P.R. Schofield, 'Extranei and the Market for Customary Land on a Westminster Abbey Manor in the Fifteenth Century', *Agricultural History Review* 49 (2001), p. 16.

57 *Military Survey*, pp. 15, 75.

poem 'Why come ye not to courte?', written in November 1522, Skelton describes the impact on the huge personal wealth of Spring of the forced loans levied by the Crown that year:

Now nothing but 'Pay, pay!'
With, 'laugh and lay down,
Borough, city and town!'
Good Spring of Lavenham
Must count what became
Of his cloth making.
He is at such taking
Though his purse wax dull,
He must tax for his wool,
By nature of a new writ.
My lord's grace nameth it
'Because it is not enough'
In spite of his tenth
He must pay again
A thousand or twain
Of his gold in store
And yet he paid before
An hundred pound and more,
Which pincheth him sore!
My lord's grace will bring
Down this high spring
And bring it so low
It shall not ever flow.[58]

Skelton's poem describes how Spring's ready money was exhausted, 'his purse wax dull', but being now assessed on all his goods and business assets, 'He must tax for his wool'. Although Spring had already been assessed for a large payment of 'An hundred pound and more', a second, larger demand was now being imposed on him.[59] In fact Spring was charged with paying £533 on his assessed wealth of £3,200, a rate of almost 17 per cent, and which he would have had to find either from among his own moveable goods of £1,800, or from the recoverable debts owing to him of £1,400. Ironically, Spring had acted as a commissioner for the collection of taxes in the preceding decade. When another tax was

[58] John Skelton, 'Why Come Ye Nat to Courte?', lines 930–52, in *John Skelton, The Complete English Poems*, ed. J. Scattergood (Harmondsworth, 1983), pp. 302–3.

[59] Greg Walker, *John Skelton and the Politics of the 1520s* (Cambridge, 1988), pp. 212–13.

levied in 1524, Alice, his widow, paid a total of £66 13s 4d, the second-largest contribution in Suffolk after the duke of Norfolk.[60]

Despite these exactions, Thomas III left a fortune on his death in 1523. His bequests and executors' distributions, including expenses, totalled £8,000. Thomas III's elder son, Sir John Spring (1498–1548), was described as a gentleman in 1524 and knighted in 1547. Thomas III's younger son, Robert, retired from the cloth trade in the mid sixteenth century and the family seat in Suffolk, then moved from Lavenham to Pakenham. This generation of the family continued to make advantageous marriages, notably Thomas's daughter, Bridget, to William Ernely, son of the lord chief justice of the common pleas, and Thomas's niece, Margaret, to Aubrey de Vere, second son of the fifteenth earl of Oxford.[61]

The Springs' cloth-making business

Thomas I was the largest producer recorded in the ulnage account for Lavenham of 1424–25, accounting for 49 cloths out of the 555 brought by thirty-two different people to be taxed. Two other members of the family were recorded in the same ulnage account: Agnes, probably Thomas's wife, and William, each producing ten cloths for sale. Over forty years later, another William Spring was commissioned in Colchester in 1470 to dye 100 lb of wool blue on behalf of John Spring of Lavenham. Seventeen years after Thomas I's death, his widow Agnes was summoned to answer for a debt owed to a merchant of Great Yarmouth.[62]

Thomas II expanded this cloth-making business further. The ulnage accounts show how either he or his son took an increasing share of cloth sales in Lavenham, from less than 10 per cent of total sales in the early 1460s to over 30 per cent ten years later, when Spring was taxed on more sales than any merchant in the previous decade. While the unchanging figures recorded in the ulnage accounts for some years suggest that some of the accounting may have been fictitious, the family's business was clearly growing. By the mid-1460s, one-fifth of the cloth sealed in Suffolk was registered in Lavenham. But although he was the leading clothier in Lavenham, Spring was still overshadowed across Suffolk by six larger producers in Hadleigh and Bildeston.[63] Thomas II left £100 each to three of his children and the large sum of 100 marks (£66 13s 4d) to 'my spinners, weavers and fullers'.[64] If we assume that Thomas II intended each of his spinners, weavers and fullers to receive the very generous bequest

[60] Hoyle, 'Taxation', p. 655; *ODNB*.
[61] *ODNB*.
[62] Britnell, *Colchester*, p. 165; *ODNB*.
[63] Britnell, 'Woollen Textile Industry', pp. 92, 98–9; Amor, 'Jack of all Trades', pp. 425–6.
[64] Betterton and Dymond, *Lavenham*, p. 12.

of 6s 8d for each individual, as John Motte of Bildeston left in 1473 for each of his spinners, weavers and fullers, the sum allocated would have provided for just over 220 workers. If Thomas II intended to leave 20d for each of his cloth-workers, the same sum as Stephen Raynham of Nayland left in 1514 to each of his weavers, that would have extended to 800 workers. If each person was intended to receive only 4d each, this could represent as many as 3,900 workers. Thomas II was clearly operating a major textile business, but exactly how many cloth-workers he was coordinating is not known.

Little is known about the business activities of Thomas III either, although after about thirty years of commercial life, he applied to the king for a general pardon. Granted in 1508, this pardon covered, among other faults, the 'illicit sale of cloth, wool, linen, and for non-payment of foreign merchants', for all 'falseness, deceptions, and offences in the making of woollen cloth and in drawing out the length and breadth of it and all false deceptions in the selling of woollen cloth'.[65] This suggests that Thomas III had become became uneasy about some of his business practices, although it should be noted that over 1,600 pardons were issued in Henry VII's reign, to recipients of all social ranks. These included many of Thomas' contemporary clothiers.[66] Thomas III's range of business contacts included John Heritage of Moreton-in-the-Marsh, from whom he bought wool, probably in London, in 1509, and John Lyard 'plomer', and Thomas Fox cloth-maker of Colchester, against whom he brought a lawsuit in Colchester in 1515–16. Thomas III still seems to have been producing cloth at the time of his death, as in his will, he left ten half balls of woad to his apprentice, Peter Gauge, and his executors paid for 411 of his cloths to be sealed for sale.[67]

It is interesting to speculate whether Thomas III's textile enterprise was so large that his death caused a short- or even longer-term economic shock in Lavenham, as at least one historian has suggested: 'The abrupt cessation of his trading cannot but have caused more or less severe dislocation until others were ready to take up the slack.'[68] Spring's fortune comprised more than 40 per cent of the combined assets of the clothiers in Babergh hundred. Between 1522 and 1524, the number of assessments of wealth in Lavenham of less than £2 rose from 40 per cent to over 56 per cent, and by 1568, the inhabitants of Lavenham paid only half as much tax in total as their counterparts in Long Melford, compared to two and a

[65] McClenaghan, *Springs of Lavenham*, p. 68.

[66] *LP*, i (1), no. 438, p. 240; K.J. Kesselring, *Mercy and Authority in the Tudor State* (Cambridge, 2003), p. 59.

[67] Dyer, *Country Merchant*, p. 117; Galloway, 'Colchester and its Region', p. 221; Betterton and Dymond, *Lavenham*, pp. 15, 100–1.

[68] Cornwall, *Wealth and Society*, pp. 72–3.

half times as much in 1524.[69] Lavenham was at the centre of disturbances in 1525, and threats of unrest were reported there in 1528 and 1536.[70] The loss of a town's leading employer, who may have paid premium rates to attract and retain labour, could have had a serious impact on the local economy. John Leland suggested that Bath was 'somewhat decayed' in 1542 after the deaths of three of its major clothiers.[71] Nonetheless, the evidence of wills reveals that successful clothiers continued to reside in Lavenham, with twenty out of the twenty-five clothiers who produced wills in the period 1530 to 1560 being sufficiently wealthy to prove them in the Prerogative Court of Canterbury, and it was not until the 1560s that Lavenham's fortunes began to wane significantly.[72]

The Springs' religious bequests

As the wealth of the Spring family grew, they made increasingly elaborate requests for their commemoration. Thomas I required a priest to be paid a stipend for four years to pray for his soul in Lavenham church. Thomas II instructed a priest to celebrate Masses for his soul for twenty years in Lavenham church and also left 10s to the rector of the parish to pray for his soul. Thomas III asked for a thousand Masses to be sung for his soul. He also left £100 for a Mass and dirge to be said in the church of every parish where he held lands, of which there were as many as 130. Thomas I bequeathed 9 marks to repair the highway between Lavenham and Bury St Edmunds; Thomas II left 200 marks and Thomas III gave 100 marks to repair broken roads around Lavenham. Thomas I left 100s for the fabric of the church, Thomas II gave 300 marks (£200) towards the building of the bell tower, and Thomas III bequeathed £200 to completing the tower.[73]

Each generation of the Spring family also requested a more prominent place of burial and commemoration in Lavenham parish church to reflect their increasing wealth and status. Thomas I asked to be buried in the cemetery of the church, Thomas II in the vestry, which he had financed and where he was commemorated with his wife and children on a memorial brass. Thomas III was buried before the altar of St Catherine, in a tomb surrounded by a parclose. Thomas II's brass depicts him and his family wearing shrouds and kneeling, emerging from two coffins (Plate 17). Above the figures were once text scrolls and a religious

[69] Cornwall, *Wealth and Society*, pp. 72–3.

[70] See above, Chapter 4.

[71] *Itinerary*, i, p. 143. See above, p. 121.

[72] Betterton and Dymond, *Lavenham*, p. 45. The Prerogative Courts of Canterbury and York proved wills of testators who left goods in more than one deanery or diocese, and therefore tended to deal with relatively wealthy individuals.

[73] Betterton and Dymond, *Lavenham*, pp. 10–15.

Plate 17 Detail of brass of Thomas Spring II, Lavenham church, Suffolk. This memorial brass depicts Thomas Spring II (d. 1486) and his children rising from a coffin in their shrouds at the Last Judgement.

device which have now been lost, although a shield containing Thomas' merchant's mark survives. Below the figures is a Latin inscription, which in translation reads:

> Pray for the souls of Thomas Sprynge, who caused this vestry to be made during his lifetime, and Margaret his wife. The said Thomas died on the 7 day of September in the year of our Lord 1486, and the aforesaid Margaret died on the _day of month_ in the year 148_ on whose souls may God have mercy, Amen.

Although the brass bears the date of Thomas' death, Margaret's dates remain blank except for the decade. Margaret was evidently alive when the brass was produced and she in fact lived until at least the first decade of the sixteenth century.

While Thomas III's will does not specifically mention a chantry, he had begun to found one as early as 1517, when a draft licence was prepared. After his death, his executors paid £200 for lands to provide an income to support two chaplains to celebrate Mass and six poor men to pray in the chantry each day. In a second licence of c.1527–28, an almshouse is also mentioned, and Alice, Thomas' wife, added seven poor women and widows, who would also attend the Masses and prayers. These would have taken place in the chantry chapel that his executors constructed on the south side of the chancel of Lavenham church. The Latin inscription running along the south parapet of the Spring chapel reads, in translation,

> [Pray for the soul of] Thomas Spring esquire, and of Alice his wife, who caused this chapel to be built in the year of our Lord 1525.

The interior and exterior of the Spring chapel are decorated with shields bearing the family's newly acquired coat of arms, and Thomas's own merchant's mark. Although most of the internal decoration and furnishing has been lost, the carved wall plates of the roof bear the Spring shield and crest, shields with the initials TS, as well as cherubs, flowers and leaves finishing with animal heads as stalks. The east window of this chapel originally contained glazing with Spring's merchant's mark, and a text asking the reader to pray for the souls of Thomas and Alice.[74]

Thomas III's tomb, enclosed by a parclose, or screen (Plate 18), which formed his mortuary chapel, lies on the other side of the church from his chantry chapel, at the east end of the north nave aisle. His chantry chapel could not have been constructed here because another clothier, Simon Branch, had already added a chantry chapel on the north side of the chancel. Thomas III's executors spent 100 marks procuring both the

[74] Tracy and Harrison, 'Spring's Chantry', pp. 224–8.

Plate 18 Detail of the Spring parclose screen, Lavenham church. Surrounding the tomb of Thomas Spring III (d. 1523), 'the rich clothier' and Alice, his wife, this richly decorated screen was intricately carved by craftsmen familiar with commissions for the royal court.

Purbeck marble tomb slab to which memorial brasses, now lost, were once attached, and the elaborately carved wooden parclose. This screen is a remarkable piece of craftsmanship: 'the superabundance and character of the applied decoration ... is not found in East Anglia, and is generally rare in England'.[75] The decoration includes a plethora of spring flowers, which may have been intended as a pun on the family's name. The craftsmen of the Spring parclose, who may have been Flemish immigrants who had settled in London, were familiar with continental joinery techniques and earlier Flemish, or Flemish-influenced, commissions for the royal court in the Henry VII Chapel in Westminster Abbey, and at St George's Chapel, Windsor. The Springs had connections through the de Vere family, earls of Oxford, which may have been used to procure these craftsmen at Lavenham, and possibly also to obtain the services of two master masons who had been engaged on royal projects. The design of Lavenham church tower has been attributed to Simon Clerk, master mason at Eton College and King's College, Cambridge, who lived about

[75] Tracy and Harrison, 'Spring's Chantry', p. 238.

eight miles from Lavenham at Hessett, and was also master mason of the abbey at Bury St Edmunds. The nave of Lavenham church is most likely to have been designed by Clerk's successor at King's College, John Wastell. The two may have collaborated at Lavenham, as they are known to have worked together on the church of St Mary the Virgin, Saffron Walden, and may also have done so at Great St Mary's, Cambridge. John de Vere, thirteenth earl of Oxford (d. 1513), who dominated East Anglian political society and enjoyed a close association with the early Tudor dynasty, acted as a quasi project-manager and fundraiser for the building programme at Lavenham's parish church, inducing local townspeople to support it.[76] It is even possible that through this family's network, Thomas Spring III met Henry VII or Henry VIII.

THE WINCHCOMBES OF NEWBURY

> In the days of King Henry the eight, that most noble and victorious prince, in the beginning of his reign, John Winchcombe, a broad-cloth weaver, dwelt in Newbury, a town in Berkshire; who for that he was a man of a merry disposition and honest conversation was wondrous well-beloved of rich and poor … Wherefore, being so good a companion, he was called of old and young Jack of Newbury'.
>
> Thomas Deloney, *Jack of Newbury* (1597)[77]

In 1597, Thomas Deloney published his work of prose fiction, *The Pleasant History of John Winchcomb, in his Younger Years called Jack of Newbury*. This popular work, appearing in sixteen editions before 1700, was dedicated 'To all famous cloth-workers in England', praising the 'long honoured trade of English clothiers'. In this rags to riches story, Jack, an exemplary worker, marries his master's widow, and runs an enormous workshop. Jack entertains Henry VIII and his entourage, leads a hundred of his own men to the battle of Flodden, and presents a petition to the royal court on behalf of clothiers. Deloney's account of Jack describes a wealthy clothier operating a workshop on a factory-sized scale, with two hundred looms housed in a single room. Entering folk memory and popular culture, Jack of Newbury was still the chief figure in the pageant of the cloth-workers of London a century later, while Daniel Defoe, writing in the 1720s, thought his story had 'almost grown fabulous'.[78]

76 Tracy and Harrison, 'Spring's Chantry', pp. 222–3. For the career of John de Vere, see Ross, *John de Vere*.

77 Deloney, *Jack of Newbury*, p. 314.

78 Deloney, *Jack of Newbury*; Lipson, *Economic History*, i, pp. 476–7; Daniel Defoe, *A Tour Through the Whole Island of Great Britain* (1724–26), quoted in Jackson, 'Boom-time Freaks', p. 166, n. 13. Defoe misdated Jack of Newbury to James I's reign.

Thomas Deloney, who died in or before 1600, was a silk-weaver and writer, probably born in Norwich. By the 1590s he was writing ballads while living in London, and became caught up in protests by the city's weavers, for which he was imprisoned.[79] *Jack of Newbury* depicts an idealised craft that is both subversive and nostalgic – one that challenges the king to change his trade policy, and looks back to an imaginary past when good management and charity earned the respect of kings. Events in *Jack of Newbury* are set in Henry VIII's reign but the concerns expressed were those particularly acute in the 1590s – poverty, the power of the guilds, and government involvement in manufacture.[80]

To what extent did John Winchcombe match the legendary Jack of Newbury? There were two John Winchcombes, father and son, both notable clothiers, who Deloney's poem appears to conflate into a single person. This has often confused subsequent accounts, and many of the achievements attributed to the elder John Winchcombe I (d. 1520) were in fact those of his son, John Winchcombe II (d. 1557). Thomas Fuller, for example, in his *Worthies of England* (1662), described John Winchcombe I as 'the most considerable clothier (without fancy and fiction) England ever beheld', and even Eric Kerridge's entry in the *Oxford Dictionary of National Biography* casts the elder John as Jack of Newbury.[81] Thanks to recent research by David Peacock, Christine Jackson and Margaret Yates though, the careers of father and son John I and John II are now much clearer, and they can be placed within the broader context of production in and around Newbury at the time.[82] While a work of fiction, there is much within *Jack of Newbury* that reflects events in the career of John Winchcombe II.

Newbury lies in the south-west corner of Berkshire on an important crossing point of the river Kennet. The road from Oxford and the Midlands to Winchester and Southampton runs north–south through the town and the road from London to Bath passes east–west just to the north. The town had an early history of cloth production, with a fulling mill documented in 1204 and the town's merchants discovered exporting wool from Southampton and Portsmouth without licence in 1275. Although the ulnage accounts suggest that Newbury's cloth trade in the late fourteenth century was relatively small, it had revived a century later, when its merchants were responsible for up to one-fifth of all cloth

[79] Paul Salzman, 'Deloney, Thomas (d. in or before 1600)', *ODNB*.

[80] Roger A. Ladd, 'Thomas Deloney and the London Weavers' Company', *Sixteenth Century Journal* 32 (2001), pp. 981–1001.

[81] Fuller, *Worthies*, p. 88; A.F. Pollard, rev. Eric Kerridge, 'Winchcombe, John (d. 1520)', *ODNB*.

[82] Peacock, 'Winchcombe Family'; Jackson, 'Boom-time Freaks'; Yates, *Town and Countryside*.

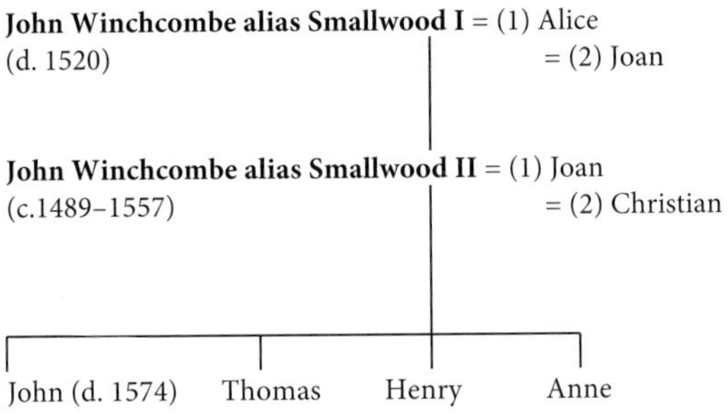

Figure 10 Winchcombe family tree
Source: *ODNB*.

sealed in Berkshire and Oxfordshire. By the early fifteenth century, many of the cloths being made in Newbury were kerseys, smaller and lighter than a broadcloth. In the customs accounts, three kerseys were usually assessed as being equivalent to one broadcloth. Newbury merchants paid brokage as they went to Southampton to export kerseys in 1439 and 1443. Other men in Newbury were known as kersey weavers or kersey makers in the mid fifteenth century.[83] It was on this established tradition of kersey production in Newbury that the Winchcombe family built their fortune.

Little is known of John Winchcombe I, who described himself in his will of 1520 as 'John Smalewoode the elder, alias John Wynchcombe'.[84] The widely accepted view that he originated from Winchcombe in Gloucestershire seems to rest solely on his surname, and a chancery case from the last seven years of the fifteenth century suggests that he may have moved to Newbury from Essex. The case, relating to property in Barking, Essex, claimed that John, son of John Smallwood of Barking, had pretended to inherit the lands of his father. It refers to Michael Winchcombe 'father in law' of John Smallwood, providing a potential explanation for the surname 'Smallwood alias Winchcombe' that both John I and John II used.[85] In the second decade of the sixteenth century, another claim was brought against John Winchcombe by Thomas and Joan Walsh, who claimed that Winchcombe had deprived them of their inheritance, a tenement, house and garden in Newbury. Around the same time, in 1518, John Winchcombe I entered into an agreement with the Dean and Canons of St George's Chapel, Windsor, to lease five pieces

[83] Yates, *Town and Country*, pp. 81–5.
[84] See Appendix 6.
[85] TNA, C 1/185/76; Peacock, 'Winchcombe Family', pp. 207–8.

of property in and around Newbury, at over £6 per year. This land had formerly belonged to Sandleford Priory, as did another sixteen acres of land that the Winchcombes held but did not pay any rent for, and did not formally declare to St George's until 1547. These three cases suggest that some of the Winchcombe's wealth may have been built on the misappropriation of property to which they did not hold title.[86]

John I left nearly £100 in cash legacies in his will of 1520, together with what must have been a substantial legacy to his son and heir, John Winchcombe II, and goods and plate to his widow Joan. The richest man in Newbury, John II was assessed on £632 6s 8d in the muster return of 1522, when his moveable possessions represented 24 per cent of Newbury's total assessment. His closest rival in the town, the clothier Robert Sewey, who had acted as a witness to John I's will, and leased Shaw Mills between 1503 and 1528, was assessed on only £133. Winchcombe subsequently paid almost a quarter of Newbury's total subsidy contribution between the years 1523 and 1527. But while Winchcombe dominated Newbury's economy, his wealth was smaller compared to that of other wealthy clothiers like Thomas Spring III (with moveable goods valued at £1,800 in the muster of 1522).[87]

John Winchcombe II served in several public offices, and some of these roles, while confused, are reflected in Deloney's account of *Jack of Newbury*. The troops that Jack provided at the battle of Flodden, for example, find parallels in the men that John Winchcombe II supplied for overseas campaigns in 1543 and 1544, and in the twenty sets of armour and two demi-lances that he left to his son. John II was also one of the gentlemen to whom it was proposed to write to provide aid against the rebels in the north of England in 1536. Jack is chosen as a member of parliament for Newbury, an office never held by John II, who did though serve as MP for the Wiltshire boroughs of Great Bedwyn in 1545, and for Cricklade in 1547.[88] Deloney describes Jack of Newbury entertaining King Henry VIII and Queen Katherine while they were on progress in Berkshire, hosting a banquet in his own house and afterwards providing the royal visitors with a tour of his business, showing them his weavers, spinners and carders, fulling mills and dye-house. Although there is no known record of Henry VIII visiting the Winchcombes, John Winchcombe II attended the reception of Henry VIII's fourth wife, Anne of Cleves, at Blackheath in January 1540. John Winchcombe II also served

[86] TNA, REQ 2/4/52; Peacock, 'Winchcombe Family', pp. 105–6, 112–13, 209–15, 222.

[87] Jackson, 'Boom-time Freaks', p. 148; Peacock, 'Winchcombe Family', p. 57.

[88] TNA, SP 1/107, fol. 47v; *LP*, xi, no. 580, p. 234. Deloney, *Jack of Newbury*, pp. 338–42; Peacock, 'Winchcombe Family', p. 121; R.L. Davids, 'WINCHCOMBE, alias SMALLWOOD, John (1488/89–1557), of Newbury, Berks.', *HoP, 1509–1558*.

as a justice of the peace appointed under the Commission of the Peace for Berkshire, and as a commissioner to collect benevolences and arrange relief.[89]

By the 1540s, John Winchcombe II was regarded as both a clothier and a gentleman. From 1540, he spent over £4,000 in six years buying and leasing manors, including those of Bucklebury and Thatcham, formerly part of Reading Abbey, from the Crown. Granted a coat of arms in 1549, John II was depicted in a portrait in the following year (Plate X). This portrays Winchcombe wearing a heavy black gown, lined with brown fur, over a black satin doublet. He is wearing a flat black Tudor cap and holds a gillyflower or carnation in his right hand and gloves in his left. Winchcombe's coat of arms is depicted above his right shoulder, and above his left is a plaque reading 'In the year of Our Lord 1550; in the year of his age 61', with his merchant's mark. Three copies of the portrait survive, possibly all contemporary, at Newbury Town Hall, Sudeley Castle and Bucklebury House. It seems likely that the original was painted by a Flemish artist, like the portrait of the London mercer Sir Thomas Gresham, completed in 1544, which also includes a merchant's mark.[90]

John Winchcombe II drew up his will on 2 December 1557 and died later that day. Although his lands only totalled £158 per annum in value, he had obtained royal licences in 1548 to settle his estates on his three sons. He was able to make cash bequests totalling about £900, as well as bestowing impressive amounts of plate, furniture and household furnishings.[91] His eldest son, the third John Winchcombe (d. 1574), moved into the ranks of the gentry, and it was his middle son, Henry (d. 1562), who took over the family cloth business, having married the daughter of the wealthy Wiltshire clothier, Thomas Horton.[92]

The Winchcombe's cloth-making business

An agreement made with the Dean and Canons of Windsor in 1519 described both John Winchcombe senior and junior as clothiers of Newbury.[93] In his will of 1520, John I reserved racks and tenters to be

[89] Deloney, *Jack of Newbury*, pp. 345–56; Peacock, 'Winchcombe Family', pp. 120, 232–4; *HoP, 1509–1558*.

[90] Peacock, 'Winchcombe Family', pp. 99–104, 125–7; Jackson, 'Boom-time Freaks', pp. 150, 159–60. The Gresham portrait, held by the Mercers' Company, London, is reproduced in Ian Blanchard, 'Gresham, Sir Thomas (*c.*1518–1579)', *ODNB*.

[91] TNA, PROB 11/40/283. Another version of the will, with slight differences in the wording, BRO, D/A1/8, fols 296v–302v, is transcribed by Peacock, 'Winchcombe Family', pp. 281–92.

[92] Gaisford, 'Elizabethan Entrepreneurs', pp. 216–17.

[93] Peacock, 'Winchcombe Family', pp. 69–70.

used by his son. The witnesses to John I's will included two wealthy textile workers of Newbury, the cloth-man Robert Sewey, and fuller Roger Benet. John I also left goods and a gift of £2 to William Dolman.[94] There is no known evidence to confirm William's reputed role as John Winchcombe I's foreman or manager, but he may have served him as an apprentice. The Dolmans became a prominent cloth-producing family in Newbury during the sixteenth century, and when William's son retired to a fine house he had built at Shaw on the outskirts of Newbury, his workers reputedly sang,

> Lord, have mercy on us miserable sinners,
> Thomas Dolman has built a new house and turned away all his
> spinners.[95]

Deloney includes a tale of a young and wealthy Italian merchant, Master Benedick, who 'coming oft from London thither to bargain for cloth', falls in love with Joan, one of Jack of Newbury's maid servants. The Winchcombes were certainly trading with Italian merchants. Antonio Bonvixi (or Bonvisi), a member of the Italian Bonvisi firm that had established a base at Antwerp, reported in a bill of complaint brought against the master of Blackwell Hall in London around 1518 that he had bought through his factor three fardels or packs of kerseys of John Winchcombe of Newbury.[96] Another member of this firm was obtaining Berkshire kerseys around the same time, as Thomas Bye of Reading brought a case against Laurence Bonvixi for payment of kerseys by a dishonoured bill. In 1526, John Winchcombe sold ninety-nine kerseys in various colours to Alexander Sepma of Venice in London, bypassing Blackwell Hall, for which they were fined £30.[97] Deloney also describes Jack of Newbury as generously supporting a London draper called Randoll Pert when he became bankrupt. Although there is no known record of Pert, the bill of £500 that he apparently owed Jack would have not been unrealistic given the volume of business that the Winchcombes conducted.[98]

Like Newbury merchants in the mid fifteenth century, the Winchcombes imported dyestuffs to Newbury and exported kerseys through Southampton. By the end of the 1530s, 70 per cent of the woad leaving Southampton was being delivered to Newbury. In 1537, John Winchcombe

[94] See below, Appendix 6.
[95] Yates, *Town and Countryside*, p. 94.
[96] Deloney, *Jack of Newbury*, pp. 366–74; LMA, COL/CA/01/01/003 (Microfilm X109/129): Court of Aldermen Repertory, vol. 3 (1515–19), fol. 198b; Peacock, 'Winchcombe Family', pp. 71–2, 302. See also above, pp. 96, 233.
[97] TNA, C 1/280/8; LMA, COL/AD/01/013 (Microfilm X109/028), Letter Book N (1515–26), fol. 316.
[98] Deloney, *Jack of Newbury*, pp. 379–83.

II brought 676 of the 878 balettes (small bales) of woad imported to Newbury through Southampton. He appears to have collaborated with two Southampton merchants to monopolise this trade in woad, Robert Ronanger and Thomas Bore. Recorded as 'Master Wynskome' in the Southampton brokage books, John II sent cloth from Newbury to Southampton 'delivered at the merchants' adventure (risk)' in 1539–40 and received seven dozen cards through the port the previous year. His trade with Southampton was on such a large scale that in 1538 he managed to negotiate a reduced rate of custom with the mayor, paying duty on woad at half price as long as he continued to export kerseys through Southampton.[99] He also sourced woad through Bristol, Exeter and London. John Smythe of Bristol supplied Winchcombe with over £20 in woad from the Azores in October and December 1549, and he paid for half the following June, via John Pernell, mercer of Bristol. An Exeter merchant was involved in a consignment of woad delivered to Winchcombe in 1546, and the London mercer Thomas Gresham supplied over 541 cwt of woad to him in 1549.[100]

Winchcombe's kerseys established an enviable reputation for quality, as the correspondence of an Antwerp commission house demonstrates. Pieter Van der Molen and brothers shipped large quantities of English, Flemish and Dutch cloths and acted as selling agents for goods sent to them from Italy. Their letters to Italian merchants in Ancona, Genoa and London for the years 1538 to 1544 reveal that this firm of international merchants graded the kerseys that it purchased into three classes, designating those supplied by Winchcombe as the highest grade. The firm's letters contain phrases such as 'kerseys below Winchcombe' (*Carisee sotto Winsicon*) and 'kerseys almost as good as Winchcombe' (*Carisee apresso Winsicon*).[101] The house paid consistently more for Winchcombe kerseys than for the others. The firm purchased these kerseys at the cloth fairs at Antwerp and Bergen-op-Zoom, and through Italian merchants in London, like Martino de Federico, who bought directly from John Winchcombe. Demand for Winchcombe kerseys was so great that English merchants at the Whitsuntide Fair of Antwerp in 1538 agreed among themselves to sell Winchcombe kerseys only to those purchasers who would take an equal number of other kerseys, and at the same fair in 1540 they agreed to sell Winchcombes only to customers who would purchase twice as many of the other kinds of kersey.[102]

[99] Hicks, ed., *Inland Trade*, pp. 7, 74, 96, 108, 127, 156. *Third Book of Remembrance of Southampton 1514–1602*, i: *(1514–40)*, ed. A.L. Merson, Southampton Records Society 2 (Southampton, 1952), pp. 61–2.

[100] *Ledger of John Smythe*, pp. 142, 297; *LP*, xxi (1), no. 24, p. 12; Yates, *Town and Countryside*, p. 93.

[101] Edler, 'Winchcombe Kerseys', p. 58.

[102] Edler, 'Winchcombe Kerseys', pp. 57–62.

Winchcombe clearly struggled on occasion to supply sufficient kerseys to keep up with demand, as in 1539, when Thomas Cromwell, Henry VIII's chief minister, ordered one thousand kerseys from him, and Winchcombe had to advise that time was short but he would make five hundred pieces ready for Easter. Winchcombe was committing to making five hundred kerseys in probably only two months. He may have diverted kerseys from other customers, as Martino de Federico ordered one hundred kerseys in May 1539, but sixty were sent late in July, after Federico had seen John Winchcombe personally while he had been in London. Winchcombe seems to have met with his major customers in person, as he suggested in his correspondence with Cromwell that he would meet with him shortly to discuss the price of the kerseys that Cromwell had ordered.[103]

Other royal advisers looked to sales of Winchcombe's kerseys in the Netherlands as a reliable source of profit. Stephen Vaughan (d. 1549), the crown's chief financial agent in the Low Countries, advised the Privy Council in December 1544 that

> if your honours send forth Winchcombe kerseys they will, with great gains, make great heaps of money, and besides that, neither cloth, lead nor other thing will be trusted unto.[104]

William Dansell, Vaughan's successor as royal agent in the Netherlands, advised in 1546 that, although there was 'wondrous little profit to be had presently in cloths or kerseys, it shall be best to have hither [to Antwerp] 1,000 of Winchcombe kerseys.'[105] Protector Somerset also sent over 'a thousand of Winchcombe's kerseys' in discharge of a debt.[106] The London Merchant Adventurer, Thomas Gresham, who replaced Dansell as royal agent, also bought from Winchcombe. Between November 1546 and November 1549, Gresham purchased 4,300 kerseys from Winchcombe. These were supplied in a variety of colours, described as watchets, blues, reds, azure, plunkets, greens and violet.[107] Thomas Dolman I and William Bennett were also supplying sizeable quantities of kerseys to Gresham, and with Winchcombe, these three Newbury clothiers provided almost 10,000 cloths in the four years between 1546 and 1550.[108] Although

[103] TNA, SP 1/143, fol. 185: *LP*, xiv (1), no. 396, p. 151; Edler, 'Winchcombe Kerseys', p. 60.

[104] TNA, SP 1/195, fol. 193: *LP*, xix (2), no. 723, p. 435.

[105] *HoP, 1509–1558*.

[106] Lipson, *Economic History*, i, p. 477.

[107] Watchet: light blue; plunket: grey or light blue (*OED*).

[108] Peacock, 'Winchcombe Family', pp. 16–26, 35–7; Peacock, 'Dyeing', pp. 190–1.

overall estimates of Winchcombe's production range from over 3,000 to 6,000 kerseys per annum, he was clearly producing large volumes.[109]

Deloney famously described Jack of Newbury as employing over one thousand skilled and unskilled workers. The reader is shown Jack's factory with 200 weavers, 100 carders, 200 spinners, 150 children picking wool, 50 shearmen, 80 rowers, and 40 men in his dye-house and 20 at his fulling mill, with descriptions given in rhyming couplets for additional effect:

> Within one room, being large and long,
> There stood two hundred looms full strong;
> Two hundred men, the truth is so,
> Wrought in these looms all in a row.[110]

Although the numbers are clearly rounded, they may not be exaggerated given that other clothiers appear to have employed large workforces. If John II was producing 3,000 kerseys per annum, he would need to have employed over 420 workers. If he was producing 6,000 kerseys in a year, the workforce required would have approached Deloney's figures.[111] When Edward Seymour (later duke of Somerset) visited Winchcombe's home in Newbury in 1537, he gave 17s 6d to John II's carders. If this had been a gift of 2d each, it could have been given to all the 'hundred women merrily were carding hard' described in *Jack of Newbury*.[112]

The Winchcombes' workshops and warehouses occupied a substantial site. An inventory of Henry Winchcombe's goods taken in 1562 records the presence of workrooms for picking, sorting, carding and weighing wool, and storage lofts for wool and dyestuffs, which may have been located alongside his father's house on Northbrook Street.[113] The Winchcombes also owned Rack Close, which was sold by John II to his apprentice Philip Kistell, for £15 in 1557. This lay between a stream and the river Kennet, adjoining the West Mill and land occupied by a Newbury dyer. Rack Close contained 'four winches called Racks' and a conduit house over the river. The conduit served a tenement in Northbrook Street, held by Winchcombe, and subsequently by Kistell, and would have provided a piped water supply, useful for washing wool and dyeing cloth. The use of winches, however, for stretching cloths, had been forbidden by statute

109 Jackson, 'Boom-time Freaks', p. 149; Peacock, 'Winchcombe Family', pp. 20–3.

110 Deloney, *Jack of Newbury*, pp. 334–5.

111 Based on Oldland's estimate that one broadcloth took 978 hours to produce, and that cloth-workers worked 230 ten-hour days a year. The total has been adjusted to reflect the late-sixteenth-century estimate that a kersey took one-third of the time to produce compared with a broadcloth: Oldland, 'Economic Impact', pp. 236–8.

112 Peacock, 'Winchcombe Family', pp. 32–3.

113 Peacock, 'Winchcombe Family', pp. 178–80.

in 1552. The inventory accompanying John Winchcombe II's will shows that he had a flock of 454 sheep. Winchcombe also sourced wool from considerable distances, including, in 1550, from John Yate of Buckland in north Berkshire and William Dormer of Wing in Buckinghamshire.[114]

Jack of Newbury describes a clothiers' petition presented to the king at a time of crisis in the cloth trade, when foreign merchants were prevented from coming to England and English merchants were forbidden to trade with France or the Low Countries. This embargo led, we are told, to weavers and other workers becoming unemployed, and halved the size of the industry. In response, Jack organises a petition, and fifty-six cloth-making towns, employing over 60,000 people in the cloth trade, sent two men each to London, to make their case to Henry VIII and Cardinal Wolsey.[115] It seems likely that Deloney was conflating the crises in the cloth trade in the 1520s with a clothiers' petition that John Winchcombe II coordinated around 1540. This seems to have been drawn up in protest at a statute of 1536 that had regulated the breadth and length of kerseys and broadcloths. Under the title 'Names of all the clothiers which make fine kerseys', the petition lists eighty clothiers from central southern England. This includes men from Newbury, Wallingford, Winnersh and Wokingham in Berkshire; Alton, Basing, Greywell, Havant, Kingsclere, Mattingley, Odiham, Overton, Petersfield, Romsey, Sherfield on Loddon, Whitchurch and Winchester in Hampshire; Chiddingfold, Farnham, Godalming and Guildford in Surrey; and Midhurst and Petworth in Sussex.[116] The Privy Council recorded that 'Winchcombe of Newbury and sundry other clothiers did make suite unto the king's highness that the statute … for the making of broad cloths and kerseys might be dissolved, or at the least the execution of the same deferred.'[117] Winchcombe's petition helped secure the suspension of the act of 1536 regulating the manufacture of woollen cloth. 'An Act for true making of kerseys' in 1541 removed the regulations on the length and breadth of kerseys that had been introduced in 1536.[118] As well as being a leading producer of kerseys, John Winchcombe II was an effective lobbyist.

[114] BRO, D/EW T49/3; 5 & 6 Edward VI, c. 6: *SR*, iv (1), p. 139; Peacock, 'Winchcombe Family', pp. 29–31, 63–4, 155–6.

[115] Deloney, *Jack of Newbury*, pp. 362–6.

[116] TNA, E 101/347/17. This has been misdated to Edward VI's reign in The National Archives catalogue, see Peacock, 'Winchcombe Family', pp. 80–7, 313–16.

[117] TNA, PC 2/1, fols 155–6; *Proceedings and Ordinances of the Privy Council of England*, ed. N. Harris Nicolas, 7 vols (London, 1834–37), vii, p. 156.

[118] 27 Henry VIII, c. 12, 33 Henry VIII, c. 18: *SR*, iii, pp. 545, 854.

The Winchcombe's religious bequests

John Winchcombe I left £40 in his will of 1520 to the 'building and edifying' of Newbury parish church. Although this was the largest of his individual cash bequests, it was small compared to the gifts of Thomas Spring II or III. John I asked his son as his executor to keep an obit for twenty-two years, distributing 10s every year to priests and clerks, and to find an honest priest to sing for him and his friends for one year. He was buried in the chancel of St Nicolas' church, Newbury, with his first wife Alice. Their monumental brass, now moved to the north wall of the tower, depicts them both with two sons and a daughter, or weepers. John wears a long gown with deep fur-edged sleeves, with a pouch attached to his girdle. Alice has a headdress, a close-fitting fur-edged gown and ornamental girdle. At each corner of the brass are roundels, two with his monogram and two with the figure of St John the Baptist carrying the lamb, a suitable clothier's emblem.

John Winchcombe II's will suggests that his religious beliefs were traditional, as he requested an obit to be kept for twenty years in the church at Newbury. He had been a substantial donor to the rebuilding of Newbury parish church in the 1520s and 1530s, where the roof bosses in the nave carry alternatively the 'IS' monogram of John Winchcombe I, and the 'IO' merchant's mark of John Winchcombe II.[119] He was rewarded with a pension of £10 by Queen Mary for 'service at Framlingham'. More controversially, he was a visitor at the trial of the protestant martyr Julins Palmer at Newbury on 15 July 1556, apparently telling Palmer to 'take pity on thy golden years, and pleasant flowers of lusty youth, before it is too late'. The trial condemned Palmer to be burnt, a sentence carried out the next day.[120] Ironically John II's son, the third John Winchcombe, was an early supporter of reform, and had been sent as a confidential messenger from Newbury in 1539 to Thomas Cromwell by the Bible translator Miles Coverdale, concerning the suppression of papal books.[121]

John Winchcombe II's house

Reflecting the status and wealth of John Winchcombe II was his house in Newbury. Built around two courtyards, with a street frontage of at least 96 feet (29 metres), it covered a larger footprint than the present-day Marks and Spencer store that now occupies much of the site. John Winchcombe

[119] *HoP, 1509–1558*. Peacock, 'Winchcombe Family', p. 67. The date of 1532 over the tower arch may mark the completion of rebuilding.

[120] *The Acts and Monuments of John Foxe*, ed. J. Pratt, 4th edn, 8 vols (London, 1877), viii, pp. 214–19.

[121] T.F.T. Baker / R.L. Davids, 'WINCHCOMBE, John (by 1519–74), of Bucklebury and Thatcham, Berks.', *HoP, 1509–1558*.

Plate 19 Panelling from John Winchcombe's house, Newbury, now in Sudeley Castle, Gloucestershire. The faces on this panel may represent John Winchcombe I and his two wives. In the centre is John II's merchant's mark.

II's will reveals that the house had a hall, little parlour, gallery, nine chambers or bedrooms, and a cellar. There was also a buttery, brewing house, kitchen, boulting house, bakehouse, cheese house and stables. Also mentioned in the will, although not necessarily all on the same site, were rooms connected with cloth-making: a brushing chamber, weighing house and dye-house. The house was richly furnished. The hall had wood panelling and wall hangings, and John Winchcombe II's own chamber contained a four-poster bed with white curtains and tester or canopy over it, walls decorated with hangings, and red and green window curtains.[122]

One small part of the building survives, still known as 'Jack of Newbury's house', on the corner of Northbrook Street and Marsh Lane. It includes several elaborate decorative features that would have marked the status of this house. On the side facing Marsh Lane, with three stories, there is close-studding timberwork infilled with herringbone brickwork (or brick nogging) on the first floor and gable, and the two upper stories are jettied out. Other surviving Tudor features include an oriel window, a bargeboard on the west side of the gable, and a decorated wooden beam or bressumer on the jetty between the ground and first floor,

[122] Peacock, 'Winchcombe Family', pp. 129–33.

decorated with stylised foliage within a row of lozenges.[123] Carvings from the house survive in a ten-frame panel hanging at Sudeley Castle near Winchcombe and in panels made into a sideboard now held by West Berkshire Museum at Newbury. The frame of ten panels at Sudeley Castle comprise a crudely carved face, possibly of John Winchcombe I, between linenfold panels. Below are two stylised birds; two women, suggested as representing the wives of John Winchcombe I; and in the centre, a leather buckler[124] with straps bearing John Winchcombe II's merchant's mark (Plate 19). These panels were discovered in situ within the house before 1833, and sold to Sudeley Castle in 1894. The panels on the sideboard in West Berkshire Museum include heraldic birds similar to those at Sudeley, and the Winchcombe initials on bucklers, one of which has John II's merchant's mark with a small 'y' below, probably indicating John Winchcombe the younger.[125] These panels confirm the wealth and status of John Winchcombe II. The many rooms and opulent furnishings reinforce Deloney's description of Jack of Newbury's grand household, which supported a butcher, brewer, baker, five cooks and six scullion boys.

Thanks to Deloney's work, the Winchcombes have long been remembered as innovators who put their workers together in a single workshop. Given the many parallels between Deloney's tale and John Winchcombe II's career, the substantial site that his house, workshops and warehouses occupied in Newbury, and the richness of his domestic accommodation, the workforce described in *Jack of Newbury* is not as fanciful as might be perceived, and the scale of production described by Deloney can no longer be dismissed as poetic licence.[126]

WILLIAM STUMPE OF MALMESBURY

William Stumpe, the son of a weaver and parish clerk, rose to become the leading clothier in Wiltshire, as well as an MP, sheriff and gentleman. Residing in Malmesbury, Stumpe was a tenant of the local Benedictine abbey, around which the town had developed. On its dissolution, Stumpe was able to use his position as a royal official to acquire the monastery site. Although the abbey church, cloister, and other monastic buildings were scheduled to be demolished, thanks to his efforts, the nave of the abbey church was saved to become the town's parish church. Stumpe

123 NHLE 1290211 (24 Northbrook Street, Newbury); West Berkshire Historic Environment Record, No. MWB15953; Peacock, 'Winchcombe Family', pp. 137–9.

124 A small round shield, usually carried by a handle at the back, but sometimes fastened by straps to the arm: *OED*.

125 Peacock, 'Winchcombe Family', pp. 140–8.

126 As dismissed by Kerridge in *Textile Manufactures*, p. 192.

filled the other monastic buildings with his weaving looms, and built his own residence in the precinct. The Stumpe family were less conscientious though, in caring for those parts of the monastery's archive and library that came into their possession, and which had probably been left in the abbey buildings. A century later, William Stumpe's great-grandson and namesake, the rector of Yatton Keynell (Wiltshire), tore leaves from manuscript books to stop the bung holes of his ale casks, and his sons used the parchment to scour their guns. Other manuscripts were taken to cover books or by local glove-makers to wrap their gloves.[127] Aside from this, the residents of Malmesbury have much to thank Stumpe for.

Malmesbury lay within the cloth-making region of west Wiltshire. While there was some textile production occurring in this area before the Black Death, and a rental dating from Edward I's reign records two weavers, two fullers and four dyers in Malmesbury, the industry flourished in the fifteenth century. Cloth-making could be found from Malmesbury in the north to Westbury and beyond in the south, and from Devizes in the east to Bradford-on-Avon in the west. Malmesbury also appears to have been an important wool market, attracting cloth-makers from Salisbury. By the mid sixteenth century the area was home to substantial clothiers like Thomas Bailey, Thomas Horton and Alexander Langford, all mentioned by the antiquary John Leland when he visited in the 1540s, together with William Stumpe of Malmesbury.[128]

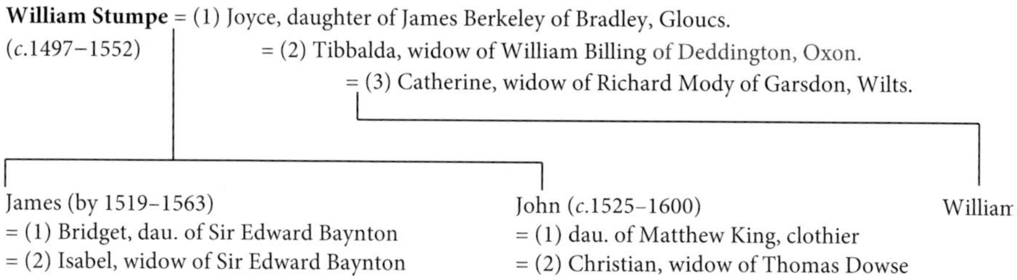

Figure 11 Stumpe family tree
Source: HoP, 1509–1558, 1558–1603.

William Stumpe's father is said to have been a weaver and served as parish clerk of North Nibley in east Gloucestershire. His brother Thomas described himself as a husbandman of North Nibley in his will of 1551. Close to this village was Berkeley Castle, and William joined a branch of

[127] John Aubrey, *The Natural History of Wiltshire*, ed. J. Britton (London, 1847), pp. 78–9.
[128] *VCH Wiltshire*, iv, pp. 141–7; Bridbury, *Clothmaking*, p. 71.

this ancient family when he married Joyce, daughter of James Berkeley of nearby Bradley. It was, perhaps, William's first step on the road to fame and fortune. By 1524, William was living in Malmesbury, where he was one of the town's four richest residents. He was sufficiently wealthy to represent the borough in parliament in 1529.[129]

The *Valor Ecclesiasticus*, the survey of church finances compiled in 1535, recorded that Stumpe paid 63s a year to Malmesbury Abbey as a tenant of Winyard Mill in Whitchurch, Malmesbury. In the same year, he paid £200 for property in Malmesbury, Chippenham and surrounding villages, and took a sixty-year lease of Cowbridge water mill from the abbey.[130] The abbot of Malmesbury surrendered his monastery to the Crown in December 1539. Sir Edward Baynton was given custody of the buildings 'to remain undefaced', while Stumpe received those buildings 'deemed to be superfluous'. These included the church, cloister, chapter house, dormitory, refectory and infirmary. In 1541, Thomas Cranmer, archbishop of Canterbury, recounting that 'the worthy Master William Stumpe Esq … hath granted all the nave of the late conventual church to be perpetually converted to the use of divine service', licensed this building as the parish church for the town.[131] Stumpe secured his title by paying over £1,500 for a royal grant of the whole monastery site in 1544.[132]

Visiting Malmesbury in 1542, John Leland observed:

> All the abbey buildings are now the property of a man named Stumpe, who bought them from the king. He is an exceptionally rich clothier, whose son has married Sir Edward Baynton's daughter. Stumpe was largely responsible for turning the abbey church into a parish church, and its main benefactor. At the present time every corner of the vast houses of office which belonged to the abbey is full of looms for weaving cloth, and it is Stumpe's intention to build one or two streets for cloth-makers in the open ground at the back of the abbey inside the town walls. At present three thousand cloths are made annually in Malmesbury.[133]

[129] Aubrey, *Natural History of Wiltshire*, p. 112; F.H. Manley, 'William Stumpe of Malmesbury, his Descendants and Relatives', *Wiltshire Notes and Queries* 8 (1914–16), pp. 385–95; T.F.T. Baker, 'STUMPE, William (by 1498–1552), of Malmesbury, Wilts.', *HoP, 1509–1558*.

[130] Wiltshire and Swindon Archives, 88/1/22–23; *HoP, 1509–1558*.

[131] E. Wilton, 'Malmesbury Abbey. License for its Conversion into a Parish Church', *Wiltshire Archaeological and Natural History Magazine* 1 (1854), pp. 249–50.

[132] *LP*, xix (ii), no. 690 (34), p. 414. Youings, *Dissolution*, pp. 238–41.

[133] Based on Chandler, *John Leland's Itinerary*, pp. 488–9 and *Itinerary*, i, p. 132. Chandler uses the term 'enormous domestic buildings' rather than 'vast houses of office'.

In a small church adjoining the south transept of the abbey, Leland also found 'Weavers have now looms in this little church.' The abbey church that Stumpe granted to the townspeople remains, but none of the other monastic buildings now survive. These stood on the north side of the church and comprised a cloister with frater or refectory beyond, a chapter house and dormitory stretching east into the area now occupied by Abbey House.[134] Stumpe's proposal to build streets for clothmakers on vacant plots of the former abbey land never seems to have been carried out, although Stumpe's will refers to his weavers and tenants living within the precincts of the former monastery.[135]

Stumpe also negotiated with the city of Oxford to establish a similar cloth-making workshop in the former Osney Abbey. Paying a yearly rent of £18 for the premises, Stumpe bound himself to

> find work for 2,000 persons from time to time, if they may be gotten, that will do their work well continually in cloth-making, for the succour of the city of Oxford and the country about it, for the which intent the mills were made.[136]

The scheme was unsuccessful, possibly due to the size of the workforce that Stumpe had committed himself to finding in a city with a population of little more than 3,000. Although Christ Church leased the site with the mills to Stumpe, he assigned his lease only a few years later to another clothier, James Atwood, who does not seem to have operated any scheme to employ the poor.[137] Plans to develop textile workshops in other former monasteries were put forward around the same time, and were generally unsuccessful, as production was based largely around the putting-out system.[138]

Leland suggests that Stumpe was using the former monastic buildings as workshops for his cloth-making. The economic historian Eric Kerridge raised a note of scepticism, arguing that the 'vast houses of office' were privies, which could hardly have been large edifices, and that the little church could not have housed many looms either. In fact, 'houses of office' could also mean 'a building or outhouse for some

[134] Pevsner, *Wiltshire*, pp. 322, 327; NHLE 1010136 (Benedictine monastery known as Malmesbury Abbey), 1269325 (Abbey House and attached rear wall, Malmesbury).

[135] See below, Appendix 7.

[136] *Selections from the Records of the City of Oxford: With Extracts from Other Documents Illustrating the Municipal History: Henry VIII to Elizabeth*, ed. William H. Turner (Oxford, 1880), p. 185.

[137] *VCH Oxfordshire*, iv, pp. 110, 464.

[138] See above, pp. 176–7.

domestic purpose, as a pantry, brewery, storehouse'.[139] Kerridge also suggested that as it was not stated that the looms in the houses of office were being worked, they may have been stored there pending delivery to weavers. Stumpe's will though, as noted above, refers to his weavers and tenants living within the former monastic precincts. Kerridge notes that nowhere was it ever suggested that the abbey was converted into a weaving shop. [140] Indeed Stumpe permitted the abbey church to become the parish church, and constructed his own residence, known as Abbey House, in the abbey precinct.

The grounds of Abbey House may have been planned by Oliver Boweseke, 'a good gardener' and priest, from Morlaix in Brittany, who became a denizen in 1544 after living in Stumpe's household for twelve years.[141] The arms of Stumpe and Baynton on the entrance porch of Abbey House were probably added by his son. One room within the house was formerly known as Henry VIII's banqueting room, as there is a story of the king paying an unexpected visit after hunting in Braydon forest and of Stumpe entertaining him at the expense of his own work-people, who had to fast so that the king and court might be fed.[142]

While this story of entertaining the king may not have any firm basis, it has been suggested that it was due to royal influence that Stumpe was appointed one of the seventeen receivers of the newly established Court of Augmentations, founded to administer monastic properties and revenues confiscated by the crown at the dissolution of the monasteries. As receiver, Stumpe gained a yearly salary of £20, profits and a travel allowance, and probably the opportunity to obtain former monastic sites like Malmesbury on preferential terms. The Court of Augmentations had leased lands of the former abbey at Conway to him in 1537–38, shortly after he had become the court's receiver for that area. Stumpe was also appointed to a succession of other public offices, including justice of the peace in Wiltshire in 1538 and Gloucestershire from 1539–44, escheator of Gloucestershire from 1545–46, and sheriff of Wiltshire in 1551. Representing Malmesbury in parliament in 1529 and 1547, Stumpe may also have served in intervening parliaments where the names of the members for this borough are missing.[143] Described as a gentleman in an assessment of the borough in 1541 and granted arms in 1549,

[139] *OED*.

[140] Kerridge, *Textile Manufactures*, p. 196.

[141] Westminster Abbey Muniments, WAM 12261, letters of denization 1544, quoted in England's Immigrants 1330–1550, http://www.englandsimmigrants.com/person/61383

[142] Manley, 'Stumpe', pp. 336, 388–9.

[143] *HoP, 1509–1558*.

Stumpe rose to enter that select oligarchy of a dozen or so country gentlemen to whom the king committed the government of Wiltshire – no mean achievement for a self-made man and a clothier.[144]

In addition to his purchase of the site of Malmesbury Abbey, Stumpe acquired extensive properties, concentrated in an area stretching from Tewkesbury southwards to Wootton Bassett and from Woodchester eastwards to Warminster. In extending his property portfolio though, he faced litigation by others. He was sued in Chancery by Richard Vaugham for possessing five former monastic mills at Lower Barns farm and Bushford bridge, which Vaugham, who lived in Essex, claimed were his. He also faced cases in Chancery brought by copyhold tenants whom he had evicted at Brinkworth and Brokenborough. Stumpe does not seem to have been restrained by any traditional customs that may have existed regarding these lands, and it might be argued, he exploited them with 'the harshness attributed to so many of the newly rich'. Stumpe was also charged with conspiring with his second wife to defraud her son John Billing of his inheritance of £400 and plate bequeathed by Billing's father, suggesting 'sharp practice even within his family circle'.[145]

Stumpe's cloth-making business

We know relatively little about Stumpe's business as a clothier. By the time of his death, the scale of his production must have been reasonably significant, as in his will he bequeathed ten broadlooms to one son and the remainder to another.[146] How he built up this business is difficult to trace. One case in the Court of Common Pleas suggests that he may have been trying to sell cloth in London even before he left the village of his birth, as in 1523 he brought a plea against Thomas Nycollys, smith of 'Nynnysfield' in Gloucestershire, who had contracted to carry six woollen cloths safely and securely from North Nibley to London but had looked after them badly. The same year, he also brought pleas of debt against John Mabson, weaver of Old Sodbury (Gloucestershire), for £15, and William Dorney, mercer of Berkeley, for £10.[147] Stumpe was pursuing further debts in 1531 for the larger sum of £40 against John Vyall of Charlton near Malmesbury, and in 1533 against husbandmen William Osbourn of Sherston (Wiltshire) for £23, and John Hancokke of Luckington (Wiltshire) for £4.[148] Like most clothiers, Stumpe must have relied on a network of credit with his suppliers and workers, and

144 Ramsay, *Wiltshire*, p. 34.
145 Ramsay, *Wiltshire*, p. 32; *HoP, 1509–1558*.
146 See below, Appendix 7.
147 TNA, CP 40/1038, m. 475, 475d (AALT 887d, 962).
148 TNA, CP 40/1068, m. 508 (AALT 1099); CP 40/1076, m. 196d (AALT 5670d).

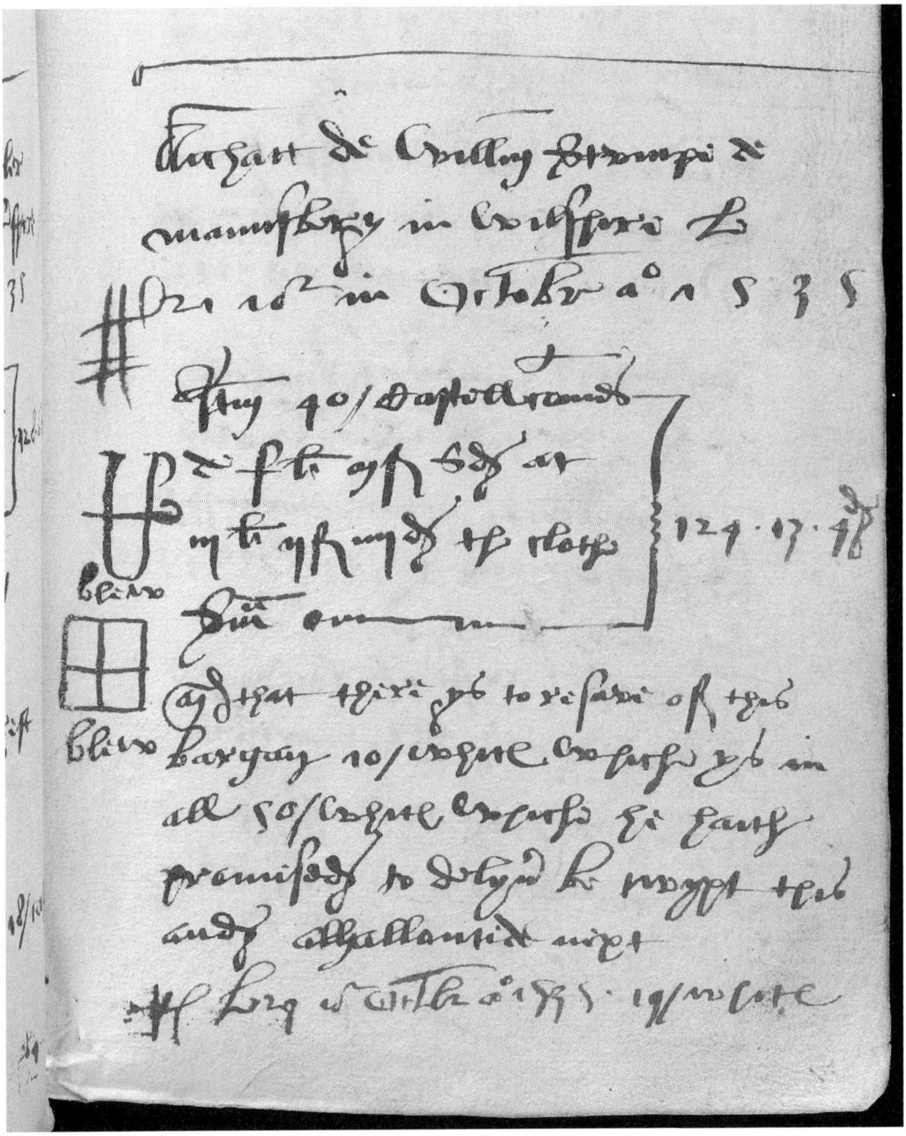

Plate 20 Thomas Kitson's purchases from William Stumpe of Malmesbury, 1535. (CUL, Hengrave Hall MS 78(2), fol. 142).
Kitson records the purchase of forty Castlecombes from Stumpe, paying £3 2s 4d for each cloth. Images of two of Stumpe's merchant's marks are drawn in the left-hand margin.

in his will, he forgave his weavers their debts. He marketed cloth to London mercers and Merchant Adventurers, including nineteen 'whites' and forty 'Castellcomes' that he sold to Thomas Kitson in 1535 (Plate 20), and he also supplied Thomas Gresham.[149] To supply such major exporting merchants, Stumpe must have built a reputation for quality, although Ralph Porter, a clothier of Cherington in Berkshire, claimed that Stumpe had supplied him with £117 worth of cloths that were 'not so good and substantial as Stumpe promised and affirmed'.[150] It seems likely that some of Stumpe's cloth was dyed and finished for him in London, like the thirty-two red cloths 'called stopp listes' that Stumpe asked a London cloth-worker to sell for him in 1541. Stumpe kept his own factor in London to find a market for his cloth.[151] Like several of the wealthier clothiers, William Stumpe also retained a large and valuable sheep flock. In 1548 he leased eight hundred of his sheep to Tristrum Pistor of Boyton, gentleman, for £23 6s 8d, a sum calculated on the basis of 7d for every sheep hired. At the end of the lease, Pistor was to deliver the sheep back to Stumpe, or else pay £160, which worked out at 4s for every sheep he had borrowed.[152]

Stumpe brought a suit against the townsmen of Tetbury over the tolls of their market, which he claimed through a lease. The man who had served as bailiff of Tetbury in 1543/4 claimed that the borough, one of the best markets for wool and yarn in Gloucestershire, was only about three miles from Malmesbury, and that it was clearly Stumpe's intention, 'if he might obtain and get the tolls and weights of the said town of Tetbury in his own hands, so to use the said tolls that by his crafty means he would utterly destroy the said market at Tetbury'. If the assertion is correct, it suggests that Stumpe was attempting to control supplies of wool and yarn to local spinners and weavers.[153]

Stumpe's religious bequests

William Stumpe died in 1552. In respect of his religious beliefs, his will is very different from the expressions of late medieval Catholicism found in the wills of Thomas Paycocke of Coggeshall and the Springs of Lavenham.[154] He committed his soul to Christ, through whose passion 'I do verily trust to be saved … and by none other means nor ways that ever was or that ever I did say or do'. In terms of charitable bequests, he left

149 CUL, Hengrave Hall MS 78(2), fol. 142; Ramsey, *Tudor Economic Problems*, p. 89.

150 TNA, STAC 2/17/374, dated to between 1538 and 1544.

151 TNA, REQ 2/11/60; Carus-Wilson, 'Woollen Industry', p. 146.

152 Wiltshire and Swindon Archives, 88/1/26.

153 *HoP, 1509–1558*.

154 See below, Appendix 7.

£40 for the poor of Malmesbury. His business interests within his will, though, were remarkably similar to the early-sixteenth-century clothiers. He gave ten looms to his second son John, and to every woman servant 20s and to every manservant 40s. He left his remaining looms to William, his infant son by his third wife Catherine, and forgave all his debtors, including his weavers and tenants residing within the precincts of the former monastery. One of his witnesses was a former monk of the abbey, John Horsleye, who had held the office of 'chaunter' and at the dissolution received a pension of £6.[155]

William left bequests to his three sons. His eldest son, Sir James, took his father's place in the shire. As Leland noted, James' first marriage had been to Bridget, daughter of Sir Edward Baynton, who had risen rapidly in Henry VIII's favour. Through his activity at court, on campaign and in local administration, Sir Edward had lifted his family above his neighbours within the county. He also profited enormously from the dissolution of the monasteries.[156] Sir James' second marriage was to Isabel, the widow of Sir Edward. It was William's second son, John, who succeeded him as a clothier, and married a daughter of Matthew King, who had become Malmesbury's leading clothier after William Stumpe's death.[157]

CONCLUSION

Examining these four families of leading clothiers reveals several common threads. All operated large-scale production, although exactly how large must remain a matter for discussion. Paycocke left a lump sum in his will that may have been intended for between 80 to 240 workers, while Thomas Spring II bequeathed an even larger sum that could have supported 220 to 3,900 workers. Deloney described Jack of Newbury as employing over 1,000 workers. While Paycocke and Spring appear to have operated their large-scale production through the putting-out system, Winchcombe and Stumpe seem to have been innovators in the use of centralised workshops. All four family businesses relied on the London market. Thomas Paycocke made a London draper his executor and his brother Robert sold cloth to a London merchant. Both Robert Paycocke and Thomas Spring III purchased wool in London. The Winchcombes traded through London, as well as Southampton, Bristol and Exeter, and like William Stumpe, supplied cloth to London mercers.

155 Manley, 'Stumpe', p. 391, n.1.

156 T.F.T. Baker, 'BAYNTON, Sir Edward (by 1495–1544), of Bromham, Wilts.', and 'STUMPE, Sir James (by 1519–63), of Malmesbury and Bromham, Wilts.', *HoP, 1509–1558*.

157 S.T. Bindoff, 'STUMPE, John (*c*.1525–1600), of Malmesbury, Wilts.', *HoP, 1558–1603*; Manley, 'Stumpe', 484–5.

Money and reputation potentially brought royal connections, with Winchcombe and Stumpe reputedly entertaining the king, and Thomas Spring III's executors drawing on craftsmen familiar with royal commissions for the screen surrounding his tomb. Wealth also led to disputes though, including claims that Thomas Paycocke had embezzled the legacies left to his sisters-in-law, and that the Winchcombes had falsely claimed an inheritance. The Springs possibly used coercion to obtain the Birdbrook lands on a favourable lease, and Stumpe allegedly seized the Tetbury market tolls, evicted tenants, and tried to defraud his stepson of his inheritance. While some of these accusations of sharp practice may have been inspired by the jealousy of less successful rivals and lacked substance, we know that the Winchcombes occupied land without paying the required rent and possessed winches, which had been banned for use in cloth-making.

Historians have taken a mixed view of the leading clothiers, but while they were untypical of the majority of cloth producers, their achievements should not be diminished. New research challenges the scepticism that some commentators have expressed over the scale of their operations. Building their fortunes over decades and generations, these families identified opportunities, took calculated risks, and were perhaps sometimes unscrupulous in their dealings. Their wealth was expressed through imposing residences, lavish furnishings, and extensive landed estates, but also in providing elaborate memorials and commemoration after death. It is only through taking a multi-disciplinary approach, including an exploration of buildings, stylistic influences and religious bequests, that we can assemble an impression of the wider significance of the leading clothiers.

Conclusion

Writing in 1597, Thomas Deloney was clear about the benefits that clothiers and cloth-making brought to the wider economy and society, particularly through providing employment.

> Among all manual arts used in this land, none is more famous for desert [deserving] or more beneficial to the commonwealth than is the most necessary art of clothing; and therefore as the benefit thereof is great, so are the professors of the same to be both loved and maintained. Many wise men therefore having deeply considered the same, most bountifully have bestowed their gifts for upholding of so excellent a commodity which hath been and yet is the nourishing of many thousands of poor people. Wherefore to you, most worthy clothiers, do I dedicate this my rude work, which hath raised out of the dust of forgetfulness a most famous and worthy man, whose name was John Winchcomb, alias Jack of Newbury.[1]

There were faint local echoes of these sentiments in summer 2017 when Newbury Town Council applied for planning permission to install a life-sized bronze statue of Jack of Newbury, or John Winchcombe II, the subject of Deloney's work. Depicting Jack holding a yard of cloth on his right arm while raising his left hand, 'as if to dramatically capture the moment he conceived the idea to scale up the process of dyed-cloth production', the statue is intended to draw the eye to the remains of the Winchcombe's Tudor residence in Northbrook Street and, according to the planning application, celebrate the town's rich cultural heritage and promote 'a greater sense of civic pride among the whole community'. One online respondent, however, posted that they would not want this 'Tudor fat-cat industrialist', 'Newbury's most notorious social climbing despot', and 'the town magistrate who executed the Newbury martyrs by having them burned alive', to be commemorated in this way.[2]

1 Deloney, *Jack of Newbury*, p. 313.

2 Newbury Today, 'Statue for Local Hero Jack?', 11 Aug 2015, and 'Plans Submitted for Life-size Jack of Newbury Statute', 4 Aug 2017, https://www.newburytoday.co.uk

While historians usually tend to shy away from making moral judgements, they have also been uncertain about the impact that clothiers made in the wider economy and society. It has been argued, for instance, that the statistics available from the customs accounts give the cloth trade 'a degree of significance in terms of the national economy that has never been fully justified', particularly given the paucity of evidence available for domestic markets and the home economy.[3] Changes in the organisation or distribution of cloth-making, and particularly the concentration of manufacturing in the hands of larger producers, could arise from restructuring rather than being the result of overall economic growth. Leading clothiers like John Winchcombe have even been dismissed as 'boom-time freaks'.[4] Recent research, however, has argued that the growth of the late medieval cloth industry has been significantly underestimated, and thereby lend some support to Deloney's claims. While it is well-known that cloth exports increased dramatically, over thirty-fold between the early fourteenth and mid sixteenth centuries, what has only recently been recognised is that the average cloth nearly doubled in weight over the same period. Whereas in 1311–14, just over 1 lb of cloth was being produced for every person in England, by the 1540s, this had risen to 7 lb of cloth per person. By the 1540s, therefore, it has been suggested that around 15 per cent of the adult workforce were making cloth, and one in four households were practising spinning.[5] The cloth industry formed a key part of the late medieval English economy and at its centre was the clothier.

THE RISE OF THE MEDIEVAL CLOTHIER

Some historians see the English clothier as emerging during the sixteenth century, a product of the individualistic and acquisitive mentalities of the Tudor age. Others have argued that these individuals first appeared in the larger cloth-making towns of the late fourteenth century, while some would look back even further to the thirteenth century for their origins. This book has argued that the clothier emerged in the particular circumstances of the late fourteenth and early fifteenth centuries. While the century after the Black Death was a period of generally tough economic conditions, with labour scarce and expensive and prices of agricultural commodities, particularly corn, low, there were economic opportunities available. Land could be leased cheaply from lords, and cultivated using household labour. Craftworkers, perhaps also employing family

[3] Goldberg, 'Urban Identity', p. 214.
[4] Coleman, *Industry*, p. 27. See also above, Introduction.
[5] Oldland, 'Economic Impact'; Muldrew, 'Early Industrial Workforce'.

members, could meet growing domestic demand from wage earners and the peasantry, as well as from overseas markets. These were the circumstances in which the yeoman, the butcher-grazier, the chapman, the wool dealer, and the clothier emerged. Many came from the upper ranks of the peasantry, and these farmers, craftworkers and traders often did business together. Although they were mostly below the level of the gentry, they operated their own networks based on wealth and political influence.[6] Many clothiers must have had their origins as aspiring craftworkers: 'The clothier was merely a more go-ahead man than the rest, who began to buy extra wool and to employ a few spinners and weavers outside his own family, himself taking the finished cloth to market.'[7]

Another key influence was the increasing economic ascendancy of London mercantile interests, particularly during the very difficult trading conditions of the mid-fifteenth-century 'great slump'. London merchants purchased finished or semi-finished cloths from clothiers, supplied them with dyestuffs, and were able to offer preferential terms of credit. The money shortages of the mid fifteenth century seem to have given Londoners a major advantage over merchants in provincial towns. Following disruption to other markets, cloth exports increasingly focused on the London to Antwerp route, to the detriment of other English ports.

The mid-fifteenth-century crisis also intensified a number of other trends that were already underway. Cloth production was moving from large towns to smaller centres. These more rural locations lacked the regulations imposed by guilds and borough governments on employment, production standards and marketing, as well as the financial contributions that these institutions levied to support their infrastructure and their administrations. Cloth production was also becoming concentrated in fewer hands. In more difficult trading conditions, those with lower production costs were better able to withstand the crisis.[8] Attempts to reduce the costs of production and marketing in this period of severe commercial downturn and monetary shortage favoured the emergence of the clothier and the associated system of outworking. Larger entrepreneurs were able to adjust their industrial output in a more flexible way to meet peaks or troughs in demand, by subcontracting to more craftworkers or fewer as required.[9]

The clothier emerged in England in different regions at different times.

[6] Dyer, *Country Merchant*, p. 225.

[7] Ella Pontefract and Marie Hartley, *Yorkshire Tour* (London, 1939), p. 93.

[8] Lee, 'Crises', pp. 331–9.

[9] Peter Stabel, 'Guilds in Late Medieval Flanders: Myths and Realities of Guild Life in an Export-oriented Environment', *Journal of Medieval History* 30 (2004), pp. 208–9.

He, or occasionally she, had their origins in the entrepreneurs who had engaged with several aspects of cloth production, sometimes supplying raw materials, sometimes employing cloth-workers, and usually selling finished cloth. Such individuals appear in the records from at least the late twelfth century in England, France, Italy and the Low Countries, and were often weaver-drapers. The Flemish migrants who came to England during the fourteenth century may have provided the initial stimulus for more coordinated production. Capitalist relationships between merchants and cloth-workers were much more prominent in the Low Countries than in England, and many of the immigrants had enjoyed a high economic status in Flanders. These migrants established a successful foreign weavers' guild in London, and a number became active wool exporters from Yarmouth and London.[10] They provided labour, expertise and finance for developing the cloth industry in several English towns and may have stimulated the expansion of the putting-out system and the rise of the clothier.

Such entrepreneurs become apparent in the thriving cloth-making centres of the late fourteenth century, including Colchester, Exeter, Winchester and York. The copious quantities of cloth presented by some traders from these and other towns in the ulnage accounts of the 1390s are insufficient evidence alone for the existence of major cloth producers coordinating production. The individuals in question may have been buying cloth manufactured by others, or the returns may simply have grouped together the output of smaller producers with their larger and wealthier neighbours. Evidence from court cases and wills though, suggests that merchants in some towns like Exeter and York were coordinating cloth-making between wool producers, weavers, fullers and dyers in the late fourteenth century. The evidence is not straightforward, because the Latin term *pannarius* can be translated as either clothier or draper. This fact in itself, though, helps to point to the origins of the clothier. The English word clothier, used interchangeably with cloth-maker and cloth-man, first appears in literature in the late fourteenth century and in the catalogued plea rolls in the early fifteenth century.[11]

The earliest documented clothiers so far discovered are to be found in Somerset, in the textile village of Croscombe and the small town of Wells, in the plea rolls of 1418. As the clothier was usually a resident of a small town or village, rather than a large city, it is not surprising to find the earliest references in these places, and a higher proportion of production was already taking place outside large towns in Somerset in

[10] Lambert and Pajic, 'Drapery in Exile'; Pajic, 'Migration of Flemish Weavers'. See also above, Introduction.

[11] See above, pp. 22–3, 123.

the 1390s than in other cloth-producing counties. The cloth industry in medieval Somerset has not yet benefitted from detailed studies such as those produced for Wiltshire or Suffolk, but it is clear that at this date cloth-making accounted for over a quarter of the share of employment in Wells, and had led to the emergence of an entirely new community at Pensford.[12] It was appropriate therefore, that Chaucer described his fictional cloth-making pilgrim as coming from 'beside Bath'.

The clothier rose to prominence in Suffolk between 1470 and 1500. Hanseatic merchants had moved out of Ipswich and Colchester and as the quantities of cloth exported and dyestuffs imported from these ports fell, the clothier, with his network of contacts and credit in London, became the key figure in textile production in this region. In Colchester this was also the period in which townspeople first began to style themselves as cloth-makers.[13] In the Kentish Weald, the clothier appeared a little later, reflecting the emergence of the textile industry in this region, in the early sixteenth century.

THE SKILLS OF THE MEDIEVAL CLOTHIER

The clothier required multifarious skills. These included a knowledge of wools and an overall understanding of the process of manufacture. Many also knew the art of dyeing. The crucial skills though, were managerial and entrepreneurial. The clothier controlled and invested in the whole production process, unlike urban drapers who financed trade but generally invested only in the finishing and dyeing of fabrics. The clothier had to recruit, organise and supply a range of independent workers and craftspeople with specialist skills in order to produce cloth from the raw materials he provided. Spinners, weavers, fullers and shearmen processed the materials put out to them, usually in their own homes or workshops. The clothier sourced supplies, arranging for materials to be transported from one worker to the next, and sold the finished cloths.

Cloth-making became more efficient during the course of the Middle Ages through both technological and organisational change. The spinning wheel, the horizontal loom, and the fulling mill all brought significant increases in efficiency, each potentially achieving a threefold improvement in productivity. These technologies were already in use though, to varying extents, in the fourteenth century. Some clothiers invested in looms and fulling mills, but many of their workers would have used their own equipment. More important than technological advance was the organisational change that the clothier achieved. The

12 Shaw, *Wells*, p. 79; Hare, 'Pensford'.

13 Amor, *From Wool to Cloth*, p. 217; Britnell, *Colchester*, p. 184.

clothier used labour more efficiently. He paid piece rates, used female and child labour, and even possibly adjusted his use of labour to meet the seasonal demands of agriculture. Combing, carding and spinning were the longest processes in cloth-making, so clothiers needed to recruit as many spinners as possible, and hold down the costs of spinning. Of all the textile workers, the services of a dyer was the most expensive on a daily basis, so if the clothier could learn these skills himself, he could reduce labour costs and still produce a product of equivalent value. Alternatively cloth could be sold undyed for a lower price.

The clothier also had to engage with the market to buy his raw materials and sell the cloth that he or she had produced. This required forging relationships with merchants from provincial towns and cities, London, and even from overseas. Some clothiers took their cloth to local markets or fairs but an increasing number travelled to London, to the great weekly market at Blackwell Hall or to the annual St Bartholomew's Fair in Smithfield. Clothiers developed reciprocal trading relationships with merchants who supplied oil, dyestuffs and alum in return for cloths. The clothier tended to specialise in producing a particular type of cloth for a national and international market, rather than making a broader range of cloths, like many urban drapers, to suit a more limited regional market.[14] The clothier also had to manage his cash flow by using credit to his advantage. Whether he was buying wool or other raw materials, paying his workers, or selling his cloth, credit underpinned virtually all these transactions. Offering extended credit where required on cloth sales, but taking credit where possible from suppliers or workers by paying them in arrears, the clothier would have been well aware of the modern business mantra: 'turnover is vanity, profit is sanity, cash is reality'.

THE ENVIRONMENT OF THE MEDIEVAL CLOTHIER

Clothiers and cloth-workers transformed the landscape. Up and down the country, communities resounded to the clacking of looms and the pounding of fulling-mill hammers. Cloths hung on tenters, stretched out to dry. Watercourses were channelled and diverted to provide for washing, scouring, fulling and finishing, and were coloured by polluting waste from dyeing activities. More and more land was turned over to grazing for sheep to meet the demand for wool, and in more marginal areas, whole villages might be abandoned. Most cloth-making centres grew organically, but a handful were master-planned with new streets of housing for cloth-workers, like Mells and Sutton Coldfield. A few

[14] Oldland, 'Economic Impact', p. 232.

entirely new communities emerged, based around cloth-making, like Pensford in Somerset and Stroudwater in Gloucestershire. The poorer clothier or cloth-worker simply extended a living space or added an extra room to the house to accommodate looms, spinning wheels, raw materials and finished cloths. The wealthiest clothiers built elegant new homes that emulated the finest manor houses or mercantile residences. Clothiers filled the buildings of former religious houses in Malmesbury, Gloucester and elsewhere with looms to become early textile factories. They enlarged, enriched, or entirely rebuilt churches. Cloth-making brought wider wealth to communities, expressed in civic projects like the market crosses and market houses of the south-west midlands, of which the octagonal covered cross, with stone vaulting and rich ornamentation at Malmesbury, provides a surviving example.[15] The wealthy clothier could expend his profits on conspicuous consumption, such as the ostentatious timber-carving on Paycocke's, Coggeshall – a fine example of late medieval Essex bling.

The leading clothiers continue to provide a legacy to their localities. Their homes and workshops shaped the built and natural environments of their locales, and this heritage is now being used to help promote tourism and civic pride. Visitors have long flocked to the village of Castle Combe or to Paycocke's House at Coggeshall, but new efforts are now being made in other cloth-making centres to raise awareness of their local cultural heritage. Tourist trails are helping to regenerate local economies in the Culm Valley of Devon and around West Yorkshire.[16] Many of the churches that clothiers reshaped, although often denuded by later reformers, still provide places of worship for their parishioners and historic assets for their communities. Even a few of the charitable works endowed by clothiers continue to offer support. Dunton's Almshouses in Dedham owe their origins to the seven cottages that the clothier Stephen Dunton left in his will of 1518 for the use of the poor, and the extensive property portfolio of cloth merchant John Greenway forms the foundation on which the Tiverton Almshouse Trust still operates.[17]

Across England by the 1540s, as many as one working adult in seven may have been engaged in cloth-making, and potentially one household

[15] Lee, 'Leland's *Itinerary*', p. 19.

[16] Cullompton and the Cloth Trade, https://cullomptonclothtrade.wordpress.com/; and West Yorkshire Textile Heritage Project, http://westyorkshiretextileheritage.org.uk/

[17] *VCH Essex*, x, p. 185; Tiverton Almshouse Trust website, http://www.tivertonalmshouse.org.uk

in four received earnings from spinning.[18] Such earnings played a crucial part in the expansion of the English economy:

> some added prosperity earned through the work of women and children, from a fairly large proportion of the peasant population, paid by wealthy clothiers, must have played a role in advancing the resurgent commercialisation of the early sixteenth century.[19]

Other jobs in manufacturing and services were created. Cloth-making transformed Lavenham from a village to a town that supported twenty different trades beyond textiles, including in 1522 a barber, a baker, a scrivener and a surgeon.[20] At the macro level, the economic impact of the cloth industry can be seen in the growth in wealth in cloth-making areas between the taxation returns of the fourteenth and sixteenth centuries, whether at the level of the counties, districts, or individual communities.[21] The other major beneficiary was London, which by 1550 'owed its economic ebullience and its aldermen their wealth to virtually one thing only – the traffic in English woollen cloths'.[22]

THE MEDIEVAL CLOTHIER AND GOVERNMENT

The clothier predominantly resided in the small town and village. Forerunners of the clothier can be found in the city merchants and drapers of the late fourteenth century and even earlier, and examples of urban clothiers can be found in the fifteenth and sixteenth centuries, but the medieval clothier was largely a rural figure. The clothier's organisation of cloth-making was a crucial factor in drawing the cloth industry from the town to the countryside. Finding themselves with declining urban industries, derelict properties and high civic overheads, national and local governments confronted challenges not dissimilar to those faced by their modern successors with the relocation of industry, housing and retailing out of town centres into more rural locations.

The changes brought by clothiers and other cloth producers impacted on national and local governments. Rising cloth exports brought customs revenue. London's share of English cloth exports grew from around 50 per cent in the 1390s to over 90 per cent by the 1560s. With preferential access to finance, London was able to exert a disproportionate influence

18 Oldland, 'Economic Impact', p. 235; Muldrew, 'Early Industrial Workforce', p. 86.

19 Muldrew, 'Early Industrial Workforce', p. 87.

20 Patten, 'Village and Town', p. 13.

21 *CUHB*, pp. 765–6; Darby et al., 'Changing Geographical Distribution of Wealth'.

22 Ramsay, 'Cloth Trade', p. 379.

on government policy in the later Middle Ages, as it still can today, and this spatial and economic imbalance between London and the provinces is something with which governments continue to grapple. Similarly, the difficulties that national governments have subsequently encountered in industries such as coal mining, shipbuilding, and steel-making, were foreshadowed by the crises in the overseas cloth trade in the 1450s and 1520s. In each case, communities and regions dependent on single industries competing in foreign markets experienced unemployment and unrest when these markets became disrupted. These communities could also be associated with religious and political dissent. Cade's revolt did not lead to political concessions in 1450, but in 1525 rebels forced the Amicable Grant to be abandoned. Indeed it may well have been the collective memory of these crises a generation later that prompted the Tudor statesman Sir William Cecil to warn: 'the people that depend upon the making of cloth are of worse condition to be quietly governed than the husbandmen'.[23]

THE MEDIEVAL CLOTHIER AS AN EARLY CAPITALIST

Clothiers have been identified as early capitalists. If capitalism is defined as a system in which the ownership of the means of production (the facilities and resources for producing goods) is concentrated in the hands of a few entrepreneurs, and by a labour force working for contractual wages and separated from the means of production, then only a few medieval clothiers would probably fit this bill. The evidence for clothiers owning capital assets and employing labour is patchy. Most had weights, scales, baskets and boards, many had spindles, looms, vats and tenter frames, some owned wool stores, dye-houses and fulling mills, and a few even possessed workshops for weavers. Many clothiers though, probably invested in little more than their raw materials, and relied on the equipment that their workers provided themselves. Clothiers might employ household servants and apprentices, but they rarely kept large numbers of employees. Even bequests in wills to spinners, weavers and fullers were relatively unusual. The clothier generally used outworkers, based in their own homes, who received work when the clothier put it out to them, but had no right to a regular wage. If they did not have alternative means of employment, they were particularly vulnerable at times of economic downturn in the cloth trade, as the unrest during the 1520s demonstrated.[24] Such economic relationships were not those of

[23] *TED*, ii, p. 45.

[24] Dyer, 'Were There Any Capitalists?', p. 306; Britnell, 'Commerce and Capitalism', p. 369; Amor, *From Wool to Cloth*, pp. 208–10.

employer and employee. Whether we view this putting-out system as an intermediate form of capitalism, or describe it as proto-industrialisation, is really a matter of definition.

Were clothiers benevolent and paternalistic or ruthless and exploitative employers? Were they pious patrons of the church, or rich men trying desperately to pass through the eye of a needle?[25] Generations of historians have grappled with these questions and arrived at different conclusions. The evidence is difficult to interpret, as a few examples illustrate. Casual wage-earners working for clothiers formed the basis of the putting-out system, which like the modern 'gig' economy, may be viewed as providing either a flexible working environment or a form of exploitation with little protection. Was the payment of cloth-workers in 'pins, girdles, and other unprofitable wares', rather than in cash, prohibited in 1464, an example of such exploitation, or a response to a shortage of low-denomination coins? Were the Suffolk and Essex weavers who complained in 1539 of 'the rich men, the clothiers', who had agreed among themselves to pay one price for weaving, voicing legitimate concerns about price-fixing or simply bemoaning a new method of organising the industry that reduced their independence?[26] Clothiers relied on credit to underpin all their cloth-making operations, and paid outworkers and independent artisans who did work for them in arrears, but it does appear that spinners bore an unequal share of the credit that sustained the cloth industry. We may perceive that clothiers were organising production to maximise efficiency, thereby generating wealth. Alternatively, we might regard them as engaging in practices that were, to borrow a modern phrase, the 'unacceptable face of capitalism'. Ultimately, these are subjective judgements based on our own beliefs and principles. What is clear is that medieval clothiers were at the forefront of an industry that transformed a number of areas in England during the later Middle Ages and left legacies to their communities that can still be found today.

[25] Matthew 19:24: 'And again I say unto you, It is easier for a camel to go through the eye of a needle, than for a rich man to enter into the kingdom of God.'

[26] 4 Edward IV, c. 1: *SR*, ii, p. 406; TNA, SP 1/151, fol. 70; *LP*, xiv (1), no. 874, p. 408.

Appendix 1
Cloths taxed by county, 1356–58 to 1468–73

	1356–58		*1394–98*		*1468–73*	
County	*Cloths*	*Rank*	*Cloths*	*Rank*	*Cloths*	*Rank*
Bedfordshire & Buckinghamshire	18	22			137	20
Berkshire & Oxfordshire	252	10	2,128	9	1,494	7
Cambridgeshire & Huntingdonshire	56	20	186	19	71	25
Devon & Cornwall *	114	16	1,461	11	1,067	10
Dorset			460	15	708	16
Essex & Hertfordshire	102	17	2,796	6	2,877	6
Gloucestershire & Bristol	2,805	2	4,426	3	4,875	4
Hampshire	4,412	1	2,333	8	1,451	8
Herefordshire	144	14	160	21	340	18
Kent	1,034	6	1,348	12	1,027	11
Leicestershire			113	24	66	26
Lincolnshire	1,242	5	545	13	286	19
London and Middlesex	1,551	3	1,548	10	983	12
Norfolk	211	11			830	13
Northamptonshire & Rutland	137	15	196	18	791	14
Northumberland	36	21	121	23	120	21
Nottinghamshire & Derbyshire	12	23	370	16	109	23
Shropshire	148	13	510	14	110	22
Somerset **	1,305	4	12,376	1	4,982	2
Staffordshire			140	22	109	24
Suffolk ***	576	8	2,792	7	5,188	1

	1356–58		1394–98		1468–73	
County	*Cloths*	*Rank*	*Cloths*	*Rank*	*Cloths*	*Rank*
Surrey and Sussex	285	9	283	17	769	15
Warwickshire	82	18	3,242	5	1,200	9
Westmorland	1	24				
Wiltshire	181	12	7,292	2	4,310	5
Worcestershire	60	19	182	20	478	17
Yorkshire	846	7	4,295	4	4,972	3
Total	15,610		49,303		39,345	

Source: H.L. Gray, 'The Production and Exportation of English Woollens in the Fourteenth Century', *English Historical Review* 39 (1924), pp. 13–35; Heaton, *Yorkshire Woollen*, pp. 84–5.

Notes: The ulnage accounts should be used cautiously, and it is safer when comparing fourteenth- and fifteenth-century figures, to compare *relative* rather than *absolute* changes in totals. Totals have been averaged from surviving ulnage accounts to produce totals for one year in each of the three periods.

Kerseys, straits and other narrow cloths were not included in the 1350s ulnage accounts but were included in the 1390s accounts. The increase in sealed cloths between these two decades exaggerates the increase in the actual number of cloths produced (Amor, *From Wool to Cloth*, pp. 219–21).

* The Devon and Cornwall figures for 1394–98 omit cloths sealed in Exeter, and production was closer to 2,500 cloths each year (Kowaleski, *Exeter*, p. 23).

** Somerset totals for 1356–58 include Dorset.

*** As the West Country accounts become fraudulent and understated during the fifteenth century, it has been argued that it is unlikely that Suffolk production was ever greater than the counties of Gloucestershire, Somerset and Wiltshire (Oldland, 'Book Reviews').

Appendix 2
Cloths taxed by locality

Berkshire 1395–97 (78 weeks)	*Cloths*	*% of county*
Steventon	576	23
East Hendred	483	19
Abingdon	386	15
Welford	192	8
Wantage	186	7
West Hendred	138	6
Benham	129	5
Boxford	108	4
Aldermaston	106	4
Newbury	53	2
Reading	45	2
Windsor	39	2
Maidenhead	30	1
Wallingford	13	1
Other places	15	1
Total	2,496	

Devon 1395–96 (56 weeks)	*Cloths*	*% of county*
Barnstaple	977	34
Exeter	714	25
Honiton	254	9
Culmstock	186	6
Bampton	160	6
Torrington	116	4
Plympton	56	2
South Molton	53	2

Totnes	48	2
Crediton	42	1
Tavistock	39	1
Plymouth	37	1
Okehampton	36	1
Chulmleigh	28	1
Other places	120	4
Total	2,866	

Essex 1394–95 (71 weeks)	*Cloths*	*% of county*
Colchester	850	35
Braintree	631	26
Coggeshall	362	15
Dedham	191	8
Maldon	186	8
Chelmsford	182	8
Total	2,402	

Essex 1467–68	*Cloths*	*% of county*
Colchester	1,393	58
Coggeshall	324	14
Dedham	322	13
Braintree	210	9
Chelmsford	46	2
Springfield	28	1
Thaxted and Saffron Walden	27	1
Other places	49	2
Total	2,399	

Hampshire 1394–95	*Cloths*	*% of county*
Winchester	2,500	77
Isle of Wight	221	7
Romsey	204	6
Southampton	69	2
Andover	65	2

Fareham	61	2
Alton	59	2
Alresford	53	2
Havant	32	1
Total	3,264	

Hampshire 1466–67	*Cloths*	*% of county*
Winchester	874	53
Romsey	221	14
Isle of Wight	190	12
Alton, Headley, Petersfield and East Meon	116	7
Andover and Whitchurch	100	6
Basingstoke and Odiham	78	5
Southampton	52	3
Fawley, Lymington and Christchurch	5	0
Total	1,636	

Kent 1476–77	*Cloths*	*% of county*
Biddenden, Egerton, Headcorn	426	40
Cranbrook	171	16
Benenden and Tenterden	153	14
Canterbury	89	8
Maidstone	71	7
Milton Hundred	35	3
Elham	30	3
Faversham	24	2
Dartford	17	2
Sandwich	17	2
Dover	17	2
Leeds	11	1
Total	1,061	

Somerset 1396–97 (43 weeks)	*Cloths*	*% of county*
Pensford	4,161	19
Frome	3,755	17
Wells	2,022	9
Bath	1,921	9
Bruton	1,479	7
Croscombe	1,261	6
Taunton	801	4
Shepton Mallet	759	3
Beckington	723	3
Mells	616	3
Rode	464	2
Bridgwater	456	2
Batcombe	444	2
Harptree	288	1
Nunney	272	1
Wellington	270	1
Kilmersdon	221	1
Norton St Philip	220	1
Other places	1,561	7
Total	21,694	

Somerset 1470	*Cloths*	*% of county*
Frome and Compton	1,300	26
Pensford and Harptree	940	19
Wells	420	8
Bath	420	8
Shepton Mallet	400	8
Taunton	379	8
Axbridge	300	6
Bridgwater	300	6
Langport and Yeovil	220	4
Ford	200	4
Bruton	100	2
Total	4,979	

Suffolk 1467–68	*Cloths*	*% of county*
Lavenham	1,120	22
Hadleigh	998	20
Bildeston	660	13
Bury St Edmunds	612	12
Nayland	428	9
Sudbury	318	6
Little Waldingfield	239	5
Long Melford	172	3
East Bergholt	137	3
Stratford St Mary	77	2
Clare	69	1
Boxford	67	1
Glemsford	59	1
Ipswich	35	1
Total	4,991	

Wiltshire 1414–15 (26 weeks)	*Cloths*	*% of county*
Salisbury	1,309	70
Devizes	140	7
Warminster hundred	129	7
Mere	80	4
Melksham hundred	73	4
Castle Combe	71	4
Wilton	67	4
Total	1,869	

Yorkshire 1468–69 (46 weeks)	*Cloths*	*% of county*
Ripon	888	21
Halifax	853	20
Wakefield	231	5
Almondbury	160	4
Leeds	177	4
Bradford	89	2

Pontefract	106	2
Barnsley	89	2
Doncaster	36	1
Selby	27	1
City of York total	1,596	38
Total	4,252	

Note: From the ulnage accounts. Unless stated otherwise, each account covers one year.

Sources: TNA, E 101/339/20, E 101/343/30; Yates, *Town and Countryside*, p. 82, n. 67; Kowaleski, *Local Markets*, p. 24; Britnell, *Colchester*, pp. 80, 189, 191; Keene, *Survey of Medieval Winchester*, i, p. 312, n. 1, p. 316, n. 4; Hare, 'Regional Prosperity', pp. 114–15; Hare, *Prospering Society*, p. 181; Heaton, *Yorkshire Woollen*, pp. 69–76.

Appendix 3
Cloth types, as defined by statute in 1552

Cloth type	*Minimum dimensions (yards)*	*Minimum weight (lb)*
Kent, Sussex and Reading broadcloths	28 x 1¾	90
White cloths called Long Worcesters & those made in Coventry	29 x 1¾	84
Coloured cloths of Coventry and Worcester	29 x 1¾	80
White cloths called Short Worcesters	23 x 1¾	60
Coloured Long cloths of Suffolk, Norfolk and Essex	28 x 1¾	80
Coloured Short cloths of Suffolk, Norfolk and Essex	23 x 1¾	64
Coloured cloths called Handywarps of Suffolk, Norfolk and Essex	23 x 1¾	Every yard weigh 3 lb at least
Whites being Coxhall Whites, Glemsford Whites and other Handywarps	Various x 1¾	Every yard weigh 3 lb at least
Whites and Reds of Wiltshire, Gloucestershire and Somerset, and all other Whites made in other parts of the realm, not mentioned above	26 x 1¾	64 White 60 Coloured
Broad Plunkets, Azures, Blues and other Coloured cloths of Wiltshire, Gloucestershire and Somerset	25 x 1¾	68
Kerseys called Ordinaries	17	20
Kerseys called Sorting Kerseys	17	23
Devonshire Kerseys called Dozens	12	14
Broadcloths called Tauntons and Bridgwaters and other cloths made in Taunton and Bridgwater	12* x 1¾	34
Narrow cloths made in Taunton and Bridgwater	23* x 1	34
Check Kerseys and Straits	17 x 1	24

Cloth type	*Minimum dimensions (yards)*	*Minimum weight (lb)*
Welsh Cottons	32 goads† x ¾	46
Welsh Friezes made in Cardiganshire, Carmathenshire and Pembrokeshire	36 x ¾	48
Northern cloths	23 x 1¾	46
Half pieces called Dozens	12 x 1¾	33
Penistones or Forest Whites	12 x 1 5/8	28
Manchester, Lancashire and Cheshire Cottons	22 goads† x ¾	30
Manchester Rugs or Friezes	36 x ¾	48

Source: Act for the Making of Woollen Cloth, 1552, 5 & 6 Edward VI, c. 6: *SR*, iv (1), pp. 136–7.

Notes: * The text of the statute appears to have transposed the dimensions of these types of broadcloths and narrow cloths.

† Goad: a measure of cloth, in the late seventeenth century said to equal 4½ feet (*OED*).

Appendix 4
Will of Thomas Paycocke of Coggeshall

1. In the name of God Amen. The 4th day of September in the year of our Lord God 1518. I Thomas Paycoke of Coxhall[1] with a whole and good memory set my testament and last will in this wise:
2. First I recommend my soul to God and to Our Lady Saint Mary and to all saints, and my body to be buried in the church of Coxhall afore the altar of Saint Catherine.
3. Item I bequeath to the high altar of Coxhall church in recompense of tithes and all other things forgotten total £4.
4. Item I bequeath to a tabernacle of the Trinity at the High Altar, and another of Saint Margaret in Saint Catherine's aisle there as the great lady stands for carving and gilding of them, total 100 marks sterling.
5. Item to the reparations of the church and bells and for my lying in the church, total 100 nobles.[2]
6. Item I will and give to a chantry for to pray for me and my wife, my father and mother John and Emma, and for my father-in-law Thomas Horrold of Clare, and for all my friends' souls that I am bound for the purchase and mortessyng[3] to the king, and also to the same chantry, six poor men to keep the same Mass three days in the week, that is for to say Monday, Wednesday and Friday, to pray for the souls afore rehearsed, and therefore to have 18d among them every week to fulfil this, and also every year 100 wood apiece of them and my priest to sing in Coxhall church afore Saint Catherine altar, total 500 marks.
7. Item I will that mine executors bestow upon my burying day, seven days and month day after this manner, at my burial to have a trental[4] of priests and to be at *Dirige*, *Lawdis* and Commendations[5] as many

[1] Coggeshall

[2] Noble: an English gold coin worth 6s 8d (*OED*).

[3] Mortmain: the permission of the king was required to alienate property in mortmain (to give in perpetuity to the Church).

[4] Trental: a set of thirty requiem Masses (*OED*).

[5] *Dirige*: the first word of the antiphon at Matins in the Office of the Dead, used as a name for that service; *Lawdis*: Lauds, the first of the day-hours of the Church, derived from the three last psalms of the psalter; Commendations: an office originally ending with the prayer *Tibi, Domine, commendamus*, in which the souls of the dead were commended to God (*OED*).

of them as may be purveyed that day to serve the trental, and if any lack to make it up the seventh day, And at the month day another trental to be purveyed whole of mine executors and to keep *Dirige*, *Lawdis* and Commendations as is afore rehearsed with three high Masses be note, one of the Holy Ghost, another of Our Lady, and another of Requiem, both burial, seventh day and month day. And priests being at this observance singing of these trentals to have 12d every time and other priests being there and not singing the trental to have 8d and every other man being at this observance 4d at every time, and children at every time 2d with torches at the burial twelve, and six at the seventh day, and twelve at the month day, with twenty-four or twelve small children in rochets with tapers in their hands and as many as may be of them let them be my godchildren and they to have 6s 8d apiece, and every other child 4d apiece, and every man that holds torches at every day he to have two apiece, and every man woman and child that holds up hand at any of these three days to have 1d apiece. And also every godchild beside 6s 8d apiece, and to the ringers for all three days 10s, and for meat drink and for two sermons of a doctor, and also to have a *Dirige* at home or I be borne to the church, total £50.

8. I will also that my Lord Abbot and convent have a broadcloth and £4 in money for to have a *Dirige* and Mass and their bells ringing at my burial when it is done at church likewise the seventh day and month day with three trentals upon the same days if they can serve them or else when they can at more leisure, total £10.
9. Also I will the Friars of Clare have for two trentals 20s, and at Lent after my decease a cade[6] of red herring.
10. Also I will the Grey Friars of Colchester have for a trental 10s and 3s 4d for the reparations of their house.
11. Also I will the Friars of Maldon have for a trental 10s and 3s 4d for the reparations of their house.
12. Also I will the Friars of Chelmsford have for a trental 10s and 3s 4d for the reparations of their house.
13. Also I will the Friars of Sudbury have for a trental 10s and 3s 4d for the reparations of their house.
14. Item I will and give to the Old Warke in Pawlis and to Powlis Pardone[7] 6s 8d. I bequeath to the church of Stoke Nayland 13s 4d.
15. Item [I] will and give to Clare church and Poslingford church each of them 10s total 20s.

[6] Cade: barrel (*OED*).
[7] St Paul's Cathedral and Pardon churchyard, London.

16. Item I will and give to Ovington and Belchamp churches to each of them 6s 8d, total 13s 4d.
17. Item I will and bequeath to Bradwell, Pattiswick and Markshall to every each of them 6s 8d, total 20s.
18. Item I bequeath to foul ways in West Street from Harsbryg to Pyssyng Gutter[8] warde after as it will perform £20.
19. Item I bequeath to the foul way between Clare and Overton £20 and £20 between Ovington and Potts Belchom[9] total £40.
20. Item I bequeath to be laid on the foul ways between Coxhall and Blackwater where as most need is £20.
21. Item I bequeath to Anne my good wife 500 marks sterling, and I bequeath my child that my wife got with all 500 marks to be paid when it comes to the lawful age and if it happen to decease I will mine executors dispose it.
22. Item I will my said child if it be a son have my house that I dwell in and all my houses with all my lands to him and to his heirs when he comes to the age of 21 years, and if he decease without heirs male to remain to John the son of my brother John Paycocke and to his heirs male of his body begotten.
23. And if he decease without heirs male of his body begotten then I will the said houses and lands remain to Thomas Paycocke the son of my brother Robert Paycocke and to his heirs male of his body begotten. And if the said Thomas decease without heirs male of his body then I will Robert Paycocke his brother have it to him and to heir heirs male of his body begotten. Provided always that my wife Anne have my house I dwell in while she lives at her pleasure and my dove house with the garden it stands in.
24. Item I bequeath to every child of my brother John and Robert Paycocke £10 apiece total £60.
25. Item I bequeath to Robert and Margaret Uppcher my sister's children £10 apiece, total £20.
26. Item I bequeath to every child my cousin Thomas Perpoint has 6s 8d apiece.
27. Item I will mine executors purvey a marble stone with mine image thereon and both my wives and they to bestow £5 thereupon.
28. Item I will also that they purvey another stone to be had to Clare church and laid on my father-in-law Thomas Horrold with his picture and his wife and children thereon. And they to bestow £5 thereupon.

[8] Hare Bridge to Pissing Gutter

[9] Possibly Belchamp St Paul

29. Item I bequeath to Clare church to keep and maintain my father-in-law Thomas Horrold's obit six kine[10] or else £3 in money.
30. Item I bequeath to the Crossed Friars in Colchester for me and for them that I am bound to pray for total £5 to the box for I am brother of them.
31. Item I bequeath to Richard Cotton and to William Cotton, my wife's brethren, to each of them £10.
32. Item I bequeath to Eleanor Cotton, my wife's sister £6 13s 4d.
33. Item I bequeath to my wife's father George Cotton and to his wife 26s 8d each of them.
34. Item I bequeath to Thomas Horrold of Clare £5, and to Margery and Margaret the sisters to the said Thomas Horrold to each of them £10 apiece, and if the foresaid Margery or Margaret die or they come to marriage I will mine executors dispose it for my soul, and if the said Margery make any business and trouble with mine executors I will her part be otherwise bestowed by mine executors.
35. Item I bequeath to Henry Perpoint of London 20s and to his sister Agnes Burton 20s, and I will that Agnes Burton's children have 3s 4d a piece of them.
36. Item I will that Robert Wyndlove of Halstead have 10s.
37. Item I bequeath to John Freman of Byely[11] 10s and each of his children 3s 4d apiece.
38. Item I give to John Freman his brother 10s and to each of his children 3s 4d apiece.
39. Item I bequeath to Richard Cavyll's wife of Stratford to have 10s and every child 3s 4d apiece.
40. Item I bequeath to John Aylward of Poynthyll Street[12] 40s to each of his children 3s 4d.
41. Item I bequeath to Edward Aylward of the Dragon to have 10s and each of his children 3s 4d.
42. Item I bequeath to Robert Gooday of *Sappysford*[13] to have 20s.
43. Item to John Gooday his brother 6s 8d, and to every sister of the said Robert I give 3s 4d apiece save to Grace Gooday my god-daughter I give 6s 8d.
44. Item I bequeath to Thomas Gooday shearman 20s and each of his children 3s 4d apiece.
45. Item I bequeath to Edward Gooday shearman 16s 8d and to his child 3s 4d.

[10] Kine: cows (*OED*).
[11] Beeleigh, Maldon
[12] Pointell Street, Coggeshall
[13] Place not identified.

46. Item to Nicholas Gooday of Stysted 10s and to each of his children 3s 4d.
47. Item to Robert Gooday of Coxhall and to his children 10s and to Sir John Gooday of Byeley[14] 10s for a trental.
48. Item I bequeath to Humfrey Stoner sometime my apprentice total 6s 8d.
49. Item I bequeath to John Beycham my weaver £5 and there be so much between 5s and else to make it up £5 and a gown and a doublet.
50. Item I bequeath to Thomas Man my tenant a gown or else 20s.
51. Item I bequeath to Robert Lamberd 20s.
52. Item to John Sponer my tenant at the chapel 20s.
53. Item I bequeath to John Reyner my man 20s and a gown 20s.
54. Item I bequeath to John Porter and Thomas Trewe 6s 8d apiece.
55. Item I bequeath and forgive Robert Taylor fuller all that is betwixt us and more I give him 3s 4d.
56. Item I bequeath to Henry Breggs my servant total 40s.
57. Item I bequeath to all my weavers, fullers and shearmen that be not afore rehearsed by name 12d apiece. And will they that have wrought me very much work have 3s 4d. apiece.
58. Item I bequeath to be distributed among my combers, carders and spinners total £4.
59. All the residue of my goods unbeset[15] I put it at the discretion of mine executors for where it is much out of my hands to perform the will I put all to your discretion for if it fortune well there is enough beside and if it miscarry so much that you have scant enough to perform this will I pray you with that you have and can get to your hands to perform everything according to the substance, and I ordain and make mine executors my brother John Paycocke and Robert Paycocke and Thomas Perpoint draper and I give to each of them £40 apiece for their labours.

Proved at Lambeth, 16 February 1519.

Source: TNA, PROB 11/19/207, printed in G.F. Beaumont, 'Paycocke's House, Coggeshall, with Some Notes on the Families of Paycocke and Buxton', *Transactions of the Essex Archaeological Society*, new series 9 (1903–06), pp. 311–24.

[14] Beeleigh, Maldon

[15] Unbeset: not bestowed or apportioned (*OED*).

Appendix 5
Will of Thomas Spring III of Lavenham

1. In the name of God Amen. The 13th day of June in the year of Our Lord God 1523 and in the 15th year of the reign of King Henry VIII, I, Thomas Spring of Lavenham in the county of Suffolk and in the diocese of Norwich, cloth-maker, being of whole mind and memory and perfect remembrance and verily knowing that there is nothing more sure or more certain to any creature in this wretched world than death, which every creature living inevitably must suffer, and nothing more unsure and uncertain than the dreadful hour thereof, fully disposing and purposing myself by the mercy, grace and help of the most merciful Lord Christ Jesus to be at all and every time and hour ready, do make my last will and testament in manner and form following:
2. First I annul and revoke all other wills and testaments ever afore this day made and declared, and will that every of them shall be of no strength nor effect.
3. Item, I bequeath my soul to Almighty God, to his Blessed Mother Mary, and to all the holy company of heaven, and my body to be buried in the church of Lavenham before the altar of Saint Katherine where I will be made a tomb with a parclose thereabout by the discretion of mine executors.
4. Item, I bequeath to the high altar of Lavenham for my tithes and offerings negligently forgotten and not paid 100s.
5. Item, I will that satisfaction and restitution be made to every person complaining and duly proving any injury, wrong, extortion, oppression, deceit or any misbehaving or demeaning against reason and conscience by me to them done in any wise.
6. Item, I will that immediately after my decease in as hasty time as it may be conveniently done, there shall be a thousand Masses sung for the wealth of my soul.
7. Item, I give and bequeath to every of the houses of friars of Clare, Sudbury, Babwell, two houses of friars in Thetford and the nuns of Thetford to pray for my soul and all my benefactors' souls and to every of them 40s.
8. Item, I will that there be disposed the 30th day after my decease and

departing out of this world £100 in all such towns and parishes as I have any lands and tenements, that is to say, to have a Mass with dirge in every church, and the money to be disposed to the priests, clerks and poor folks to pray for my soul and all my benefactors' souls.

9. Item, I give and bequeath to the finishing of the steeple of Lavenham £200.
10. Item, I give and bequeath to the reparation of highways to be disposed where mine executors shall think most necessary about the town of Lavenham 100 marks.
11. Item, I bequeath and give to Alice, my wife, all her apparel with jewels, and 1,000 marks in money and pennyworths[1] over and beside 600 marks that she brought to me at the time of her marriage, which 600 marks I will that be paid her over and beside the said 1,000 marks.
12. Item, I will that all my plate, ornaments and implements of household as bedding, napery, hangings, brass, pewter and all other hustlements[2] of house be divided between my wife and John Spring, my son, by mine executors.
13. Item, I give and bequeath to Alice, my wife, two of my best horses and three kine[3] such as she will choose.
14. Item, I will that the wood in my yards and my corn and malt upon the sollars[4] be equally divided between my wife and John, my son, except such as shall be spent by mine executors about my interment and other things touching the ministration of my goods.
15. Item, I give and bequeath towards the marriage of Bridget Spring, my youngest daughter, 500 marks to be delivered to her at the age of 16 years. And if it happen the said Bridget to die afore she come to the age of 16 years, then I will the said 500 marks be divided equally between my children's children then living.
16. Item, I give and bequeath to John Spring, mine oldest son, £200.
17. Item, I give to Frances, his daughter, 100 marks.
18. Item, I give and bequeath to Robert Spring, my son, £200.
19. Item, I give to every of the children of Thomas Jermyn now living £20. And if any of them die before the age of 16 years, then I will the part or parts of them so departed or deceased be evenly divided amongst the other then living.
20. Item, I give and bequeath to every child of my daughter, Rose Guybon, now living £20. And if any of them die before the age of

[1] Pennyworth: in goods, wares (*OED*).
[2] Hustlement: household furniture (*OED*).
[3] Kine: cows (*OED*).
[4] Sollar: upper room in a house; a loft, attic (*OED*).

16 years, then I will that the part or parts of them so departed or deceased be evenly divided amongst the other then living.

21. Item, I will that mine executors do pay unto my wife's daughter, Alice May, when she shall be of the age of 16 years, £26 13s 4d which I recovered for her of May's executors.
22. Item, I will that if Robert Newman and William Goding of Bocking do not pay the said Alice May £40 at the age of 16 years, that then mine executors shall sue a certain obligation in which they be bound to me.
23. Item, I give and bequeath to every of my godchildren 3s 4d.
24. Item, I will there be distributed among my household servants so much money as shall be thought necessary by the discretion of mine executors.
25. The residue of all my goods and chattels not given nor bequeathed I give it to the disposition of mine executors whom I ordain and make Sir William Waldegrave, knight, and Thomas Jermyn, my son-in-law, desiring and requiring them in the way of charity to order and dispose the same in charitable deeds as they shall think most expedient to the pleasure of God and for the wealth of my soul.
26. Item, my mind and will is that if my wife or any of my children do interrupt, let or trouble any article comprised in this my last will and testament, so that this my last will cannot take effect according to the true intent thereof, then I will that all legacies and bequests to them before given that so do interrupt be void and of none effect, and that such person or persons so interrupted or troubled shall have and enjoy the same legacy and bequest which was bequeathed to him or them that shall make such trouble, vexation and business.
27. And further I require and charge John Spring, mine eldest son, upon my blessing that he hinder not, disturb nor let this my testament and last will in no point, but that he endeavour himself as much as in him is to perform and accomplish the same according to the truth.
28. Item, I give to the bailiff of Lavenham William Betryn one hundred pounds, whereof I will that John his son have £20.
29. Item, I give and bequeath to Peter Gawge mine apprentice, 10 half balls of woad.
30. In witness of the truth I have sealed and delivered this as my last will and testament in the presence of William Betryn bailiff of Lavenham, Henry Symond, William Wooder and Peter Turnour.

Proved at St Paul's, London, 3 July 1523.

Source: TNA, PROB 11/21/179, printed in Betterton and Dymond, *Lavenham*, pp. 14–15.

Appendix 6
Will of John Smallwood the elder alias John Winchcombe I of Newbury

1. In the name of God Amen. The fourth day of January in the year of Our Lord God 1519 [1520] I John Smalwoode the elder alias John Wynchecombe of the parish of St Nicholas in Newbury in the diocese of Salisbury of whole and perfect mind make my testament and last will in manner and form following.
2. First I bequeath my soul to Almighty God to our blessed lady Saint Mary the Virgin and to all the holy company of heaven and my body to be buried in our lady chancel within the parish church of Newbury aforesaid by Alice my wife and a stone to be laid upon us both.
3. Also I bequeath to our mother church of Salisbury 12d.
4. Also I bequeath to the high altar of the said church of Newbury for my offerings negligently forgotten 12d.
5. Also I bequeath to Jesus altar within the said parish church 8d.
6. Also I bequeath to Our Lady altar in the said church 8d.
7. Item I bequeath to St Thomas altar in the same church 8d.
8. Also I bequeath to every altar besides in the said parish church 4d.
9. Also I give and bequeath of Joan my wife 100 marks sterling and my stuff of household.
10. Also I give and bequeath to Joan my wife all my cattle and the wood that lies in the midst of the Culverhouse[1] with all my corn and hay.
11. Also I give and bequeath unto her half my plate.
12. Moreover, I will that the said Joan shall have during her natural life all such lands and tenements with their appurtenances as I hold by indenture of the College of Windsor except and only reserved to John my son all the racks and tenters as there now stand within a close called the Culverhouse with free liberty and passage in and out to him and to his assigns in and for the occupying of the same and after the decease of the said Joan I will that the said lands and tenements with their appurtenances wholly remain to the said John my son during the terms comprised in the said indentures thereof made.

[1] Culver: dove or pigeon (*OED*).

13. Also I give and bequeath to the said parish church of Newbury towards the building and edifying of the same £40 sterling.
14. Also I bequeath to John Tunnell £3 6s 8d.
15. Also I bequeath to Richard Coke 20s.
16. Also I bequeath to Thomas Harryson 20s.
17. Also I bequeath to Margaret Beiche 40s.
18. Also I bequeath to Kateryn West 20s.
19. Also I bequeath to Alice Marsshe 20s.
20. Also I bequeath to Agnes Holmes 6s 8d.
21. And to every of my women servants besides 20d.
22. Item I bequeath to every of my men servants in my house 20d.
23. Also I bequeath to William Dolman besides all things of his covenants 40s.
24. Also I bequeath to Sir John Waite parson of Newbury for the recompense of my tithes negligently forgotten 40s.
25. Also I will that mine executor do keep an obit for me and my friends to the sum of 10s once every year to be distributed among priests and clerks during the terms of 22 years.
26. Also I will that mine executor do find an honest priest to sing for me and my friends by the space of one whole year.
27. The residue of all my goods not given and bequeathed my funeral debts and legacies paid and fulfilled, I give and bequeath wholly to John my son whom I ordain and make my true lawful and sole executor of this my present testament and last will to dispose for the health of my soul as he shall think most expedient.
28. Also I make and ordain Robert Sheway overseer of this my present testament and last will, and I will that he have for his labour 20s.
29. Witness Sir John Wayte parson of the said church of Newbury, Sir Robert Wright curate of the same, Robert Sheway, Roger Benet, John Tunnell and Thomas Harrison with many others.

Proved at Lambeth, 24 March 1520.

Source: TNA, PROB 11/19/384.

Appendix 7
Will of William Stumpe of Malmesbury

1. In the name of God, Amen. I, William Stumpe, do make my testament and last will in manner and form following the 15th day of October in the 4th year of our dread sovereign Lord King Edward VI [1550] by the grace of God King of England, France, and Ireland, and in earth Supreme Head of the Church of England and also of Ireland.
2. First I do give thanks to God that I am in good mind and memory as ever I was and not sick in body thereof.
3. First of all I do bequeath my soul to our Lord Jesus Christ, I do verily trust to be saved by His blessed passion that He did suffer for me and for all mankind, and by none other means nor ways that ever was or that ever I did say or do but by Him only. My body to be buried wheresoever that God will have the body as He please.
4. I do give and bequeath to John Stumpe, my second son, my leases that I have of Gale's house, John Wyndowe's house and Richard Smith's house at Charlton, with ten broad looms and in money £500, all this to be delivered after my departing, when he will have it.
5. And I do give and bequeath to Richard Stumpe, William Stumpe, and Thomas Stumpe, my brother John's children, £10 apiece, to be delivered to them when they come to the ages of 21 years, and if any of them do die before that ages then I would their part that do die shall be delivered to the other. And if they do die all before the ages of 21 years then it shall remain to my executors.
6. And I do give and bequeath to every woman servant 20s above their wages and to every man servant in my house 40s, that is John Chappell 40s, and to Robert Saunson £4.
7. My debts paid, all the rest of my goods unbequeathed I do give to James Stumpe my son, who I do make my executor.
8. Witnesses: Robert Cove, David Serney, Robert Rowles with others more, Thomas Nele. This is my last will written with my hand and sealed with my seal the date above written William Stumpe.

1. Memorandum that the 22nd day of July in the year of our Lord God 1552, the foresaid William Stumpe being in perfect mind and of

good remembrance, acknowledged and ratified his testament above written and declared and willed the same to stand and be for his true testament and last will in the presence of the witnesses underwritten, and further declaring and adding unto the said testament did then will and bequeath these legacies particularly ensuing.

2. First he willed and bequeathed to Edith Bendall his servant £10.
3. Item to Mergery Stowle his servant £6 13s 4d.
4. Item, to Eve [1] his servant £5.
5. Item, to William Stumpe his youngest son the residue of his broad looms not bequeathed above.
6. Item, he did forgive Robert Saunson 20 nobles he did owe him.
7. Item, he did forgive John Bocher all such debts as he did owe[2] him except £7 which he willed that he should pay to his executor.
8. Item, he did forgive his brother Thomas Stumpe and Agnes Lyppet, widow, his sister, all such debts as they did owe unto him.
9. Item, he did forgive George Darbye £14 which he did owe unto him.
10. Item, he did forgive all his weavers and tenants dwelling within the precincts of the late monastery of Malmesbury all such debts as they did owe unto him.
11. Item, he bequeathed £40 to be distributed amongst poor people of the town of Malmesbury according to the discretion of his executor.
12. Witnesses hereof Sir John Horsleye, priest, Thomas Frauncsom, Robert Cole, John Lawrence with divers others.

Proved before the Archbishop's Court of Canterbury, London, 18 October 1554, and administration granted to James Stumpe, executor.

Source: TNA, PROB 11/35/323, printed in Manley, 'Stumpe', pp. 390–1.

[1] There is a blank space in the document for Eve's surname.
[2] This line is missing in Manley's transcript.

Gazetteer of surviving buildings

Most of these sites are accessible to the public, but visitors are recommended to check before making a long journey, and to respect those marked private. Opening hours of National Trust and English Heritage sites can be found on their websites and an admission charge is made. Churches are frequently open unless services are taking place (though this is not always the case), and rarely charge for admission. However, as the responsibility for upkeep falls mainly on the local congregations, donations are strongly encouraged. Further information about these buildings can be found in the relevant county volume of Pevsner's *Buildings of England* series and in the National Heritage List for England, available on the Historic England website.

Beckington, Somerset
St George's Church, Church Street, BA11 6TG

South chancel aisle, originally dedicated to the Virgin Mary, and now known as Compton's Aisle, probably built by the bequest of the clothier John Compton (d. 1484). Brass to John and Edith Compton (d. 1505) with five sons in prayer, and circular plates on each side with angels holding Compton's rebus, a barrel or tun inscribed 'J.Com'. In the south aisle, set in the wall is John Compton's merchant's mark, which consists of a gridiron with handle in the form of a cross and his initials JC. This aisle also contains the brass of the clothier Thomas Webb (d. 1585) which was originally in the north aisle.

Bildeston, Suffolk
Chapel Street (private)

Early-sixteenth-century row of four identical houses, half-timbered and jettied, possibly built by a clothier for his weavers.

Bradford-on-Avon, Wiltshire
Holy Trinity Church, Church Street, BA15 1LW

Former chapel in the north aisle with brass of Thomas Horton (d. 1530) and wife Mary (d. 1544), with representation of the Trinity and merchant's mark. This brass was engraved during the couple's lifetime as neither date has been filled in.

Horton's House, Church Street (private)

Built around 1496 by Thomas Horton and recorded by Leland in 1538. Extension added to the west, probably soon afterwards, for a cloth workshop, the walls and stonework of which are now incorporated into a modern extension. The house is linked to a late-eighteenth-century building known as Abbey House.

Masonic Hall (Former Church Hall), Church Street (private)

Stone building built by the clothier Thomas Horton and recorded by Leland in 1538.

Bristol

St Mary Redcliffe Church, Redcliffe Way, BS1 6NL

Brass in the chancel of John Jay, sheriff (1472) in civilian dress, and Joan c.1480 with sons and daughters, merchant's marks and two shields with carding combs.

Castle Combe, Wiltshire

St Andrew's Church, Market Place, SN14 7HP

Construction of the tower started in 1434 supported by money from the wool and cloth trades and a bequest from John Fastolf, lord of the manor. The fan vaulting is reminiscent of Bath Abbey. The tower contained a faceless clock, one of the oldest working clocks in the country, now standing in the base of the tower. Additions to the tower are commemorated by a carving below the string course depicting a weaver's shuttle, shears and a teasel card, with the inscription 'VIVAT REGINA (Long live the Queen) 1576'.

Colchester, Essex

Marquis of Granby Inn, 24 North Street, CO1 1EG

A building of c.1520, heavily restored in 1914. Timber-framed and plastered, with jettied upper storey. Exceptionally finely carved interior detail in the east wing, including a beam bearing a shield with the initials HW, indicating this was probably the house of the clothier Henry Webb.

Coggeshall, Essex

Paycocke's House, 25 West Street, CO6 1NS (National Trust)

Impressive half-timbered house of five bays, originally three storeys. Built in 1509 for the clothier Thomas Paycocke (d. 1518). This may have been Thomas' salesroom, workshop and residence. Carriageway at the east end. Elaborate wood carvings both outside and inside that include Paycocke's merchant's mark and initials, and those of his first wife, Margaret.

St Peter ad Vincula Church, Church Green, CO6 1UD

The church was constructed to one plan in the fifteenth century and may have been rebuilt from wealth generated by the local cloth industry. The Paycockes are buried in St Catherine's Chapel in the north chancel aisle. Thomas Paycocke (d. 1461) and wife Christina are recorded as buried here but their tomb has been lost. Tomb of Thomas Paycocke (d. 1518) and wives Margaret and Anne without its brasses. John (d. 1533) and Joan Paycocke in brass on tomb in centre. Robert Paycocke and wives Elizabeth and Joan on tomb to right, with brasses missing. Thomas (d. 1580), grandson of this Robert, buried in tomb with brass above that of John. Tombs of the elder Thomas and Robert carry the Paycockes' merchant's mark.

Cranbrook, Kent

St Dunstan's Church, Stone Street, TN17 3HA

Brass to civilian c.1520 with a child in swaddling clothes, merchant's mark with initials TS, inscription lost, in the south chapel. This probably commemorates Thomas Sheefe, clothier (d. 1520).

Cullompton, Devon

St Andrew's Church, Church Street, EX15 1JU

Lane's Aisle, built between 1526 and 1529, for the clothier John Lane (d. 1528) as his chantry chapel. Lane and his wife were buried inside at the east end of the aisle. An indent marks their brass, which depicted John and his wife Thomasine, four lozenges, and a marginal inscription inscribed in stone. Elaborate fan vaulting includes images of cloth-making, with fulling stocks on a roof boss and angels holding cloth shears, teasel frames, and his merchant's mark on corbels. Exterior buttresses decorated with ships, cloth shears, Lane's initials and merchant's mark.

Dedham, Essex

Church of St Mary the Virgin, High Street, CO7 6DE

Church rebuilt in the late fifteenth and early sixteenth centuries, reflecting the prosperity of the local cloth trade. The tower, in progress in 1494, has a passage vault with Tudor roses, portcullises, shields, and the initials IW and TW for John and Thomas Webb, with their merchant's mark. Two small portraits in lozenge-shaped panels are thought to be of John and his wife Joan. John Webb erected a monument to his father Thomas (d. 1506), a traceried altar tomb, now in the north aisle of the church, probably moved from the chancel. It contains their initials and merchant's mark and has indents marking where a brass would have been fixed.

Southfields The Flemish Cottages, The Drift (private)

Clothier's house with late-fifteenth- or early-sixteenth-century rooms built around a courtyard capable of accommodating workshops as well as warehousing. Carriageway with gable over on the north side.

East Hendred, Oxfordshire (formerly Berkshire)
Church of St Augustine of Canterbury, Church Street, OX12 8LA

Brass inscription to William Whitwey, *pannarius et lanarius* (clothier or draper and woolman), 1479, on wall of north transept. Brass on the floor of the north transept depicting Henry (effigy now lost) and Roger Eldysley, merchants, dated 1439. Three merchants' marks (another lost). According to tradition, they lived in a house in a meadow behind the church.

Glemsford, Suffolk
Church of St Mary the Virgin, Churchgate, CO10 7QE

South aisle chapel with inscription to founders, the clothier John Golding and wife Joan, 1497. North aisle chapel with inscription to founders, the clothier John Mundys, wife Margaret, son John and his wife Elizabeth, 1525.

Gloucester
Blackfriars, Ladybellegate Street, GL1 2HS (English Heritage)

A former Dominican friary acquired by the clothier and capmaker Thomas Bell who converted the church into his mansion and used the other buildings as workshops for his weavers.

Ipswich, Suffolk
St Margaret's Church, Soane Street, IP4 2BT

Late-fifteenth-century clerestory commemorating John Hall (d. 1503), dyer, his wife Katherine (d. 1506), and son William (d. 1526), clothier and dyer. The family's monograms and merchant's mark are displayed, the latter formed of a dyer's posser and pair of tongs.

Lavenham, Suffolk

Numerous surviving timber-framed buildings, mostly dating from c.1460–1530 in this cloth-making town. Although some of the largest houses were demolished in the seventeenth century, fine examples of clothiers' houses survive, including Molet House (probably originally part of a larger house), and the Old Grammar School, both on Barn Street.

Guildhall of Corpus Christi, Market Place, CO10 9QZ
(National Trust)

Close studded and jettied, with exuberant carving, dating to c.1530. Two adjacent properties, 26 and 27 Market Place, were domestic houses, with No. 26 containing a shop at one end.

Church of St Peter and St Paul, Church Street, CO10 9QT

Rebuilt in the late fifteenth and early sixteenth centuries by John de Vere, thirteenth earl of Oxford, and local clothiers. The Rector's Vestry, to the east of the sanctuary, was built in 1444 by Thomas Spring II (d. 1486), who gave 300 marks towards building the tower. The vestry contains the memorial brass to Thomas Spring II, his wife Margaret and their children, all in shrouds rising from tombs, and merchant's mark. Thomas Spring III (d. 1523) bequeathed money to complete the tower, build a south chapel, and erect a finely carved wooden parclose screen around his tomb. The Lady Chapel or Spring Chapel, built in 1525, has an external inscription to pray for the souls of Thomas III and his wife Alice. The Spring's merchant's mark decorates the base of the tower, and Thomas III's shields are carved on the parapet. The Spring's merchant's mark and monogram can also be found on bosses on the rood canopy of honour at the east end of the nave. Simon Branch, another local clothier, built the Branch Chapel on the north side of the church, around 1500. An external inscription asks to pray for the souls of Simon and his wife Elizabeth. Memorial brass to Allaine Dister, clothier (d. 1534) with wife Agnes, three sons and three daughters, of c.1560, in the north aisle.

Little Waldingfield, Suffolk
St Lawrence's Church, Church Road, CO10 0SP

Memorial brasses to John Colman (d. 1506) with wife Katherine, sons and daughters, and to John Wyncoll, clothier (d. 1544).

Malmesbury, Wiltshire
Malmesbury Abbey, Gloucester Street, SN16 0AA

Former Benedictine monastery, whose buildings were used after the dissolution by the clothier William Stumpe as workshops for weavers. The surviving nave of the abbey church was granted by Stumpe to the townspeople of Malmesbury for use as their parish church.

Abbey House, Market Cross, SN16 9AS
(private house, but gardens open to the public)

Built by William Stumpe, upgraded in the later sixteenth century and subsequently extended. The house has a half H plan with two storeys and gabled attics. The central range is built over a thirteenth-century undercroft and may include part of the abbey dormitory. The arms of Stumpe are in one of the spandrels of the doorway arch.

Mells, Somerset
St Andrew's Church, New Street, BA11 3PW

The vestry was largely paid for by a London draper named Garland, in 1485.

New Street, to the south of the church, was built c.1490 by Abbot Selwood of Glastonbury, with two rows of houses probably for cloth-workers. These are of two storeys, with squared and coursed stone. Nos. 4, 7/8 and 9 have undergone the least change.

Minchinhampton, Gloucestershire
Holy Trinity Church, Bell Lane, GL6 9BP

Memorial brass to Edward Haliday of Rodborough, cloth-maker (d. 1519) and wife Margery, with merchant's mark, at the west end of church.

Nayland, Suffolk
Alston Court, High Street (private)

House with fully enclosed sixteenth-century courtyard behind the hall, and on the west side, a service wing that included workshops and probably a dye-house. Hall contains oriel window with carved sill, added c.1520.

Newbury, Berkshire
St Nicolas' Church, West Mills, RG14 5HG

John Winchcombe I left £40 to the building of the church and was buried in the chancel with his first wife, Alice. Their brass, now moved to the north wall of the tower, also depicts their two sons and a daughter or weepers. John Winchcombe II helped to fund the rebuilding of the church in the 1520s and 1530s. The nave roof bosses bear the 'IS' monogram of John I and the 'IO' merchant's mark of John II.

'Jack of Newbury's house', 24 Northbrook Street

A small surviving part of John Winchcombe II's house on the corner of Northbrook Street and Marsh Lane. Some decorative features remain, including close studding timberwork infilled with herringbone brickwork on the side facing Marsh Lane, an oriel window, and a decorated wooden beam or bressumer on the jetty between the ground and first floor. Winchcombe's house was built around two courtyards, and the Marks and Spencer store now occupies much of the rest of the site. A life-size bronze statute of John Winchcombe II holding a yard of cloth on his right arm has been commissioned for the street corner.

North Warnborough, Odiham, Hampshire
Castle Bridge Cottages, Bridge Road (private)

Long range of jettied houses, built in 1476 and extended in 1534–35, possibly as a row of weavers' cottages with heated accommodation for an overseer.

Norton St Philip, Somerset
The George Inn, High Street, BA2 7LH

Purpose-built as an inn to accommodate travellers and merchants coming to fairs, apparently part of a planned settlement established by Carthusian monks in the neighbouring parish of Hinton Charterhouse. The earliest surviving parts of the building date to around 1370. Goods were stored in the inn before being sold at fairs, linen cloth was sold at the inn and woollen cloth sold at a field outside.

Otterburn, Northumberland
Otterburn Mill, NE19 1JT

An eighteenth-century tweed mill, with fulling hammer, dam and leat, and tenter field. Two rows of early-nineteenth-century tenters stand south-east of the mill. They are made of wood and iron and each row measures about 40 feet long and were used to stretch and dry out newly fulled cloth. These are claimed to be the last surviving set of tenters.

Seend, Wiltshire
Church of the Holy Cross, High Street, SN12 6NR

The north aisle added by the clothier John Stokes (d. 1498) with a west window with a crowned Virgin Mary and cloth shears in the window mouldings inside, and shears and scissors depicted in the carvings outside. The aisle also contains his memorial brass, now mutilated, depicting John and his wife Alys.

Steeple Ashton, Wiltshire
Church of St Mary the Virgin, Church Street, BA14 6EW

A brass tablet at the west end records that the church was built between 1480 and 1500, with the north aisle built by Robert and Edith Long, and the south aisle by Walter and Maud Lucas, both clothiers. This was copied from an inscription on a painted board previously fixed to the gallery in the tower.

Stratford St Mary, Suffolk
Church of St Mary, CO7 6LS

North aisle built by Thomas Mors, clothier, and wife Margaret in 1499, and extended eastwards to add a north chapel by their son Edward and his wife Alys, 1530, with donor inscriptions and shields with their merchant's mark. The porch is dated 1532 and carries the initials of merchant John Smith.

Tiverton, Devon
St Peter's Church, St Peter Street, EX16 6RP

Chantry chapel on south side of the church added in 1517 by the cloth merchant John Greenway. It has elaborate exterior carvings including merchant vessels and Greenway's coat of arms and his merchant's mark. Brass of John Greenway with wife Joan, 1529, with arms of the Merchant Adventurers' and Drapers' Companies, two other shields, and the Trinity.

Almshouses, Gold Street (private)

Founded by the cloth merchant John Greenway in 1517 for five men and now managed by the Tiverton Almshouse Trust. The almshouses have been rebuilt, but the chapel survives.

Westwood, near Bradford-on-Avon, Wiltshire
Church of St Mary the Virgin, Farleigh Lane, Lower Westwood, BA15 2AF

Tower built by the clothier Thomas Horton (d. 1530), who was tenant of Westwood Manor (see below). His initials appear on the spandrels above the west door of the tower. The window on the north side of the west entrance contains medieval fragments that were removed from Westwood Manor and include part of a rebus on Horton with the letters HO. Horton may also have built the north aisle chapel, where in the nineteenth century the initials TH were visible on the wooden ceiling.

Westwood Manor, Farleigh Lane, Lower Westwood, BA15 2AF (National Trust)

This stone manor house, built in the fifteenth century, extended in the sixteenth century and adapted in the seventeenth century, was the home of the clothier Thomas Horton. Thomas built the dining room as a parlour and the panelled bedroom above, which joined the existing hall to a small house to form the west wing, to which he added an oriel window. In the dining room his initials are carved above the fireplace, although now very worn, and there are moulded oak ceiling ribs. The dining room and panelled bedroom both have stained glass containing the Horton family's rebus.

Worcester

The Commandery, Sidbury, WR1 2HU

The Hospital of St Wulstan, purchased in 1544 by the clothier Thomas Wild (c.1508–59), and converted into his residence. Subsequently used as the Royalist headquarters, a college, and printing works, it is now a museum. The earliest buildings, which are fifteenth century, include the hall range. There have been considerable additions and modifications to the buildings, many of which are timber-framed, with much brick infill.

Glossary

alum an astringent mineral salt used as a mordant to fix dyes on fabrics.

aulnage see ulnage.

barbing see shearing (2).

bastards a type of woollen cloth, possibly named because the **warp** and **weft** yarns were different.

Black Death the most severe epidemic of the last one thousand years, which occurred in 1348–49.

borough urban centre with charters granted by the Crown or a lord to a group of residents (known as **burgesses**) to exercise certain rights and privileges.

broadcloth size fixed by statute in 1465 as 24 yards long and 1¾ yards wide; the statute of 1552 specified different dimensions for types of regional broadcloths (cf. **narrow cloth**).

burgesses residents of a **borough** who were entitled to its rights and privileges.

carding the process of dressing wool with a pair of cards (hand-held instruments with iron teeth) to separate and straighten the fibres, and remove impurities. Unlike **combing**, carding separated the strands without removing the short fibres. It also provided a way of blending together a variety of wools (cf. **combing**).

carder a person **carding** wool.

Castlecombes a type of woollen cloth, usually dyed red, made in and around Castle Combe in Wiltshire.

chantry an endowment in perpetuity or for a term of years, to maintain one or more priests to say Masses for the souls of the founder and others nominated by him or her.

Coggeshalls also known as Coxhall whites, Glemsford whites, **handy-warps** and baizes. A broad and heavy type of woollen cloth, typically white, having its **warp** thread spun on a **distaff** and **spindle** rather than a spinning wheel, made particularly in and around Coggeshall in Essex.

combing the process of dressing wool with a comb, to separate and straighten the fibres, and remove impurities (cf. **carding**).

Commendations A liturgical office originally ending with the prayer *Tibi, Domine, commendamus*, in which the souls of the dead were commended to God.

cotton a type of woollen cloth similar to **frieze**, made largely in Lancashire and in Wales.

cropping see shearing (2).

Dirige (Latin), **dirge** the first word of the antiphon at Matins in the Office of the Dead, used as a name for that service.

distaff a cleft staff that held the unspun wool fibres during **spinning**.

domestic system see **putting-out system**.

dozens half-cloth, known as *duodena* or dozen.

ell a measure of length. The English ell was equivalent to 45 inches.

fair annual trading event lasting from a few days to a fortnight or more. Fairs usually sold a wider range of goods and attracted a wider range of traders than at a weekly **market**.

flocks coarse tufts and refuse of wool and cloth shearings.

freeman see **burgess**.

frieze a type of coarse woollen cloth, with a **nap** usually on one side only.

fuller a person **fulling** cloth, also known as a **tucker** or **walker**.

fuller's earth clay minerals (hydrous aluminium silicates) used in cleansing cloth.

fulling the process of cleansing and thickening cloth by beating and washing.

fulling mill a mill in which cloth is fulled by being beaten with wooden hammers, which fall upon it, and cleansed with soap or **fuller's earth**.

gig mill a machine for raising a **nap** on cloth by the use of teasels or wire-cards.

goad a measure of cloth, in the late seventeenth century said to equal 4½ feet.

guild (gild) (1) an economic association of craftspeople to enforce trading regulations relating to their craft or trade, known as a craft guild, craft or mystery. (2) a religious and social association committed to pious purposes and to the welfare of its members, also known as a fraternity. In practice, guilds often had a mixture of economic, religious and social functions.

handles hand-held wooden frames containing teasels, which were drawn across the cloth, to raise the **nap**.

handywarps see **Coggeshalls**.

kempster a worker involved in the **combing** of wool.

kersey a type of woollen **narrow cloth**, with twice as many **weft** as **warp** threads, and woven with a twill (a kind of weave where the **weft** does not pass over and under the **warp** threads singly, but in a different pattern), giving elasticity. In the fourteenth century they were inexpensive cloths, but by the sixteenth century the finest, known as sorting kerseys, were as valuable, by surface area, as a quality **broadcloth**. Their size was fixed by statute in 1465 as 18 yards long and a yard in width (the same width as **straits** but half as long again), and in 1552 at 17 yards long (or 12 yards long for Devon kerseys). Produced largely in Berkshire, Hampshire and Devon.

Lawdis (Latin), **Lauds** the first of the day-hours of the Church, derived from the three last psalms of the psalter.

linen cloth woven from flax.

loom a machine in which yarn or thread is woven into fabric by the crossing of threads called the **warp** and **weft**.

manor (1) a house where property was administered, rents collected, and where the lord could be accommodated. (2) a group of lands usually attached to a particular house, not necessarily in a single block. Manors had courts with varying degrees of authority over their tenants.

market (1) a place in the centre of the town or village set aside for trade. (2) a formally regulated meeting of buyers and sellers, in a specific marketplace, on a specific day or days of the week, and at set times.

mark a sum of money equivalent to two-thirds of a **pound**, 13s 4d.

mercer a merchant, originally dealing in fine fabrics like silk, who might be a member of the London Mercers' Company.

merchant adventurer a merchant engaged in trading overseas, and a member of an association of such merchants, found in London and other towns. Originally applied to any trader not exporting wool, the term later became concentrated on those exporting cloth.

medley a type of cloth made of wools dyed (often in different shades or colours) and mixed before being spun.

musterdevillers a type of mixed grey woollen cloth, modelled on the fine grey cloths produced in Montivilliers in Normandy.

narrow cloth cloth under 52 inches wide, including **straits** and **kerseys**.

nap a rough layer of projecting threads or fibres on the surface of a cloth.

napping the process of raising the **nap** by brushing the cloth with **handles** containing teasels, both while the cloth was wet and when dry. The nap was then removed by **shearing**.

noble an English gold coin worth 6s 8d, one-third of a **pound**.

penny (plural - **pence**) a small sum of money (d.) equivalent to 1/240 of a **pound**. In 1971 this was replaced in Britain by the new penny (p) equivalent to 1/100 of a pound.

Penistone a kind of coarse woollen cloth used for garments and linings. Made around Penistone in Yorkshire, and in Lancashire and Cheshire.

plunket a type of woollen cloth usually of grey or light blue colour.

pound (1) a sum of money (£) equal to 20 **shillings** or 240 **pence**. (2) a unit of weight (lb) usually equivalent to 16 ounces.

putting-out system (also known as the domestic system). Merchant-entrepreneurs such as clothiers 'put out' materials to rural producers, who usually worked in their homes but sometimes in workshops. Finished products were returned to the clothier for payment on a piecework or wage basis. The workers neither bought their materials nor sold their products, relying on the clothier to do this.

rays cloths with stripes woven into the pattern, produced particularly in Salisbury.

reed part of a **loom** consisting of evenly spaced wires (originally slender pieces of reed) fastened between two parallel horizontal bars and used for separating the **warp** threads, and for beating the **weft** threads into place.

rowing see **napping**.

russet originally a type of coarse woollen cloth. During the fourteenth century Colchester specialised in making a middle-value russet cloth of grey-brown colour.

rug a type of coarse woollen cloth, made particularly in and around Manchester.

sack a measure of wool, usually weighing 364 lb.

shearing (1) the process by which the woollen fleece of a sheep is cut off. (2) the process of finishing a cloth by cutting off the **nap**.

shearman a person **shearing** woollen cloth.

shilling a sum of money (s) equivalent to 12 **pence** and 1/20 of a **pound**.

slay see **reed**.

spindle an instrument used for **spinning** by hand, consisting of a short wooden stick, weighted at one end by a spindle **whorl**, which is made to revolve and twist wool fibres into thread or **yarn**.

spinning the process of converting fibres into thread or yarn, using either a **distaff** and **spindle** or a spinning wheel.

strait a **narrow cloth**. Size fixed by statute in 1465 as 12 yards long and a yard in width. Produced largely in Essex, Suffolk and Devon.

Stroudwaters a type of woollen cloth, usually dyed red, made in the Stroudwater district of Gloucestershire along the river Frome from Chalford to Stroud.

teasing see **napping**.

tenter a wooden frame on which cloth is stretched after **fulling**, so that it can dry evenly without shrinking.

tentering the process of stretching cloth on **tenters**.

trental a set of thirty requiem Masses.

tucker a **fuller**.

ulnage (also aulnage) a subsidy levied by the Crown on cloth sold.

ulnager official who checked the measurements and quality of cloth sold, affixing a seal and collecting the **ulnage** subsidy.

vesses or set-cloths, a type of lower-quality woollen cloth produced as both a **strait** and a **broadcloth** in Suffolk.

walker a **fuller**.

warp the threads that extend lengthways on the loom, crossed with the **weft** threads in **weaving**.

weaving the process of forming cloth by the interlacing of **yarn** on a **loom**.

weft the threads that pass from side to side at right angles to the **warp** thread in **weaving**, also known as the woof threads.

whites white cloth, often sold undyed and unfinished.

worsted a woollen fabric made from well-twisted **yarn** spun from long-staple wool combed to lay the fibres parallel.

yarn spun wool fibres used in **weaving** and knitting.

Sources: Glossary definitions are largely drawn from the *OED*, supplemented by details on cloth types from Oldland, 'Variety and Quality of English Woollen Cloth', pp. 215–29, and Kerridge, *Textile Manufactures*.

Bibliography

MANUSCRIPT SOURCES

Berkshire Record Office, Reading (BRO)

D/A1 Wills and inventories, Archdeaconry of Berkshire
D/EZ104/1/1–2 Will of William Martyn of Wokingham clothier, 1541
D/EW T49/3 Deed to Rack Close, Newbury, 1557
R/IC2/1 Inspeximus by Henry VIII of articles for the regulation of cloth-making in Reading, agreed by the cloth-makers and the weavers, fullers and tuckers, 1520

Birmingham Archives and Heritage, Library of Birmingham

Z Lloyd 51/1 William Mucklowe of Worcester's account book, 1511

Borthwick Institute for Archives, York (YBIA)

York Prob. Reg. 1–5 Will registers of the Exchequer and Prerogative Court of York

British Library, London (BL)

Add MSS
Cotton MSS

Cambridgeshire Archives, Cambridge Record Office

City/PB Box III/10A, part 1 Lease of the Coventry booth to drapers Thomas and John Ryley at Stourbridge Fair, Cambridge, 1550

Cambridge University Library (CUL)

Hengrave Hall MS 78(2) Thomas Kitson's Boke of Remembraunce (1529–39)

Drapers' Company, London

Ledger of Thomas Howell (1517–28)

Gloucestershire Archives, Gloucester

D674b/T8 Deeds, Cirencester, new house and mills called St Mary's Mills (1533–82)

The Huntington Library, San Marino, California

Ellesmere MS 2652

Kent History and Library Centre, Maidstone (KHLC)

PRC 17 Will registers, Archdeaconry Court of Canterbury
PRC 32 Will registers, Consistory Court of Canterbury
U1044/F1 Thomas Hendle of Otham's book, including memoranda of contracts for the construction of a fulling mill (1545–46)

King's College, Cambridge

KCAR/3/3/1/1/1 College Ledger Book I

London Metropolitan Archives (LMA)

COL/AD/01/013 (Microfilm X109/028) Letter Book N (1515–26)
COL/CA/01/01/003 (Microfilm X109/129) Court of Aldermen Repertory, vol. 3 (1515–19)
COL/CC/01/01/011 (Microfilm X109/053) Journal of the Court of Common Council of London, vol. 11 (1507–19)

The National Archives, London (TNA)

Chancery
C 1 Chancery proceedings
Court of Common Pleas
CP 40 Plea rolls. The AALT number corresponds to the respective image on the Anglo-American Legal Tradition website in the image folder 'fronts' or 'dorses' for the relevant common plea roll
Duchy of Lancaster
DL 25/3371 Deeds, Series L
Exchequer, Records of King's Remembrancer
E 101 Ulnage accounts
E 159 Memoranda Rolls
Privy Council
PC 2 Registers
Records of the Prerogative Court of Canterbury
PROB 2 Inventories
PROB 11 Will registers
Court of Requests
REQ 2 Pleadings
Records of various departments, formerly entitled Special Collections
SC 8 Ancient Petitions
State Papers
SP 1 Henry VIII: General Series
SP 11, SP 14 Secretaries of State: State Papers Domestic, Mary I, James I
Records of the Court of Star Chamber
STAC 2 Proceedings, Henry VIII

Surrey History Centre, Woking

LM/1535 Lease to John Perkyns of Guildford, clothier, of the profits of the ulnage in Guildford and the hundred of Woking, 1510

LM/1536/1 Agreement between deputy ulnager for Sussex and William Yonge of Petworth, clothier regarding sealing of cloths

West Yorkshire Archive Service, Bradford

SpSt/4/11/66/53 Award, William Gelles and James Wrose of Horsforth, clothier, 1538

SpSt/6/6/3/5 Will of John Mitchell of Colne, clothier, 1552

Wiltshire and Swindon Archives, Chippenham

88/1/22 Bargain and Sale of land in Malmesbury, Chippenham, and elsewhere to William Stumpe, 1535

88/1/23 Lease of Cowbridge Mill. Robert, abbot of Malmesbury to William Stumpe, 1535

88/1/26 William Stumpe hires 800 sheep to Tristrum Pistor of Boyton, copy of 1548 agreement

York Explore Library and Archive (YELA)

Y/COU/1/1 York City House Books vols 7–9, 20, 23 (1490–96, 1496–1503, 1503–19, 1549–52, 1561–65)

PRINTED PRIMARY SOURCES

Acts of Court of the Mercers' Company, 1453–1527, eds L. Lyell and F.D. Watney (London, 1936)

Aubrey, John, *The Natural History of Wiltshire*, ed. J. Britton (London, 1847)

The Black Death, ed. R. Horrox (Manchester, 1994)

Calendar of Close Rolls, 1272–1485, 45 vols (London, 1892–1954)

Calendar of Inquisitions Miscellaneous, 7 vols (London, 1916–68)

Calendar of Letter-books Preserved Among the Archives of the Corporation of the City of London at the Guildhall, ed. R.R. Sharpe, 11 vols (London, 1899–1912)

Calendar of Patent Rolls, 1232–1509, 52 vols (London 1891–1916)

Chaucer, Geoffrey, *The Wife of Bath*, ed. Peter G. Beidler (New York, 1996)

Chronicon Henrici Knighton vel Cnitthon, monachi Leycestrensis, ed. Joseph Rawson Lumby, 2 vols (London, 1889–95)

The Coventry Leet Book, ed. M. Dormer Harris, Early English Text Society, O.S., 4 vols, 134, 135, 138, 146 (London, 1907–13)

Deloney, Thomas, *Jack of Newbury*, in *An Anthology of Elizabethan Prose Fiction*, ed. Paul Salzman (Oxford, 1987)

De Engelse Natie te Antwerpen in de 16e Eeuw (1496–1582), ed. O. De Smedt, 2 vols (Antwerp, 1950–54)

Fitzherbert, John, *The Boke of Husbandry* (London, 1533), STC (2nd edn)/10995.5

Fox, Richard, *Letters of Richard Fox, 1486–1527*, eds P.S. Allen and H.M. Allen (Oxford, 1929)

Foxe, John, *The Acts and Monuments of John Foxe*, ed. J. Pratt, 8 vols, 4th edn (London, 1877)

Fuller, Thomas, *The History of the Worthies of England* (London, 1662)

Halifax Wills: Being Abstracts and Translations of the Wills Registered at York from the Parish of Halifax. Part I, 1389 to 1514, ed. J.W. Clay (Halifax, 1904)

Hall, Edward, *The Union of the Two Noble and Illustre Famelies of Lancastre and Yorke* (London, 1809)

Journal of the House of Commons, i: *1547–1628* (London, 1802)

Langland, William, *Piers Plowman. A Parallel-Text Edition of the A, B, C and Z Versions*, ed. A.V.C. Schmidt, 2 vols (London, 1995)

Langland, William, *Will's Vision of Piers Plowman. An Alliterative Verse Translation by E. Talbot Donaldson*, eds E.D. Kirk and J.H. Anderson (New York, 1990)

The Ledger of John Smythe, 1538–1550, eds John Angus and Jean Vanes, HMC, Joint Publication Series 19 (London, 1974)

Leland, John, *The Itinerary of John Leland in or about the Years 1535–1543*, ed. Lucy Toulmin Smith, 5 vols, 2nd edn (London, 1964)

Leland, John, *John Leland's Itinerary: Travels in Tudor England*, ed. John Chandler (Stroud, 1992)

Letters and Papers, Foreign and Domestic, of the Reign of Henry VIII, eds J.S. Brewer, J. Gairdner and R.H. Brodie, 2nd edn, 23 vols in 38 (London, 1862–1932)

The Little Red Book of Bristol, ed. F.B. Bickley, 2 vols (Bristol, 1900)

Middle English Dictionary, eds Hans Kurath, Sherman M. Kuhn and Robert E. Lewis (Ann Abor, 1952–2001)

The Military Survey of 1522 for Babergh Hundred, ed. John Pound, Suffolk Records Society 28 (Woodbridge, 1986)

Political Poems and Songs Relating to English History, Composed During the Period from the Accession of Edw. III to that of Ric. III, ed. T. Wright, 2 vols (London, 1859–61)

Prince, John, *Danmonii orientales illustres: or, the worthies of Devon* (Exeter, 1701)

Probate Inventories of the York Diocese 1350–1500, eds P.M. Stell and Louise Hampson (York, 1998)

Proceedings and Ordinances of the Privy Council of England, ed. N. Harris Nicolas, 7 vols (London, 1834–37)

Rotuli Parliamentorum, 6 vols (London, 1777–1832)

Royal Commission on Historical Manuscripts, *The Manuscripts of Lord Kenyon*, HMC, Fourteenth Report, Appendix, Part 4 (London, 1894)

—— *The Manuscripts of Lincoln, Bury St Edmunds and Great Grimsby Corporations*, HMC, Fourteenth Report, Appendix, Part 8 (London, 1895)

—— *Report on Manuscripts in the Welsh Language*, 2 vols (London, 1898–9)

Selections from the Records of the City of Oxford: With Extracts from Other Documents Illustrating the Municipal History: Henry VIII to Elizabeth, ed. William H. Turner (Oxford, 1880)

Smith, Thomas, *A Discourse of the Common Weal of this Realm of England*, ed. E. Lamond (Cambridge, 1893)

Smyth, John, *The Berkeley Manuscripts. A Description of the Hundred of Berkeley in the County of Gloucester and of its Inhabitants*, ed. John Maclean, 3 vols (Gloucester, 1883)

Skelton, John, *The Complete English Poems*, ed. J. Scattergood (Harmondsworth, 1983)

Somerset Medieval Wills 1383–1500, 1500–1530, 1531–1538, ed. F.W. Weaver, Somerset Record Society 16, 19, 21 (1901–05)

Statutes of the Realm (1101–1713), Record Commission, 11 vols (London, 1808–28)

Stow, John, *A Survey of London*, ed. C.L. Kingsford, 2 vols (Oxford, 1908)

Third Book of Remembrance of Southampton 1514–1602, i: *(1514–40)*, ed. A.L. Merson, Southampton Records Society 2 (Southampton, 1952)

Tudor Economic Documents, eds R.H. Tawney and E. Power, 3 vols (London, 1924)

Tudor Royal Proclamations, eds Paul L. Hughes and James F. Larkin, 3 vols (New Haven, 1964–9)

York Mercers and Merchant Adventurers, 1356–1917, ed. M. Sellers, Surtees Society 79 (Durham, 1918)

SECONDARY SOURCES

Alston, Leigh, 'The Old Grammar School. The Finest Merchant's house in Lavenham', *Historic Buildings of Suffolk: The Journal of the Suffolk Historic Buildings Group* 1 (1998), pp. 31–49

—— 'Late Medieval Workshops in East Anglia', in Barnwell, Palmer and Airs, eds, *The Vernacular Workshop*, pp. 38–59

Ammannati, Francesco, 'Francesco di Marco Datini's Wool Workshops', in Giampero Nigro, ed., *Francesco di Marco Datini. The Man the Merchant* (Florence, 2010), pp. 489–514

Amor, N.R., 'Merchant Adventurer or Jack of all Trades? The Suffolk Clothier in the 1460s', *Proceedings of the Suffolk Institute of Archaeology and History* 40 (2004), pp. 414–36

—— *Late Medieval Ipswich: Trade and Industry* (Woodbridge, 2011)

—— *From Wool to Cloth. The Triumph of the Suffolk Clothier* (Bungay, 2016)

Andrews, David, ed., *Discovering Coggeshall 2: The 1575 Rental Survey and the Dated Buildings* (Coggeshall, 2013)

Armitt, M.L., 'Fullers and Freeholders of the Parish of Grasmere', *Transactions of the Cumberland and Westmorland Antiquarian and Archaeological Society*, new series 8, (1908), pp. 136–205

Ayers, Brian, *Norwich: 'a fine city'* (Stroud, 2003)

Badham, Sally and Cockerham, Paul, eds, *'The beste and fayrest of al Lincolnshire': The Church of St Botolph, Boston, Lincolnshire, and its Medieval Monuments*, British Archaeological Reports, British series 554 (Oxford, 2012)

Bailey, Mark, *A Marginal Economy?: East Anglian Breckland in the later Middle Ages* (Cambridge, 1989)

—— *Medieval Suffolk: An Economic and Social History, 1200–1500* (Woodbridge, 2007)

—— 'Technology and the Growth of Textile Manufacture in Suffolk', *Proceedings of the Suffolk Institute of Archaeology and History* 42 (2009), pp. 13–20

Bailey, M. and Rigby, S., eds, *Town and Countryside in the Age of the Black Death: Essays in Honour of John Hatcher* (Turnhout, 2012)

Baker, Nigel, 'The Archaeology of the Larger Medieval Towns', *West Midlands Regional Research Framework, Research Papers* (Birmingham, 2003)

Barron, Caroline, *London in the Later Middle Ages: Government and People, 1200–1500* (Oxford, 2004)

Barron, Caroline M. and Sutton, Anne F., eds, *Medieval London Widows 1300–1500* (London, 1994)

Barron, Caroline, Coleman, Christopher and Gobbii, Claire, 'The London Journal of Alessandro Magno 1562', *London Journal* 9 (1983), pp. 136–52

Barnwell, P.S., 'Workshops, Industrial Production and the Landscape', in Barnwell, Palmer and Airs, eds, *The Vernacular Workshop*, pp. 179–82

Barnwell, P.S., Palmer, M., and Airs, M., eds, *The Vernacular Workshop: From Craft to Industry, 1400–1900*, Council for British Archaeology Research Report 140 (York, 2004)

Basing, Patricia, *Trades and Crafts in Medieval Manuscripts* (London, 1990)

Bateman, Nick, 'From Rags to Riches: Blackwell Hall and the Wool Cloth Trade, *c*.1450–1790', *Post-Medieval Archaeology* 38 (2004), pp. 1–15

Beresford, M.W. and St Joseph, J.K.S., *Medieval England. An Aerial Survey*, 2nd edn (Cambridge, 1979)

Bernard, G.W., *War, Taxation, and Rebellion in Early Tudor England: Henry VIII, Wolsey, and the Amicable Grant of 1525* (Brighton, 1986)

Beaumont, G.F., 'Paycocke's House, Coggeshall, with Some Notes on the Families of Paycocke and Buxton', *Transactions of the Essex Archaeological Society*, new series 9 (1903–06), pp. 311–24

Bennell, John, 'Shop and Office in Medieval and Tudor London', *Transactions of the London and Middlesex Archaeological Society* 40 (1989), pp. 189–206

Betterton, A. and Dymond, D., *Lavenham: Industrial Town* (Lavenham, 1989)

Bettley, James and Pevsner, Nikolaus, *The Buildings of England: Essex* (London, 2007)

—— *The Buildings of England: Suffolk: West* (London, 2015)

Bindoff, S.T., 'Clement Armstrong and his Treatises of the Commonweal', *EcHR* 14 (1944), pp. 64–73

Blatchly, John and Northeast, Peter, 'Discoveries in the Clerestory and Roof Structure of St Margaret's Church, Ipswich', *Proceedings of the Suffolk Institute of Archaeology* 38 (1996), pp. 387–408

Bolton, J.L., *The Medieval English Economy 1150–1500* (London, 1980)

—— *Money in the Medieval English Economy, 973–1489* (Manchester, 2012)

Bowden, Peter, *The Wool Trade in Tudor and Stuart England* (London, 1962)

Bratchel, M.E., 'Italian Merchant Organization and Business Relationships in Early Tudor London', *Journal of European Economic History* 7 (1978), pp. 5–32

Braudel, Fernand, *The Wheels of Commerce* (London, 1982)

Brenner, R., 'Agrarian Class Structure and Economic Development in Pre-Industrial Europe', *Past and Present* 70 (1976), pp. 30–75

Brett, C.J., 'The Fairs and Markets of Norton St Philip', *Somerset Archaeology and Natural History Society: Proceedings* 144 (2002 for 2000), pp. 165–96

—— 'Thomas Kytson and Somerset Clothmen 1529–1539', *Somerset Archaeology and Natural History Society: Proceedings* 143 (2001), pp. 29–50

—— 'Thomas Kytson and Wiltshire Clothmen, 1529–1539', *Wiltshire Archaeology and Natural History Magazine* 97 (2004), pp. 35–62

Bridbury, A.R., *Economic Growth: England in the Later Middle Ages* (London, 1962)

—— 'English Provincial Towns in the Later Middle Ages', *EcHR*, 2nd series 34 (1981), pp. 1–24

—— *Medieval English Clothmaking: An Economic Survey* (London, 1982)

Briggs, Chris, *Credit and Village Society in Fourteenth-Century England* (Oxford, 2009)

Britnell, R.H., *Growth and Decline in Colchester, 1300–1525* (Cambridge, 1986)

—— 'Commerce and Capitalism in Late Medieval England: Problems of Description and Theory', *Journal of Historial Sociology* 6 (1993), pp. 359–76

—— *The Commercialisation of English society 1000–1500*, 2nd edn (Manchester, 1996)

—— *The Closing of the Middle Ages? England, 1471–1529* (Oxford, 1997)

—— 'The English Economy and the Government, 1450–1550', in J.L. Watts, ed, *The End of the Middle Ages? England in the Fifteenth and Sixteenth Centuries* (Stroud, 1998), pp. 89–116

—— 'Urban Demand in the English Economy, 1300–1600', in Galloway, ed, *Trade*, pp. 1–21

—— 'The Woollen Textile Industry of Suffolk in the Later Middle Ages', *The Ricardian* 23 (2003), pp. 86–99

—— *Britain and Ireland 1050–1530: Economy and Society* (Oxford, 2004)

—— 'Markets, Shops, Inns, Taverns and Private Houses in Medieval English Trade', in Bruno Blondé, Peter Stabel, Jon Stobart and Ilja Van Damme, eds, *Buyers and Sellers: Retail Circuits and Practices in Medieval and Early Modern Europe* (Turnhout, 2006), pp. 109–24

Brown, A.D., *Popular Piety in Late Medieval England: The Diocese of Salisbury, 1250–1550* (Oxford, 1995)

Brown, Sarah and MacDonald, Lindsay, eds, *Fairford Parish Church. A Medieval Church and its Stained Glass* (Stroud, 2007)

Brunskill, R.W., *Vernacular Architecture. An Illustrated Handbook*, 4th edn (London, 2000)

Burgess, Clive, 'Obligations and Strategy: Managing Memory in the Later Medieval Parish', *Transactions of the Monumental Brass Society* 18 (2012), pp. 289–310

—— 'Making Mammon Serve God: Merchant Piety in Later Medieval England', in Caroline M. Barron and Anne F. Sutton, eds, *The Medieval Merchant* (Donington, 2014), pp. 183–207

Camille, M., 'At the Edge of the Law: An Illustrated Register of Writs in the Pierpoint Morgan Library', in N. Rogers, ed., *England in the Fourteenth Century. Proceedings of the 1991 Harlaxton Symposium* (Stamford, 1993), pp. 1–14

Campbell, B.M.S., 'Nature as Historical Protagonist: Environment and Society in Pre-Industrial England', *EcHR* 63 (2010), pp. 281–314

Carruthers, Mary, 'The Wife of Bath and the Painting of Lions', *PMLA:*

Publications of the Modern Language Association of America 94, No. 2 (1979), pp. 209–22

Carus-Wilson, E.M., 'The Aulnage Accounts: A Criticism', *EcHR* 2 (1929), pp. 39–60, reprinted in Carus-Wilson, *Medieval Merchant Venturers*, pp. 279–91

—— 'An Industrial Revolution of the Thirteenth Century', *EcHR* 11 (1941), pp. 39–60, reprinted in Carus-Wilson, *Medieval Merchant Venturers*, pp. 183–210

—— 'The English Cloth Industry in the Twelfth and Early Thirteenth Centuries', *EcHR* 14 (1944), pp. 32–50, reprinted in Carus-Wilson, *Medieval Merchant Venturers*, pp. 211–38

—— 'Trends in the Export of English Woollens in the Fourteenth Century', *EcHR*, 2nd series 3 (1950), pp. 162–79, reprinted in Carus-Wilson, *Medieval Merchant Venturers*, pp. 239–64

—— 'The Significance of the Secular Sculptures in the Lane Chapel, Cullompton', *Medieval Archaeology* 1 (1957), pp. 104–17

——'Evidences of Industrial Growth on Some Fifteenth-Century Manors', *EcHR*, 2nd series 12 (1959), pp. 190–205

—— *The Expansion of Exeter at the Close of the Middle Ages* (London, 1963)

—— *Medieval Merchant Venturers*, 2nd edn (London, 1967)

—— 'The Woollen Industry', in Edward Miller, Cynthia Postan and M.M. Postan, eds, *The Cambridge Economic History of Europe*, ii: *Trade and Industry in the Middle Ages*, 2nd edn (Cambridge, 1987), pp. 613–90

—— and Coleman, Olive, *England's Export trade 1275–1547* (Oxford, 1963)

Carlton, Richard and Jones, David, 'A Medieval Fulling Mill at Barrowburn on the River Coquet: Evidence and Context', *Archaeologia Aeliana* 43 (2014), pp. 221–40

Casson, Catherine, 'Reputation and Responsibility in Medieval English Towns: Civic Concerns with the Regulation of Trade', *Urban History* 39 (2012), pp. 387–40

Casson, Mark and Casson, Catherine, *The Entrepreneur in History From Medieval Merchant to Modern Business Leader* (Basingstoke, 2013)

Casson, Mark and Lee, John S., 'The Origin and Development of Markets: A Business History Perspective', *Business History Review* 85 (2011), pp. 9–37

Clark, David, 'The Shop Within?: An Analysis of the Architectural Evidence for Medieval Shops', *Architectural History* 43 (2000), pp. 58–87

Chatwin, P.B. and Harcourt, E.G., 'The Bishop Vesey Houses and Other Old Buildings in Sutton Coldfield', *Birmingham Archaeological Society Transactions and Proceedings* 64 (1941–2), pp. 1–19

Childs, Wendy, *Anglo-Castilian Trade in the Later Middle Ages* (Manchester, 1978)

Coleman, D.C., 'Textile Growth', in N.B. Harte and K.G. Ponting, eds, *Textile History and Economic History. Essays in Honour of Miss Julia de Lacy Mann* (Manchester, 1973), pp. 1–21

—— *Industry in Tudor and Stuart England* (London, 1975)

Colson, Justin, 'Commerce, Clusters and Community: A Re-evaluation of the Occupational Geography of London, *c.*1400–*c.*1550', *EcHR* 69 (2016), pp. 104–30

Connell-Smith, G., 'The Ledger of Thomas Howell', *EcHR*, 2nd series 3 (1950–1), pp. 363–70

Cornwall, J.C.K., *Wealth and Society in Early Sixteenth Century England* (London, 1988)

Cowper, H.S., 'Two Headcorn Cloth Halls', *Archaeologia Cantiana* 31 (1915), pp. 121–30

Craig, John, 'Reformers, Conflict, and Revisionism: The Reformation in Sixteenth-Century Hadleigh', *Historical Journal* 42 (1999), pp. 1–23

Cruickshank, John Louis, *Headingley-cum-Burley, c.1540–c.1784*, Thoresby Society, 2nd series 22 (Leeds, 2012)

Crump, W.B. and Ghorbal, Gertrude, *History of the Huddersfield Woollen Industry*, Tolson Memorial Museum Publications 10 (Huddersfield, 1935)

Cunningham, W., *The Growth of English Industry and Commerce during the Early and Middle Ages* (Cambridge, 1890)

Darby, H.C., Glasscock, R.E., Sheail, J. and Versey, G.R., 'The Changing Geographical Distribution of Wealth in England: 1086–1334–1525', *Journal of Historical Geography* 5 (1979), pp. 247–62

Davies, Matthew and Saunders, Ann, *A History of the Merchant Taylors' Company* (Leeds, 2004)

Davis, James, '"Men as March with Fote Packes": Pedlars and Freedom of Movement in Late Medieval England', in P. Holden, ed., *Freedom of Movement in the Middle Ages: People, Ideas, Goods* (Donington, 2007), pp. 137–56

—— *Medieval Market Morality: Life, Law and Ethics in the English Marketplace, 1200–1500* (Oxford, 2011)

—— 'Selling Food and Drink in the Aftermath of the Black Death', in Bailey and Rigby, eds, *Town and Countryside*, pp. 351–406

Davis, J.F., 'Lollard Survival and the Textile Industry in the South-east of England', *Studies in Church History* 3 (1966), pp. 191–201

Dickens, A.G., *Lollards and Protestants in the Diocese of York, 1509–1558* (Oxford, 1959)

—— *The English Reformation* (London, 1964)

Dobb, Maurice, *Studies in the Development of Capitalism* (London, 1946)

Dodds, Ben and Britnell, Richard, eds, *Agriculture and Rural Society after the Black Death: Common Themes and Regional Variations* (Hatfield, 2008)

Duffy, E., *The Stripping of the Altars. Traditional Religion in England 1400–1580*, 2nd edn (London, 2005)

Dunn, Penelope, 'Trade', in Carole Rawcliffe and Richard Wilson, eds, *Medieval Norwich* (London, 2004), pp. 213–34

Dyer, Alan D., *The City of Worcester in the Sixteenth Century* (Leicester, 1973)

—— *Decline and Growth in English Towns 1400–1640* (Cambridge, 1991)

Dyer, Christopher, *Standards of Living in the Later Middle Ages: Social Change in England, c.1200–1520* (Cambridge, 1989)

—— 'Were There Any Capitalists in Fifteenth-Century England?' in Christopher Dyer, *Everyday Life in Medieval England* (London, 1994), pp. 305–27

—— 'Villages and Non-villages in the Medieval Cotswolds', *Transactions of the Bristol and Gloucestershire Archaeological Society* 120 (2002), pp. 11–35
—— *An Age of Transition?: Economy and Society in England in the Later Middle Ages* (Oxford, 2005)
—— *A Country Merchant, 1495–1520: Trading and Farming at the End of the Middle Ages* (Oxford, 2012)
—— 'Poverty and its Relief in Late Medieval England', *Past and Present* 216 (2012), pp. 41–78
—— Richard Britnell obituary, *The Guardian*, 26 December 2013.
—— 'A Golden Age Rediscovered: Labourers' Wages in the Fifteenth Century', in M. Allen and D. Coffman, eds, *Prices, Money and Wages* (London, 2014), pp. 180–95
Dymond, David, 'The Famine of 1527 in Essex', *Local Population Studies* 26 (1981), pp. 29–40
—— 'Socio-religious Gilds of the Middle Ages', in Livia Visser-Fuchs, ed., *Richard III and East Anglia: Magnates, Gilds and Learned Men* (Stroud, 2010), pp. 91–104
Edler, Florence, 'Winchcombe Kerseys in Antwerp (1538–44)', *EcHR* 7 (1936), pp. 57–62
Edwards, John, *The History of Woad and the Medieval Woad Vat* (Chalfont St Giles, 1998)
Elton, Stuart F., *Cloth Seals. An Illustrated Reference Guide to the Identification of Lead Seals Attached to Cloth* (Oxford, 2017)
Epstein, Steven A., *An Economic and Social History of Later Medieval Europe, 1000–1500* (Cambridge, 2009)
Ferguson Mann Architects and Rodwell, Kirsty, *The George Inn Norton St Philip Somerset* (Bristol, 1999)
Finberg, H.P.R., *Tavistock Abbey, a study in the Social and Economic History of Devon* (Cambridge, 1951)
Fisher, F.J., 'Commercial Trends and Policy in Sixteenth-Century England', *EcHR* 10 (1940), pp. 95–117
Fletcher, A. and MacCulloch, D., *Tudor Rebellions*, rev. 5th edn (London, 2008)
Fradley, Michael, 'Water Street, Lavenham, Suffolk. A Desk-based Assessment of a Brick Culvert', *English Heritage Research Department Report Series* 7/2007 (2007)
Friis, Astrid, *Alderman Cockayne's Project and the Cloth Trade: Commercial Policy of England in its Main Aspects, 1603–1625* (Copenhagen, 1927)
Fryde, E.B., *Peasants and Landlords in Later Medieval England,* c.1380–c.1525 (Stroud, 1996)
Fudge, John D., *Cargoes, Embargos, and Emissaries: The Commercial and Political Interaction of England and the German Hanse, 1450–1510* (Toronto, 1995)
Gaisford, John, 'Elizabethan Entrepreneurs: Three Clothiers of the Frome Valley, 1550–1600', in J.P. Bowen and A.T. Brown, eds, *Custom and Commercialisation in English Rural Society: Revisiting Tawney and Postan* (Hatfield, 2016), pp. 203–24
Galloway, James A., ed., *Trade, Urban Hinterlands and Market Integration*

c.*1300–1600*, Centre for Metropolitan History Working Paper Series 3 (London, 2000)
Galloway, James A., Keene, Derek and Murphy, Margaret, 'Fuelling the City: Production and Distribution of Firewood and Fuel in London's Region, 1290–1400', *EcHR* 49 (1996), pp. 447–72
Giles, Colum, *Research Agenda: Historic Buildings in West Yorkshire (Medieval & Post-Medieval to 1914)* (West Yorkshire Joint Services, West Yorkshire Archaeology Advisory Service, 2013)
Girling, F.A., *English Merchants' Marks. A Field Survey of Marks Made by Merchants and Tradesmen in England between 1400 and 1700* (London, 1964)
Goddard, R., 'Small Boroughs and the Manorial Economy: Enterprise Zones or Urban Failures?', *Past and Present* 210 (2011), pp. 3–31
—— 'Medieval Business Networks: St Mary's Guild and the Borough Court in Later Medieval Nottingham', *Urban History* 40 (2013), pp. 3–27
—— 'Surviving Recession: English Borough Courts and Commercial Contraction: 1350–1500', in R. Goddard, J. Langdon and M. Muller, eds, *Survival and Discord in Medieval Society: Essays in Honour of Christopher Dyer* (Turnhout, 2010), pp. 69–87
Goldberg P.J.P., 'Urban Identity and the Poll Taxes of 1377, 1379, and 1381', *EcHR* 43 (1990), pp. 194–216
—— *Women, Work, and Life Cycle in a Medieval Economy: Women in York and Yorkshire* c.*1300–1520* (Oxford, 1992)
—— 'The Fashioning of Bourgeois Domesticity in Later Medieval England: A Material Culture Perspective', in Maryanne Kowaleski and Jeremy Goldberg, eds, *Medieval Domesticity* (Cambridge, 2008), pp. 124–44
Gough, J.W., *The Rise of the Entrepreneur* (London, 1969)
Gould, J.D., *The Great Debasement: Currency and Economy in Mid-Tudor England* (Oxford, 1970)
Gray, H.L., 'The Production and Exportation of English Woollens in the Fourteenth Century', *English Historical Review* 39 (1924), pp. 13–35
Gunn, S.J., 'Wolsey's Foreign Policy and the Domestic Crisis of 1527–8', in S.J. Gunn and P.G. Lindley, eds., *Cardinal Wolsey: Church, State and Art* (Cambridge, 1991), pp. 149–77
Hanham, A., *The Celys and their World: An English Merchant Family of the Fifteenth Century* (Cambridge, 1985)
Hare, J.N., 'The Wiltshire Risings of 1450: Political and Economic Discontent in Mid-Fifteenth Century England', *Southern History* 4 (1982), pp. 13–31
—— 'Growth and Recession in the Fifteenth-Century Economy: The Wiltshire Textile Industry and the Countryside', *EcHR* 52 (1999), pp. 1–26
—— 'Regional Prosperity in Fifteenth-century England: Some Evidence from Wessex', in M. Hicks, ed., *Revolution and Consumption in Late Medieval England* (Woodbridge, 2001), pp. 105–26
—— 'Pensford and the Growth of the Cloth Industry in Late Medieval Somerset', *Somerset Archaeology and Natural History Society: Proceedings* 147 (2003), pp. 173–80
—— *A Prospering Society: Wiltshire in the Later Middle Ages* (Hatfield, 2011)

—— 'Inns, Innkeepers and the Society of Later Medieval England, 1350-1600', *Journal of Medieval History* 39 (2013), pp. 477–97
—— *Basingstoke: A Medieval Town, c.1000–c.1600* (forthcoming)
Harper-Bill, Christopher, 'The English Church and English Religion after the Black Death', in Mark Ormrod and Phillip Lindley, eds, *The Black Death in England* (Donington, 2003), pp. 79–123
Harrison, David, *The Bridges of Medieval England: Transport and Society, 400–1800* (Oxford, 2004)
Harry, David, 'A Cadaver in Context: The Shroud Brass of John Brigge Revisited', *Transactions of the Monumental Brass Society* 19 (2015), pp. 101–10
Harman, Ruth and Pevsner, Nikolaus, *The Buildings of England: Yorkshire West Riding: Sheffield and the South* (London, 2017)
Harvey, I.M.W., *Jack Cade's Rebellion of 1450* (Oxford, 1991)
Hatcher, John, *Plague, Population and the English Economy, 1348–1500* (London, 1977)
—— 'England in the Aftermath of the Black Death', *Past and Present* 144 (1994), pp. 3–35
—— 'The Great Slump of the Mid-Fifteenth Century', in R.H. Britnell and J. Hatcher, eds, *Progress and Problems in Medieval England: Essays in Honour of Edward Miller* (Cambridge, 1996), pp. 237–72
—— 'Unreal Wages: Long-Run Living Standards and the "Golden Age" of the Fifteenth Century', in B. Dodds and C.D. Liddy, eds, *Commercial Activity, Markets and Entrepreneurs in the Middle Ages: Essays in Honour of Richard Britnell* (Woodbridge, 2011), pp. 1–24
—— and Bailey, Mark, *Modelling the Middle Ages: The History and Theory of England's Economic Development* (Oxford, 2001)
Heaton, Herbert, *The Yorkshire Woollen and Worsted Industries from the Earliest Times up to the Industrial Revolution*, 2nd edn (Oxford, 1965)
Hicks, Michael, ed., *English Inland Trade 1430–1540* (Oxford, 2015)
Hilton, R.H., *The English Peasantry in the Later Middle Ages: The Ford Lectures for 1973 and Related Studies* (Oxford, 1975)
History of Parliament: The House of Commons 1386–1421, 1509–1558, 1558–1603, eds J.S. Roskell, L. Clark, C. Rawcliffe, S.T. Bindoff, P.W. Hasler (London, 1981–93)
Hoskins, W.G., 'English Provincial Towns in the Early Sixteenth Century', *Transactions of the Royal Historical Society*, 5th series 6 (1956), pp. 1–19
Hoyle, R.W., 'Taxation and the Mid Tudor Crisis', *EcHR* 51 (1998), pp. 649–75.
Hunting, Penelope, *A History of the Drapers' Company* (London, 1980)
Jack, Ian, R., 'The Cloth Industry in Medieval Wales', *Welsh History Review* 10 (1980), pp. 443–60
Jackson, C., 'Clothmaking and the Economy in Sixteenth-Century Abingdon', *Oxoniensia* 67 (2002), 59–78
—— 'Boom-Time Freaks or Heroic Industrial Pioneers? Clothing Entrepreneurs in Sixteenth- and Early Seventeenth-Century Berkshire', *Textile History* 39 (2008), pp. 145–71
James, Margery K., 'A London Merchant of the Fourteenth Century', *EcHR*, 2nd series 8 (1956), pp. 364–76

Jenkins, David, ed., *The Cambridge History of Western Textiles*, 2 vols (Cambridge, 2003)

Jenkins, J. Geraint, *The Welsh Woollen Industry* (Cardiff, 1969)

Jennings, Bernard, ed., *A History of Harrogate and Knaresborough* (Huddersfield, 1970)

—— *A History of Nidderdale*, 3rd edn (York, 1992)

Johnson, A.H., *The History of the Worshipful Company of the Drapers of London*, 5 vols, (Oxford, 1914–22)

Jones, B.C., 'Westmorland Pack-Horsemen in Southampton', *Transactions of the Cumberland and Westmorland Antiquarian and Archaeological Society*, 59 (1960), pp. 65–84.

Jones, D.W., 'The "Hallage" Receipts of the London Cloth Markets, 1562–*c.*1720', *EcHR* 25 (1972), pp. 567–87

Jones, W.H., 'Terumber's Chantry at Trowbridge, with Deed of Endowment 1483', *Wiltshire Archaeological and Natural History Society* 10 (1867), pp. 240–52

Keene, Derek, *Survey of Medieval Winchester*, 2 vols (Oxford, 1985)

—— 'Changes in London's Economic Hinterland as Indicated by Debt Cases in the Court of Common Pleas', in Galloway, ed., *Trade*, pp. 59–81

Kerridge, Eric, *Textile Manufactures in Early Modern England* (Manchester, 1985)

Kermode, Jennifer, *Medieval Merchants: York, Beverley and Hull in the Later Middle Ages* (Cambridge, 1998)

Kesselring, K.J., *Mercy and Authority in the Tudor state* (Cambridge, 2003)

Kowaleski, Maryanne, *Local Markets and Regional Trade in Medieval Exeter* (Cambridge, 1995)

Ladd, Roger A., 'Thomas Deloney and the London Weavers' Company', *Sixteenth Century Journal* 32 (2001), pp. 981–1001

Lambert, Bart and Pajic, Milan, 'Drapery in Exile: Edward III, Colchester and the Flemings, 1351–1367', *History* 99 (2014), pp. 733–53

—— 'Common Profit versus Corporate Protectionism: The London Weavers and the Crown's Economic Immigration Policy in the Fourteenth Century', *Journal of British Studies* 55 (2016), pp. 633–57

Langdon, John, 'Horse-hauling: A Revolution in Vehicle Transport in Twelfth- and Thirteenth-Century England', *Past and Present* 103 (1984), pp. 37–66

Lee, John S., 'Tracing Regional and Local Changes in Population and Wealth during the Later Middle Ages Using Taxation Records: Cambridgeshire, 1334–1563', *Local Population Studies* 69 (2002), pp. 32–50

—— 'Feeding the Colleges: Cambridge's Food and Fuel Supplies, 1450–1560', *EcHR* 56 (2003), pp. 254–64

—— *Cambridge and its Economic Region, 1450–1560* (Hatfield, 2005)

—— 'The Functions and Fortunes of English Small Towns at the Close of the Middle Ages: Evidence from John Leland's *Itinerary*', *Urban History* 37 (2010), pp. 3–25

—— 'Grain Shortages in Late Medieval Towns', in B. Dodds and C.D. Liddy, eds, *Commercial Activity, Markets and Entrepreneurs in the Middle Ages: Essays in Honour of Richard Britnell* (Woodbridge, 2011), pp. 63–80

—— 'The Role of Fairs in Late Medieval England', in Bailey and Rigby, eds, *Town and Countryside*, pp. 407–37

——'Piped Water Supplies Managed by Civic Bodies in Medieval English towns', *Urban History* 41 (2014), pp. 369–93
—— 'Medieval Local History from Published Records: A Case-study of the Medieval Manor, Market and Church of Masham, Yorkshire', *The Local Historian* 45 (2015), pp. 54–67
—— 'Decline and Growth in the Late Medieval Fenland: The Examples of Outwell and Upwell', *Proceedings of the Cambridge Antiquarian Society* 104 (2015), pp. 137–48
——'Crises in the Late Medieval English Cloth Trade', in A.T. Brown, Andy Burn and Rob Doherty, eds, *Crises in Economic and Social History: A Comparative Perspective* (Woodbridge, 2015), pp. 325–49
—— "'Tis the sheep have paid for all": Merchant Commemoration in Late Medieval Newark', *Transactions of the Monumental Brass Society* 19 (2017), pp. 301–27
——'Monuments and Memory: A University Town in Late Medieval England', in John S. Lee and Christian Steer, eds, *Commemoration in Medieval Cambridge* (Woodbridge, 2018).
——Lipson, E., *The History of the Woollen and Worsted Industries* (London, 1921)
—— *The Economic History of England*, i: *The Middle Ages*, 12th edn (London, 1959)
Lowe, Norman, *The Lancashire Textile Industry in the Sixteenth Century* (Manchester, 1972)
MacCulloch, D., *Suffolk and the Tudors. Politics and Religion in an English County, 1500–1600* (Oxford, 1986)
Mackie, J.D., *The Oxford History of England*, vii: *The Earlier Tudors, 1485–1558* (Oxford, 1952)
McClenaghan, B., *The Springs of Lavenham and the Suffolk Cloth Trade in the XV and XVI Centuries* (Ipswich, 1924)
Manley, F.H., 'William Stumpe of Malmesbury, his Descendants and Relatives', *Wiltshire Notes and Queries* 8 (1914–16), pp. 385–95
Marx, K., *Capital*, 3 vols (1867–94)
McGarvie, Michael, *St George's Church Beckington* (Beckington, 1990)
McSheffrey, S. and Tanner, N., eds, *Lollards of Coventry, 1486–1522*, Camden Fifth Series 23 (London, 2003)
Mendels, F.F., 'Proto-Industrialization: The First Phase of the Industrialization Process', *Journal of Economic History* 32 (1972), pp. 241–61
Merrick, Phoebe, 'Taxing Medieval Cloth', *The Local Historian* 32 (2002), pp. 218–33
Miller, Edward, 'The Fortunes of the English Textile Industry during the Thirteenth Century', *EcHR* 18 (1965), pp. 64–82
——ed., *The Agrarian History of England and Wales*, iii: *1348–1500* (Cambridge, 1991)
——and Hatcher, John, *Medieval England: Towns, Commerce and Crafts 1086–1348* (London, 1995)
Morrison, Kathryn A., *English Shops and Shopping* (London, 2003)
Muldrew, Craig, "'Th'ancient Distaff" and "Whirling Spindle": Measuring the

Contribution of Spinning to Household Earnings and the National Economy in England, 1550–1770', *EcHR*, 2nd series 65 (2012), pp. 498–526
—— 'An Early Industrial Workforce: Spinning in the Countryside, *c.*1500–50', in Richard Jones and Christopher Dyer, eds, *Farmers, Consumers, Innovators. The World of Joan Thirsk* (Hatfield, 2016), pp. 79–88
Munro, John H., 'Wool-Price Schedules and the Qualities of English Wools in the Later Middle Ages *c.*1270–1499', *Textile History* 9 (1978), pp. 118–69
—— 'The 1357 Wool-Price Schedule and the Decline of Yorkshire Wool Values', *Textile History* 10 (1979), pp. 211–19
—— 'The Symbiosis of Towns and Textiles: Urban Institutions and the Changing Fortunes of Cloth Manufacturing in the Low Countries and England, 1270–1570', *Journal of Early Modern History* 3 (1999), pp. 1–74
—— 'The Anti-Red Shift – To the Dark Side: Colour Changes in Flemish Luxury Woollens, 1300–1550', in Robin Netherton and Gale R. Owen-Crocker, eds, *Medieval Clothing and Textiles* 3 (Woodbridge, 2007), pp. 87–91
Murray, James M., *Bruges, Cradle of Capitalism, 1280–1390* (Cambridge, 2005)
National Trust, *Guildhall of Corpus Christi Lavenham* (Swindon, 2004)
—— *Westwood Manor* (Swindon, 2014)
Newman, Christine M., *Late Medieval Northallerton* (Stamford, 1999)
Newman, John, *The Buildings of England: Kent: West and the Weald* (London, 2012)
Nightingale, Pamela, *A Medieval Mercantile Community: The Grocers' Company and the Politics and Trade of London 1000–1485* (New Haven and London, 1995)
—— 'Gold, Credit, and Mortality: Distinguishing Deflationary Pressures on the Late Medieval English Economy', *EcHR* 63 (2010), pp. 1081–1104
—— 'The Rise and Decline of Medieval York: A Reassessment', *Past and Present* 206 (2010), pp. 1–42
—— 'The Impact of Crises on Credit in the Late Medieval English Economy', in A.T. Brown, Andy Burn and Rob Doherty, eds, *Crises in Economic and Social History: A Comparative Perspective* (Woodbridge, 2015), pp. 261–82
Norris, M., *Monumental Brasses: The Memorials*, 2 vols (London, 1977)
North, Susan, '"Galloon, incle and points": Fashionable Dress and Accessories in Rural England, 1552–1665', in Richard Jones and Christopher Dyer, eds, *Farmers, Consumers, Innovators. The World of Joan Thirsk* (Hatfield, 2016), pp. 104–23
Oldland, John, '"Fyne worsted whech is almost like silke": Norwich's Double Worsted', *Textile History* 42 (2011), pp. 181–99
—— 'Making and Marketing Woollen Cloth in Late-Medieval London', *London Journal* 36 (2011), pp. 89–108
—— 'The Variety and Quality of English Woollen Cloth Exported in the Late Middle Ages', *Journal of European Economic History* 39 (2011), pp. 215–29
—— 'Wool and Cloth Production in Late Medieval and Early Tudor England', *EcHR* 67 (2014), pp. 25–47
—— 'The Economic Impact of Clothmaking on Rural Society, 1300–1550', in Martin Allen and Matthew Davies, eds, *Medieval Merchants and Money. Essays in Honour of James L. Bolton* (London, 2016), pp. 229–52

—— 'Book Reviews: Nicholas Amor, *From Wool to Cloth*', *EcHR* 70 (2017), pp. 662–3
Orme, Nicholas, *Medieval Schools from Roman Britain to Renaissance England* (New Haven, 2006)
Pajic, Milan, *Immigration and Economic Development. Flemish Textile Workers in England, 1331–1400* (forthcoming)
Palliser, D.M., ed., *The Cambridge Urban History of Britain*, i: *600–1540* (Cambridge, 2000)
Palmer, C.F.R., 'The Friars-Preachers, or Black Friars, of Gloucester', *Archaeological Journal* 39 (1882), pp. 296–306
Pantin, W.A., 'Chantry Priests' Houses and other Medieval Lodgings', *Medieval Archaeology* 3 (1959), pp. 216–58
Patten, John, 'Village and Town: An Occupational Study', *Agricultural History Review* 20 (1972), pp. 1–16
Peacock, David, 'Dyeing Winchcombe Kersies and Other Kersey Cloth in Sixteenth-Century Newbury', *Textile History* 37 (2006), pp. 187–202
Perry, R., 'The Gloucestershire Woollen Industry, 1100–1690', *Transactions of the Bristol and Gloucestershire Archaeological Society* 66 (1945), pp. 49–137
Pevsner, N, *The Buildings of England: North Somerset and Bristol* (Harmondsworth, 1958)
—— and Cherry, B., *The Buildings of England: Wiltshire* (Harmondsworth, 1975)
—— *The Buildings of England: Devon*, 2nd edn (London, 1989)
Phythian-Adams, Charles, 'Urban Decay in Late Medieval England', in Philip Abrams and E.A. Wrigley, eds, *Towns in Societies: Essays in Economic History and Historical Sociology* (Cambridge, 1978), pp. 159–85
—— *Desolation of a City. Coventry and the Urban Crisis of the Late Middle Ages* (Cambridge, 1979)
Pirenne, Henri, *Economic and Social History of Medieval Europe* (London, 1936)
Pollard, A.J., *North East England during the Wars of the Roses: Lay Society, War, and Politics, 1450–1500* (Oxford, 1990)
Poos, L.R., *A Rural Society after the Black Death: Essex, 1350–1525* (Cambridge, 1991)
Pontefract, Ella and Hartley, Marie, *Yorkshire Tour* (London, 1939)
Postan, M.M., 'The Economic and Political Relations of England and the Hanse from 1400 to 1475', in E. Power and M.M. Postan, eds, *Studies in English Trade in the Fifteenth Century* (London, 1933), pp. 91–153
—— 'The Fifteenth Century', *EcHR* 9 (1938–9), pp. 160–7
Pound, J.F., 'Rebellion and Poverty in 16th Century Suffolk: The 1525 Uprising against the Amicable Grant', *Proceedings of the Suffolk Institute of Archaeology* 39 (1999), pp. 317–30
Power, E., *The Paycockes of Coggeshall* (London, 1920)
—— 'Thomas Betson: A Merchant of the Staple in the Fifteenth Century', and 'Thomas Paycocke of Coggeshall: An Essex Clothier in the Days of Henry VII', in E. Power, *Medieval People* (London, 1924), pp. 120–73
—— *The Wool Trade in English Medieval History: Being the Ford lectures* (Oxford, 1941)

Prestwich, Michael, *The Three Edwards: War and State in England 1272–1377* (London, 1980)

Quiney, Anthony, *Town Houses of Medieval Britain* (London, 2003)

Ramsay, G.D., 'The Distribution of the Cloth Industry in 1561–2', *English Historical Review* 57 (1942), pp. 361–9

—— *The Wiltshire Woollen Industry in the Sixteenth and Seventeenth Centuries*, 2nd edn (London, 1965)

—— 'The Cloth Trade at London in Mid-sixteenth Century: The Merchant Adventurers and Their Rivals', in M. Spallanzani, ed., *Produzione, commercio e consume dei panni di lana* (Florence, 1976), pp. 377–83

—— *The English Woollen Industry, 1500–1750* (London, 1982)

Ramsey, Peter, *Tudor Economic Problems* (London, 1963)

Rigby, Stephen, ed., *Historians on Chaucer. The 'General Prologue' to the* Canterbury Tales (Oxford, 2014)

Roberts, Edward and Miles, Daniel, 'Castle Bridge Cottages, North Warnborough, Hampshire', *Vernacular Architecture* 28 (1997), pp. 117–18

Robertson, D.W., '"And for my land thus hastow mordred me?" Land Tenure, the Cloth Industry, and the Wife of Bath', *Chaucer Review* 14 (1980), pp. 403–20

Rollison, David, *The Local Origins of Modern Society: Gloucestershire, 1500–1800* (London, 1992)

Ross, James, *John de Vere, Thirteenth Earl of Oxford, 1442–1513: 'The foremost man of the kingdom'* (Woodbridge, 2011)

Royal Commission for Historical Monuments England, *Rural Houses of West Yorkshire 1400–1830* (London, 1986)

Ruddock, A.A., *Italian Merchants and Shipping in Southampton, 1270–1600* (Southampton, 1951)

Ryder, Michael L., 'Fascinating *Fullonum*', *Circaea, The Journal of the Association for Environmental Archaeology* 11 (1994 for 1993), pp. 23–31

Salzman, L.F., *English Industries of the Middle Ages*, 2nd edn (London, 1923)

Saul, N., 'The Wool Merchants and their Brasses', *Transactions of the Monumental Brass Society* 17 (2006), pp. 315–35

Schofield, Peter and Vannan, Alastair, *Windermere Reflections: Fulling Mills in Easedale, Grasmere, Elterwater, Great Langdale and Graythwaite*, Oxford Archaeology North (Lancaster, 2012)

Schofield, Phillipp R., '*Extranei* and the Market for Customary Land on a Westminster Abbey Manor in the Fifteenth Century', *Agricultural History Review* 49 (2001), pp. 1–16

Schofield, R.S., 'The Geographical Distribution of Wealth in England, 1334–1649', *EcHR*, 2nd series 18 (1965), pp. 483–510

Shaw, D.G., *The Creation of a Community: The City of Wells in the Middle Ages* (Oxford, 1993)

Sheils, William and Sheils, Sarah, 'Textiles and Reform: Halifax and its Hinterland', in Patrick Collinson and John Craig, eds, *The Reformation in English Towns, 1500–1640* (Basingstoke, 1998), pp. 130–43

Slack, P., 'Mortality Crises and Epidemic Disease in England, 1485–1610', in C. Webster, ed., *Health, Medicine and Mortality in the Late Sixteenth Century* (Cambridge, 1979), pp. 9–59

Simpson, J.J., 'The Wool Trade and the Woolmen of Gloucestershire', *Transactions of the Bristol and Gloucestershire Archaeological Society* 53 (1931), pp. 65–97

Smith, R.B., *Land and Politics in the England of Henry VIII. The West Riding of Yorkshire: 1530–1546* (Oxford, 1970)

Spufford, Margaret, 'The Importance of Religion in the Sixteenth and Seventeenth Centuries', in Margaret Spufford, ed., *The World of Rural Dissenters, 1520–1725* (Cambridge, 1995), pp. 1–102

Stabel, Peter, 'Guilds in Late Medieval Flanders: Myths and Realities of Guild Life in an Export-oriented Environment', *Journal of Medieval History* 30 (2004), pp. 187–212

Steer, Christian, 'The Language of Commemoration', in Mary Carruthers, ed., *Language in Medieval Britain: Networks and Exchanges* (Donington, 2015), pp. 240–50

—— '"For quicke and deade memorie masses": Merchant Piety in Late Medieval London', in Martin Allen and Matthew Davies, eds, *Medieval Merchants and Money: Essays in Honour of James L. Bolton* (London, 2016), pp. 71–89

Stenning, D.F., 'Timber-Framed Shops 1300–1600: Comparative Plans', *Vernacular Architecture* (1985), pp. 35–9

—— *Discovering Coggeshall. Timber-framed Buildings in the Town Centre* (Coggeshall, 2013)

Stevens, Matthew, 'London Creditors and the Fifteenth-century Depression', *EcHR* 69 (2016), pp. 1083–1107

Sutton, Anne F., *The Mercery of London. Trade, Goods and People, 1130–1578* (Aldershot, 2005)

—— 'London Mercers from Suffolk *c.*1200 to 1570: Benefactors, Pirates and Merchant Adventurers (Part II)', *Proceedings of the Suffolk Institute for Archaeology and History* 42 (2010), pp. 162–84

Swain, John T., *Industry Before the Industrial Revolution: North-east Lancashire, c.1500–1640*, Chetham Society, 3rd series 32 (Manchester, 1986)

Swanson, Heather, *Medieval Artisans* (Oxford, 1989)

Tarbutt, William, *The Annals of Cranbrook Church* (Cranbrook, 1870)

Tawney, R.H., *Religion and the Rise of Capitalism* (Harmondsworth, 1938)

Thirsk, Joan, 'Industries in the Countryside', in F.J. Fisher, ed., *Essays in the Economic and Social History of Tudor and Stuart England* (London, 1961), pp. 70–86

Thornton, G.A., *A History of Clare Suffolk* (Cambridge, 1928)

Thrupp, S.L., *The Merchant Class of Medieval London* (London, 1948)

Tracy, C., Harrison, H. and Wrapson, L., 'Thomas Spring's Chantry and Parclose at Lavenham, Suffolk', *Journal of the British Archaeological Association* 164 (2011), pp. 221–59

Unwin, George, *Industrial Organization in the Sixteenth and Seventeenth Centuries*, 2nd edn (London, 1957)

The Victoria History of the Counties of England (London, 1900–in progress)

Walker, Greg, *John Skelton and the Politics of the 1520s* (Cambridge, 1988)

Walker, Muriel and Guy, Simon, *The Church of Saint Mary the Virgin and the Parish of Westwood, Wiltshire* (Westwood, 1989)

Ward, Jennifer, 'Townswomen and their Households', in Richard Britnell, ed., *Daily Life in the Late Middle Ages* (Stroud, 1998), pp. 27–42

—— 'Merchant Families and Religion in Later Medieval Colchester', in Caroline M. Barron and Anne F. Sutton, eds, *The Medieval Merchant* (Donington, 2014), pp. 242–58

Welsford, A.E., *John Greenway, 1460–1529. Merchant of Tiverton and London. A Devon Worthy* (Tiverton, 1984)

Whittle, Jane, *The Development of Agrarian Capitalism: Land and Labour in Norfolk 1440–1580* (Oxford, 2000)

Williams, E.H.D., Penoyre, J., Penoyre, J. and Hale, B.C.M., 'New Street, Mells. A Building Survey of an Uncompleted Late Medieval Planned Development', *Somerset Archaeology and Natural History Society: Proceedings* 130 (1985–86), pp. 115–25

Wilton, E., 'Malmesbury Abbey. License for its Conversion into a Parish Church', *Wiltshire Archaeological and Natural History Magazine* 1 (1854), pp. 249–50

Wolff, Philippe, 'Three Samples of English Fifteenth-Century Cloth', in N.B. Harte and K.G. Ponting, eds, *Cloth and Clothing in Medieval Europe. Essays in Memory of Professor E.M. Carus-Wilson* (London, 1983), pp. 120–5

Woodward, D., 'Wage Rates and Living Standards in Pre-industrial England', *Past and Present* 91 (1981), pp. 28–46

Yates, Margaret, *Town and Countryside in Western Berkshire,* c.*1327*–c.*1600: Social and Economic Change* (Woodbridge, 2007)

Youings, J., *The Dissolution of the Monasteries* (London, 1971)

Zell, Michael, 'The Exchequer Lists of Provincial Cloth-makers Fined in London during the Sixteenth Century', *Bulletin of the Institute of Historical Research* 57 (1984), pp. 129–30

—— *Industry in the Countryside: Wealden Society in the Sixteenth Century* (Cambridge, 1994)

—— 'Credit in the Pre-Industrial English Woollen Industry', *EcHR*, 2nd series 49 (1996), pp. 667–91

—— 'Parliament, the Textile Industry and the Mid-Tudor Crisis', in Charles Carlton, ed., *State, Sovereigns and Society in Early Modern England: Essays in Honour of A.J. Slavin* (Stroud, 1998), pp. 71–84

UNPUBLISHED THESES

Egan, Geoffrey, 'Provenanced Leaden Cloth Seals', University of London, Ph.D. thesis, 1987

Galloway, James A., 'Colchester and its Region, 1310–1560: Wealth, Industry and Rural–Urban Mobility in a Medieval Society', University of Edinburgh, Ph.D. thesis, 1986

Gibbs, Samuel, 'The Service Patterns and Social-economic Status of English Archers, 1367–1417: The Evidence of the Muster Rolls and Poll Tax Returns', University of Reading, Ph.D. thesis, 2015

Jones, Amanda, '"Commotion time": The English Risings of 1549', University of Warwick, Ph.D. thesis, 2003

Oldland, John R., 'London Clothmaking, *c.*1270–*c.*1550', University of London, Ph.D. thesis, 2003

Pajic, Milan, 'The Migration of Flemish Weavers to England in the Fourteenth Century: The Economic Influence and Transfer of Skills 1331–1381', University of Strasbourg and University of Ghent, Docteur thesis, 2016

Peacock, David, 'The Winchcombe Family and the Woollen Industry in Sixteenth-Century Newbury', University of Reading, Ph.D. thesis, 2003

Pilgrim, J.E., 'The Cloth Industry in Essex and Suffolk 1558–1640', University of London, MA thesis, 1939

Quinton, Eleanor Jane Powys, 'The Drapers and the Drapery Trade of Late Medieval London, *c.*1300–*c.*1500', University of London, Ph.D. thesis, 2001

UNPUBLISHED REPORTS

Alston, L., 'Paycocke's Coggeshall, Essex. Historical Analysis of Structure', unpublished report, 2005

Thornton, C., 'Paycocke's House, Coggeshall. Historical report', unpublished report for the National Trust, 2011

ONLINE SOURCES

[all accessed 13 May 2017]

Anglo-American Legal Tradition: Documents from Medieval and Early Modern England from The National Archives in London, http://aalt.law.uh.edu

Bradford-on-Avon – History, http://www.freshford.com/10_horton_house.htm

Court of Common Pleas: The National Archives, CP40 1399–1500 (London, 2010), British History Online, http://www.british-history.ac.uk/no-series/common-pleas/1399-1500

Cullompton and the Cloth Trade, https://cullomptonclothtrade.wordpress.com/

eChaucer: Chaucer in the Twenty-First Century, http://echaucer.machias.edu/formage/

England's Immigrants 1330–1550, https://www.englandsimmigrants.com

History of Parliament, http://www.historyofparliamentonline.org

Monumental Brass Society, http://www.mbs-brasses.co.uk

National Heritage List for England, Historic England, https://historicengland.org.uk/listing/the-list

Newbury Today, https://www.newburytoday.co.uk

Overland Trade Project: People, Places, and Commodities 1430–1540, http://overlandtrade.org

Oxford Dictionary of National Biography, http://www.oxforddnb.com

Oxford English Dictionary, http://www.oed.com

Tiverton Almshouse Trust, http://www.tivertonalmshouse.org.uk/

West Yorkshire Textile Heritage, http://westyorkshiretextileheritage.org.uk/

Index

Abeck, Ann, of Manchester, cloth-maker 80, 194
Abeck, Thomas, of Manchester, cloth-maker 80, 194
Abel, Thomas, of Manchester, clothier 61
Abergavenny (Monmouthshire) 103
Abingdon (Berkshire) 16, 19, 133, 222, 284
  Abbey 74, 176, 177, 209
Acre (Israel) 94
Adlam, Roger, of Devizes, clothier 89
Afternewell, Nicholas 205
Aiscough, William, bishop of Salisbury 179
Alake, Thomas, of Tewkesbury 111
Alderley (Gloucestershire) 121
Aldermaston (Berkshire) 284
Aldham (Essex) 229
Alexandria (Egypt) 94
All Cannings (Wiltshire) 123 n.26
Allen, Richard, of London, Merchant Taylor 86
Allen, Sir John, mayor of London 103, 187
Allen, William, of Calne, clothier 159, 207
Allerthorpe (Yorkshire) 207
Almondbury (Yorkshire) 132, 208, 288
almshouses 210, 219, 225
  Dedham 221, 278
  Lavenham 215, 248
  Tiverton 136, 221, 278, 311
  Trowbridge 126, 180, 220–1
Alresford (Hampshire) 286
Alton (Hampshire) 122, 259, 286
Alyward, Edward 295
Alyward, John, of Coggeshall 295
Amyot, Benet, of Benenden 192
Amyot, Gervase, of Benenden, clothier 192
Amyot, Stephen, of Benenden 192
Amyot, Thomas, of Benenden 192
Andover (Hampshire) 122, 134, 285, 286
Andrew, John, of Cranbrook, clothier 184
Anne of Cleves, wife of Henry VIII, queen of England 253
Ancona (Italy) 256
Antwerp 3, 11, 79, 84, 154, 233, 255, 274
  cloth merchant 87
  commission house 95, 256
  fairs 91, 99, 256
apprentice 125, 223, 245, 258, 280, 299
apprenticeship 68, 141, 171, 172, 191, 193
Appulford, John, of Thaxted 108
Appulford, William, of Thaxted 108
Aragon (Spain) 8
Archer, Henry, of London 152
Archer, John 211
Ardsley (Yorkshire) 207
Armeys, William 123
Armstrong, Clement, of London, grocer 93, 102, 170
Ashton-under-Lyme (Lancashire) 139
Atwood, James, clothier 265
aulnage *see* ulnage
Avon, River 120
Axbridge (Somerset) 287
Ayelmar, John, of Colchester, brewer 104–5
Azores 256
Babergh hundred (Suffolk) 68, 70, 130, 245
Babwell, friars 297
Bailey, Christopher, of Stowford, clothier 126
Bailey, Thomas, of Trowbridge, clothier 89, 126, 204, 208, 263
Bailey, William, of Keevil, clothier 126

Baisbrown manor (Westmorland) 192
Baker, John, of London, merchant 110
Ball, William, of Dewsbury, shearman 193, 222
Ballingdon (Essex) 183
Baltic 10, 92, 154
Bampton (Devon) 284
Banester, John, of Halifax 139
Banwell, Thomas, of Coventry, draper 100
barbing *see* shearing
Barker, John, of Lavenham, clothier 199
Barker, Robert, of Colchester, cloth-maker 57
Barking (Essex) 252
Barnard, Richard 21
Barnsley (Yorkshire) 289
Barnstaple (Devon) 21, 134, 135, 284
Barre, Richard, of Cranbrook, clothier 109
Barton (Gloucestershire) 53
Barton, John 15
Barton, Walter, of Reading 133
Basing (Hampshire) 259
Basingstoke (Hampshire) 3, 46, 105, 122, 134, 286
Batcombe (Somerset) 287
Bath (Somerset) 121, 128, 194–5, 305
  clothiers 89, 119, 121, 194, 246
  cloth-making 120, 122
  cloths taxed in 115, 287
  cloth-workers 17, 116
  see also Wife of Bath
Bathhurst, clothier 176
Batt, Richard, of Westbury, clothier 89
Bawden, John, of Horsmonden, clothier 71
Bayly, Nicholas, of Baskingstoke 134
Baynton, Bridget 263
Baynton, Isabel 263, 270
Baynton, Sir Edward 263, 264, 270
Beauchamp, John, of Sudbury, cloth-maker 83
Beaumont, Elizabeth, of Whitley Beaumont 208
Beaumont, Thomas, of Whitley Beaumont 208
Beccles (Suffolk) 202
Beckington (Somerset) 94, 121, 194
  church of St George 212–14, 304
  clothiers 45, 89, 107, 112, 118, 123 n.26, 212–14, 217, 221
  cloths taxed in 287
Beckley (Oxfordshire) 19
Bedfordshire 282
Beeleigh, Maldon (Essex) 295
Beiche, Margaret 301
Beirut (Lebanon) 94
Belchamber, John, of Basingstoke, mercer 105
Belchamp St Paul (Essex) 234, 293, 294
Bell, Thomas, of Gloucester, clothier and capmaker 36, 126, 159, 176, 209, 307, Plate VII
Bene, William, of London, grocer 61
Benedick, Master 255
Benenden (Kent) 137, 192, 286
Benet, John, of Cirencester, clothier 68, 125, 200
Benet, Roger, of Newbury, fuller 61, 255, 301
Beneyt, John, of Canterbury, weaver 51
Benham (Berkshire) 284
Bennet, William, of Newbury, clothier 257
Benson family of Grasmere 140, 192
Benson, John, of Grasmere 192
Benson, William, of Kendal 192
Bergen (Norway) 92
Bergen-op-Zoom (Netherlands) 91, 99, 154, 256
Bergholt 70, 232
  see also East Bergholt, West Bergholt
Berkeley (Gloucestershire) 121, 125, 263, 267
Berkeley, James, of Bradley 263–4
Berkeley, Lord Thomas 186
Berkshire 11, 16, 29, 96, 165, 315
  cloths taxed in 115, 133, 282, 284
  kerseys 11, 96, 134, 226, 252, 255–9
  protests in 181, 182, 186
Bertyn, William, bailiff of Lavenham 299
Beste, Robert, of Essex, cloth-maker 110
Betson, Thomas 14
Beverley (Yorkshire) 8, 18, 65
  cloth-making in 33, 131
  merchants 21, 30, 87
  weavers 149, 158
Bewdley (Shropshire) 103
Beycham, John, weaver 231, 296
Biddenden (Kent) 85, 137, 286
Bigge, John, of Goudhurst 71

Bildeston (Suffolk) 69, 128, 245
Chapel Street houses 204, 304
clothiers 83, 85, 95–6, 130, 244
cloths taxed in 128, 288
cloth-workers 69, 96
Billing, John 267
Binegar (Somerset) 106
Birdbrook (Essex) 242, 271
Bishopstrow (Wiltshire) 59
Bishopthorpe (Yorkshire) 48
Bisley (Gloucestershire) 125, 146
Black Death 4–6, 10, 12, 13, 41, 99, 151, 313
Blackburn (Lancashire) 138
Blackdon, Roger, of Farleigh Hungerford, clothier 89, 194
Blackwater, River 227
Blanket, Thomas, of Bristol 19
Blome, John 206
Blundell, Peter, of Tiverton, clothier 136
Bocher, John 303
Bocking (Essex) 151, 180, 299
Boinebroke, Jehan, of Douai 18
Bolton (Lancashire) 98, 138
Bolton-in-Craven priory (Yorkshire) 211
Bomer, Robert, of Croscombe, clothier 123
Bonde, Henry, of Salisbury, weaver 122
Bonvisi, Antonio 93, 233, 255
Bonvisi, family 43
Bonvixi *see* Bonvisi, Antonio; Bonvisi, family
Bore, Thomas, of Southampton, merchant 256
Borham, Henry, of Clare, cloth-maker 52
Boroughbridge (Yorkshire) 132
Boston (Lincolnshire) 18, 92, 99, 187
Boswell, John, of Colchester, clothier 102, 184
Bothe, of Halifax 81
Boweseke, Oliver 266
Boxford (Berkshire) 284
Boxford (Suffolk) 85, 242, 288
Boxted (Essex) 198
Boyton (Wiltshire) 269
Brabant 16, 53, 91, 174
Bradford (Yorkshire) 33, 96, 99, 100, 131–2, 288
Bradford-on-Avon (Wiltshire) 105, 121, 152, 304–5
church of Holy Trinity 304
church house 221, 305
clothiers 32, 94–5, 193
Horton's house 198, 204, 305
Bradford-on-Tone (Somerset) 99
Bradley (Gloucestershire) 263–4
Bradwell (Essex) 234, 294
Braintree (Essex) 127, 129, 285
Bramley (Surrey) 151
Brampton (Huntingdonshire) 61
Branch, Elizabeth, of Lavenham 197, 219, 308
Branch, Simon, of Lavenham 219, 248, 308
brasses, monumental 36, 210
clothiers 107, 125, 133, 212–14, 218, 225, 230, 234, 304–11, Plate IX
Compton 212–14, 304
Horrold 230, 234
Paycockes 234, 306
Springs 245, 247–9, 308
Winchcombe 260, 309
Braybrooke, Thomas, of Abingdon, clothier 133
Braydon forest (Wiltshire) 266
Breggs, Henry, servant 296
Brent Eleigh (Suffolk) 182
Brett, River 239
Brickenden, Richard, clothier 217
Brickles, John, of London, draper 84
Bridbury, A.R. 27, 153
Bridgwater (Somerset) 120, 122, 152, 186, 287
cloth 105, 154, 290
Bridport (Dorset) 95, 180
Briggs, John, of Salisbury, clothier 68, 122
Bright, Thomas, of Canterbury, fuller 180
Brikles, John, of London, draper 71
Brinkworth (Wiltshire) 267
Bristol 79, 93, 96, 140, 256
church of St Mary Redcliffe 212, 305
cloth 11, 72, 161
cloth hall 98
cloth-making 19, 153
regulation 51, 158, 167, 168, 173
cloths taxed in 116, 120
cloth-workers 61, 80
drapers 106
Flemings 16–17
fullers 61, 180, 193

mercers 33, 61, 64, 80, 107, 109, 194, 256
merchants 82, 85, 99, 100
water conduit 222
Britnell, Richard 24, 27–8, 68, 75, 238–9
Brittany 79, 135, 266
Brograve, William 71
Brokenborough (Wiltshire) 267
Bromsgrove (Worcestershire) 142–3
Brown, John, of Manchester, cloth-maker 138
Browne, Mr, of London 121
Browtun, Mr, of Manchester 139
Bruges (Netherlands) 91
Brussels 79
Bruton (Somerset) 80, 109, 121, 207
Bruyn, John, of Ghent, cloth-maker 19
Bryket, Patrick, Kendalman 100
Buchar, William, clothier 61
Buckfast Abbey (Devon) 209
Buckinghamshire 282
Buckland (Berkshire) 259
Bucklebury (Berkshire) 254
Budde, Thomas, of Wellington, cloth-man 105
Bungay (Suffolk) 202
Burford (Oxfordshire) 43, 74, 133, 176, 199, 209
Burges, Philip, of North Molton, merchant 161
Burgundy 57, 178, 184
Burin, Henning, of Cologne 93
burling 40, 53, 60, 198
Burnley (Lancashire) 138
Burton, Agnes 295
Burwood (Shropshire) 113
Bury (Lancashire) 138
Bury St Edmunds (Suffolk) 42, 49, 119, 128, 171, 202
abbey of 147, 250
cloths taxed in 288
protests in 188
Buxton, Noel 227
Bydfeld, Robert, of Tewkesbury 111
Bye, Thomas, of Reading 255
Byland Abbey (Yorkshire) 208
Bysee, John, of Stoke, clothier 89
Cade, Jack's revolt 179–80, 280
Calais 14, 42
Calderdale (Yorkshire) 43, 195
Calley, William, of London, draper 84
Calne (Wiltshire) 159, 207
Cam (Gloucestershire) 223
Cambini firm 43
Cambridge 2, 6, 145, 182
church of Great St Mary 250
King's College 207, 249
Queens' College 220
Stourbridge Fair 100, 139
university of 220
Cambridgeshire 63, 145, 207, 242
cloths taxed in 282
protests in 182
worsted 141
Canterbury (Kent) 51, 116, 137, 176, 180
cathedral priory 147
cloths taxed in 115, 286
friaries 176, 209
Canterbury Tales 35, 194
see also Wife of Bath
capital 6–8, 151–3, 156, 159, 191, 280
clothiers' use of 29, 76
credit 108–11
investment 46, 49, 52, 54, 139
capitalists 17–28, 38, 148, 275
clothiers acting as 2, 24–8, 280–1
cap-making 122, 126, 142, 178
Cardemakere, John 197
carding 18, 22, 37, 40, 44, 45–6, 49, 65, 139, 142, 169, 176, 258, 313, Plate I, Plate III
carder 39, 150, 169, 170, 178, 313
employed by clothiers 46, 181, 183, 232, 253, 258, 296
carding combs 45–6, 197, 212, 305
cardmaker 116, 197
timescales and costs 73, 75, 277
Cardiganshire 291
Carewe, Sir William 41
Carmarthen 140
Carmarthenshire 291
carriers *see under* transport
Carruthers, Mary 194
Carter, John, of York, tailor 80
Cartere, Michael 20
carts *see under* transport
Carus-Wilson, Eleanora 25, 32, 53, 194
Cary, Richard, of Bristol 100
Castle Combe (Wiltshire) 2, 179, 278, 313
cloth-making 59, 121, 123–5, 148, 204, 305
cloths taxed in 288

see also Castlecombes *under* cloth types
Catalonia 8
Catterick bridge (Yorkshire) 221
Cavyll, Richard, wife of 295
Caype, William, of Northallerton 65
Cecil, Sir William 280
Cely family 14
Chacombe, Henry, of London, draper 103
Chalford (Gloucestershire) 124
Chans, William, of Pendine 141
Chapman, John, of Minchinhampton, woolman 106
Chapman, Roger, of Coggeshall 104
Chapman, Thomas, of Bath, clothier 121
chapmen 34, 80, 151–2, 155
Chappell, John 302
Charlton (Wiltshire) 267, 302
Chasty, John, of Exeter, carrier 113
Chaucer, Geoffrey 12, 35, 275
Chellow, Alice, of York, widow 49
Chelmsford (Essex) 234, 285, 293
Cheltenham (Wiltshire) 123 n.26
Cherington (Berkshire) 269
Cheshire
  cloth 89, 138, 154, 315, 291
  wool 44
Chester (Cheshire) 96, 138
Chew Magna (Somerset) 121
Chick, Stevyn, of Bruton 109
Chiddingfold (Surrey) 259
Chippenham (Wiltshire) 113, 205, 264
Chipping Camden (Gloucestershire) 42
Christchurch (Hampshire) 286
Christmas, Thomas, of Colchester, clothier 50, 52, 56
Chulmleigh (Devon) 285
churches
  bequests by clothiers 216, 225, 278, 304–11
  chantries 37, 126, 136, 192, 211, 214, 219–21, 225, 230, 233–4, 248, 292, 306, 311, 313
Cirencester (Gloucestershire) 42, 59
  abbot of 54, 126
  clothiers 68, 72, 121, 125, 200
Clare (Suffolk) 127, 197, 222, 294
  clothiers 52–3, 55, 192, 193–4, 230, 233
  cloths taxed in 288
  fair 100
  friars 234, 293, 297
Clerk, Simon, master mason 249
Clerke, John, of Hadleigh, clothier 130, 224
Clerke, Walter 224
Clevelod, John, of Beckington, clothier 45, 89, 112, 194, 217
Clevelod, Mary, of Beckington 194
Cliddesden (Hampshire) 105
cloth
  colours 165–6
  domestic market 9, 11
  exports 9, 78, 92, 155, 181, 184, 273–4, 276
    from London 11, 81–3, 87, 279
cloth types
  bastards 154, 313
  blanket 12, 96, 121, 153
  burrel 18, 143, 173
  Castlecombes 87, 89, 123, 153–4, 268–9, 313
  Coggeshalls 87, 96, 154, 233, 313
  cotton 153, 314
    Lancashire 80, 89, 98, 138, 291
    Welsh 140, 291
  dozens 82, 122, 135, 136, 153, 154, 290–1, 314
  frieze 84, 153, 314
    Lancashire and Cheshire 138–9, 291
    Welsh 84, 89, 141, 291
  Glemsford whites 129, 290, 313
  harden 39, 64, 132
  kerseys 45, 65, 89, 95, 100, 103, 153, 283, 290, 314–15
    Berkshire 11, 96, 134, 226, 252, 255–9
    Devon 135, 136, 154, 165, 175, 290, 315
    Essex 164
    kerseyman 133
    kersey makers 165
    kersey-making scheme 175
    Kent 137, 154
    Lancashire 138
    Suffolk 116, 128, 164
    Wiltshire 122
    Yorkshire 43, 81, 116, 154
  musterdevillers 128, 315
  linen 39, 50, 64–5, 86, 98, 100, 107, 138–40, 175, 177, 245, 315

medleys 85, 122, 167, 315
northern cloths 291
Penistones 89, 140, 154, 291, 315
plunkets 257, 290, 315
rays 11, 122, 153, 164, 316
rugs 138, 291, 316
russets 12, 13, 85, 161, 316
Colchester 11, 127, 128, 153, 154
costs of making 74–5
Halifax 80
Kent 71, 89, 137
straits 39, 45, 116, 153–4, 283, 290, 314–16
Devon 135, 160
Essex 228
Suffolk 128–9
Stroudwaters 123, 153, 316
vesses 93, 128, 153, 154, 165, 316
worsted 10, 11, 39, 45, 117, 141, 173, 177, 317
exports of 82, 86
sales of 97, 104
cloth-making
costs 20, 52, 73–5
advantage of English cloth 10 n.23, 11
employment in 75–6, 273, 278–9
innovation 153
organisation of 65–6, 276
processes *see* burling; carding; combing; fulling; napping; shearing; spinning; weaving
proposals to encourage 15–17, 175–7
restricted to towns 173–5
technology 51, 53, 76, 276
timescales 50, 72–3, 75
cloth-workers 15, 16, 19, 20, 24, 39, 49, 65, 69, 76, 115–17, 129, 144, 150, 151, 155, 156, 192, 193, 225, 250, 273
bequests to 31, 46, 49, 245, 270
houses 204, 232, 277–8, 304, 309, 310
protests 93, 180, 184, 186–90, 240
see also carding; combing; dyeing; finishing; fulling; napping; outworkers; shearing; spinning; weaving
Clynt, Thomas, of York 20, 49
Coggeshall (Essex) 104
abbey 228–9, 231, 234, 293
church of St Peter ad Vincula 217, 229, 230, 233–4, 292, 306
clothiers 84, 118, 156
see also Paycocke, Thomas
cloth-making 57, 127, 145, 228–9
cloths taxed in 285
houses 30, 204, 230, 232, 237–8
fairs 43, 228
White Hart Inn 238
see also Coggeshalls *under* cloth types
coinage, shortage of 71, 151–2, 170, 181
Coke, John 174, 206
Coke, Richard 301
Colbrond, Walter, of Gussage St Michael 123
Colbrooke 223
Colchester (Essex)
church of St Peter 211
cloth 84, 148, 153, 316
clothiers 24, 50, 52, 57, 70, 85, 102, 119, 184, 211, 245, 275–6
see also Hervey, Robert; Webb, Henry
cloth-making 11, 20, 21, 28, 52, 68, 72, 86, 127–30, 145, 229, 244
cloths taxed in 129–30, 285
costs 74–5
Flemings 16–17, 19, 144
New Draperies 177
regulation 169, 170, 173
trade 92–3, 99, 102, 104–5, 113, 127–8, 148
fairs 99
friars 234, 293, 294
Marquis of Granby Inn 198, 203, 305
Moothall 98
protests in 70, 179, 232
Cole, Robert 303
Coleman, D.C. 27, 153
Collet, William, of London, mercer 152
Collinson, Robert, of York, mercer 21, 211, 221
Colman, John, of Great Cornard, weaver 100
Colman, John, of Little Waldingfield 308
Colman, Katherine, of Little Waldingfield 308
Colman, Robert, of Coggeshall 229
Colne (Lancashire) 138, 139, 207
Colne, River 198
Cologne 6, 92, 93
combing 18, 22, 37, 40, 45–6, 139, 277, 313

combs 45, 49, 132, 197, 212, 305
combers 39–40, 45, 46, 116, 178, 314
employed by clothiers 46, 169, 170, 232, 296
timescales and cost 73–4
Compton (Somerset) 287
Compton, Edith, of Beckington 213–14
Compton, John, of Beckington, clothier (father and son) 107, 212–14, 221, 304
Conishead Priory (Lancashire) 192
Conway Abbey 207
Copynger, William 42
Cornwall 44, 136, 282, 283
Corsham (Wiltshire) 106
Cotswold wool 13, 44
Cotton, Eleanor 295
Cotton, Richard 295
Cotton, William 295
Court of Common Pleas 22–3, 34, 42, 81, 83, 86, 110, 117–20, 123, 229, 267, 275
Courthop, Alexander, of Cranbrook, clothier 137, 217
Courthop, Richard, of Cranbrook, clothier 86, 137
Cove, Robert 302
Coventre family of Devizes 159
Coventry (Warwickshire) 79
clothiers 119, 123
cloth-making 11, 79, 87, 115, 142, 152
cloths 11, 154, 167, 290
cloth-workers 116–17, 119, 142, 222
drapers 100, 103, 142
Drapery 97
heresy prosecutions 222
protests in 179
regulation 160 n.10, 166–7, 169, 171, 173
Coverdale, Miles 260
Cowley (Oxfordshire) 19
Cowpere, William 113
Coxhall whites *see* Coggeshalls *under* cloth types
Cranbrook (Kent) 137, 217, 286, 306
clothiers 85, 86, 109, 111, 137, 184, 187, 193
protests in 184
Craven (Yorkshire) 44, 80
Crawley (Hampshire) 179
credit 7–8, 34, 216
clothiers use of 37, 71–2, 76, 93, 104, 108–11, 151–2, 267–9, 276, 281
Londoners dominate 11, 34, 83, 152, 274
wool sales 14, 18, 139, 238
Crediton (Devon) 135, 285
Creswell, Thomas, cloth-man 61
Cricklade (Wiltshire) 253
Critoft, Roger of Lavenham 197
Cromwell, Thomas 134, 176, 257, 260
cropping *see* shearing
Croscombe (Somerset) 23, 84, 111, 122–3, 275, 287
Crosseby, William, of York, dyer 46
Crossley, John, of Huddersfield, clothier 103
Crytott, Roger, of Lavenham, weaver 52
Cuff, William, of Salisbury, cloth-maker 72, 122
Cullompton (Devon) 113, 135, 136, 217, 278
Lane chapel 55, 57, 58, 61, 136, 218, 219, 306
Culm, River 135, 278
Culmstock (Devon) 284
Cumberland 43, 44, 211
Cunningham, William 25
Curtas, Thomas 20–1
customs 10, 14, 15, 77, 92, 144, 157, 188, 279
accounts of 10, 25, 33, 82, 252, 273
farm of 136
local rates 138, 228
rates paid by overseas merchants 92, 188
Dacres, Robert, of Beverley, weaver 65
Damascus (Syria) 94
Dansell, William 257
Darbye, George 303
Dartford (Kent) 137, 286
Dartmouth (Devon) 79, 136
Datini, Francesco di Marco 18
Davy, Richard, of Nayland, clothier 55
Davy, William, of Haverfordwest 141
De Federico, *see* Federico
De Ibarra, *see* Ibarra
De Pape *see* Pape
De Vere *see* Vere
Dedham (Essex) 70, 232, 285
Brook House 218
church of St Mary the Virgin 36, 218, 306
clothiers 85, 93, 127, 148, 167

Dunton's Almshouses 221, 278
Marlborough Head Inn 197
Southfields 197, 307
Defoe, Daniel 250
Deloney, Thomas 1, 35, 134, 207, 226, 250, 251, 253, 270, 272–3
Denby Grange (Yorkshire) 208
Denton, John, of Oxford, weaver 51
Derby 116
Derbyshire 282
Devizes (Wiltshire) 89, 121, 288
members of parliament 159
protests in 179, 186
Devon 80, 87, 183, 278
cloth 113, 154
kerseys 135, 136, 154, 165, 175, 290, 315
clothiers 119, 135–6
cloths taxed in 21, 282–3, 284–5
cloth-making 11, 20, 79, 134–6, 153
regulation 160, 165, 167
wool 44, 165
Dewsbury (Yorkshire) 132, 193, 222
Diss (Norfolk) 242
Dister, Allaine 308
Dobb, Maurice 26
Dolman, Thomas, of Newbury, clothier 134, 255, 257
Dolman, William, of Newbury, clothier 255, 301
domestic system *see* putting-out system
Doncaster (Yorkshire) 131, 210, 289
Donne, Bartholomew, of London, tailor 86
Dorewarde, William 229
Dormer, William, of Wing 259
Dormer, William, of West Wycombe, woolman 71
Dorney, William, of Berkeley, mercer 267
Dorset 94, 282, 283
Douai (France) 18
Doudyng, William, of Salisbury, draper 164
Dover (Kent) 286
Dowe, Laurence, of Long Melford, clothier 193
Draner, Stephen, of Cranbrook, clothier 111, 137, 187, 217
Draper, Henry, of Mytholmroyd 196
Draper, Nicholas, of Basingstoke 134
draperies, wet and dry 45
Draperies (cloth markets) 97
Draperies, New 177
drapers 19, 22, 29, 42, 78, 80–1, 82–3, 94, 116, 140, 163, 175, 216, 279
Basingstoke 134
Bocking 151
Bramley 151
Bristol 106
Colchester 98
Coventry 100, 103, 142
Doncaster 210
East Hendred 307
London 33, 64, 71, 77, 82, 83–7, 96, 103, 111, 123, 143, 152, 184, 200, 203, 219, 232, 255, 270, 276–7, 296, 309
Drapers' Company 80, 83–6, 102, 136, 212, 219, 311
Hadleigh 128, 151
Salisbury 164
Tiverton 136
York 21, 49, 206
Yorkshire 151
see also weaver-drapers
drawer 59
Droitwich (Worcestershire) 143
Dulverton (Somerset) 99
Dunton, Stephen, of Dedham, clothier 218, 221, 278
Durham, County 43, 44, 156, 242
Dursley (Gloucestershire) 121, 223
clothiers 72, 111, 125, 199, 203
Durston, William 41
dyeing 18, 40, 44, 61–4, 73–5, 80, 89, 124, 141–3, 149, 167, 176, 193, 198, 276
alum 63, 64, 79, 82, 84, 85, 94, 199, 277, 313
dyers 15, 16, 20, 39, 42, 61, 63, 64, 65, 74, 82, 84, 119, 130–1, 133, 135, 142–3, 168, 178, 188, 263, 275
dyestuffs 2, 18, 20, 45, 62–3, 64, 74, 75, 80, 94, 136, 144, 176, 197, 274, 276–7
cinnabar 62
grain 62, 85, 94
madder 13, 62, 64, 79, 80, 83, 86, 199
saffron 62–3
weld 12–13, 62
see also woad
dye-houses 36, 61, 152, 175, 232

clothiers 52, 63, 64, 76, 122, 125, 198, 253, 258, 261, 280, 309
fuel supply 145, 206
tools 24, 217, 307
water supply 145, 198, 258, 277
Dyes, Franciso, Spanish merchant 96
Dyffryn Clwyd lordship (Wales) 140
Earls Colne (Essex) 229
East Bergholt (Suffolk) 93, 127, 288
see also Bergholt
East Budleigh (Somerset) 57
East Hendred (Berkshire) 133, 284, 307
East Meon (Hampshire) 286
Edington (Wiltshire) 179
Edwardstone (Suffolk) 206–7
Egerton (Kent) 286
Eldysley, Henry, of East Hendred 133, 307
Eldysley, Roger, of East Hendred 133, 307
Elham (Kent) 286
Elland (Yorkshire) 132
Ely (Cambridgeshire) 100
entrepreneurs 2, 3, 17–22, 27–28, 38, 46, 49, 128, 130, 143, 156, 157, 274, 275, 280
clusters 120
costs and margin 75
merchant-entrepreneurs 65, 67
Erith (Kent) 180
Ernely, William 244
Essex 81, 145, 183, 207, 237, 242
cloth 84, 94, 101, 128–9, 153–4, 290, 315–6
cloth trade 96, 101, 110
clothiers 85, 118–20, 129–31, 183
cloth-making 16, 31, 87, 120, 127–31, 146, 218
cloths taxed in 32, 115, 148, 228, 282, 285
cloth-workers 117, 129–31
protests in 69–70, 76, 171, 179–80, 182, 232, 281
regulation 164
saffron 63
wool 44
Eton College (Buckinghamshire) 249
Evesham (Worcestershire) 143
Exe, River 135
Exeter (Devon) 256, 270
carriers 113, 136
cloth merchants 20, 152, 275
clothiers 23, 135
cloth-making 19, 34, 79, 135, 149
cloths taxed in 283, 284
fair 99
inns 104
Exyng, Matilda 104
Exyng, Thomas 104
factories 2, 26, 27, 38
advantages of 67
clothiers' workshops as 1, 69, 232, 250 258, 278
early examples of 19
see also workshops
factors (intermediaries) 101, 105, 110, 172, 269
Fairford (Gloucestershire) 42
fairs 6–7, 29, 175, 314
cloth 96, 97, 99–100, 103, 105–7, 158, 277, 310
Low Countries 79, 90–1, 99, 256, Plate V
wool 43, 228
Fareham (Hampshire) 286
Farleigh Hungerford (Somerset) 41, 89, 194
farming 4, 5, 13–14, 42
combined with cloth-making 35, 51, 67, 130, 146, 151
by clothiers 132, 139, 200, 205–6, 209
see also sheep farming
Farnham (Hampshire) 259
Farnley Moor (Yorkshire) 208
Farrer, Henry, of Halifax, clothier 103
fashion 12, 13, 16, 154
Fastolf, Sir John 124, 148, 305
Faversham (Kent) 286
Fawley (Hampshire) 286
Federico, Martino de 95, 256
Felsted (Essex) 197
Fenny Bridges (Devon) 135
Fermor, Emmot, of Witney, wool trader 42, 199
Fermor, Thomas, of Witney 42
Ferrour, William, of Norwich, dyer 103
Ferrybridge (Yorkshire) 221
finishing 21, 40, 59–61, 73, 80, 130, 238
costs 73–4
specialist centres 133, 137, 140, 142, 143, 168, 180
see also napping; pressing cloth; shearing
firewood 104, 144–5, 150, 206

Flanders 174, 185, 194
cloth-making in 8, 17, 51
immigrants from 16, 19, 177, 275
trade with 7, 79, 89, 91, 153
see also Flemings
flax 39, 64–5, 92, 315
Flemings, in cloth industry 15–17, 19–20, 69, 95–6, 144, 177, 275
other artists and craftworkers 147, 235, 249, 259
flocks (waste wool and cloth shearings) 132, 165, 167, 169
Flodden, battle of 250, 253
Florence 43, 94
Flower, John, of Potterne, clothier 41, 52
fraternities *see* guilds
Foglia (Italy) 63
Ford (Somerset) 287
Forest of Dean 80
Fornham St Genevieve (Suffolk) 49
Fortey family 42
Forthe, Robert, of Hadleigh, clothier 130
Forthe, William of Hadleigh, clothier 81, 113, 130
Fountains Abbey (Yorkshire) 211
Fowler, Robert, of Stonehouse 54
Fox, Richard, bishop of Winchester 186
Fox, Thomas, of Colchester, cloth-maker 245
Framlingham (Suffolk) 260
France 174, 235, 185, 206
cloth-making in 8, 18, 145, 177, 275
England at war with 3, 10, 15, 124, 148
trade with 7, 62, 91, 259
Frauncsom, Thomas 303
Freman, John, of Beeleigh 295
Frere, William, of Clare 222
Freshford (Somerset) 126, 221
Frome (Somerset) 114, 152
clothiers 23, 118, 121, 204
cloths taxed in 122, 287
protests in 188, 222
Frome, River 120, 124, 208, 221, 316
fulling 20, 40, 49, 53–9, 67, 73, 75, 139, 198, 314, Plate I
fullers 15, 18, 20–1, 37, 40, 42, 49, 53–7, 61, 68, 70, 71, 72, 83–4, 116, 120, 122, 263, 275, 280, 314
Bristol 178, 193
Colchester 129
Coggeshall 228–9, 231–2
Devon 135
engaged by clothiers 31, 52, 232, 296
Flemings 16
Kent 137
London 143
protests involving 180, 181, 186, 188
Reading 133
regulations 98, 158, 166, 168–74, 178, 222
Winchester 142
Yorkshire 131
fuller's earth 75, 145, 314
fulling mills 8, 19, 26, 36, 76, 121, 124–6, 132, 135–6, 140, 142, 145, 175–7, 192, 196, 203, 205, 209, 219, 223, 251, 253, 258, 276–7, 280, 306, 310, 314
held by clothiers 24, 54–6, 208
Fulsnape, Thomas, of Hadleigh, clothier 130, 211
Fyllype, George, of Tenterden, clothier 193
Gascony 10, 79, 127, 135, 153, 154
Gauge, Peter, apprentice 63, 245, 299
Gawter, John, of Beckington 94
Genoa 6, 94, 256
Genoese 63, 94, 95, 180
gentry
clothiers joining ranks of 207–8, 244, 254, 262, 266
engaging in cloth-making 208, 224
owning fulling mills 54, 208
reacting to protests 185–6
relations with clothiers 207–8
Ghent 6, 19, 194
gig mill 54, 57–9, 124, 148, 205, 314
use prohibited 59, 168
Gilbert, William, of Clare, clothier 52–3
Gisze, Georg, Hanseatic merchant 92, 201, Plate VI
Glastonbury (Somerset)
Abbot John Selwood of 127, 205, 309
Stranger Church 177
Glaswright, Robert, of Great Waldingfield, cloth-maker 100
Glasyer, Richard, of London, mercer 88
Glemsford (Suffolk) 74, 288, 307
clothiers 50, 130
see also Glemsford whites *under* cloth types

Gloucester
  Blackfriars 126, 176, 209, 278, 307
  cap-making 122, 126
  clothiers 126, 159, 175, 176
  protests in 180
Gloucestershire
  cloths 290, 316
  cloth-making 11, 31, 223
  clothiers 118–20
  cloth-workers 93
  cloths taxed in 115–16, 120, 282, 283
  gentry 185, 186
  protests in 93, 185, 186
  regulation 175, 208
  wool 44
Godalming (Surrey) 175, 259
Goding, William, of Bocking 299
Goldling, John, of Glemsford, clothier 50, 307
Golding, Joan 307
Goldney, Henry alias Fernell, of Chippenham 205
Goodbarne, William, servant 113
Goodday, Edward, shearman 231, 295
Goodday, Grace 295
Goodday, John 295
Goodday, Nicholas 295
Goodday, Robert, of Coggeshall 295
Goodday, Sir John, of Beeleigh 295
Goodday, Thomas, shearman 231, 295
Goodwyn, Matthew, of Ipswich 100
Goudhurst (Kent) 71, 85, 137, 184
Gower, John 12
Grasmere (Westmorland) 140, 192
Great Bedwyn (Wiltshire) 253
Great Coggeshall *see* Coggeshall
Great Cornard (Suffolk) 100
Great Englebourne (Devon) 209
Great Tey (Essex) 180
Great Torrington (Devon) 135, 284
Great Waldingfield (Suffolk) 100
Great Yarmouth (Norfolk) 11, 202, 239, 244
  immigrants in 16, 19, 275
Greatham (County Durham) 221
Greenway, Joan 219, 221
Green, John 190
Greenham (Berkshire) 205
Greenway, John, of Tiverton, cloth merchant 79–80, 136, 212
  almshouses 221, 278, 311
  chantry chapel 136, 219, 311
Gresham, Sir Thomas, of London, mercer 109, 134, 254, 256, 257, 269
Greville, William 42
Grey, John 20
Greywell (Hampshire) 259
Griffith, Ellis, chronicler 182
Grimston (Yorkshire) 13
Grinton (Yorkshire) 98
Grom, John, of Colchester 72
Grome, Robert, of Lavenham, clothier 110
Guildford (Surrey) 163, 259
Guildford, Sir Henry 186
guilds 314
  craft 18, 68, 82, 86, 148–50, 157–9, 166, 168, 171–2, 251, 274
    merchants *see* merchant adventurers
    weavers 8, 16, 65, 131, 142, 275
  religious 210, 211, 214–16, 215–17, 225,
  halls 147, 150, 197, 214–16, 240, 308
Gussage St Michael (Dorset) 123
Guybon, Rose 240, 298
Hadleigh (Suffolk) 69, 127, 147, 202, 223, 224, 232
  clothiers 81, 83, 85, 100, 113, 130
  cloths taxed in 128, 130, 244, 288
  drapers 82, 128, 151
  wealth of 2
  wool from 41
Haliday, Edward, of Rodborough, cloth-maker 125, 309
Haliday, Margery, of Rodborough 309
Halifax (Yorkshire) 8, 132, 139, 150, 224
  act 43, 132
  cloth 80, 99, 161
  clothiers 43, 59, 81, 103, 118
  cloths taxed in 33, 131, 288
  houses 195–6
Hall, Edward, chronicler 181–4
Hall, John, of Ipswich, dyer 62, 217, 307
Hall, Katherine, of Ipswich 217, 307
Hall, William, of Ipswich, clothier 62, 217, 307
Halstead (Essex) 295
Halwey, Richard, of Castle Combe 204
Hampshire
  cloth production 11, 115, 120, 122, 134, 154, 315
  clothiers 186
  cloths taxed in 282, 285

protests in 186
Hancokke, John, of Luckington, husbandman 267
handles 57–8, 61, 200, 314
handywarps 290, 313
Hanse merchants 78, 86, 91–4, 102, 126, 127, 130, 148, 153–4, 276
privileges 92, 187–8
see also Gisze, Georg
Harberton (Devon) 209
harbicks 36, 59
Harding family, of Cam 223
Harding, John, of Tidbury, cloth-maker 110
Hardy, John, of Halifax, clothier 43
Hardy, William, of Heptonstall, clothier 103
Harptree (Somerset) 287
Harrison, Thomas 301
Harrogate (Yorkshire) 132
Harry, John, of Lavenham, clothier 205, 215
Harryes, John, of Croscombe, clothier 123
Harryson, Thomas 301
Harset, Robert, of Long Melford, cloth-maker 220
Hart, Davy, of Bristol, shearman 61
Hartrege, Matthew, of Benenden 192
Hasche, Thomas, clothier 61
Hatter, John, of Hendred 133
Havant (Hampshire) 259, 286
Haverfordwest (Pembrokeshire) 141
Haynes, Marjorie, of Castle Combe 148
Haynes, William, of Castle Combe 59, 148
Headcorn (Kent) 202, 286
Headingley-cum-Burley (Yorkshire) 145
Headley (Hampshire) 286
Heaton, Herbert 24, 149
heckle 65
Hedges, John, of Malmesbury, clothier 159
Hedon (Yorkshire) 8
hemp 39, 64–5, 132
Hemyock (Devon) 103
Hengrave Hall (Suffolk) 91
Henry VIII, king of England 182, 250, 259
entertained by Jack of Newbury 207, 250, 253
entertained by William Stumpe 207, 266
Heptonstall (Yorkshire) 103, 132
Hereford 140
Herefordshire 282
wool 13, 44, 144
heretical ideas 77, 222–4, 225
Heritage, John, of Moreton-in-Marsh, wool merchant 33, 42, 71, 112, 232, 245
Hertfordshire 282
Hervey, Robert, of Colchester, cloth-maker 211
Hessett (Suffolk) 61, 250
Hewet, William, of Colchester, dyer 86
Higham (Suffolk) 59
Hillam (Yorkshire) 132
Hindon (Wiltshire) 179
Hinton Charterhouse (Somerset) 105, 203, 310
Holbein, Hans, the younger 92, 200, Plate VI
Holme (Nottinghamshire) 15
Holme, Robert 20
Holmes, Agnes 301
Holton, Thomas, of Nayland, shearman 100
Honiton (Devon) 284
Honley (Yorkshire) 208
Hoocke, Thomas, of London, dyer 64
Horewood, John, of Wells 123
Horewood, Margery, of Wells 123
Horndon, John 93
Horner, John, of Stoke, clothier 89
Horrold, Agnes, of Clare 194
Horrold, John, of Clare, clothier 192, 193–4, 230
Horrold, Margaret (first wife of Thomas Paycocke) *see* Paycocke, Margaret
Horrold, Margaret (II, sister of Margaret Paycocke) 230–1, 295
Horrold, Margery (sister of Margaret Paycocke) 230–1, 295
Horrold, Thomas (brother of Margaret, Margaret II and Margery) 295
Horrold, Thomas (father-in-law of Thomas Paycocke) 231, 234, 239, 292, 294
Horsforth (Yorkshire) 207
Horsleye, John, priest 270, 303
Horsmonden (Kent) 71

Horton, Austin, of Cullompton 136
Horton, Thomas, of Bradford-on-Avon, clothier 126, 254, 263, 304
  bridge 221
  chantry and school 220
  church of Holy Trinity, Bradford-on-Avon 304
  church of St Mary the Virgin, Westwood 311
  church house 221
  fulling mills 126
  houses
    Bradford-on-Avon 198, 305
    Westwood 35, 126, 202–3, 204, 311
  wealth 32
Houghton-le-Spring (County Durham) 242
Houhil, Henry 18
houses
  clothiers 195–209
    Bradford-on-Avon 198, 305
    Coggeshall 30, 35, 127, 199, 200, 201, 234–9, 278, 305, Plate VIII
    Dedham 218
    Gloucester 126, 176, 209, 307
    Lavenham 112, 199, 200, 307
    Malmesbury 35, 203, 204, 209, 266, 308
    Nayland 198, 309
    Newbury 37, 44, 260–2, 272, 309–10
    Westwood 35, 126, 202–3, 204, 311
  cloth-workers 204, 232, 277–8, 304, 309, 310
  extensions for cloth-making 195, 224
  furnishings 203, 261
Howard, John, duke of Norfolk 208
Howell, Thomas, of London, draper
  accounts 33, 85, 108
  cloth dyed and finished for 64, 143
  cloth supplied to 71–2, 85, 137, 154, 203–4
Huddersfield (Yorkshire) 33, 103, 131, 132, 208
Hull (Yorkshire) 30
  cloth hall 98
  Hanseatic warehouses 92
  Marie of 161
  mercers 87
  regulation at 172
  trade of 11, 21, 79
Hungerford (Berkshire) 179
Hunte, John, of Lavenham, clothier 110
Huntingdonshire 16, 282
Hykeman, Richard 99
Hythe (Essex) 11, 79, 127
Ibarra, Fernando de, Spanish merchant 96
Iberia 153
  see also Spain
Iford (Wilts) 126
inns 104–7, 197, 223, 310
Ipswich (Suffolk) 82, 223, 228
  church of St Margaret 62, 217, 307
  cloth exported from 11, 52, 79
  cloth taxed in 208, 288
  clothiers 85, 100, 217
  Hanse at 92, 130, 276
  merchants 128, 200
  Moot Hall 97, 98
  protests in 69, 232
Ireland 138, 153
Isle of Wight (Hampshire) 285, 286
Islip (Oxfordshire) 19
Italians 6, 18, 180, 275
  cloth-workers 69 n.120
  merchants 4, 42, 62, 63, 78, 94–6, 153–4, 188, 255–6
  trade 79, 83, 127, 154
  see also Bonvisi family; Cambini firm; Orlandini firm
Jack of Newbury see Winchcombe family of Newbury
Jackson, Christine 251
Jackson, John 13
Jacob, William, of Lavenham, clothier 147, 211, 221–2
Jacob, William, of Sudbury, cloth-maker 100
Jay, John, of Bristol 212, 305
Jermyn, Sir Thomas 184, 187, 240, 241, 298, 299
Jonys, Thomas 163
journeymen 68, 122, 171, 172, 223
  protests by 186, 188
Justinian, Bernard, Venetian merchant 94–5
Kaye, Arthur, of Woodsome Hall 208
Kaye, John 208
Kaye, Laurence, of Woodsome Hall 208
Keevil (Wiltshire) 126
Keighley, John, of Scriven 132
Kelsall, Henry, of Reading, clothier 216
Kelstern, Walter de 20

Kelvedon (Essex) 145
Kempe, John 16, 19
kempster *see* combers *under* combing
Kempston, John, of Hadleigh, draper 82, 128
Kendal (Westmorland)
  cloth 81, 99, 112, 140, 144, 154
  cloth market 98, 140
  cloth-making 11, 140
  Kendalmen 100, 105
  merchants 139, 192
Kendall, John of Bridgwater, cloth merchant 152
Kennet, River 133, 199, 251, 258
Kent
  cloth 81, 89, 133, 153–4, 165, 290
  clothiers 85, 118–19, 120, 137, 145, 176, 191–3, 206, 276
  cloths taxed in 115, 282, 286
  cloth-making 11, 29, 31, 87, 137, 146, 175
  cloth-workers 50, 51, 56
  protests in 70, 170, 179, 180, 181, 182, 183, 186, 188
  wool from 44
Kent, John, of Bath, clothier 89, 121, 194
Kerridge, Eric 27, 251, 265–6
Kersey (Suffolk) 98, 128
kerseys *see under* cloth types
Kett, Robert 188
Keynsham Abbey (Somerset) 208
Kidderminster (Worcestershire) 69, 142–3
Kilburn, Thomas de, of York, draper 206
Kilmersdon (Somerset) 287
King, Anne *see* Spring, Anne
King, Matthew, of Malmesbury, clothier 159, 263, 270
King's Lynn (Norfolk) 52, 92
King's Stanley (Gloucestershire) 125
Kingsclere (Hampshire) 259
Kingsmill, Richard, of Basingstoke, innkeeper 105
Kingswood (Gloucestershire) 121
Kirkby, Elizabeth, of Harrogate 132
Kistell, Philip, apprentice 258
Kitson, Thomas, of London, mercer 45, 88–91
  accounts 33, 108, 167, 268–9
  purchases by 109, 112, 113, 121, 126, 134, 136, 137, 138, 140, 141, 194, 205, 268–9
Knaresborough (Yorkshire) 64, 81, 99, 132
Knighton, Henry 12
Knottingley (Yorkshire) 132
Kryt, Eberhard, of Cologne 93
Kyng, John, clothier 83
Kyng, Robert, of Edwardstone, cloth-maker 206
Lake District, cloth-making in 11, 36, 100, 140, 192
Lamberd, Robert 296
Lancashire
  cloth 138, 154, 291, 314, 315
    cottons 80, 89, 98, 138, 291
  clothiers 43, 138–40
  cloth-making 138, 173, 175
  cloths taxed in 163
  wool from 44
Lane, John, of Cullompton, clothier 113, 135–6, 217
  Lane chapel 55, 57, 58, 61, 136, 218, 219, 306
Lane, John atte, apprentice 171
Lane, Thomas, of London, grocer 80
Lane, Thomasyn, of Cullompton 218
Langdale (Westmorland) 140, 192
Langford, Alexander, senior and junior of Trowbridge, clothier 89, 126, 263
Langford, Edward 126
Langland, William 22
Langport (Somerset) 287
Lavenham (Suffolk) 30, 35, 49, 61, 69, 93, 147, 149, 155, 156, 197, 217, 222, 239, 307–8
  26 and 27 Market Place 196, 308
  church of St Peter and St Paul 30, 36, 217, 226, 240–1, 246–50, 297–8, 308
  cloth 61
  clothiers 52, 57, 64, 71, 74, 84, 110, 130, 147, 198, 199, 205, 216, 222
    see also Spring, Thomas I; Spring, Thomas II; Spring, Thomas III
  cloths taxed in 130, 241, 244, 288
  cloth-making 127–8, 239–42, 244
  cloth-workers 52, 182, 220, 279
  guildhall of Corpus Christi 147, 215–16, 240, 308
  market cross 222

Molet House 307
Old Grammar School 112, 199, 200, 307
'project' 220
protests in 69, 181–3, 187–8, 232, 246
rector of 223
wealth in 2, 32, 239, 245–6
wool supplies to 41
Lawrence, John 303
Lawrence, John, of Bristol 64
Lawrens, John, of Westbury, clothier 89
Leake, John 96
Leeds (Kent) 286
Leeds (Yorkshire) 3
cloth 99
clothiers 132
cloths taxed in 33, 288
cloth-making 131, 145–6, 150
Leicester (Leicestershire) 8, 18–19, 100, 228
Leicestershire 282
Leland, John, antiquarian 35, 98, 135, 138, 204, 221, 263, 270
cloth markets 78, 138, 140
cloth-making 107, 121, 131, 133, 142
cloth-making workshops 27, 126, 264–5
clothiers 123, 126, 193, 246, 305
Leman, John 231
Leyham, Thomas, of Colchester 104
Lifton hundred (Devon) 165
Limendous (France) 108
Lincoln (Lincolnshire) 8, 18, 19, 175–6
Lincolnshire
cloths taxed in 115, 282
protests in 186–7
wool from 13, 43, 44
Lindley, John, of Harrogate 132
Lingards (Yorkshire) 208
Little Coggeshall (Essex) 229
Little Ribston (Yorkshire) 206
Little Waldingfield (Suffolk) 212, 288, 308, Plate IX
Liverpool (Lancashire) 65
Liversedge (Yorkshire) 208
Lodsworth (Sussex) 163
Lollardy 222
Lombardy 8
London 6, 16, 29, 46, 92, 94, 96, 112, 153, 155
Blackwell Hall 36, 84, 86, 92, 95, 98 101–3, 183–5, 223, 255, 277
regulations 101, 104
Blossom's Inn 104
brass workshop 212
Christ's Hospital 101
cloth exports 11, 81–2, 87, 279
cloth-making 19, 115, 143, 177
cloth-workers 16 ,18
dyers 64
finishers 84, 269
fullers 158
weavers 5, 65, 143, 158, 251, 275, 236, 238
cloths taxed in 282
Cornhill 200
Crosby Place, Bishopsgate Street 96
drapers 71, 78, 80, 82, 83–5, 96, 101, 103, 111, 123, 152, 200, 232
see also Greenway, John; Howell, Thomas; Monmouth, Humfrey
economic growth 34, 279
fishmongers 83, 130
Gracechurch Street 113
grocers 30, 61, 78, 80, 82–4, 93, 100, 109, 140, 152
Guildhall 101
haberdashers 84, 100, 139
Holborn 105, 112
ironmonger 82
Limestreet 121
members of parliament 161
mercers 30, 78, 80, 82, 83, 86–8, 100, 109, 152, 254, 269
merchant adventurers 82, 86, 87, 89, 109, 110, 113, 187, 269
see also Thomas Kitson
merchants 42, 63, 81, 93, 100, 108, 110, 113, 152, 160, 206, 207, 274
regulation 107–8, 158, 168
St Bartholomew's Fair 86, 100, 103, 187, 277
St Paul's 234, 293
Steelyard, Thames Street 92, 201
Stocks market 101
tailors 78, 85–6
see also Southwark; Westminster
London, Dr John 176
Long Melford (Suffolk) 245
clothiers 118, 193, 220
cloth-making 127, 128, 147, 152
cloths taxed in 288
protests in 182
Long, Edith 217, 310

Long, Henry 113
Long, Robert, of Steeple Ashton, clothier 126, 217, 310
Longley (Wiltshire) 205
looms 19, 35, 48, 50–3, 67, 67, 76, 128, 132, 138–41, 143, 165, 172, 173, 188, 223, 232, 275, 278, 280, 315–17, Plate IV
  bequeathed 59, 65, 194, 197, 205, 267, 270, 302–3
  broadlooms 39, 51, 72, 131, 138, 141, 208
  narrow looms 10, 39, 51, 138, 141
  owned by clothiers 24, 70, 72, 122, 171, 250, 258, 263–6, 302–3
Loughborough (Leicestershire) 139
Loughrigg (Westmorland) 192
Low Countries 154, 257, 275
  immigrants from 16, 19, 177
  trade with 7, 8, 10, 79, 87, 90, 180, 186, 259
Lübeck (Germany) 91
Lucas, Matilda 217
Lucas, Maud 310
Lucas, Walter, of Steeple Ashton, clothier 126, 217, 310
Lucca 94, 96, 233
Luckington (Wiltshire) 267
Ludlow (Shropshire) 113, 140
Lyard, John, 'plomer' 245
Lymington (Hampshire) 286
Lynch, William 137
Lyppet, Agnes 303
Mabson, John, of Old Sodbury, weaver 267
Maghfeld, Gilbert, of London, ironmonger 82, 128
Magno, Alessandro, of Venice 103
Maiden Bradley (Wiltshire) 106
Maidenhead (Berkshire) 284
Maidstone (Kent) 286
Maldon (Essex) 234, 285, 293
Malmesbury (Wiltshire) 156, 207, 308
  Abbey 27, 52, 126, 177, 203, 209, 226, 262–4, 270, 278, 303, 308
  Abbey House 35, 203, 204, 209, 266, 308
  clothiers 126, 270
  see also Stumpe, William
  cloth-making 263
  cloth-making workshop 26–7, 52, 66, 69, 126, 203, 208–9, 232, 264–5, 270, 308
  Cowbridge mill 264
  market cross 278
  members of parliament 159
  protests in 179
  Whitchurch 264
  Winyard Mill 264
Man, Thomas 296
Manchester (Lancashire)
  cloth 194
    cottons 291, 310
    rugs 291, 310
  clothiers 61, 80, 138–9, 194
  cloth-making 138–9
Manhode, William of Thaxted 108
Manningham (Yorkshire) 103
Manwyche, John 94
Marcanova company 94
Markshall (Essex) 234, 294
Marlborough (Wiltshire) 18, 122
Marsham (Norfolk) 141
Marshe, John, MP for London 161
Marsshe, Alice 301
Martyn, William, of Wokingham, clothier 203
Marx, Karl 25–6
Masham (Yorkshire) 8–9
Mathewe, John 41
Mattingley (Hampshire) 259
Mawdleyn, John, of Wells, clothier 123
Mawdleyn, Richard, of Croscombe, clothier 84, 123
May, Alice (step-daughter of Thomas Spring III) 299
Maynard, Nicholas, of Colchester 198
Maynard, Thomas, of London, grocer 109
Mayow, Walter, of Chew (Somerset), clothier 111
Mediterranean 10
Melcombe Regis (Dorset) 152
Melksham hundred (Wiltshire) 288
Mellors, Robert 168
Mells (Somerset) 217
  church of St Andrew 309
  cloths taxed in 287
  cloth-workers' houses 127, 205, 277, 309
members of parliament, clothiers serving as 159, 264
merchant adventurers 25, 78, 82, 86,

87–8, 92, 113–14, 154, 160, 168, 187, 206, 315
see also Greenway, John; Gresham, Thomas; Kitson, Thomas
merchants' marks
clothiers' 62, 89, 166, 217–19, 234, 240, 248, 254, 262, 268, 304–11
on brasses 36, 133, 212, 305,
on cloth 79, 166–7
Mere (Wiltshire), cloths taxed in 288
Middleburg fair 99
Middleham (Yorkshire) 161
middlemen 21, 41–3, 143
Middlesex 115, 282
Midhurst (Sussex) 259
Midsomer Norton (Somerset) 106
Midwinter, William, of Northleach, wool trader 14
Milan 94
mill *see* fulling mill; gig mill
Milton hundred (Kent) 286
Minchinhampton (Gloucestershire) 106, 125, 146, 309
Mitchell, Christopher, of Colne, clothier 139
Mitchell, John, of Colne 207
Molen, Pieter Van der 256
Molton cloth 154, 161
Monmouth, Humfrey, of London, draper 77, 184, 223
More, Christopher 163
More, Thomas 184
Morebath (Devon) 103
Moreton-in-Marsh (Gloucestershire) 33, 42, 112, 233, 245
Morlaix (Brittany) 266
Morrys, John 163
Mors, Alys, of Stratford St Mary 311
Mors, Edward, of Stratford St Mary 311
Mors, Margaret, of Stratford St Mary 311
Mors, Thomas, of Stratford St Mary, clothier 311
Motte, John, of Bildeston 83, 130, 245
Mucklowe, William, of Worcester, merchant 79
Mundys, Elizabeth, of Glemsford 307
Mundys, John, of Glemsford, clothier 307
Mundys, John, son of John 307
Mundys, Margaret, of Glemsford 307
Mytholmroyd (Yorkshire) 196
Nabbs, John, of Manchester, cloth-maker 139
napping 40, 57–9, 315, Plate I
Nayland (Suffolk)
Alston Court 198, 309
clothiers 55, 85, 130–1, 245
cloths taxed in 288
shearman 100
Needham Market (Suffolk) 147
Nele, Thomas 302
Netherlands 183
Nethermill, Julian, of Coventry, draper 100
Neville, John, of Liversedge 208
Neville, Robert, of Liversedge 208
Newark-on-Trent (Nottinghamshire) 15
Newbury (Berkshire) 11, 46, 155–6, 272
church of St Nicolas 36, 260, 300–1, 309
clothiers 61, 83, 134, 253, 255, 259
see also Winchcombe, John I; Winchcombe, John II
cloth-making 11, 95, 133–4, 251–2
cloths taxed in 251, 284
dyers 258
fullers 61, 255
Marsh Lane 261
martyrs 260, 272
protests in 179
Shaw Mills 253
West Mill 61, 258
Newcastle-upon-Tyne 8, 87, 92
Newman, Robert 299
Newton, John, of Lavenham, clothier 147
Newton, Thomas, Somerset ulnager 106
Nicholls, Walter of Burwood, clothier 113
Nicholson, William 168
Norfolk 80, 81, 202, 207, 242
cloth 290
see also worsted *under* cloth types
cloth-making 86, 129, 141, 146, 164
cloth-workers 117
cloths taxed in 282
Norfolk, duke of 182–5, 187, 189–90, 208, 244
Norland (Yorkshire) 100
Normandy (France) 8, 135, 315

North Bradley (Wiltshire) 123 n.26
North Molton (Devon) 161
see also Molton cloth; South Molton
North Muskham (Nottinghamshire) 15
North Nibley (Gloucestershire) 263, 267
North Walsham (Norfolk) 117, 141
North Warnborough (Hampshire) 204, 310
Northallerton (Yorkshire) 65
Northampton 8, 97, 176, 209
Northamptonshire 282
Northe, William, of Bruton 109
Northleach (Gloucestershire) 14, 43, 199
Northumberland 282
Norton St Philip (Somerset) 106, 121, 287
George Inn 105–7, 310
Norwich 6, 87, 103, 152, 251
church of St Peter Mancroft 202
cloth-making in 11, 141
Dragon Hall 201–2
dyer's workshop 36, 61
immigrants in 16, 177
protests in 179, 180, 181–2
regulations at 98, 141, 170, 173
wool supplies to 41
Worsted Seld 97
Nottingham 168
Nottinghamshire 282
Novgorod (Russia) 92
Nunney (Somerset) 287
Nycollys, Thomas, of 'Nynnysfield', smith 267
Nycolyne, Master 114
Odiham (Hampshire) 134, 204, 259, 286
oil (for cloth-making) 2, 45, 185, 199, 205
imports of 80, 84, 85, 96
sales 89, 104, 139, 233, 277
scarcity of 185
Okeford Fitzpaine (Dorset) 217
Okehampton (Devon) 285
Okle, William 20, 75
Old Sodbury (Gloucestershire) 267
Olyver, John, of London, draper 84
Orcheston (Wiltshire) 123 n.26
Ore, William, of Canterbury, weaver 51
Orlandini firm 43
Osbourn, William, of Sherston, husbandman 267
Osemond, Thomas, of Frome 114
Oswestry (Shropshire) 140
Otham (Kent) 54
Otterburn (Northumberland) 56, 310
Ottery St Mary (Devon) 135
outworkers 69, 71, 141, 190, 274, 280
overseas trade *see* exports *under* cloth
Overton (Hampshire) 259
Ovington (Essex) 234, 293
Oxford 18, 19, 51
Christ Church 265
clothworkers in 116
Osney abbey 176–7, 209, 265
university of 220
Oxfordshire 165, 282
packhorses *see under* transport
Padiham (Lancashire) 138
Pakenham (Suffolk) 244
Palmer, Julins 260
Pape, Frans de, of Antwerp, cloth merchant 87
Parks, William, of Worcester, carrier 113
Parle, John, of London, merchant 108, 233
Parman, John 21
Parsons, Robert 215
Paston, John 112
Pattenden, Stephen, of Rolvenden, clothier 193
Pattiswick (Essex) 234, 294
Paxton (Huntingdonshire) 53
Paycocke, Anne (née Cotton, second wife of Thomas) 228, 294, 306
Paycocke, Christina (wife of Thomas, d.1461) 228–9, 306
Paycocke, Elizabeth (sister-in-law of Thomas) 228, 234
Paycocke, Joan (sister-in-law of Thomas) 228, 234, 306
Paycocke, John (d. 1506, father of Thomas) 41, 192, 228, 229–30, 238
Paycocke, John (d. 1533, brother of Thomas) 228, 231, 234, 294, 296, 306
Paycocke, John (d. 1584, great-nephew of Thomas) 204, 228, 230
Paycocke, John (fl. 1575, relationship unclear) 204, 232, 238
Paycocke, Margaret (first wife of Thomas) 201, 306

Paycocke, Margaret (née Horrold, first wife of Thomas Paycocke) 201, 228, 230, 231, 234, 235, 238, 306
Paycocke, Robert (d. 1520, brother of Thomas) 228, 234, 237, 294, 296, 306
  wool purchased by 33, 42, 233, 238, 270
Paycocke, Thomas (d. 1461, grandfather of Thomas) 41, 192, 228–9, 238
Paycocke, Thomas (d. 1518)
  cloth-making business 231–3
  historians' view of 25, 28, 238–9
  merchant's mark 226–7, 236–7
  Paycocke's House 30, 35, 127, 199, 200, 201, 234–9, 278, 305
    workshop 232, 305
  will 46, 210–11, 217, 230–1, 233–4, 292–6
  workforce 31, 46, 68, 270, 296
Paycocke, Thomas (d. 1580, great-nephew of Thomas) 228, 234, 306
payment in kind (truck) 70, 170, 281
Peacock, David 251
Pembrokeshire cloths 291
Pendine (Carmarthenshire) 141
Penistone (Yorkshire) 315
  see also under cloth types
Pensford (Somerset) 120, 121, 122, 146, 276, 278, 287
Percy family 180
Percy, John, of Erith, tailor 180
Perkyns, John, of Guildford, clothier 163
Pernell, John, of Bristol, mercer 256
Perpoint, Henry 295
Perpoint, Thomas, of London, draper 231–2, 294, 296
Person, John, of Lavenham, cloth-maker 71
Pert, Randoll, of London, draper 255
Petersfield (Hampshire) 259, 286
Pettor, Thomas, shearman 143
Petworth (Sussex) 163, 259
Peverell, Thomas, of East Bergholt, clothier 93
Pevnser, Nikolaus 218, 227, 304
Philipson, John, of Doncaster, draper 210
Picardy 79
Pickering, John, of London, mercer 87
Pilgrimage of Grace 187
Pilton (Devon) 135
Pistor, Tristrum, of Boyton, gentleman 269
Place, John, of Lavenham, clothier 205
Plomer, Richard, of Colchester, cloth-maker 70
Plymouth (Devon) 79, 285
Plympton (Devon) 284
Poland 92
Pontefract (Yorkshire) 20, 131, 289
Porter, John 296
Porter, Ralph, of Cherington, clothier 269
Poslingford (Suffolk) 234, 293
Potterne (Wiltshire) 41, 52
Poullain, Valérand 177
Power, Eileen 25, 226–7, 238
Prato (Italy) 18
Prentys, John, of Colchester 104
pressing cloth 40, 59–60, Plate I
Preston (Lancashire) 138
Preston (Suffolk) 242
Priddy (Somerset) 106
proto-industrialisation 27, 146, 281
Prussia 87, 92, 127
Prysshton, John, of Pensford 122
Prysshton, Thomas, of Pensford 122
Pulham Market (Norfolk) 82
putting-out system 2, 17, 25, 28, 37, 65–9, 72, 75–6, 129, 139–40, 142–3, 151, 155–6, 168–9, 173, 177, 270, 275, 315–16
  extent of 68
  impact on workers 69, 160, 190, 281
Pypere, Richard 104
Raynham, Stephen, of Nayland 245
Reading (Berkshire) 216, 255
  Abbey 254
  cloth 84, 165, 290
  cloth-making in 133, 149
  cloth-workers' agreement 70, 133–4, 166, 170
  cloths taxed in 284
reed 50, 316
Reve, John, weaver 104
Reyner, John 296
Rhineland 8
Rich, Richard 176
Richards, Mother, spinner 71
Richardson, John, of Chippenham, common carrier 113

Richmond (Yorkshire) 211
Richmondshire (Yorkshire) 43
Ripon (Yorkshire) 33, 44, 131–2, 288
  cloth 99, 161
Risby, Thomas, of Lavenham, clothier 147
roads, bequests for 130, 221
Robertson, David 194
Roborough hundred (Devon) 165
Rochdale (Lancashire) 43, 138
Rochester (Kent) 184
Rodborough (Gloucestershire) 125, 200, 309
Rode (Somerset) 287
Rolvenden (Kent) 54, 193
Romsey (Hampshire) 46, 95, 180, 259, 285–6
Ronanger, Robert, of Southampton, merchant 256
rowing *see* napping
Rowles, Robert 302
Royston (Hertfordshire) 155
Russell, Lord 188
Russia 92
Ruthin (Denbighshire) 140
Rutland 282
Rychard, Robert, of Dursley, clothier 72, 111, 125, 199, 203
Ryley, Thomas, of Coventry, draper 100
Rysby, John, of Lavenham, clothier 216
Sadler, Katherine, of York, carder 46
saffron 62–3
Saffron Walden (Essex) 63, 155, 250, 285
Salisbury (Wiltshire) 34, 46, 112, 152, 222, 300
  cloth 84, 94
    rays 11, 122, 153, 164, 316
  clothiers 68, 72, 122, 263
  cloths taxed in 94, 115, 120, 288
  cloth-making 11, 115, 120, 122, 164
  cloth-workers 82, 116
  drapers 82
  fair 99
  protests in 179, 180
  weavers 51, 122, 222
Sammys, Thomas 184
Sandleford Priory (Berkshire) 253
Sandwich (Kent) 96, 286
Sandys, William Lord 186, 189
Saricold *see* Sorocould
Saunson, Robert 302–3
Savage, Edward, of London, grocer 140
Savey, John, of Colchester 104
Scarborough (Yorkshire) 87
Schecher, Agnes, of Wells 194
schools 136, 175, 193
  founded by clothiers 136, 220
Scotton (Yorkshire) 20
Scottow (Norfolk) 141
Scriven (Yorkshire) 132
Seend (Wiltshire) 61, 219, 310
Selby (Yorkshire) 103, 289
Selwood, Abbot John, of Glastonbury 204, 309
Selwood, Henry, of Wells, chapman 80
Semur-en-Auxois (France) 57, 61, Plate I
Sergeaunt, Robert, clothier 208
Serney, David 302
servants 49, 51, 64, 65, 74, 139, 140, 270
  of clothiers 45, 68, 69, 125, 192, 195, 231, 280
    bequests to 231, 296, 299, 301–3
    laid off 185, 186, 188, 190
  of Flemings 19–20
  of lords 12
  of weavers 51, 122
set-cloths *see* vesses *under* cloth types
Sewey, Robert, of Newbury, clothier 253, 255
Seymour, Edward, first duke of Somerset 177, 257, 258
‘s-Hertogenbosch, Brabant 91, Plate V
Shakespeare, William 180, 181
Sharpe, John, of Cranbrook, clothier 193
Shavelock, Roger, of London, tailor 86
shearing (cloth) 36, 40, 57–9, 61, 71, 72, 139, 141, 142, 167, 316, Plate I
  shearman 59–61, 100, 116, 143, 172, 193, 222, 295, 316
  shears 59, 60–1, 219, 310
Sheefe, Thomas, clothier 306
sheep farming 4, 5, 14, 42
  by clothiers 41, 132, 192, 205–6, 242, 259, 269
Shelley (Suffolk) 83
Shepton Mallet (Somerset) 287
Sherborne (Dorset) 120, 121, 179
Sherfield on Loddon (Hampshire) 259
Sherston (Wiltshire) 267
Sheway, Robert 301
Shilton, Richard of 18
Shipley, William, of York, draper 49

Shipman, William 64
ships *see under* transport
shops 103, 136, 196–7, 200, 224, 308
  see also showrooms, workshops
Shorthose, Janna, of Wells 194
showrooms 104, 196, 201–2, 237
  see also shops
Shrewsbury (Shropshire) 140
Shropshire 101, 282
  wool 13, 44, 144
Silvester, Richard, of Colchester 68
Sixpenny Handley (Dorset) 123 n.26
Skarlet, William, of Coggeshall, weaver 229
Skelton, John, poet 1, 242–3
Skipton (Yorkshire) 73
Slaithwaite (Yorkshire) 208
slay *see* reed
Smallwood, John
  see also Winchcombe, John I and Winchcombe, John II
  son of John, of Barking 252
Smarden (Kent) 179
Smith, Edmund, of Odiham 134
Smith, Richard 302
Smith, Robert, of Odiham 134
Smith, Roger, of Rolvenden, fuller 54
Smith, Sir Thomas 174, 178
Smyth, John, of Nibley 223
Smyth, Thomas, of London, merchant tailor 85
Smyth, William, of Colchester 72
Smyth, William, of Higham, merchant 59
Smythe, John, of Bristol, mercer 33, 61, 64, 80, 85, 107, 109, 194
Somerset 99, 106, 208
  cloth 89, 153–4, 167, 290
  clothiers 80, 89, 118–20, 123, 175, 275
  cloths taxed in 94, 115–16, 120, 122, 282–3, 287
  cloth-making 115, 120–1, 135, 151, 275–6
  cloth-workers 20
  protests in 186, 188
Sorocould, Edward, of Manchester 138
Sorocould, Gilbert of Manchester, cloth-maker 138
South Molton (Devon) 284
  see also North Molton; Molton cloth
Southampton (Hampshire) 2, 11, 105, 165, 177
  brokage books 33–4, 111–12, 114
  cloth 94, 161
  cloths taxed in 285, 286
  protests in 180, 186
  trade 46, 63, 79, 94–6, 134, 139–40, 144, 251–2, 255–6
Southwark 103, 143
Spain 45, 63, 79, 80, 83, 85, 96, 135, 183, 185
  Spanish merchants 96, 100, 154
  see also Iberia
Spaxton (Somerset) 57, 60
Spema, Alexander of Venice 255
spinning 6, 22. 29, 35, 37, 40, 46–50, 67, 71, 76, 89, 139, 142, 169, 173, 273, 277, 316, Plate II, Plate III
  costs 73–5
  spindles 47, 76, 169, 280, 313, 316, Plate II
  spinners 39, 47–50, 51–2, 72, 137, 140, 150, 169, 175, 178,
    bequests to 21, 31, 46, 53, 130, 211, 232, 244–5, 280, 296
    clothiers 65, 70, 73–4, 181, 183–4, 255, 258, 274, 277
    payments to 70–1, 170–1, 281
  spinning wheels 47–9, 72, 104, 132, 139, 233, 276, 278, Plate III
  whorls 36, 47–8, 316
Spinola, Antonio 95
spinsters *see* spinners *under* spinning
Sponer, John 231, 296
Springs of Lavenham 156, 226, 239–50
Spring, Agnes (wife of Thomas I) 240, 244
Spring, Alice May (second wife of Thomas III) 218, 240, 242, 248, 298
  wealth 32, 239, 244
Spring, Anne (née King, first wife of Thomas III) 240, 242
Spring, Bridget (daughter of Thomas III) 240, 244, 298
Spring, Margaret (niece of Thomas III) 147, 244
Spring, Margaret (née Appleton, wife of Thomas II) 212, 240, 246–8, 308
Spring, John (son of Thomas III) 184, 187, 207, 240, 241, 244, 298, 299
Spring, Robert (son of Thomas III) 240, 244, 298
Spring, Thomas I 192

cloth-making business 244
will 211, 220, 246, 270
workforce 270
Spring, Thomas II
brass 212, 246–8, 308
cloth-making business 244–5
will 244–5, 246, 260
workforce 68, 130, 244–5, 270
Spring, Thomas III 240
church, commemorated in 30, 147, 218, 246, 248–50, 308
cloth-making business 245–6, 270
historians' view of 27
landholdings 111, 207
wealth 111, 127, 131, 181, 242–4, 253
will 63, 205, 220, 246, 260, 297–9
wool purchased by 33, 42
Spring, William (relationship unclear) 244
Springfield (Essex) 85
Sprunte, Thomas, of Lavenham, dyer 182
St David's Cathedral (Pembrokeshire) 235
St Neots (Huntingdonshire) 152
Staffordshire 14, 282
Stamford (Lincolnshire) 2, 161
Stamford Bridge (Yorkshire) 21
Stanesby, John, of Bildeston, clothier 69, 83, 95–6, 130
Stansby, Thomas, of Lavenham, clothier 199, 216
Staple, Company of 14
Stede, John, of Norland 100
Steeple Ashton (Wiltshire) 113, 121, 126, 217, 310
Steventon (Berkshire) 133, 284
Stoby, John, of Cirencester 72
Stockhouse, Dr Thomas, rector of Lavenham 223
Stoke Lane (Somerset) 89
Stoke Michael (Somerset) 89
Stoke-by-Clare (Suffolk) 55, 74
Stoke-by-Nayland (Suffolk) 85, 93, 185, 220, 234, 293
Stokes, Alys, of Seend 310
Stokes, John, of Seend, clothier 219, 310
Stokton, John 23
Stoner, Humphrey, apprentice 231, 296
Stonehouse (Gloucestershire) 54
Stonor, Sir William 14
Stourbridge Fair *see under* Cambridge
Stow, John 101, 103
Stowford (Wiltshire) 55, 126, 208
Stowford, William, of Stowford, clothier 55
Stowmarket (Suffolk) 183
Stratford St Mary (Suffolk) 93, 288, 295, 311
Strete, Thomas, of Mells 217
Striklond, James, of Kendal, cloth-man 140
Stroud (Gloucestershire) 11, 145, 146
clothiers 125
fullers 72
protests in 180
see also Stroudwater
Stroudwater (Gloucestershire) 3
cloth-making 74, 120, 121–2, 124–5, 278
cloth-workers 69
exemption from regulation 175
see also under cloth types
Stubbard, Agnes, of Bury St Edmunds 49
Stumpe, Bridget (daughter-in-law of William) 263, 270
Stumpe, Catherine (third wife of William) 263
Stumpe, Isabel (daughter-in-law of William) 263, 270
Stumpe, Sir James (son of William) 207, 263, 270, 302, 303
Stumpe, John (son of William) 263, 270, 302
Stumpe, Joyce (née Berkeley, first wife of William) 263, 264
Stumpe, Richard (nephew of William) 302
Stumpe, Tibbalda (second wife of William) 263
Stumpe, Thomas, of North Nibley, husbandman (brother of William) 192, 263, 303
Stumpe, Thomas (nephew of William) 302
Stumpe, William 226, 262–70
Abbey House 35, 203, 204, 209, 266, 308
cloth-making business 89, 109, 267–9
family tree 263
father of 192, 263
historians view of 26–7

member of parliament 159, 264, 266
offices held 266–7
will 269–70, 302–3
workers engaged 69
workshop at Malmesbury 26–7, 52, 66, 69, 126, 203, 208–9, 232, 264–5, 270, 308
workshop at Oxford 176–7, 209, 265
Stumpe, William (nephew of William) 302
Stumpe, William (son of William) 263, 270, 303
Sturmyn, Alan, of Lavenham, cloth-worker 220
Sturmyne, Thomas, of Lavenham, clothier 74
Style, Thomas, of Bath, clothier 121
subsidies *see* taxation
Sudbury (Suffolk) 183
clothiers 83, 100, 241
cloth-making 127, 128
cloths taxed in 288
friars 234, 297
protests in 181, 182
Sudeley Castle (Gloucestershire) 254, 261–2
Suffolk 35, 80, 141, 145, 207, 218
clothiers 29, 54, 81, 83, 85, 86, 100, 118–19, 120, 127–31, 171, 203, 207, 211, 220, 270
cloths 290
straits 128–9, 153–4, 316
vesses 93, 128, 153, 154, 165, 316
cloths taxed in 115–16, 244, 282–3, 288
cloth-making 11, 28, 48, 77, 127–31, 145, 147, 241
regulations 165, 175
wealth 2, 31, 32, 68, 239, 244
cloth-workers 16, 117, 129–31, 171, 193
protests in 65, 69–70, 76, 179–80, 181–9, 190, 232, 281
woolmen 42
Suffolk, duke of 182
sumptuary legislation 12
Surrey 154, 163, 165, 283
Sussex 133, 154, 163, 165, 283, 290
Sutton Coldfield (Warwickshire) 175, 277
Swan, Richard 20
Swansea 140
Swayne, Henry, of Salisbury, cloth-maker 122
Swetyng, John, of Coggeshall, dyer 84
Swindon (Wiltshire) 123 n.26
Symond, Henry 299
Sympson, Robert 72
Tadcaster (Yorkshire) 20
Taillour, Richard, of Colchester 72, 104
Tallmage, Robert, of London, merchant tailor 103
Tame, John, of Fairford 42
Tanner, Roger, of Westbury, clothier 45, 89
Tarrant Hinton (Dorset) 123 n.26
Taunton (Somerset) 120, 186, 287, 290
Tavistock (Devon) 135, 154, 165, 285
Tawney, Richard 26, 148
taxation 31–2, 69, 181–2, 187, 240, 279
see also customs duties, ulnage
Taylor, Robert, fuller 231, 296
teasels 2, 46, 57, 79,
handles 57–9, 60, 136, 200, 218, 305, 306, 314
Temple Newsam (Yorkshire) 53
Tenterden (Kent) 137, 193, 286
tentering 40, 56–7, 59, 73, 316
tenter hooks 20, 36, 60, 75
tenters 52, 131, 167, 198, 237, 254, 277, 280, 300, 310, 316
Terumber, Alice 221
Terumber, James of Bradford on Avon and Trowbridge, clothier 126, 179–80, 193
almshouse and chantry 126, 220–1
cloth sold 94–5
house 204
wool purchased 41
water conduit 222
Terumber, Johanne 221
Tetbury (Wiltshire) 180, 269, 271
Tetley, Richard 139
Tetlow, Richard 139
Tewkesbury (Gloucestershire) 111
Thames Valley 133–4, 179
see also Berkshire, Oxfordshire
Thatcham (Berkshire) 254
Thaxted (Essex) 108, 155, 285
Thetford (Norfolk) 297
Thomas, John, of Worcester 83
Thornbury (Gloucestershire) 121

Thornton, Richard, of Ashton-under-Lyme 139
Tidbury (Gloucestershire) 110
Tillington (Sussex) 163
Tilshead (Wiltshire) 123 n.26
Tippar, Richard, of Bristol, tucker 61
Tiverton (Devon) 103, 135
  church of St Peter 212, 219, 221, 311
  grammar school 136
  Greenway's Almshouses and Chapel 136, 219, 221, 278, 311
  see also Greenway, John
Tolfa (Italy) 63, 79
Tooley, Henry, of Ipswich, merchant 200
Toppes, Robert, of Norwich, mercer 201
Tortworth (Gloucestershire) 121
Totnes (Devon) 154, 209, 285
Touker family, of Castle Combe 123
Touker, Thomas, of Castle Combe 123
Toukere, Philip 20
Toulouse 62, 108
Towker *see* Terumber
Townshend, Roger II 41
Trafford, Margaret 163
Trafford, Ralph 163
transport
  carriers 111–13, 136
  carts 7, 33, 102, 104, 111–12
  packhorses 72, 112, 144
  ships 90–1, 136, 202, 219, 306
Trewe, Thomas 296
Trippe, Robert, of Lavenham, clothier 198
Trotman, Henry 223
Trotman, Richard 223
Trotman, Thomas, of Cam, clothier 223
Trowbridge (Wiltshire) 105, 179
  cloth-making 121, 126
  clothiers 41, 89, 94–5, 193, 204, 221
truck *see* payment in kind
Truxton, Oliver, common carrier 113
Tucker of Burford, cloth-maker 74, 176
tuckers *see* fullers *under* fulling
Tunbridge Wells (Kent) 137
Tunnell, John 301
Turnour, Hugh, of Stoke-by-Clare, clothier 55
Turnour, Peter 299
Turnour, William, of Hadleigh, weaver 100
Tuscany 8
Twyne, William, of Newbury, clothier 83
Tyler, John, of Wells, cloth-maker 56
Tyndale, John 223
Tyndale, Katherine 223
Tyndale, William, religious reformer 223
Typpyng, Ralph 41
ulnage accounts 21, 24, 32–3, 105, 316
  changing distribution of cloth-making 115–16, 120, 122–3, 127, 128, 129, 282–3
    Berkshire 133, 251, 284
    Devon 135, 284–5
    Essex 129–30, 229–30, 285
    Hampshire 285–6
    Kent 286
    Somerset 122, 123, 194, 287
    Suffolk 127–8, 129, 208, 244, 288
    Wiltshire 288
    Yorkshire 131, 288–9
  limitations of 32, 116, 283
  trade at fairs 99, 100
Uppcher, Robert and Margaret 294
Usburn, John, of York 64
Vaugham, Richard 267
Vaughan, Stephen 257
Venetians 94, 103, 154, 161, 180, 255
Vere family, earls of Oxford 147, 187, 240, 249
Vere, Aubrey de 147, 244
Vere, John de, thirteenth earl of Oxford 147, 241, 250, 308
Vere, John de, fifteenth earl of Oxford 147
Veysey, John, bishop of Exeter 175
Vyall, John, of Charlton 267
wages
  cloth-making trades 73–4
  legislation 149, 170–1
  trends 5–6, 13, 150–1
  wage-earners 18, 24, 28, 46, 67–71, 151, 182–3, 188, 190, 274, 280–1
Waite, John, parson of Newbury 301
Wakefield (Yorkshire) 207
  cloth 99
  clothiers 118
  cloth-making in 51, 131, 132, 150
  cloths taxed in 33, 288
Waldegrave, Sir William 299
Waldingfield (Suffolk) 182, 223

see also Great Waldingfield; Little Waldingfield
Wales 79, 80
cloth
cottons 140, 291, 314
frieze 84, 89, 141, 291
cloth-making in 11, 140–1, 175
tailor 152
wool 44
walkers *see* fullers *under* fulling
Walker, Mark, of London grocer 83
Wallingford (Berkshire) 259, 284
Walsh, Joan 252
Walsh, Thomas 252
Wantage (Berkshire) 284
Wareham, Archbishop of Canterbury 183
warehouses 102
clothiers 125, 197, 199–200, 201, 207, 216, 258, 262
Hanseatic 92
tailors 86
Waren, Christopher, of Coventry, draper 100
Warminster (Wiltshire) 105, 288
Warton (Lancashire) 88
Warwickshire 115, 153, 181, 182, 283
Wastell, John, master mason 250
water supplies 145, 198–9, 222, 258, 277
Waterhouse, Gilbert, of Halifax, cloth-maker 59
Waterhouse, Robert, of Halifax 196
weaving 19, 35, 40, 50–3, 76, 129, 132, 139, 140, 142, 149, 150, 193, 195, 317, Plate I, Plate IV
costs 70, 73–5, 281
weavers 19–21, 39, 40, 49, 50–3, 68–72, 75, 76, 100, 104, 120, 132, 135, 141–2, 143, 158, 165, 168–70, 177–8, 180, 181, 186, 192, 204, 222, 223, 230, 250, 252, 259, 263, 265, 266–7, 281
act (1555) 171, 173–4, 188
apprenticeship 172–3
becoming clothiers 192–3
bequests to 31, 52–3, 83, 130, 211, 232, 244–5, 269, 270, 280, 296, 303
clothiers use of 274
Flemish 15–17, 19
guilds 8, 16, 65, 131, 142, 275
London Company of 236–8
weaver-drapers 17–18, 28, 275
see also looms
Webb family of Dursley, clothiers 125
Webb, Henry, of Colchester, clothier 198, 203, 305
Webb, John, of Dedham, clothier 167, 218, 306
Webb, Thomas, of Dedham, clothier 167, 218, 306
Webb, Thomas, vicar of Dedham 218
webster *see* weavers *under* weaving
Welford (Berkshire) 284
Welles, John, of Salisbury, weaver 51
Wellington (Somerset) 105, 287
Wells (Somerset) 23
chapman 80
clothiers 23, 56, 99, 123, 275
cloth-making 121, 152, 194, 276
cloths taxed in 115, 120, 122, 287
protests in 179
Wenman, Henry 42
West Bergholt (Essex) 56
West Hendred (Berkshire) 284
West Wycombe (Buckinghamshire) 71
West, Kateryn 301
Westbury (Wiltshire) 121, 222
clothiers 45, 89, 123 n.26
protests in 186, 190
western cloth 80, 94, 96, 100, 154
blankets 121, 153
dozens 136
Westminster 6, 22, 23
Abbey 242, 249
fair 97, 164
Westmorland 183, 283
cloth 43, 112, 154, 175
Westoneys, Matilda 20, 75
Westwood (Wiltshire) 35, 126, 202–3, 311
Whelespynner, Isabella, of Bishopthorpe 48
Whitby (Yorkshire) 8
Whitchurch (Hampshire) 259, 286
White, Robert, fuller 180, 222
Whitley Beaumont (Yorkshire) 208
Whitwey, William, of East Hendred 133, 307
Wickwar (Gloucestershire) 121
Wife of Bath 35, 194–5, 276
Wild, Robert 209
Wild, Thomas, of Worcester, clothier 161, 209, 220, 312

Willinson, James, of Knaresborough, mercer 81
Wilton (Wiltshire) 41, 105, 179, 288
Wiltshire
- clothiers 24, 80, 89, 118–20, 123, 126, 183
- cloth-making 11, 29, 31, 120–2, 146, 151, 154
- cloth-workers 117
- cloths taxed in 94, 95, 115–16, 120, 163, 283, 288
- legislation 175, 208
- members of parliament 159, 253
- protests in 179, 181, 186, 188

Winchcombes of Newbury 134, 156, 226, 250–62
- cloth-making business 57, 95, 134, 254–60
- family tree 252
- historians' view of 26–7

Winchcombe, Alice (wife of John I) 252, 260, 300
Winchcombe, Christian (second wife of John II) 205, 252
Winchcombe, Henry (son of John II) 252, 254, 258
Winchcombe, Joan (first wife of John II) 252, 300
Winchcombe, John (son of John II) 252, 254, 260
Winchcombe, John I
- brass 260, 309
- will 253, 260, 300–1

Winchcombe, John II 198–9, 207, 252–3
- dye-house 63–4
- farm 205
- Jack of Newbury's House 37, 44, 260–2, 272, 309–10
- lobbyist 161, 259
- oppose rebels 187, 253
- portrait 36, 254, Plate X
- sheep 41
- statute 272
- wealth 133, 253–4
- will 254, 260
- workforce 69, 258
- workshop at Newbury 26, 66, 69, 134, 232, 250, 258, 262, 270

Winchcombe, Michael ('father-in-law' of John I) 252
Winchcombe (Gloucestershire) 252
Winchester (Hampshire) 105
- cloth 84
- cloth sellers 18, 21, 32, 135, 275
- clothiers 119, 159, 170, 259
- cloth-making 8, 16, 19, 46, 115, 120, 142,
- cloths taxed in 115, 120, 285, 286
- fair 99
- regulation 173
- protests in 179

Windsor (Berkshire) 284
- St George's Chapel 249, 252, 254, 300

Wing (Buckinghamshire) 259
Winnersh (Berkshire) 259
Witney (Oxfordshire) 42, 43, 199
woad 62–3
- bequeathed in wills 199, 214, 245, 299
- imports of 79, 82, 85, 94, 255–6
- sales of 71–2, 80, 84, 89, 139, 140, 208
- store 62, 72

Wokingham (Berkshire) 203, 259
Wolf, Thomas, of Coventry, draper 103
Wolford, Adam, Kendalman 100
Wolsey, Cardinal Thomas 77, 182, 184–6, 259
- and London merchants 103, 185

Wolverhampton (Staffordshire) 123
Wood, John, clothier 198
Woodchester (Gloucestershire) 267
Wooder, William 299
Woodsome Hall (Yorkshire) 208
wool
- dealers 5, 14–15, 18, 26, 33, 83, 112, 131–2, 139, 170, 229, 233, 245, 259, 274
  - woolmen 42–3, 71, 133, 212, 223, 225
- exports 4, 10, 14–15, 19, 82, 92, 99, 138, 144, 275
- markets and fairs 98, 103, 106–7, 228, 263, 269
- preparing 44–5, Plate I
- price 11, 13, 74–5, 127, 144, 154
- quality 13, 44, 135, 144, 165, 228
- stores 43, 125, 199–200, 237, 256, 280
- supplies 21–2, 41–3, 71, 144

Woolpit, Robert, of Fornham St Genevieve 49
Wootton Bassett (Wiltshire) 267
Worcester 145
- bishop of 113
- carrier 113
- cathedral 220

cloth 87, 113, 154, 160, 290
clothiers 83, 113, 119, 123, 143, 159, 161, 209, 220
cloth-making 142–3, 149
regulation of 160, 169, 170, 173
cloth-workers 116
Commandery 209, 312
Free School 220
hospital of St Wulstan 209, 312
merchants 79, 83
protests in 188
Worcestershire 44, 69, 143, 160, 173, 283
workshops 197, 237, 278, 315
clothiers' 52, 63, 72, 133, 176–7, 195–8, 208–9, 280
Bradford-on-Avon 305
Boxted 198
Coggeshall 305
Dedham 306
Gloucester 126, 307
Malmesbury 26–7, 52, 66, 69, 126, 203, 208–9, 232, 264–5, 270, 308
Nayland 309
Newbury 26, 69, 134, 250, 258, 262, 270
Oxford 176–7, 265
cloth-workers 204, 276
dyers 36, 61
fullers 61
tailors 80–1
weavers 141
monumental brasses 212
selling cloth in 97, 103–4
wool-processing 18
see also shops
Worstead (Norfolk) 117, 141
worsted *see under* cloth types
Wotton, John, of Totnes, merchant 209
Wotton, William, of Harberton, clothier 209
Wotton-under-Edge (Gloucestershire) 121
Wright, Richard, curate of Newbury 301
Wrose, James, of Horsforth 207
Wycliff, John 22
Wyllymot, Elizabeth 64
Wyllymot, Robert 64
Wyllymot, Thomas, of Lavenham 64
Wylye, River 120
Wyncoll, John, of Little Waldingfield, clothier 212, 308, Plate IX
Wyndlove, Robert, of Halstead 295
Wyndowe, John 302
Wytham, William 171
Wytton, Miles 215
Yarcombe (Devon) 41
yarn 18, 20, 65, 71, 153, 173, 317
bequests 132, 199, 205
dyeing 40, 61
faulty 44
markets 41, 98, 138, 143, 269
preparing 46, 73–4, 197
spinning 47–50, 96, 167, 169, 232
supplies 20, 129, 142, 269
weaving 50–3, 166, 169
weights 133
Yate, John, of Buckland 259
Yates, Margaret 251
Yatton Keynell (Wiltshire) 263
Yeldham (Essex) 229
Yeovil (Somerset) 287
Yerbery, John, of Bruton, cloth-maker 61, 80, 109
Yonge, William, of Petworth, clothier 163
York 8, 30, 64
cloth-making 11, 131, 153
decline of 150
merchants engaging in 19–21, 49, 135, 151, 211, 221, 275
monopoly of coverlet manufacture 173
regulation of 168
cloth sales at 97, 98, 99, 105, 132
cloths taxed in 33, 115, 289
cloth-workers 116–17, 119
carder 46
dyer 46
draper 49, 206
guild fees 172
tailor 80
weavers 8, 51, 131, 149
immigrants in 16–17
fair 99
Merchant Adventurers 87
protests in 180
wool sales 42
Yorkshire 72, 80, 100, 146, 211, 278
cloth 154, 315
clothiers 24, 43, 103, 118
houses in 196–7

cloths taxed in 33, 115–16, 283, 288–9
cloth-making 8, 11 ,16, 31, 131–2
exemption from regulations 165, 175
protests in 180
wool 44
Youle, Robert, of Worcester, clothier 159, 220
Young, Roger 123
Ypres (Belgium) 194
Yurle, Peter 20
Zeeland (Netherlands) 110